The Bloomsbury
Companion to Heidegger

Bloomsbury Companions

The *Bloomsbury Companions* series is a major series of single volume companions to key research fields in the humanities aimed at postgraduate students, scholars, and libraries. Each companion offers a comprehensive reference resource giving an overview of key topics, research areas, new directions, and a manageable guide to beginning or developing research in the field. A distinctive feature of the series is that each companion provides practical guidance on advanced study and research in the field, including research methods and subject-specific resources.

Aesthetics, edited by Anna Christina Ribeiro
Analytic Philosophy, edited by Barry Dainton and Howard Robinson
Aristotle, edited by Claudia Baracchi
Continental Philosophy, edited by John Mullarkey and Beth Lord
Epistemology, edited by Andrew Cullison
Ethics, edited by Christian Miller
Existentialism, edited by Jack Reynolds, Felicity Joseph, and Ashley Woodward
Hegel, edited by Allegra de Laurentiis and Jeffrey Edwards
Hobbes, edited by S. A. Lloyd
Hume, edited by Alan Bailey and Dan O'Brien
Kant, edited by Gary Banham, Dennis Schulting, and Nigel Hems
Leibniz, edited by Brandon C. Look

Locke, edited by S.-J. Savonious-Wroth, Paul Schuurman, and Jonathan Walmsley
Metaphysics, edited by Robert W. Barnard and Neil A. Manson
Philosophical Logic, edited by Leon Horston and Richard Pettigrew
Philosophy of Language, edited by Manuel Garcia-Carpintero and Max Kolbel
Philosophy of Mind, edited by James Garvey
Philosophy of Science, edited by Steven French and Juha Saatsi
Plato, edited by Gerald A. Press
Political Philosophy, edited by Andrew Fiala and Matt Matravers
Pragmatism, edited by Sami Pihlström
Socrates, edited by John Bussanich and Nicholas D. Smith
Spinoza, edited by Wiep van Bunge

THE BLOOMSBURY
COMPANION TO HEIDEGGER

EDITED BY

François Raffoul and
Eric S. Nelson

Bloomsbury Academic
An imprint of Bloomsbury Publishing Plc

B L O O M S B U R Y
LONDON · OXFORD · NEW YORK · NEW DELHI · SYDNEY

Bloomsbury Academic

An imprint of Bloomsbury Publishing Plc

50 Bedford Square
London
WC1B 3DP
UK

1385 Broadway
New York
NY 10018
USA

www.bloomsbury.com

BLOOMSBURY and the Diana logo are trademarks of Bloomsbury Publishing Plc

First published 2013

Expanded paperback edition published 2016

British Library Cataloguing-in-Publication Data
A catalogue record for this book is available from the British Library.

ISBN: HB: 9781441199850
PB: 9781474245104
ePDF: 9781441175045
ePub: 9781441141613

Library of Congress Cataloging-in-Publication Data
The Bloomsbury companion to Heidegger / edited by François Raffoul and Eric S. Nelson.
pages cm. – (Bloomsbury companions)
Includes bibliographical references and index.
ISBN 978–1–4411–9985–0 – ISBN 978–1–4411–7504–5 (pdf) – ISBN 978–1–4411–4161–3 (epub)
1. Heidegger, Martin, 1889–1976. I. Raffoul, François, 1960- editor of compilation.
II. Nelson, Eric S., 1968- editor of compilation.
B3279.H49B588 2013
193–dc23
2013005645

Typeset by Newgen Imaging Systems Pvt Ltd, Chennai, India
Printed and bound in Great Britain

CONTENTS

CONTENTS

CONTENTS

ACKNOWLEDGMENTS

Organizing an edited volume such as this requires the cooperation and assistance of many individuals from family and friends to colleagues, contributors, editors, and external reviewers. An anthology is the most social form of publishing and we are each thankful to all those individuals—first and foremost our contributors—who have directly and indirectly made its publication possible. We would particularly like to express our gratitude to Iain Thomson for suggesting that we pursue this volume and our editors at Continuum/Bloomsbury, David Avital, Sarah Campbell, and Rachel Eisenhauer. We thank them for their patience and confidence. Our gratitude to Delbert Burkett, Seynaeve Professor of Biblical Studies and Chair of the Department of Philosophy and Religious Studies at Louisiana State University, for his advice and support. We also want to thank Alice Frye for her patient encouragement and assistance as well as Meli Badilla for her generous support and lively spirit.

LIST OF ABBREVIATIONS

GERMAN EDITION

(GA):   Martin Heidegger's *Gesamtausgabe* (Frankfurt am Main: Vittorio Klostermann, 1978–)

GA 1:   *Frühe Schriften*, ed. Friedrich-Wilhelm von Herrmann, 1978

GA 2:   *Sein und Zeit* (1927), ed. Friedrich Wilhelm von Herrmann, 1977

GA 3:   *Kant und das Problem der Metaphysik* (1929), ed. Friedrich-Wilhelm von Herrmann, 2nd edn, 2010

GA 4:   *Erläuterungen zu Hölderlins Dichtung* (1936–68), ed. Friedrich-Wilhelm von Herrmann, 1981

GA 5:   *Holzwege*, ed. Friedrich-Wilhelm von Hermann, 1977

GA 6.1: *Nietzsche* I (1936–9), ed. Brigitte Schillbach, 1996

GA 6.2: *Nietzsche* II (1939–46), ed. Brigitte Schillbach, 1997

GA 7:   *Vorträge und Aufsätze* (1936–53), ed. Friedrich-Wilhelm von Herrmann, 2000

GA 8:   *Was heißt Denken?* (1951–2), ed. Paola-Ludovika Coriando, 2002

GA 9:   *Wegmarken*, ed. Friedrich-Wilhelm von Hermann, 1976

GA 11: *Identität und Differenz* (1955–7), ed. Friedrich-Wilhelm von Herrmann, 2006

GA 12: *Unterwegs zur Sprache*, ed. Friedrich-Wilhelm von Herrmann, 1985

GA 13: *Aus der Erfahrung des Denkens*, ed. Hermann Heidegger, 1983

GA 14: *Zur Sache des Denkens*, ed. Friedrich-Wilhelm von Herrmann, 1962

GA 15: *Seminare*, ed. Curd Ochwadt, 1981

GA 16: *Reden und andere Zeugnisse eines Lebensweges*, ed. Hermann Heidegger, 2000

GA 18: *Grundbegriffe der aristotelischen Philosophie*, ed. M. Michalski, 2002

GA 19: *Platon: Sophistes*, ed. Ingeborg Schüßler, 1992

GA 20: *Geschichte des Zeitbegriffs. Prolegomena zur Phänomenologie von Geschichte und Natur*, ed. Petra Jaeger, 3rd edn, 1994

GA 21: *Logik. Die Frage nach der Wahrheit*, ed. Walter Biemel, 2nd edn, 1995

GA 22: *Die Grundbegriffe der antiken Philosophie*, ed. Franz-Karl Blust, 1993

GA 23: *Geschichte der Philosophie von Thomas von Aquin bis Kant*, ed. H. Vetter, 2006

GA 24:   *Die Grundprobleme der Phänomenologie*, ed. Friedrich-Wilhelm von Hermann, 3rd edn, 1997

GA 25:   *Phänomenologische Interpretation von Kants Kritik der reinen Vernunft*, ed. I. Görland, 3rd edn, 1995

GA 26:   *Logik. Metaphysische Anfangsgründe der Logik im Ausgang von Leibniz*, ed. Friedrich-Wilhelm von Herrmann, 1990

GA 27:   *Einleitung in die Philosophie*, ed. O. Saame et I. Saame-Speidel, 2nd edn, 2001

GA 28:   *Der deutsche Idealismus (Fichte, Schelling, Hegel) und die philosophische Problemlage der Gegenwart*, Claudius Strube, 2nd edn, 2011

GA 29/30: *Die Grundbegriffe der Metaphysik. Welt—Endlichkeit—Einsamkeit*, ed. Friedrich-Wilhelm von Herrmann, 3rd edn, 2004

GA 31:   *Vom Wesen der menschlichen Freiheit. Einleitung in die Philosophie*, ed. H. Tietjen, 2nd edn, 1994

GA 32:   *Hegels Phänomenologie des Geistes*, ed. I. Görland, 3rd edn, 1997

GA 33:   *Aristoteles, Metaphysik J 1–3. Von Wesen und Wirklichkeit der Kraft*, ed. H. Hüni, 3rd edn, 2006

GA 34:   *Vom Wesen der Wahrheit. Zu Platons Höhlengleichnis und Theätet*, ed. Hermann Mörchen, 1988

GA 35:   *Der Anfang der abendländischen Philosophie: Auslegung des Anaximander und Parmenides*, ed. Peter Trawny, 2012

GA 36/37: *Sein und Wahrheit*, ed. H. Tietjen, 2001

GA 38:   *Logik als die Frage nach dem Wesen der Sprache*, ed. G. Seubold, 1998

GA 39:   Hölderlins Hymnen *"Germanien"* und *"Der Rhein,"* ed. Susanne Ziegler, 1980

GA 40:   *Einführung in die Metaphysik*, ed. Petra Jaeger, 1983

GA 41:   *Die Frage nach dem Ding*, ed. Petra Jaeger, 1984

GA 42:   *Schelling: Vom Wesen der menschlichen Freiheit*, ed. Ingrid Schüssler, 1988

GA 43:   *Nietzsche: Der Wille zur Macht als Kunst*, ed. Bernd Heimbüchel, 1985

GA 44:   *Nietzsches metaphysische Grundstellung im abendländischen Denken: Die ewige Wiederkehr des Gleichen*, ed. Marion Heinz, 1986

GA 45:   *Grundfragen der Philosophie: Ausgewählte "Probleme" der "Logik,"* ed. Friedrich-Wilhelm von Herrmann, 1984

GA 46:   *Zur Auslegung von Nietzsches II. Unzeitgemäßer Betrachtung "Vom Nutzen und Nachteil der Historie für das Leben" (1938–39)*, ed. Hans-Joachim Friedrich, 2003

GA 47:   *Nietzsches Lehre vom Willen zur Macht als Erkenntnis*, ed. E. Hanser, 1989

GA 48:   *Nietzsche: Der europäische Nihilismus*, ed. Petra Jaeger, 1986

GA 49:   Die Metaphysik des deutschen Idealismus. Zur erneuten Auslegung von Schelling: *Philosophische Untersuchungen über das Wesen der menschlichen Freiheit und die damit zusammenhängenden Gegenstände (1809)*, ed. G. Seubold, 1991

GA 50:   *Nietzsches Metaphysik*, ed. Petra Jaeger, 1990

GA 52:   *Hölderlins Hymne "Andenken,"* ed. Curd Ochwadt, 1982

GA 53:   *Hölderlins Hynme "Der Ister,"* ed. Walter Biemel, 1982

GA 54:   *Parmenides*, ed. Manfred S. Frings, 1982

GA 55: *Heraklit*, ed. Manfred S. Frings, 1994

GA 56/57: *Zur Bestimmung der Philosophie*, ed. Bern Heimbüchel, 1987

GA 58: *Grundprobleme der Phänomenologie*, ed. Hans-Helmuth Gander, 1992

GA 59: *Phänomenologie der Anschauung und des Ausdrucks. Theorie der philosophischen Begriffsbildung*, ed. C. Strube, 1993

GA 60: *Phänomenologie des religiösen Lebens*, ed. Matthias Jung, Thomas Regehly, and Claudius Strube, 1995

GA 61: *Phänomenologische Interpretationen zu Aristoteles. Einführung in die phänomenologische Forschung*, ed. Walter Bröcker and Käte Bröcker-Oltmanns, 2nd edn, 1994

GA 62: *Phänomenologische Interpretation ausgewählter Abhandlungen des Aristoteles zu Ontologie und Logik*, ed. G. Neumann, 2005

GA 63: *Ontologie. Hermeneutik der Faktizität*, ed. K. Bröcker-Oltmanns, 1988; 2nd edn, 1995

GA 64: *Der Begriff der Zeit (1924)*, ed. Friedrich-Wilhelm von Herrmann, 2004

GA 65: *Beiträge zur Philosophie (vom Ereignis)*, ed. Friedrich-Wilhelm von Herrmann, 1989

GA 66: *Besinnung*, ed. Friedrich-Wilhelm von Herrmann, 1997

GA 67: *Metaphysik und Nihilismus*, ed. H.-J. Friedrich, 1999

GA 68: *Hegel*, ed. I. Schüssler, 1993

GA 69: *Gedachtes. Die Geschichte des Seyns*, ed. Peter Trawny, 2012

GA 70: *Über den Anfang (1941)*, ed. Friedrich-Wilhelm von Herrmann, 2005

GA 71: *Das Ereignis*, ed. Friedrich-Wilhelm von Herrmann, 2009

GA 72: *Die Stege des Anfangs (1944)*, ed. Friedrich-Wilhelm von Herrmann, forthcoming

GA 73: *Zum Ereignis-Denken*, ed. Hans-Joachim Friedrich, 2013

GA 74: *Zum Wesen der Sprache und Zur Frage nach der Kunst*, 2010

GA 75: *Zu Hölderlin / Griechenlandreisen*, ed. C. Ochwadt, 2000

GA 77: *Feldweg-Gespräche (1944/45)*, ed. Ingrid Schüssler, 1995

GA 78: *Der Spruch des Anaximander (1942)*, ed. Ingeborg Schüßler, 2010

GA 79: *Bremer und Freiburger Vorträge*, ed. P. Jaeger, 1994

GA 86: *Seminare Hegel—Schelling*, ed. Peter Trawny, 2011

GA 87: *Seminare Nietzsche*, ed. P. von Ruckteschell, 2004

GA 88: *Seminare (Übungen) 1937/8 und 1941/2:*
    1. *Die metaphysischen Grundstellungen des abendländischen Denkens*, ed. Alfred Denker, 2008;
    2. *Einübung in das philosophische Denken*, ed. Alfred Denker, 2008

GA 89: *Zollikoner Seminare*, ed. Medard Boss, 2006

GA 90: *Zu Ernst Jünger "Der Arbeiter,"* ed. Peter Trawny, 2004

GA 94: *Überlegungen II–VI (Schwarze Hefte 1931–1938)*, ed. Peter Trawny, 2014

GA 95: *Überlegungen VII–XI (Schwarze Hefte 1938/39)*, ed. Peter Trawny, 2014

GA 96: *Überlegungen XII–XV (Schwarze Hefte 1939–1941)*, ed. Peter Trawny, 2014

GA 97: *Anmerkungen I–V (Schwarze Hefte 1942–1948)*, ed. Peter Trawny, 2015

OTHER TEXTS

EM: *Einführung in die Metaphysik*, 5th edn (Tübingen: Max Niemeyer, 1987)

N1: *Nietzsche. Erster Band*, 5th edn (Pfullingen: Neske, 1989)

N2: *Nietzsche. Zweiter Band*, 5th edn (Pfullingen: Neske, 1989)

SZ: *Sein und Zeit* (Tübingen: Max Niemeyer Verlag, 1953)

VA: *Vorträge und Aufsätze*, 7th edn (Pfullingen: Neske, 1994)

WhD: *Was heißt Denken?* 4th edn (Tübingen: Max Niemeyer, 1984)

Z: *Zollikoner Seminare : Protokolle—Zwiegespräche—Briefe* (Frankfurt am Main: Klostermann, 1997/2006)

ZSD: *Zur Sache des Denkens*, 3rd edn (Tübingen: Max Niemeyer, 1988)

ENGLISH TRANSLATIONS

AM: *Aristotle's Metaphysics Theta 1–3 On the Essence and Actuality of Force*, trans. Walter Brogan and Peter Warnek (Bloomington: Indiana University Press, 1995)

BAT: *Being and Truth*, trans. Gregory Fried and Richard Polt (Bloomington: Indiana University Press, 2010)

BCAP: *Basic Concepts of Ancient Philosophy*, trans. Richard Rojcewicz (Bloomington: Indiana University Press, 2007)

BCAR: *Basic Concepts of Aristotelian Philosophy*, trans. Robert D. Metcalf and Mark B. Tanzer (Bloomington: Indiana University Press, 2009)

BFL: *Bremen and Freiburg Lectures: Insight into That Which Is and Basic Principles of Thinking*, trans. Andrew J. Mitchell (Bloomington: Indiana University Press, 2012)

BH: *Becoming Heidegger: On the Trail of His Early Occasional Writings, 1910–1927*, ed. Theodore J. Kisiel and Thomas Sheehan (Evanston: Northwestern University Press, 2007)

BP: *The Basic Problems of Phenomenology*, trans. A. Hofstadter (Bloomington: Indiana University Press, 1982; rev. edn, 1988)

BQP: *Basic Questions of Philosophy: Selected "Problems" of "Logic,"* trans. Richard Rojcewicz and Andre Schuwer (Bloomington: Indiana University Press, 1994)

BT: *Being and Time*, trans. Joan Stambaugh. Revised and with a Foreword by Dennis J. Schmidt (Albany: SUNY Press, 2010)

BTMR: *Being and Time*, trans. John Macquarrie and Edward Robinson (New York: Harper, 1962)

BW: *Basic Writings*, rev. and exp. edn, ed. David Farrell Krell (San Francisco: Harper, 1993)

CP1: *Contributions to Philosophy (From Enowning)*, trans. Parvis Emad and Kenneth Maly (Bloomington and Indianapolis: Indiana University Press, 1999)

CP2: *Contributions to Philosophy: Of the Event*, trans. Richard Rojcewicz and Daniela Vallega-Neu (Bloomington: Indiana University Press, 2012)

CPC: *Country Path Conversations*, trans. Bret W. Davis (Bloomington: Indiana University Press, 2010)

CT: *The Concept of Time*, trans. William McNeill (Oxford: Blackwell, 1992)

DT: *Discourse on Thinking*, trans. John M. Anderson and E. Hans Freund (New York: Harper & Row, 1966)

EGT: *Early Greek Thinking*, trans. David F. Krell and Frank A. Capuzzi (New York: Harper & Row, 1975)

EHF: *The Essence of Human Freedom*, trans. Ted Sadler (London: Continuum, 2002)

EHP: *Elucidations of Hölderlin's Poetry*, trans. and introduction by Keith Hoeller (Amherst, NY: Humanity Books, 2000)

ET: *The Essence of Truth. On Plato's Cave Allegory and Theaetatus*, trans. Ted Sadler (London: Continuum, 2002)

FCM: *The Fundamental Concepts of Metaphysics: World, Finitude, Solitude*, trans. William McNeill and Nicholas Walker (Bloomington: Indiana University Press, 1995)

FS: *Four Seminars*, trans. Andrew Mitchell and François Raffoul (Bloomington: Indiana University Press, 2003)

HCT: *History of the Concept of Time: Prolegomena*, trans. Theodore Kisiel (Bloomington: Indiana University Press, 1985)

HHTI: *Hölderlin's Hymn "The Ister,"* trans. William McNeill and Julia Davis (Bloomington: Indiana University Press, 1996)

HPS: *Hegel's Phenomenology of Spirit*, trans. Parvis Emad and Kenneth Maly (Bloomington: Indiana University Press, 1988)

HR: *The Heidegger Reader* (Bloomington: Indiana University Press, 2009)

HS: *Heraclitus Seminar, 1966/67* (Tuscaloosa, AL: University of Alabama Press, 1979)

ID: *Identity and Difference*, trans. Joan Stambaugh (New York: Harper & Row, 1969)

IM: *Introduction to Metaphysics*, trans. Gregory Fried and Richard Polt (New Haven, CN: Yale University Press, 2000)

IPTP: *Introduction to Philosophy—Thinking and Poetizing*, trans. Phillip Jacques Braunstein (Bloomington: Indiana University Press, 2011)

KPM: *Kant and the Problem of Metaphysics*, trans. Richard Taft (Bloomington: Indiana University Press, 1997)

LEL: *Logic as the Question Concerning the Essence of Language*, trans. Wanda Torres Gregory and Yvonne Unna (Albany: SUNY Press, 2009)

MFL: *The Metaphysical Foundations of Logic*, trans. Michael Heim (Bloomington: Indiana University Press, 1984)

NI: *Nietzsche I: The Will to Power as Art*, ed. and trans. David F. Krell (New York: Harper & Row, 1979)

NII: *Nietzsche II: The Eternal Recurrence of the Same*, ed. and trans. David F. Krell (New York: Harper & Row, 1984)

NIII: *Nietzsche III: The Will to Power as Knowledge and Metaphysics*, ed. David F. Krell, trans. Joan Stambaugh (New York: Harper & Row, 1987)

NIV: *Nietzsche IV: Nihilism*, ed. David F. Krell, trans. Frank A. Capuzzi (New York: Harper & Row, 1982)

OBT: *Off The Beaten Track*, ed. and trans. Julian Young and Kenneth Haynes (New York: Cambridge University Press, 2002)

OHF: *Ontology: The Hermeneutics of Facticity*, trans. John van Buren (Bloomington: Indiana University Press, 1999)

OWL: *On the Way to Language* (New York: Harper & Row, 1971)

P: *Parmenides*, trans. Andre Schuwer and Richard Rojcewicz (Bloomington: Indiana University Press, 1992)

PA: *Pathmarks*, ed. William McNeill (Cambridge: Cambridge University Press, 1998)

PIA: *Phenomenological Interpretations of Aristotle: Initiation into Phenomenological Research*, trans. Richard Rojcewicz (Bloomington: Indiana University Press, 2001)

PIA2: *Phenomenological Interpretations in Connection with Aristotle: An Indication of the Hermeneutical Situation*, trans. John van Buren, in Heidegger, ed. John van Buren, *Supplements: From the Earliest Essays to Being and Time and Beyond* (State University of New York Press, 2002)

PICPR: *Phenomenological Interpretation of Kant's Critique of Pure Reason*, trans. Parvis Emad and Kenneth Maly (Bloomington: Indiana University Press, 1997)

PIE: *Phenomenology of Intuition and Expression: Theory of Philosophical Concept Formation*, trans. Tracy Colony (London: Continuum, 2010)

PLT: *Poetry, Language, Thought*, trans. Albert Hofstadter (New York: Harper & Row, 1971)

PRL: *The Phenomenology of Religious Life*, trans. Matthias Fritsch and Jennifer Anna Gosetti-Ferencei (Bloomington: Indiana University Press, 2004)

PS: *Plato's Sophist*, trans. Richard Rojcewicz and Andre Schuwer (Bloomington: Indiana University Press, 1997)

PT: *The Piety of Thinking*, trans. James G. Hart and John C. Maraldo (Bloomington: Indiana University Press, 1976)

QCT: *The Question Concerning Technology and Other Essays*, trans. William Lovitt (New York: Harper & Row, 1977)

S: Supplements, ed. John Van Buren (Albany: SUNY Press, 2002)

STEHF: *Schelling's Treatise on the Essence of Human Freedom*, trans. Joan Stambaugh (Athens: Ohio University Press, 1984)

TB: *On Time and Being* (New York: Harper & Row, 1972)

TDP: *Towards the Definition of Philosophy*, trans. Ted Sadler (London: Continuum, 2002)

WCT: *What Is Called Thinking?* trans. Fred D. Wieck and J. Glenn Gray (New York: Harper & Row, 1968)

WIP: *What Is Philosophy?* trans. Jean T. Wilde and William Kluback (New Haven: College and University Press, 1958)

WIT: *What Is a Thing?* trans. W. B. Barton, Jr. and Vera Deutsch (Chicago: Henry Regnery Company, 1967)

ZS: *Zollikon Seminars*, ed. Medard Boss, trans. Franz K. Mayr and Richard R. Askay (Evanston, IL: Northwestern University Press, 2001)

NOTES ON CONTRIBUTORS

Kevin Aho is Professor of Philosophy at Florida Gulf Coast University. He has published widely on Heidegger, phenomenology, and hermeneutics and is the author of *Heidegger's Neglect of the Body* (Albany: SUNY Press, 2009), coauthor (with James Aho) of *Body Matters: A Phenomenology of Sickness, Illness, and Disease* (Lanham: Lexington Books, 2008), and coeditor (with Charles Guignon) of a new edition of Dostoevsky's *Notes from the Underground* (Indianapolis: Hackett, 2009). He recently published *Existentialism: An Introduction* (Cambridge: Polity Press, 2014).

Emilia Angelova is Associate Professor of Philosophy at Concordia University, Montreal. Her research is in Twentieth-Century Continental Philosophy and Kant, including Nineteenth-Century Continental Philosophy. Her recent work has been directed at the study of themes raised by Kant and transformed by Heidegger, interpreting selfhood, temporality, freedom, and the imagination. Her publications include articles in *Idealistic Studies, Symposium, Journal of Contemporary Thought*, and "Hegel and Deleuze on Life, Sense and Limit," in *Hegel and Deleuze* (Evanston: Northwestern University Press); and "Time's Disquiet and Unrest: Affinity Between Heidegger and Levinas," in *Between Heidegger and Levinas* (Albany: State University of New York Press). She is completing a book manuscript on Heidegger's reading of Kant from *Kant and the Problem of Metaphysics* and is the editor of an anthology, *Hegel, Freedom, and History* (Toronto: University of Toronto Press).

Robert Bernasconi is Edwin Erle Sparks Professor of Philosophy at Pennsylvania State University. He is the author of *The Question of Language in Heidegger's History of Being* (Amherst: Humanity Books, 1985), *Heidegger in Question* (Atlantic Highlands: Humanities Press, 1993), and *How to Read Sartre* (New York: W.W. Norton & Co., 2007). In addition to his work on Heidegger and Sartre he has published extensively on Kant, Hegel, Levinas, Derrida, Sartre, Fanon, and numerous topics on the critical philosophy of race. Together with Paul Taylor and Kathryn Gines he is the editor of the journal *Critical Philosophy of Race*.

Peg Birmingham is Professor of Philosophy at DePaul University. She is the author of *Hannah Arendt and Human Rights* (Bloomington: Indiana University Press, 2006) and coeditor (with Philippe van Haute) of *Dissensus Communis: Between Ethics and Politics* (Kampen: Koros, 1995). She has published in journals such as *Research in Phenomenology, Hypatia* and *The Graduate Faculty Philosophy Journal* on topics that include radical evil, human rights, and the temporality of the political. She is currently working on a manuscript tentatively titled "Hannah Arendt and Political Glory: Bearing the Unbearable."

Andrew Bowie is Professor of Philosophy and German at Royal Holloway, University of London. He has published very widely on modern philosophy, music, and literature, and is a jazz saxophonist. His books are *Aesthetics and Subjectivity: From Kant to Nietzsche* (2nd edn Manchester: Manchester University Press, 2003); *Schelling and Modern European Philosophy* (London: Routledge, 2002); Introduction to, edition and translation of *F.W.J. von Schelling: "On the History of Modern Philosophy"* (Cambridge: Cambridge University Press, 1994); *From Romanticism to Critical Theory. The Philosophy of German Literary Theory* (London; New York: Routledge, 1997); Introduction to and Editor of *Manfred Frank: "The Subject and the Text"* (Cambridge: Cambridge University Press, 1997); Introduction to, edition and translation of *F.D.E. Schleiermacher, "Hermeneutics and Criticism" and Other Writings* (Cambridge: Cambridge University Press, 1998); *Introduction to German Philosophy from Kant to Habermas* (Cambridge: Polity Press, 2003); *Music, Philosophy, and Modernity* (Cambridge: Cambridge University Press, 2007); *Philosophical Variations: Music as Philosophical Language* (Malmö: NSU Press, 2010); *The Very Short Introduction to German Philosophy* (Oxford: Oxford University Press, 2010); and *Adorno and the Ends of Philosophy* (Cambridge: Polity Press, 2013).

Lee Braver is Associate Professor of Philosophy at the University of South Florida. He is the author of *A Thing of This World: A History of Continental Anti-Realism* (Evanston: Northwestern University Press, 2007), *Heidegger's Later Writings: A Reader's Guide* (London: Continuum, 2009), and *Groundless Grounds: A Study of Wittgenstein and Heidegger* (Cambridge: MIT Press, 2012), as well as a number of articles and book chapters. He is presently working on two books: *Heidegger: Thinking of Being* and *Unthinkable*.

Scott M. Campbell is Professor and Chair of the Philosophy Department at Nazareth College in Rochester, New York. He has written on issues in education and communication, especially as these relate to the notion of the practical in the early work of Martin Heidegger. He has published *The Early Heidegger's Philosophy of Life* (New York: Fordham University Press, 2012) and a translation of Heidegger's *Basic Problems of Phenomenology* from the Winter Semester of 1919/1920 (London: Continuum, 2012). Together with Paul W. Bruno, he has coedited a volume of essays titled *The Science, Politics, and Ontology of Life-philosophy* (London: Continuum, 2013).

Tina Chanter is the Head of School of Humanities at Kingston University. She is author of *Whose Antigone? The Tragic Marginalization of Slavery* (Albany: SUNY Press, 2011),

The Picture of Abjection: Film Fetish and the Nature of Difference (Bloomington: Indiana University Press, 2008), *Gender* (London: Continuum Press, 2006), *Time, Death and the Feminine: Levinas with Heidegger* (Stanford: Stanford University Press, 2001), *Ethics of Eros: Irigaray's Re-writing of the Philosophers* (London: Routledge, 1995). She is also the editor of *Feminist Interpretations of Emmanuel Levinas* (University Park: Penn State University Press, 2001), and coeditor of *Revolt, Affect, Collectivity: The Unstable Boundaries of Kristeva's Polis* (Albany: SUNY Press, 2005), and of *Sarah Kofman's Corpus* (Albany: SUNY Press, 2008). In addition, she edits the Gender Theory series at SUNY Press. Her current book, forthcoming with Polity Press, is *Art, Politics and Rancière: Seeing Things Anew*.

Daniel O. Dahlstrom is Professor of Philosophy at Boston University. In addition to trans-lating Heidegger's first Marburg lectures, *Introduction to Phenomenological Research* (Bloomington: Indiana University Press, 2005), he is the editor of *Interpreting Heidegger: Critical Essays* (Cambridge: Cambridge University Press, 2011) and the founding editor of *Gatherings*, The Heidegger Circle Annual. His book-length publications on Heidegger include *Heidegger's Conception of Truth* (Cambridge: Cambridge University Press, 2001, 2009) and *The Heidegger Dictionary* (London: Bloomsbury, 2013).

Françoise Dastur is an honorary professor of philosophy and attached to the Husserl Archives of Paris (ENS Ulm). She taught at the University of Paris I (Sorbonne) from 1969 to 1995, at the University of Paris XII (Créteil) from 1995 to 1999, and at the University of Nice–Sophia Antipolis from 1999 to 2003. She is the honorary president of the Ecole Française of Daseinsanalyse, which she founded in 1993. She is the author of several books in French from which three have been translated into English: *Heidegger and the Question of Time* (Amherst: Humanity Books, 1998), *Telling Time, Sketch of a Phenomenological Chronology* (New Brunswick: Athlone Press, 2000), and *Death, An Essay on Finitude* (New Brunswick: Athlone Press, 1996). Her latest publications include *Heidegger. La question du logos* (Paris: Vrin, 2007), *La mort. Essai sur la finitude* (Expanded edition, Paris: PUF, 2007), *Daseinsanalyse. Phénoménologie et psychiatrie*, coauthored with Ph. Cabestan (Paris: Vrin, 2011), and *Heidegger et la pensée à venir* (Paris: Vrin, 2011).

Bret W. Davis is Associate Professor of Philosophy at Loyola University, Maryland. He received his PhD in philosophy from Vanderbilt University and has spent 13 years studying and teaching in Japan, during which time he completed the coursework for a second PhD in Japanese philosophy at Kyoto University. He is the author of *Heidegger and the Will: On the Way to Gelassenheit* (Evanston: Northwestern University Press, 2007), translator of Martin Heidegger's *Country Path Conversations* (Bloomington: Indiana University Press, 2010), editor of *Martin Heidegger: Key Concepts* (Durham: Acumen, 2010), coeditor of *Japanese and Continental Philosophy: Conversations with the Kyoto School* (Bloomington: Indiana University Press, 2011), and coeditor of *Sekai no naka no Nihon no tetsugaku* [Japanese Philosophy in the World] (Kyōto: Showado, 2005). He has also written more than 40 articles in English and in Japanese. Among his current projects are two monographs on Zen and the Kyoto School respectively, and *The Oxford Handbook of Japanese Philosophy*.

Alfred Denker is Director of the Martin-Heidegger-Archive and the Martin-Heidegger-Museum in Messkirch, Baden-Württemberg, Germany. He has edited and coedited numerous anthologies as well as works and letters of Heidegger, including the "Heidegger-Jahrbuch" (Freiburg: Karl Alber, 2004–ongoing) and the "Martin-Heidegger-Briefausgabe" (Freiburg: Karl Alber, 2010–ongoing). His publications also include the recent book *Unterwegs in Sein und Zeit. Einführung in sein Leben und Werk* (Stuttgart: Klett-Cotta, 2011).

Andrew Feenberg is Canada Research Chair in Philosophy of Technology in the School of Communication, Simon Fraser University, Canada, where he directs the Applied Communication and Technology Lab. His books include *Heidegger and Marcuse: The Catastrophe and Redemption of History* (London: Routledge, 2005), *Between Reason and Experience: Essays in Technology and Modernity* (Cambridge: MIT Press, 2010), and a coedited collection titled *The Essential Marcuse* (Boston: Beacon, 2007). A book on Feenberg's philosophy of technology titled *Democratizing Technology* appeared in 2006 with the SUNY Press. *Realizing Philosophy: Marx, Lukács and the Frankfurt School* was published by Verso Press in 2014.

Gregory Fried received his BA from Harvard College and his MA and PhD from the University of Chicago. He is the chair of the Philosophy Department at Suffolk University, and he has taught at the University of Chicago, Boston University, and UCLA. His research has focused on defending the classical Enlightenment tradition against some of its most serious critics, most particularly Martin Heidegger. He is the author of *Heidegger's Polemos: From Being to Politics* (New Haven: Yale University Press, 2000). With Richard Polt, he is also the translator of two of Heidegger's works, *Introduction to Metaphysics* (New Haven: Yale University Press, 2000) and *Being and Truth* (Bloomington: Indiana University Press, 2010); they have a third Heidegger translation that appeared in 2013: *Nature, History, State*. Together with his father, Fried is the author of *Because It Is Wrong: Torture, Privacy and Presidential Power in the Age of Terror* (New York: W.W. Norton & Co., 2010), an exploration of moral, legal, and political questions in the post-9/11 world. Fried is also Director of The Mirror of Race Project (www.mirrorofrace.org), an online, interdisciplinary project exploring the meaning of race in America's history.

Wayne J. Froman teaches philosophy at George Mason University where he served as Department Chair from 1989 to 1999. In 1995–6 he held a Fulbright Research Professorship at the Hegel Archive, Ruhr Universität, Bochum. He has published numerous articles in phenomenology and related topics. He has also edited and coedited a number of volumes, including, most recently, *Merleau-Ponty and the Possibilities of Philosophy: Transforming the Tradition* (Albany: State University of New York Press, 2009). He is currently working on a comparative study of the thought of Franz Rosenzweig with that of Martin Heidegger.

Trish Glazebrook received a PhD in philosophy from the University of Toronto. She has taught at Colgate University, Syracuse University, and Dalhousie University. She is Professor of Philosophy and Director of the School of Politics, Philosophy, and Public Affairs at

Washington State University. She has published *Heidegger's Philosophy of Science* (New York: Fordham University Press, 2000), and edited *Heidegger on Science* (Albany: State University of New York Press, 2012). She is coeditor of a 2012 issue of *Inflexions* on the architecture of Arakawa and Gins, and has published numerous papers in Heidegger studies, ecophenomenology, ancient philosophy, climate ethics, and international development studies. Her current research addresses impacts of climate change on women farmers in Ghana, and governance and policy issues in Ghana's oil industry.

Peter E. Gordon is Amabel B. James Professor of History and Harvard College Professor at Harvard University. A faculty affiliate of the Minda de Gunzburg Center for European Studies, Gordon is also cofounder of the Harvard Colloquium for Intellectual History. His books include: *Rosenzweig and Heidegger: Between Judaism and German Philosophy* (Berkeley: University of California Press, 2003) and *Continental Divide: Heidegger, Cassirer, Davos* (Cambridge: Harvard University Press, 2010). He is coeditor of several books, including: *The Cambridge Companion to Modern Jewish Philosophy* (Cambridge: Cambridge University Press, 2007), *The Modernist Imagination: Critical Theory and Intellectual History Essays in Honor of Martin Jay* (New York: Berghahn Books, 2009), and *Weimar Thought: A Contested Legacy* (Princeton: Princeton University Press, 2013). He is the recipient of numerous fellowships and awards, including the Jacques Barzun Prize from the American Philosophical Society.

Ullrich Haase is Principal Lecturer and Head of Philosophy at the Manchester Metropolitan University. He is also the editor of the Journal of the British Society for Phenomenology. Over the last years his research has been turning around the relation between Heidegger's and Nietzsche's thought in order to open an understanding of the question of modern science in the twenty-first century. He has published various essays on these two authors as well as on Hegel, Merleau-Ponty, Blanchot, and Bataille. In 2008 he published an introduction to the work of Friedrich Nietzsche with Continuum Publishers. His translation of Heidegger's lecture course on Nietzsche's second *Untimely Meditation* (GA 46) will appear with Indiana University Press in 2016.

Kirsten Jacobson is Associate Professor of Philosophy at the University of Maine. Her research interests include the study of spatiality, existential psychology, and, more generally, the philosophical significance and status of the phenomenological method. She has developed novel interpretations of spatial neglect, agoraphobia, hypochondria, and anorexia, and explored the political significance of our spatial inhabitation. Her recent publications include "Embodied Domestics, Embodied Politics: Women, Home, and Agoraphobia" (*Human Studies*, 34(1), 2011), "The Experience of Home and the Space of Citizenship" (*The Southern Journal of Philosophy*, 48(3), 2010), and "A Developed Nature: A Phenomenological Account of the Experience of Home" (*Continental Philosophy Review*, 42, 2009). Currently, she is developing a holistic view of health that is demanded, but not yet provided, by long-standing efforts in phenomenology to overcome the dualism of self and world.

Sean D. Kirkland is Associate Professor in the Department of Philosophy at DePaul University. He works in the areas of ancient Greek philosophy and contemporary continental philosophy. He published a monograph with SUNY Press in 2012 titled *The Ontology of Socratic Questioning in Plato's Early Dialogues* and he is currently finishing his second book, tentatively titled *Aristotle and the Ecstatic Present*, which undertakes a study of temporality in Aristotle's *Physics, Ethics, Politics, Rhetoric, and Poetics*. He has written articles on subjects ranging from Plato and Aristotle to Greek tragedy, from Heidegger's phenomenological thought to Nietzsche's philosophy of history.

Theodore Kisiel is Distinguished Research Professor emeritus of philosophy at Northern Illinois University, author of *The Genesis of Heidegger's Being and Time* (Berkeley: University of California Press, 1993), and coeditor, with Tom Sheehan, of *Becoming Heidegger: On the Trail of his Early Occasional Writings, 1910–1927* (Evanston: Northwestern University Press, 2007), which has been published in a second revised edition as *The New Yearbook for Phenomenology and Phenomenological Philosophy IX* (Seattle: Noesis Press, 2009). He is currently working on a sequel volume titled *The Demise and Destruction of Heidegger's Being and Time*.

Leonard Lawlor is Edwin Erle Sparks Professor of Philosophy at Penn State University. He is the author of seven books: *Early Twentieth Century Continental Philosophy* (Bloomington: Indiana University Press, 2011); *This is not Sufficient: An Essay on Animality in Derrida* (New York: Columbia University Press, 2007); *The Implications of Immanence: Towards a New Concept of Life* (New York: Fordham University Press, 2006); *Thinking Through French Philosophy: The Being of the Question* (Bloomington: Indiana University Press, 2003); *The Challenge of Bergsonism: Phenomenology, Ontology, Ethics* (London: Continuum, 2003); *Derrida and Husserl: The Basic Problem of Phenomenology* (Bloomington: Indiana University Press, 2002); and *Imagination and Chance: The Difference Between the Thought of Ricoeur and Derrida* (Albany: SUNY Press, 1992). He is one of the coeditors and cofounders of *Chiasmi International: Trilingual Studies Concerning the Thought of Merleau-Ponty*. He has translated Merleau-Ponty, Derrida, and Hyppolite into English. He has written dozens of articles on Derrida, Foucault, Deleuze, Bergson, and Merleau-Ponty. He is currently working on two books: *Is it Happening?* (for Edinburgh University Press), and (coauthored with Vernon Cisney) a *Guide to Derrida's Voice and Phenomenon* (for Edinburgh University Press).

Leslie MacAvoy is Associate Professor of Philosophy and Chair of the Department of Philosophy and Humanities at East Tennessee State University. She works on issues pertaining to phenomenological conceptions of subjectivity and meaning. Her essays include "On the Unity of Intelligibility in Heidegger: Against Distinguishing the Practical and the Discursive," *Philosophy Today* 55 (2011); "Meaning, Categories, and Subjectivity in the Early Heidegger," *Philosophy and Social Criticism* 31(1) (2005); "The Other Side of Intentionality," in *Addressing Levinas. Ethics, Phenomenology and the Judaic Tradition*, eds Eric Nelson, Antje Kapust, and Kent Still (Evanston, IL: Northwestern University Press, 2005); "Thinking through Singularity and Universality in Levinas," *Philosophy Today* 47(5) (2003), and "Overturning Cartesianism and the Hermeneutics of Suspicion: Rethinking Dreyfus on Heidegger," *Inquiry* 44(4) (December 2001). She is currently doing research on the concept of meaning and its relationship to temporality in the phenomenological work of Husserl, Heidegger, and Levinas.

John McCumber is Professor of Germanic Languages at UCLA. His PhD is in Philosophy and Greek from the University of Toronto, and he has taught in philosophy departments there and at the University of Michigan-Dearborn, the Graduate Faculty of the New School for Social Research, Northwestern University, UCLA, and John Carroll University. He has also taught in the German Departments of Northwestern University and UCLA and in the Classics and Political Science Departments at UCLA. He is the author of many books and articles on the history of philosophy, including most recently *Time and Philosophy: A History of Continental Thought* (Durham: Acumen, 2011) and *On Philosophy: Notes from a Crisis* (Stanford: Stanford University Press, 2013). He is currently preparing a book on American philosophy in the early Cold War.

Iain Macdonald is *professeur agrégé* (Associate Professor) in the Department of Philosophy, Université de Montréal, and president of the Canadian Society for Continental Philosophy. He is the author of many articles in English and French on Hegel, Adorno, Heidegger, Nietzsche, Terrence Malick, and Paul Celan, among others—in the areas of metaphysics, epistemology, and aesthetics. He is coeditor of *Adorno and Heidegger: Philosophical Questions* (Stanford: Stanford University Press, 2008) and of *Les normes et le possible: héritage et perspectives de l'École de Francfort* (Éditions de la maison des sciences de l'homme, 2013). His current work deals with the relation of possibility to actuality, especially in Hegel, Marx, Critical Theory, and Heidegger.

William McNeill is Professor of Philosophy at DePaul University in Chicago. He is author of *The Glance of the Eye: Heidegger, Aristotle, and the Ends of Theory* (Albany: SUNY Press, 1999) and *The Time of Life: Heidegger and Ēthos* (Albany: SUNY Press, 2006). He has translated or cotranslated a number of Heidegger's works, including (with Julia Davis) the lectures on *Hölderlin's Hymn "The Ister"* (Bloomington: Indiana University Press, 1996) and (with Julia Ireland) Heidegger's first Hölderlin lecture course, *Hölderlin's Hymns "Germania" and "The Rhine"* (Bloomington: Indiana University Press, 2014).

Andrew J. Mitchell is Associate Professor at Emory University where he specializes in nineteenth- and twentieth-century continental philosophy and the philosophy of literature. He is the author of *Heidegger Among the Sculptors: Body, Space, and the Art of Dwelling* (Stanford: Stanford University Press, 2010) and *The Fourfold: Reading the Late Heidegger* (Evanston: Northwestern University Press, 2015), translator of Martin Heidegger's *Bremen and Freiburg Lectures* (Bloomington: Indiana University Press, 2012), and coeditor with Sam Slote of *Derrida and Joyce: Texts and Contexts* (Albany: SUNY Press, 2013).

Dermot Moran holds the Professorship of Philosophy (Metaphysics & Logic) at University College Dublin and is a Member of the Royal Irish Academy. Prof. Moran has published widely on medieval philosophy (especially Christian Neoplatonism) and contemporary European philosophy (especially phenomenology). His books include: *The Philosophy of John Scottus Eriugena* (Cambridge: Cambridge University Press, 1989; reissued 2004), *Introduction to Phenomenology* (Routledge, 2000), *Edmund Husserl. Founder of Phenomenology* (Cambridge & Malden, MA: Polity, 2005), *Husserl's Crisis of the European Sciences: An Introduction* (Cambridge: Cambridge University Press, 2012), and, coauthored with Joseph Cohen, *The Husserl Dictionary* (London: Continuum, 2012). He has edited *Husserl's Logical Investigations*, 2 vols. (London: Routledge, 2001), *The Shorter Logical Investigations*, *The Phenomenology Reader*, coedited with Tim Mooney (London: Routledge, 2002), *Phenomenology. Critical Concepts in Philosophy*, 5 Volumes, coedited with Lester E. Embree (London: Routledge, 2004), *Eriugena, Berkeley and the Idealist Tradition*, coedited with Stephen Gersh (South Bend: University of Notre Dame Press, 2006), and *The Routledge Companion to Twentieth Century Philosophy* (London: Routledge, 2008). Professor Moran is Founding Editor of *The International Journal of Philosophical Studies*.

Eric S. Nelson is Associate Professor of Philosophy at the Hong Kong University of Science and Technology. He is interested in the encounter, interaction, and conflict among different forms of life, systems of practice and belief, and styles of thought. His areas of research include hermeneutics, ethics, and the philosophy of culture, nature, and religion. He has published over 60 articles and book chapters on European and Asian philosophy, including many on Heidegger. He is the coeditor, with François Raffoul, of *Rethinking Facticity* (Albany: SUNY Press, 2008); with John Drabinski, of *Between Levinas and Heidegger* (Albany: SUNY Press, 2015); with G. D'Anna and H. Johach, of *Anthropologie und Geschichte. Studien zu Wilhelm Dilthey aus Anlass seines 100. Todestages* (Würzburg: Königshausen & Neumann, 2013); and, with Antje Kapust and Kent Still, of *Addressing Levinas* (Evanston: Northwestern University Press, 2005). His monograph *Chinese and Buddhist Philosophy in early Twentieth-Century German Thought* is forthcoming with Bloomsbury Academic.

Anne O'Byrne is Associate Professor of Philosophy at Stony Brook University. Her work is in political philosophy and ontology, and engages a number of thinkers in the twentieth century and contemporary continental philosophy—Heidegger, Arendt, Dilthey, Derrida, and Jean-Luc Nancy—on a range of issues—identity, natality, embodiment, education, history, gender, and genocide. Publications include *Natality and Finitude* (Bloomington: Indiana University Press, 2010), a variety of articles, and translations of Nancy's *Being Singular Plural* (translated with Robert Richardson, Stanford: Stanford University Press, 1996) and *Corpus II* (New York: Fordham University Press, 2013).

Richard Polt is Professor of Philosophy at Xavier University in Cincinnati. He is the author of *Heidegger: An Introduction* (Ithaca: Cornell University Press, 1999) and *The Emergency of Being: On Heidegger's "Contributions to Philosophy"* (Ithaca: Cornell University Press, 1999). With Gregory Fried, he has translated Heidegger's Introduction to Metaphysics (New

Haven: Yale University Press, 2000) and Being and Truth (Bloomington: Indiana University Press, 2010), and edited A Companion to Heidegger's *"Introduction to Metaphysics"* (New Haven: Yale University Press, 2001). Fried and Polt have also translated Heidegger's 1933–4 seminar "On the Essence and Concept of Nature, History, and State," which was published together with essays about the text by several scholars (Bloomsbury, 2013).

François Raffoul is Professor of Philosophy at Louisiana State University. He is the author of *Heidegger and the Subject* (Amherst: Prometheus Books, 1999), *A Chaque fois Mien* (Paris: Galilée, 2004), and *The Origins of Responsibility* (Bloomington: Indiana University Press, 2010). He is the coeditor of several volumes, *Disseminating Lacan* (Albany: SUNY Press, 1996), *Heidegger and Practical Philosophy* (Albany: SUNY Press, 2002), *Rethinking Facticity* (Albany: SUNY Press, 2008), and *French Interpretations of Heidegger* (Albany: SUNY Press, 2008). Author of more than 45 articles, he has also cotranslated several French philosophers, in particular Jean-Luc Nancy, *The Title of the Letter* (Albany: SUNY Press, 1992), *The Gravity of Thought* (Albany: SUNY Press, 1998), *The Creation of the World or Globalization* (Albany: SUNY Press, 2007), and *Identity* (New York: Fordham University Press, 2014). His co-translation of Dominique Janicaud's *Heidegger in France* appeared with Indiana University Press in 2015. He is the coeditor of a book series titled *Contemporary French Thought* (Albany: SUNY Press, ongoing). He is currently preparing a monograph on the question of the event in contemporary philosophy.

Hans Ruin is Professor in Philosophy at Södertörn University. He has published approximately 40 articles and chapters in peer-reviewed journals and books, mainly on Heidegger, phenomenology, and hermeneutics. Monographs include: *Enigmatic Origins. Tracing the Theme of Historicity through Heidegger´s Works* (Stockholm: Almqvist & Wiksell, 1994), *Herakleitos Fragment* (Lund: Propexus, 1997), *Inledning till Heideggers Varat och tiden* (2006), and *Frihet, ändlighet, historicitet. Essäer om Heidegger filosofi* (2012). Edited books include: *Fenomenologiska Perspektiv* (with A. Orlowski, Stockholm: Thales, 1997), *Metaphysics, Facticity, Interpretation. Phenomenology in the Nordic Countries* (with D. Zahavi och S. Heinämaa, Dordrecht: Kluwer Academic Publishers, 2003), *The Past's Presence* (with Marcia Cavalcante, Huddinge: Södertörns högskola, 2006), *Phenomenology and Religion: New Frontiers* (with Jonna Bornemark, Huddinge: Södertörn University, 2010), *Rethinking Time. History, Memory and Representation* (with Andrus Ers, Huddinge: Södertörns högskola, 2011), *Fenomenologi, Teknik och Medialitet* (with Leif Dahlberg, Huddinge: Södertörns högskola, 2011), *Ambiguity of the Sacred. Phenomenology, Aesthetics, Politics* (with Jonna Bornemark, Stockholm: Södertörns högskola, 2011). He translated into Swedish Derrida's *The Origin of Geometry and Schibboleth for Paul Celan* (with Aris Fioretos Stockholm: Symposion, 1990), and the Heraclitean fragments from Greek (with Håkan Rehnberg, Lund: Propexus, 1997).

John Russon is Professor of Philosophy at the University of Guelph. He is the author of three original works in the tradition of existential phenomenology: *Human Experience: Philosophy, Neurosis, and the Elements of Everyday Life* (Albany: SUNY Press, 2003), *Bearing Witness* to *Epiphany: Persons, Things, and the Nature of Erotic Life* (Albany: SUNY Press, 2009), and *Sites of Exposure: A Philosophical Essay on Politics, Art, and the Nature of Experience* (Bloomington: Indiana University Press, forthcoming). He is also the author of three books on Hegel: *The Self and Its Body in Hegel's Phenomenology* (Toronto: University of Toronto Press, 1997), *Reading Hegel's Phenomenology* (Bloomington: Indiana University Press, 2009), and *Infinite Phenomenology: The Lessons of Hegel's Science of Experience* (Evanston: Northwestern University Press, 2015). He is currently at work on a book titled *Adult Life*.

Frank Schalow is University Research Professor at the University of New Orleans. He has published numerous books, including *Departures: At the Crossroads between Heidegger and Kant* (Berlin: Walter de Gruyter, 2013), *The Incarnality of Being: The Earth, Animals and the Body in Heidegger's Thought* (Albany: SUNY Press, 2006), *Heidegger and the Quest for the Sacred: From Thought to the Sanctuary of Faith* (Dordrecht: Kluwer Academic Publishers, 2001), *The Renewal of the Heidegger-Kant Dialogue* (Albany: SUNY Press, 1992), along with the edited volume *Heidegger, Translation, and the Task of Thinking: Essays in Honor of Parvis Emad* (Dordrecht: Springer, 2011). Currently, he is coeditor of the international journal *Heidegger Studies*.

Dennis J. Schmidt is Research Professor at Western Sydney University. He has been a visiting professor of Classics and Philosophy at the Universität Freiburg (Germany) and a visiting professor of the humanities at the Universitá Roma (La Sapienza). Recently he authored *Idiome der Wahrheit* (Frankfurt am Main: Klostermann Verlag, 2014), *Between Word and Image* (Bloomington: Indiana University Press, 2012), *Lyrical and Ethical Subjects* (Albany: SUNY Press, 2005), *On Germans and Other Greeks* (Bloomington: Indiana University Press, 2001). He publishes in the areas of Ancient Greek philosophy and tragedy, aesthetics, German Idealism and Romanticism, and Contemporary Continental Philosophy.

Gregory Schufreider is Professor of Philosophy at Louisiana State University, where he was the founding director of the Program for the Study of the Audio-Visual Arts. His publications on Heidegger include: "Art and the Problem of Truth" (*Man and World*, 13(1), 1980); "Heidegger on Community" (*Man and World*, 14(1), 1981); "Heidegger's Contribution to a Phenomenology of Culture" (*JBSP*, 17(2), 1986); "Heidegger's Hole: The Space of Thinking" (*Research in Phenomenology*, 31(1), 2001); "Sticking Heidegger with a Stela: Lacoue-Labarthe, Art and Philosophy" (in *French Receptions of Heidegger*, Albany: SUNY Press, 2008); "Re:Thinking Facticity" (in *Rethinking Facticity*, Albany: SUNY Press, 2008) as well as "The Art of Truth" (*Research in Phenomenology*, 40(3), 2010). He is currently completing a two-volume study of Heidegger and Mondrian.

Andrea Janae Sholtz is Assistant Professor of Philosophy at Alvernia University in Reading, Pennsylvania. She completed her PhD in philosophy at University of Memphis and her MA in philosophy at New School for Social Research. She researches primarily in Nineteenth- and Twentieth-Century Continental Philosophy, Feminism, and Philosophy of Art. Dr. Sholtz is writing a book titled *The Invention of A People Art and the Political in Heidegger and*

Deleuze on the intersections between ontology, art, and the political in Martin Heidegger and Gilles Deleuze, situating this discussion in the larger context of contemporary philosophical conversation concerning community. She is a coauthor of "What is Philosophy for Deleuze and Foucault?" (with Leonard Lawlor) to be published in *Between Deleuze and Foucault* and published "Reflections on Continental and Feminist Pedagogy: Heidegger and Anzaldua" in *PhiloSOPHIA: A Journal of Continental Feminism*, 2(1), 2012.

Thomas Sheehan is Professor of Religious Studies and, by courtesy, Philosophy and German at Stanford University and Professor Emeritus of Philosophy at Loyola University Chicago. He is the author of *The First Coming: How the Kingdom of God Became Christianity* (New York: Random House, 1986), *Karl Rahner: The Philosophical Foundations* (Athens: Ohio University Press, 1987) and the editor and translator of *Martin Heidegger, Logic: The Question of Truth* (Bloomington: Indiana University Press, 2010), *Becoming Heidegger: On the Trail of his Early Occasional Writings, 1910–1927* (Evanston: Northwestern University Press, 2011), *Edmund Husserl, Psychological and Transcendental Phenomenology, and the Confrontation with Heidegger* (Dordrecht: Kluwer Academic Publishers, 1997), and *Heidegger, the Man and the Thinker* (Chicago: Precedent, 1981), as well as the author and translator of numerous works on Heidegger. He recently published *Making Sense of Heidegger: A Paradigm Shift* (New York: Rowman & Littlefield, 2014).

P. Christopher Smith is Professor Emeritus of Philosophy at the University of Massachusetts, Lowell. He has translated numerous books of Hans-Georg Gadamer and is the author of *Hermeneutics and Human Finitude: Toward a Theory of Ethical Understanding* (New York: Fordham University Press, 1991) and *The Hermeneutics of Original Argument: Demonstration, Dialectic, Rhetoric* (Evanston: Northwestern University Press, 1998).

Jill Stauffer is Associate Professor of Philosophy and Director of the Concentration in Peace, Justice and Human Rights at Haverford College. Her edited volume (with Bettina Bergo), *Nietzsche and Levinas: After the Death of a Certain God*, was published by Columbia University Press in 2009. She has published articles in journals such as *Law, Culture and the Humanities, Theory and Event, Humanity,* and *Australian Feminist Law Journal*. She recently published a book titled *Ethical Loneliness: The Injustice of Not Being Heard* (New York: Columbia University Press, 2015).

Robert D. Stolorow is a founding faculty member at the Institute of Contemporary Psychoanalysis, Los Angeles, and at the Institute for the Psychoanalytic Study of Subjectivity, New York. Absorbed for more than three decades in the project of rethinking psychoanalysis as a form of phenomenological inquiry, he is the author of *World, Affectivity, Trauma: Heidegger and Post-Cartesian Psychoanalysis* (London: Routledge, 2011) and *Trauma and Human Existence: Autobiographical, Psychoanalytic, and Philosophical Reflections* (London: Routledge, 2007) and coauthor of eight other books. He received his PhD in Clinical Psychology from Harvard in 1970 and his PhD in Philosophy from the University of California at Riverside in 2007.

Iain Thomson is Professor of Philosophy at the University of New Mexico. He is the author of two books: *Heidegger on Ontotheology: Technology and the Politics of Education* (Cambridge: Cambridge University Press, 2005) and *Heidegger, Art, and Postmodernity* (Cambridge: Cambridge University Press, 2011), as well as dozens of articles in philosophical journals, essay collections, and reference works. A recipient of the Gunter Starkey Award for Teaching Excellence, Thomson is well-known for his ability to bring Heidegger's difficult ideas to life for contemporary readers. He is currently working on a philosophical biography of Heidegger as well as on a book on the philosophical influence of Heidegger's understanding of death.

Peter Trawny studied Philosophy, Musicology, and History of Art in Bochum, Freiburg, Basel, and Wuppertal. He taught at universities in Shanghai, Vienna, and Stockholm. Today he teaches at the Bergische Universität Wuppertal, where he is also the director of the Martin-Heidegger-Institut. He is an editor of several volumes of the *Martin-Heidegger-Gesamtausgabe*. His latest publications include *Adyton. Heideggers esoterische Philosophie* (Berlin: Matthes & Seitz, 2010); *Medium und Revolution* (Berlin: Matthes & Seitz, 2011); *Ins Wasser geschrieben. Versuche über die Intimität* (Berlin: Matthes & Seitz, 2013); *Irrnisfuge* (Berlin: Matthes & Seitz, 2014); and *Technik—Kapital—Medium* (Berlin: Matthes & Seitz, 2015).

Alejandro A. Vallega is Associate Professor of Philosophy at the University of Oregon. He is the author of *Heidegger and the Issue of Space: Thinking On Exilic Grounds* (American and Continental Philosophy Series, University Park: Pennsylvania State University Press, 2003) and of *Sense and Finitude: Encounters at the Limits of Art, Language, and the Political* (Contemporary Continental Philosophy Series, Albany: SUNY Press, 2009). He is head editor for the Latin America of the World Philosophies Series published by Indiana University Press. His work focuses on aesthetics, Latin American philosophy, decolonial thought, and Continental philosophy.

Daniela Vallega-Neu is Associate Professor at the University of Oregon. Among her book publications are *Heidegger's Contributions to Philosophy: An Introduction* (Bloomington: Indiana University Press, 2004) and *The Bodily Dimension in Thinking* (Albany: SUNY Press, 2005). She translated (together with) Martin Heidegger's *Contributions to Philosophy: Of the Event* (Bloomington: Indiana University Press, 2011) and coedited (with Charles E. Scott, Susan Schoenbohm, and Alejandro Vallega) *A Companion to Heidegger's Contributions to Philosophy* (Bloomington: Indiana University Press, 2001). Her current research includes a book project on Heidegger's "poietic writings" from 1936 to 1942, as well as investigations on embodiment and time.

Ben Vedder studied Theology in Utrecht and Philosophy in Leuven. He wrote his dissertation on Heidegger and Scheler. He was university teacher in Amsterdam and had a special chair for philosophy at Wageningen University. He was full professor for Systematic Philosophy at Tilburg University and, from 2002 onward he serves as Professor of Metaphysics and Philosophy of Religion at Radboud University Nijmegen. He published, among others,

Was ist Hermeneutik? Ein Weg von der Textdeutung zur Interpretation der Wirklichkeit
(What is Hermeneutics? From Interpretation of Texts to Interpretation of Being, Stuttgart:
Kohlhammer, 2000), *De voorlopigheid van het denken, Over Heideggers hermeneutisering van de filosofie* (The Provisionality of Thinking, Dudley: Peeters Leuven, 2004), and
Heidegger's Philosophy of Religion, From God to the Gods (Pittsburgh: Duquesne University
Press, 2007). At present he works on Paul in contemporary philosophy together with other
colleagues, and is preparing a book on hermeneutics and religion.

Holger Zaborowski is professor of philosophy and philosophical ethics at the
Philosophisch-Theologische Hochschule Vallendar in Germany. He has edited several volumes on Heidegger and is the author of *Wie machbar ist der Mensch?* (Mainz: Matthias-
Grünewald-Verlag, 2003), *Spielraume der Freiheit: Zur Hermeneutik des Menschseins*
(Freiburg: Alber, 2009), *Robert Spaemann's Philosophy of the Human Person: Nature,
Freedom, and the Critique of Modernity* (Oxford: Oxford University Press, 2010), and *Eine
Frage von Irre und Schuld?: Martin Heidegger und der Nationalsozialismus* (Frankfurt am
Main: Fischer Taschenbuch Verlag, 2010).

EDITORS' INTRODUCTION
François Raffoul and Eric S. Nelson

I

The Bloomsbury Companion to Heidegger provides succinct and lucid essays introducing the thinking of Martin Heidegger (September 26, 1889–May 26, 1976), one of the twentieth century's most striking, innovative, and controversial philosophers. Heidegger's groundbreaking works have had a notable impact on twentieth- and twenty-first-century thought through their extensive reception, appropriation, critique, and polemical rejection and condemnation. Heidegger's impact can be traced in the responses of philosophers as diverse as Adorno, Arendt, Deleuze, Derrida, Foucault, Gadamer, Levinas, Merleau-Ponty, Rorty, and Sartre, among others.

In addition to Heidegger's formative role in intellectual movements such as phenomenology, hermeneutics, existentialism, structuralism and post-structuralism, deconstruction and postmodernism, he has had a transformative effect on diverse areas of inquiry such as political theory and historiography, cultural studies and literary criticism, architecture and art theory, theology and religious studies, gender theory and feminism, and technology and environmental studies.

It is the ambition of this volume to offer a definitive reference guide to Heidegger's path and thought by presenting 59 original essays written for this volume by an international group of prominent Heidegger scholars. This collection offers a detailed, extensive, and comprehensive resource for introductory and more advanced audiences to explore and further reflect on Heidegger's thought, key writings, themes and topics, and reception and influence.

II

Heidegger was born on September 26, 1889 in the small, provincial, conservative village of Meßkirch. The young Heidegger's initial intellectual development was shaped by the rhythms and rituals of everyday rural Catholic life and informed by his religious and theological studies. After initially focusing on theology, Heidegger studied philosophy and worked with the neo-Kantian philosopher Heinrich Rickert and the phenomenologist Edmund Husserl. Heidegger narrates later in life how his philosophical journey began with the question of being posed in Brentano

1

and Aristotle, a question to which he would repeatedly return. Despite his early interests in Catholic scholasticism, his philosophical training was in the modern epistemological traditions of German academic philosophy, and his habilitation work on the philosophy of Duns Scotus (1915) reflects the intersection of both.

During the First World War, and increasingly as it came to an end, Heidegger was inspired not only by Husserl's phenomenological method but by the existential and life-philosophical crises and tendencies of his time. Unlike his teachers Rickert and Husserl, who wrote polemically of these trends in this period, the early Heidegger attempted to make life-philosophy philosophical while at the same articulating philosophy immanently from out of life. In contrast with prevalent popular or vulgar conceptions of life-philosophy, the early Heidegger focused on the temporal event character of life (the *es ereignet sich* of 1919 in GA 56/57, 73–5) and increasingly the hermeneutical situation and historical intersection of meaning and life. Under Dilthey's influence, among others, "life" is understood as fundamentally historical and interpretive rather than as biological life (whether mechanistically or vitalistically understood) or as intuitively self-transparent life.

Heidegger perceived the philosophical significance of a life-philosophy that had failed to think through the issue of life radically enough. This insight was unfolded in Heidegger's developing project of a "hermeneutics of factical life," which foreshadowed many of the concerns and strategies of *Being and Time*.[1] The task is to articulate life in its questionability even more primordially than life-philosophy itself could (GA 60, 50). This radicalization of life surpasses even Dilthey, who inspired the task of articulating

life—and the historical, immanent, and already meaningful "categories of life"—from out of life itself, by realizing Husserl's demand of returning to the things themselves and phenomenologically allowing each phenomenon to show itself from itself.

In this context, Heidegger formulated two objections to "life-philosophy" that would motivate the modification of his thinking through a sustained engagement with the philosophical tradition, in particular Aristotle and Kant, in the mid-1920s. First, existential and life-philosophy is absorbed in the life that it should clarify. Second, life-philosophy was insufficient to address life's basic disquiet (*Unruhe*, GA 60, 30–54), that is, the inner tendencies of life toward its own self-ruination (GA 61, 2). Life is encountered not only in the intuitive self-certainty and egotistical security of the vulgar life-philosopher but as dispersed and ruinated (103). "Care" (*Sorge*) emerges as a defining practical—as care for one's "daily bread" (90)—and communicative—as a "vox media" (GA 62, 357)—lived category enacted in human existence.

In the lectures-courses of the mid-1920s and *Being and Time*, Heidegger developed an "analytic of Dasein" in which Dasein ("being-there") was defined as the site of an understanding of being (*Seinsverständnis*). This attention to the entity that we are led some—notably Husserl—to accuse Heidegger of developing a philosophical anthropology and falling back into subjectivist metaphysics. Heidegger recognized this possibility when, evoking the interruption of the "path" opened by *Sein und Zeit*, he later admitted: "The reason for the disruption is that the attempt and the path it chose confront the danger of unwillingly becoming merely another entrenchment of subjectivity" (GA 6.2, 194/N III, 141). In the same passage, Heidegger explained that far from subjectivism or anthropology, *Being and Time* was an ontological questioning of the human being, who was interrogated solely in terms of its *being*; that is to say, in terms of being itself. This interrogation occurs on the basis of the question concerning the truth of being itself, as "an attempt is made to determine the essence of the human being solely in terms of his relationship to Being (*aus seinem Bezug zum Sein*). That essence was described in a firmly delineated sense as *Da-sein*" (ibid.). The term Dasein is hyphenated as Da-sein in order to stress this sheer relatedness to being.

The understanding of being is not one property of humans among others, but it is that which defines the human being. This is why such understanding is *not* a "human" determination, but a *characteristic of being*. The "privilege" of Dasein is not ontic or anthropological, but ultimately *ontological*: "*Understanding of being is itself a determination of being of Dasein [Seinsverständnis is selbst eine Seinsbestimmtheit des Daseins*]. The ontic distinction of Dasein lies in the fact that it *is* ontological" (SZ, 12/BT, 11). Humans are thus made possible by the understanding of being and not the inverse: "*Accordingly, the understanding of being is the ground of the possibility of the essence of the human being*" (GA 31, 125/EHF, 87, modified). To this extent, the understanding of being is not posited by us, much less by consciousness or the subject, but is an event in which we find ourselves among and in the midst of other beings.

Therein lies the turn from a thinking centered in Dasein's openness to being to a thinking that meditates on the openness of being to Dasein:

The thinking that proceeds from *Being and Time*, in that it gives up the word "meaning of being" in favor of "truth of being," henceforth emphasizes the openness of being itself, rather than the openness of Dasein in regard to this openness of being. This signifies "the turn," in which thinking always more decisively turns to being as being. (FS, 41)

In the later stage of his corpus, Heidegger's thinking turned toward the truth of being as such (and no longer beingness), as it moved from a thematic of the understanding of being to that of a happening of being. This opened the way to new directions in his work, which focused more on the various modes of givenness of being in its happening, in its historical "sendings" and "epochs." This led Heidegger, in a *Seynsgeschichtliche Denken* or "beyng-historical thinking," to stress the historicality of being itself, understood as "history of being."

In this situation, Heidegger carried out a project of overcoming metaphysics in dialogue with Nietzsche, returned to the Greek dawn of philosophy, and engaged in a dialogue with Hölderlin and other poets. In that historical meditation on the destiny of the West (and its confrontation with the East, explored by Bret Davis in this volume), Heidegger was able to further develop the thematization of technology, of nihilism and the *Gestell*, of the "end of philosophy" and of the possibility of an other beginning. As Richard Polt reminds us, in contrast with the "first beginning" of Western thought, which asks: what are beings? the "other beginning" would ask: "How does beyng occur essentially? [*Wie west das Seyn?*]" (GA 65, 75, 7/ CP2, 60, 8).

The thinking of being, from the Dasein-centered analyses of *Being and Time* to the happening of being as such, led Heidegger to a further reflection on the very event of givenness of being, or *Ereignis*. This

3

reflection (*Besinnung*) on the event (*Ereignis*) of being (*Sein*) that emerged in the 1930s, as well as his support of National Socialism and its disastrous consequences, informs his later lectures and writings on topics that encompass architecture and art, animals and humanism, the body and psychology, language and listening, letting, releasement (*Gelassenheit*) and the thing, the poetic word and technology, space and sense of place, among others.

In Heidegger's later work, the emphasis shifts from a questioning of being to one that gestures toward the dimension from which being is given; that is, the event of givenness of being, or *Ereignis*. That focus on the "*es gibt*" of being led Heidegger to rethink the meaning of being as "letting" (FS, 59). Beginning from a reflection on the sense of *Ereignis* as an event of the givenness of presence, Heidegger states that it "is a matter here of understanding that the deepest meaning of being is *letting* [lassen]" (ibid.). Being is not the horizon of beings, nor the "there is" of beings. Rather, being means now: letting the being be (*Das Seiende sein-lassen*). This letting is not a cause, for causality still depends on the logic of beings and their "sufficient" grounding. It is also not a "doing," which draws from the philosophy of the acting subject. Letting is to be thought instead in the context of "giving." The giving here in question should not refer primarily to a present being, or even to the *presence* of beings. The "giving" should be separated from presence itself; for the issue is to give thought to the "*es gibt*," to giving, from an interpretation of "letting" itself. The "*es gibt*" is then the gift of a giving as such, a giving that withdraws in the very movement of its event: it lets being (*Es läßt Sein*). In this sense, releasement (*Gelassenheit*) is engaged from the question of *Ereignis*.

Heidegger makes the important point that being is to be thought from *Ereignis*, that in fact "Being is appropriated through the appropriative event [*Sein ist durch das Ereignis ereignet*]" (60, modified). We read a few lines further: "The appropriative event appropriates being [*das Ereignis ereignet das Sein*]." One of the most important contributions of Heidegger's later work is the way in which he distinguishes between *Ereignis* and being, showing how *Ereignis* exceeds being and its economy. In *On Time and Being*, Heidegger went so far as to state, in a provocative and enigmatic saying, that "Being vanishes in *Ereignis* (*Sein verschwindet im Ereignis*)" (GA 14, 27/TB, 22). One should thus not think *Ereignis* with the help of the concepts of being or of the history of being. *Ereignis* is said to exceed the ontological horizon, as it exceeds the Greek "sending" in the history of being. It appears then that Heidegger's thought is not contained within the horizon of ontology nor limited to the thought of being. Heidegger in fact explains that his thinking of the ontological difference—especially in the period from 1927 to 1936, which is taken to be the crux of this work—was a "necessary impasse" (*Holzweg*) (FS, 61).

Furthermore, there is no destinal epoch of *Ereignis*. *Ereignis* is *not* an epoch of being, and nor is it the end of the history of being, in the sense in which the history of being would have "reached its end." Rather, the history of being is able to appear *as* history of being from *Ereignis*. In fact, the historical sendings of being are to be thought *from Ereignis*. "Sending is from the appropriative event [*Das Schicken ist aus dem Ereignen*]" (ibid.). Heidegger's own summations of his path of thought shift us from the early focus on the "meaning of being" all the way to his late notion of a "topology of being" and "tautological thinking." Heidegger also characterized his final thinking as a "phenomenology of the inapparent" [*Phänomenologie des Unscheinbaren*] (80).

III

PART I: LIFE AND CONTEXTS

This volume encompasses 5 parts viz. an extensive list of entries on Heidegger's life and contexts (7 essays), his sources, influences, encounters, and students (13 essays), his key writings (10 essays), themes and topics (15 essays), and his impact on philosophical movements and major contemporary continental thinkers in "Reception and Influence" (13 essays).

The seven essays in the first part, *Life and Contexts*, examine Heidegger's thought with respect to the conditions of his life, the trajectory of his work, and his career as a whole, including his involvement with National-Socialist politics. As Theodore Kisiel reminds us in "Heidegger and the Question of Biography," Heidegger was skeptical of biographies when it came to the work of thought. He notably declared in an early lecture course, when introducing Aristotle, "As for the personality of a philosopher, our only interest is that he was born at a certain time, that he worked, and that he died. The character of the philosopher, and issues of that sort, will not be addressed here" (GA18, 5/BCAR, 4). However, what is salient is the history, trajectory, and—in a sense—the "biography" of the thinking itself; in other words, it is the story and history "of Heidegger's philosophical development within his particular historical and hermeneutical context" that is the task of the first part to articulate.

The part is structured according to the defining periods of Heidegger's intellectual life. It begins with Kisiel's reconsideration of the very notion of biography itself in terms of Heidegger's approach to the hermeneutic character of life in its facticity; that is, the fact that life interprets itself, explicates itself, and articulates itself; that is, that it has a hermeneutic structure. In turn, the work of sense ultimately refers to factical life: "The very idea of facticity implies that only *authentic and proper* [*eigentliche*] facticity—understood in the literal sense of the word: one's *own* [*eigene*] facticity—that is, the facticity of one's own time and generation, is the genuine object of research" (GA 62, 366/BH, 167). In this sense, thinking leads us back to life—to "bio-graphy," understood as the concrete and hermeneutic existing of human Dasein.

Dermot Moran concentrates on Heidegger's Freiburg and Marburg lecture courses to *Being and Time*. Claiming that Heidegger's development was not as "monolithic" as presented by Heidegger retrospectively, Moran unmasks a number of myths concerning that period, myths presumably entertained by Heidegger himself (for instance, Moran stresses that the question of being was not central in these early writings, and that Heidegger was instead occupied with factical life and the nature of philosophy, as well as noting that Heidegger was never a *student* of Husserl). Moran shows that in addition to a critique of the primacy of theoretical knowledge—"the primacy of the theoretical" (*Primat des Theoretischen*, GA 56/57, 87/ TDP, 73), the analysis of such factical life led Heidegger to understand it as a hermeneutic notion comprising a world and a self. In such a widening, "Heidegger is envisaging that phenomenology must incorporate a new and expanded kind of intuition—'hermeneutic intuition'" (*die hermeneutische Intuition*, GA 56/57, 117/TDP, 98). Moran identifies Heidegger's writings on the phenomenology of religious life as prefiguring the themes of his existential analytic. Indeed, the notion of a phenomenological destruction (*Destruktion*) originates in the early project of a destruction of the "metaphysical edifice encrusted on religious experience." Following the Marburg years with its interpretations of Aristotle and Kant, among others, the road is paved for the appearance of Heidegger's magnum opus, *Being and Time*, in 1927.

Thomas Sheehan's essay focuses on the scope and significance of the turn (*die Kehre*) in Heidegger's work. Beginning with the claim that "Heidegger's main topic was not 'being,'" but initially meaning or significance understood as "the *significance to us* of whatever we meet in the world," Sheehan points out that not even significance was Heidegger's key concern. Rather, "Heidegger's ultimate purpose was . . . to move beyond such meaningfulness to the '*X*' *that makes it possible*." Sheehan contends that the turn includes at least three distinct but interrelated senses: the first, and primary, sense of the turn refers to what Heidegger calls the *reciprocity* (*Gegenschwung*) between human existence (*Dasein*) and the clearing: "Without human being, there is no clearing, and without the clearing, there is no human being." The second sense of the turn, usually taken—mistakenly, according to Sheehan—by Heideggerians as its proper signification, is the shift that occurs from the 1930s, from the earlier question on meaningfulness to the question of the provenance of such meaningfulness. The third sense of the turn is the conversion, or transformation, of the self-understanding of human Dasein, known in the Heideggerian lexicon as *resolve* (*Entschlossenheit*) and *releasement* (*Gelassenheit*).

The following two essays are devoted to Heidegger in the 1930s. Richard Polt investigates the problematic of Heidegger's thinking of the "people" and the question "who are we?" in this period. The 1930s are marked, according to Polt, "by Heidegger's attempt to leap actively into a singular, transformative event that would bring Germany into its own." In this process, the question "who are we?" takes on a central role, and it can be taken as a guiding thread to understand Heidegger's thought during these years. Polt insists that Heidegger's orientation toward the question of the people includes a radical critique of biologism. What matters is how our own being is put into question and how, "Our own proper Being is grounded in our belonging to the truth of Being itself" (GA 65, 51/CP2, 42). This implies that the question of "who we are" remains *as a question*, the question of human uncanniness. As Heidegger writes in *Introduction to Metaphysics,* "The determination of the essence of the human being is *never* an answer, but is essentially a question" (GA 40, 107/IM, 149).

Robert Bernasconi examines Heidegger's relation to Nietzsche and his troubled involvement with National-Socialism. He contends that Heidegger's metaphysical concern was "uppermost in his treatment of Nietzsche's relation to Darwinism and biologism" and that when "it came to readings of Nietzsche, Heidegger's 'resistance' was directed primarily against those among the Nazis whom he suspected of promoting both the Darwinian struggle for existence and a biologistic conception of race." Bernasconi shows how the distinction between the biological and the metaphysical, as well as the distinction between the political and the metaphysical, "was proving more fluid than Heidegger had at first suspected." With respect to Nietzsche, Bernasconi states that Heidegger initially defended Nietzsche against the charge of biologism "only subsequently to locate him within the history of Western metaphysics." However, in this account of Western metaphysics as destiny, Heidegger "deprived himself philosophically of a basis for a moral condemnation of National Socialism."

Françoise Dastur examines Heidegger's later thought and work. She considers Heidegger's thought from the Bremen Lectures after the war to the late seminars of The Thor in France in the late 1960s and early 1970s by way of his various essays on art, technology, and psychotherapy. Her essay elaborates on the theme of the end of philosophy that emerged in Heidegger's latest writings, particularly in his 1964 lecture on "The End of Philosophy and the Task of Thinking."

In the last contribution to this part, Alfred Denker explores an oft-neglected aspect of scholarship on Heidegger, his correspondence, which offers fascinating insights into Heidegger's private thoughts, his ties to his contemporaries, and with his own work. Providing an overview of Heidegger's correspondence, which comprises an estimated 10,000 letters, Denker reveals the extent of Heidegger correspondence: with philosophers (Heinrich Rickert, Edmund Husserl, Karl Jaspers, Karl Löwith, Hans-Georg Gadamer, Hannah Arendt, Hans Jonas, Max Scheler, Jean-Paul Sartre, and Ernst Tugendhat); scholars in the humanities (Kurt Bauch, Beda Allemann, and Emil Staiger); scientists (Werner Heisenberg and Carl-Friedrich von Weizsäcker); psychiatrists (Medard Boss and Ludwig Binswanger); theologians (Conrad Gröber, Karl Rahner, and Johannes Baptist Lotz); authors and poets (René Char, Paul Celan, and Ernst and Friedrich-Georg Jünger), and artists (such as Eduardo Chillida, Bernhard Heiliger,

Georges Braque, Otto Dix, or Hans Kock). Heidegger's largest correspondence was with his wife Elfride (over 1,100 letters). Since these letters provide clarifications of his own thinking, they can be taken as genuine additions to Heidegger's work.

PART II: SOURCES, INFLUENCES, AND ENCOUNTERS

The second part investigates Heidegger's sources, influences, students, and encounters in 13 essays. Heidegger understood his own work as a conversation with tradition. He declared, in a response to a question about so-called Heideggerian philosophy: "There is no Heideggerian philosophy; and even if it existed, I would not be interested in that philosophy . . ." Rather, he characterized his thought as being engaged in a "dialogue with the tradition."[2] Heidegger insisted on the historicity of the question of being, and his thought has been formed through rigorous readings and bold interpretations of the corpus of Western philosophy. This historical character of the question of being would be further radicalized in his later thinking of history of being and its "sendings."

This part explores such links with the philosophical tradition with essays examining Heidegger's reading and responses to Greek and medieval philosophy (Sean Kirkland and Holger Zaborowski), Descartes and Kant (Emilia Angelova and Frank Schalow), Hegel, Schelling, and German Idealism (Peter Trawny), Nietzsche (Ulrich Haase), Husserl (Leslie MacAvoy), Dilthey's hermeneutics and Carnap's logical positivism (Eric S. Nelson), his encounters and confrontations with philosophical movements such as neo-Kantianism and Cassirer (Peter Gordon), as well as his reception by his early students such as Arendt (Peg Birmingham), Gadamer

(Emilia Angelova), and Marcuse (Andrew Feenberg).

Sean Kirkland shows the necessity for Heidegger and for contemporary thought to engage Greek philosophy. Heidegger's attempt to reopen the question of being occurs in direct dialogue with the ancients, as the opening paragraphs of *Being and Time* testify. The "entire project" of *Being and Time* can be said to unfold "explicitly within a space opened up and delineated by ancient Greek thought." Kirkland explores Heidegger's relation with Greek thought as provenance of our history, which is not a simple return to the Greeks but indeed an engagement with "the ancients' unthought and unsaid as such." Holger Zaborowski explores the often-neglected relation of Heidegger to medieval philosophy. Heidegger's response to medieval thought and the scholastic tradition "is closely tied up with his relation to Christianity," and to that extent was determinative of Heidegger's early work. Through these early works, Heidegger made "a considerable move towards . . . key insights of his later hermeneutics of facticity, of his phenomenology of Dasein, and also of his being-historical thinking." In her essay, "Heidegger and Descartes," Emilia Angelova contrasts Heidegger's early lecture courses with the later period. Whereas in the early period, the focus was on the ambiguity of Descartes' problematic, the later writings (in particular in the Nietzsche courses, *What is a Thing? The Age of the World Picture*, and the final seminars) show a much more pronounced critical stance with respect to Descartes' subjectivism. Angelova retraces that trajectory and appraises its significance.

Reflecting on how Kant's destructive-retrieval of transcendental philosophy illuminates the ostensible impasse surrounding the unpublished, third division of part I of *Being and Time*, Frank Schalow suggests that Heidegger's interpretation of Kant could shed light on the "turn" in his thinking. Essays on Heidegger's responses to German Idealism—concentrating on Hegel and Schelling (Peter Trawny)—and to Nietzsche (Ullrich Haase) follow, giving a unique perspective on Heidegger's treatment of post-Kantian and nineteenth-century philosophy, and their role in his understanding of the history of being. Eric Nelson considers the import of Heidegger's understanding of Dilthey's hermeneutical life-philosophy. This is followed by an essay by Leslie MacAvoy on Husserl and Heidegger in which she articulates their respective conceptions of phenomenology.

Peter E. Gordon takes on Heidegger's relationship with neo-Kantianism by considering the key themes of Kantian and neo-Kantian philosophy that "left their mark on Heidegger's early thought." After Eric Nelson's chapter on Heidegger and Carnap, which contrasts their conceptions of nothingness, Peg Birmingham challenges the common understanding of the relation between Heidegger and Arendt in terms of contrast (if not opposition) and shows their proximity with respect to the notions of world and community. Emilia Angelova examines Gadamer's exposition of philosophical hermeneutics with Heidegger's project of fundamental ontology and clarifies how Gadamer distanced himself from the later Heidegger. In the last chapter of Part II, Andrew Feenberg engages Marcuse and Heidegger, discussing the various stages of Marcuse's appraisal of Heidegger's thought, and confronting their respective conceptions of technology.

PART III: KEY WRITINGS

The third part offers ten essays bearing on Heidegger's key writings, following a chronological order and highlighting the most influential writings: the early lecture courses (Scott Campbell), the early lecture courses on Aristotle (P. Christopher Smith), *Being and Time* (Dennis Schmidt), *The Origin of the Work of Art* (Gregory Schufreider), *Introduction to Metaphysics* (Gregory Fried), *Contributions to Philosophy* (Peter Trawny), the Hölderlin lectures (William McNeill), *The Letter on Humanism* (Andrew Mitchell), *The Bremen Lectures* (Andrew Mitchell) and later essays and seminars (Lee Braver).

Scott Campbell approaches Heidegger's early writings in terms of three main foci: the meaningfulness of life; religious experience; and language and the Greeks. P. Christopher Smith discusses what he calls the early Heidegger's "revolutionary rehabilitation of rhetoric," showing how Heidegger considered human existence to be fundamentally rhetorical in a transformed sense. Dennis Schmidt considers that unique text that is *Being and Time*, marking its irreducible character with respect to the history in which it is otherwise situated. Schmidt remarks that, "In its efforts to set itself apart from philosophical traditions and languages, and to resist any easy appropriation into well-established contexts, *Being and Time* quietly announces the radicality of its own intentions." It is that extraordinary originality of the work that makes it a promise still to come. While noting that there are about half a dozen versions of the "The Origin of the Work of Art," if not more if one takes into account the various transcripts of the lectures taken by students who attended them, Gregory Schufreider argues that Heidegger's aim in turning his attention to the work of art in the 1930s "is to provide a new model of philosophy."

Gregory Fried notes that *Introduction to Metaphysics* is one of Martin Heidegger's most widely read works, second perhaps only to *Being and Time*, and one of his more controversial works. Fried explains how *Introduction to Metaphysics* "occupies a transitional position in Heidegger's path, between the fundamental ontology and the analytic of Dasein in *Being and Time* and the efforts in *Contributions to Philosophy* (1936–38)," a volume considered in an entry by Peter Trawny. Trawny insists on the "style" of this work, referring to "the will and the style of thinking" (CP1, 15), the "style of inceptual thinking" (24) and the "reservedness" evoked by Heidegger. The "experimental character of Heidegger's scripturality" is stressed. William McNeill provides an account of Heidegger's relation to and dialogue with Hölderlin, elaborating on Heidegger's Hölderlin lectures and their prominent place in his path of thinking. McNeill considers the first Hölderlin Lecture Course, that is, *The Hymns "Germania" and "The Rhine"* (1934–5), the "Remembrance" lectures (1941–2), and the last Hölderlin Lecture Course: "The Ister" (1942).

Andrew J. Mitchell contextualizes the writing of Heidegger's "Letter on Humanism," demonstrating that at the heart of the essay is a profound thinking of "the interrelation between the human, being, and language." This essay is followed by Mitchell's text on the 1949 Bremen Lectures, a volume that he recently translated into English. He considers these lectures to be "a third, decisive milestone along Heidegger's path of thought," alongside the early *Being and Time*, and the mid-period *Contributions to Philosophy*. In the last contribution of Part III, Lee Braver reflects on what distinguishes what is known as the "later Heidegger." In addition to the question of style, Braver suggests that Heidegger has added some new motifs, such as "artworks and technology, for example, and what he calls 'things,' which are very different from objects."

Part IV: Themes and Topics

The 15 essays of the fourth part focus on key notions and themes found in Heidegger's work. They enact and perform this task in diverse ways by clarifying key notions and questions in Heidegger's corpus. In this part, François Raffoul illuminates Heidegger's conception of *Dasein* ("being-there"); Daniela Vallega-Neu carefully explicates the complex fundamental notion of *Ereignis* (the "event"); Andrew Mitchell reflects on Heidegger's meditations on the fourfold (*das Geviert*); Hans Ruin inquires into the role of technology in Heidegger's thought; Daniel Dahlstrom describes the event and structure of truth in Heidegger's philosophy; Gregory Schufreider turns to the question of the Nothing (*das Nichts*); Anne O'Byrne investigates the elemental significance of both birth and death in Heidegger's works; Iain Thomson elucidates Heidegger's important discussions of ontotheology; while Kevin Aho pursues the question of the extent to which Heidegger adequately addressed the thematic of the body.

Other essays explore Heidegger's relation to various disciplines or domains of theory and practice. These include Trish Glazebrook's detailed analysis of Heidegger's approach to science; Andrew Bowie's thoughtful commentary on Heidegger's relation to art and aesthetics; François Raffoul's interrogation of Heidegger's import for ethics; John Russon and Kirsten Jacobson's examination of space in Heidegger's texts; Ben Vedder's explication of Heidegger's thinking of religion and theology; and John McCumber's clarification of Heidegger's meditations concerning the question of language. The essays in this part serve to illuminate Heidegger's thinking by presenting Heidegger's key technical notions as well as his transformation of our understanding of a wide-range of domains and topics.

Part V: Reception and Influence

The fifth part consists of 13 essays that investigate the influence of Heidegger's thought on various thinkers and contemporary philosophical movements. Heidegger has had a major impact on late modern and postmodern philosophy. Just to mention the French example, one can list: Levinas' first commentaries on Heidegger's early works (Levinas was the first one to introduce Heidegger in France); Sartre's magisterial (mis)appropriation of the key moments and vocabulary of *Being and Time* in *Being and Nothingness*; the fame, after the war, of existentialism and the celebrated "Letter on Humanism" addressed to Jean Beaufret, a key figure in the French reception of Heidegger; Heidegger's visit to France in the mid-1950s to attend the Cerisy meeting and his encounter with Lacan, his lecture at Aix-en-Provence in 1958; the seminars held in the 1960s in France, in Provence at the Thor, near the house of René Char; and finally the reappropriation of Heidegger's *Destruktion* in the thought of Jacques Derrida and deconstruction, a work further pursued by Jean-Luc Nancy and Philippe Lacoue-Labarthe.[3]

A number of essays review Heidegger's relation to these individual French thinkers, whether Wayne Froman on Merleau-Ponty, Jill Stauffer on Emmanuel Levinas, Robert Bernasconi on Jean-Paul Sartre, François Raffoul on Jacques Derrida, Leonard Lawlor and Janae Sholtz on Gilles Deleuze, and also Leonard Lawlor on Michel Foucault. These detailed synthetic studies shed a unique light on the ways in which Heidegger has helped shape twentieth-century French philosophy.

Beyond the French case, Iain Macdonald's essay focus on Adorno's critical reading and diagnosis of Heidegger's thought. Leslie MacAvoy's incisive contribution concentrates on Heidegger's reception in the Anglo-American philosophical world, particularly in Hubert Dreyfus, Mark Okrent, and Richard Rorty. Bret Davis's entry depicts the profound response to Heidegger's work in Chinese, Indian, and Japanese philosophy. Alejandro Vallega's chapter portrays the noteworthy reception of Heidegger's thinking in Latin American philosophy.

Moreover, Heidegger's writings have informed the formation of new discourses on the environment, gender, and psychology. In further contributions, Trish Glazebrooke measures and evaluates Heidegger's impact on philosophical movements such as ecology and environmental philosophy. Tina Chanter pursues the question of gender in Heidegger via a discussion of Sophocles' Antigone and its retrieval in Hegel, Heidegger, and feminist philosophers such as Luce Irigaray and Judith Butler. Robert D. Stolorow investigates Heidegger's thought-provoking links with psychology and psychoanalysis and new possibilities for thinking the psychological in existential, phenomenological, and post-Cartesian ways.

In addition, there is a new appendix on the recently published *Black Notebooks* (*Schwarze Hefte*) especially written for this new paperback edition by Eric Nelson.

In the time since Heidegger's death on May 26, 1976, his thought and life have continued to inspire philosophical reflection and argumentation as well as controversy and polemic. Our hope is that this volume, with its 59 contributions from a range of notable researchers of Heidegger's thought and life from the United Kingdom, the United States, Germany, France, and Canada, will offer an expansive and detailed scope of analysis, and serve as one of the most comprehensive guides available to approach and explore Heidegger's works. This is a work that is still to be discovered insofar as we do not cease to confront the mystery—and wonder—of being.

NOTES AND REFERENCES

[1] On the notion of facticity and its role in Heidegger's early philosophy, see our introduction to *Rethinking Facticity*, ed. François Raffoul and Eric S. Nelson (Albany, NY: SUNY Press, 2008), 1–21.

[2] In a session from August 31, 1955 in Cerisy, cited in Dominique Janicaud. *Heidegger in France*, vol. 1 (Paris: Albin Michel, 2001), 154.

[3] On that reception of Heidegger's thought in France, in addition to Dominique Janicaud's *magnum opus*, see *French Interpretations of Heidegger*, ed. D. Pettigrew and F. Raffoul (Albany, NY: SUNY Press, 2008).

PART I:
LIFE AND CONTEXTS

1

HEIDEGGER AND THE QUESTION OF BIOGRAPHY

Theodore Kisiel

In order to exemplify Heidegger's dismissive attitude toward the role of biography in philosophy, it has long been the custom to cite or paraphrase the remark he made on the opening day of his lecture course of Summer Semester 1924 on the *Basic Concepts of Aristotelian Philosophy*:

> As for the personality of a philosopher, our only interest is that he was born at a certain time, that he worked, and that he died. The character of the philosopher, and issues of that sort, will not be addressed here. (GA 18, 5/BCAR, 4)

To his students, Heidegger recommends instead a book on the (hi)story of Aristotle's development by the "classical philologist" Werner Jaeger that bears the title, *Aristotle: Fundamentals of the History of his Development*. In short, what is of interest to Heidegger is not so much the story of Aristotle's life as the story of the development of his philosophy. In the terms of the minimalist biography presented above, the focus therefore falls on the fact/facticity "that he worked" as a philosopher and thinker "at a certain time," and in the course of that lifetime produced "works" that were then handed down to us as part and parcel of the "classical" tradition of philosophy. Our "question of biography" then becomes: what, if any, elements of biography, of the story of the life of a philosopher like Aristotle, enter into the story of his philosophical development within his particular historical and hermeneutical context.

Jaeger's book was preceded by a set of "Studies toward the *Entstehungsgeschichte* of Aristotle's Metaphysics," a (hi)story of the origin (genesis, emergence, and development) of his philosophy. In his course, Heidegger accordingly embarks on a study of the formation of the basic concepts that shape and contextualize Aristotle's philosophy. The most telling of his discoveries is that Aristotle's word for being, *ousia*, in the Greek language ordinarily means property, possessions and goods, and real estate. This customary meaning is constantly present and simultaneously accompanies its terminological meaning. And "terminologically, *ousia* is 'a being in the how of its being'" (GA 18, 24/BCAR, 19). As property and possessions, this how of being is being in its being-available. This becomes the paradigm example of Aristotle's way of philosophical concept-formation: drawing on an expression that was prevalent in the everyday language of his world, Aristotle shapes it into his term for beings and their being. In living in the native language that imparts intelligibility to his world and all that is experienced within it, he draws on that natural intelligibility of experience to form his philosophical concepts that accordingly remain indigenous (*bodenständig*) to that intelligible world wherein they are rooted and from which they are drawn.

A related concept that Heidegger draws from Aristotle and makes central is the concept of life, *zoe*, as drawn from the Aristotelian definition of the human being as *zoon logon echon*, the living being possessing, and possessed by, speech. Likewise here, *zoe* is a concept of being, a particular how of being:

> "Life" refers to a mode of being, indeed a mode of *being-in-a-world*. . . . The being-in-the-world of the human being is defined in its ground through speaking. The fundamental mode of being in which the human being is in its world is in speaking with it, about it, of it. (GA 18, 18/BCAR14) "Living, for the human being, means [*heisst*] speaking." (GA 18, 21/BCAR, 16)

We are not too far removed here from Dilthey's sense of the pan-hermeneutic character of human life, expressed succinctly by Hans-Georg Gadamer: "Das Leben selbst legt sich aus. Es hat selbst hermeneutische Struktur. [Life itself lays itself out, interprets itself, explicates itself, articulates itself. Life itself has a hermeneutic structure]."[1] This pan-hermeneutic dimension is especially relevant to the life of a philosopher, who in his conceptual labor naturally draws his concepts from the meaningful context of life-experience already articulated in the native language into which he happens to

have been thrown. In short, each and every philosopher necessarily lives and works, in Heidegger's terms, out of his very own hermeneutic situation in its already prepossessed, previewed, and preconceptualized form. In fact, at one point in his development of an ontology of being-here, Heidegger identifies one's own temporally particular hermeneutic situation as the sole object of philosophical research of a time and a generation (BH, 153). "The very idea of facticity implies that only *authentic and proper* [*eigentliche*] facticity—understood in the literal sense of the word: one's *own* [*eigene*] facticity—that is, the facticity of one's own time and generation, is the genuine object of research" (GA 62, 366/BH, 167). "Resolved to speak radically to the world—to question and to research" (GA 18, 40/BCAR, 29), each generation of philosophers is called upon to radically retake its unique hermeneutic situation for its own time, to appropriate its own past in order to recover its precedent possibilities that are especially appropriate for its time and generation. It is incumbent upon each generation of philosophers, by way of radical questioning, to explicate and interpret that situation for its own time. And by its very nature, it is something that a time "can never borrow from another time" (GA 62, 348/BH, 156). So identified are we with our particular historical time that Heidegger does in fact identify them, in existential assertions such as "I myself AM my time" and "We ourselves ARE history," to be sure, not an objectified history but rather a history-in-actualization (*Vollzugsgeschichte*).

Acknowledging one's own hermeneutic situation as the proper matter of philosophy and the proper arena of philosophical concept formation marks a considerable step beyond ordinary unthinking life. It in fact marks a transition into the more intense life of thought. The tradition of philosophy has called it the transcendental move. But a flag of caution must now be quickly raised, since we are dealing here with a uniquely nontraditional domain of transcendence. The young Heidegger is quick to rule out any sort of transcendental ego or theoretical I abstracted in Cartesian fashion from its vital context, denouncing such an ego as thoroughly denuded of its world and therefore wholly devoid of concrete meaning, dehistoricized, and, last but not least, thoroughly devitalized. The phenomenological return back to our most original life-experience, methodologically called a reduction, can perhaps be better characterized as a movement of transdescendance into our most original concretion of experience. It is a return back to our most original factic life experience, where the very act of living spontaneously articulates and contextures itself into the manifold of vitally concrete and meaningful basic relations that constitute the fabric of human concerns that we call our historical life-world, which in turn constitutes the tacit background context of meaningfulness within and against which all of factic life necessarily takes place and is thereby understood. In explicating the implicit background of meaningfulness that underlies all of our experience, this move can be called the hermeneutic-phenomenological re-duction.

But in this uniquely transcendental domain of meaningfulness in which the life of thought now operates, where, if at all, is there room for the entry of anything like the biographical elements of a life? The answer resides in our inescapable starting point from a temporally particular (*je-weiligen*) hermeneutic situation unique to an historical individual and an historical generation, in the distinction made above between a purely transcendental ego and an historically situated I, and in Dasein's

essential nature of being in each instantiation mine (*je meines*), yours (*je deines*), and ours (*je unsriges*). Finding ourselves situated in existence, thrown into an historical world that in fact is very much our own, we, each of us, are called upon to overtly own up to this situation as a whole and properly make it our very own. This call (solicitation, challenge, or demand) elicited by the existential situation into which we find ourselves thrown is the function of the formally indicative concepts of philosophy. "The meaning-content of these concepts does not directly intend or express what they refer to, but only gives an indication, a pointer to the fact that anyone seeking to understand is called upon by this conceptual context to *actualize* [*vollziehen*] a transformation of themselves into their Dasein" (GA 29/30, 430/FCM, 297, trans. modified). Because such concepts—Heidegger's terse examples are "death, resolute openness, history, existence"—can only convey the call for such a transformation to us without being able to bring about this transformation themselves, they are but *indicative* concepts. They, in each instance, point to Dasein itself, which in each instantiation is my (your, our) Dasein, as the locus and potential agent of this transformation. "Because in this indication they in each instance point to a *concretion of the individual Dasein* in the human being, yet never bring the content of this concretion with them, such concepts are *formally indicative*" (GA 29/30, 429/FCM, 296, trans. modified).

These formally indicative, properly philosophical concepts thus only evoke the Dasein in human being, but do not actually bring it about. There is something penultimate about philosophizing in all of its conceptuality. Its questioning brings us to the very brink of the possibility of Dasein, just short of "restoring to Dasein its *actuality*, that is, its *existence*" (GA 29/30, 257/FCM, 173). There is a very fine line between philosophizing and *actualizing* over which the human being cannot merely slip across, but rather must overleap in order to dislodge its Dasein. "Only individual action itself can dislodge us from this brink of possibility into actuality, and this is the *moment* of decision and of holistic insight [into the concrete situation of action and be-ing]" (GA 29/30, 257/FCM, 173, trans. modified). It is the protoaction (*Urhandlung*) of resolute openness to one's own concretely unique situation of be-ing, of letting it be in its wholeness and ownness, in each instantiation concretely reenacted in accord with one's own unique situation and particular "while" of history that authenticates our existence and properizes our philosophizing. It is in such originary action, repeatedly reenacted from one generation to the next, that ontology finds its ontic founding. Just as Aristotle (and so the metaphysical tradition) founded his *prote philosophia* in *theologia*, so Heidegger now founds his fundamental ontology upon "something ontic— the Dasein" (GA 24, 26/BP, 19).

And it is this ontic founding that is actualized by "individual [proto]action" that allows for the entry of selected biographical elements at least at the threshold of the trans[des]cendental level of philosophy. In the same vein, this individual protoaction brings in the content of the "*concretion of the individual Dasein*" in the human entity that is left undecided because of the *formal* character of the indication. It is the individual Dasein itself, which, as the *being* (*Seiendes*) that in its be-ing is concerned with this very be-ing, in its very nature straddles the ontological difference between be-ing and beings, the ontological and the ontic, that in its transcending/ transforming move from the human being to its Dasein, from the ontic to the ontological,

brings with itself certain elements of its ontic background that it regards as indispensable and irrevocable to its very identity as a self. This can be readily exemplified through the testimony of Heidegger himself in a letter to Karl Löwith in August 1921 in which he spells out the vital identity out of which he himself does his own philosophizing:

I work concretely and factically out of my "I am"—out of my spiritual and thoroughly factic provenance [*Herkunft*], my milieu, my life contexts, and whatever is available to me from these, as the vital experience in which I live. This facticity, as existentiell, is no mere "blind existence"—this Dasein is one with existence, which means that I live it, this "I must" of which no one speaks. The act of existing seethes with this *facticity of being-thus*, it surges with the historical just as it is—which means that I live the inner obligations of my facticity and do so as radically as I understand them. This facticity of mine includes—briefly put—the fact that I am a "Christian theo*logian*." This implies a certain radical self-concern, a certain radical scientificity, a rigorous objectivity [*Gegenständlichkeit*] *in* this *facticity*; it includes the historical consciousness, the consciousness of the "history of spirit." And I am all this in the life context of the *university*. (BH, 99–100)

"Ich bin 'christlicher Theo*loge*.'" Such deeply personal declarations of who "I am" are clear-cut statements of self-identity in which Heidegger is owning up to the deep Christian roots that ineradicably belongs to his factic provenance, and so an admission of where he is in fact coming from (*Her-kunft*) in his thinking. Eventually this provenance will assume a note of necessity, of the inalterability and inescapability of a person's situation that cannot be denied without "denying who I am," and so being untrue to oneself. "I cannot do otherwise without rejecting myself and denying who I am" (BH, 102). The note of possibility comes into play in how one takes up this inevitability and develops it further. "I cannot make my 'I am' into something different, but can only take hold of it and be it in this or that way" (BH, 101). In confessing where he is in fact coming from, Heidegger is at once translating "the inner obligations of my facticity" into "must do" tasks and projects, e.g., by assuming the self-confessed role of "Christian theo*logian*" in his courses on the phenomenology of religion and on Augustine and Neoplatonism in 1920–21.

The letter continues with Heidegger contrasting himself with his two best students at the time, Löwith and Oskar Becker, first of all in regard to where each is coming from and how starkly divergent these concrete backgrounds are. "It has always been clear to me that neither you nor Becker would accept the Christian side of me" (BH, 100). But in spite of the disagreements and misunderstandings that such radically divergent backgrounds are bound to promote and the radically different paths that may therefore be taken, Heidegger nevertheless looks forward to a "meeting of minds" provided that each comes to terms with his temporally particular existential situation in its ownness and wholeness in full propriety and authenticity.

Only one thing is decisive: that we understand each other well enough so that each of us is radically devoted to the last to what and how each understands the *unum necessarium* ["one thing necessary" (namely, our respective facticities)]. We may be far apart in "system,"

"doctrine," and "position,"—but we are *together* in the one way in which humans are able to be genuinely together: in *Existenz*. (BH, 102)

What particularly distinguishes Heidegger from Becker, the scientifically oriented philosopher, and Löwith, the existentielly inclined thinker, in their respective facticities (concrete backgrounds) is that "the fact that I am a 'Christian theo*logian*'" is a side of Heidegger that neither one of them could be expected to empathize with. Behind this admission of identity lies an ontic-existentiell background experience that finds itself deeply embedded in a facticity of Christian religiosity that developed into the (here left unsaid and clearly ontic-existentiell) autobiography of a former Catholic seminarian who had broken with the religion of his youth to become a nondenominational "free Christian" and was now on the verge of proclaiming the atheism of philosophy in close conjunction with the rigorous fideism of Protestant theology. Thus the admission implies a "particular radical personal concern" (Löwith's forté) and pathos that stems from this past life, but it also involves a "particular radical scientificity" (Becker's inclination) being cultivated by a university philosopher who had just completed two courses on the phenomenology of religion that had developed formal schemata that prefigure the concrete historical actualization of Christian life (its Da-sein!) as it is depicted respectively in Paul's letters and Augustine's *Confessions*.

Heidegger's admission provides the warrant for further biographical probes into the Heideggerian opus during this early phase. And over the decades there has been a proliferation of documents that have surfaced that testify to the interplay of life and thought, biography and philosophy, in the early period of Heidegger's existentiell rootedness in Christian religiosity. Let me venture one such probe that brings out his deep Catholic roots, "the religion of my youth." 1915 is the year in which Heidegger writes his dissertation on Duns Scotus, where its Introduction in its concluding lines first announces a major personal project of a hermeneutic phenomenology of religious life.

For the decisive insight into [the nonpsychologistic character of scholastic psychology's concept of intentionality], I regard the philosophical, more precisely, the phenomenological elaboration of the mystical, moral-theological, and ascetic literature of medieval scholasticism to be of special urgency. (GA 1, 205)

In short, what is needed here is a phenomenology of the full spectrum of religious experience in the Middle Ages, in order to capture the "living spirit" of the medieval worldview, a goal that Heidegger sets for himself in the penultimate lines of the 1916 Conclusion of the Scotus dissertation: "It is by such means that we shall first penetrate into the vital life of medieval scholasticism and see how it decisively founded, vitalized, and strengthened a cultural epoch." For the medieval life-world, the "form of its inner existence," is anchored in the "transcendent primal relationship of the soul to God—an inner existence that was alive in the Middle Ages with rare concentration and intensity. The manifold of vital relations between God and the soul, the world beyond and this world, varies according to the particular distance or proximity between them" (GA 1, 409/BH, 84). That is why "scholasticism and mysticism essentially belong together in the medieval worldview" and so mutually offset

the extremes to which each by itself might be carried. "Philosophy as a rationalistic system detached from life is impotent, mysticism as an irrational experience is aimless" (GA 1, 410/BH, 85).

It should be noted that when Heidegger speaks of the vitality of the medieval worldview, he is speaking from the personal life-experience of his own boyhood in his hometown of Messkirch as a son of the sextant of the nearby parish church. His later reminiscences in a talk to a hometown crowd entitled "The Mystery of the Bell Tower" recalls for them the daily medieval rhythm of the daily ringing of the Angelus and the seasonal rhythms of the liturgical year that still defined daily life in his boyhood home at the turn of the century. [I myself experienced the same medieval rhythms still being practiced as late as 1965 during an extended stay in the Catholic village of St. Peter bei Freiburg]. This nostalgia for a medieval way of life and its worldview is only reinforced and amplified by the presence of the Benedictine monastery at Beuron within hiking distance of Messkirch. His hermeneutic tour of the devotional manuals of the Middle Ages by way of the phenomenological guideline of intentionality, while being philosophical in intent, assumes in part the character of a personal itinerary, thus becoming both a personal and philosophical appreciation as well as confrontation of his boyhood faith, and be-ing.

But by 1917, it becomes clear to Heidegger that the excessive dogmatizing and theorizing of medieval scholasticism drains *all* of the vitality from religious life and that its rationalistic structures instigate a radical divorce from life. In a note to himself in mid-1917 out of the context of a neo-Kantian philosophy of culture and religion nuanced by Schleiermacher's experiential sense of the religious a priori, he writes in no uncertain terms that:

... dogmatic casuistic pseudo-philosophies, which pose as philosophies of a particular system of religion (for instance Catholicism) and presumably stand closest to religion and the religious, are the least capable of promoting the vitality of the problem [of the religious a priori]. One is at a loss even to find the problem, since such [scholastic] philosophies are not familiar with anything like a philosophy of religion. For one thing, in the environment and context of such systems, the capacity to experience the different domains of value, in particular religious value, stagnates, owing to the complete absence of an original consciousness of culture. For another, the structure of the system has *not* grown out of an *organic* cultural deed. Hence, the inherent worth of the religion, its palpable sphere of meaning, must first be experienced through a tangled, inorganic, dogmatic hedgerow of propositions and proofs that are left *totally unclarified* theoretically, which as an ecclesiastical and canonical statute backed by police power in the end serves to overpower and repress the subject and to encumber it in darkness. In the end, the system

totally excludes an original experience of genuinely religious value. . . . This is already implicit in the heavily scientific, naturalistic, and theoretical metaphysics of being of Aristotle and its radical exclusion and misconstrual of Plato's problem of value, a metaphysics that is revived in medieval scholasticism and that sets its norm in the predominantly theoretical. Accordingly, scholasticism, within the totality of the medieval Christian life-world, severely jeopardized the immediacy of religious life and forgot religion for theology and dogma. The theorizing and dogmatizing influence was exercised by church authorities in their institutions and statutes already in the time of early Christianity. [In a situation like this,] a phenomenon like that of mysticism is to be understood as an elementary countermovement. (GA 60, 313f./PRL, 237f.)

NOTES AND REFERENCES

[1] Hans-Georg Gadamer, *Wahrheit und Methode: Grundzüge einer philosophischen Hermeneutik* (Tübingen: J.C.B. Mohr, 1965), 213. Revised translation: Joel Weinsheimer and Donald G. Marshall *Truth and Method* (New York: Continuum, 1994), 226.

2

THE EARLY HEIDEGGER
Dermot Moran

In this chapter I shall discuss the work of Martin Heidegger from 1912 to 1927, but I shall concentrate especially on the Freiburg and Marburg lecture courses leading up to *Being and Time*.

Heidegger's intellectual origins are extremely important for his overall philosophical outlook but he also tended to a degree of self-mythologization in later retrospective writings. Heidegger's intellectual development was less monolithic and focused that his later assertions to William Richardson[1] and others might lead one to think. For instance, it is clear that the "question of Being" (*die Seinsfrage*) is not the dominant theme of his early writings, which are more concerned in making precise his understanding of the very nature of *philosophy* and to articulate the nature of historical *human existence* (what he first called "life" and then "Dasein") in facticity and finitude. Secondly, contrary to his later 1963 account in "My Way to Phenomenology" (TB, 74) it is not at all clear that Franz Brentano's *On the Several Senses of Being in Aristotle*,[2] the first philosophical text Heidegger read while still in the Gymnasium, really did offer much of an inspiration.[3] At best, it led him to distinguish the *existentialia* of Dasein from the categories that apply to other entities. Finally, despite their close friendship

and collaboration for more than a decade (1916–27), Heidegger was never a *student* of Husserl's. Heidegger had already completed both his doctorate and his Habilitation thesis before he first met Husserl in Freiburg shortly after the latter's arrival there in April 1916. Husserl himself had just lost his son in the war and it seems that, at least in Husserl's eyes, Heidegger gradually began to fit the role of Husserl's adopted son. Heidegger himself displayed less than filial loyalty in his public and private evaluations of the "old man."

Largely because of the poverty of his parents, Heidegger had begun his studies as a Catholic seminarian and theology student. His 1914 doctoral thesis, an analysis of the nature of judgment in which he criticized both Rickert and Lask, was entitled *Die Lehre vom Urteil in Psychologismus* (*The Doctrine of Judgment in Psychologism*, GA 1, 59–188),[4] written under the direction of Arthur Schneider, who held the Chair of Christian Philosophy in Freiburg. It is a somewhat pedestrian critical discussion of psychologism that shows few hints of his later genius.

Heidegger's Habilitation thesis was entitled *Die Kategorien- und Bedeutungslehre des Duns Scotus* (*The Categories and the Doctrine of Meaning in Duns Scotus*, reprinted GA 1, 189–412), under the direction of Heinrich Rickert. This thesis was on a text supposedly by Duns Scotus, but in fact written by Thomas of Erfurt. Already in his *Habilitation* (1915), Heidegger had claimed that philosophy had to be not just about values but about "the value of life (*Lebenswert*)." Furthermore, he maintained that the formal study of Scholastic thought needed to be balanced by a phenomenological exploration of religious experience:

I hold the philosophical, more exactly, the phenomenological handling of the mystical, moral-theological, and ascetic writings of medieval scholasticism to be especially crucial in its decisive insight into this fundamental characteristic of Scholastic psychology. (GA 1, 205, my translation)

In his efforts to gain an academic position, Heidegger tailored his curriculum vitae and interests. Thus he presented himself as someone interested in the neo-Scholastic revival of medieval philosophy. Later Karl Jaspers would record in his *Autobiography* that in conversation with Heidegger he expressed his surprise that "The dedication of Heidegger's first book to Rickert, of his second to Husserl, emphasizes a connection with people of whom he had spoken to me with contempt."[5] Heidegger was certainly career oriented.

On January 21, 1919, benefitting greatly from the support of Husserl, Heidegger officially became a salaried member of the Freiburg philosophy seminar.[6] Four days later, on January 25, the "War Emergency Semester" (*Kriegnotsemester*) commenced, and Heidegger offered his first lecture course, "The Idea of Philosophy and the Problem of Worldview," in which he explored his own understanding of the true method of philosophy and its relation to phenomenology (GA 56–7/TDP). The influence of Rickert is clearly visible. In this first course, his question is: what is involved in the very idea of philosophy? Or, as he puts it, he wants to identify the "essential elements of the idea of philosophy" (GA 56/57, 39/ TDP, 32). Heidegger presents philosophy as a scientific attitude that breaks through the natural attitude and heightens the sense of *life*. Philosophy is presented as a "primordial science" (*Urwissenschaft*) that should not be allowed degenerate into a "worldview" (*Weltanschauung*). Phenomenology cannot be understood as a standpoint at all. Philosophy is unique in that it contemplates itself through its history and in this way awakens to a higher spiritual life:

Every history and history of philosophy *constitutes* itself in life in and for itself, life which is itself *historical* in an absolute sense. (GA 56/57, 21/ TDP, 18)

It is clear that Heidegger is interested in a way of capturing *life*, while still having sympathy for it. Heidegger questions the manner in which Rickert and other neo-Kantians had misunderstood the nature of value and validity, but he is also critical of phenomenology—saying the concept of "lived experience" (*Erlebnis*) has now been devalued to the point of meaninglessness (GA 56/57, 66/ TDP, 55) but he is still trying to remain true to the experience and attend to what is given in it, filtering out all misinterpretation.

This first lecture course gives the impression of a young philosopher struggling to articulate intuitions that are not yet clear to him. The primary sense is of someone resisting and attempting to throw off the existing academic tradition in Germany, especially the neo-Kantian emphasis on epistemology and theory of science. There are foreshad-owings—when the circular nature of philo-sophical understanding is mentioned, or the meaning of the "questioning comportment" (GA 56/57, 66/TDP, 56), the manner in which humans always belong to an "environing world" (*Umwelt*), the way in which things are always experienced as worldly, such that one can say "it worlds" (*es weltet*, GA 56/57, 73/TDP, 61). Perhaps most intriguingly, Heidegger is already trying to distinguish between objective knowledge that involves distance from things and a kind of "event of appropriation" or "happening" (*Ereignis*) in which one is self-involved. Most importantly Heidegger is envisaging that phenomenol-ogy must incorporate a new and expanded kind of intuition—"hermeneutic intuition" (*die hermeneutische Intuition*, GA 56/57, 117/TDP, 98). Already in 1919 Heidegger is attempting to fuse hermeneutical interpret-ing with phenomenological intuiting.

One of the early Heidegger's major con-cerns is the meaning of realism. He diag-noses critical realism and critical idealism as both suffering from the same defect—in believing our sense of world and of objects are somehow constituted out of "sense data" (*Sinnesdaten*). Both idealism and realism pre-sume the primacy of theoretical knowledge— "the primacy of the theoretical" (*Primat des Theoretischen*, GA 56/57, 87/TDP, 73) and assume its stance toward the world as being simply the way things are. The problem is: what is to be understood as the immediately given? (GA 56/57, 85/TDP, 71) Realism and idealism fail to grasp what being-in-the-world really means. Heidegger wants to understand how the "environmental" (*das Umweltliche*) is experienced: "how do I live and experi-ence the environmental?" (GA 56/57, 88/ TDP, 74). Heidegger is already stressing that our primary engagement with things is

practical. We should not even say the envi-ronment is "given" because givenness already presupposes the theoretical. "Thingliness [*Dinghaftigkeit*] marks out a quite original sphere distilled out the environmental" (GA 56/57, 89/TDP, 75). Once we grasp things, their worldliness disappears. The expression "it worlds" is supposed to convey the char-acter of pre-theoretical experience. In this first lecture course, Heidegger is interested in the manner in which the world as such is presupposed in various kinds of encounters with things.

Heidegger continued to lecture at Freiburg from 1919 to 1923 and his courses show him developing an independent critical perspective on the then contemporary philosophical scene, specifically neo-Kantian philosophy (particu-larly Rickert, Natorp, Windelband, and Emil Lask), phenomenology (Husserl and Scheler), hermeneutics, and life-philosophy (Dilthey and Simmel). No matter what the announced course title was, Heidegger always used the occasion to think deeply about the nature of philosophy as such (What is it? What kind of science? How do we reach it?) and more spe-cifically to interrogate the meaning and value of phenomenology as a mode of approach to the issues (and, in passing, treated in his lectures of issues such as the nature of phi-losophy as a science, the meaning of "world-view," the "externalities" of the current study of philosophy in the university, the need for university reform, and so on).

Husserl's own opinion of Heidegger at that time is instructive. At first Husserl saw Heidegger as a "confessionally bound" Catholic, but he came to appreciate the seri-ousness with which Heidegger appeared to have embraced Protestantism and regarded him as something of an expert on Martin Luther. For, on January 9, 1919, just prior to taking up his post as Husserl's assistant,

Heidegger himself, in a letter to his former confessor Fr. Krebs, signaled his departure from "the *system* of Catholicism" and talks of his own "phenomenological studies in religion" (S, 69–70). Similarly, he wrote to his friend Elizabeth Blochmann in May 1919, stating that he was making preparations toward a "phenomenology of religious consciousness."[7] In these early Freiburg lectures Heidegger constantly emphasizes that religion as a way of life has its own "entirely originary intentionality" (*ganz originäre Intentionalität*, GA 60, 322/PRL, 244), its own structural categories—already described in his 1920/21 lecture course as "existentialia" (*Existenzialien*, GA 60, 232/PRL, 173), its own "worldliness and valuableness" (*Welt- und Werthaftigkeit*, GA 60, 322/PRL, 244), and its own basic conceptions on which philosophy must not try to impose its own conceptual schemes from without:

> Real philosophy arises not from pre-conceived concepts of philosophy and religion. Rather the possibility of its philosophical understanding arises out of a certain religiosity [*Religiosität*]—for us the Christian religiosity. . . . The task is to gain a real and original relationship to history, which is to be explicated from out of our own historical situation and facticity. (GA 60, 124–5/PRL, 89)

Heidegger claims that no real religion "allows itself to be captured philosophically" (GA 60, 323/PRL, 244).[8] Unfortunately, in this 1920–1 course—as in the Freiburg lecture courses generally—Heidegger is somewhat vague and promissory in his approach to the kind of temporality enjoyed by Christian life and how it orients itself to the eternal. His confidence in describing temporality grows over the years such that, in his 1924

lecture to the Marburg Theological Society, Heidegger is much more detailed in terms of explaining the relation between Dasein and temporality, now deliberately employing his own technical jargon. Here he laments that previous Christian thinkers (paradigmatically Augustine) have always taken their orientation from the eternity (*aei*) enjoyed by God and measured time in some respect as offset against eternity, whereas he wants to clear the foreground by analyzing how time is lived in its everyday sense. Dasein itself *is* time (GA 64/CT, 20E). Heidegger does recognize that the distinctive claim of Christianity is that time is in some sense "fulfilled" (e.g. St Paul, Gal. 4.4), but his own account concentrates on the manner the self disperses itself in the everyday and flees from facing futurity, which is the real essence of human temporality.

Heidegger's interest is to find a way to understand "life in and for itself" (GA 56/57, 125/TDP, 106) as he puts it in his 1919 lecture course "Phenomenology and Transcendental Philosophy of Value." In his 1919/1920 lecture course "Basic Problems of Phenomenology" (*Grundprobleme der Phänomenologie*, GA 58), he speaks of an "original exploration of life" (*Ursprungserforschung des Lebens*, GA 58, 155). Heidegger suggests that phenomenology has to describe the special kind of non-objectifying, nontheoretical self-awareness of original experience (GA 58, 155–7; see also 257–8). This nonreflective awareness belongs to the immediate experience of life. This theme remains—self-reflection is not the best way to grasp the meaning of Dasein. Thus, in his 1927 lecture course, Heidegger emphasizes, against Husserlian phenomenology, that self-reflection is not the primary mode in which Dasein is with itself or "for itself":

> Dasein, as existing, is there for itself, even when the ego does not expressly

direct itself to itself in the manner of its own peculiar turning around and turning back, which in phenomenology is called inner perception as contrasted with outer. The self is there for the Dasein itself without reflection and without inner perception, *before* all reflection. Reflection, in the sense of a turning back, is only a mode of self-*apprehension*, but not the mode of primary self-disclosure. (GA 24, 226/BP, 159)

In his 1920 lecture course *Phenomenology of Intuition and Expression*, Heidegger presents one of the chief tasks of philosophy as the attempt to awaken and appreciate the sense of *facticity* (*die Faktizität*): "Philosophy has the task of preserving the facticity of life and strengthening the facticity of Dasein" (GA 59, 174/PIE, 133). In notes for this course, he writes: "life—the primary phenomenon!" (*Leben Urphänomen*, GA 59, 176). Similarly, in his 1921–2 lecture course *Phenomenological Interpretations of Aristotle* he writes: "'Factical life': 'life' expresses a basic phenomenological category; it signifies a basic phenomenon" (*Grundphänomen*, GA 61, 80/PIA, 61). Life, however, is also a vague and ambiguous concept. The key to life is its "facticity": "This facticity is something life is, and whereby it is, in its highest authenticity" (GA 61, 87/ PIA, 66). Facticity is the basic sense of the being of life (ibid.). Furthermore, "philosophy is historiological cognition of factical life" (GA 61, 1/PIA, 3). Life is also, Heidegger affirms, "world-related" (GA 61, 85/PIA, 65). Thus, in his early lecture courses in Freiburg, Heidegger is concerned less with issues of Being (*Sein*) and more with the concrete sense of factical human existence.

From 1920 to 1923 Heidegger identifies and explores the existential structures that will receive full scale thematization in *Being and Time* (1927). For example, it is in reflection on the existential structures of Christian living that Heidegger develops his particular conceptions of "everydayness" (*Alltäglichkeit*), where time is experienced primarily as the present, and "fallenness" (*Verfallen*), the manner in which human life finds itself captivated by the world.[9] When Heidegger writes that "Christian experience lives time itself" (GA 60, 82/PRL, 57), he seems to be suggesting that Christianity has a certain stance toward life in its temporal unfolding, one that emphasizes a future that has in some sense already arrived, *parousia*, which in traditional Greek means "arrival" (GA 60, 102/PRL, 71), and in the Old Testament signifies the arrival of the Lord on the day or Judgment and, in Jewish texts, refers to the arrival of the Messiah. But, Heidegger claims that in Christianity it means the arriving again of the already appeared Messiah and hence its entire conceptual structure has changed. *Parousia* is not characterized by "waiting" or "hope," rather the issue is a question about the manner of carrying out one's life, the "enactment of life itself" (*Vollzug des Lebens*, GA 60, 104/PRL, 73). Living life constitutes different senses of temporality. Similarly faith (*pistis*) is not interpreted as a kind of believing, a "taking to be true" (*Fürwahrhalten*, GA 60, 108/ PRL, 76) but rather as a "complex of enactment" (*Vollzugszusammenhang*) of sense, a way of experiencing capable of "increase" or greater intensity and hence testifying to something like authenticity. Christian hope, as Heidegger interprets it, is not about some future event to come but rather about enduring, coping, and resilience in relation to the insecurity of life (GA 60, 151/PRL, 107). Heidegger is interpreting religious life not in terms of its supposed transcendent meaning but in terms of an historically determined style of living in and through time, a way of coping with the fundamental insecurity. Christian life involves "enactment" (*Vollzug*); "Christian facticity is enactment" (GA 60, 121/PRL, 86). The challenge for Christian factical life is to remain "awake and sober" in relation to the enormous challenge of life.

For Heidegger, early Christian religious life has already been Hellenized or "Greecicized" (Heidegger's word is *Gräzisierung*) due to the influence of "the specifically Greek interpretation of Dasein and through Greek conceptuality" (GA 61, 6/PIA, 6). Heidegger here explicitly speaks of "the Greek worldview" (*die griechische Lebenswelt*) and he is deeply aware—in the spirit of Dilthey—of the manner in which worldviews wither away and are replaced by different worldviews. He wants then to uncover the meaning of historical everyday existence before it is obscured by worldviews—this is *Daseinsanalyse*.

It is a noteworthy feature of this period of Heidegger's intellectual formation that the activity of removing the metaphysical edifice encrusted on religious experience is referred to, already in 1920, as "destruction" (*Destruktion*, also *Zerstörung*, GA 60, 311/PRL, 236). Heidegger's model here is Martin Luther's reading of St. Paul.[10] In his 1920 lecture course he articulates the notion of "phenomenological *Destruktion*" (GA 59, 35) or "phenomenological-critical destruction" (GA 59, 30), which should be thought of as not so much "demolition" (*Zertrümmern*) but rather as "de-structuring" (*Abbau*, GA 59, 35). In his *Phenomenology of Religious Life* lectures, he also speaks of the need to subject modern history of religion to a "phenomenological destruction" to allow the evidence of its "fore-conception" to manifest itself (GA 60, 78/PRL, 54).

Alongside theses explorations of religious life, the early Heidegger was also deeply immersed in Aristotle's account of ethical living. He offered a course on "Phenomenological Interpretations of Aristotle" in 1921/1922 (GA 61/PIA) and also prepared a text with a similar title that he submitted as a writing sample to Paul Natorp for consideration for a post in Marburg for which Husserl had recommended him. This writing sample—the so-called *Natorp Bericht*—was rediscovered and published for the first time in 1989.[11] It is a fascinating document that many—including Hans-Georg Gadamer—see as the first step toward *Being and Time*.[12] Heidegger is now explicitly linking phenomenology to a kind of Aristotelian inquiry. He is seeking "the *being* of factical life" (S, 121). The object of research is "factical human Dasein" (115). Life has a tendency to make things easy for itself (113). It has a tendency for "falling" (117). Life is always experienced as "*having-been-interpreted*" (116). "Life is always mired in inauthentic traditions and customs of one sort or another" (118). It is only when one brings one's own death into explicit focus that life as such becomes visible (119). This is genuinely anticipatory of *Being and Time* in that Heidegger now speaks of a "fundamental ontology" (121) of factical Dasein.

In these years Heidegger is also elaborating on the meaning of *hermeneutics*. In his 1921/22 course on Aristotle he is already speaking of "phenomenological hermeneutics" (GA 61, 187/PIA, 141; see also S, 122) and the fundamental intentional movement of life as *care* (*curare*). By 1923, he is characterizing hermeneutics not as any kind of interpretative *method* but rather as Dasein's own "wakefulness" (*Wachsein*) with regard to its own existence; hermeneutics is the *self-interpretation* of facticity (GA 63, 15/

OHF, 12). As Heidegger writes in his *Natorp Bericht*:

> ... philosophy is not an artificial occupation that merely accompanies life and deals with "universals" ... but rather is a knowing that questions, that is, as research, simply the explicit and genuine actualizing of the tendency towards interpretation that belongs to the basic movements of life in which what is at issue is this life itself and its being ... (S, 121)

In other words, humans live through self-interpretative engagement with their lives and philosophy is that illumination of that self-interpreting historical living in facticity.

In Autumn 1923 Heidegger moved to Marburg. Heidegger now comes into close contact with neo-Kantian philosophers such as Nicolai Hartmann, distinguished classicists such as Natorp, and theologians such as Rudolf Otto and Bultmann.[13] But he himself seemed to find more affinity in the writings of Dilthey and Scheler. In 1924, he offered "Basic Concepts of Aristotelian Philosophy" (*Grundbegriffe der aristotelischen Philosophie*, GA 18), which focused on the *Nicomachean Ethics*. The theme is practical life. In 1925, Heidegger was nominated by the Philosophy Faculty for the Chair at Marburg recently vacated by Hartmann. However, his nomination was turned down by the Education Ministry because of insufficient publications. To remedy this gap, he was pressured by the Dean of the Marburg Faculty to hasten into print the still uncompleted manuscript of *Being and Time*. Heidegger promised to have the typescript to Niemeyer by April 1, 1926. Over the term break, from February to April 1926, Heidegger retired to his hut in Todtnauberg and brought together some 240 pages of *Being*

and Time that he arranged—with Husserl's help—to have printed. Husserl himself even visited Todtnauberg that Spring to assist Heidegger with the proofreading.[14] However, in December 1926, the Education Minister in Berlin declared the publication inadequate and the Chair in Marburg was not offered to Heidegger. Heidegger then went on to publish the full text of *Being and Time, Part I* in Spring 1927 both as a separate book and as part of Husserl's *Jahrbuch*.[15] Heidegger's magnum opus had finally appeared in print, an uneven work that manifests the enormous efforts Heidegger had made to impose a system (transcendental phenomenological ontology) and even an architectonic (see § 8 "Design of the Treatise," GA 2, 52–3/BTMR, 63–4) on what had been his diverse concrete explorations of human historical existence (his "preparatory fundamental analysis of Dasein," GA 2, 53/BTMR, 64) over the preceding decade.

NOTES AND REFERENCES

[1] See Heidegger's Letter to Richardson, in William J. Richardson, *Heidegger: Through Phenomenology to Thought* (The Hague: Nijhoff, 1963), viii–xxiii.

[2] Franz Brentano, *Von der mannigfachen Bedeutung des Seienden nach Aristoteles* (Freiburg: Herder, 1862; reprinted, Darmstadt: Wissenschaftliche Buchgesellschaft, 1960), translated by Rolf George as *On the Several Senses of Being in Aristotle* (Berkeley: University of California Press, 1975).

[3] Theodore Kisiel, *The Genesis of Being and Time* (Berkeley: University of California Press, 1993), 229, has rightly pointed out that both "My Way to Phenomenology" and the letter to Richardson stress only Heidegger's involvement with phenomenology and hence are not reliable guides to his overall intellectual development.

[4] M. Heidegger, *Die Lehre vom Urteil in Psychologismus. Eik kritisch-positiver Beitrag zur Logik* (Leipzig: Barth, 1914).

[5] Quoted in Elizabeth Hirsch, "Remembrances of Martin Heidegger in Marburg," *Philosophy Today* (Summer 1979), 160–9.

[6] See Karl Schuhmann, *Husserl-Chronik. Denk- und Lebensweg Edmund Husserls* (The Hague: Nijhoff, 1977), 231. For the significance of Husserl's achievement in gaining funding for a paid assistantship, see Hugo Ott, *Martin Heidegger. A Political Life*, trans. Allan Blunden (Oxford: Blackwell, 1993), 115–16. Heidegger had been a *Privatdozent* but Husserl secured funding for him. It is not clear that Heidegger was actually Husserl's assistant in the formal sense.

[7] See *Martin Heidegger-Elizabeth Blochmann Briefe 1918–1969*, hrsg. Joachim W. Storck (Marbach am Necker: Deutsches Literatur-Archiv, 1989), 16; 2nd edn, 1990.

[8] Heidegger was not alone in wanting to free religion from its philosophical superstructure. Ernst Troeltsch and Rudolf Bultmann were proposing something similar.

[9] In his "Letter on 'Humanism,'" Heidegger emphasizes that *Verfallen* does not signify the theological Fall of humanity but rather an essential relation of human being to Being, see, GA 9, 163/PA, 253.

[10] John van Buren, *The Young Heidegger* (Bloomington: Indiana University Press, 1994), 167, has suggested that Heidegger's first use of the term "destruction" is in GA 58, 139, in connection with Luther's attack on Aristotle and Scholasticism. However, I believe van Buren overstates the case when he claims: "The young Heidegger saw himself at this time as a kind of philosophical Luther of Western metaphysics" (ibid., 167). In fact, Heidegger's tone in his lecture courses is still one of trying to come to terms with the meaning of the various competing philosophical methods (neo-Kantian, phenomenological, hermeneutic, life-philosophy) that were current in contemporary Germany. It is true, if a little odd, that Heidegger arrived in Marburg with a reputation as an expert on Luther!

[11] See M. Heidegger, "Phänomenologische Interpretationen zu Aristoteles. Anzeige der hermeneutischen Situation," *Dilthey-Jahrbruch für Philosophie und Geschichte der Geisteswissenschaften* 6 (1989), 237–74; reprinted in *Phänomenologische Interpretationen zu Aristoteles. Ausarbeitung für die Marburger und die Göttinger Fakultät (1922)* (Stuttgart: Reclam, 2003). There is a new English translation by John van Buren "Phenomenological Interpretations in Connection with Aristotle. An Indication of the Hermeneutical Situation" (S, 111–45).

[12] Indeed Husserl had even planned to publish a version of it in Volume VII of his *Jahrbuch* (1924/1925).

[13] On Heidegger's time in Marburg see Elisabeth Hirsch, "Remembrances of Martin Heidegger in Marburg," *Philosophy Today*, 23(1979), 160–9.

[14] In the tradition of proofreading, it is customary to read the text backward so that typographical errors are more visible as one is not disrupted by the flow of the text. It is possibly for this reason that Husserl did not at that time realize how far Heidegger had departed from his own transcendental phenomenology until he sat down to read and comment on the book in 1929.

[15] In later years Heidegger recalled that *Being and Time* was published in February 1927, whereas Theodore Kisiel, *The Genesis of Being and Time*, 489, dates it to April 1927. On April 8, 1926—Husserl's birthday—Heidegger presented Husserl with a handwritten dedication page for the book.

3

THE TURN: ALL THREE OF THEM
Thomas Sheehan

Heidegger's main topic was not "being"—and that for at least two reasons. First of all, when Heidegger uses the phrase "the being of beings" (*das Sein des Seienden*), he understands the phrase as *das Anwesen des Anwesenden*, the meaningful presence of things to human concerns. In other words, despite Heidegger's employment of the surpassed ontological lexicon of "being," there is, underlying all of his work, a phenomenological reduction of "being" to "meaning." In his mature work, in fact, Heidegger shied away from the word *Sein*. "I no longer like to use the word 'being,'" he said.

> "Being" remains only the provisional term. Consider that "being" was originally called "presence" [*Anwesen*] in the sense of a thing's staying-here-before-us in unconcealment [i.e. in meaningfulness].[1]

Thus Heidegger does not read the phrase "the being of beings" in terms of things existing "out there in the world," so to speak, apart from human beings, as does classical realist metaphysics. Rather, he understands "the being of beings" *phenomenologically*, as referring to the meaningful presence of things to our corresponding needs and interests, whether practical or theoretical. At least initially, Heidegger focused on the *correlation* between whatever we encounter and the corresponding human concerns and intentions. Which is to say that the early Heidegger concentrated on the *significance to us* of whatever we meet in the world.

The second reason why being is not Heidegger's main topic is the same reason why meaningfulness (*Anwesen*) was not his final goal but only his initial concern. Heidegger's ultimate purpose was not to analyze the meaningfulness of things but to move beyond such meaningfulness to the "X" *that makes it possible*. Using the tradition's ontological lexicon, he named this project the quest for the "essence" of being (*das Wesen des Seins*). This means not the definable "whatness" of being but, rather, what brings being about. To state the matter more properly in phenomenological terms, Heidegger's sights were ultimately set on what *allows for or makes possible* meaningfulness (*das Anwesenlassen*), that is, the *source and provenance* of meaningfulness (*die Herkunft des Anwesens*).[2] He called that enabling source "the clearing" (*Lichtung*), understood as the primal opening up of intelligibility at all (*Verstehbarkeit*) that lets us make sense of whatever we encounter.[3]

These two moments of Heidegger's project—the analysis of the meaningfulness of things and the discovery of the source of that meaningfulness—correspond to what we may distinguish as his "lead-in question" and his "basic question." In turn we might align those two moments with the earlier (1919–29) and the later (1930–76) periods of his philosophy.

* * *

Like many of Heidegger's key terms, "the turn" (*die Kehre*) is analogical rather than univocal: it refers, by way of an analogy of attribution (πρὸς ἕν), to at least three distinct but interrelated issues in Heidegger's thought. We may call them (1) reciprocity, (2) reversal, and (3) resoluteness.[4]

The first and primary issue that bears the title "the turn" is what Heidegger calls the *reciprocity (Gegenschwung)*[5] or back-and-forth oscillation between human existence (*Dasein*) and meaning. We can express that reciprocity in a chiasmic formula: Without human being, there is no meaning, and without meaning, there is no human being. This reciprocity of need is the core of Heidegger's thinking, what he called "the thing itself." Meaning needs us if things are to be intelligible; and we need meaning if we are to exist at all and as *das Da,* the locus of all possible sense. Especially in his *Contributions to Philosophy* (1936–8; published 1989), Heidegger declares that this reciprocity is in fact the proper sense of the turn, "the hidden ground of all other subordinate turns. . . ."[6] It is the prime analogue that lends meaning to the other, subordinate usages of the term *Kehre*. Therefore, let us call this reciprocity *Kehre*-1.

The second and quite distinct issue that also bears the title "the turn" is "the reversal," the de facto shift in focus that Heidegger carried out in his work from the 1930s onwards, a shift from his lead-in question about meaningfulness to his basic question about the "X" that makes meaningfulness possible. Most Heideggerians wrongly take this second and secondary meaning of the turn as the proper sense of *die Kehre*. As against that, and in order to emphasize its secondary nature, I will call this reversal *Kehre*-2.

A third and analogous meaning of the "turn" (*Kehre*-3) refers to the radical conversion in one's self-understanding that ideally follows from realizing that *Kehre*-1/reciprocity is the basis of all meaningfulness and thus of human existence itself.[7] This personal ("existentiel") conversion in how one understands and lives out one's life is discussed by the early Heidegger under the rubric of "resoluteness" (*Entschlossenheit*) and by the later Heidegger under that of "releasement" (*Gelassenheit*), understood as taking "the turn into *Ereignis*."[8] Both of these are understood as the entrée to what Heidegger called "authenticity" in the sense of living in terms of one's true selfhood.

Among these three analogical meanings of the word *Kehre*—the *reciprocity* of man and meaning, the *reversal* of perspective worked out in the 1930s, and the *resoluteness* that ideally follows from an awareness of the finitude of reciprocity—it is the first one, the chiasm of man and meaning, that ultimately controls the other two. On the one hand, the reversal of perspective (*Kehre*-2) that was planned for the unpublished part of *Being and Time* and that was de facto carried out in the mid-1930s, is only a *means* to arriving at a clear understanding of the reciprocity of man and meaning: *Kehre*-1. On the other hand, the resoluteness or releasement that can follow from insight into the reciprocity is the way that we personally enact the consequences of that reciprocity in our own lives. Thus, as is the case with the analogy of attribution, the second and third meanings of the turn gather around and derive their sense from the first and primary meaning, the prime analogue that is *Kehre*-1. In fact this reciprocity of man and meaning is the core of Heidegger's thought, the "thing itself" (*die Sache selbst*).

We now take up the main characteristics of each of these three "turns."

* * *

Kehre-1, reciprocity. Only with the posthumous publication of Heidegger's *Contributions to Philosophy* did it become clear that the primary meaning of "the turn" was the chiasmic reciprocity of human existence's need of meaning and meaning's need of human existence. The thesis underlying this position is that the very nature of human being is to make discursive sense of things, that is, to understand their meaning (to deny this thesis is willy-nilly to make sense of it and thus to confirm it). We do not first exist and only then, as an add-on, make sense of things. Rather, we are pan-hermeneutical: sense-making *is* our very existence. Even madness is a way of making sense.

To begin with the first moment of this chiasmic reciprocity: *Contributions* speaks of human existence as necessarily belonging (*zugehörend*) to meaning in the sense of *sustaining the openness* that is the condition of all discursive intelligibility. Meaningfulness requires a "space"—a possibilizing dimension—within which we can perform the twofold act of making sense of something, namely, distinguishing S and P (διαίρεσις: keeping distinct a thing and its possible meanings) while taking S in terms of P (σύνθεσις: unifying the thing and its meaning). The primordial openness of the clearing is what makes possible such distinguishing and synthesizing. Without that possibilizing

"space" there could be no meaningfulness at all, whether practical (using this tool for that task) or theoretical (taking Socrates as an Athenian). The primary function of human existence, its raison d'être, is to hold open that space and to belong to meaning. Or to put it in terms of the second half of the chiasm: meaning requires (*braucht*) human existence to sustain the openness within which meaning can occur.

Heidegger often speaks of meaning as such ("being itself") as taking the initiative of "calling" human existence to itself and as awaiting a "response" or "correspondence" to that call.[9] He will sometimes say that being itself "throws itself forth" to human existence while at the same time "claiming" existence as its own "property" (*Eigentum*).[10] Such metaphors risk serious misunderstanding, not only because they hypostasize being itself into an "other" that stands over against human existence but also because they attribute anthropomorphic agency to meaning ("being itself"), as if it had a mind and will of its own. The same anthropomorphizing hypostatization persists in Heidegger's use of the *faux* reflexive voice when he speaks of being "hiding *itself*" from and "revealing *itself*" to human beings. The way to avoid these gross misunderstandings is first of all to read "being" phenomenologically in terms of meaningfulness and its enabling source, and then to understand man's "thrown" nature (*Geworfenheit*) as the necessity of holding open the space for meaning.

In *Contributions to Philosophy*, Heidegger equates such thrown-openness with what he calls the "appropriation" (*Ereignis* or *Ereignetsein*) of human being to sustaining the clearing. The term *Ereignis*/appropriation means the same thing as thrownness and has to do with human existence being "brought into its own."[11] Appropriation is the later Heidegger's preferred term for the chiasmic reciprocity that is *Kehre*-1. One's appropriation to holding open the clearing *is* one's thrown-openness (with emphasis on the thrownness) *as* the clearing. *Ereignis* is thus the "thing itself" of Heidegger's philosophy. It is the the opening of the openness that allows for meaningful presence (*Anwesenlassen*) and thus answers the question of how meaningfulness "is given." Heidegger's key phrase *Es gibt Sein* ("being is given") now translates as: "Appropriation/thrown-openness is what makes meaningfulness possible."

* * *

Kehre-2, the reversal. Heidegger's shift of focus from meaningfulness to its source was already programmed into the 1927 outline of *Being and Time*. The book was projected in two parts, which we may abbreviate as BT I (fundamental ontology) and BT II (historical deconstruction), but only BT I interests us here. The first two divisions of part one (= BT I.1–2) were focused on how human existence is thrown open as the locus of all possible meaningfulness. The third division (= BT I.3) was then going to effect a shift in focus, a "reversal" (*Kehre*-2) *from* human thrown-openness as the locus of meaning *to* the question of how meaningfulness "is given" within the space of that openness. Whereas BT I.1–2 concentrated on human existence, BT I.3 would reverse things and concentrate on meaningfulness itself, with special emphasis on its source. In that sense, *Kehre*-2 was to be the "reversal" (William J. Richardson) of the trajectory of BT I.1–2.

However, BT I.3 was never published, partly because Heidegger found the transcendental approach, with human existence as its centerpiece, inadequate to carry out the full project of *Being and Time*. The book remained a torso, and the reversal, at least in the transcendental form in which Heidegger had originally planned to carry it out, remained a road not taken. Nonetheless, still intent on carrying out the turn to meaningfulness and its source, Heidegger in the 1930s adopted a different approach to his project, one that he characterized as *seinsgeschichtlich*, which is best paraphrased as the "giving-of-meaning" approach.

Thus from 1930 on, we notice a remarkable shift in Heidegger's lectures and publications. If his early work emphasized the first half of the chiasm—no human being = no meaning—his later work shifted its focus to the second half: no meaning = no human being. The focus now in *Kehre*-2 was on how the clearing, which it is our very nature to hold open, makes possible the meaning of all we encounter. But even with this shift, what remained constant throughout the earlier and the later work was the core of Heidegger's thought: the reciprocity of need that we have called *Kehre*-1. In fact, *Kehre*-2, the reversal, was only a means to spelling out *Kehre*-1, the reciprocity that is the goal of Heidegger's thought. So once again we state the chiasm—but now in the reverse order: The clearing-for-meaning is human existence's raison d'être (in that sense the clearing has priority over existence); and human existence is the sine qua non of the clearing-for-meaning (in that sense, existence is the ground of the emergence of meaning).

* * *

Kehre-3, resoluteness. Above I said that *Kehre*-1—the reciprocity of need between man and meaning—is the final goal of Heidegger's thinking. But that is not exactly right. First of all, the final goal of his entire project is not theoretical but practical: a transformation in human being itself (*eine Verwandlung des Menschseins selbst*).[12] Secondly, an effective and not merely theoretical understanding of the reciprocity of man and meaning issues in that very transformation. In the text cited below, Heidegger speaks of the "truth of being," by which he means the *opening for* (or "dis-closure of") meaningfulness, which equates with the appropriated clearing as the source that enables all meaning. The phrase "the meaning-process" in the following text translates the German *Seyn*. Note the relation between all three senses of the "turn."

> We must insist over and over that what is at stake in the question of the openness [of the meaning-process] as raised here is . . . *a transformation in human being itself* [*Kehre*-3: resoluteness]. . . . We are questioning human being in its relation to the meaning-process, or in the perspective of *Kehre*-2 [i.e. the reversal], the meaning-process and its openness in relation to human being. Determining the essence of openness [*Kehre*-1] is accompanied by a necessary transformation of human being [*Kehre*-3]. Both are the same.[13]

The whole of Heidegger's work is a protreptic to accept and become what one already is: thrown open for the sake of meaningfulness. This means taking the reciprocity, with all its finitude, upon oneself as the basis for a new, authentic way of living. Before the reversal *Being and Time* culminated in an exhortation to resoluteness, to becoming oneself by taking over one's thrownness (*Übernahme der Geworfenheit*).[14] After the reversal Heidegger's work is an exhortation to become oneself by taking over one's appropriation (*Übernahme der Er-eignung*).[15] In both cases (which are coequal) the issue is an

effective acceptance of the "mystery" of one's inexorable way of being, namely thrownness or appropriation for the sake of sustaining the clearing for meaning. The point of Heidegger's exhortation is to "love our fate," that is, to take upon ourselves (= *Kehre*-3) our finite appropriation (= *Kehre*-1) and to live in accord with it.

Thus *Kehre*-3 or resoluteness not only depends on insight into *Kehre*-1 but also is related to it in three other ways. The first deals with the threefold hiddenness of *Ereignis* (hiddenness, too, is an analogical term) and thus with the difficulty of personally realizing one's thrownness as the basis of a possible conversion. The second concerns Heidegger's so-called "history of being," which he presents under the rubric of appropriation/thrown-openness as the giving of "epochs of meaningfulness" (*die Geschicke des Seins*). The third is the virtual obliteration of all traces of *Ereignis* in the present age. In what follows, I gather these three issues together.

The three analogical levels of the hiddenness of appropriation, and thus of the clearing, are (1) their *intrinsic* hiddenness, (2) the *overlooking* of that hiddenness, and (3) the present age's *virtual obliteration* of both the intrinsic hiddenness and its overlooking. The second level corresponds to the history of metaphysics and the third to the current age of techno-think (*Technik*).

As regards the first level of hiddenness. Because our thrown-openness is the presupposition of all sense-making, it is opaque to any attempt to find out why that is the case. Heidegger expresses this opacity as the "intrinsic hiddenness" of the bond of man and meaning. Because that bond of appropriation is the presupposition of all sense-making, one cannot make sense of *it*—for example, trace it back to a reason or cause—without presupposing it and thus falling into circular reasoning. We can experience *the fact* that thrown-openness-for-the-sake-of-meaning is as far back as we can go, but we are unable to peek over its edge to find out *why* thrownness/appropriation is the case. We can discern *that* but not *why* we are thrown into the need to sustain the clearing-for-meaning. To try to make sense of this thrownness requires that we already use it as the basis of our effort to make sense of it—which comes down to the logical fallacy called "begging the question" (*petitio principii*), that is, already assuming and utilizing what we say we are trying to explain.[16] This complete opacity to questions about the what and why of thrown-openness is what Heidegger means by the intrinsic hiddenness of the man-meaning reciprocity. It is the prime analogue for the other two meanings of hiddenness.

Metaphysics and the second level of hiddenness. Given its intrinsic hiddenness, the reciprocal man-meaning bond is easily overlooked and forgotten, and this constitutes the second level of hiddenness. For Heidegger, the history of Western philosophy is a history of overlooking human thrownness and the open region of possible intelligibility that it sustains. Metaphysics (1) has focused on the meaningfulness ("being") of whatever is encountered within the clearing, while forgetting the clearing itself; and (2) has traced meaningfulness back to an ultimate ontic cause or reason, usually but not necessarily called "god."

Thus for metaphysics the clearing is bracketed out (is subject to an epoché), that is, the fact of its intrinsic hiddenness is overlooked. Hence the history of meaning is parceled out as a series of metaphysical formations of meaning. These formations are distinct "gifts" (*Geschicke*) of the "giving of meaning" (*Schenkung*) that is made possible by thrown-openness. These individual formations—called "epochs" insofar as appropriation and the clearing are under epoché—can be distinguished by seeing how select Western philosophers, from Plato through Nietzsche, construed the basic sense of "being"/meaningfulness: for example, εἶδος in Plato, ἐνέργεια in Aristotle, *esse* in Aquinas, and so on. In all such historical cases—as well as in individuals today who are unable to see through their fallenness to the thrown-open clearing—the intrinsic hiddenness of *Ereignis* is doubled: *Ereignis*, the source of the clearing that allows for all meaningfulness, is not only ineluctably hidden, but that hiddenness is also overlooked and forgotten.

The result is that the ideal of traditional Western humanism is a conversion to a metaphysical understanding of man as the rational animal, capable of comprehending the meaning of things and its ultimate entitative cause, but blocked from an insight into, much less a conversion to, the mortal thrown-openness that is *Kehre*-1.

The present age and the third level of hiddenness. Heidegger holds that the current epoch of meaningfulness is characterized by techno-think (*Technik*) and its compulsion to construe everything, including human beings, as a resource to be exploited for capitalization and consumption. The danger haunting this age is that techno-think virtually blots out all traces of both the intrinsic hiddenness *and* the overlooking of *Ereignis* and thus leads to a "tripling" of the hiddenness of our appropriation. The age of techno-think and global exploitation is characterized by a virtually complete *obliteration* (third level) of our *overlooking and forgetting* (second level) of the *intrinsic hiddenness* of the reciprocity (first level).

However, Heidegger sees a glimmer of hope that at least some people ("the few") could, at opportune moments, enjoy "a brief glimpse into the mystery"[17]—a moment of epiphany—and even further, might "turn into *Ereignis*." In his 1949 lecture "*Die Kehre*," Heidegger held out the prospect that, in this age that virtually obliterates *Ereignis*, some might sense their profound alienation from the source of meaning. In a moment of sudden but decisive epiphany (*Blitz, Blick*),[18] they might experience their mortal bondedness to meaning and thereby be drawn to a transformation of themselves and of the current oppressive formation of meaning.

* * *

In summary: (1) A proper, *phenomenological* understanding of "the turn" begins with the realization that Heidegger's discourse about "being" is to be understood as a discourse about meaningfulness, one that is ultimately focused on the *source* of meaningfulness. The traditional and easily misunderstood *ontological* terms for that source include "being itself," "the essence of being," and "the truth of being." Phenomenologically that source is to be understood as "the clearing," that is, our appropriation or thrown-openness for the sake of discursive meaningfulness. (2) The reciprocity of need—meaning requires us, and we require meaning, both moments at the service of our making sense of things—is what Heidegger calls the primary "turn" at the heart of his thinking (*Kehre*-1), an effective insight into which would constitute a resolute conversion to living an authentic life based on one's radical finitude (*Kehre*-3). Heidegger's change of perspective from human existence as the locus of meaningfulness to the clearing as the locus of human existence (= *Kehre*-2) was carried out in the 1930s and finally fulfilled the project that was announced for part one

of *Being and Time*. (3) Heidegger's history of philosophy reads all of Western metaphysics as oblivious of the intrinsic hiddenness of the reciprocity that is *Kehre*-1. While the present age of techno-think harbors the danger of obliterating any trace even of our obliviousness, Heidegger holds out the hope of a personal insight into the source of meaning and human existence, and a corresponding turn or transformation in how we lead our lives.

NOTES AND REFERENCES

1. GA 15, 20.8–9/HS 8.34–5: "Obwohl ich dieses Wort nicht mehr gern gebrauche"; and GA 7, 234.13–17/EGT, 78.21–4: ". . . her-vor-währen in die Unverborgenheit."
2. GA 14, 45.29–30/TB, 37.5–6: "Anwesen*lassen*." GA 6.2, 304.10–11 = NIV, 201.13–15: "Wesensherkunft," "Herkunft von Anwesen." See GA 2, 53.34–5: "Das Anwesen aus dieser Herkunft."
3. GA 16, 424.18–22: "der Bereich der Unverborgenheit oder Lichtung (Verstehbarkeit)." See GA 9, 199.21/PA, 152.24: ". . . ins Offene des Begreifens."
4. In this paper I put aside the hapaxlogomenon of the "metontological" turn that leads to metontology *qua* "metaphysical ontics" (GA 26, 201.28–35/MFL, 158.29–35). As far as I can see, Heidegger never again mentions this "turn." I disagree with Theodore Kisiel that the metontological turn is referenced in Heidegger's preparatory notes to GA 29/30: See Bret Davis, (ed.), *Martin Heidegger: Key Concepts* (Durham: Acumen, 2009), 28.17.
5. GA 65, 251.24/CP2, 198.14; see ibid., 261.26/206.3: "gegenschwingende." The new translation of CP (CP2) uses "oscillation" for "Gegenschwung."
6. GA 65, 407.7–11/CP2, 322.32–4: "der verborgene Grund aller anderen, nachgeordneten . . . Kehren."
7. Heidegger speaks of the goal of his work as the transformation of a person into *Dasein*, that is, into accepting oneself as thrown-open as the clearing for the sake of meaning. This, he says, is the same as *Kehre*-1. Hence I

name this transformation *Kehre*-3. This turn is referred to in Heidegger's lecture "The Turn" at GA 79, 76.3–4/BFL, 71.31–2: "sich ent-wirft, ent-spricht."

[8] GA 14, 50.23 and 51.33/TB, 41.24 and 42.30–1: das Einkehr in das Ereignis.

[9] GA 9, 322.30–1/PA, 246.15–16; "Noch wartet das Sein, daß Es selbst dem Menschen denk-würdig werde."

[10] GA 65, 263.14/CP2 207.16.

[11] GA 65, 239.5/CP2 188.25: ". . . geworfener . . . d.h. er-eignet"; ibid., 304.8/240.16: "Dasein ist geworfen, ereignet"; ibid., 34.9/29.7: "die Er-eignung, das Geworfenwerden in das eigentliche Innestehen in der Wahrheit von der *Kehre im Ereignis.*"

[12] GA 45, 214.18/BQP, 181.7–8, italicized in the original. See the next note.

[13] GA 45, 214.15–26/BQP, 181.5–15. Heidegger's emphasis.

[14] GA 2, 431.13/BT, 226.13–14.

[15] GA 65, 322.7–8/CP2, 169.14.

[16] Aristotle, *Prior Analytics* II 16, 64b 28–65a 9: τὸ ἐν ἀρχῇ αἰτεῖσθαι: On circular reasoning, ibid., II 5, 57b 18—59b 1.

[17] GA 65, 11.21ff./CP2, 11.38ff: die Wenige. GA 9, 198.21–2/PA, 151.36: "Der Ausblick in das Geheimnis."

[18] See GA 79, 74–5/BFL, 70–1. Note the equivalence of Einblitz der Welt, Lichtblick von Welt, Blitz der Wahrheit, and Blitz des Seyns.

4

HEIDEGGER IN THE 1930s: WHO ARE WE?

Richard Polt

The decade of the 1930s is a distinctive and troubled period in Heidegger's philosophical career, marked by a shift "from the understanding of Being to the happening of Being" (GA 40, 219). That is, instead of analyzing Dasein's capacity to understand the meaning of Being, as he intended to do in *Being and Time*, Heidegger now looks to the happening by virtue of which Dasein comes into its own as the entity who stands in the truth of Being. The emphasis is no longer on our own constitution—human nature, in traditional terms—but on a transformative event that seizes us and thrusts us into the condition of being-there.

Such an event could involve the founding of a new political order—and in fact, the 1930s are notoriously the decade of Heidegger's overt political engagement, including his 1933–4 tenure as Nazi rector of the University of Freiburg. For several years, he is intensely concerned with action, decision, and an authentic gathering of the German *Volk*. By the end of the decade, however, Heidegger's view of politics is considerably jaundiced; in the 1940s he will develop a philosophy of *Gelassenheit* or "release-ment" that lays aside power and will in order to await the gift of Being. The 1930s, then,

are marked by Heidegger's attempt to leap actively into a singular, transformative event that would bring Germany into its own.

A detailed survey of this period would have to review Heidegger's intricate interpretations of a variety of thinkers, his passionate but ambivalent connection to National Socialism in thought and practice, and the relationship of his academic lecture courses and seminars to his voluminous private texts. In this brief overview we can only scratch the surface, but one recurring question can serve as our guiding thread: "Who are we?" For a time Heidegger believed that Hitler could answer this question in practice, but with his increasing distance from the Nazi party, he comes to see the question as a deeper and more difficult one, requiring a philosophical and poetic struggle that may never eventuate in a solution.

THE PREDICAMENT OF "WHO?"

Heidegger lays the basis for the question, "Who are we?" in the 1920s, when he develops a conception of human temporality that culminates in the individual's choice of how to exist. Each of us is thrown into a concrete heritage, inhabits a meaningful world, and projects possible ways to act in terms of some ultimate "for-the-sake-of-which"—a possibility that provides the raison d'être for one's choices and in terms of which one's meaningful world is structured (SZ, 84). However, we ordinarily forget and even avoid this ultimate possibility; it is easier to sink into everyday inauthenticity, and simply take one's world and one's identity for granted.

Being and Time formalizes this human predicament by defining Dasein as the entity whose own Being is an issue for it (41–2). That is, we are always, either deliberately or by default, taking a stand on our own Being and deciding how to exist. We thus have a relation to our own Being that other entities seem to lack. But our relation to ourselves also affects our relation to all other entities: we exist by Being-in-the-world, and we encounter other entities within the world, so the question of how to exist marks our interpretation of entities other than ourselves (12–13). In short, I care about the Being of all beings in terms of how I care about my own Being. What beings signify to me depends on *who* I take myself to be.

One can gain insight into one's own Being, and ultimately into Being as such, only by lifting oneself out of everyday, anesthetized comfort and coming to grips with *who* one is. Heidegger thus says that Dasein is a "who," not a "what" (45). A general definition of the human species fails to yield insight into how any individual is existing; we must ask who the person is, that is, which defining possibility he or she is pursuing. Furthermore, because Dasein is always Being-with, we can infer that the question "Who am I?" implies the further question, "Who are we?"—a decision about the destiny of a people. Every generation must discover its destiny, Heidegger

writes laconically, through "communicating and struggling" (384).

Heidegger begins to address the communal dimension of identity more explicitly in the 1929–30 lecture course *The Fundamental Concepts of Metaphysics*. Here he carries out an exhaustive first-person-singular phenomenology of boredom, and then makes a surprising leap into the first person plural: he identifies "profound boredom" as the defining mood of "our" time (GA 29/30, 239–49/FCM, 160–7). In this condition, nothing seems urgent; the question of who we are has not come alive for the community. Heidegger's bold step into cultural critique anticipates the hazardous commitments of the decade to come, when he will often refer to *die Not der Notlosigkeit*, the urgency of the lack of urgency (e.g. GA 45, 183/BQP, 158).

The courses of the next few years evince Heidegger's desire to address the question of who "we" are on the basis of a concrete place, time, and community rather than in the name of an abstract "humanity" or "Dasein."

In *The Essence of Human Freedom* (1930), Heidegger argues that the concepts of negative and positive freedom both invite reflection on the general question of what it means to be (GA 31, 6–7, 30–1/EHF, 4–5, 22–3). But he does not subordinate the problem of freedom to the problem of Being: to the contrary, the question of Being itself is a "problem of freedom," not only theoretically but in a concrete sense, since it requires one to "become essential in the actual willing of [one's] own essence" (GA 31, 303/EHF, 205).[1]

The philosophical tradition, in Heidegger's view, has failed to engage the problems of freedom and Being deeply enough. He attempts to reveal "what remained *un-happened*" in the tradition (GA 34, 322/ET, 228) through readings of key texts such as the *Critique of*

Pure Reason (GA 31/PICPR; GA 41/WIT) and Book Theta of Aristotle's *Metaphysics*, which establishes the priority of actuality over potentiality (GA 31, 107/EHF, 75; GA 33/AM). Heidegger, in contrast, affirms the possible over the actual: it is only in terms of possible ways to be—which are always shadowed by the possibility of death—that we can encounter any actualities (SZ, 262).

Our own essence must be chosen from *finite* possibilities. Accordingly, in his 1930-1 reading of the *Phenomenology of Spirit*, Heidegger asks: are "we," with Hegel, those who presume to possess absolute knowledge (GA 32, 71/HPS, 50-1), or are knowledge and being not absolute, but finite (GA 32, 55, 145/HPS, 38, 100-1)? If being is finite, Heidegger implies that "we" must also recognize our finitude by thinking and acting from a unique historical situation. Accordingly, true freedom is not the absence of limits, but the right kind of self-binding (GA 34, 59/ET, 44). Even God, Heidegger suggests, must be finite, not omnipotent (GA 33, 158/AM, 135).

Heidegger's account of the history of Western philosophy is deepened through readings such as these and by the beginning of his intense interest in pre-Socratic thought (GA 35). The common thread in these interpretations is the need for a free but situated decision that would reorient our own Being and, in this way, establish a fresh relation to Being as such.

GERMAN DESTINY AND THE POLITICS OF BEING

For Heidegger, the triumph of National Socialism in 1933 seems to have provided, for a while, an answer in practice to the question, "Who are we?" and the opportunity to find the liberating bond. According to Rector Heidegger's inaugural address of May 1933, by taking its place in the new order, the university is performing an act of "self-assertion." This kind of self-assertion is not arbitrary license, but positive commitment: labor service, military service, and knowledge service (GA 16, 113-14/HR, 113-14).

At this time, Heidegger puts his own thought into the service of dictatorship. According to his 1933-4 seminar on "Nature, History, and State," the state is the very Being of the people: in the state, the *Volk* finds its identity and endurance.[2] The people naturally feels *eros* for the state, just as every individual wills to exist. And since the state essentially depends on the "soaring will" of a born leader, it is ultimately the *Führer* who decides who the German people is.[3] The only alternative, as Heidegger sees it, is confusion and collapse. A "higher bond," such as a bond to the *Volk*, "creates the highest freedom, whereas lack of commitment is negative freedom. One has sometimes understood political freedom in this latter sense, and thus misunderstood it."[4]

The course "On the Essence of Truth," from the same semester, glorifies the darkest element of Nazism: glossing Heraclitus on *polemos* or war, Heidegger proposes that in order to avoid losing its edge, a people must find—or even fabricate—its inner enemies and pursue them ruthlessly, to the point of elimination (GA 36/37, 91/BAT, 73). One way to answer the "who" question, in practice, is to annihilate those among us who "we" are not.

The same course includes a vehement attack on biological interpretations of Nazism. Heidegger insists that human beings cannot be understood biologically precisely because they are a "who." Only an entity whose own Being is at issue for it faces a destiny and is capable of freedom and sacrifice (GA 36/37, 210–11, 214–15/BAT, 161, 163–4).

Heidegger's lectures on *Logic as the Question Concerning the Essence of Language* in 1934 unfold as a series of questions, with the "who" question at the center (GA 38, 78, 97/LEL, 67, 81–2). What is logic? Logic is rooted in language, so we must inquire into humans as the beings who have language. To be human is to be a self, an entity that is thrown into the questions, "Who am I?" and "Who are we?" We are a people—but what is that? Belonging to the people is a matter of decision: we decide to testify that "We are here!" and we affirm the will of a state that wills that the people become its own master. Decision brings us into history—but what is history? If history is temporal, what is time? We must realize that we ourselves are time's "temporalizing" (GA 38, 120/LEL, 100). Heidegger concludes by pointing to the world-building power of poetic language.

It is to poetry that Heidegger turns in search of a deeper understanding of the German essence. His first lecture course (1934–5) on Hölderlin, the enigmatic poet who muses on Germany's relation to the Greeks and the departed gods, emphasizes the difficulty of "the free use of the national," the challenge of discovering and even of asking who we are, and the enigma of the fatherland (GA 39, 4, 49, 290–4). The riddle of national identity calls for an elite who can participate in the poetic founding of a secret Germany. Such themes will recur in further courses on Hölderlin in 1941 and 1942 (GA 52, GA 53/HHTI; see below, chapter 26).

Poetic founding is not necessarily peaceful. At the same time as he is discovering Hölderlin, Heidegger embraces the language of power and conflict in a way that blends politics with ontology. This is evident in the 1935 course *Introduction to Metaphysics* (see Chapter 24 in this volume). As he puts it there, human beings struggle to affirm their power in the face of the overpowering violence of Being; in this way they take a stand on who they are and what difference it makes that there are beings instead of nothing (IM, 160–76). "The Origin of the Work of Art," also from 1935, presents the artwork as the site of a revealing struggle between the meaningful world of a people and the opaque earth on which it rests (see Chapter 23).

This violent imagery gradually fades as Heidegger tries to work through the metaphysical dimension of National Socialism by way of Nietzsche (GA 43–4, GA 46–8, GA 87; see Chapter 5) and Ernst Jünger (GA 90). He concludes that Jünger's concept of the worker as a new human type is only a one-sided Nietzscheanism, and that Nietzsche himself is "the last metaphysician" (GA 47, 10/NIII, 8).

Nietzsche's struggle against traditional metaphysics ended up as a mere "inverted Platonism." His thoughts of eternal recurrence and the will to power were the ultimate metaphysical representation of beings as such and as a whole, instead of an opening to the question of Being itself. By the late 1930s, Heidegger's reflections on the will to power as metaphysics will lead him to declare that Being has nothing to do with either power or powerlessness (GA 66, 83).[5]

SELFHOOD AND APPROPRIATION

These tumultuous thoughts and events begin to crystallize in a series of private texts begun in 1936 (GA 65–72), where Heidegger develops a new way of thought that circles around *Ereignis*. Interpretations of these texts and of *Ereignis* itself vary considerably (see also Chapters 25 and 35). For present purposes we will focus on the most clearly structured text and the first in the series, the *Contributions to Philosophy* of 1936–8, paying special attention to its treatment of the question, "Who are we?"[6]

According to the *Contributions*, the "first beginning" of Western thought asks: what are beings? "The other beginning" will ask, "How does beyng occur essentially? [*Wie west das Seyn?*]" (GA 65, 75, 7/CP2, 60, 8). One could take the old-fashioned spelling *Seyn* as indicating the granting of significance and unconcealment—a granting that is more fundamental than any general representations of what is. In other words, whereas the philosophical tradition has sought principles and patterns that characterize all entities, Heidegger now wants to ask how we are given any meaning of Being in the first place.

The central proposal of the text is that beyng essentially occurs as *Ereignis*, the appropriating event (GA 65, 260/CP2, 205). This proposal is not simply a statement of fact, but a new mode of thinking and existing into which we may shift. The *Contributions* are structured around this transitional movement (GA 65, 6/CP2, 7): we must feel the shock of Being's "abandonment" and hear its echo in the history of the first beginning before making a leap into a new grounding of the "there"—led, perhaps, by the few "future ones" who will follow the trace of the Hölderlinian "last god." In all this, our own Being is put into question, or thrown into a state of emergency—and only in this way can we enter genuine selfhood or "the *domain of what is proper*" (GA 65, 320/CP2, 253). The word *Ereignis* deliberately echoes *eigen*, "own"—hence translations such as "appropriation," "appropriating event," or

"enowning." *Ereignis* initiates us into selfhood, allowing us to belong to a site and time where beings can have significance.

This brings us back to the "who" question. According to the *Contributions*, philosophy necessarily involves a meditation on the self, but not Cartesian self-certainty; the Cartesian ego is an underlying, thing-like entity whose selfhood is not genuinely at stake. Furthermore, the "who" question must be asked in the first-person-plural—but Heidegger recognizes that the reference or extension of "we" is problematic. Who gets to ask "who are we" in the first place? "*Which ones* do we mean in speaking of 'we'? . . . do we mean 'the' human being as such? Yet 'the' human being 'is' unhistorical only as being historical" (GA 65, 48/CP2, 40). Human historicity implies that our identity cannot be some ahistorical abstraction; it also implies that we are in constant danger of failing to exist in an authentically historical way.

One might affirm that "we" are the *Volk*, but Heidegger now insists on the problematic character of this concept: "How is the essence of a people determined?" (GA 65, 48/CP2, 40). He rejects the supposition that we should simply decide who we are by willfully organizing the people; busy activity may or may not indicate genuine selfhood (GA 65, 49–50/CP2, 40–1). Thought is essential: in the absence of any meditation on who we are, we may even fail to *be* in the proper sense at all (GA 65, 51/CP2, 41).

It is this complacent self-certainty, devoid of genuine selfhood, that Heidegger diagnoses as the fatal trait of his time. The self-assured subject willfully plans and manipulates the world, turning itself into the center of all meaning. "This (namely, such self-certainty) is the innermost essence of 'liberalism,' which precisely for that reason can apparently unfold freely" and march on in its unstoppable "progress."

The predominant racial ideology is nothing but "biological liberalism" (GA 65, 53/CP2, 43), and Marxism is an equally thoughtless outgrowth of Judeo-Christian egalitarianism (GA 65, 54/CP2, 44). Heidegger is coming to see all the established political and religious options as forms of bankrupt subjectivism, whether on the individual, the national, or the international scale.

What is the alternative? Selfhood, writes Heidegger, is "a realm of occurrences, a realm in which human beings are appropriated to themselves only if they themselves reach the open time-space wherein an appropriation can occur." Our own proper Being is grounded in our belonging to the truth of Being itself (GA 65, 51/CP2, 42). To find ourselves, then, we have to look beyond any narrow and self-centered identity and turn to the gift of the meaning of Being, a gift that can be granted only in a distinctive site or situation: the time-space of the "flight of the gods" (GA 65, 52/CP2, 42, translation modified). Absence, departure, denial, and longing thus point more genuinely to our selfhood than any easily ascertainable, present-at-hand characteristics. Here as elsewhere in the *Contributions*, Heidegger points to the instability and problematic character of all meaning: meaning depends on a mysterious event that cannot itself be understood in terms of the meaning that it grants. Significance hovers over an "abyssal ground" (*Ab-grund*: for example, GA 65, 379/CP2, 299).

Heidegger never accepted liberal democracy, and he may never have abandoned his faith in the "inner truth and greatness" of Nazism (IM, 213)—the movement's secret potential. However, his reflections on the difficulty of genuine selfhood and the questionable character of the *Volk* did lead him to reject the form that Nazism actually took. By 1939, he is attacking Hitler by name in his private writings. When the Führer declares in a speech that every attitude must be judged by its utility for the whole, Heidegger asks: Why should only utility count? What is utility? And who is the whole? (GA 66, 122). The Nazis had never genuinely allowed themselves to ask the question, "Who are we?" In "The Age of the World Picture" (1938), Heidegger characterizes modernity as an age that objectifies beings and represents them in terms of willfully affirmed principles. The modern subject blocks off the event that might call into question what it means to be and who we ourselves are. Heidegger apparently concluded that actual Nazism was another form of modern subjectivity (GA 5, 92–3/HR, 220).[7]

Texts such as these indicate that Heidegger came to see his own political actions as rash, and that his thought cannot be reduced to a rigid ideology. By the late 1930s, the urgency of his questioning has won out over any fixed answers. Even if we decide that we cannot forgive him for supporting Hitler, this is a decision not only about Heidegger but about ourselves—and in this way it testifies that Heidegger was at least correct to insist on the importance of the question: *Who are we?*[8]

THE PERSISTENT QUESTION

We can conclude with a few suggestions on how we might judge the politics of this crucial decade.

NOTES AND REFERENCES

[1] Similar claims are found in the 1930 essay "On the Essence of Ground," in PA. Heidegger was

44

to explore the question of freedom further in his lectures on Schelling: GA 42 (1936) and GA 49 (1941).

2 "Über Wesen und Begriff von Natur, Geschichte und Staat," in Alfred Denker and Holger Zaborowski (eds), *Heidegger und der Nationalsozialismus I: Dokumente*, Heidegger-Jahrbuch 4 (Freiburg/Munich: Karl Alber, 2009), 76. A translation of this text by Gregory Fried and Richard Polt is forthcoming from Bloomsbury under the title *Nature, History, State*.

3 Ibid., 86–7.

4 Ibid., 88.

5 See Fred Dallmayr, "Heidegger on *Macht* and *Machenschaft*," *Continental Philosophy Review* 34 (2001), 247–67; Richard Polt, "Beyond Struggle and Power: Heidegger's Secret Resistance," *Interpretation* 35.1 (Fall 2007), 11–40.

6 See François Raffoul, "Rethinking Selfhood: From Enowning," *Research in Phenomenology* 37.1 (2007), 75–94; Richard Polt, *The*

Emergency of Being: On Heidegger's "Contributions to Philosophy" (Ithaca: Cornell University Press, 2006), 156–80. Readers can also find relatively accessible presentations of some of the central ideas of the *Contributions* in GA 45/BQP.

7 There are discrepancies between the 1938 manuscript of this text and its 1950 published version. In particular, the original lacks a passage that describes the human self-conception as "nation or people" as a type of subjectivity. See Sidonie Kellerer, "Heideggers Maske: 'Die Zeit des Weltbildes'— Metamorphose eines Textes," *Zeitschrift für Ideengeschichte* 5.2 (Summer 2011), 111. However, passages such as GA 65, 488 indicate that Heidegger was already critical of "the communal subject" by the late 1930s.

8 For a good introduction to further secondary literature on this period of Heidegger's career, see James Risser (ed.), *Heidegger toward the Turn: Essays on the Work of the 1930s* (Albany: SUNY, 1999).

5

HEIDEGGER, NIETZSCHE, NATIONAL SOCIALISM: THE PLACE OF METAPHYSICS IN THE POLITICAL DEBATE OF THE 1930s

Robert Bernasconi

When in 1961 Heidegger presented his lectures on Nietzsche in a two-volume edition running to over 1,100 pages, he insisted on their centrality for an understanding of his path of thought from 1930 to 1947 (GA 6.1, xii/NI, xvi). It was an oblique reference to the Nazi period and its immediate aftermath, but what was not understood in 1961 was that in the course of editing the lectures for publication he had omitted a number of significant passages. It was only when these lectures were republished in the *Gesamtausgabe* between 1985 and 1990, using Heidegger's own lecture notes as well as student transcripts, that this became clear. Many readers were slow to recognize the significance of the differences between the lectures as Heidegger delivered them and the versions published in 1961 (GA 43; GA 44; GA 47; GA 48; GA 50), just as they have been slow to recognize the invaluable assistance given by the recently published notes from Heidegger's seminars in 1937, 1937–8, and 1944 (GA 46; GA 87). A careful comparison reveals that Heidegger did much more than simply omit passages in which he repeated himself for the sake of his students or add some clarificatory remarks in hindsight. Some scholars, such as Charles Bambach, believe that in 1961 Heidegger had doctored the lectures to conceal compromising passages, whereas others, such as Tracy Colony, find another significance in those same passages and argue that when they impinge on political issues they express, albeit very discreetly, his rejection of National Socialism.[1] In any event, to the extent that the secondary literature on Heidegger's relation to Nietzsche is still shaped by the version of the Nietzsche lectures published in 1961, it is inadequate to the task of addressing the question of Heidegger's philosophical and political development. And because the 1961 edition is the basis for the only English translations of Heidegger's writings on Nietzsche, it is especially important to know the problems with that edition when passing judgment on Heidegger's relation to National Socialism.

After the Second World War, Heidegger claimed that his lectures and seminars on Nietzsche from 1936 until 1940 constituted a form of intellectual or spiritual resistance to National Socialism (GA 16, 402).

But if there is a problem determining what Heidegger meant when in 1935 he referred to the "inner truth and greatness" of the movement (GA 40, 208/IM, 213), it is even less clear what he was claiming to have resisted. In order to address that question we need to begin with the Nazi interpretation of Nietzsche. Nevertheless, a problem immediately presents itself: what is meant by *the* Nazi conception of Nietzsche? For those within Nazi Germany who were sympathetic to Nietzsche, his name served almost as a surrogate for the National Socialist movement itself, but that simply means that there was no standard Nazi assessment of Nietzsche any more than there was a uniform understanding of National Socialism.[2] Ernst Krieck was an opponent of Nietzsche and, although Alfred Rosenberg did not reject Nietzsche, he clearly favored Kant. To be sure, one major reason for these differences was uncertainty as to how to respond to the fact that the biology of race had undergone a decisive shift since Nietzsche's day. Heidegger had no such uncertainty, albeit he only expressed his reservations in a manuscript that remained unpublished until 2004. Heidegger wrote: "'Race researchers' play the part of admirers of the teacher of the will to power without caring that Nietzsche, precisely at the time of his work on *The Will to Power* in 1886-7, wrote in his notebook: 'Maxim: Deal with nobody who participates in the fake race-swindle'" (GA 90, 254).[3]

There was, it seems, an attempt to produce "the Nazi interpretation of Nietzsche" when Heinrich Härtle's *Nietzsche und der Nationalsozialismus* was published under the imprint of the NSDAP. Härtle attributed to Nietzsche a "materialist biologism" but largely limited himself to locating in Nietzsche's texts passages that reflected Nazi positions on such topics as war, Jews, breeding, and so on.[4] Härtle's Nietzsche was no doubt an extreme case, but it should not be forgotten that in 1930 Nietzsche was often seen throughout the world as an advocate of breeding programs and other forms of eugenics.[5] In 1920 Heinrich Rickert, one of Heidegger's early teachers, explicitly denied that Nietzsche was a philosopher of the first rank and proposed that it would be better to consider him an influential biologist instead.[6] Heidegger disagreed in his 1921-2 lecture course at Freiburg University (GA 61, 80/PIA, 62), but it was not until the 1930s that the decisive shift in Nietzsche's reputation took place.[7] Today Karl Jaspers is usually given credit for establishing Nietzsche's philosophical stature,[8] but at that time Alfred Baeumler was a more influential reader of Nietzsche. In 1931 he wrote a book on Nietzsche with the intention of proving that Nietzsche belonged alongside Descartes, Leibniz, and Kant "as a thinker of European rank."[9] When Heidegger put Nietzsche in dialogue with Descartes, Leibniz, and Kant, among others, he would have been understood as following Baeumler's lead. Heidegger was presumably thinking about Baeumler when in 1932 he acknowledged that there were a few German thinkers, albeit only a few, who had begun to have a sense that they were under an obligation to make Nietzsche's destiny the fundamental event of their innermost history (GA 35, 45-56).[10] This is indeed what Baeumler was attempting, but his argument for Nietzsche's philosophical stature was based in large part on a political reading. Indeed in 1934 Baeumler quoted Nietzsche's call for the extinction of misfits, weaklings, and degenerates and argued that he provided the foundation for a new policy that would ground the state on race.[11] At the end of this second essay, which was entitled "Nietzsche and National

Socialism," Baeumler proclaimed that "if today we shout 'Heil Hitler' . . . at the same time we are also hailing Nietzsche."[12]

Heidegger characterized his own interpretation of Nietzsche as metaphysical and dismissed Baeumler for being political (GA 6.1, 20/NI, 22). This was in the context of a discussion of Baeumler's decision to ignore the doctrine of the eternal recurrence as of no consequence for Nietzsche's system.[13] Heidegger—unlike Baeumler, Jaspers (G 6.1, 19–20/NI, 22), and Ernst Bertram (GA 50, 99/IPTP, 9)—placed the doctrine of eternal recurrence at the summit of Nietzsche's reflections. And when Heidegger addressed Baeumler's 1931 book directly in 1939 in the reworked version of the final lecture of *The Will to Power as Knowledge* that was never delivered as such, he praised Baeumler's essay for attempting to set the interpretation of Nietzsche free from a psychologizing and existential misinterpretation of his work, but complained that he had failed to see the metaphysical essence of justice (GA 47, 297).[14] Heidegger explained that it is only with the insight into the essence of justice as the essential ground of life that it can be decided whether, how, and within what limits Nietzsche's thinking is biologistic, and this formulation was repeated almost word for word in the final lecture (GA 6.1, 580/NIII, 145).[15] In other words, Baeumler, contrary to his own claim in *Nietzsche, der Philosoph und Politiker*, had failed to identify Nietzsche's metaphysics, because, even though he highlighted justice, he read it politically and not metaphysically.

But if Heidegger wanted his interpretation to be understood as metaphysical, as opposed to political, that would limit the degree to which one could think of it as resisting National Socialism as he claimed. It would simply amount to a refusal to read Nietzsche a

certain way. Heidegger seems to have intended something more than this. Indeed, as Jaspers noted in a letter to Heidegger, the Rectoral Address had Nietzschean resonances.[16] That Heidegger himself read Nietzsche with an eye to politics is also clearly in evidence in his seminar from the Winter semester 1938–9, largely devoted to tracking the concept of life in Nietzsche's "The Use and Abuse of History." He also used the opportunity to explore the question of culture in the formation of German identity. Heidegger's claim that in Nietzsche "*Volk*" was a metaphysical concept far distant from *Volkskunde* was part of his tendency to dismiss *Volkskunde* as superficial (GA 46, 281). This is another way in which his metaphysical reading of Nietzsche, understood roughly as a reading that attended to the ontological status of the concepts employed, bleeds into politics.

Heidegger's metaphysical concern was uppermost in his treatment of Nietzsche's relation to Darwinism and biologism. When it came to readings of Nietzsche, Heidegger's "resistance" was directed primarily against those among the Nazis whom he suspected of promoting both the Darwinian struggle for existence and a biologistic conception of race. This was clearly stated in 1944 when Heidegger evoked Nietzsche's account of the Germans and described it as reflecting "a world for which 'Darwinism' is the only philosophy with its doctrine of the 'struggle for existence' and the natural selection and choice of the stronger" (GA 50, 120/IPTP, 28). By this time the proper name "Nietzsche" had become for Heidegger "the name for an age: the epoch of the development and installation of the mastery of the human over the earth" (GA 50, 84/IPTP, 64–5). However, Heidegger had employed a different strategy earlier and this raises the question as to whether this earlier approach was equally pointed politically.

It is clear that already in 1939 Heidegger directly challenged the dominant reading of Nietzsche as a Darwinist. He claimed that Darwin thought "metaphysically-sociologically," whereas Nietzsche thought "metaphysically-ontologically" (GA 47, 91). Initially Heidegger's argument was that, in contrast to Darwin's focus on self-preservation in the "struggle for existence," Nietzsche was concerned with the self-transcending enhancement of life (GA 6.1, 439/NIII, 15). Heidegger at one time believed that Nietzsche had taken this point from the biologist Wilhelm Rolph who had opposed the notion of a struggle for the increase of life to the Darwinian struggle for life (GA 87, 193).[17] But Heidegger subsequently was forced to acknowledge that the two terms—preservation and enhancement—could not be separated in Nietzsche. The following semester he referred to their "necessary interconnection" (GA 6.2, 91/NIV, 65), and a couple of years later, following aphorism 715 from *The Will to Power*, he insisted there should be no "and" between them, only a hyphen joining them (GA 6.2, 242/NIII, 196).[18] By 1939 Heidegger conceded that Nietzsche thought "in a concretely biological way [. . .] without misgivings" (GA 6.1, 532/NIII, 101), but he argued that Nietzsche's apparently biological explanation of the categories moves into the area of metaphysical thinking (GA 6.1, 535–6/NIII, 104). The distinction between the biological and the metaphysical, like the distinction between the political and the metaphysical, was proving more fluid than Heidegger had at first suspected.

Heidegger learned the same lesson when he sought to use the term "biologism" as a weapon. There has been a longstanding tendency for defenders of Heidegger to want to believe that "biologism" was a code word for National Socialism and especially National Socialist racial policies, but things are more complicated. Some Nazis did adhere to biologism, but this represented only one way of being a Nazi, albeit one to which Heidegger was resolutely opposed.[19] And it was possible to support most, if not all, of the Nazi's racial policies without accepting the biological theories that some used in an attempt to justify them. Heidegger's initial claim was that biologism arose when the prevailing views about living beings are transferred from biology to other realms of being, for example, to history (GA 6.1, 472/NIII, 45). However, Heidegger quickly dropped this argument borrowed from Rickert,[20] choosing instead to issue the modified claim that Nietzsche would only have been guilty of biologism if he had adopted certain concepts and key propositions from biology without realizing that they already implied certain metaphysical decisions. The proper defense against biologism was to be conducted in terms not of protecting the borders between disciplines but in terms of metaphysics: "Biological thinking [. . .] can only be grounded and decided in the metaphysical realm and can never justify itself scientifically" (GA 6.1, 472/NIII, 45). In a twenty-six page so-called Repetition that was omitted by Heidegger from the first publication of *The Will to Power as Knowledge and as Metaphysics*, he emphasized that the main thrust of his account was to displace from the realm of biology to that of metaphysics (GA 47, 68–93, esp. 85). At the time he clearly believed that this issued a challenge to contemporary readers of Nietzsche. Indeed, he wrote that "the many writers who whether consciously or unconsciously expound and copy Nietzsche's treatises invariably fall prey to a variety of biologism" (GA 6.1, 474/NIII, 46).

Nevertheless, Heidegger had earlier acknowledged a significant exception to this account. In 1936 he judged Baeumler to be among the few who rejected Klages's "psychological-biologistic interpretation of Nietzsche" (GA 6.1, 20/NI, 21). But whereas Heidegger declared Nietzsche innocent of biologism, Baeumler in his 1931 study had actually criticized Nietzsche for his biologism, which he judged had its roots in Darwin.[21] According to Heidegger, in 1939, biologism was ignorance of the fact that "all biology that is genuine and restricted to its field points beyond itself" (GA 6.1, 472/NIII, 45). Heidegger had said the same thing in a different idiom in 1927 when he maintained that in the philosophy of life there was an implicit tendency toward understanding the being of Dasein (SZ, 46). According to Baeumler, by contrast, biologism is the doctrine that everything, including consciousness, can be traced back to life-processes.[22] By excluding consciousness from this process, he believed that he could avoid extreme forms of biologism and so he argued that "life" in Nietzsche must be understood not "empirically-physiologically" but metaphysically, that is to say, as a Dionysian or divine phenomenon.[23]

In lectures from the late 1930s, Heidegger maintained that the critique of biologism did not apply to Nietzsche. He claimed that the latter recognized the metaphysical character of the propositions in which he employed biological concepts, concepts borrowed, as Heidegger well knew, from William Rolph, Herbert Spencer, and Wilhelm Roux (GA 87, 193–4. That at least is what Heidegger said in public. In private, matters were different. In *Contributions to Philosophy* he not only complained that the fact that Nietzsche stressed life was a clear indication of the lack of originality of his questioning (GA 65, 326/CP2, 258), but he also presented contemporary biologism in historical perspective and

associated it specifically with Nietzsche (GA 65, 315/CP2, 249). The fact that Heidegger was more inclined to associate Nietzsche unambiguously with biologism in private than in his public lectures could be used as an indication that the attempt to critique biologism in the course of a reading of Nietzsche was a way of being political, even if the political work was limited to an attack on only one group within the Nazi Party. But it was an attack only in the sense that he was marking his own distance from biologism. It did not have a critical edge beyond that. In a manuscript contemporary with the Nietzsche lectures, *Die Geschichte des Seyns*, Heidegger conceded that all attempts to refute biologism are worthless (GA 69, 71). By this time he no longer understood biologism as an error to be corrected but as something to be traced back to its source in the Western metaphysical concept of life as developed especially by Leibniz, Hegel, and Nietzsche. To relate Nietzsche to Descartes, Leibniz, and Kant now meant to circumscribe all of them together within the unity of Western metaphysics. This constituted a second sense in which Heidegger used the word "metaphysics," one that came to dominate his use of the term. "Metaphysics" as the history of Western metaphysics extending from Plato to Nietzsche was to be overcome. Whereas Heidegger had initially looked to National Socialism to assist in this task, at a certain point, the precise date of which is hard to determine, he came to see National Socialism in its realization as a symptom of Western Metaphysics. In other words, he came to see it as a symptom of the problem and not a contribution to its solution.

There are clear indications of this shift already in 1939. The governing thesis of Heidegger's *The Will to Power as Knowledge* is not explicitly stated in the lecture course, but is announced in a note included only in an appendix to the *Gesamtausgabe* version of the lecture course. The thesis was that Nietzsche avoided mere biologism only by virtue of the fact that his biologism was a necessary consequence of a metaphysical interpretation of beingness as will to power (GA 47, 321). Metaphysical thinking as the thinking of the Being of beings was thus the prescribed way to avoid biologism, but at the same time, insofar Nietzsche was also metaphysical in the sense that his name stood for the consummation of Western metaphysics (GA 6.1, 429/NIII, 6), this was no longer a thinking to which Heidegger himself aspired. Nietzsche did not offer Heidegger a way of resisting National Socialism, although it did offer him an opportunity to be critical of all those who sought to "plunder Nietzsche merely for the sake of some contemporary spiritual counterfeit" (GA 6.1, 593/NIII, 157). Instead, he used Nietzsche to offer his diagnosis of why one must look to the history of Western metaphysics to understand the decline he saw everywhere he looked and not just in Nazi Germany.

This background is fundamental to understanding the much misunderstood passage from "Nietzsche's Metaphysics" where Heidegger wrote: "Only where the absolute subjectivity of will to power comes to be the truth of beings as a whole is the *principle* of a program of racial breeding possible; possible, that is, not merely on the basis of naturally evolving races, but in terms of the self-conscious thought of race. That is to say, the principle is metaphysically necessary" (GA 6.2, 278/NIII, 231). The next sentence is missing from the manuscript written in 1940 and so was presumably added only in 1961: "Just as Nietzsche's thought of will to power was ontological rather than biological, even more was his racial thought metaphysical

rather than biological" (ibid. Compare GA 50, 57). If one understands the two uses in this passage of the term "metaphysical" in the positive sense of a thinking of the Being of beings, then it might seem that Heidegger was legitimating a thinking in terms of "race," including eugenics or racial hygiene (*Rassenhygiene*). But although this reading is popular among Heidegger's harshest critics, it arises from a failure to see that he is speaking here of metaphysics as understood from the history of Being understood as a destiny (*Geschick*). Heidegger's argument, as he explained elsewhere, was that eugenics with its project of racial breeding and race ranking had to be seen as a manifestation of Western metaphysics (GA 69, 70–1 and 223). Indeed, it was an inevitable consequence of Western metaphysics which is why he refers to it as "metaphysically necessary."

By initially defending Nietzsche against the charge of biologism only subsequently to locate him within the history of Western metaphysics, Heidegger in a double movement elevated Nietzsche above his biologistic contemporaries the better to circumscribe him more forcefully in another way. Heidegger rescued Nietzsche from a Darwinist reading, including Baeumler's appropriation of him, but only to associate him with the worst Nazi policies at a more fundamental level. This means that the sense in which Heidegger could claim that his attempt to save Nietzsche from biologism amounted to a form of resistance to National Socialism is extremely limited. Heidegger offered a powerful diagnosis of the ills of his time, but it left little or no room for a political response that was capable of combating it. By embracing an account of Western metaphysics as destiny Heidegger deprived himself philosophically of a basis for a moral condemnation of National Socialism.

NOTES AND REFERENCES

1 Charles Bambach, *Heidegger's Roots, Nietzsche, National Socialism, and the Greeks* (Ithaca: Cornell University Press, 2003), 266–72 and Tracy Colony, "Heidegger's Early Nietzsche Lecture Courses and the Question of Resistance," *Studia Phaenomenologica*, 4 (2004), 151–72. See also Tracy Colony, "The Death of God and the Life of Being: Heidegger's Confrontation with Nietzsche," *Interpreting Heidegger*, ed. Daniel O. Dahlstrom (Cambridge: Cambridge University Press, 2011), 197–216.

2 Steven E. Aschheim, *The Nietzsche Legacy in Germany 1890–1990* (Berkeley: University of California Press, 1994), 255. See also Martha Zapata Galindo, *Triumph des Willens zur Macht. Zur Nietzsche-rezeption im NS-Staat* (Hamburg: Argument, 1995) and especially the list of courses on Nietzsche taught during the Nazi period, pages 210–18.

3 The quotation from Nietzsche can now be found in Friedrich Nietzsche, *Sämtliche Werke. Kritische Studienausgabe* (Berlin: De Gruyter, 1980), vol. 12, 205.

4 Heinrich Härtle, *Nietzsche und der Nationalsozialismus* (Munich: Zentralverlag der NSDAP, 1937), 77.

5 For example, see Dan Stone, *Breeding Superman. Nietzsche, Race and Eugenics in Edwardian and Interwar Britain* (Liverpool: Liverpool University Press, 2002). The French reading of Nietzsche in this period was more antagonistic because of anti-German senti- ments. See Douglas Smith, *Transvaluations: Nietzsche in France 1872–1972* (Oxford: Oxford University Press, 1992), 56–81.

6 Heinrich Rickert, *Die Philosophie des Lebens. Darstellung und Kritik der Philosophischen Modestromungen unserer Zeit* (Tubingen: J.C.B. Mohr, 1920), 179n. and Heinrich Rickert, "Lebenswerte und Kulturwerte," *Logos* II.2 (1912), 136.

7 For a contemporary review of the German literature on Nietzsche, see Karl Löwith, *Nietzsche*, Sämtliche Schriften 6 (Stuttgart: J.B. Metzler, 1987), 345–80; trans. J. Harvey Lomax, *Nietzsche's Philosophy of the Eternal Recurrence of the Same* (Berkeley: University of California Press, 1997), 195–225

8 It might be true that Jaspers wrote the first sanitized book on Nietzsche by describing a Nietzsche for whom biologism was not central. Karl Jaspers, *Nietzsche. Einführung in das Verständnis seines Philosophierens* (Berlin: Walter de Gruyter, 1936); trans. by Charles F. Wallraff and Fredrick J. Smith, *Nietzsche. An Introduction to the Understanding of His Philosophical Activity* (Tucson: University of Arizona Press, 1965).

9 Alfred Baeumler, *Nietzsche der Philosoph und Politiker* (Leipzig: Philipp Reclam, 1931), 5.

10 Another possible candidate was Kurt Hildebrandt, a member of Stefan George's circle. See "Nietzsche als Richter: Sein Schicksal" in Ernst Gundolf and Kurt Hildebrandt, *Nietzsche als Richter unsrer Zeit* (Breslau: Ferdinand Hirt, 1923), 63–104.

11 Alfred Baeumler, "Nietzsche und der Nationalsozialismus," in *Studien zur deutschen Geistesgeschichte* (Berlin: Junker und Dünnhaupt, 1937), 292.

12 Baeumler, "Nietzsche und der Nationalsozialismus," 294.

13 Baeumler, *Nietzsche der Philosoph und Politiker*, 80.

14 Heidegger is referring to Baeumler, *Nietzsche der Philosoph und Politiker*, 77–8.

15 Heidegger explained in a passage that was excised from the first publication that justice is the how in which the livingness of the living holds itself (GA 47, 303).

16 Karl Jaspers to Martin Heidegger, August 23, 1933, *Briefwechsel 1920–1963* (Frankfurt: Klostermann, 1990), 155.

17 See W. H. Rolph, *Biologische Probleme zugleich als Versuch zur Entwicklung einer rationellen Ethik* (Leipzig: Engelmann, 1884), 97.

18 For the original version of this text, see GA 50, 18.

19 Further on this topic, see Robert Bernasconi, "Heidegger's Alleged Challenge to the Nazi Concepts of Race," in *Appropriating Heidegger*, eds James E. Faulconer and Mark A. Wrathall (Cambridge: Cambridge University Press, 2000), 50–67.

20 Heinrich Rickert, *Die Philosophie des Lebens. Darstellung und Kritik der Philosophischen Modestromungen unserer Zeit* (Tübingen: J.C.B. Mohr, 1920), 75.

21 Baeumler, *Nietzsche der Philosoph und Politiker*, 28.

22 Ibid.

23 Ibid., 35.

6

THE LATER HEIDEGGER: THE QUESTION OF THE OTHER BEGINNING OF THINKING

Françoise Dastur

A long time before the lecture Heidegger gave in 1964 on "The End of Philosophy and the Task of Thinking," the theme of the end of philosophy had already emerged in some of the texts he had published. One of the notes he wrote between 1936 and 1946 that have been published under the title "Overcoming metaphysics" says that, if with Nietzsche's metaphysics, philosophy is accomplished, which means that it has covered up to the end the circle of its prescribed possibilities, "this end of philosophy is not the end of thinking, which is going over to another beginning" (VA, 83). The transition from the Greek beginning to another beginning is Heidegger's main concern in the middle of the 1930s, in a time when in his manuscripts, and especially in *Beiträge zur Philosophie*, "Contributions to Philosophy," written between 1936 and 1938, the word *Ereignis*, which will become a key one for the last part of Heidegger's work, appears for the first time. Until then, the question had rather been, instead to begin in another manner, to begin again, that is, to repeat the question of being as a question that is the leading question of philosophy. Such a repetition does not mean however to follow the

path that had been cleared 2,000 years ago by Plato and Aristotle, but on the contrary requires the "destruction" of the history of ontology in order to go back to "the original experiences" (SZ, 22), which are at the basis of the meaning of the being concept that is still ours. In 1927 the question was nevertheless to renew with the Greek beginning from which it was necessary to bring back, to retrieve—this is the proper meaning of the German word *wiederholen*—what could give a new life and future to a tradition that had become sclerotic. Heidegger's purpose was then to revive philosophy in rooting it again in its true beginning. But in 1927 the Greek beginning is understood in the light of what Heidegger will call later "its initial end" (EM, 137), that is, in the light of the *gigantomachia peri tès ousias*, the battle of giants concerning being (SZ, 1), which defines Plato's and Aristotle's ontological investigation. Heidegger, taking up again the Aristotelian discovery of the nongeneric character of Being was led to the idea of the ontological difference, which was explicitly expounded in his 1927 lecture course on *The Basic Problems of Phenomenology*, but which constitutes already the implicit horizon of *Being and Time*, where Being is defined as the *transcendens pure and simple* (38). On the basis of the definition of ontology as "transcendental science" (GA 24, 460) Heidegger could therefore identify, as Kant already did, metaphysics and human nature in his 1929 inaugural lecture on "What is metaphysics?" whose conclusion is : "So long as man exists, philosophizing of some sort occurs" (BW, 110). The concept of transcendence is still at that time the horizon into which metaphysics, according to the current meaning of the expression *meta ta physica*, is defined as "inquiry beyond or over beings, which aims to recover them as such and as a whole for our grasp" (107). But as a general questioning on beings, metaphysics does not think the ontological difference, at least as long as it has not thematized in an explicit manner Being and Nothingness as such, which is the case of traditional metaphysics. It is only, as Heidegger emphasizes, when nothingness becomes a problem that "it awakens for the first time the proper formulation of the metaphysical question concerning the Being of beings" (108), because the Being of beings is truly questioned only when it is thought in his difference with the beings, that is, as what is not a being, not a thing or in the literal sense of the word, as nothing. We have therefore to deal with two concepts of metaphysics here that are opposed in the same manner as traditional ontology and what Heidegger calls in *Being and Time* "fundamental ontology," that is, ontology of Dasein. The condition of possibility of metaphysics in its "proper formulation"—in other words "authentic" metaphysics—as explicit questioning can be found in human existence insofar as the human being can have a relationship with beings only on the basis of a preliminary openness to nothingness, that is, to the Being of beings. Metaphysics is thus Dasein

itself, since existing means nothing else than to perform the ontological difference, as Heidegger explains in *The Basic Problems of Phenomenology* (GA 24, 454). Philosophy itself can therefore only be "metaphysics getting under way" (BW, 110), that is, an explicit metaphysics that can be accomplished only through a "leap" bringing us outside of what Heidegger names *Verfallenheit*, fallenness. For fallenness is what defines a way of existing that is completely absorbed by the tasks of the everyday, on the basis of which we have to open ourselves to what constitutes in the proper manner *Dasein*, which is Being in the world as such. This is possible, as Heidegger showed in *Being and Time* and again in *What is metaphysics?* only through the experience of this no-thing that is a world that takes place in *Angst*, anxiety. Philosophy seems therefore to be the expression of "authentic" Dasein, of a Dasein that exists on the modus of *epekeina*, that is, transcendence (GA 24, 425); and at that time it is precisely this transcendental essence of philosophy that has to be renewed and accomplished, without questioning the Platonic origin of such a project. On the contrary, Heidegger declares in *The Basic Problems of Phenomenology*, that "philosophy, in its cardinal question, has made no progress since Plato" (399–400), so that when we ask the apparently abstract question of the condition of possibility of the comprehension of Being, "we want nothing else than searching how to get out of the cave and find an access to light" (404).

Heidegger has elaborated under the name of "fundamental ontology" this metaphysics of *Dasein* on the basis of which philosophy as explicit metaphysics is founded. It is therefore not surprising to see him developing the project of a repetition of Kant's foundation of metaphysics in his 1929 book on Kant. Kant is for Heidegger the first thinker after

Aristotle who has tried to give to traditional metaphysics, to this *metaphysica generalis* that is nothing else than Aristotle's *prote philosophia*, the foundation of which it is deprived and which alone can make it possible, that is, the ontological difference as the modus of existence of the human being, that Heidegger calls "transcendence." Kant has indeed seen the necessary connection between the Being-question and the finite ontological constitution of man. But because Kant remained prisoner of the Cartesian way of thinking, in particular of the modern determination of man as subject, the question is for Heidegger to repeat in a more originary manner the Kantian foundation of metaphysics. To give a foundation to metaphysics does not mean however only to add to the already existing metaphysical edifice the basis that is missing, but this implies on the contrary to designing the plan of the future metaphysical edifice.[1] Heidegger's purpose is consequently to determine in a concrete manner the essence of the metaphysics to come: this is the full meaning of fundamental ontology, which aims at elaborating a new metaphysics.

It seems therefore that with the project of a repetition of the Being-question, a project that guided Heidegger's thought until 1929, we are very far from the theme of the end of philosophy. However this theme is not completely absent during the 1920s, insofar as Heidegger, in a very insistent manner, situates his own philosophical project in connection with Hegel's philosophical accomplishment. He writes in *The Basic Problems of Phenomenology*: "With Hegel, philosophy, i.e. antic philosophy, is in a way thought to its end. Hegel was completely right when he formulated this awareness of an accomplishment" (GA 24, 400). But if after Hegel a new beginning is not only possible but necessary, it is because he has not used up all the possibilities contained in the Greek beginning (ibid.). Heidegger developed this idea in his 1935 lecture course *An Introduction to Metaphysics*, when differentiating in the Greek beginning itself a beginning and an end: "In order to overcome Greek philosophy as the beginning of Western philosophy, it is necessary to grasp this beginning at the same time in its initial end; for it is only this end that became for the following times the 'beginning,' a beginning which at the same time concealed the initial beginning" (EM, 137). Hegel has only brought to its end the initial end of the great beginning, that is, Plato's and Aristotle's philosophies, which are the determination of *physis* as *idea* (144), and not the thinking of Being as *physis* of the so-called Presocratics. Thus, the possibility of a more originary repetition of the beginning is still preserved as our only chance to overcome Hegel and to give a future to philosophy.[2] But beginning anew in a more originary manner the beginning and not considering it as a thing of the past that it would be sufficient to imitate, this already means to transform it in another beginning (29). It is in fact not possible to limit oneself to the perpetuation of a beginning, because the beginning, by essence, and not only because of the incapacity of those who are watching over it, can only decline and collapse, without being ever able to conserve by itself the immediacy of its upheaval. It can be "conserved" only if it is repeated in a more originary manner (145–6). Heidegger develops this reflection on the notion of beginning, which has to be put in connection with what he called his political "mistake" in the same period, in the first version, written also in 1935, of "The Origin of the Work of Art." It is even possible to think that what characterizes the Greek beginning can reveal itself in a more essential manner in art, in Greek tragedy and architecture, than in Heraclitus' and Parmenides' thought, which are also, in this same period, explicitly questioned. In fact the Presocratics have never been absent from Heidegger's horizon of thought, and it has to be recalled that one part of his very first lecture course was dedicated in 1915–16 to the Presocratics, and more particularly to Parmenides. His last seminar, in 1973, ends up in the same manner with a meditation on *eon emmenai,* Parmenides' tautology. But if the Presocratics are summoned to come in the foreground after 1935 and if from now on Platonism has to be situated in relation to their thoughts, it is perhaps because what has been preserved in Heraclitus' saying *physis krypthestai philei* and in Parmenides' notion of *aletheia* reveals itself at first and in a privileged manner in the work of art. Hölderlin, to whom Heidegger dedicated a first lecture course in 1934–5, was the one from whom he learnt that tragedy is a way in which truth occurs and the sacred opens itself. For the work of art gives a testimony of what is really a beginning: a happening of truth (BW, 162), which, because it lets appear the antagonism of world and earth, of what opens itself and of what is secluded in itself, can subsist only as a conflict maintained in a work. Heidegger declares however that the work of art as the truth of being setting itself in work is only one of the ways for truth to happen: another way is questioning and saying (186–7). But we can wonder whether this work of language that is thought possesses as much initiating power as this work of language that is poetry (EM, 146), especially in regard to its capacity of grounding history (BW, 202).

A beginning, because it happens suddenly, can be maintained only if it is repeated, that is, begun anew. And beginning anew is always beginning in another manner. This is why repetition did not mean for Heidegger in 1927 to become Aristotelian again, and did not mean so either ten years later, as Heidegger himself later underlined, "to philosophize only in a Presocratic manner and declare that all the rest is misunderstanding and decline" (WhD, 175). The question is rather to "master" the beginning of Western philosophy, which means to understand how initial beginning and initial end are related to each other in it. The question is precisely to situate Plato in regard to the thinkers of *physis.* This is the reason why Heidegger was led to speak of a "mutation" (*Wandel*) of the essence of truth in *Plato's Theory of Truth*—a text published in 1942, but which was already the subject of two lectures in 1930—and, in a less explicit manner, in his 1935 lecture course *An Introduction to Metaphysics.* If the word *physis* belongs to the same root as *phôs,* light, according to the etymology invoked by Heidegger more than once, for example, in his 1935 lecture course and in the first version of "The Origin of the Work of Art,"[3] the Platonic determination of being as *idea,* a word meaning look, aspect, becomes comprehensible. As Heidegger points out, the interpretation of Being as *idea* "proceeds with an inescapable necessity from the fact that Being has been experienced as *physis,* as the reign of what unfolds itself, as appearing, as what stands in light" (EM, 138–9). The *idea* is not the appearing as such, but only the appearing insofar as it is related to a look, so that it can remain stable and be understood as constant presence, that is, as *ousia.* The famous mutation of truth that Heidegger attributes to Plato comes from the preeminence given to *idea* and *idein* over *physis* and consists in submitting Being to *noein,* that is, to thinking and perception. Ideas, which are grasped by a non-sensible look, constitute the *noetos topos,* the domain of the supersensible, into which the supreme idea, the *idea tou agathou*, the idea of the Good, is considered as the cause of all that exists and therefore called *to theion*, the divine. Metaphysics that sees in the *idea* the *ontôs on*, the true being, that is situated beyond *physis*, which itself is reduced to the level of a *me on*, a nonbeing, is essentially, in the form of Platonism, an ideo-logy, a science of the ideas and no longer a physio-logy, a science of *physis*. As Heidegger points out: "Since being has been interpreted as *idea*, the thinking of the Being of beings is metaphysics, and metaphysics is theological."[4]

It is on the basis of this new definition of metaphysics that the theme of the overcoming of metaphysics can be developed, directly taken up from Nietzsche and his project of the "reversal of Platonism" that Heidegger analyzed in the first lecture course he dedicated to Nietzsche in 1936–7 (N1, 231 f). Metaphysics does not know that the clarity of the ideas comes from the light of Being. This does not mean however that metaphysics, which has legitimately been named "metaphysics of light" insofar as the metaphor of light is at the center of its self-interpretation, is totally blind to light, but it experiences light only under the form of the lighting into which the enlightened beings stand, so that the question it asks is only directed toward the state of clarity and the *permanent* source of light and never toward the *event* of light itself. This explains why Heidegger declares in the Introduction he added in 1949 to "What is metaphysics?": "Wherever metaphysics represents beings, Being has (already) lit up."[5] Metaphysics thinks only the being-lighted of beings, but not the lighting-process of Being from which the clarity that illuminates being proceeds: "Being is not thought in its revealing coming-to-presence, i.e. in its truth."[6] Metaphysics thinks therefore only the truth

of beings, not the truth of Being itself. But the expression "truth of Being" should not be misunderstood. It does not mean that Being is true, but that Being is in itself truth in the sense of *alètheia*. In this 1949 Introduction, Heidegger, in opposition to what he said in *Plato's Theory of Truth*, includes in the metaphysical epoch the Presocratics thinkers themselves: "The truth of Being remains concealed to metaphysics in the course of its history from Anaximander to Nietzsche."[7] All tentative of a rebirth of the Presocratic thought is therefore definitively discredited, as Heidegger suggested already in *Being and Time* when he declared that "the phenomenon of world was passed over at the beginning of the ontological tradition decisive for us, explicitly in Parmenides" (SZ, 100). What remains to be understood is the fact that the Presocratics did think only the truth of beings and not the truth of Being, the *alètheia* itself, in spite of the fact that they named it. To experience *aletheia* and to remain under its influence is not equivalent to mastering it by thinking. *Aletheia* is for the Presocratics beyond all questions. That the beginning cannot be mastered by thinking and opens the way to its possible future renewal belongs to the very essence of beginning. This is what Heidegger explained in 1933 in his *Rectoral address* that should not be considered in this respect only as having been required by the circumstances: "The beginning is still. It does not lie *behind* us as something long past, but it stands in front of us. The beginning has, as the greatest moment, in advance already passed over all that is coming and hence over us as well. The beginning has fallen into our future, it stands there as the distant decree that requires of us to recapture its greatness."[8]

* * *

To recapture the greatness of the beginning, this can be accomplished only through the transition to another beginning, which opens itself as soon as the truth of Being is thought. This is clearly said in 1936–8 in *Contributions to Philosophy* dedicated to the thinking of this transition. Here the ambiguous status of the ontological difference becomes manifest, because, being linked to a questioning dealing with the beings and beingness, it can be elaborated only through a going beyond of beings toward their Being. The question is now, as Heidegger declares, "no to go beyond beings (transcendence), but rather to leap over *(überspringen)* this difference and question in a more initial manner starting from Being and truth" (GA 65, § 132, 250). Heidegger writes *Seyn* now with a y, to indicate through this old spelling, that the word "Being" now means truth and no longer the Being of beings, that is, their ground. The ontological difference reveals itself as at the same time necessary and fatal: necessary, as a first step in elucidating the Being-question and as springboard for the leap into the *Ereignis*; but fatal, because it can succeed in helping us to get out of beingness (this was the virtue of Aristotle's nongeneric concept of Being) only to immediately immerse us again into it, since in the ontological difference Being is thought of only in relationship to beings. As such, the ontological difference is the structure of the domain of Western metaphysics that "names Being but means the beings as beings," so that all what it says "moves in a strange manner right from the start and until the end in a permanent confusion between beings and Being."[9]

We can however wonder if in this transition leading to this other beginning that is the truth of Being, we have not already gone out of philosophy. Here also, ambiguity remains, as shown in the title of this big manuscript that Heidegger wrote with no intention of immediate publishing, where he deals with the transition from the first to the other beginning, that is, from philosophy to thought, but still considers that he is thus "contributing" to philosophy. At that time, philosophy is considered as including in itself a double questioning: the question of the beingness of beings, which refers to philosophy as it has existed up to now, and the question of the truth of Being, which refers to the philosophy to come. This duality in the essence of philosophy is linked to the difference of two kinds of questioning: first of all, the question of the relationship between being and thinking that characterizes the entire history of Western philosophy into which the leading thread of the Being-question is *noein* and *legein*, which implies the inevitable domination of logic upon ontology and its final triumph in Hegel's *Science of Logic*; and secondly, the question of the relationship of Being and time, where time is, as Heidegger stresses, the first indication of the truth of Being (GA 65, § 91, 183). Here we have a good example of Heidegger's retrospective view on his own work that is the basis of his self-interpretation, a self-interpretation that was a way of presenting his thinking as a "path" including different landmarks, as shown in the title "*Wegmarken*" he choose in 1967 for a collection of the most important among the short texts he published between 1929 and 1964. It seems that in *Beiträge zur Philosophie*, Heidegger considers in a somewhat paradoxical manner that the other beginning *is* the other beginning *of* philosophy. However the other beginning has no longer to do with philosophy—a word that is for Heidegger synonymous with metaphysics—and it is also no longer Greek, as Heidegger explained some years later, when he began to see in *Ereignis* the unthought element of the Greek thought, unthought meaning not that which Greek thinking left aside, but what it preserved in itself as a gift to future thinkers (WhD, 72). He said in 1954 in his dialogue with Professor Tetzuka from Tokyo University that "our thinking today is charged with the task to think what the Greek have thought in an even more Greek manner," adding that "to enter into thinking this unthought element means: to pursue more originally what the Greek have thought, to see it in the source of its essence. To see it so is in its own way Greek, and yet in respect to what it sees it is no longer, is never again Greek" (OWL, 39, tr. modified). In an even more categorical manner, Heidegger declared in the last seminar he gave in Le Thor in France in 1969

> Thinking *Ereignis* with the concepts of being and the history of being will not be successful; nor will it be with the assistance of the Greek (which is precisely something "to go beyond"). With being, the ontological difference also vanishes. Looking ahead, one would likewise have to view the continual references to the ontological difference from 1927 to 1936 as a necessary impasse or blind alley. With *Ereignis*, it is no longer an issue of Greek thought at all. (FS, 60–1)

The question arises here: how should we understand what Heidegger names "*Ereignis*," if it is that which constitutes the unthought element of Greek thought? Heidegger himself declared in *Identity and Difference* that this word is "as little translatable as the leading Greek word logos and the Chinese word Tao."[10] He also insisted on the fact that this word should not be understood in the ordinary sense of "event," as it were an "event" among others, but that it is a "singulare tantum."[11] In *Contributions to Philosophy,*

whose subtitle is "*Vom Ereignis*," the word is clearly understood on the basis of its incorrect popular etymology by which it is related to the verb *eignen*, meaning to make proper, to appropriate. But in later texts, Heidegger recalled that its true etymology stems from the word "*Auge*," eye, so that *er-äugen*, which is the older form of *ereignen*, meant "to catch sight of, to see."[12] It is in fact the combination of these three meanings (event, appropriation, and sight) that renders this term properly untranslatable. It means therefore in Heidegger's view the singular event that allows the reciprocal "propriation" of Being and man by making visible. As such, as he explains in *Identity and Difference*, it names the belonging together of Being and man. But this belonging together is based on a self de-propriation, *Ent-eignis*, of *Ereignis* itself, which comes from the fact that *Ereignis* cannot reveal itself completely as such and, as Heidegger explains, "withdraws itself to the unlimited de-concealment" (ZSD, 23). This is precisely this concealed belonging together of Being and man that the Greeks did not think, because for them Being had the meaning of something subsistent, "*vorhanden*," which has no intrinsic relationship with the human being.

But if the theme of the end of philosophy could appear in the foreground in the last decades of Heidegger's "path of thinking," it was because metaphysics had been itself understood as the history of being, so that all tentative attempts to "overcome" it could begin to appear as bound to fail. Such tentative attempts can lead nowhere, either in the Kantian form of the project of a "metaphysics of metaphysics" (a project that Heidegger tried in 1929 to take up again) or in the form of the Nietzschean "reversal of Platonism," which for Heidegger is only the proof that thinking is definitively entangled into metaphysics (VA, 79). In the fragments collected under the title "Overcoming of metaphysics," which are fragments from different manuscripts (including *Beiträge*) written between 1936 and 1946, Heidegger immediately made clear that the expression *"Überwindung der Metaphysik"* was used only as an expedient, because it does not allow to experience the ground of the history of Being, which is *Ereignis* (71). If metaphysics does not think the truth of Being, it is not an omission or a mistake, and the forgottenness of Being that characterizes it is not in itself something negative, this forgottenness is on the contrary what is sent to us by Being, which, as the source of beings that are not itself a being of higher rank, has to stay in concealment for the sake of the unconcealment of beings.[13] The question is neither therefore to suppress metaphysics and to expel it from the horizon of culture nor to get rid of it as if it were a mere opinion,[14] but to *recover* from it, in what Heidegger calls no longer *"Uberwindung,"* but *"Verwindung,"* a word that implies that metaphysics has been assimilated and is no longer something that can govern the movement of thinking. However, such a recovery does not depend upon our decision, but, like the forgottenness of being, it is a sending, a destiny, which allows us to experience forgottennness as such. Such an experience can only be the experience of the "identity" of *Lichtung und Verbergung*, of clearing and concealing—Heidegger says precisely in "The Origin of the Work of Art" that "the clearing in which beings stand is at the same time concealment" (BW, 178). In the experience of forgottenness as forgottenness, the truth of being appears as that which has been concealed up to now, so that the forgottenness of Being can be accepted and included—*verwunden*—in *Ereignis* (VA, 79). What has now to be thought is not the difference between beings and being, but their double fold, *Zwiefalt*, that at the same time holds them together and separates them (ibid.). The ontological difference was identified with the transcendence of Dasein, it was then considered as a power of differentiation belonging to Dasein, whereas now it is Being that preserves in itself the difference of Being and beings, the difference being sent to the human being by Being itself and no longer unfolded by him. In *Contributions to Philosophy*, Heidegger names this reversal *die Kehre des Ereignisses* (GA 65, § 255). Such a reversal inverts the direction of the differentiating process: the human being is now the accomplishment of the differentiating process and no longer the one that accomplishes it, because if it were the case, it could make us believe that this accomplishment is his decision and the work of a transcendental subject. Now the facticity and thrownness of the differentiation process is no longer referred to Dasein, but to Being itself; and as Heidegger says in the *Letter on Humanism*, "Being is illuminated for man in the ecstatic projection *(Entwurf)*. But this projection does not create Being. Moreover, the projection is essentially a thrown projection. What throws in projection is not man, but Being itself, which sends man into the ek-sistence of Dasein that is his essence" (BW, 241). Dasein is therefore *gebraucht*, "employed" by the differentiation process and stays in its service. But in order to make possible the thinking of the *Zwiefalt*, in order to let appear the double fold of being and the beings, necessary for difference to properly happen, what is needed is the "event" of difference. This is precisely what takes place at the end of metaphysics, in the last stadium of the accomplished metaphysics, when the forgottenness of Beings reaches its culmination and when at the same time the decline of beings begins, the becoming manifest of the beings having lost its exclusiveness.

* * *

What does Heidegger mean under the expression "the end of philosophy"? We should first of all leave aside the negative representations of the end as interruption or decadence. It means rather accomplishment, completion, fulfillment of an assignment to which philosophy responds since the beginning of its history and which requires that it thinks the ground of beings, that is, the presence of what is present. Metaphysical or philosophical thinking (this is the same in Heidegger's view) is, as Heidegger says in his 1964 lecture on "The End of Philosophy and the Task of Thinking," a thinking that "starting from what is present, represents it in its presence and thus exhibits it grounded by its ground" (432). The use of the terms representing (*Vorstellen*) and exhibiting (*darstellen*) does not mean that the metaphysics in question here is only the modern metaphysics of subjectivity. Representation and exhibition are not referred here to the activity of a subject, but to thinking itself when it is taken as the leading thread of the interpretation of Being. This is exactly what happened with Plato who gave the primacy to *idein* and *noein*, to seeing and perceiving, and this is the reason why in the period of its completion, philosophy defines itself as "*die Wissenschaft*," "the Science" with Fichte and Hegel, ontology having been thus completely dissolved into logic. But if Plato's thought determines the entire history of philosophy, if indeed metaphysics is Platonism, it takes various forms corresponding to various ways of experiencing and interpreting the presence of what is present. For Heidegger, the history of philosophy is the history of the mutations of presence, which have to be thought as happening in a "free succession" and not, as Hegel wanted, in a logical and dialectical order. But this does not mean that they are the results of the arbitrary views of each philosopher, because, as Heidegger stressed in his 1955 lecture "What is philosophy?" philosophers are only responding each time to the claim of a new form of presence.[15] But if the philosophies do not proceed in a dialectical order from each other, if no necessity governs their development, in which sense is it possible to think of completion and fix a limit to such a free succession? What could allow us to see, after the determination of presence as *idea* and *ousia* in Greek thought and as objectivity in modern times, in its determination as *Bestellbarkeit*, as orderability, the ultimate phase of the history of philosophy? Is it not possible to imagine that future mutations of presence could appear after the one that is now? Heidegger explains that the mutation of presence that characterizes our time determines the presence of what is present no longer on the basis of the face to face of subject and object, but as a mere standing-reserve orderable by what is no longer a subject, that is, by the industrial society in its entirety, since it is itself subjected to the challenging power of what Heidegger calls *Ge-stell*, the gathering of all modes of *stellen*, of framing and setting in order, which "concentrates man upon ordering the actual as standing-reserve" (BW, 324). But in spite of the special character of this mutation of presence, how can we be sure that this "becoming-world" of philosophy that is for Heidegger modern technology is really the ultimate form of philosophy? Is there really in this period something that goes beyond the limits of a thinking of presence and ground? To such a legitimate question, Heidegger answers that an "insight into what is" today can perceive that the thinking of ground does no longer govern modern science, which as operative mode of thinking, makes use of the old categories of cause and ground in a pure instrumental manner. Because the domination of operative thinking is extended to the entire domain of the beings and therefore also concerns man himself, who is thus "employed" (*gebraucht*) by *Gestell*, the relationship of the human being to presence takes a form in which presence as such becomes questionable. Philosophical thinking does not question presence as such, but only what is present in its relation to presence considered as its ground. The end of philosophy is consequently double-faced, as is also *Gestell*: it means on one side the completion of the thinking of ground and presence, in the form of the thinking of orderability, and on the other side, the task of questioning presence in the light of the thinking of orderability.

But cannot such a questioning of presence be already found in Greek thought? Plato himself, when he defined the presence of what is present as *idea*, referred it at the same time to light as what alone allows us to see. Is not Greek thinking characterized by the fact that it thinks presence in relation to light, so that it can see in a being a *phainomenon*, that is, something that appears in light and shines? It is only, as Heidegger explains in his *Letter in Humanism*, in Roman thinking that the emphasis was put unilaterally on seeing, and no longer on appearing as such, so that the way was henceforth cleared for the modern transposition of *idea* into *perceptio*. Plato however sees in light only the link, the *zugon*, the yoke between seeing and what is to see,[16] without thinking the *event* of light, which happens as the simultaneity of clearing and concealment. The "metaphor" of light, because it *opposes* light to darkness,

cannot understand such a simultaneity that constitutes the very structure of *aletheia*. For that it is necessary to see in *lethe*, the heart of *aletheia* and not its opposite. It is not sufficient either to bring to language their opposition as a contra-diction, *ein Widerspruch*, but it is necessary to see the conflict, *die Widerstreit*, into which clearing does not appear only as the clearing of presence, but as the clearing of a presence that conceals itself (ZSD, 79).

This is the reason why Heidegger insists on the necessity of understanding the *Lichtung*, the lighting-process or clearing, no longer out of the idea of light and brightness but rather out of the idea of lightness, which is the meaning of the German word *lichten* that corresponds to the adjective *leicht* meaning light as opposed to heavy. As Heidegger explains in "The End of Philosophy and the Task of Thinking," "to lighten something means to make it light, free and open" and "the space thus originating is the clearing," so that "light can stream into the clearing, into its openness, and let brightness play with darkness in it, but light never creates the clearing, rather it presupposes it" (BW, 441). But this openness (*Offene*) to which Heidegger gives the old name of *Gegnet*, country (in the literal meaning of what is encountered),[17] should not be identified with space alone. It should rather be put in relationship with what Heidegger called in *Beiträge* "*Zeitraum*," time-space (GA 65, § 238, 371 f.), which constitutes a more originally mutual belonging of space and time than their metaphysical juxtaposition. The openness of time-space, the clearing, is nothing else, as Heidegger said in his "Letter on Humanism" (BW, 230), than the world itself that cannot be understood on the basis of space, but is on the contrary that what is *einräumend*, that what gives space (BT, § 24).

Thus with the thinking of *Lichtung* as clearing and no longer of the *Lichtung* as light, we have already left behind philosophy, because as Heidegger says, "philosophy does speak about the light of reason, but does not heed the clearing of Being" (BW, 443).

This new definition of *Lichtung* makes possible to measure the distance covered since 1927. In opposition to *Ereignis*, which appears as a key-word in Heidegger's writings only in the mid-1930s, the word *Lichtung* is already a key-word in *Being and Time*, where we can read in § 28 that this being that is Dasein "*is* itself the *Lichtung*" (SZ, 133), in the sense that it is in itself "lighted," and not by another being, as it is said in the ontically figurative expression "*lumen naturale.*" It is therefore still in relation to the light of reason that the disclosure of Dasein is defined in 1927. Going from the lighting that is Dasein for himself to the clearing that is Being itself requires the "leap" in *Ereignis* that is thermalized in *Contributions to Philosophy*. This is what is acknowledged by Heidegger in one of his last public lectures, in October 1965, where he declares: "The analytic of Dasein does not reach to what is properly clearing and absolutely not to the domain to which clearing for its part belongs."[18] What is thus implicitly acknowledged is the fact that Heidegger's "path of thinking" goes from what is in question in philosophy to what is in question in thinking.

Philosophy is therefore a question of light and seeing, as it has become manifest in its end, with Hegel's speculative thinking and Husserl's thought of the originary giving intuition. Is there another mode of thinking that could be neither immediate seeing nor reflective mediation? A thinking that, going beyond Greek experience—*über das Griechiche hinaus* (BW, 448)—would be a "phenomenology of the inapparent," as

Heidegger suggested in his last 1973 seminar? (FS, 82). But what can we say about the inapparent? Heidegger already asked the question in *Contributions to Philosophy* when he observed: "We can never say Being *(Ereignis)* immediately, and therefore also never say it mediately in the sense of an enhanced 'logic' of dialectic. Every saying already speaks from within the truth of Being and can never immediately leap over Being itself" (GA 65, § 38).

This is the reason why he was favoring a "logic of silence," a sigetic (GA 65, § 37) that does not exclude, but on the contrary includes the logic of beingness and substance, which is always a predicative and foundative logic. For what has to be done is not to remain silent, but to give access to silence in language itself. This is exactly what happens in the famous tautologies or self predicative sentences such as "*die Sprache ist die Sprache*"[19] or "*Die Zeit zeitigt,*" "*Der Raum räumt.*"[20]

Heidegger often says that the thinking that is no longer metaphysical is inferior in a way to philosophy, precisely because it does not raise itself to the level of a foundative way of thinking. To the dream of an absolute thinking, of this *noesis noesos*, the thinking of thinking, that Hegel thought accessible for the human being, Heidegger opposes the finitude of a thinking that is not self-centered, and which "in the poverty of its provisional essence" (BW, 256) "lets that before which it is led show itself" (FS, 82). But there should be no misunderstanding about the fundamentally provisional character of the thinking that is no longer philosophy. *Vorläufigkeit*, the provisional or preparatory character of thinking, as Heidegger stresses in the *Letter on Humanism*, is the "essence" of thinking, that which constitutes thinking as such and of which philosophy has remained unaware, in spite of the fact that it acknowledged it in its own way, since it "forgets" Being, remaining thus in a negative way faithful to the *event* of Being, which can give itself only by concealing itself.

NOTES AND REFERENCES

1 M. Heidegger, *Kant und das Problem der Metaphysik* (Frankfurt am Main: Klostermann, 1973), 2

2 GA 24, 254: «The overcoming of Hegel is the intrinsically necessary step in the development of Western philosophy which has to be accomplished if Western philosophy ought to stay alive.»

3 EM, 54; GA 5, 28.

4 M. Heidegger, *Platons Lehre von der Wahrheit*, in *Wegmarken* (Frankfurt am Main: Klostermann, 1967), 141.

5 Heidegger, *Wegmarken*, 196.

6 Ibid.

7 Ibid., 199.

8 M. Heidegger, "*Die Selbstbehauptung der deutschen Universität,*" *Reden und andere Zeugnisse eines Lebensweges*, GA 16, 110.

9 Heidegger, *Wegmarken*, 199.

10 M. Heidegger, *Identität und Differenz* (Pfullingen: Neske, 1957), 29.

11 Ibid.

12 Ibid., 28. See also M. Heidegger, *Unterwegs zur Sprache* (Pfullingen: Neske, 1959), 260.

13 Heidegger, *Wegmarken*, 199.

14 Ibid., 72.

15 M. Heidegger, *Was ist das—die Philosophie?* (Pfullingen: Neske, 1956), 29 and 31.

16 Plato, *Politeia*, 508 a

17 M. Heidegger, *Gelassenheit* (Pfullingen: Neske, 1979), 31.

18 M. Heidegger, *Zur Frage nach der Bestimmung der Sache des Denkens* (St Gallen: Erker, 1984), 19.

19 Heidegger, *Unterwegs zur Sprache*, 15.

20 Ibid., 213.

7

HEIDEGGER'S CORRESPONDENCE
Alfred Denker

Martin Heidegger is probably the last of the great letter writers in the history of philosophy. He wrote an estimated 10,000 letters in his life. If we add to this the sheer mass of his publications and other writings—the collected edition of his writings (*Gesamtausgabe*) contains approximately 100 volumes—it is hard to imagine how he found time to do other things than write. During his lifetime a number of interesting letters were published. In this chapter I will present an overview of his correspondence. In the first section I will discuss his letters in general. The second section is dedicated to the letters that were published during his lifetime with his permission and correspondences that have been published since his death. In the third section we will take a closer look at the planned publication of almost all his letters in the *Martin-Heidegger-Briefausgabe*.

MARTIN HEIDEGGER'S
CORRESPONDENCE IN GENERAL

Martin Heidegger corresponded with many important philosophers (among others Heinrich Rickert, Edmund Husserl, Karl Jaspers, Karl Löwith, Hans-Georg Gadamer, Hannah Arendt, Hans Jonas, Max Scheler,

Jean-Paul Sartre, and Ernst Tugendhat), scholars of the humanities (e.g. Kurt Bauch, Beda Allemann, and Emil Staiger), scientists (Werner Heisenberg and Carl-Friedrich von Weizsäcker), psychiatrists (Medard Boss and Ludwig Binswanger) theologians (Conrad Gröber, Karl Rahner, and Johannes Baptist Lotz), authors and poets (René Char, Paul Celan, and Ernst und Friedrich-Georg Jünger to name a few), and artists (for instance Eduardao Chillida, Bernhard Heiliger, Georges Braque, Otto Dix, and Hans Kock). Many of Heidegger's correspondences and letters are voluminous. His largest correspondence with his wife Elfride contains over 1,100 letters and we have to bear in mind that several hundred letters have been destroyed. The longest letter has over 50 manuscript pages. Heidegger's letters are first and foremost important because of their biographical and philosophical content. Heidegger often presents and clarifies his thought in his letters. Repeatedly he gives a far more detailed account of his thought than elsewhere. He is also very critical of himself and his work. And of course the letters always show glimpses of the background or context of his thought that cannot be found anywhere else. Without exaggerating we can claim that his letters are an important addition to his work and lecture courses. We could describe his correspondence as a work in its own right alongside the *Gesamtausgabe.*

The importance of his letters has been documented by the few published correspondences. They are unique and irreplaceable sources for any biographical, historical, or philosophical interpretation of Heidegger's life and work. Heidegger's correspondence with Karl Jaspers is for instance not only of great help in understanding Heidegger's relation to the university and his ideas of a reform of the Humboldt-University but also of incomparable value for an understanding of the genesis of his main work *Being and Time.* His correspondence with Karl Löwith that will be published in 2013 is of similar importance. Heidegger's correspondence with Hannah Arendt, Elisabeth Blochmann, and his wife are of great value for biographical and philosophical research. In these correspondences Heidegger shows himself in his role as philosophical mentor who not only clarifies his thought but also explains his thought in its philosophical context and against the historical background. The letters also contain numerous accounts of his travels and contacts for which we have no other sources. For the time immediately after the end of Second World War Heidegger's correspondence with Max Müller is of utmost importance. It offers many insights into the Denazification-process, university politics, and Heidegger's role.

THE LETTERS PUBLISHED BY HEIDEGGER AND CORRESPONDENCES PUBLISHED AFTER HIS DEATH

Heidegger published or gave permission to publish letters during his lifetime. The most

famous letter of them all is without doubt his letter to Jean Beaufret that was written in late 1946 and published in 1947 under the title "*Brief über den Humanismus* [Letter on Humanism]" in a small volume that also contained his "*Platons Lehre von der Wahrheit* [Plato's Doctrine of Truth]."[1] Heidegger's letter was an answer to a letter Beaufret had written to him on November 10, 1946.[2] In this letter Heidegger looked back on his path of thought from *Being and Time* until 1946 and positioned himself in the philosophical debate of the time. It is to a certain extent also an answer to the famous essay by Jean-Paul Sartre, "L'existentialisme est un humanisme" that was published earlier in Paris in 1946.

Another important letter is Heidegger's letter to William J. Richardson, SJ, that was published as a "preface" in his *magnus opus*: *Heidegger. Through phenomenology to thought.*[3] Heidegger's comments on Richardson's interpretation of his thought offers some valuable insights in the problem of the "turning" on his pathway of thought.

This is not the place to take a closer look at the contents of these letters. Instead I will provide the readers with a complete list of the letters that were published with Heidegger's permission during his lifetime. It may be of interest to note that the last letter of this list is the last thing Heidegger wrote in his life.

Letter to Max Kommerell, published in: Max Kommerell. *Briefe und Aufzeichnungen 1919–1944.* Freiburg 1967, 404–5.

To a verse of Mörike. A correspondence with Martin Heidegger from Emil Staiger. In: *Trivium* 9, Zürich 1954; reprinted in: Martin Heidegger, *Aus der Erfahrung des Denkens,* hrsg. von Hermann Heidegger, *Gesamtausgabe* 13, Frankfurt am Main 1983, 93–109.

Martin Heidegger's letter on *Einführung in die Metaphysik*. In: *Die Zeit*, Jhg. 8, Nr. 39. 15. September 1953. Reprinted in: Martin Heidegger, *Einführung in die Metaphysik*, hrsg. von Petra Jaeger *Gesamtausgabe* 40, Frankfurt am Main 1983, 232–3.

Letter of April 1962 to William J. Richardson, SJ, published as a preface in his *Heidegger. Through phenomenology to thought*. The Hague 1963, vii–xxiii.

Letter to Takehiko Kojima written July 5, 1963. In: Dino Larese (Hrsg.), *Begegnung. Zeitschrift für Literatur, bildende Kunst, Musik und Wissenschaft* 1, 1965, 2–7.

Letter of March 11, 1964 written for a discussion at Drew University in Madison (USA) from April 9 to April 11, 1964. Einige Hinweise auf Hauptgeschichtspunkte für das theologische Gespräch über "Das Problem eines nicht-objektivierenden Denkens und Sprechens in der heutigen Theologie," first published in French translation in: *Archives de Philosophie* (32) 1969, 396–416. Reprinted in: Martin Heidegger, *Wegmarken*, hrsg. von Friedrich-Wilhelm von Herrmann *Gesamtausgabe* 9, Frankfurt am Main 1976, 68–78,

Readers letter to the editor in chief of the *Spiegel* of February 22, 1966. In: *Der Spiegel*, Jhg. 20, Nr. 7, 7. February 1966, 110–12; Nr. 11, 7. März 1966. 12. Reprinted in: Martin Heidegger, *Reden und andere Zeugnisse eines Lebensweges*, hrsg. von Hermann Heidegger, Gesamtausgabe 16, Frankfurt am Main 2000, 639.

Letter to Arthur H. Schrynemakers of September 20, 1966 as greetings to the Symposium on Heidegger's Philosophy at Dusquesne University, Pittsburgh October 15–16, 1966 published in: John Sallis (ed.), *Heidegger and the Path of Thinking*. Pittsburgh 1970; reprinted in *Gesamtausgabe* 16, 650–1.

Letter to Manfred S. Frings of October 20, 1966 as greetings to the Heidegger-Symposium in Chicago, November 11–12, 1966, published in: Manfred Frings (ed.), *Heidegger and the Quest for Truth*. Chicago 1968; reprinted in: *Gesamtausgabe* 16, 684–6.

Letter to François Bondy from January 29, 1968, reprinted in: *Critique. Revue générale des publications françaisses et étrangers* (24), 1968.

Letter to Roger Munier from July 31, 1969. In: *Qu'est-ce que la métaphysique?*, précédé d'une lettre de l'auteur. Trad. Roger Munier, published in: *Le Nouveau Commerce*, cahier 14, été-automne 1969, 55–6 ; reprinted in: Martin Heidegger, *Seminare*, hrsg. von Curd Ochwadt, *Gesamtausgabe* 15, Frankfurt am Main 1983, 414–16.

Letter to Albert Borgmann from 29. October 39, 1969 as greetings and thanks to the participants of the Heidegger-Conference in Honolulu, Hawaii 17–21. November 17–21, 1969, published in: *Philosophy East and West* 20, 1970; reprinted in *Gesamtausgabe* 16, 721–2.

Letter to Jan Aler from November 1970, published in: *Zeitschrift für Ästhetik und allgemeine Kunstwissenschaft* 18, 1973; reprinted in: *Gesamtausgabe* 16, 723–4.

Letter an Henri Mongis from June 7, 1972, published in: H. Mongis. *Heidegger et la Critique de la Notion de Valeur*. The Hague 1976, vi–xi, reprinted in: *Gesamtausgabe* 16, 727–9.

Greetings to the Symposium in Beirut November 1974, in: *Extasis. Cahiers de philosophie et de littérature* (8), Beirut 1981; reprinted in Gesamtausgabe 19, 742–3.

Letter from November 19, 1974 as congratulations to the publishing of volume 500 of the journal *Risô*, published in: *Risô*, (500),

January 1975; reprinted in: *Gesamtausgabe* 16, 744–5.

Greetings to Bernhard Welte and his hometown Meßkirch from late May 1976, published in: *Stadt Meßkirch—Ehrenbürgerfeier Professor Dr. Bernhard Welte*. Meßkirch 1978; reprinted in: *Gesamtausgabe* 13, 243.

In the last 25 years important correspondences have been published. The most famous correspondence is of course the letter exchange with his onetime lover Hannah Arendt. These publications have documented the different stages of Heidegger's life and work. Some of his earliest letters—that offer insight into Heidegger's philosophical development in his student years—were published in the Heidegger-Rickert correspondence. For the 1920s and the genesis of *Being and Time* the correspondences with Karl Jaspers and Karl Löwith are of great importance. Heidegger's relation to National-Socialism in the late 1930s and early 1940s can be found in his letter exchange with Kurt Bauch. In his second letter to Bauch from March 14, 1933 for instance Heidegger writes:

In my opinion we can only try to avoid mistakes and make people conscious of the necessity of a total revolution that cannot be achieved by so-called measures alone, but only by a clarification and determination of the will and the mission of the young generation: In this respect I have already presented a proposal in the committee. If we don't want our platonic program come to nothing, we need to know first what the government is planning.[4]

From this passage we can learn several things: (1) Before Heidegger became rector of Freiburg University on April 21, 1933 he had already formulated a program

for a reform of the Humboldt-University. From the Heidegger-Jaspers correspondence we know that the necessity of a university reform was one of the main topics of their discussions in Heidelberg in the early 1930s. (2) He was actively trying to promote this proposal not only among the other professors but also in the Ministry of Education in both Karlsruhe and Berlin. (3) Heidegger's reform program was inspired by Platonic philosophy. A small citation from a letter like the one above already proves that Heidegger's involvement with National-Socialism and his ideas of university reform that he tried to put in place as rector in 1933 cannot be separated from his thought. There are not only philosophical reasons why Heidegger was attracted to National-Socialism and the charismatic leadership of Hitler but also philosophical reasons why he became ever more critical of National-Socialism. In the late 1930s he sees National-Socialism as the most extreme and terrible form of Nihilism and Hitler and his clique as the worst criminals in history.

For the convenience of the reader I have put together a list of the Heidegger correspondences that have been published so far.

Hannah Arendt/Martin Heidegger, *Briefe 1925 bis 1975 und andere Zeugnisse*, Frankfurt am Main: Vittorio Klostermann, 1998.

Martin Heidegger/Elisabeth Blochmann, *Briefwechsel 1918–1969*, Marbach am Neckar: Deutsches Literaturarchiv, 1989.

Martin Heidegger/Imma von Bodmershof, *Briefwechsel 1959–1976*, Stuttgart: Klett-Cotta, 2000.

Martin Heidegger/Edmund Husserl, *Briefwechsel 1916–1933*; in: Heidegger-Jahrbuch Bd. 6 (2012), 9–39.

Martin Heidegger/Karl Jaspers, *Briefwechsel 1920–1963*, Frankfurt am Main/München; Vittorio Klostermann/Piper, 1990.

Martin Heidegger/Erhart Kästner, *Briefwechsel 1953–1974*, Frankfurt am Main: Insel Verlag, 1986.

Martin Heidegger/Heinrich Rickert, *Briefe 1912–1933*, Frankfurt am Main: Vittorio Klostermann, 2002.

Rudolf Bultmann/Martin Heidegger, *Briefwechsel 1925–1975*, Frankfurt am Main/Tübingen: Vittorio Klostermann/J.C.B. Mohr Verlag, 2009.

Martin Heidegger/Ludwig von Ficker, *Briefwechsel 1952–1967*, Stuttgart: Klett-Cotta, 2004.

Ernst Jünger/Martin Heidegger, *Briefe 1949–1975*, Frankfurt am Main/Stuttgart: Vittorio Klostermann/Klett-Cotta, 2008.

Martin Heidegger, *Briefe an Max Müller und andere Dokumente*, Freiburg/München: Karl Alber Verlag, 2003.

Martin Heidegger/Bernhard Welte, *Briefe und Begegnungen*, Stuttgart: Klett-Cotta, 2003.

Martin Heidegger/Kurt Bauch, *Briefwechsel 1932–1975* (*Martin-Heidegger-Briefausgabe* II.1), Freiburg: Verlag Karl Alber, 2011.

Martin Heidegger/Erhart Kästner. *Briefwechsel 1953–1974*. Herausgegeben von Heinrich W. Petzet. Frankfurt am Main: Insel Verlag, 1986.

Heideggers Briefwechsel mit Max Kommerell wurde teilweise veröffentlicht in: Max Kommerell, *Briefe und Aufzeichnungen: 1919–1944*. Aus dem Nachlaß herausgegeben von Inge Jens. Freiburg: Olten, 1967.

Karl Löwith veröffentlichte Teile von seinem Briefwechsel mit Heidegger in: Karl Löwith, *Zu Heideggers Seinsfrage: Die Natur des Menschen und die Welt der Natur*; in seinen *Sämtlichen Schriften*. Bd. 8: *Heidegger—Denker in dürftiger Zeit*. Stuttgart: Metzler, 1984.

Heideggers Briefwechsel mit Paul Häberlin wurde veröffentlicht in: Paul Häberlin/Ludwig Binswanger. *Briefwechsel 1908–1960*. Herausgegeben von Jeannine Luczak. Basel: Schwabe, 1997.

Heideggers Briefwechsel mit Medard Boss wurde teilweise veröffentlicht in: Martin Heidegger, *Zollikoner Seminare. Protokolle—Zwiegespräche—Briefe*. Herausgegeben von Medard Boss. Frankfurt am Main: Vittorio Klostermann,[2] 1994.

THE MARTIN-HEIDEGGER-BRIEFAUSGABE

The *Martin-Heidegger-Briefausgabe* has been published by Verlag Karl Alber in three divisions and edited by Alfred Denker and Holger Zaborowski. Its aim is to publish Heidegger's correspondences with philosophers, scientists, artists, writers, and other personalities as well as his private and institutional correspondence with universities, ministries, publishers, and academies. The series is divided into three divisions: I. Private correspondence, II. Scientific correspondence, and III. Correspondence with institutions and publishers. Approximately 45 volumes are planned. A full list is provided below. In 2011 the first volume of the *Martin-Heidegger-Briefausgabe* was published. It contains Heidegger's correspondence with his colleague and friend, the historian of art Kurt Bauch mentioned above.

Heidegger's letters will continue to be of utmost importance for the research into his life and thought.

Volume	Correspondence	Number of letters (approx.)
I.1	Correspondence with his parents and sister	126
I.2	Correspondence with his wife Elfride	1,100
I.3	Correspondence with his brother Fritz	700
I.4	Correspondence with other family members (nephews, nieces, grandchildren, parents-in-law, etc.)	300
I.5	Correspondence with his friends Bruno and Erika Leiner	200
I.6	Correspondence with his friends Ernst Laslowski, Fritz Blum, and Theophil Reese	200
I.7	Correspondence with friends in Meßkirch, Todtnauberg, and Freiburg	150
I.8	Private correspondence	1,500
II.1	Correspondence with Kurt Bauch	144
II.2	Correspondence with Karl Löwith	115
II.3	Correspondence with Walter Bröcker, Friedrich Gundolf, Werner Jaeger, Gerhard Krüger, Walter F. Otto, Wolfgang Schadewaldt, Bruno Snell, and Julius Stenzel	200
II.4	Correspondence with Julius Ebbinghaus, Hildegard Feick, Georg Misch, Hermann Mörchen, Hermann Nohl, and Manfred Schröter	200
II.5	Correspondence with Beda Allemann, Wolfgang Binder, Ivo Braak, Max Kommerell, Paul Kremer, Paul Kuckhohn, Eduard Lachmann, Emil Staiger, Ingeborg Strohschneider-Kohrs, Leopold Ziegler, and Franz Zinkernagel	250
II.6	Correspondence with Max Müller, Gustav Siewerth, and Bernhard Welte	200
II.7	Correspondence with Elisabeth Blochmann	112
II.8	Correspondence with Jean Beaufret	250
II.9	Correspondence with Romano Guardini, Engelbert Krebs, and Karl Rahner	250
II.10	Correspondence with Medard Boss, Ludwig von Binswanger, and Victor von Gebsattel	350
II.11	Correspondence with Erich Rothacker, Eugen Fink, Paul Häberlin, Maria Scheler, Ludwig Langrebe, Paul Natorp, and Oskar Becker	200
II.12	Correspondence with Hans Kock, Bernhard Heiliger, George Braque, Hans Wimmer, Otto Dix, and Carl Orff	100
II.13	Correspondence with Jean-Paul Sartre, Otto Pöggeler, Hans Jonas, Hartmut Buchner, Helene Weiß, and Walter Biemel	250
II,14	Correspondence with Ernst Jünger, Friedrich Georg Jünger, Egon Vietta, Paul Celan, and Andrea von Harbou	120
II.15	Correspondence with Käte Victorius, Walter Schulz, Wilhelm Szilasi, and Gottfried Martin	100

Volume	Correspondence	Number of letters (approx.)
II.16	Correspondence with Edmund Husserl, Heinrich Rickert, and Jonas Cohn	150
II.17	Correspondence with philosophers and persons from Asia, South America, the USA, and Canada	250
II.18	Correspondence with philosophers and persons from Asia, South America, Canada and the USA	300
II.19	Correspondence with Heinrich Wiegand Petzet, Hans Jantzen, Marilene Putscher, and Inge Krummer-Schroth	250
II.20	Correspondence with Ludwig von Ficker and Imma von Bodmershof	120
II.21	Correspondence with Rudolf Bultmann	120
II.22	Correspondence with Clemens and Dorothea Podewils	350
II.23	Correspondence with Karl Jaspers	155
II.24	Correspondence with Hannah Arendt	169
II.25	Single letters I	300
II.26	Single letters II	300
II.27	Zusatzband	500
III.1	Correspondence with Gütnher Neske Verlag and others	300
III.2	Correspondence with Vittorio Klostermann Verlag	500
III.3	Correspondence with Academies in Berlin, Munich, and Heidelberg	400
III.4	Correspondence with universities	600
III.5	Correspondence with other institutions	250
III.6	Correspondence with the cities of Meßkirch, Todtnuberg, Marburg, and Freiburg	150

NOTES AND REFERENCES

[1] Martin Heidegger, *Platons Lehre von der Wahrheit/Brief über den Humanismus* (Bern: Verlag Francke, 1947).

[2] This letter is published in the Dutch translation of "Brief über den Humanismus." This volume contains both the Fench original and a Dutch translation (Martin Heidegger, *Over het humanisme*, transl. by Chris Bremmers (Budel: Uitgeverij Damon, 2005), 9–15)

[3] William J. Richardson, SJ, *Heidegger. Through Phenomenology to Thought* (The Hague: Martinus Nijhoff, 1963).

[4] Martin Heidegger/Kurt Bauch, *Briefwechsel 1932–1975*, herausgegeben und kommentiert von Almuth Heidegger (Freiburg/München: Karl Alber, 2010), 14.

PART II:
SOURCES, INFLUENCES, AND ENCOUNTERS

8

HEIDEGGER AND GREEK PHILOSOPHY
Sean D. Kirkland

There is need (*Es bedarf*) of a thoughtful looking back into that which an ancient (*uralt*) memory holds preserved for us, into that which through all the things that we think we know and possess nonetheless remains distorted. We can after all only seek that which is already known, even if concealedly so (*verhüllterweise*). (*Auf.*, 2/*Soj.*, 3, trans. modified)

The epigraph above has much to tell us about how Heidegger views our late-modern or postmodern relationship to ancient Greek philosophy. It is taken from *Sojourns: The Journey to Greece*, a travel-book that Heidegger composed on the occasion of his first visit to that country in 1962. We learn here that a "thoughtful looking back" to the ancient Greeks is not merely a pleasant historical diversion from more pressing contemporary problems, not the sating of an idle curiosity, and not merely a scholarly exercise. Rather, Heidegger views this is as a *Bedürfnis*, a real necessitation or compulsion for us. However, the ultimate destination toward which we find ourselves thus compelled is not located in the past, but right here in our own present. That is, Heidegger is calling for an ancient detour, by which we would ultimately arrive at what we in a certain sense already have; reading the Greeks

with Heidegger brings to light not what the ancients themselves intended or had in mind, not the factual reality of a long dead Greek culture, but what is preserved, although currently inaccessible and unthinkable, in the "originally old (*uralt*)" memory still somehow at work in our living present. Indeed, this passage indicates the motive for and the method of Heidegger's engagement with Greek philosophy, both earlier and later in his career.

To be sure, Heidegger's confrontations with ancient Greek philosophy are numerous. Taking the published works and the lecture courses together, there are multiple monograph-length studies of Heraclitus, Parmenides, Plato, and Aristotle, to which must be added the nearly countless embedded discussions of varying depth and detail in which Heidegger takes up Greek thought in general or a given Greek concept or term in particular. Anything like a comprehensive study of Heidegger and Greek philosophy would thus require volumes.[1] However, even under the constraints within which this essay must operate, what we can address is the basic "why" and the "how" of Heidegger's deep and persisting interest in ancient Greek philosophy. That is, the aforementioned necessitation and the way in which Heidegger's hermeneutic, by identifying a certain ambivalence in the original texts of our inherited tradition, aims to bring about a change in our experience of our world today.

THE NECESSITY OF LOOKING BACK TO THE GREEKS

The very first words of Heidegger's *Being and Time* are Plato's. And the projected final section of the work would have been an extensive treatment of Aristotelian physics and metaphysics. In an important sense, then, the entire project unfolds explicitly within a space opened up and delineated by ancient Greek thought. Furthermore, the central aim of all Heidegger's thinking—the recovery of the question of the meaning of Being—is introduced here as that same question that had "provided a stimulus for the researches of Plato and Aristotle, only to subside from then on *as a theme for actual investigation*" (SZ, 2/BTMR, 21). Why did this question cease to be posed thereafter, such that it is initially impossible for us to pose it again today? Because, ever since the original response to that question and on the basis of that response, Being has been and continues to be dismissed as a notion either universal and self-evident or empty and indefinable.

Even the posing of this question, therefore, requires preparation today, which is to say that Being must be first uncovered in its question-worthiness and made available once again for consideration. In our epigraph above, then, it is Being *as worthy of our attention and inquiry* to which Heidegger is referring when he speaks of what our ancient memory still preserves for us today, but as distorted and concealed. We might wonder how Being, as both inaccessible and nevertheless somehow preserved, can emerge for us as

worthy of inquiry—This is where our "ancient memory" will have a role to play, meaning our persisting relation to ancient Greek philosophical thinking and the texts that contain the trace of what was experienced there. And the compulsion to take up those ancient texts comes from a preliminary perplexity. That is, from the simple strangeness of our being incapable of asking the question of the meaning of Being today despite this question's having a certain undeniable priority with respect to every other inquiry. Once this "necessity (*Notwendigkeit*) for restating the question . . . becomes plain" (SZ, 3/BTMR, 22), it is unfolded into and imposes itself on us as that "twofold task" (SZ, 15/BTMR, 36) that organizes the projected whole of *Being and Time* into its two main parts.

Part one undertakes a *Daseinsanalytik*, a phenomenological, hermeneutical "analysis of *Dasein*," which is to say, of ourselves as "being there" in the world in such a way that we can ask or not ask the question of "what it means to be" (which ipso facto entails a certain pre-understanding of Being). However, the fact that Being appears to us as initially unworthy of any investigation at all indicates that Dasein has a tendency to "fall" away from itself on this point. That is, we treat the question of "what it means to be" as always already definitively answered in part because we reduce everything that *is*, including ourselves, to the one mode of being that belongs to the things in the world with which we are most closely and most constantly involved—Being as "being present" ("presence" here having a double valence of either *Zuhandenheit*, "present and available to be employed toward our ends," or *Vorhandenheit*, "present and available for contemplation, scrutiny, and understanding"). Heidegger then goes on to show that we, as Dasein, actually have as our mode of being a certain way of emerging out of a given past and stretching ourselves out toward a future, thereby deciding our being each and every time. This fundamentally temporalizing structure Heidegger designates as *Sorge* or "care." With this insight into our own mode of being as something other than mere "presence," we should come to suffer anew the question of the meaning of Being *tout simple*.

Although never completed, Heidegger projects Part two as an absolutely necessary corollary to the analysis of Dasein. The temporalizing movement that is Dasein's mode of being also entails an "elemental historicality" (SZ, 20/BTMR, 41), a way of taking up a certain tradition and projecting ourselves toward possibilities delineated by that tradition. We receive certain principles, concepts, and values from historical sources and we decide our future actions accordingly. Indeed, Heidegger traces the "fallenness" of our present condition to two distinct tendencies in Dasein's basic mode of being; As we remarked above, "Dasein's tendency is inclined to fall back upon its world . . . and interpret itself in terms of that world by its refracted light," but Dasein also "simultaneously falls prey (*verfällt*) to the tradition of which it has more or less explicitly taken hold" (SZ, 21/BTMR, 42). Heidegger continues,

Tradition takes what has come down to us and delivers it over to self-evidence; it blocks our access to those original "sources" (*Zugang zu den ursprünglichen Quellen*) from which the categories and concepts handed down to us have been in part genuinely drawn. Indeed, the tradition makes us forget that they have had such an origin. It teaches the needlessness (*Unbedürftigkeit*) of even understanding the necessity (*Notwendigkeit*) of any such going back. (SZ, 21/BTMR, 43)

With this insight into our own fundamental way of being as Dasein, in order to respond properly to our newly awakened perplexity at our own inability to ask the most fundamental and most all-embracing question, *it is necessitated of us* that we disrupt our traditional and inherited understanding of Being. And this we can do only by tracing our own basic ontological orientation back through the epochal moments of its development as charted by the outline of *Being and Time*'s projected second half, through Kant to Descartes, then looking back through the medieval thinkers all the way to Aristotle. It is the Greeks, most dramatically Aristotle but perhaps already Parmenides (SZ, 26/BTMR, 48), who had confronted the question of the meaning of Being to some extent and had answered it, holding that "to be" is exclusively "to be present" in the specific sense of present and available to *legein* or "speaking" for Aristotle or to *noein* or "thinking" for Parmenides. And this interpretation, the work of Greek thinking about the world as they experienced it, was dogmatically passed along as something self-evident, unworthy of questioning. By way of this "destruction" of our own tradition, what had seemed an absolute and manifest truth would come to appear as a product of human interpretation, an historical artifact, and thus something that emerged at a specific moment in our past. With this, we free up that *ursprüngliche Quelle* or "original source" from which the Greek interpretation of Being itself had originally arisen and we become able to think in relation to it, posing once again the question of the meaning of Being for ourselves. We will return to this below, for it is the aim of excavating just this source that determines Heidegger's hermeneutic with respect to Greek texts.

Having identified where the need or the necessity of looking back to the Greeks comes from in *Being and Time*, we might now just note that the call for something like this "destruction" actually appears much earlier in Heidegger's thinking. For example, in the 1922 introduction to a never-executed book project, "Phenomenological Interpretations in Connection with Aristotle," the task of analyzing the basic structures of "factical human Dasein" (PIA2, 233/S, 114), that is, the phenomenological hermeneutic of our own present existence "carries out its tasks only on the path of destruction" (PIA2, 249/S, 124). Heidegger writes,

In philosophical research, this destructive confrontation with its own history is not merely . . . an occasional overview of what others before us "came up with" . . . Rather, destruction is the authentic path upon which the present needs to encounter itself in its own basic movements. (ibid.)

Already here in this text, we are compelled to push the destruction of our tradition back to Aristotle, where Being was first firmly equated with *ousia* or "being, substance," here defined specifically as "being made present or produced" (PIA2, 272/S, 144).

[T]his sense of being has its provenance in the environing world as it is originally given in experience, but then, and this is found even in Aristotle himself, it lost the sense of this provenance due to the pressure exerted by the kind of ontology being worked out and refined. In the course of the subsequent development of ontological research, it fell into the averageness of having its vague traditional meaning of "reality" or "actuality" and as such then provided the starting point for the problems of epistemology. (PIA2, 274/S, 145)

Interesting here is the intimation that we find in the texts of Aristotle evidence of an experience of the world from which the interpretation of Being as presence arose as well as evidence that some aspect of that experience is being "lost" and put under "pressure." Again, as we shall see, it is precisely this kind of ambivalence in the text that Heidegger's method of reading the Greeks attempts to draw out.

What necessitates our looking back to the Greeks in Heidegger's earlier period is thus an initial perplexity at our own lack of perplexity, or at our own incapacity to be provoked by the question of the meaning of Being.[2] Once our fundamentally historicizing mode of being is brought to light, this initial perplexity compels us to trace our own presumed understanding back through the tradition we inherit as our own, until we expose its moment of origination in Greek thought.

Whatever the precise meaning and significance of the *Kehre* or "turn" that Heidegger diagnosed in his own thinking, it must be acknowledged that, with specific respect to the needfulness of looking back to the Greeks, the change between the earlier and later periods is minor. Let us start with the *Contributions to Philosophy (Of the Event)*, composed between 1936 and 1938, where the terminology and central themes of the later period are introduced with startling intensity and compression.

Here Heidegger reaffirms his commitment to the question of the meaning of Being—"[It] is and remains *my* question, and is my *unique* question" (GA 65, 10/CP2, 11). Indeed, it is the posing of just this question that should open the site for what Heidegger refers to as "the other beginning," a thinking that, recognizing the ontological difference, would not reduce Being to the presence of present beings. Instead, beings are to be thought from out of Being, now spelled with a "y" (*Seyn*) and identified with *Ereignis* or "event," the dynamic and always historically situated emergence or unfolding of beings into appearance, which precisely as such withdraws or remains inaccessible behind the very beings it allows to present themselves. This other beginning will only be possible, however, when it is held in an essential relation to "the first beginning," that is, the Greek interpretation of Being as presence. Heidegger calls for a "thinking in the crossing from the first beginning to the other," in which "the first beginning remains decisive as the first and yet is indeed overcome as beginning" (GA 65, 5–6/CP2, 7). That is, understanding ourselves as the inheritors of an ontological standpoint accomplished by the Greeks, we come to inhabit the space of the "crossing" between our Greek past and our present in such a way that we will become decided for the futural possibility of thinking Being otherwise.

Although Heidegger is certainly still affirming the necessity of looking back to the Greeks, his way of speaking of the source of that necessitation represents a departure from that of the earlier period. He writes, "As unavoidable as is the confrontation with the first beginning of the history of thought, just as certainly must questioning forget everything round about itself and merely think about its own distress (*Not*)" (GA 65, 10/CP2, 11, trans. modified). In order to open up this other way of thinking Being, Heidegger again introduces a "twofold task" (SZ, 15/BTMR, 36), described here as looking back to the Greek origin of our ontological commitments while attending to the *Not* or "distress, needfulness" that one should feel in our present historical moment.

This distress takes the place of the essentially epistemic perplexity provoked in *Being*

and Time's opening pages, that is, a perplexity at our own incapacity to pose the question of Being and a dissatisfaction with our own claim to already enjoy adequate knowledge of Being. Now Heidegger has recourse to a pre-epistemic register. He writes of, "the fundamental attunement (*Grundstimmung*) of thinking in the other beginning" (GA 65, 14/CP2, 14, trans. modified), a certain way of being already opened up to, in contact with, and disposed toward the world around us.[3] The attunement of our historical present is described as a combination of *Erschrecken* or "shock," *Verhaltenheit* or "restraint," and *Scheu* or "diffidence." It seems then that one is to take up the other beginning from out of the nihilistic exhaustion of Western culture today, just as philosophizing in the first beginning arose from out of the pathos of *thaumazein* or "wonder." And this necessitates our looking back to the Greeks in order to understand our late-modern moment as the end of the historical development that began with them. Indeed, by taking up the first beginning, we will intensify and concentrate our already fundamentally attuned condition until we are able to take the "leap" (see especially GA 65, 227–89/CP2, 179–227), which is how Heidegger describes the transition into the other beginning's thinking Being otherwise than as the presence of present beings.

In the 1946 essay, "The Anaximander Fragment," one finds this same necessitation at work. Heidegger begins by problematizing his readers' interest in this piece of antiquity. He asks, "Are we latecomers in a history now racing towards its end, an end which in its increasingly sterile order of uniformity brings everything to an end? . . . Do we stand in the very twilight of the most monstrous transformation our planet has ever undergone, the twilight of that epoch in which the earth itself hangs suspended?" (EGT, 16–17, GA 5, 300). That is, Heidegger wants to evoke here the disposition of the epigone, and then to intensify just that disposition with his questioning, concentrating us on our present mood of nagging doubt or outright horror at the state of things in late modernity. Whether this be the dehumanization associated with the exchangeability and reproducibility of everything or the terrifying prospect of nuclear annihilation, Heidegger seems to wager that his reader is experiencing at present a certain distress, which he then hopes will necessitate attending to the Greek beginning of that very historical, philosophical development that we feel coming to a troubling end today.

THE WAY OF LOOKING BACK TO THE GREEKS

As was already clear from the epigraph with which we began, in taking up the texts of Greek philosophers, Heidegger is not concerned about accurately retrieving the objective truth concerning events or attitudes belonging to that past reality. Rather, throughout his career, Heidegger addresses "what our ancient memory holds preserved for us." The past we take up in order to change our present is not *the* past itself but *our past*, the past that is still vital and effective in our experience of our world and ourselves today. But how does Heidegger's peculiar way of reading Greek texts accomplish this?

In *Being and Time*, he says that our task is to "*destroy* the traditional content of ancient ontology until we arrive at the original experiences (*zu den ursprünglichen Erfahrungen*) in which we achieved our first ways of determining the nature of Being—the ways which

have guided us ever since" (SZ, 22/ BT, 44, trans. modified). Throughout his career, what Heidegger hopes to bring to light in Greek texts is again and again this *transitional* or *liminal moment*, in which the interpretation of Being as presence is just emerging from an original experience that, even while generating that interpretation, nonetheless exceeds it. Early Heidegger reads the Greeks in order to get "access to those original 'sources' (*Zugang zu den ursprünglichen Quellen*) from which the categories and concepts handed down to us have been in part genuinely drawn" (SZ, 21/BTMR, 43), and later on he hopes to access precisely what was in the first beginning "*sheltered (Verborgene)*, the origin (*Ursprung*) that has not yet been misused and driven on, the one that reaches furthest ahead in constantly withdrawing" (GA 65, 57/CP2, 46). In both periods, however, it is by confronting his readers with an ambivalence or liminality in traditional texts that Heidegger hopes to reactivate that still hidden *Quelle* or *Urpsrung*, that "source" or "origin," so that our thinking can attend to it today and begin to think beings otherwise.

Over the course of his career, Heidegger does seem to locate that ambivalence, that *limen* or "threshold," at an ever earlier moment in Greek intellectual history. The younger Heidegger focused more attention on the work of Aristotle, with a number of lecture courses being devoted to him in the years prior to *Being and Time* (and even the course on *Plato's Sophist* in 1924/1925 and the more general *Basic Concepts of Ancient Philosophy* from 1926 both take Aristotle as the central figure in accessing what is there for us in ancient Greek thought). In the middle period, we see Heidegger more determined to find ambivalence in the Platonic text, especially in the 1931 essay (revised in 1940), "Plato's Doctrine of Truth," and in the lecture course from 1931/1932, *On the Essence of Truth: On the Allegory of the Cave and the Theaetetus* (not to mention Heidegger's extremely deep and illuminating treatments of the *Republic* and the *Phaedrus* in the 1936/1937 lecture course on Nietzsche entitled *The Will to Power as Art*). Finally, later still, Heidegger's attention seemed to be drawn more and more to the Pre-Socratics, for example, 1942/1943's lecture course on Parmenides and 1943's lecture course on Heraclitus, as well as the essays from 1943 to 1954 collected in the English volume, *Early Greek Thinking*, and finally the seminar Heidegger held with Eugen Fink in 1966/1967.

Let us now look for this hermeneutic of ambivalence with respect to three of the most fundamental and most frequently discussed themes in Heidegger's readings of Greek philosophy, *alêtheia*, *phusis*, and *logos*.

To be sure, Heidegger returns to the issue of truth throughout his career, almost always taking as his touchstone the Greek term *alêtheia*, commonly translated as "truth." In the opening pages of "Plato's Doctrine of Truth," Heidegger indicates that his interpretive approach will be quite unorthodox. He writes that "the 'doctrine (*Lehre*)' of a thinker is that which, within what is said, remains unsaid, that to which we are exposed so that we might expend ourselves on it" (GA 9, 109/PA, 155). What we seek in analyzing Plato's text is something inexplicit, but which we are nonetheless able to experience in what is said through Heidegger's interpretation. This "unsaid" to which we will be exposed is nothing other than "a certain change (*Wendung*) in what determines the essence of truth" (ibid.). Heidegger reads Plato's Allegory of the Cave as a meditation on the process of *paideia* or "education." There he finds a transition from a more

original notion of truth, which he associates with the word *alêtheia*, to a notion much more familiar to us, that of truth as correspondence. In Plato's description of the more *orthotês* or "correct" relation to the *eidê* or "Ideas," Heidegger sees a foreshadowing of "truth" as *adequatio intellectus et rei*. Truth in this sense would be located in the subject and would refer to the re-presentation in the mind or in speech of the reality of present objects and their relations. The more original notion of truth is named by *alêtheia*, which Heidegger understands as an abstract noun composed by adding the *alpha privativum* to *lêthê* or "forgetting, concealment" and which he thus translates as "unconcealment." This would precede and subtend the subject-object ordered relation the correspondence theory seems to presuppose. Here, truth names the emergence of beings into presentation to us, and is thus located not in the subject standing over against an object, but *between* us and beings in their appearing to us (where our relation to such appearing beings is always already secured and inviolable).[4] In Plato's discussion, thus, Heidegger reveals a moment of transition between these two conceptions of truth.

Heidegger finds a like liminality in Aristotle's thinking of *phusis* or, as it is most often translated, "nature." In "On the Essence and Concept of *Phusis* in Aristotle's *Physics* B1," we uncover a moment where the modern concept of nature is dramatically emerging into view ready to accept its opposition to civilization, spirit, history, or the supernatural, but where also there are some traces of a prior, more original experience of the world's unfolding as *phusis*, an experience of the encompassing site that precedes and invokes these later conceptual oppositions. Heidegger challenges us in reading Aristotle's *Physics* with him, saying "the distinction between nature and history must be pushed back into the underlying area that sustains the dichotomy, the area where nature and history *are*" (GA 9, 311/PA, 184).

In *Physics* B1, Aristotle begins again with his study of *ta phusika* or "natural things," now opposing them to things produced by *technê* or "skill," insofar as the former have their own *archê* or "source" of movement and emergence within themselves while the latter have their moving source external themselves in the craftsperson who produces them.

Heidegger focuses on Aristotle's hylomorphic conception of the individual being and his rejection in this text of the sophist Antiphon's claim that it is the *hulê* or "matter" of any given natural thing that must be its real *phusis*, its internal source of coming to be what it is. Aristotle ultimately seems to reject this in favor of the thing's *morphê*, "shape," or *eidos*, "form," that is, the "look" that a thing presents us with whereby it enters into intelligibility and articulability as "what it is." Although it is this position that is passed along in the substance metaphysics that arises from Aristotle, the text offers access to an experience of *morphê* and *phusis* as *dichôs* or "intrinsically twofold." If *morphê* is understood as essentially bound to its *hulê*, then it is not the static intelligible form of the natural thing that is its being, its *phusis*, but rather the dynamic emergence of the being into its form, a "being-on-the-way" according to which "each being that is *pro-duced* or put forth (excluding artifacts) is also put away, as the blossom is put away by the fruit" (GA 9, 367/PA, 227). *Phusis* would then be the movement according to which beings emerge into appearance before us, leaving obscured necessarily or withholding that movement as the being's ultimate source. With this insight, an ambivalence emerges in Aristotle's text between, on the one hand, Being as "being

produced" or "being present for articulation and intellection" and, on the other hand, Being as "self-concealing revealing, *phusis* in the original sense" (GA 9, 371/PA, 230).

And finally, we find this same hermeneutic at work again in Heidegger's treatment of the Greek term *logos*, translated variously as "language, speech, statement, argument, reason, or logic." Let us focus on the piece entitled "Logos (Heraclitus, Fragment 50)," which Heidegger delivered first in the context of a lecture course in 1944, then again as an stand-alone lecture in 1951, and finally published as a chapter of *Vorträge und Aufsätze* in 1967.

When we attempt to understand Heraclitus's claim that, "Listening not to me but to the *Logos*, it is wise to say that all is one" (DK 50), Heidegger notes that we presume to do so by means of *logos* or by letting "reason" be our guide, even though it is precisely the nature of *logos* that is at stake in the fragment. In response to this perplexing situation, Heidegger invites us instead "to meditate on the essential origin of reason and to let [ourselves] into its advent . . . paying heed to *logos* and following its initial unfolding" (GA 7, 200/EGT, 60, trans. modified). We begin to do so with Heidegger by relating *logos* back to its verbal root, *legein*, which surely means "to speak, talk," but which also has a profoundly illuminating and original sense, that of "laying out" and "gathering together." Heidegger insists that this gathering be heard not as mere "amassing," but, as with a harvest, as a kind of "letting-lie-together-before" of what comes into presence or appears to us, and specifically in such a way that the gathering undertakes a "sheltering" and a "safe-keeping" of what it gathers (GA 7, 203–4/EGT, 62–3). A profoundly different conception of *legein*, thus, opens up here beneath our own familiar conception of "speaking" or "language-usage," whereby this has been reduced to a mere juxtaposing of words that either successfully re-presents or fails to re-present the objective state of affairs to which it refers. By contrast, *legein* would now seem to have as its task the receiving of what is appearing in such a way that it is allowed to lie together before oneself and one's listener and is thus sheltered in its way of being. Note that this *legein* is inseparable from what it gathers together, unlike our modern conception of language or speech, which always stands over against and is in principle severed from the world of present objects it strives to re-present. Once *logos* has been revealed in its essential relation to this gathering, as a safe-keeping of what emerges into presence *in its emergence*, hearing becomes not fundamentally an acoustical phenomenon, but a reception of just this gathering into appearance before us.

All of this, then, Heidegger brings to bear on the interpretation of the Heraclitus fragment. We are to listen not to Heraclitus but to the *logos* itself, for what is at stake is not a subject voicing his opinion, but the gathering of "what is" into appearance, which allows it to emerge before us and present itself. Listening in this way, it is wise to *homolegein*, usually translated as "to agree" but meaning more literally "to *legein* the same, in the same way, or along with." And what is it that we wisely say along with, gather, and shelter? It is wise to say, "All is One." Here Heidegger finds not a motto or a principle articulated in *logos*, but rather what *logos* itself accomplishes. All is One, in the specific sense that everything that *is*, is by participating in the dynamic movement of emergence by which beings are gathered together and present themselves to us in a world. Heidegger thus locates in Heraclitus's fragment the transition between these two moments, where

logos in its later traditional sense arises from this original sense, of which he writes,

> Language would be the gathering letting-lie-before of what is present in its presencing. In fact, the Greeks *dwelt* in this essential determination of language. But they never *thought* it—Heraclitus included. (GA 7, 220/EGT, 77)

Heidegger's hermeneutic with respect to the Greek text, as we have seen, is aimed at drawing out that "unsaid" or "unthought," which precedes and motivates, without being taken up in or articulated by the metaphysical thinking that follows, dominated and delimited as it is by the identification of Being with presence. Having energized the tension of this liminal, transitional moment, we come to experience the source or origin of the entire tradition that emerged with the Greeks and still joins us to them. This tradition and its ontology of presence having been shown to emerge from a source it leaves behind, we are thereby placed in contact with that excessive source and become capable of questioning Being and thinking it otherwise.

CONCLUSION

In his 1958 essay, "Hegel and the Greeks," Heidegger begins by asserting that the conjunction that joins together the two subjects in his title represents not an arbitrary or accidental connection, but an essential and internal one. Our title here, "Heidegger and Greek philosophy," employs a no less essential conjunction, but of an utterly different kind. Indeed, Heidegger is linked to Greek philosophy *not by recovery or synthesis* with respect to earlier historical moments in the necessary unfolding of spirit, *but by shared excess or openness.* If Heidegger tasks us with recovery, it is of the ancients' unthought and unsaid as such, and if he tasks us with synthesis, it is only of that which must remain inaccessible, withdrawn. Both earlier and later, Heidegger hopes to expose thinking once again to that dynamic and inevitably self-withdrawing source by which beings emerge into presence before us. This necessitates today a thoughtful looking back to what our ancient memory holds preserved for us. That is, it necessitates the destruction of our tradition all the way back to the Greeks and a reading of those ancient texts that highlights their ambivalence and confronts us with a trace of the very source we are seeking.

NOTES AND REFERENCES

[1] Even excluding the hundreds of essays on these subjects and limiting ourselves to books, previous scholarship on this subject would include the first volume of Jean Beaufret's *Dialogue avec Heidegger* series, *Philosophie Grecque* (Paris: Éditions de minuit, 1973), as well as the collection, *Heidegger and the Greeks* (Bloomington: Indiana University, 2006), edited by Drew Hyland and John Panteleimon Manoussakis. On Heidegger and Aristotle, there is Franco Volpi's *Heidegger e Aristotele* (Rome: Editori Laterza, 1984), Ted Sadler's *Heidegger and Aristotle: The Question of Being* (London: Continuum, 2001), and Walter Brogan's *Heidegger and Aristotle: The Twofoldness of Being* (Albany, NY: SUNY,

2005). Heidegger's interpretation of Plato is the subject of Alain Boutot's *Heidegger et Platon: Le probleme du nihilisme* (Paris: Philosophie d'aujourd'hui, 1987), of the collection *Heidegger and Plato: Toward Dialogue* (Evanston, IL: Northwestern University, 2005), edited by Catalin Partenie and Tom Rockmore, and of Francisco Gonzalez' *Heidegger and Plato: A Question of Dialogue* (State College: Penn State University, 2009). Finally, on Heidegger and the early Greek thinkers, we have George Seidel's early *Martin Heidegger and the Pre-Socratics* (Lincoln: University of Nebraska, 1964), David Jacobs' collection of essays, *The Presocratics after Heidegger* (Albany, NY: SUNY, 1999), as well as Ivo de Gennaro's *Logos—Heidegger Liest Heraclitus* (Berlin: Duncker & Humblot, 2001).

[2] This precise form of provocation is repeated in the later period, in the lecture course from 1951–2 entitled *What is Called Thinking?* where Heidegger wants his listeners to wrestle with his claim that, "Most thought-provoking is that we are still not thinking" (GA 8, 2/WCT, 4).

[3] It might be objected that the *Stimmung* or "attunement" of *Angst* or "anxiety" already plays an important role in *Being and Time*. Although that is no doubt the case, this mood is not presented as motivating the task of destruction.

[4] Earlier, Heidegger seems to have placed some emphasis on the actual etymology of the term *alêtheia* as "unconcealment," a claim that was problematized by Paul Friedländer (*Platon*, Bd. I, Berlin: De Gruyter, 1964, 233–43), among others. Although Friedländer ultimately withdraws his original opposition to Heidegger's etymology, he does resist Heidegger's claim that prior to Plato, truth was understood as "unconcealment" rather than "correctness," and Heidegger himself seems to grant as much later on, in his 1964 essay "The End of Philosophy and the Task of Thinking."

9

HEIDEGGER AND MEDIEVAL PHILOSOPHY
Holger Zaborowski

A FORGETFULNESS OF MEDIEVAL THOUGHT?

Heidegger's reading of ancient philosophy—primarily of the pre-Socratics, Plato, and Aristotle—and of modern philosophy from Descartes to Husserl is much discussed by Heidegger scholars. It has also significantly influenced the common understanding of, and research into, both ancient and modern philosophy. With a few notable exceptions, however, scholars of medieval philosophy hardly take notice of Heidegger's thought. Furthermore, Heidegger's reading of medieval texts and its influence on his own thinking, is not a common topic among students of his thought.[1]

This does not come as a surprise. Medieval philosophy does not play a very significant role for Heidegger after 1919. The main focus of his philosophical attention lies without any question at all on ancient and modern philosophy, that is, on, roughly speaking, the very beginning and the completion of Western metaphysics. Because of his focus on the Greeks and, indeed, the Germans, who, for Heidegger, primarily shaped modern philosophy, the medieval period is very often not even mentioned where a reader would expect

at least a marginal reference to it. And if it is mentioned at all, Heidegger refers to it more often than not in a stereotypical and foreseeable manner.

Medieval philosophy thus seems to share the same fate as Roman philosophy in Heidegger's texts: It is overlooked or simplified and often not fully taken seriously as philosophy. There is, however, one crucial difference: For Heidegger's way of thought, medieval thought was much more important than the philosophy of Cicero, Seneca, or Marcus Aurelius. As is well known, Heidegger began his career as a promising scholar of scholastic philosophy.

CHRISTIANITY, SCHOLASTICISM, AND THE ORIGINS OF HEIDEGGER'S THINKING

It goes without saying that Heidegger's relation to medieval thought and the scholastic tradition is closely tied up with his relation to Christianity. For him, medieval thought is by and large a form of Christian and, more specifically, Catholic thinking (Heidegger, to be sure, did not show an interest in Jewish and Arabic medieval thought; for scarce references to Arabic philosophy see GA 23, 44; GA 24, 113f.). This is why when Heidegger lost his Catholic faith, his philosophical interests also changed significantly.

Heidegger's rereading of Aristotle as well as his turn toward Protestant theologians and figures such as St Paul and St Augustine (i.e. toward a particular, rather Protestant reading of these figures), both beginning in the late 1910s, neatly show his self-distancing from Catholicism and its intellectual heritage and thus also from medieval thought. For the Aristotle of the lecture courses that Heidegger gave at the University of Freiburg between 1919 and 1922 is a distinctly non-scholastic proto-phenomenological Aristotle. And his understanding of Christianity in this period of his way of thinking is one that favors texts that belong to the very origins of Christianity such as the letters of St Paul over later sources that already show the deteriorating effects, so Heidegger thought, of the Hellenization of Christianity (see GA 60; GA 61, 6f.). From this perspective, medieval thought appeared doubly unappealing to Heidegger: not only as a betrayal of Christianity and its distinctly nonphilosophical character but also of philosophy and its original impetus as disclosed in early Greek thought.

Heidegger's turn away from medieval thought came as a surprise to many who considered him a new voice in Catholic medieval studies. Heidegger first read Aquinas when he still went to school,[2] studied Aquinas, Bonaventure, and neo-Scholastic textbooks as a young student (GA 16, 37), and was introduced into early and high scholasticism by his doctoral supervisor Arthur Schneider and into medieval history by the Catholic historian Heinrich Finke (42). Many of Heidegger's earliest publications,

written between 1909 and 1915 when he was a student and then a young doctor of philosophy (see particularly GA 13, 1–7; GA 16, 3–36), show the great extent to which Heidegger was at some point influenced by an anti-modernistic emphasis on medieval theology and philosophy, common in early twentieth-century neo-Scholastic Catholicism:[3] While medieval thought was considered to be properly grounded in eternal truth and thus to be capable of bringing together faith and reason, the bible and the Greeks (primarily Aristotle, of course), modern philosophy from Descartes and Kant up to Nietzsche and early twentieth-century thought was regarded to be characterized by the principle of doubt, relativism, subjectivism, historicism, and, eventually, nihilism. However, Heidegger's interest in (neo-)scholasticism was characterized by a certain dissatisfaction from the very beginning (see GA 16, 37); he was, therefore, also quite critical of the narrow kind of neo-Scholasticism, favored by the Catholic church of his time. His own anti-modernistic turn toward a highly idealized medieval world was thus rather short-lived. It was the product of a young and very gifted mind that had not yet found its own voice, but was eagerly looking for it.

In his doctoral dissertation *The Doctrine of Judgment in Psychologism*,[4] Heidegger critically discussed then contemporary psychologist doctrines, using insights that he found in Husserl's phenomenology and Rickert's neo-Kantianism to defend an agenda that was at least partly motivated by his own religious persuasions: the critique of a "naturalization of consciousness" (FRS, 5), of a misconstrual of logic proper, and of a relativization of the concept of truth. There is, therefore, an indirect relation between the topic of his PhD thesis and his early interest in medieval thought. It is, however, important to note that Heidegger decided to write his PhD thesis on modern and not medieval philosophy. Furthermore, when he decided to focus on a medieval thinker in his *Habilitationsschrift*, Heidegger chose Duns Scotus (so he thought at least) and not Aquinas.[5] Even in the very early phase of his philosophical career, Heidegger was neither a Thomist nor a neo-Scholastic thinker in the narrow and exclusive sense of the word and, as we will see, was open to a serious engagement with modern thought.

HEIDEGGER'S HABILITATION ON THOMAS OF ERFURT'S DE MODIS SIGNIFICANDI

Heidegger's *Habilitationsschrift* (FRS, 131–354) was written under the guidance of his neo-Kantian teacher Heinrich Rickert (to whom the published book is dedicated "in most grateful admiration"; 132) and is entitled *Duns Scotus' Doctrine of Categories and Meaning*. In this book, Heidegger focuses on the text *De modis significandi* that at the time was thought to be written by Duns Scotus (it was, in fact, written by the Scotist logician Thomas of Erfurt, as Martin Grabmann showed a short time after Heidegger worked on this text[6]). Heidegger's study of this text is divided into two parts. Following an introduction on the "necessity of a problem-historical (*problemgeschichtlich*) examination of scholasticism," the first part discusses the doctrine of categories as a "systematic foundation of the understanding of the doctrine of meaning"; the second part focuses on the doctrine of meaning. Heidegger concludes with a short reflection on the problem of categories.

In his *Habilitationsschrift*, Heidegger did not intent to historicize the medieval period, thus turning it into an object of merely historical research, nor did he dismiss modern philosophy (even in the years prior to his *Habilitation*, he had shown a serious interest in figures such as Kant, Nietzsche, and Husserl). Already Heidegger's brief preface and introduction show that he follows a specific agenda in this book: He explicitly thanks not only Heinrich Rickert but also the neo-Kantian and neo-Fichtean Emil Lask (whose influence on the early Heidegger cannot be overestimated).[7] The introduction stands under a citation from Hegel, that is, his idea, that "with respect to its inner essence, there are neither predecessors nor successors in philosophy" (FRS, 135)—as if Heidegger, focusing on philosophical problems rather than merely historical relations, wanted to distance himself from an understanding of the history of philosophy as a decline or, alternatively, as a progress from the medieval to the modern period.

Heidegger is, on this basis, interested in rereading texts from the medieval period with respect to logical problems discussed by then contemporary neo-Kantianism and phenomenology—and also with respect to the history of German idealism and Protestant theology. In 1922, he wrote retrospectively about his interests after completing his PhD that his

> initial intention inclined toward an investigation of late scholasticism, above all Ockham, in order to obtain [. . .] a concrete and broad infrastructure for the scientific understanding of the history of the genesis of Protestant theology and thereby of the central contexts of problems of German idealism. My preoccupation with Ockham made a return to Duns Scotus urgent for me.[8]

Heidegger is, however, well aware of the differences between the different periods of the history of philosophy. He notes, for example, that the medieval period lacks a "consciousness of methods, this strongly developed *desire and courage to question*, the permanent control of every step of thinking" (FRS, 140). According to Heidegger's interpretation, the "idea of authority" and the "high esteem for all tradition" are "clear signs" for this. Unlike the medieval human being, Heidegger reasons, the modern person is liberated from his or her background (141; see also 206). These comments show very nicely the transitional character of this book: While he criticized the modern "liberation" from tradition and authority quite radically in his previous occasional writings, his approach to it is now positive; it is an achievement. And what he now notes about medieval thought in a rather concluding manner will later become on object of his severe criticism: its dependence on something that is not philosophy, that is, its doctrinal presuppositions.

It is, in the context of this discussion of the transitional character of the book, important to note that Heidegger makes a considerable move toward (not more, of course) key insights of his later hermeneutics of facticity, of his phenomenology of Dasein, and also of his being-historical thinking (see GA 66, 411f. for Heidegger's retrospective interpretation of this text and its focus) not some years after the *Habilitation*, as some scholars have argued, but already in the published version of it (the version that he submitted to the faculty is lost). If nothing else, the reader can find such a prelude to his later thought in Heidegger's choice of topic—the doctrine of categories and meaning—as well as in his choice of a text by Duns Scotus/Thomas of Erfurt: Heidegger explicitly emphasizes his

modern character and his "greater and finer proximity (haecceitas) to real life" (FRS, 145) and stresses his focus on the concrete individual as really existing: "The individual is *an irreducible ultimate*" (194f.), so Heidegger writes both commenting on Duns Scotus/Thomas of Erfurt and anticipating his own later phenomenology of Dasein.

The transitional and anticipatory character of the book perhaps becomes most apparent in the afterword that Heidegger wrote in 1916 for the publication of his book. It is not only Hegel who plays an important role in Heidegger's concluding remarks but also Dilthey and the emphasis on life, history, and the irresolvable relation between philosophy and both life and history (see particularly 352f.). Thus, particularly in concluding this book, Heidegger goes beyond the medieval world. His examination of a text by Duns Scotus/Thomas of Erfurt was a stepping stone toward thinking about the problem of the meaning of historical life/existence in its concrete individuality and temporality.

AFTER HIS HABILITATION— TOWARD BEING AND TIME VIA THE HERMENEUTICS OF FACTICITY

After his *Habilitation*, Heidegger's main focus, both in his research and in his teaching, was on other periods of the history of philosophy than on the medieval period. Heidegger continues to be interested in Kant and, primarily, Husserl, does extensive work in the area of modern philosophy of religion, most notably on Schleiermacher in these years, and slowly rediscovers Aristotle as a proto-phenomenologist. In 1916, Heidegger gave a lecture course on "Kant and 19th century German philosophy" and cotaught a seminar with the Catholic priest and scholar Engelbert Krebs about Aristotle's logical writings. He only once lectured on medieval philosophy in the years following his *Habilitation*. In the winter semester 1915/16, Heidegger gave a lecture course on "The History of Ancient and Scholastic Philosophy" (there are no written notes left either from this course or from the Kant and the Aristotle courses). In 1918 and 1919, Heidegger prepared a lecture course on "The Philosophical Foundation of Medieval Mysticism" (GA 60, 303–37); but he abandoned the idea of delivering this lecture course. It seems that Heidegger was at some point also preparing, or at least thinking about, a comparative study of Aquinas and Scotus;[9] but he must have dropped the idea of such a study relatively early, if he ever followed it seriously.

One reason for Heidegger's loss of interest in the medieval tradition may be the influence of Husserl (and of his lack of interest for the medieval tradition) on him, particularly since Husserl took over Rickert's chair at the University of Freiburg in 1916. There is, however, another reason that has already been briefly mentioned: The focus of Heidegger's interest in the late 1910s and early 1920s is also closely related to Heidegger's religious crisis, his increasing distance to the Catholicism of his youth and its philosophical underpinnings, and the eventual break with it. In a famous letter to Engelbert Krebs, written on January 9, 1919, Heidegger wrote that the "*system* of Catholicism," that is, particularly the neo-Scholastic system of Catholicism, had become "problematic and unacceptable to me" due to "epistemological insights that extend to the theory of historical knowledge."[10] Even though he confesses that he "believe[s] that I—perhaps more than those who work on the subject

officially—have perceived the values that the Catholic Middle Ages holds within itself, values that we are still far from truly exploiting,"[11] he did not continue to exploit these "values." In this letter, he further mentions that his "research into the phenomenology of religion, which will draw heavily on the Middle Ages [. . .] should prove beyond dispute that, even though I have transformed my basic standpoint, I have refused to be dragged into abandoning my objective high opinion and regard for the Catholic lifeworld." This promise, however, should remain unfulfilled. After 1919, he left his possible career not just as a Catholic philosopher, but also as an expert in medieval philosophy behind.

Neither does his lecture course "Introduction into the Phenomenology of Religion," held in the winter semester of 1920/21, seem heavily indebted to the Middle Ages (quite the opposite, one can argue, is the case; see GA 60, 3–125, 127–56). Nor did he *not* abandon his "high opinion" and "regard" for the Catholic lifeworld and thus for the medieval world. Under the particular influence of Luther and other Protestant theologians, he now strongly emphasized the radical difference between Christian theology and philosophy and thus also the intrinsic problems of medieval thought as a distinctly Christian kind of thinking that did not take this difference seriously. As a consequence of this view, the medieval world disappeared rapidly from his sight.

There is, however, one important exception (if we disregard two seminars: the first on "High Scholasticism and Aristotle. Thomas, *De ente et essentia*, Cajetan, *De nominum analogia*," taught during the summer semester of 1924, and the second on "On the Ontology of the Middle Ages [Thomas, *De ente et essentia*, *Summa contra gentiles*]," taught during the winter semester of 1924/5; no written notes from these seminars are known). In the winter semester of 1926/7, when he was finishing *Being and Time*, Heidegger gave a lecture course entitled "History of Philosophy from Thomas Aquinas to Kant" (see GA 23; during this semester, he offered a seminar on the same topic). The topic and content of this lecture course are rather unusual for Heidegger: He discusses not only Aquinas and Descartes (he did not reach the goal of examining Kant at any length) but also Spinoza, Leibniz, Wolff, and Crusius. A note that accompanied the manuscript of this lecture course suggests that the topic of the lecture course was due to a "teaching necessity" (243), that is to say that Heidegger himself did not chose the very topic of this lecture course. Given these circumstances, it does not surprise that the manuscript of the lecture course shows the lack of time and enthusiasm on Heidegger's side in preparing it.

Nonetheless, this lecture course is an important source for an understanding of Heidegger's view of medieval philosophy in the late 1920s. Two important features can be singled out for special attention: First, Heidegger discusses Aquinas in the context of his interest in the origins of modernity and in the development of Western metaphysics. He criticizes the common reading of Descartes as the first modern thinker and argues instead that the foundations of modernity were already laid in the medieval period. There is, then, not such a great gap between the medieval world and the modern period as many readings of the history of philosophy, both the Catholic anti-modernistic and the modernistic anti-Catholic, for example, suggest. Heidegger also highlights Aquinas' significance for an appropriation and transformation of ancient philosophy so that from this perspective the unity of the history of

Western philosophy is emphasized (this idea stands clearly in the background of *Being and Time* and its thesis of the forgetfulness of the question of Being in Western philosophy since its very beginning). Second, Heidegger finds the center of Aquinas' thought in the doctrine of creation (see 56). This implies, as he argues, that philosophy and theology are extremely closely intertwined in the Middle Ages (see 60f.). First philosophy is therefore for Aquinas, as Heidegger points out, always already theology and dependent on the "dogmatic presupposition of God" (60). "What was a problem for Aristotle," that is, the relation between first philosophy and theology, Heidegger argues, is in Aquinas "a dogma" (ibid.). Heidegger interprets Aquinas' thought, particularly his concept of truth, therefore, as dependent on dogmatic presuppositions and thus as eventually falling back behind the ancient philosophy of Aristotle (see 63). His later comments on medieval philosophy in general and on Aquinas in particular are, as we will see, variations of this theme.

MEDIEVAL THOUGHT IN BEING AND TIME

At first sight, medieval thought does not play a prominent role at all in *Being and Time*. Aquinas is explicitly mentioned twice in the very beginning (see SZ, 3/ BT, 2, where Heidegger refers to Aquinas' *Summa theologiae*; SZ, 14/BT, 13, where he refers to Aquinas' *Quaestiones de veritate* and his *De natura generis*). He notes that in Aquinas' *Quaestiones de veritate*, "the priority of 'Dasein' over and above all other beings, which emerges here without being ontologically clarified, obviously has

nothing in common with a vapid subjectivizing of the totality of beings" (SZ, 14, BT,
13).[12] This is a rather important statement:
Heidegger seems to read Aquinas as a kind
of predecessor with respect to his own
view of the "ontico-ontological priority" of
Dasein. Heidegger, however, does not examine this historical link any further in *Being
and Time*, presumably because of the lack
of ontological clarification in Aquinas and
also because of the very differences between
Aquinas' thought and the overarching interests of *Being and Time* (and not the least
also because of the dogmatic character of
Aquinas' thought). Duns Scotus and Meister
Eckhart (or Thomas of Erfurt for that matter) are not mentioned at all in *Being and
Time*. It is almost as if the history of Western
thinking between Augustine on the one hand
and Luther, Calvin, Zwingli, Cajetan, and
Scaliger (and then Descartes) on the other
did not exist for Heidegger, when he wrote
his masterwork.

There is, however, a little more to be said,
as there is clearly a Scotist dimension of
Being and Time (as there is such a dimension in his writings on the way to *Being and
Time*). One can argue, for example, that
Heidegger's fundamental ontology and his
existential analysis of Dasein in *Being and
Time* shows an often striking similarity with
key ideas of the Scotist tradition such as the
understanding of, and emphasis on, *haecceitas* (thisness), the priority of possibility over
actuality, or the *distinctio formalis*. In many
cases, the Scotist dimension may be mediated
through later philosophies so that one has to
be very careful in determining the extent to
which medieval thought had a *direct* impact
on *Being and Time*. In other cases, Heidegger
significantly transformed the Scotist tradition and conflated it with other traditions
or ideas. It needs to be said, though, that

even though there are very important and
promising beginnings, more research into the
Scotist dimension of *Being and Time* and its
relation to its other dimensions (particularly
its Aristotelian, Augustinian, Husserlian, and
Kantian dimensions) is needed.

AFTER BEING AND TIME:
PHILOSOPHY, CHRISTIAN FAITH,
AND THE METAPHYSICAL IMPACT
OF MEDIEVAL THOUGHT

In the period after *Being and Time*, Heidegger
mentions medieval thought in passing, if at
all. The student of his writings misses a reference to medieval thought particularly in his
frequent considerations about the course of
Western metaphysics and the forgetfulness of
Being. It is fair to argue that he is now very
often fully ignorant of medieval thought.
In *Introduction to Metaphysics* (1935), we
find an explanation for this ignorance that
stands in the tradition of some of his earlier
comments on Aquinas (for this and the following see EM, 5f., see also 147). It has to
do with his radical emphasis on the difference between theology and faith on the one
hand and philosophy on the other. There is,
according to Heidegger, Christian theology,
but no "Christian philosophy" (for this view
see also NI, 14f.). Philosophy is according
to Heidegger concerned with the ultimate
why question, the question why there is anything at all and not rather nothing. However,
the believer, as Heidegger argues, for whom
"the Bible is divine revelation and truth,"
has already found an answer to the ultimate
why question in the doctrine of creation:
"What is, insofar as it is not God himself, has
been created by him." Thus, the believer cannot ask the ultimate why question "without

93

abandoning himself as a believer." He is not only pursuing a totally different intellectual enterprise, but lives differently. Faith is therefore according to Heidegger "an own way of standing in truth" with its own "safety" from which the philosopher needs to distance himself (EM, 4). Thus, as one can conclude on the basis of this and other texts, medieval thought is for Heidegger either medieval theology, substantially dependent on the doctrine of creation, and, because he no longer shared the Christian faith, therefore uninteresting to Heidegger and his concern with what he considered philosophy proper, or, if it claims to be philosophy, a misunderstanding of what philosophy ought to be and therefore even more uninteresting. It remains surprising, though, that Heidegger even disregarded medieval contributions to logic, for example, in his later works. For he did not only know these contributions very well because of his earlier interest in them, they are also not simply forms of Christian theology. But Heidegger no longer makes the distinctions that he could, and should, have made with respect to the rich variety of medieval texts.

Even in his work of the 1950s and 1960s (when he gave up the radically anti-Christian position that characterized some of his writings of the 1930s), Heidegger would not substantially revise his account of medieval thought. In a seminar held in Le Thor in 1968, Heidegger discussed the ontological difference and also examined medieval philosophy in this context. Heidegger emphasized that "all metaphysics indeed moves within the difference (this is constantly stressed, in particular by Aquinas), but that no metaphysics recognizes this difference as difference in the dimension that it unfolds" (GA 15, 310/FS, 24). For Heidegger, Aquinas, too, fully remains in the metaphysical tradition and its forgetfulness of Being even though he

deserves special attention for his insight in the nature of metaphysics. Furthermore, the metaphysical character of Aquinas' thought had in Heidegger's view a lasting impact on the history of modern philosophy:

> Having on the one hand reduced ἐνέργεια to the ontic determination of *actualitas*, and, on the other hand, with Aquinas, having identified the *Summum Ens* with the *Ipsum esse*, ontology suppresses every possibility for a question of being. The entirety of modern philosophy is burdened by this ontic stamp inherited from Christian ontology of the middle ages. (GA 15, 311/FS, 25)

This claim about Aquinas, taken as representative of the medieval tradition, explains why medieval thought does not play a role for Heidegger any longer. For he is now mainly concerned with the question and the history of Being. Furthermore, he *had* to forget medieval thought as a synthesis of Athens and both Jerusalem and Rome, as it were, in order to save philosophy: "To restore philosophy to its own essence means to purge it of its Christian element, and to do this out of concern for the Greek element—not for its own sake, but insofar as it is the origin of philosophy" (ibid.).

His emphasis on a radical distinction between philosophy and Christianity led Heidegger to overlook the possibility of an encounter with medieval thought from which he may have benefitted. There is, however, one important exception: the medieval mystical tradition, most notably Master Eckhart. In his "Country Path," Meister Eckhart is the only thinker who is explicitly mentioned (GA 13, 89). Already the *Habilitationsschrift* shows Heidegger's interest in the German theologian and mystic (FRS, 160, 344); the published version of the public *Habilitation* lecture "The Concept of Time in the Science of History" (355–75), stands under a citation from Meister Eckhart (358).[13] There is no question at all about the high esteem with which Heidegger treated Meister Eckhart during his whole way of thinking (see also GA 24, 127f.). In a letter to Bernhard Welte, written on February 29, 1968, Heidegger briefly compared Aquinas and Eckhart and found "really a new step" in Eckhart.[14] According to Heidegger, Meister Eckhart has a unique position because "a sentence such as Sed etiam Deus quod Deo non convenit esse nec est ens, sed est aliquid altius ente [...] cannot be found anywhere else as far as I know."[15] In arguing that God is "something higher than (a) being" and that Being does not belong to him, nor is he a being, Meister Eckhart, not Aquinas (as Welte suggested[16]), shows for Heidegger a "hidden agenda that points beyond metaphysics," that is, to the possibility of an alternative to metaphysics. Heidegger therefore encouraged an "extensive account of the 'problem of Being' in Thomas Aquinas and Meister Eckhart."[17]

All important differences notwithstanding, there is no doubt that Meister Eckhart is one important (not the only) source of Heidegger's own later discourse about letting-be as a way beyond the metaphysic of the will to power (see particularly GA 16, 517–29; see also GA 77). Heidegger did not, however, examine Meister Eckhart's writings with the kind of scrutiny that characterizes his writings on other important thinkers.

READING AND DISCUSSING MEDIEVAL THOUGHT—AFTER HEIDEGGER

Given the significance of Heidegger's interpretation of the history of ancient and modern philosophy, one must pity the fact that, after his encounter with the medieval world in his very early work, Heidegger did not continue to pay similar attention to medieval philosophers, theologians, and mystics. Some of Heidegger's students, however, have reinterpreted the medieval tradition in the light of his thought. They took Heidegger's thought and its challenges seriously while at the same time not sharing his very critical, if not even often dismissive attitude toward medieval thought. The group of these thinkers includes what one could call the Catholic Heidegger school of notable figures such as Johannes B. Lotz, Gustav Siewerth, and, to a different degree, Karl Rahner and Hans Urs von Balthasar. Bernhard Welte, too, belongs to this group of mediators between Heidegger's thought and the medieval tradition. Welte wrote not only an essay about "Thomas Aquinas and Heidegger's Idea of the History of Being" (this is one of many essays about Heidegger's thought that he wrote), he also wrote a book-length study of Meister Eckhart that clearly shows the influence of Heidegger on his own thought and methodological self-understanding.[18] Many more scholars could be mentioned who have continued the dialogue between the medieval world and Heidegger's thought. In the English-speaking context, John Caputo's early work on Heidegger and Aquinas and on Heidegger and mystical thinking may be singled out for special reference.[19] More work can, and should, be done along these lines. The question of Heidegger's relation to medieval thought and of his legacy for our reading of medieval texts not only remains open, it is one of the most challenging (even though often unnoticed) questions both for students of medieval thought and for students of Heidegger's way of thinking.

NOTES AND REFERENCES

1 The number of secondary sources on Heidegger's relation to medieval thought is limited. The following studies or collections of essays are particularly helpful (and contain further bibliographical references to earlier works on this topic): Sean McGrath, *The Early Heidegger and Medieval Philosophy. Phenomenology for the Godforsaken* (Washington, DC: The Catholic University of America Press, 2006); Constantino Esposito (ed.), *Heidegger e i medievali*. Atti del colloquio internazionale, Cassino 10/13 maggio 2000 (Turnhout: Brepols, 2001); Helmuth Vetter, *Heidegger und das Mittelalter*. Wiener Tagungen zur Phänomenologie 1997 (Frankfurt am Main: Peter Lang, 1999).

2 SZD, 81–90, esp. 81Here and in the following, all translations, if not otherwise indicated, are my own.

3 For the early Heidegger's life and thought see particularly Alfred Denker, Hans-Helmuth Gander and Holger Zaborowski (eds), *Heidegger und die Anfänge seines Denkens*. Heidegger-Jahrbuch 1 (Freiburg/München: Karl Alber, 2004).

4 Martin Heidegger, *Frühe Schriften* (Frankfurt am Main: Klosterman, 1972), 1–129. Hereafter cited as FRS, followed by page number.

5 For the Scotist dimension of the early Heidegger's thought see Theodore Kisiel, *The Genesis of* Heidegger's *Being and Time* (Berkeley: University of California Press, 1995); Sean J. McGrath, *The Early Heidegger and Medieval Philosophy*, 88–119; Sean J. McGrath, "*Die scotistische Phänomenologie des jungen Heidegger*," in Alfred Denker, Hans-Helmuth Gander and Holger Zaborowski (eds), *Heidegger und die Anfänge seines Denkens*. Heidegger-Jahrbuch 1 (Freiburg/ München: Karl Alber, 2004), 243–58.

6 See Martin Grabmann, "Die Entwicklung der mittelalterlichen Sprachlogik [Tractatus de modis significandi]," *Philosophisches Jahrbuch* 35 (1922), 121–35, 199–214 (for a revised and expanded version see Martin Grabmann, *Mittelalterliches Geistesleben. Abhandlungen zur Geschichte der Scholastik und Mystik* (München: Max Hüber, 1926), 104–46).

7 For an insightful discussion see Theodore Kisiel, "Why Students of Heidegger Will Have to Read Emil Lask," in Theodore Kisiel, *Heidegger's Way of Thought. Critical and Interpretative Signposts*, ed. Alfred Denker and Marion Heinz (New York/London: Continuum, 2002), 101–36.

8 Martin Heidegger, "Vita," in Theodore Kisiel and Thomas Sheehan (eds), *Becoming Heidegger. On the Trail of His Early Occasional Writings, 1910–1927* (Evanston, IL: Northwestern University Press, 2007), 106–9, 107 (GA 16, 41–5, 42). See also 7–9 (GA 16, 37–9).

9 See his letter to Martin Grabmann, written on January 7, 1917, in Denker et al., *Heidegger und die Anfänge seines Denkens*, 73–4, esp. 74.

10 Denker et al., *Heidegger und die Anfänge seines Denkens*, 67/Kisiel and Sheehan (eds), *Becoming Heidegger*, 96.

11 Theodore Kisiel and Thomas Sheehan (eds), *Becoming Heidegger*, 96.

12 For this see also Kisiel, *The Genesis of Heidegger's Being and Time*, 426f.

13 For an English translation see Kisiel and Sheehan (eds), *Becoming Heidegger*, 61–72.

14 Martin Heidegger and Bernhard Welte, *Briefe und Begegnungen. Mit einem Vorwort von Bernhard Casper, herausgegeben von Alfred Denker und Holger Zaborowski* (Stuttgart: Klett-Cotta, 2003), 29

15 Ibid.

16 In his "Thomas von Aquin und Heideggers Gedanke von der Seinsgeschichte (1967)," in Bernhard Welte, *Denken in Begegnung mit den Denkern II. Hegel—Nietzsche—Heidegger, eingeführt und bearbeitet von Holger Zaborowski, Freiburg, Basel* (Wien: Herder, 2007), 139–55, particularly 145ff.

17 Heidegger and Welte, *Briefe und Begegnungen*, 30.

18 Bernhard Welte, "Meister Eckhart. Gedanken zu seinen Gedanken (2nd edition, 1992)," in Bernhard Welte, *Denken in Begegnung mit den Denkern I. Meister Eckhart—Thomas von Aquin—Bonaventura, eingeführt und bearbeitet von Markus Enders, Freiburg, Basel* (Wien: Herder, 2007), 21–215. Welte mentions that, when he last met Heidegger on January 14, 1976, a few months before Heidegger died, he and Heidegger "spoke primarily and forcefully about the thing of Meister Eckhart" (21).

19 John Caputo, *The Mystical Element in Heidegger's Thought* (Athens: Ohio University Press, 1978); *Heidegger and Aquinas. An Essay on Overcoming Metaphysics* (New York: Fordham University Press, 1982).

10

HEIDEGGER AND DESCARTES
Emilia Angelova

Heidegger shifts between two contrasting interpretations of Descartes. While discussion around the time of the project of fundamental ontology emphasizes rather the unavoidable ambiguity of Descartes' views, the later texts (the courses on Nietzsche, *What is a Thing?*, *The Age of the World Picture*, the final seminars) more clearly express a critique of the extreme subjectivism of the Cartesian system and Cartesian method. Reception dates since the early lecture course 1921–2 in Freiburg[1] and the *Prolegomena* from summer 1925 in Marburg, into the best known engagements from *Being and Time* (esp. sections 6, 10, 18b–21, 43) and in 1927, *Basic Problems of Phenomenology* (esp. sections 11, 12, 13a, 15a).

From *Prolegomena*, Descartes' figure looms large, symptomatic of the forgetting of Being that marks the modern epoch itself: he is the "example of the passing over of the phenomenon of the worldhood of the world" (GA 20, 230–1/171). The *sum* is the mode of being, which as such orientates a turning around to the subject, and yet: "It is not the *cogito sum* which formulates a primary finding but rather *sum cogito*" (296/216). As will be critically clarified, the *sum cogito* is disclosive rather of Dasein's being as a mode of interpretation—it is a determination of the manner in which the self and the subject "is," comports itself in the world: "And this *sum* is not taken in the ontological indifference in which Descartes and his successors took it, as the extantness of a thinking thing. *Sum* here is the assertion of the basic constitution of my being: I-am-in-the-world and therefore I am capable of thinking it" (ibid.).

The modern epoch marks the "conscious reversion of the ego," an orientation that "determines the philosophical tradition, and beginning with Descartes, starts from the ego, the subject" (GA 24, 173–4/123). Heidegger finds himself at odds with the modern epoch's "return" to the subject, since a critical appropriation will only show that and how Descartes "leaped over the subject" (220–1/155). The onset of a "philosophical revolution of modern philosophy" in the end "was not a revolution at all" (175/124), causing disappointment in two ways. One, taking over Descartes' classical ontology is a challenge standing before Heidegger and his contemporaries. Modern philosophy allegedly revived, as the contemporaries claim, has only been one-sidedly appropriated. So Heidegger finds disturbing the "historical construction" of the "Neo-Kantianism of recent decades," which heralds Descartes as the foundation with which a "completely new epoch of philosophy begins." He cautions against a "total turnabout" centered on philosophy of the ego, including Husserl: through to contemporary phenomenology in Husserl's *Ideen I*, philosophy remains precisely one-sidedly subjectivist, "in the form in which Descartes expressed it: *res cogitans—res extensa*" (175–6/124–5). Two, Descartes' own relationship to the predecessors is steeped in ambivalence. Descartes works within the tradition, namely, the ancient metaphysics of God, soul, and nature, back to Plato, and basic ontological concepts, drawn directly from Suarez, Duns Scotus, and Thomas Aquinas. Heidegger praises the heightened sensitivity to the unity of the subject that preserves continuity with the metaphysics of substance (see discussion 165–73/117–23): an "ontology of nature" leads Descartes to conceive of the subject— for ancient ontology "the ontologically exemplary entity . . . is nature in the broadest sense" (173/123). Still, modern philosophy works only on the "ancient metaphysical problems," even "the newly posed problems were posed and treated on the foundation of the old" and "everything in principle remained as it was"; and yet, this inertia notwithstanding modern philosophy nevertheless marked and accentuated the subject: "shifting the distinction between subject and object in some way to the center," "in conceiving with greater penetration the peculiar nature of subjectivity" (175/124).

Heidegger engages Descartes on immanent critical grounds. In the 1920s Heidegger takes over the fundamental-ontological orientation to the subject, awakening the problematic of the self and the modern "subject," and awakening philosophy itself: arriving at an "understanding" of Being, it "necessarily looks back to the Dasein" (172/122). Recognizing Descartes' primary findings demands that Heidegger "takes aim at a problem of principle" (i.e. Dasein's "distinctive

function for making possible an adequately founded ontological inquiry in general"). The gleaned problematic of Being in Descartes hence undergoes a threefold reworking: the "basic ways of being," which are the being of nature (*res extensa*); the being of mind (*res cogitans*); and "the subject's way of being," which now "becomes an ontological problem" (174/123). The findings give the "clue" to the "intentional structure of [Dasein's] comportments and the understanding of being at each time immanent in each comportment," and as well, the question of the meaning of "actuality, or of thingness and actuality"—for they enable the questioner to ask "about the constitution of the being to which in each instance the comportment comports: the perceived of perception in its perceivedness, the product (producible) of production in its producedness" (173/122).

From *Being and Time*, Descartes opens certain "distinctive domains of Being": "The *ego cogito* of Descartes, the subject, the 'I,' reason, spirit, person"; even as he fails to determine the "ontological foundation" of subjectivity and leaves "uninterrogated," according to it, the "categorial content" of substance (GA 2, 22/44). The project of fundamental ontology dictates but a new reversion, one directed outside of the ego— "If the *cogito sum* is to serve as the point of departure for the existential analytic of Dasein, then it needs to be turned around": when it is turned around, the "'*sum*' is then asserted first, and indeed in the sense that 'I am in the world'" (211/254). Crucially, it is the mode of Being that determines the existential structure of the entity of Dasein opening up the "I am" to more than thought: "As such an entity, 'I am' in the possibility of Being toward various ways of comporting myself—namely, *cogitationes*—as ways of Being alongside entities within-the-world" (ibid.). Descartes is a possible ally but only "if we recall that spatiality is manifestly one of the constituents of entities-within-the-world, then in the end the Cartesian analysis of the 'world' can still be 'rescued'" (101/134). The turn to the subject is to be "rescued" but one has to carry it through primarily out of fundamental-ontological motives, thus against Descartes' analysis that "*cogitationes* are present-at-hand, and that in these the ego is present-at-hand too as a worldless *res cogitans*" (211/254).

Strikingly Heidegger disengages Descartes from the dogmatism of the Middle Ages and Greek influence, on the issue of produced-ness—in what way are subject and object distinguished ontologically? Clearly, Descartes depends on the ancient-medieval classical ontology, he posits the inherited concept of *realitas* and this becomes a first and main point of Heidegger's distancing, as we note in section 43: Care is the meaning of the real.[2] But despite faithfulness to medieval thought, Descartes' novel foundation of idealism strikes a kinship rather with the meaning of just what Greek ontology already thinks in its deepest underlying presuppositions. Descartes understands what takes place in Christianity's ex nihilo creation to be ideas inscribed in the Greek ontology of production (see GA 24, 149–75/106–21). Descartes gestures to the projective understanding of existential life that is the subject's doing/thinking; he grasps that projection is always already underway. And yet, while he agrees that "the division into *ens increatum* and *creatum* is decisive" (115/82), Heidegger's account of this division runs on very different reasons than Descartes' "seemingly new beginning" and "'radical' way": "But createdness [*Geschaffenheit*] in the widest sense of something's having been produced [*Hergestelltheit*], was an essential item in the

structure of the ancient conception of Being" (GA 2, 24–5/46; also see GA 24, 151–3/108). Heidegger here neglects—pace Descartes and the medieval tradition debate—that since production means always producing something *from* something, material, the implied issue that remains is the assimilation of creation to production. The homogenization of the two domains (GA 24, 167/118) tracks back to the interpretation of Being: "Nevertheless, the question remains whether the *whole universe* [as Leibniz also asks] of beings is exhausted by the present-at-hand"; and "[T]he Dasein, which in each instance we ourselves are, is just that to which all understanding of being-at-hand, actuality, must be traced back" (169/119).[3] The medieval interpretation of Being, which orients Descartes ("the implantation of a baleful prejudice" (GA 2, 25/46)), is "not radical enough": to take up reductively *res cogitans* as *ens creatum* just means to close off the subject and its ontology of production.[4] A radicalized Descartes emerges out of this critique: "All entities other than God need to be 'produced' in the widest sense and also to be sustained" (92/125).

Being and Time infamously charges Descartes with "evasion" of the "question of Being" (94/126), a "failure to master the basic problem of Being" and the "ontological difference" (94/127), above all targeting Descartes' ambiguous reception of ancient ontology, it "kept later generations from making any thematic ontological analytic of the 'mind'" (25/46). And yet Heidegger will demonstrate that "Being is included in each case" in phenomenologically elaborating expressions underlying Descartes' utmost concern, such as "God is" and "the world is." As Heidegger claims, the clue to the existential-ontological problematic tracks back but to the scholastic tradition, which first places beyond debate "the positive sense in which Being signifies" (93/126). Despite "problems lost," there remains in Descartes nevertheless an "ontology of the 'world'" (89/122) and a characterization of the problem of Being. He preserved the difference of Being, albeit in evasion, for he continued to enunciate—to repeat, not to alter—an equivocation: the meaning of "is," existence, cannot be the same for God and for created things.

In a large sense, Heidegger elaborates Descartes' question: How can the meaning be the same for a created entity that "is" and for God who also "is"? The emphasis is on "same," for Descartes shows that the elucidation of substantiality applies to two kinds of "things"—*res cogitans* or thinking things, and *res extensa* or corporeal things. It even applies to "three kinds of substances"—of God, too, we admit that he "is" (93/126). So Heidegger reiterates: "The name 'substance' is not appropriate to God and to these *univocally*, as they say in the schools; that is, no signification of this name which would be common to both God and his creation can be distinctly understood" (ibid.). It is here that one must investigate into the holding off of meaning: the withdrawal of the "meaning of Being which the idea of substantiality embraces" behind the entity (ibid.). The inaccessibility of substance that withholds meaning—substance is not clarified, it cannot be clarified—attests to the impossibility that substance be discovered merely from the fact that it is a "thing" that exists. By itself alone substance, as Descartes knows, does not affect us.

Heidegger thus aptly translates Descartes: "Being itself does not affect us, and therefore cannot be perceived" (94/127). Focus shifts to an "infinite difference of Being" (93/126) that separates finite being and infinite being.

From here to Heidegger's existential analytic is a short distance: Existence, the Being of the entity which is Dasein, is the constitution on whose basis Being's own interpretation appears. The substantiality of substance—Heidegger's expression for the Being of being that is veiled in Descartes, and whose correlate is the theory of preeminent attributes—is able to be grasped only on the basis of "definite characteristics of the entities under consideration [*seiende Bestimmtheiten des betreffenden Seienden*]—attributes" (94/127). This is why he says: "the expression '*substantia*' functions sometimes with a signification which is ontological, sometimes with one which is ontical, but mostly with one which is hazily ontico-ontological" (94/127). Notably, Descartes ought to conceive of the being of the subject, *res cogitans*, within the horizon of substance:

> To determine the nature of the *res corporea* ontologically, we must explicate the substance of this entity as a substance—that is, its substantiality. What makes up the authentic Being-in-itself [*das eigentliche An-ihm-selbst-sein*] of the *res corporea*? How is it at all possible to grasp a substance as such, that is, to grasp its substantiality? (90/123)

Descartes opposes *res extensa* to *res cogitans*, claiming that *res cogitans* is better known, and even conceives of the Being of the subject, *res cogitans*, on the model of *res extensa*: "On the contrary, [Descartes] takes the Being of 'Dasein' (to whose basic constitution Being-in-the-world belongs) in the very same way as he takes the Being of *res extensa*—namely, as substance" (98/131). The model of *res extensa* is constitutive of the substantiality of matter, *res corporea*. Taking over this reasoning critically (the ancient ontology of Nature), Heidegger rescues the indispensable presupposition that *res cogitans*, the ego cogito, is disclosive but out of the basic principles of determination of "Worldhood" (sections 19 and 20). The promised phenomenological destruction of the *cogito sum*, which was never published, will have justified this analysis.[5]

Descartes, then, positively prepares ways of the grounding of the interpretation of Being. (1) Sensible qualities, reduced in their ontical properties alone, are not sufficient to define the substantiality of the *res corporea* (e.g. force, hardness, smell, coldness of bodies, as in the example of the piece of wax, as was discussed by the second meditation and *Principles of Philosophy*). Descartes is "oriented ontologically by these principles": "Sensatio (*aisthesis*), as opposed to *intellectio*, still remains possible as a way of access to entities by a beholding which is perceptual in character" (96/129). (2) The preeminent attribute of *res corporea* (subsuming the substantial property that belongs most preeminently to the particular substance) is extension, but this means that for the integrity of the body it is the property that is presupposed by all else: "For everything else that can be ascribed to the body presupposes extension." That is, extension is positively distinct, remains intelligible, after everything else has been removed; the modes of extension retained in this logic anticipate Kantian conditions of possibility (92/125). *Res extensa* constitute the substantiality of the *res corporea*, providing to this entity the possibility of substantiality. (3) The intellect is the privileged mode of access to entities, on the model of mathematical-physical knowledge. But in grasping the nature of the body, of which only the understanding is able, *intellectio* is mathematical knowledge: "apprehending entities which can always give assurance that their Being has been securely grasped" (95/128). Securely grasping

a thing equates to "an idea in which Being is equated with constant presence-at-hand [*ständige Vorhandenheit*]" (96/128–9): this is how (anticipating Kant) Descartes firmly "prescribes" for the world its "real" Being. In summary, *Being and Time* directs its "criticisms" against the ways in which the Being of the "world" remains covered over and veiled in the concept of substantiality—Descartes does not "let" what entities within-the-world "they themselves" "might have been permitted to present." The Cartesian circle (between "I am" and "God is") revisited, Heidegger remarkably argues that *res extensa* emerge as a horizon of meaning already in the world: "world" founds existence upon Being, in the same way in which entities of the present-to-hand, *Vorhandenheit*, found upon the Being-in-the-world of the "I am."

In the mid-1930s, starting with the lecture courses on Nietzsche, Heidegger palpably shifts the tone, perhaps in recognition as well of his own growing awareness of the difficulty of twisting free from subjectivity. Not even a doubt is left that in Nietzsche's "doctrine of the Overman," Descartes "celebrates his supreme triumph" (*Nietzsche*, vol. IV: *Nihilism*, 28).[6] And even so, in typical manner, ambiguity remains:

No matter how sharply Nietzsche pits himself time and again against Descartes, whose philosophy grounds modern metaphysics, he turns against Descartes only because the latter still does not posit man as *subiectum* in a way that is complete and decisive enough. The representation of the *subiectum* as ego, the I, thus the "egoistic" interpretation of the *subiectum*, is still not subjectivist enough for Nietzsche. (ibid., 28)

In Nietzsche—despite attention, as Heidegger continues to hold back, on a conception of "anthropology" as the "metaphysics of man," and the more essential content to be detected in referrals to "'cosmos', beings as a whole"—the very essence of modern metaphysics becomes a "psychology." It assigns to "man" the basic character of being: in a definite preeminence man becomes the measure and center of beings, and in this subjectivist interpretation of *subiectum* man is at the "bottom of all objectification and representability" (ibid.). Western history culminates, or consummates the "truth" of Being in the doctrine of the "will to power." To hear transformatively the sending or *Schickung* of Being, what now calls for thinking, need is to attend more carefully to how and that "the Cartesian *Meditations* on man as *subiectum*"[7] is the path to the fundamental problems of metaphysics implying "nothing less than the way in which man is historical" (ibid., 29)—not an extrinsic form of communication, therefore, but a "nihilism," "inherently viewed as a configuration of the *will to power*, as the occurrence in which man is historical" (ibid., 28) (i.e. the "question of the 'psychical'" "what is living, in that particular sense of life that determines becoming as 'will to power'" (ibid.).[8]

NOTES AND REFERENCES

[1] For Heidegger's earliest engagement see, GA 61: *Phenomenological Interpretations of Aristotle*, English trans. Rojcewicz. This confrontation develops in *Der Beginn der Neuzeitlichen Philosophie* (WS 1923–4)/*Introduction to Modern Philosophy*. As Marion (68) observes, here for Heidegger, Descartes "already poses the question of the mode of being of the *sum*, precisely in overlooking it in favour of a question about the status and the power of the *ego*." Support for this comes from *Wegmarken*, GA 9, 79: about the course in SS 1928, *The Metaphysical*

Foundations of Logic, Heidegger recollects that it "attempted to come to terms with Leibniz . . ."; and also recollects that the course in Marburg 1923–4 "sought to adopt a corresponding position with regard to Descartes"; "this latter [position] that was then incorporated into *Sein und Zeit* (sections 19–21)." As Jean-Luc Marion, Bernasconi, and others note, there may be a stronger and more sustained discussion of Aristotle and Kant, but Descartes is no secondary figure for Heidegger, the reception Husserl-Descartes is a preoccupation from the beginning, and to the very end. For Heidegger on Descartes, including in the *Thor Seminars* (1969), the *Zäringen Seminar* (1973), and 1974 text "*Der Fehl heiliger Namen*" ("The lack of sacred names"), see Marion in *Critical Heidegger*, 67–96. Marion offers a more original interpretation of Descartes and Heidegger stressing the proximity with Husserl (and Levinas) along alterity and ethics: "So Heidegger does not question the *ego cogito* with regard to the primacy of its cognitive origin but rather the ontological indeterminateness of the *esse*, that which it conceals from view rather than that which it proclaims" (69). Marion's further explanation of why Descartes left undetermined and undiscussed the meaning of Being, is found in: *Sur le prisme metaphysique de Descartes* (Paris: Presses Universitaires de France, 1986), 177–80. Also see F.-W. Herrmann, *Husserl und die Meditationen des Descartes* (Frankfurt, Vittorio Klostermann,1971). Along similar lines with Marion, but different, see Robert Bernasconi, *Heidegger in Question* (New Jersey: Humanities Press, 1993), 150–70.

[2] "Of course as long as Dasein is (that is, only as long as an understanding of Being is ontically possible), 'is there' Being [*es gibt Sein*]" (GA 2, 212/255). A footnote to this passage points out that in *Letter on Humanism* Heidegger will insist that "*es gibt*" here is used deliberately— "[f]or the 'it' which here 'gives' is Being itself. The 'gives', however, designates the essence of Being . . ."

[3] "And even if creation out of nothing is nothing identical with producing something out of a material that is found already on hand, nevertheless, this creating of the creation has the general ontological character of producing. . . .

as if ancient ontology in its foundations and basic concepts were cut to fit the Christian world-view" (GA 24, 168/118–19).

4 Heidegger claims, "Our Interpretation will not only prove that Descartes had neglected the question of Being altogether; it will also show why he came to suppose that the absolute 'Being-Certain [*Gewisssein*] of the *cogito* exempted him from raising the question of the meaning of Being which this entity possesses" (GA 2, 24/46).

5 For more on Heidegger's critique, appropriation and interpretation of Descartes, see François Raffoul, *Heidegger and the Subject*, trans. David Pettigrew and Gregory Recco (Amherst: Humanity Books, 1998), 54–70; P. Ricoeur, *Le conflit des interprétations* (Paris: Seuil, 1969), 222–32; trans. *The Conflict of Interpretations*, ed. D. Ihde (Evanston: Northwestern, 1974), 223–35. Also see Jean-Luc Nancy, "Mundus est fabula," *Ego sum* (Paris: Flammarion, 1979), 95–127; trans. Daniel Brewer, "Mundus est fabula," *MLN* 93.4, 1978, 635–53.

6 A sustained new reading of Descartes begins here, to continue to the very end. This new tone marks the lectures on European Nihilism, in *Nietzsche* volume iv, esp. in Sections 13–21. Heidegger grows increasingly aware of this need, as he himself sees *Being and Time* as more Cartesian and more bound to subjectivity than he realized. See J. Taminiaux, "Heidegger lecteur de Descartes," in ed. W. Biemel and

F.-W. Herrmann, *Kunst und Technik* (Frankfurt: Klostermann, 1989), 109–23.

7 Heidegger's critique of Descartes is directed much more against the successors, the ones who have developed a metaphysics of subjectivity. See, for example, GA 24, 178/127, 217/153; see *Nietzsche* vol. ii, 48; also *Nietzsche* vol. iv, 179, where the link with Leibniz is made clear: "Descartes' metaphysics is indeed a metaphysics of will to power (. . . Leibniz begins the interpretation of *subiectum* (*substantia* as *monas*))." From the late lecture on Kant, *What is a Thing?* of 1935–6, comes the verdict on Descartes: "at best it is only a bad novel, and anything but a story in which the movement of Being becomes visible"—citing from the revised translation by David Farrell Krell, appearing in *BW*, 298 ff.

8 From the early period onwards, Heidegger returns to Descartes as the one who initiates the shift toward modern mathematical physics in modern philosophy, which shift is continually stressed everywhere; this return is even more incessant in the later texts. Even so, what cannot be stressed enough is that the ambiguity of "critique" will remain, notably in *QT*, *AWP* (*Holzwege*, GA 5, 108–9 (n. 9)), and to the very last texts. See also 1936–46, *Verwindung der Metaphysik*, in *Vorträge und Aufsätze*, I, 65. This completes the remaking of Descartes as a thinker (with Leibniz) in the subjectivist tradition of *cogito me cogitare* (*rem*).

11

HEIDEGGER AND KANT: THREE GUIDING QUESTIONS

Frank Schalow

Because the philosophies of Martin Heidegger and Immanuel Kant are of legendary complexity, unraveling the *Auseinandersetzung* between them poses an enormous challenge. In *Kant and the Problem of Metaphysics* (1929), Heidegger emphasizes the "violence" of his interpretation of Kant's *Critique of Pure Reason*. Rather than provide an authoritative commentary of this work, Heidegger undertakes a destructive-retrieval of transcendental philosophy, in order to elicit its "unsaid" ontological implications for re-asking the question of being (GA 3, 249/KPM, 175). He thereby brings to fruition his earlier revelation that Kant "opened my eyes" to how temporality makes possible our understanding of being and yields the idioms for its expression (GA 25, 430/PICPR, 292). Yet, in order to develop parallels between Kant's thinking and his own, Heidegger must first "cross" a terminological gulf separating them. The language that provides a common thread between these two thinkers develops, on the one hand, the reciprocal concern each places on human finitude, and, on the other, makes possible being's disclosure through temporality.

In retrospect, Heidegger provides the key to developing this language and thereby "cracking the code" of a complementary mode of expression governing his exchange with Kant. In his lecture-course on Heraclitus (1943), Heidegger suggests that his radical reinterpretation of transcendental philosophy hinges on first "translating" the *Critique* (GA 55, 63). In other words, the reciprocal interest each thinker has in temporality will provide a crossing, allowing Heidegger to transpose the key motifs of Kant's thought within a broader, ontological context and thereby amplify the question of being. Conversely, by appropriating Kant's thinking in terms of his own, Heidegger underscores the originality of his project, and consequently recasts his hermeneutic inquiry of *Being and Time* within a wider historical orbit. The inaugural of three questions shaping Heidegger's exchange with Kant emerges into the foreground. First, what are the key steps by which Heidegger transposes the *Critique* and allows it to become a "sounding board" to echo the central themes of *Being and Time*? Second, why did Heidegger appeal to Kant's account of "schematism," in order to develop the unspoken connection between being and temporality? Third, how does Heidegger continue to develop his conversation with Kant in light of the "turning" and the transition of thinking to the "other beginning"?

I

Ironically, the central philosophical issue that Heidegger embraced, namely, the question of being, assumed only peripheral importance to Kant. When in 1929 Heidegger titles his seminal work *Kant and the Problem of Metaphysics*, it is not metaphysics that constitutes this problematic conventionally understood. In questioning metaphysics, Kant asks about its "possibility," while emphasizing that it is a "natural predisposition" of human nature. Kant's attempt to root the problem of metaphysics in human finitude provides Heidegger with a springboard to his own methodological innovation, namely, that the inquiry into being is inextricably interwoven with *who* raises it. Accordingly, that inquiry must proceed by examining the inquirer's capacity to understand being, in such a way that the crucial philosophical problematic becomes: how is an understanding of being (*Seinsverständnis*) possible? The concern for "possibility" not only points back to the intimate connection between metaphysics and "human nature" but also how our capacity to understand is shaped, structured, and developed by our temporal finitude.

Kant coined the term "Copernican revolution" to describe his innovative approach to philosophy, which for Heidegger poses the subsequent challenge of unfolding the circular dynamic of our understanding. For Kant, the Copernican revolution seeks in human finitude a new axis to anchor the possibility of human understanding/knowledge and thereby delineate its preconditions (i.e. for determining what can be known as a possible object). The centering of knowledge in this way suggests (to Heidegger) that whatever the content of its categorial determinations may be, they (i.e. in Kantian terminology, the pure concepts or categories) must derive from

a common origin. By arising from this origin, the categories acquire their power to signify the universal determinations of any possible object. If it can be shown that our temporal finitude constitutes this origin, then time must also provide the key for understanding and expressing what is first in universality, that is, being. A clue is then given to the hidden reciprocity between being and temporality, such that the latter not only provides the possibility for our understanding the former but also yields the vocabulary for expressing its meaning.

The manner in which we can "speak of" being with words that exhibit a temporal character, simultaneously suggests that there is an inherent dynamic to being and its capacity for self-manifestation. Our understanding as well must also unfold within a temporal arc, in order to project the horizon "upon-which" (*worhaufin*) being can manifest itself and thereby convey its "meaning." The universality of any concept of being must be wedded to the singularity of its manifestation, in order that its meaning can be transmitted and disclosed through language. The so-called problem of metaphysics, to which our finitude is central, transforms itself into a hermeneutic concern in the most originary way. That is, in its etymology hermeneutics stems from Hermes, the messenger or "go-between." In this originary sense, hermeneutics renders meaningful what is otherwise arcane, elusive, and indeterminate, thereby opening up a new horizon for finite, human understanding. Due to our finitude (and the fact that being withdraws from disclosure), our understanding must be constructed on the basis of this "intermediary" or go-between. In undertaking a destructive-retrieval of Kant's transcendental philosophy, Heidegger unveils temporality as this basis, that is, as holding the key to the transmission of its "meaning" and determination in words. In harmony with the dynamic of being's manifestation, the meaning of being must be conveyed in equally concrete terms, that is, through temporal idioms.[1]

Can we identify specific texts, in conjunction with his reading of Kant, by which Heidegger begins to develop this hermeneutic breakthrough? In his 1925 lecture-course *Plato's Sophist*, Heidegger provides an important clue to the role that time plays in formulating the question of being and in suggesting a vocabulary to express its "meaning." He characterizes being as a "tense-word" (*Zeitwort*), specifically pointing to the "grammar" of a distinctive linguistic practice, the declension of the verb "to be" (GA 19, 592/PS, 410). In *The Basic Problems of Phenomenology* (1927), in which his interpretation of Kant begins to take center stage, Heidegger states that "all propositions of ontology are *temporal propositions*" (GA 24 460/BP, 323). With this remark, he illustrates the double role that temporality assumes both in shaping the possibility of our understanding of being, and in dictating the grammar for its expression. This grammar must heed the verbal form "to be," that is, in a way that calls forth the unique temporal idioms that evoke the dynamic of being's manifestation. Only when the inquiry into being reaches this level of concreteness, and develops a *logos* in concert with the dynamics of being's manifestation, can an ontology or the science of being arise that is truly "phenomenological." Conversely, this phenomenological ontology retains its "transcendental" ancestry, precisely by accenting the temporal determinations or the lexicon of being, which incorporates human finitude as its central "problematic."

As Heidegger states at the conclusion of the *Basic Problems*, ontology is essentially a "temporal or transcendental science" (GA 24, 466/BP, 327). With this statement, he brings Kant's sense of the transcendental, as a way of considering the preconditions for the knower's "passing over" to encounter what is knowable, in line with his own: the ecstatic trajectory of projecting forth the horizon for any understanding of being. In either case the movement of "going beyond," or surpassing to, is propelled by the "whereto" of temporality. As Heidegger illustrates in *Basic Problems*, the act of finite transcendence equals temporality, that is, as the ecstatic horizon "upon-which" to project (the understanding of) being, and thereby formulate a *logos* in harmony with the singularity of its disclosure. With this observation, Heidegger's initial strategy for "translating" the *Critique of Pure Reason* becomes evident: that is, rendering Kant's transcendental philosophy (of knowledge) into a phenomenological ontology (of the possibility of understanding being via the lens of temporality).

Throughout *Kant and the Problem of Metaphysics*, Heidegger translates the key motifs of transcendental philosophy into terms commensurate with his own inquiry into being. In order to implement this strategy, Heidegger reconstructs Kant's account of schematism or the procedure (*Verfahren*) for graphically depicting the meaning of the categories in temporal terms.[2] As Heidegger states in *Being and Time*: "Kant is the first and only one who traversed a stretch of the path toward investigating the dimension of temporality [*Temporalität*]—or allowed himself to be driven there by the compelling force of the phenomena themselves" (GA 2, 32/BT, 22). With this directive, we then proceed to the second question: why did Heidegger appeal to schematism in order to establish the connection between being and temporality?

II

Heidegger recognized that while metaphysics has persistently overlooked the question of being, the withdrawal of that concern also preserves the possibility of renewing interest in it. For him, Kant's transcendental philosophy harbored the vestige of such a point of departure, the opportunity for a "hermeneutic foothold" in lieu of all other foundations, for example, God, reason, the "I think," or even the consummation of all these metaphysical positions in the Hegelian absolute. Only given such a foothold would it be possible to address the "possibility of metaphysics," and begin to map the historical landscape for re-asking the question of being in terms of the dynamic of temporality (GA 25, 427/PICPR, 289). When viewed within this wider context, Heidegger turns to Kantian schematism; for it is the first and foremost harbinger of this multidimensional dynamic of being's manifestation, the signpost along the way to its hidden reciprocity with temporality, such that "there is" being only insofar as "there is" time. In a retrospective glance toward the end of his career, Heidegger offers an illuminating remark in his seminar from 1973 that schematism "is the Kantian way of discussing being and time" (GA 15, 380–1/FS, 69).

Given this context, Heidegger casts a new spotlight on what is perhaps one of the most nebulous of all philosophical doctrines, Kant's schematism of the pure concepts of the understanding. Kant may have proceeded uncritically when he adopted the categories from Aristotle. Indeed, from Heidegger's perspective, Kant did not fully appreciate how he also adopted Aristotle's legacy that being can be spoken in many ways. For Heidegger, however, the diversity of these ways must be taken back into and adduced from the possibility of understanding being in general, and its origin in temporality. For Kant, the temporal character of our finitude yields the common root for legitimately employing the categories. The role of schematism is to uncover this deeper temporal origin, and thereby uproot reason in favor of a new form of creativity for engendering the nuances, distinctions, and determinations of the categories, that is, the power of imagination. Heidegger was attracted to schematism because of these radical implications, but most of all because of its "tactical" role in developing a new linguistic usage or grammar for the categories, which could elicit a common root of determination from a pre-predicative source, that is, the synthesis of time. In this regard, to follow the path of "translating" the *Critique of Pure Reason* is to reach the archway of a crossing, the "trans-literating," iconic power of imagination (*Einbildungskraft*) through which time emerges as the figure to transcribe pure concepts into a distinctly ontological vocabulary, that is, words capable of signifying (the meaning) of "being."

Accordingly, Kant calls this procedure "schematism," which yields a new precedent for the use of pure concepts by "indexing" them to the conditions of our finitude and providing a nexus of interlocking patterns of signification. In its "strategic" role, temporality provides the creative nexus for engendering new "distinctions," reconfiguring the pure concepts so that (through their synthetic unities) they can elicit precisely those (transcendental) "time-determinations" to define objects "for us" (GA 25, 431/PICPR, 292) Within the overall procedure of schematism, time serves as the "proxy" of our finitude, and, by bearing this insignia, provides the common ancestry to shape the content of each of the pure concepts. Through the strategic role that time plays, however, the formative power of imagination can graphically exhibit a genre of distinctions— as etched through a temporal nexus—which prefaces the development of language in its predicative form. We appeal to this "pre-predicative" level to suggest a "novelty" of linguistic practice, which, by graphically portraying each of the pure concepts through images, *simultaneously implicate the precise vocabulary for their expression.* Time, then, forms the universal character of the lexicon, because its chief idioms, for example, "succession," "permanence," "presence," cultivate an awareness that is common to all human beings, precisely because it is *"emblematic" of our finitude* as such.

By forming a new grammar of articulation, the "prefixical" character of the schemata sculptures or carves out in advance the finite horizon in which whatever can appear does so in accord with precisely those "temporal" determinations. To clarify the ontological import of this "schematism," as outlining the temporal backdrop for whatever can manifest itself, Heidegger characterizes the ecstatic character of these schemata as "horizonal" (GA 24, 436/BP, 307). As the impetus and trajectory of finite transcendence, ecstatic-horizonal temporality projects-open the expanse of manifestation and thereby outlines the possibility of understanding being. This understanding, however, is intimately tied to the grammar for expressing it, that is, its "meaning," in terms of the priority of the verbal form of the "is." The horizonal schemata outline the simplest form in which the temporalization of being can emerge into language via the idiom "to be." That is, we return to the dynamism of the verbal form; we do not say something "is," but, in referring back to the hidden connection between being and time, say instead: *"es gibt."*

Why, then, did Heidegger turn to Kantian schematism? He did so because the procedure of schematism yields temporal idioms capable of signifying the meaning of being. Thus, our understanding must take a detour through temporality, through the pre-orientation of the directionality of the horizonal schema, in order to avail itself of the precise determinations to express the meaning of being in conceptual terms. Once again, the basic thrust of Heidegger's destructive-retrieval of transcendental philosophy is to extend the hermeneutic arc of questioning and carry that forward within this dynamic of translating the key message of the *Critique.* Insofar as the question of being is inherently historical, he broadens the arc of that inquiry in and through his *Auseinandersetzung* with his predecessors, most notably, Kant. Let us proceed to our third question and ask how Heidegger's conversation continues to unfold in light of the turning.

III

In all of Heidegger's extensive writings on transcendental philosophy, there is one section of the Kant-book whose importance has been vastly underestimated: section 44 of part IV. In his "Notes" to the Kant-book, later published in the "Preface to the Fourth Edition" (1973) of that work, Heidegger calls attention to "Part IV," and its importance in alleviating the "misinterpretation" surrounding the so-called unpublished third division (of part I) of *Being and Time,* as well as the task of "*Destruktion*" in part II, calling special attention to the conclusion (part IV) of the Kant-book (GA 3, xiii/KPM, xvii). In alluding to the "real question" left open in the third division of the first part of *Sein und Zeit,*

Heidegger then concludes his personal reflection with this enigmatic remark: "*Beiträge*: beginning to a new beginning" (*Anfang zu neuem Anfang*) [GA 3, xiii/KPM, xvii]. As we will see, in *Contributions to Philosophy (From Enowning)* [1936–8], he briefly reexamines his conversation with Kant. At issue is how Kant's destructive-retrieval of transcendental philosophy illuminates the so-called impasse surrounding the unpublished, third division of part I of *Being and Time*, to be titled "Time and Being."

Whatever may have been the various scenarios for addressing being at the inception of Western thought, relative to its influence on the subsequent tradition, one approach in particular assumes prominence: Aristotle's concept of *ousia* as permanent presence. And, while some scholars argue that Heidegger simply rejects Aristotle's interpretation of being, his criticism targets instead the ambiguity surrounding the birth of the ancient concept of *ousia*. What exactly is this ambiguity? In conceiving of being as permanent presence, the ancients implicitly allude to time, but they do not question why this linkage should be inevitable. But once the ancients forgo this initial line of questioning, the *first* level of neglect for the question of being arises. Given the lack of insight into the inevitable conjunction of being and time, the ancients then "fall" victim to a *second* level of neglect when the occasion arises to address the constitution of temporality. Rather than make the concern for time the priority for any investigation into being, the ancients proceed in an inverse way: they adopt an understanding of being that is already thematized through time, and then, once being has been conceived as permanent presence, redefine time, as if by an afterthought, on the basis of this permanence. But how does this dissimulation subsequently impact the genesis of the traditional concept of time? The problem with preconceiving being as permanent presence is that it "prejudices" any subsequent view of time in terms of the single temporal ecstasies to which it gives rise, for example, the "present." "The being of beings obviously is understood here as permanence and constancy [*Beständigkeit und Ständigkeit*]" (GA 3, 240/KPM, 168). On the basis of a preconception of being in terms of permanence, a controversy then irrupts as to which temporal model can salvage the priority of the present: the continuance of the present under the ideal of eternity, or, in, recognition of the coming to be and passing away of nature, the opposite concept of transitoriness. Eternity and the "immediate and always present" [*gegenwärtigen*] are two sides of the same coin (GA 3, 240/KPM, 168). As the flip side of this vision of eternity, a linear concept of time as a sequence of "nows," which segments the movement of time into "before" and "after," is born. The philosophical tradition must then juggle two conflicting views of time, as permanence and transitoriness, each of which, however, stems from the same derivative root of time that privileges the temporal dimension of the "present." A double dissimulation occurs, in short, the tradition's forgottenness of its forgottenness.

In the occurrence of this forgottenness, Heidegger locates the historical juncture where Western *metaphysics* arises. If metaphysics begins by "inverting" the projection of being upon time, falling prey to forgottenness, then how can this inertia be counteracted through an alternative possibility of recollection? Through his *Auseinandersetzung* with Kant, Heidegger seizes upon this possibility and rediscovers the origin of his own inquiry through the "turning" (*die Kehre*), that is, the "turning around" of the question from *Being and Time* to "time and being." In the turning around of the question, the emphasis on the conjunction "and" first comes to light (GA 31, 126 /EHF, 87). For it is the grammar of this connective that redirects Heidegger's inquiry back to the "giving" of each, being/time, in reciprocity with one another, as enunciated through the most primeval of all gestures: "there is/it gives" (*es gibt*) being, and, correlatively, "there is/it gives" (*es gibt*) time (GA 15, 363–4/FS, 59–60). These locutions help to carry out the turning as Heidegger describes it, by allowing an attunement to language to intervene and introduce the basic *experience* by which being can first become "understandable" to us and we can participate in its openness. *The Kantian legacy is such that the conceptualization of being must always be linked to the experience thereof, with temporality serving as the "go-between," the mid-point of intermediation.*

After the Kant-book, Heidegger would periodically renew his *Auseinandersetzung* with Kant. A brief remark from *Contributions to Philosophy* offers a retrospective glance on his own Kant-interpretation. In justifying his initial attempt to "use force against Kant" in order to "*work out the transcendental power of imagination*," Heidegger states: "And so the Kant-book is necessarily ambiguous . . . because Kant continues to be the only one since the Greeks who brings the interpretation of beingness into a certain relation to 'time'. . . ." (GA 65, 253–4 /CP1, 178–9). "Indeed: As thrown projecting-opening grounding, Da-sein is the highest actuality in the domain of imagination, granted that by

this term we understand not only a faculty of the soul and not only something transcendental (cf. Kant-book) but rather enowning itself, where all transfiguration reverberates. 'Imagination' as occurrence of the *clearing* itself" (GA 65, 312/CP1, 219).

CONCLUSION

Heidegger's *Auseinandersetzung* with Kant extends over the course of four decades, carving out a *Denkweg* the many twists and turns of which lead to the crossroads of the other beginning. Perhaps more than any philosopher within the Western tradition, Kant offers Heidegger a blueprint for developing his own fundamental ontology and thereby the key for rediscovering the hidden connection between being and time.

NOTES AND REFERENCES

[1] For a discussion of this topic, in connection with schematism, see Frank Schalow, *Departures: At the Crossroads between Heidegger and Kant* (Berlin: de Gruyter, 2013), pp. 49–61. For a discussion of the role that translation, understood "broadly," plays in transmitting the meaning of the most basic philosophical terms, see See Parvis Emad, *Translation and Interpretation: Learning from Beiträge*, ed. F. Schalow (Bucharest: Zeta Books, 2012), 61–9.

[2] See Immanuel Kant, *Critique of Pure Reason*, trans. Norman Kemp Smith (New York: St. Martin's Press, 1965), 182 (A 140 / B 179).

12

HEIDEGGER AND GERMAN IDEALISM
Peter Trawny

German Idealism is for Heidegger a certain constellation and context of certain philosophers and poets in the history of metaphysics, that is, of being. The constellation and context of German Idealism are not always the same, but they are ultimately stable. It is remarkable that Heidegger, with the exception of the lecture course "German Idealism" of summer semester 1929, ignores the canonical accentuation in the study of German Idealism on the names of Fichte, Schelling, and Hegel.[1] German Idealism for Heidegger is primarily the thinking of Hegel and Schelling, its being-historical location is the "Absolute" in its relation to "subjectivity." On the one hand, it is set up by the philosophy of Kant, which is at the same time decidedly notable (GA 42, 62, 72; GA 86, 193). On the other hand, Hölderlin's poetry, insofar as it in a certain respect belongs to German Idealism, is dehistoricized (yet *not* understood as unhistorical), and its specific significance for the history of being beyond German Idealism is emphasized (GA 65, 421–2).

We will accordingly consider German Idealism in the following order:

(1) Hegel and German Idealism
(2) Schelling and German Idealism
(3) German Idealism in the history of metaphysics, that is, of being

HEGEL AND GERMAN IDEALISM

In a later text Heidegger speaks of the "superficial talk of the breakdown of Hegelian philosophy" (GA 7, 74).[2] This opinion is rejected, because "in the 19th Century only this philosophy has determined reality," and indeed it has as "metaphysics." And then he claims: "Since Hegel's death (1831) everything is only a countermovement, not only in Germany, but also in Europe."

Heidegger's engagement with Hegel begins early and ends late. Heidegger dealt with no other philosopher perhaps as continuously as Hegel.[3] When later he introduces certain notations simply with "Hegel | Heidegger" (GA 11, 105–7), the proximity and distance is clearly marked. Heidegger's philosophy is also the attempt, by "overcoming metaphysics," to overcome that "counter movement."

Already in his habilitation treatise, *Duns Scotus's Doctrine of Categories and Meaning* (1916), Heidegger speaks of the "great task" of bringing about a "thorough confrontation [*Auseinandersetzung*] with the abundance and depth, richness of experience and conceptualization of the most powerful system," that is "with Hegel" (GA 1, 410–11). This task, formulated under the influence of Dilthey, was realized in the coming decades of Heidegger's thinking.

113

This begins in summer 1923, in the lecture course *Ontology (Hermeneutics of Facticity)*, where Heidegger separates phenomenology and dialectics in the Hegelian sense for the first time (GA 63, 43–7). If "today it is attempted to connect the authentic underlying tendency of phenomenology with dialectics," then this is as if "someone would like to connect fire and water" (42). Fire and water build an antagonism resulting in the annihilation of each other. This demonstrates that phenomenology is not indifferent to dialectics.

In *Being and Time*, Heidegger appears to distance himself from German Idealism. While Plato and Aristotle challenged him at the beginning of the 1920s to further his philosophical development, Hegel still remains present. In the famous passage, where Heidegger reminds us of the γιγαντομαχία περὶ τῆς οὐσίας, the "question for the meaning of being," "which provided a stimulus for his researches of *Plato* and *Aristotle*," Heidegger also speaks of Hegel. For what was "achieved" in this research, "was to persist through many alterations and 'retouchings' down to the 'logic' of Hegel" (GA 2, 3). Hegel's understanding of time then becomes so important that Heidegger announces a comparative lecture of Hegel's *Jena Logic* and Aristotle's *Physics* and *Metaphysics* (570). In the summer semester of 1927, he ventured such an interpretation (in fact not on the *Jena Logic*, but on the *Science of Logic* (see GA 86)).

In the summer of 1929, Heidegger interprets Hegel further in a lecture course on *German Idealism* (GA 28, 195–232). In this lecture course, he returns to the "confrontation [*Auseinandersetzung*] with Hegel" (214). Initial expressions of this confrontation are crystallized, which remain in place. A "confrontation with Hegel" is one with "absolute idealism and therefore with western metaphysics." It pushes "in totally concealed dimensions, which we primarily have to obtain in a deep elaboration of the problem of metaphysics." But still something different emerges. Heidegger in his readings of Hegel will notably refer to the "central work" of the "Phenomenology of Spirit," but also to the "Science of Logic." He attempts his first extended readings of Hegel's "Phenomenology" in the winter-semester 1930/31. It is "abandoned" in the interpretation of "self-consciousness" (GA 32, 215). "Everything" should "remain unsettled."

Heidegger taught a seminar four years later (1934/35) about Hegel's *Philosophy of Right* with the well-known theorist of jurisprudence Erik Wolf at the university of Freiburg. This seminar testifies to how the philosopher seeks to unfold a political philosophy in recourse to Hegel's thought. A concept of National-Socialism, and its coherence with political realities is questionable, serves as a pathmark. This attempt to answer National-Socialism with Hegel's *Philosophy of Right* is not resumed. Hegel's *Elements of the Philosophy of Right* remained the only classical work of political philosophy that Heidegger publically interpreted.

At the end of the 1930s we see Heidegger addressing Hegel's understanding of "negativity," renewing the appeal for a "philosophical confrontation" with Hegel (GA 68, 3). For Hegel's philosophy "*stands definitively in the history of thinking*," that is, "of Beyng" as a "unique and still not *conceived* demand." "Every thinking" that comes "*after*" Hegel, "or also only primarily wants to arrange the presuppositions of philosophy," cannot avoid this "demand." The "uniqueness of Hegel's philosophy" consists "*primarily* in the fact that a *higher* standpoint of the self-consciousness of spirit beyond this philosophy is no longer possible." Therefore, there is no philosophy that "*still* could be superordinated on a higher level than Hegel's systematics." But the "standpoint of a necessary confrontation" with Hegel's philosophy has "nonetheless to cope with it, and thus to be superior in an essential aspect." This "standpoint" cannot be "brought and convinced from outside," but must be found "*in* Hegel's philosophy" as an "essentially inaccessible and indifferent ground for it." A true critique of a philosophy has to confront its main ideas. An external interpretation of Hegel's philosophy remains shallow.

The *second* presupposition of a "philosophical confrontation" with Hegel challenges the systematic standard of his thinking. As the "principle of his philosophy" (4–5) conceives the "whole of beings," thus that philosophy has to dispose of the "principle" that shows itself in the "whole of beings" because it is "the actual." A "basic confrontation with Hegel" can only succeed if it fulfills "*at the same time* and *consistently both* demands" (6). In the introduction of the notes of 1938/39, Heidegger begins to deal with Hegel's "fundamental determination" of "negativity."

The 1942 summer term seminar represents a further intense interpretation of Hegel's "Phenomenology of Spirit." This turned out to be a very fertile exploration. The outcome of this seminar was the essay *Hegel's Concept of Experience* (GA 5, 115–208) and *Elucidation of the "Introduction" of the "Phenomenology of Spirit"* (GA 68). *Hegel's Concept of Experience*, published in *Off the Beaten Track* (1950), belongs to the context of examining the problem of "experience" in general. For Hegel, "experience concerns the present in its presence" (GA 5, 186). Insofar as "consciousness" exists by exposing itself

to its own "inquiry" (*Prüfung*), it "moves out of its presence to arrive in this presence." "Experience" is the "representation" of the "appearance of the appearing knowledge."

During this period, Hegel's philosophy found its place in the context of the history of metaphysics. The "desertification of the earth" (GA 7, 97) begins "as a process which is willed, but unknown in its essence, and also not knowable at the time," where "the essence of truth is projected as certainty." It is Hegel who conceives "this moment of the history of metaphysics as the moment in which absolute self-consciousness becomes the principle of thinking."

Heidegger confirmed this idea immediately after the war. In his *Letter on Humanism* (1946) Hegel's thinking appears in the history of beyng (GA 9, 335, 360), the key to Heidegger's later philosophy. Those who wish to understand the accomplishment of modernity with its far-reaching consequences in the twentieth century cannot avoid a "confrontation" with Hegel's philosophy.

Hegel's thinking is furthermore the starting point for the interpretation of the "onto-theo-logical constitution of metaphysics" (1957). The "philosophical confrontation" has become a "thinking dialogue" about the "matter of thinking" (GA 11, 55). If we want to enter into such a dialogue "with Hegel," we not only have "to talk with him about the same matter, but to talk with him about the same matter in the same way." Hegel thinks the "being of beings in a speculative-historical way" (spekulative-geschichtlich). Heidegger responds to this "way" of thinking by "being-historical" thinking.

The outcome of this correspondence is differences that Heidegger roughly contrasts: "For Hegel" (56) "the matter of thinking is being in reference of the being-thought in absolute thinking and as absolute thinking."

In contrast "for us the matter of thinking is the same, thus being, but being in reference to its difference to beings." Heidegger then adds: "For Hegel, the matter of thinking is the idea as the absolute concept. For us, formulated in a preliminary fashion, the matter of thinking is difference *as* difference."

Heidegger's exhortation to speak with Hegel "about the same matter in the same way" continues in a lecture given in 1958 in Heidelberg and Aix-en-Provence with the title "Hegel and the Greeks." In this text Heidegger interrogates the originality of Hegel's philosophy of history insofar as he is also concerned with "philosophy in the totality of its historical destiny" (GA 9, 429). The question is whether Hegel is able to recognize the "enigma of Ἀλήθεια" in his consideration of "truth" (442). For with Ἀλήθεια "our thinking is addressed by something"; "what *before* the beginning of 'philosophy' and through the whole course of its history has already drawn thought to itself" (444).

The relation "Hegel | Heidegger" was so precarious that Heidegger, at the instigation of Jean Beaufret in 1962, accepted the necessity of distinguishing his thinking from Hegel with even more emphasis. It is stated in the *Protocol of a Seminar about "Time and Being"*: "Thus in France the impression was widely predominant that Heidegger's thinking was a recapitulation—as a deepening and an expansion—of Hegel's philosophy" (GA 14, 57). "From Hegel's point of view" (59), one could say that *"Being and Time"* gets caught in being, because it is not developed "to the 'concept.'" On the other hand, one could ask from the perspective of *Being and Time*, why Hegel considers "being as indeterminate immediacy," just "to place it from the very beginning in relation to determination and mediation." For Hegel, the "identity of being and thinking" is "really an equivalence" (59). Therefore, it does not come to a *"question* of being." Furthermore, the human being is interpreted as a "coming-to-itself of the Absolute," what "leads to a sublation of the finitude of the human being." In the thinking of Heidegger the "finitude" of the human being is what "comes to view."

In the Le Thor seminars (1968/69), Heidegger attempts to formulate the "great task" of a "philosophical confrontation" with Hegel. Heidegger thinks the *"finitude of being"* (GA 15, 370–1). Being can "not be absolutely for itself." Even if Hegel says that the "Absolute is not 'without us,'" he says this in reference to the Christian God, who in a certain sense is reliant on the human being. But for Heidegger "being is not without its relation to Dasein" and "Nothing is further away from Hegel and all idealism."

SCHELLING AND GERMAN IDEALISM

Heidegger became acquainted with Schelling at the same time as Hegel (GA 1, 56), in the years before the First World War. This might not be a coincidence. Heidegger always read Schelling with Hegel and Hegel with Schelling; Hegel and Schelling build the essential constellation and core of German Idealism.

Heidegger offered a seminar about Hegel's logic in the summer semester of 1927. He taught *Schelling's Philosophical Inquiries into the Nature of Human Freedom* for the first time in the winter of 1927/28. The notations as they are handed down to us do not reveal a special interest, but the discussion of "love" of "evil" reveal a change in Heidegger's interpretation of Hegel.

In the lecture course *German Idealism* from the summer of 1929, Heidegger discussed Schelling rather briefly. He is interpreted as a critic of Fichte, and Heidegger refers more or less superficially to Schelling's philosophy of nature. Heidegger claims that Schelling "primarily in a countermovement [*Gegenspiel*] to Hegel's phenomenology came to himself" (GA 28, 197). Nonetheless, somebody different "has brought him to himself, i.e., has freed the whole of philosophizing in him," namely "Caroline"[4] (193). She has "by the impact [*Wucht*] of her existence," which took place "beyond convention, moralism, and prevailing taste and the dwarfishness of everyday life, accomplished her great life." This was undoubtedly an opportunity for Heidegger to identify himself with Schelling.

A half-dozen years later Heidegger returns to Schelling. In the context of the being-historical lecture courses Heidegger now allows Schelling a special meaning. In the Schelling-lecture course (summer 1936), Schelling has freed himself of his dependency on Hegel. He is now the "real creative and farthest reaching thinker of this whole era of German philosophy," that is, of German Idealism. He is this thinker "to *such* an extent that he drives German Idealism from within right past its own fundamental position" (GA 42, 6). It is difficult to say what this means.

Heidegger offers an initial clue when he emphasizes that the "innermost center" of Schelling's thinking is the "essence of human freedom," that is, "the question for freedom" (ibid.). Hegel did not see "that just this single thing, freedom, was not isolated for Schelling, but was thought and developed as the essential foundation of the whole, as a new foundation for a whole philosophy" (21). Heidegger becomes even more definite

in *Mindfulness*. Schelling has projected "the deepest form of the spirit within the history of German metaphysics." Indeed, the "spirit and the Absolute" remain "'Subjectum'; but if it [spirit] has its essence in freedom, thus in this freedom a determination of the capability of good and evil is present, which says something more essential than Hegel's 'absolute concept'" (GA 66, 264).

It is plain that Schelling transcends German Idealism, because he is able to confront Hegel with an own understanding of spirit and the Absolute. Heidegger elucidates this event in the history of being in an explanation entitled *The Difference of Hegel's and Schelling's System*. The philosopher emphasizes immediately that this difference builds an aspect of the history of being. The difference between Hegel and Schelling lies in the "determination of 'being'" (GA 86, 212). It is only possible to speak of a difference, when "in advance unanimity in the essential" is given. This is the case insofar as for Hegel and Schelling being is "subjectivity—reason—spirit."

For Schelling and Hegel, "spirit" is "absolute—that is it unifies everything in himself." If this is true, then the "non-spiritual" or "*the sensuous*" belongs to it. Here, in the determination of the relation between the "sensuous" and "reason," lies the difference. For Hegel, the "sensuous" is the "one-sided—abstract." It is not "negated," but considered irrational. Schelling in contrast understands the "sensuous emerging from will and appetite." This is also recognized by Hegel, but the "*unity*" as "unity of ground (base) and existence is nevertheless different"; Schelling's "idea of *identity* and *un-ground* as *in*-difference" is "more original *within* the absolute metaphysics of subjectivity," but "only within." Schelling consequently does not project a thinking that crosses German Idealism's historical borders.

This is articulated again in another context. The "fundamental movement to the *positive*" (GA 88, 149) is decisive for Schelling. Heidegger calls this "Schelling's ἔρως." The "positive" consists: (1) in the fact that "it is not able to be content with the negative of the Fichtian *non-I*, but that it has to conceive *nature* out of itself as the visible spirit"; (2) that it does not integrate "the identity of intelligence and nature" in a "mutual dialectics of both," but that it goes back in a "ground of both," their "*absolute indifference*"; and (3) the "fundamental movement into existence as first" testifies that "the freedom and the will as such" is "the first, what comes forward *from itself*" and "thus becomes beings." With this Schelling reaches "the *highest stage* of his philosophy and perhaps of *western* metaphysics in general" (141). Of course, the "fundamental movement to the existing" unfolds "in a final, highly Christian-theological restorative way." The "growing antagonism to Hegel" renders Schelling "more and more dependent on him, and makes the *positive* more and more rude and backwards oriented." Therefore, "the real exciting moment of Schelling's thinking" lies "*not* in his late philosophy." Especially in this philosophy, Schelling reveals less of "what is necessary for the overcoming of real 'rationalism.'"

The status of Schelling's late philosophy is consequently evident. The "difference between the negative and positive philosophy" is "the reflection of the onto-theological essence of metaphysics—within absolute idealism" (GA 86, 520). But the "onto-theological essence of metaphysics" has its basis in the "ontological difference" (517). Whereas Hegel has "*dissolved*" the "ontological difference" in

"speculative idealism," Schelling has "reconstructed" it in the "difference of *negative and positive* philosophy." In the identity of identity and difference, "ontological difference" has disappeared yet is *not* overcome, as it returns again in the difference of negative and positive philosophy.

THE GERMAN IDEALISM IN THE HISTORY OF METAPHYSICS AND BEING

Heidegger considered German Idealism to be an era in the history of being. In *Contributions to Philosophy*, he allocated it its own place in the third "joining" of "Playing-Forth." Localizing an era in the history of being requires that its descent from the "first beginning" be made visible.

This descent consists in the fact that idealism interprets the ὄν as ἰδέα, and that ἰδέα is understood as "being-seen, re-presentedness—and of course re-presented[ness of] κοινόν and ἀεί" (GA 65, 202). Hence idealism goes back to its Platonic genesis, where the idea is thought as the general and the eternal. The idea is "re-presented" already in Plato. Thus Plato's idealism became "an anticipation of the interpretation of beings as ob-jects for representation."

This place in the history of being is the beginning of the modern age. Here the "*representation* is *ego percipio*, the representedness as such for the *I think*." This representation is at the same time an "*I think myself*," which means that the I gains "certainty." But this certainty is apparently not a consequence of representation, but the "origin of the priority of the *ego*" that lies "in the will to certainty" to be "*certain of itself*."

But this place in the history of being is still not the place of German Idealism. For this first "*self*-representation" still remains in the "particularity of precisely each particular I." In this sense, *this* version of idealism does not even reach Platonic idealism for "what is *thus represented*" "is not yet κοινόν and ἀεί." Therefore, the "self-representation" has to become a "*self*-knowing in the absolute sense." This "absolute" "*self*-knowing knows the necessity of the relation of the object to the I *and* of the I to the object." It has freed itself from the "one-sidedness" of Cartesian philosophy.

This "absolute knowledge" in German Idealism is connected "with divine knowing of the Christian God." It can look back on a tradition in which St. Augustine has already determined "what is represented in the representation of God," that is, as "ideas." Nevertheless, Heidegger insists that such idealism, which can invoke the whole history of metaphysics since Plato, was "developed" "only since Descartes."

"*German Idealism*" (202) is this idealism, which was "delineated in advance in Leibniz," and "attempts to conceive the *ego cogito* on the basis of Kant's transcendental step beyond Descartes at the same time as it moves in direction of Christian dogma." The "aberrance" (203) of German Idealism therefore lies in the combination of "modern Dasein and Christianity," which finally hindered its thinking of the "question of being." In this sense, German Idealism was "*too 'true'-to-life*" and produced countermovements like "positivism, which now celebrates its biologistic triumphs."

In the context of German Idealism's allocation in the history of metaphysics, the following can be understood: Truth as being is thought differently in metaphysics and becomes "the *certainty* that unfolds into an unconditioned trust in spirit and thus unfolds first as spirit in its absoluteness." Now "beings" are "completely displaced into objectness." What Heidegger has in mind with this unusual interpretation becomes more evident in his reference to "machination." For "machination" as the "basic character of beingness" becomes a "subject-object-dialectics, which, as absolute, plays out and arranges together all possibilities of all familiar domains of beings [in the system]."

From this position "there is no bridge to the other beginning." Nevertheless it is important "to know particularly this thinking of German Idealism"; for here "the machinational power of beingness" comes into its "utmost, unconditioned unfolding." Hence the "end is prepared."

The end of metaphysics is prepared in this way that the "self-evidence of being," that is, the neglect of the question of being, "is now systematically extended to the richness of the historicity of spirit and its forms" (203–4). It is Hegel's system appearing as *one* end of philosophy or metaphysics. Schelling's "treatise on freedom" attested to "individual thrusts," but it "nevertheless does not lead to any decision" (204). Hegel and Schelling are nearly codified, as German Idealism remains in its "richness" a location of the history of metaphysics.

NOTES AND REFERENCES

[1] Daniel O. Dahlstrom places more emphasis on Heidegger's reading of Fichte in Dahlstrom, *Heidegger and German Idealism*. In: *A Companion to Heidegger*, ed. Hubert L. Dreyfus and Mark A. Wrathall (Malden, MA: Blackwell Publishers, 2005), 65–79.

[2] The quotations are related to the *Gesamtausgabe* (GA), but, if possible, oriented to existing English translations.

[3] Rockmore writes about Heidegger's reading of Hegel: "Although he prepared a number of texts on aspects of Hegel's thought, he seems finally not to have made much progress toward understanding Hegel's position as a whole" (*Heidegger, German Idealism, and Neo-Kantianism*, ed. by Tom Rockmore (Amherst: New York, 2000), 13). This judgment is based on many hermeneutic presuppositions. Perhaps the most problematic one lies in this question: what does it mean to "understand Hegel's position as a whole"?

[4] Caroline Michaelis (1763–1809), since 1803 married to Schelling, formerly married to August Wilhelm Schlegel, was a woman with a very unusual biography in the early nineteenth century.

13

HEIDEGGER AND NIETZSCHE
Ullrich Haase

One cannot underestimate the influence that Nietzsche had on Heidegger from his early to the very end of his career. While readers often stress the extensive thematic interpretation of Nietzsche from the mid-1930s to the mid-1940s, one should be careful not to overlook that Heidegger's reading of Nietzsche in the early years of the twentieth century have influenced the very beginning of his philosophical development and that it does so even and especially where Nietzsche is not explicitly mentioned. From the question of metaphysics, to the question of the meaning of being, to his reflections on art and nihilism, right down to the fact that when asking *What is Called Thinking* in the years 1951 and 1952, Heidegger very quickly turns toward a reflection on the thought of Friedrich Nietzsche, the latter's philosophical influence is ubiquitous in Heidegger's writings. Where Nietzsche said that "there are no truths, there are only interpretations and interpretations of interpretations," Heidegger, already in *Being and Time*, develops the essentially hermeneutic essence of truth. Where Nietzsche speaks of "the death of God," Heidegger demands the complete extrication of Christian theology from the philosophical problematic. Where Nietzsche thinks of the potential of the doctrine of the *Eternal Return of the Same* to overcome

European Nihilism, Heidegger sees the overcoming of the "metaphysics of presence" by means of the temporal dimension of the existential understanding of the human being. Where Nietzsche thinks the *Overhuman* as the historical potential of human life after the end of the Platonic understanding of human being, Heidegger thinks the possibility of an insertion into *Dasein* as its historical potentiality.

One might say that as Heidegger has taught many of us to think, so Nietzsche has taught Heidegger to think, whatever other influences there might have been in the form of Husserlian Phenomenology, nineteenth-century neo-Kantianism, or the extensive interpretations of Hölderlin's poetry, among others. This makes reading Heidegger on Nietzsche for us about as difficult as it was for him. In the end, thinking "thematically" about a thought that has given rise to one's own, always means thinking against oneself; it means putting into question the very foundation of one's own thinking. As Heidegger said himself, Nietzsche is the thinker who is closest to him and the whole of Heidegger's career is characterized variously by meditations on Nietzsche's thought or the attempt to distance himself from it.

But the relation between these thinkers is not only complicated by way of Heidegger's personal philosophical development. Rather, the reason for which Heidegger puts so much emphasis on Nietzsche's philosophy is not only in this sense "personal," but rests on the conviction that Nietzsche's thought constitutes the historical fulfillment and exhaustion of metaphysical thought as it has reigned over two millennia of European history. Or, rather, it is "metaphysics which by means of Nietzsche deprives itself in a specific way of its own essential potentialities" [HW, 193]. To be able to understand Nietzsche is thus not only a philological endeavor but the attempt at making a historical difference. As Heidegger says in a lecture course on Schelling:

Nietzsche . . ., has been ruined over his main work, the *Will to Power*. Whoever would truly come to understand the reason for this failure would have to become the founder of a new beginning of occidental philosophy. (GA 42, 4)

As this was precisely Heidegger's aim as a philosopher, everything for him depended on such an essential understanding of Nietzsche's philosophy and, consequently, his ability finally to separate his thinking from Nietzsche's.

Thus to understand Heidegger's philosophy it is necessary to follow two alternative and contradictory moments in which Nietzsche and Heidegger, first, are made to say the same thing, if in rather different words—a method complicated by the fact that especially Nietzsche makes his readers aware of the question of style in the presentation of philosophical thinking—in order then to move from here to make the difference between Nietzsche and Heidegger, in such a way that Heidegger comes to say, not the opposite of Nietzsche, but something new

beyond the limits of metaphysical thought. Such an interpretive strategy is supported by Heidegger's own stance, which sometimes involves Nietzsche's thought with the utmost affirmation, while then turning to its clearest condemnation. It is this ambivalence that confuses many readers, especially if they are looking for a critical judgment on a thinker. What is it now? Is Nietzsche the last metaphysician, oriented backwardly by being lost in his reversal of Platonism? Or is Nietzsche the thinker who still waits for us in our future (NI, 340)? In any case, if trying to understand the philosophical stakes in the confrontation of Nietzsche and Heidegger, one needs to avoid the rather meaningless escape route of claiming that the contradictions in Heidegger's statements concerning Nietzsche's philosophy are due to him changing his mind a few times. Great philosophers as they are, neither Nietzsche nor Heidegger ever change their minds.

Indeed, Heidegger's own approach has often followed this ambiguous strategy. It could be useful here to pick up Rita Casale's distinction between the time of Heidegger's encounter with Nietzsche's philosophy from 1910 to 1928, his unthematic critical disengagement [*Auseinandersetzung*] from 1929 to 1935 and his thematic, critical disengagement from 1936 to 1946,[1] as long as one adds Heidegger's later work to this distinction. One will have to bear in mind, though, that these are just strategic differences, which do not allow for a very precise differentiation of his work. Thus, for example, the lecture course from 1938/39, *Towards an Interpretation of Nietzsche's 2nd Untimely Meditation*, while certainly thematic, belongs more to the elaborations of Heidegger's philosophy closer to *Being and Time*, than to the contemporaneous *Nietzsche Lectures*. Yet in all these cases the aim of reading Nietzsche is not to ascertain an abstract "philological truth" of Nietzsche's text. Indeed, philologically speaking, Heidegger's approach might sometimes appear violent if not even unjust. As many interpreters have tried to object: can one not find more in Nietzsche's text? Could one not read him with more hermeneutic generosity? And yet, for Heidegger, Nietzsche is certainly too great a thinker to be in need of such generosity, while his greatness is reflected in his value for our openness to the future. As Heidegger puts this, locating the Nietzsche lectures within the context of his wider "historical lectures": "Nietzsche: to dare the critical dis-engagement [*Auseinandersetzung*] with him who is closest to us and to realize that he is furthest away from the question of being. To understand Nietzsche as the end of metaphysics is the historical approach to the future of occidental thought" (GA 65, 176). In such an engagement with Nietzsche, one should never fall for the impression that Heidegger assumes the chair of the judge who can or should condemn Nietzsche's thought from above, and this not only because of the greatness of Nietzsche's thinking but also because of the historical nature of philosophical thought:

We too have to take a previous thought into view and interpret it from the perspective of our own thinking. As little as Nietzsche and as little as Hegel are we able to posit ourselves outside of history and of "time" and to pretend to an absolute position from which to regard that which has been, as if independent from a determined and therefore necessarily one-sided optic. This holds for us as much as for Nietzsche and Hegel; but also this: that the horizon of our thinking might not even have the essentiality and certainly not the greatness of the question posed by these thinkers. (NI, 115)

To understand this rather exalted place that Nietzsche finds in Heidegger's universe, one needs to make an attempt to understand the essentially historical [*geschichtliche*] nature of Nietzsche's and Heidegger's understanding of philosophy.

* * *

When Heidegger spoke above of the greatness of Hegel's and Nietzsche's thought, then this has to be understood on account of both of these realizing the essential nature of history as to philosophical thought. Where Hegel had ended in the claim that the history of philosophy is identical to the philosophy of history, Nietzsche's maybe most pivotal reflection came in the *2nd Untimely Meditation*,[2] when considering the essentially historical nature of all thinking. In this text Nietzsche does not merely ponder the nature of history, but wonders about the possibility of historical intervention, that is, the creation of the new, the conservation of the given and the destruction of the old. But more than that, Nietzsche asks in this text for the historical task that philosophy is allotted in our age, and, therefore, he also asks for the very possibility of his own thinking. At the end of this text he sketches out a historical methodology of philosophical thinking, which attempts to deal with the historical reality of thought after the death of God, that is, once it has been demonstrated to the philosopher that he cannot take up a position in a purely logical domain outside of historical reality. Philosophical thinking, itself a part of this world, has to address the essentially temporal dimension of thought and, therefore, has to address this in its methodological foundations. When he speaks in subsequent texts about the destruction of Idealism he really has in mind any philosophical stance that presents itself in a theoretical fashion, that is, that adheres to the traditional notion of truth as a thought correctly representing a state of affairs, or, as the philosophers say, as *adequatio intellectus et rei*. Consequently, the question is no longer which one of a set of competing theories is the true one, but what is truth itself? For there to be any promise of a future, Nietzsche says, knowledge must turn its sting against itself, that is, the philosopher has to ask what knowledge is good for and how an answer to this question might change our very understanding of what truth is. From here stems Heidegger's insight into the fact that philosophers have for too long taken the meaning of truth for granted and from here also follows the famous discussion of truth in § 44 of *Being and Time*.

But what has Nietzsche in mind when he speaks of a historical method by means of which history itself must solve the problem of history? In the second half of the text, Nietzsche makes clear that of the three forms of history, the monumental, the antiquarian and the critical; we live in an age characterized by a one-sided prevalence of critique, that is, in an age of essential change that, in its inception, is purely negative, that is, destructive. This idea of a historical malady will later become Nietzsche's thought of nihilism as the truth of European history. It is here in the *2nd Untimely Meditation* that Nietzsche outlines the phases of his work as it is to be developed over the next decades, from the radicalization of critical philosophy in what has come to be called his critical phase, up to the later writings beginning with *Thus Spoke Zarathustra*. The critique of critical history cannot for Nietzsche lead to an affirmation of its opposite, as thought has to engage with what is given, which is to say, derive itself from the given. The critical age can thus only be overcome by a radicalization of critique

and nihilism can thus only be engaged by a more active nihilism.

As thought is to be understood as an action within the historical world, or as Heidegger will later say, as philosophizing is a handicraft, it can no longer appear in the form of a theory representing a present state of affairs. Nietzsche therefore does not present theories of the *Eternal Return of the Same* or the *Will to Power*, but sees these as doctrines or "teachings" [*Lehre*]. Such a doctrine, as Nietzsche says, has more than one "face." It, on the one hand, has to look backwards in order to comprehend the present, while, on the other hand, it has to make a difference with respect to the future. A teaching like the *Eternal Return of the Same* thus incorporates a movement from critique to creation. This is especially clear in the famous passage from the *Zarathustra*, "Of the Face and the Riddle," in which Nietzsche demonstrates the modern nature of the thought as arising from the development of modern physics and the philosophical discourse from Leibniz to German Idealism, while trying to draw the consequences from such a thought in order to transform it into a promise of the future. In such a process the thought changes as does the thinker, while the thinker who does not change with thinking the thought is left behind, failing to understand anything.

Thus the tripartite methodology of Nietzsche's text, separating the moments of creation, preservation, and destruction in history, becomes in Heidegger's work the sequence of the "destruction" [*Destruktion*] of metaphysics in *Being and Time* and the "critical disengagement" [*Auseinandersetzung*] not only from Nietzsche, but throughout the historical lecture courses and always in unison with the "critical disengagement" from metaphysics itself, as Heidegger develops these between *Being and Time* and the mid-1940s, especially in the three books, *Contributions to Philosophy* (GA 65), *Meditation* (GA 66), and *The History of Beyng* (GA 69), but also later on in the question concerning technology. This is how Heidegger characterizes the idea of an *Auseinandersetzung*:

> The historial critical disengagement [*Auseinandersetzung*] . . . moves us into those fundamental attunements [*Grundstimmungen*], in which and from out of which the thinkers are no longer "mutually intelligible" [*verständigt*], where "agreement" is essentially declined, because no agreement of opinions within the same are able to bear whatever truth. . . . For this reason an *Auseinandersetzung* never concerns a calculation of the correctness and incorrectness of doctrines or opinions; the ideas of a schoolmaster, thinking about the "mistakes" which a thinker might have "made" and which are to be eradicated, might have a place in the setting of a "school," but not in the history of being and never in the conversation between thinkers. (GA 66, 69)

I have translated *Auseinandersetzung* here as a "critical disengagement," in order to bring out the methodological idea of Heidegger, insofar as this word, otherwise translated as confrontation, literally refers to "the setting oneself apart from," and it is for this reason that as to the thematic interpretation of Nietzsche in the famous lecture courses Heidegger insists that, insofar as Nietzsche's thought marks an historical transition,

only a dialogue whose own path prepares for a transition can be commensurate to it. Yet in terms of such a transition, Nietzsche's thought will need to be brought to stand wholly on that side

away from which the transition moves towards the other side. (GA 8, 21)

As we have seen above, it is this methodological demand that legitimates the violence of Heidegger's reading of Nietzsche.

Being and Time, the "repetition of metaphysics with the intent of its destruction," as Heidegger describes it, attempts to bring out the historical foundation of contemporary ontology. In this respect it reflects, for example, on the true foundation of our understanding of truth. It is for this reason that many commentators are much happier with the period of *Being and Time* than with the later work, as they often do not quite see the sense of the destruction of metaphysical ontology as intended by Heidegger. In a similar way as the initial step of the doctrine of the *Eternal Return of the Same* is to make the nihilism of our contemporary age palpable and to do so especially where there seems not to be any explicit nihilism at stake, *Being and Time* demonstrates an age that drifts along the path toward the loss of history [*Geschichtslosigkeit*] as which Heidegger understands the Nietzschean notion of nihilism in his famous dictum that "the desert grows." Such *Geschichtslosigkeit* is, therefore, *Ver-wüstung*, that is, desertification. History proper exists therefore not where there is a high value placed on historical science, but only where there is a passing down of decisions and of resoluteness (see GA 66, 167).

It is, then, first with the famous *Turning* of Heidegger, that he attempts to move toward the understanding of a new thinking, which would no longer be metaphysical. The development from asking the question of the meaning of being toward that of the history of Beyng does not accidentally fall into the time in which Heidegger begins his critical engagement with Nietzsche in quite an explicit form, namely by a sustained set of lecture courses lasting from the mid-1930s to the mid-1940s..

* * *

From *Being and Time* onwards, the underlying thread of Heidegger's work can be seen as a critique of science, culminating in his later question of technology. This question, as he makes clear in a text on the *Bedrohung der Wissenschaft*[3] has become possible and necessary with Nietzsche's meditation on science as it started with the *Birth of Tragedy*. It is first with the end of metaphysics that we can understand the question of science properly and as this has been opened with Nietzsche's work, Heidegger can claim that

> the fact that Nietzsche left the university [of Basel] is the sharpest decision of those days against its "science." Seen from this perspective any contemporary reflection on science is only a more or less adequate and modified renewal of the task assigned to us by Nietzsche. (ibid. 7)

Still in 1943, in a text on *Nietzsche's Word God is Dead*, Heidegger understands the essentially important task set by Nietzsche's work as enabling us to think in the midst of the sciences, "to pass by them without disdaining them" (GA 5, 207). Heidegger thus again credits Nietzsche with the insight that the interpretation of nihilism necessarily leads us to a critique of science in the appearance of modern technology. The "sciences" here are always thought of in the more essential sense of *Wissenschaft*, rather than only in terms of the more narrow idea of the "natural sciences."

Thus it is by means of science itself that the essential relation of true knowledge to beings is destroyed and, insofar as the true, essential knowledge is the ground of all science, the modern sciences create themselves the menace to their being by means of a ground- and unfoundedness [*Grund und Bodenlosigkeit*]. (Bedrohung., 8)

This *Grund und Bodenlosigkeit* is explained by the "prevalence of method and its consolidation as technology," an analysis that Heidegger quotes verbatim from Nietzsche who said in § 466 of the *Will to Power* that "it is not the victory of science which characterizes our 19th century, but the victory of scientific methods over the sciences." While Nietzsche does not use the word technology to clarify his critique of science, Heidegger can thus still build his case on Nietzsche's insight.

In these few pages I cannot do this question of the destiny of the modern natural sciences and their reflection by Nietzsche and Heidegger any justice at all. So all I will do here is to point to Nietzsche's reflection, especially in the *Antichrist* as a preparation for Heidegger's critique of technology and quickly to circumscribe Heidegger's argument that finally Nietzsche's critique remains wholly on the side of metaphysics. To do so, let us see if we can find a short quotation clarifying what Heidegger expects from a historical reflection on science if it then is to overcome the metaphysical delimitation of philosophy, thereby putting the critique of Nietzsche into perspective:

> The normative delimitation of the essence of place and of time for all metaphysics is found in a "physics." Roughly speaking, this entails that place and time are not

conceived in terms of their relation to history or to human beings as historical, but rather are thought with respect to mere processes of movement in general. As such, the places and sequences of events in human history also fall into "dimensions," that is, into those realms in which space and time can be measured numerically. The representations of space and time that have held reign for almost two and a half thousand years are of a metaphysical kind. (GA 53, 65f)

This, for Heidegger, is the essential delineation of metaphysics as instituted by Aristotle's *Physics*, and he claims that this idea of physics determining metaphysics holds equally for Thomas Aquinas' doctrine of the *actus purus*, of Hegel's absolute notion, as of Nietzsche's thinking of *Eternal Recurrence* and *Will to Power* (GA 40, 14), especially as both have been developed from the fundamental essence of our understanding of the physical universe since Leibniz and Newton. While Heidegger grants that this is not what Nietzsche has intended (NI, 134), he claims that it was using the language of physiology and biology, which hold him back in the metaphysical context of his time. Already the central reflection of Nietzsche under the title of the physiology of art would therefore condemn him to biologism (NI, 109), in such a way that all further reflections concerning possibility and necessity would reduce these to modes of the real (GA 66, 187). Yet this thinking from out of "reality" is what Heidegger conceives of as the forgetting of the question of being as separate from beings, while Nietzsche, even in his later work still affirms, as Heidegger claims, the primacy of beings (NI, 477).

According to Heidegger, it is for the same reason that Nietzsche's understanding of nihilism remains short of enabling us to experience its metaphysical essence (NII, 336). Nietzsche says that nihilism holds sway when the highest values devalue themselves. While the introduction of the notion of values seems to place the question of science on a ground independent from the presumably value-free methodology of the sciences, thereby opening up a critique of science that, as Nietzsche argued, needs to locate the problem of science outside of its own territory (BT, 5), on closer inspection these values seem themselves derived from the fundamentally "physical" foundation of the doctrines of *Eternal Recurrence* and *Will to Power*. In other words, Nietzsche understands values generally with respect to a "so much, to quantum and number," as Heidegger argues in *Nietzsche's Word: God is Dead* (GA 5, 223). In the same way as Nietzsche's main doctrines are derived from the foundation of modern physics, Nietzsche argues that one would have to make an "attempt to base a scientific order of values on a *numerical scale of measures of forces* . . .—all—other '*values*' are prejudices, naiveties, misunderstandings . . .—they are always *reducible* to that numerical scale of measures of forces."[4]

It is on this account that Heidegger claims that Nietzsche does not exceed the experience of modern metaphysics. Or, the misunderstanding of the origin of values is the reason for which he fails to reach into the true essence of philosophy (GA 40, 152). And this not reaching, according to Heidegger, is philosophically due to his self-proclaimed aim of "reversing Platonism." While Nietzsche was the first thinker properly to have understood the importance of Plato in the history of philosophy, more so than even Hegel, who understood his philosophy as the realization of Platonic *logos*-philosophy, it is exactly for this reason that he cannot proceed to overcome Platonism. Accordingly, insofar as Nietzsche's thought is and was always a consistent but also ambiguous dialogue with Plato (NII, 221), he interprets pre-Socratic thought from a Platonic perspective (GA 65, 219).

The difference between the thought of Nietzsche and Heidegger, then, essentially goes back to the fundamental estimation of the role of philosophical thinking. While Nietzsche keeps himself within the philosophical tradition that since Aristotle sees truth as a determination and a result of thinking (362), Heidegger argues that from all the above follows Nietzsche's misunderstanding of the role of philosophy. Indeed, as Heidegger claims, no doctrine will ever be able to change the fate of our existence. Rather any change has to arise from *Dasein* itself (GA 54, 81). This explains the rather contrary understanding that Nietzsche and Heidegger have concerning the role of philosophy. While Nietzsche thinks of the philosopher as the author of history, and therefore as the most active individual—following the major outlines of Platonic and Leibnizean thought—in Heidegger's understanding the philosopher has a much more modest role to play. It is breaking with the identity of Being and Thinking that finally makes Heidegger say that "only a God can save us" (GA 16, 671).

As we have seen by means of the above confusion of arguments, Heidegger, after decades of reflection on Nietzsche's philosophical thought, a thought that lies at the foundation of his own, will never quite come to a decision concerning its location in the history of European thought. Thus we are still wondering whether Nietzsche is the last metaphysician or whether, in his last steps, Nietzsche has left metaphysics behind (NI, 618). Finally, thus, Nietzsche remains, even after Heidegger's extensive meditation on his thought, the philosopher who is still to come (340).

NOTES AND REFERENCES

[1] Rita Casale, *Heideggers Nietzsche: Geschichte einer Obsession* (Bielefeld, Transcript Verlag, 2010), 21.
[2] Friedrich Nietzsche, "On the Uses and Disadvantages of History for Life," in *Untimely Meditations* (Cambridge: CUP, 1997), ed. Daniel Breazeale, 57–144.
[3] Martin Heidegger, "Die Bedrohung der Wissenschaft," in: *Zur philosophischen Aktualität Heideggers*, vol I, edited by Dietrich Papenfuss und Otto Pöggeler, Frankfurt a. M.: Klostermann 1991.
[4] Friedrich Nietzsche, *Der Wille zur Macht*, Kröner Verlag: Stuttgart 1964, § 710.

14

HEIDEGGER AND DILTHEY: A DIFFERENCE IN INTERPRETATION

Eric S. Nelson

INTRODUCTION

It is arguable how extensively the historically and hermeneutically oriented "life-
philosophy" (*Lebensphilosophie*) of Wilhelm
Dilthey (1833–1911) influenced Heidegger's
intellectual development between the end
of the First World War and the publication of *Being and Time*. There is a strong
thesis maintaining that there was a whole
period in the early and/or mid-1920s and
even a draft of *Being and Time* inspired
by Dilthey.[1] A more minimalistic interpretation supports the claim that the scope
and depth of Dilthey's impact is exaggerated, highlighting instead an intellectual
formation shaped by modern German
Scholasticism, neo-Kantianism, Husserl's
phenomenology, and the general existential
and life-philosophical intellectual climate of
the postwar years.

Others, like Hans-Georg Gadamer, emphasize the importance for Heidegger of Count
Paul Yorck von Wartenburg (1835–97),
Dilthey's more politically conservative,
philosophically speculative, and theologically oriented friend and correspondent
over Dilthey's more humanistic, liberal,
and scientifically oriented articulation of

hermeneutical and life-philosophical themes.[2]
Nonetheless, Heidegger did not disregard
Dilthey in *Being and Time* as he continued
to draw on concepts and strategies from
Dilthey's writings. Heidegger's conclusion
that "the preparatory existential and temporal analytic of Dasein is resolved to cultivate the spirit of Count Yorck in the service
of Dilthey's work" (SZ, 404; BT, 369) indicates both a critical "spiritual" distance from
Dilthey as well as a concern with continuing, in some sense, Dilthey's project, which
Dilthey portrayed as a "critique of historical
reason."

LIFE-PHILOSOPHY AND HISTORICAL LIFE

Dilthey is credited with motivating the introduction of the language of "hermeneutics"
into Heidegger's early thought. Yet, in
addition to hermeneutics and historicity,
Heidegger stresses in his earliest remarks
concerning Dilthey the priority of the question of life, and particularly the being and
reality of the life that poses this question and
he continues this theme in "Wilhelm Dilthey's
Research and the Struggle for a Historical

Worldview" (1925). Heidegger describes here how this question of life and human life reflects a crisis in knowledge and life that has shaken the sciences and ordinary life itself and created the conditions of a "struggle for a historical world view" (S, 148).

What distinguished Dilthey's conception of life from other conceptions, and intrigued the early Heidegger, was the threefold articulation of life in Dilthey's mature magnum opus *The Formation of the Historical World in the Human Sciences* (1910) as (1) experientially lived (*Erlebnis*), (2) structured through and embodied in its expressions and objectifications (*Ausdruck*), and (3) interpretively enacted and understood (*verstehen*). All three modalities are fundamentally historical insofar as they encompass relations of resistance, conflict, and the fullness of a greater life-context or connectedness (*Lebenszusammenhang*).

Heidegger differentiated Dilthey's interpretation of life as historically mediated from the immediacy of both biological—whether mechanistic and vitalistic—conceptions of life as well as appeals to the self-intuitive certainty or introspective transparency of life or consciousness to itself in early lecture courses such as the *Phenomenology of Intuition and Expression* (PIE, 1–29/GA 59). Dilthey's life is consequently fundamentally that of the historian (S, 152); that is, a kind of external, formal, ultimately aesthetic construction of life even if it is does not attain that presumed objectivity of the natural scientist (PIE, 128).

Despite Heidegger's suspicions throughout the 1920s of the exteriority and distance of life to itself in Dilthey, which is indeed what makes human life intrinsically interpretive and hermeneutical for Dilthey, Heidegger recognized at the same time the primordiality of the question of life in Dilthey's thought. In 1925, Heidegger claimed that "Dilthey penetrated into that reality, namely, human Dasein which, in the authentic sense, is in the sense of historical being. He succeeded in bringing this reality to givenness, defining it as living, free, and historical" (S, 159). This is not "pure life," however, as Heidegger notes how Dilthey elucidates the "structures" of "the primary vital unity of life itself" (156). What Heidegger gestures to here is Dilthey's articulation of the "categories of life" (such as selfsameness, doing and undergoing, and essentiality) that are dynamically given in reality and constituted and enacted in the interpretive processes of life itself rather than grasped as abstract and fixed categories or forms of the understanding (*Verstand*). Dilthey's model of an immanent, self-generative, and worldly formation of sense and meaning informed Heidegger's rethinking of categories as existentiell and existenzial structures.

THE ONTIC AND THE ONTOLOGICAL

According to Dilthey, a specifically modernistic conception of life-philosophy calls for interpreting life from out of itself.[3] Dilthey confronted the idealization of the nonconceptual with the unavoidability of conceptual mediation and self-reflection.[4] However, despite Dilthey's hermeneutical approach to the categories of life and the generation of meaning, Heidegger rejects the modernistic epistemological focus of Dilthey's writings while also contending that Dilthey—even if coming closest, but failing like all "life-philosophy" in the end—did not adequately attain the categorical-conceptual clarity and ontological character of the self-articulation of life (GA 21, 216; SZ, 46).

Whereas the turn toward the immanence of life led to empirical and interpretive work in psychology, anthropology, and human scientific inquiry in Dilthey's thought, Heidegger demanded a more radical distinction between ontic inquiry into entities (whether in the human or natural sciences) and the ontological task of phenomenology and philosophy. Accordingly, Heidegger concludes that Dilthey "did not pose the question of historicity itself, the question of the sense of being, i.e., concerning the being of beings. It is only since the development of phenomenology that we are in a position to pose this question clearly" (S, 159).

Heidegger repeats the charge in *Being and Time* as he credits Yorck with prefiguring the ontological difference by distinguishing, in contrast with Dilthey, the historical-ontological and the historiological-ontic (SZ, 399–400).[5] This distinction is not entirely absent in Dilthey, where it entails the unbreakable relation between history as science and history as facticity. For Heidegger, it constitutes the difference between the ontic science of history or historiography (*Historie*) and history as ontological enactment, occurrence, and event (*Geschichte*). Heidegger separates *Historie* from *Geschichte*, a tendency that culminated in his history of being (*Seinsgeschichte*), whereas Dilthey emphasized the mediated intertwinement of historical lived-experience (the lived history that we are) and historical research (the academic history that we study) through self-reflection and interpretation.

Heidegger revisits this issue once again when he argues that in Dilthey's orientation toward the sciences and worldviews, being (*Sein*) is lost in beings (*Seiende*), the world vanishes in a plurality of worlds, and the ontological difference disappears in unending ontic differences (GA 27, 367–8, 382–90).[6] Dasein primordially understands and intuits the world *as* world; it does not first ontically observe and inquire, as Dilthey's hermeneutical experientialism suggests.

The lack of unity, the inductive incompleteness, and the danger of relativity that Heidegger criticizes in Dilthey is a consequence of Dilthey's pre-phenomenological methodology. Heidegger noted that Dilthey prefigured phenomenology and was one of the first to appreciate the radical nature of Husserl's project. Nonetheless, Heidegger consistently maintained throughout his active reception of Dilthey's work from 1918 to 1927 that "we are indebted to him for valuable intuitions, which, however, do not reach down to ultimate and primordial principles and to radical purity and novelty of method"; that is, the self-evidence of things disclosed only by phenomenology (TDP, 140; S, 160).

RESISTANCE AND FACTICAL LIFE[7]

According to Dilthey, the phenomenon of resistance is what enables the formation of a worldly self; that is, a self that cannot purely be itself to the extent that it is always thrown and entangled in relations with others and objects. Self and resistant world are neither independent nor derivative of the other, they are co-given or equiprimordial. It is accordingly a kind of difference that is the condition of self-identity. Resistance is a primary feature of Dilthey's thought for the early Heidegger. Its significance is to some extent underestimated in the reception of Heidegger due to his critique of "reality as resisting" in *Being and Time* (SZ, 209). In that context, Heidegger rejected resistance as proving the externality of the world, arguing that resistance already presupposes world. Despite his suspicion of an epistemological and ontic conception of resistance, which he associated with Dilthey, resistance arguably remains operative at various levels of Heidegger's thinking—from the resistance of things in the breakdown of their instrumental and pragmatic purposiveness to the resistance of existence to human projects and understanding in the impossibility of mastering and appropriating one's own death.

Worldly resistance continues to inform Heidegger's early hermeneutics of factical life, as experience is still related to the "resistant" insofar as experience is both passive and active and implies a differentiating setting-apart-with (*Sich-Auseinander-setzen-mit*) and the self-assertion of what is experienced (GA 60, 9). The origin and goal of philosophy is factical life understanding and articulating itself, as thinking springs from its facticity in order to return to it (8, 15). The resistance of facticity not only opens access to the world through differentiation, it equally resists and blocks access to itself in its everyday indifference (12, 15–16).

Heidegger further transformed Dilthey's conception of resistance as the ruination, counter-movedness, and transversal of life (GA 61, 185). The "there" in and from which the "I" occurs is primordially resistant and ruinating (ibid.). Thus, despite Heidegger's suspicion of resistance as an argument for the self-existence of the external world, Dilthey's notion of resistance is appropriated and transformed in Heidegger's thinking of life's facticity.

In contrast to this account of resistance as (1) the key to individuation and (2) the counter-movement of life, which is immanent to life insofar as it is life itself that presents us with its own ruination and questionability, we can compare (3) Heidegger's critical interpretation of Dilthey's account of resistance in *Being and Time* (GA 61, 130–1; SZ, 209–11). Magda King notes how resistance "characterizes beings within the world, and by no means explains the phenomenon of the world."[8] Resistance occurs from out of the world rather than being the how or way in which the world can be grasped *as* world. It is significant though that Heidegger provides an ontological basis for resistance while rejecting its apparent ontic and empirical character in Dilthey: Resistance "gives a factical existence to understand his exposedness to and dependence upon 'a world of things' which, in spite of all technical progress, he can never master."[9]

Heidegger perceived in his Kassel lectures that the epistemological and methodological aspects of Dilthey's thinking need to be considered in light of the centrality of the question and conception of life. Historical knowledge is self-reflexive, and thus turns on the self relating to itself as well as to its worldly context. The life that reflects upon itself is confronted by its own historicity and conditionality in attempting to know itself. Accordingly, the self is a world to itself along with an environing world and a world of others. For Heidegger, this "self-world in factical life is neither a thing nor an ego in the epistemological sense," rather it has the character of "a definite significance, that of possibility" (GA 58, 232; GA 61, 94). The self-world is not a denial of others, it indicates how the "I" is always referred to others and the world in the equiprimordiality of the self-world, with-world, and environing world (GA 61, 95). These three overlapping co-constitutive worlds make up the "life-world" such that they cannot be separated from each other or interpreted as self-sufficient (96). Hence, despite the constitutive but cogiven significance of the self-world in these early lecture courses, Heidegger problematized the primacy of the subject as separate from life. Life can neither be understood as merely an object or a subject (GA 58, 236).

Dilthey's primary concern is with the historically embedded self and its potential for self-knowledge in which the being who questions is at the same time addressed by and included in the question of "who" it is. Life confronts me as personal in being my own life to live even as the "subject" of that life is inevitably differentiated from itself by living in a historical and worldly context (GS 19, 346–7).[10] Life is then not only the ground of knowledge, it resists it and is thus in the last instance unknowable. The facticity of life is the "last ground of knowledge," such that knowledge cannot penetrate behind its own facticity.[11] Life endeavors to understand itself while remaining non-transparent and ineffable to itself; human life is consequently necessarily interpretive or hermeneutical. Such alterity, excess, and remainder that restlessly pulls life out of itself is a concern in Heidegger's early thinking from the singular thisness (*haecceitas*) of his early work on Duns Scotus to the thisness and mineness (*Jemeinigkeit*) of my existence in *Being and Time*. As Dilthey explicated lived-experience as an exposure to life's facticity in its singularity and contingency, he should be considered a primary source for interpreting Heidegger's early philosophical project of a hermeneutics of factical, or resistant, life (GS 19, 348).

DIVERGENT LEGACIES: HEIDEGGER, MISCH, AND PLESSNER[12]

Heidegger was less influenced by Dilthey's personalist interpretive psychology, even as he appreciated Dilthey as a thinker of human life as immanently self-interpretive, affective, historical, and worldly (GA 20, 161).[13] Dilthey's project was, however, a flawed anti-naturalist personalism and a failed phenomenology that gave the naturalistic and scientistic perspective too much authority (ibid.). Dilthey's works are consequently an ambiguous source for the new phenomenology. Heidegger's criticisms of Dilthey did not go unanswered, as some of Heidegger's earliest critics were former students of Dilthey, such as Georg Misch (1878–1965), or scholars who were in part inspired by his philosophical project, such as Helmuth Plessner (1892–1985). Georg Misch's *Lebensphilosophie und Phänomenologie: Eine Auseinandersetzung der Diltheyschen Richtung mit Heidegger und Husserl* (1929/1930) is one of the first sustained critiques of Heidegger, which he responded to in his lecture-courses and correspondence.

Based on Misch and Plessner's arguments, it could well be argued that Dilthey's full hermeneutical legacy only partially resonates in the ontologically oriented hermeneutics of Heidegger and Gadamer, as neither of them further articulated the emergence and individuation of the biographical human individual immanently from the mediating contexts of a natural-biological and social-historical life. In contrast to Dilthey's historical-anthropological approach to human life, Heidegger asserts the dignity of the ontological and the transcendent over against the complex mediations of life that call for continuing empirical inquiry and interpretive understanding.

From Dilthey's perspective, as Misch argued, Heidegger marginalized the discourses of the natural and human sciences as ontic from the tasks of a fundamental ontology. Heidegger did not recognize or allow for the basic role that Dilthey gave the particular sciences in interdisciplinary research and critical self-reflection. According to Misch, the "dispersion" in ontic multiplicity that Heidegger criticizes in Dilthey's thought is not the negation of the essence and dignity of philosophy, if it is the arena in which philosophy takes place as an event and enactment not of impersonal being and neutral

Dasein—a formal neutrality that is derived "after the fact" from the partiality and perspectivality of historical life in Misch's estimation—but, extending Dilthey's interpretive individualism, of individual and personal biographical life.[14]

It was not in Heidegger's phenomenology then, but in the bio-hermeneutical anthropology of Plessner and hermeneutical logic of Misch that the historically mediated character of nature and spirit continues to be analyzed. Echoing Dilthey's elucidation of an individuated self in the midst of the conditions and forces of natural and historical life, Plessner corrected the partiality of naturalism and an anti-naturalistic personalism by clarifying their immanent consistency in the formation of a relational self: that is, the naturally eccentric and artificial constructive animal called human occurring in the midst of historical life.

NOTES AND REFERENCES

[1] Compare Theodore Kisiel, *The Genesis of Heidegger's Being and Time* (Berkeley: University of California Press, 1993), 313; Otto Pöggeler, "Historicity in Heidegger's Late Work," ed. J. N. Mohanty and R. W Shahan, *Thinking about Being: Aspects of Heidegger's Thought* (Norman: University of Oklahoma Press, 1984), 56.

[2] Hans-Georg Gadamer, "Martin Heidegger's One Path," ed. Theodore Kisiel and John van Buren, *Reading Heidegger from the Start: Essays in His Earliest Thought* (Albany: SUNY Press, 1994), 23.

[3] Wilhelm Dilthey, GS 5, *Die Geistige Welt: Einleitung in die Philosophie des Lebens. Erste Hälfte* (Göttingen: Vandenhoeck und Ruprecht, 1957), 370.

[4] I develop this point in Eric S. Nelson, "Self-Reflection, Interpretation, and Historical Life in Dilthey," ed. H.-U. Lessing, R. A. Makkreel, und R. Pozzo, *Recent Contributions to Dilthey's Philosophy of the Human Sciences* (Stuttgart: Frommann-holzboog, 2011), 105–34.

[5] See Eric S. Nelson, "The World Picture and its Conflict in Dilthey and Heidegger," *Humana.*

Mente: Journal of Philosophical Studies, 18 (2011), 33. Also compare Eric S. Nelson, "Life and World," ed. J. Malpas and H.-H. Gander, *Routledge Companion to Philosophical Hermeneutics* (London: Routledge, 2015), 378–389.

[6] See Eric S. Nelson, "History as Decision and Event in Heidegger," *Arhe*, IV.8 (2007), 102–4; compare Eric S. Nelson, "Heidegger, Levinas, and the Other of History," ed. J. Drabinski and E. S. Nelson, *Between Levinas and Heidegger* (Albany: SUNY Press, 2014), 51–72.

[7] This section draws on Nelson, "The World Picture and its Conflict in Dilthey and Heidegger," 19–38.

[8] Magda King, *A Guide to Heidegger's Being and Time* (New York: SUNY Press, 2001), 261.

[9] Ibid., 261.

[10] Wilhelm Dilthey, *Gesammelte Schriften* 19: *Grundlegung der Wissenschaften vom Menschen, der Gesellschaft und der Geschichte Ausarbeitungen und Entwürfe zum zweiten Band der Einleitung in die Geisteswissenschaften* (ca. 1870–95), edited by Helmut Johach & Frithjof Rodi (Göttingen: Vandenhoeck & Ruprecht, 1982), 346–7.

[11] Wilhelm Dilthey, *Leben Schleiermachers: Auf Grund des Textes der 1. Auflage von 1870 und der Zusätze aus dem Nachlaß*, ed. M. Redeker (Göttingen: Vandenhoeck und Ruprecht, 1970), 53.

[12] I examine this issue further in Eric S. Nelson, "Between Nature and Spirit: Naturalism and Anti-Naturalism in Dilthey," in G. D'Anna, H. Johach, and E. S. Nelson, *Anthropologie und Geschichte. Studien zu Wilhelm Dilthey aus Anlass seines 100. Todestages* (Würzburg: Königshausen & Neumann, 2013), 141–160. Also see Eric S. Nelson, "Biological and Historical Life: Heidegger between Levinas and Dilthey," ed. S. M. Campbell and P. Bruno, *The Science, Politics, and Ontology of Life-Philosophy* (London: Bloomsbury Press, 2013), 15–29.

[13] Compare E. von Aster, *Die Philosophie der Gegenwart* (Leiden: A. W. Sijthoff, 1935), 149, 155.

[14] Georg Misch, *Lebensphilosophie und Phanomenologie* (Leipzig: Teubner, 1931), 47; on Misch's pluralistic and life-immanent personalism, in contrast with Heidegger's history of being, see Eric S. Nelson, "Heidegger, Misch, and the Origins of Philosophy," *Journal of Chinese Philosophy*, 39, Supplement (2012), 10–30.

15

HEIDEGGER AND HUSSERL
Leslie MacAvoy

Although Martin Heidegger engaged with a great many thinkers and philosophical positions in the early part of his career, his relationship to Husserl's phenomenology occupies a place of special importance. In 1916 Edmund Husserl came to the University of Freiburg, where Heidegger was a lecturer, to occupy the senior chair in philosophy. Heidegger had become interested in Husserl's phenomenology several years earlier and was already familiar with *Logical Investigations*, and within the next couple of years, a philosophical friendship developed between them. In time Husserl came to view Heidegger as one of his most talented and promising students, and expected him to play an important role in his phenomenological research program. Indeed, Husserl thought so highly of Heidegger that he exerted considerable effort in advancing the young philosopher's career. He made Heidegger his assistant in 1919 and supported him for an associate professorship at Marburg. Most significantly, Husserl advocated for Heidegger to succeed him in the philosophy chair at Freiburg when he retired in 1928.[1]

Husserl and Heidegger were very close for about a decade, but signs that Heidegger was drifting further from "orthodox" phenomenology became apparent during the Marburg years, though it may not have become apparent to Husserl until about 1927 when *Being and Time* was published and when he invited Heidegger to collaborate with him on an article on phenomenology for the *Encyclopedia Brittanica*. In the course of this (failed) collaboration, the extent of Heidegger's departure from Husserl's approach became evident.[2] Husserl was disappointed by the direction Heidegger's work was taking, and their philosophical relationship deteriorated after 1928 and was broken irremediably when Heidegger became rector of the university and joined the National Socialist party in 1933.

Although Husserl thought that Heidegger had drifted away from phenomenology, Heidegger understood himself to be engaging with important philosophical questions using its approach. This is evident throughout much of his work during the 1910s and 1920s. While direct discussion of Husserl's work rarely appears in Heidegger's texts, the 1925 lecture course *The History of the Concept of Time* is a particularly important exception. This essay will consider Heidegger's claims about the contributions of phenomenology and the way he appropriates these contributions to develop his existential phenomenology and fundamental ontology. Though clearly influenced by Husserl's phenomenology, Heidegger is also critical of it, and a clear understanding of how he responds to Husserl can facilitate a deeper understanding of his own philosophy.

For Husserl phenomenology is a method for studying phenomena by analyzing the intentional acts of which they are correlates and through which they are given. This intentional analysis is meant to yield a logic of experience that can then be used to ground the sciences and epistemology. In *Logical Investigations* the project is to uncover the a priori logical principles that guide thought, which turn out to be principles for the constitution of objects.[3] These objects are validly formed wholes exhibiting a propositional structure. Thus, Husserl likens these logical principles, derived through an analysis focused on the structure of intentional acts and their objects, to an a priori logical grammar.

Husserl argues against a psychologistic approach to logic in *Logical Investigations,* and he attempts to distinguish his position from psychologism by arguing that the objects and content of intentional acts are ideal. However, critics of *Logical Investigations* argued that his approach, which he characterized as a "descriptive psychology," results in its own kind of psychologism. It is generally thought that Husserl introduces the phenomenological reduction in *Ideas* in order to respond to these objections.[4] The reduction functions to suspend the empirical components of an intentional act in order to arrive at its ideal content. The first moment suspends the natural attitude to enable the assumption of the phenomenological attitude. In the natural attitude, we simply live through our intentional relations and focus on the objects with which we are absorbed. By suspending this attitude, we can focus on the acts through which these objects are given. A second moment of the reduction, which is particularly important for responding to the psychologism objection, involves bracketing the empirical ego in order to direct the intentional analysis away from the psychological states of the particular person and toward the meaning content of the experience as it belongs to a transcendental ego. This ideal meaning content can then be analyzed with regard to its structure.

Although Husserl understands phenomenology as contributing to epistemology, Heidegger argues that phenomenology is instead a method for doing ontology. He justifies this claim through an etymological analysis of the term "phenomenology."[5] "Phenomenon" means "that which shows itself in itself" or "that which shows itself as what it is" while "logos" means "what lets something be seen." This yields a definition of phenomenology as a discourse that lets things be seen as what they are. It is, to put it in Husserl's terms, a way of going "to the things themselves." But since to see something as what it is is to see it in its being, Heidegger claims that phenomenology aims to unpack the being of something and thus is a method for doing ontology.

In *History of the Concept of Time* Heidegger maintains that the three most important contributions of phenomenology are intentionality, categorial intuition, and a particular view of the a priori. While this claim signals the importance of Husserl's work, particularly *Logical Investigations*, for Heidegger, closer examination of his discussion of each of these three items reveals that he is already radicalizing Husserl's concepts.

The first concept that Heidegger emphasizes is intentionality. In *Logical Investigations*, Husserl holds that intentionality is the structure of consciousness and indicates that consciousness always has an object, though that object need not be an actual object. Rather, consciousness is always "of" something, and what it is conscious of is the intentional object. Further, Husserl notes that a given object might be intended in different ways, and so he draws a distinction between the object that is intended and the object as it is intended, or between the intentional object strictly speaking and its intentional sense. For instance, Napoleon might be intended either as victor at Jena or as vanquished at Waterloo.[6] Examples of this sort suggest that how something is intended is a function of the predication that is performed in a judgment.

Heidegger's discussion of intentionality is consistent with Husserl's treatment up to a point. He stresses that intentionality is the structure of lived experience (GA 20, 36/ HCT, 29), and like Husserl he rejects the view that intentionality is a kind of psychic directedness toward a physical object. On such a view an act is only intentional if it is in fact directed toward a real object, and this would yield the result that false perceptions or hallucinations would not be intentional. Heidegger dismisses such objections as based on a misunderstanding of intentionality and argues that false perceptions and hallucinations still contain a directedness toward an object. If I think I see a pink elephant, and subsequently realize that I was hallucinating, my hallucination was still directed at an object; it was still "of" something, namely a pink elephant. Any comportment whatsoever has a "directing-itself-toward" as its structure (GA 20, 39–40/HCT, 31).

In other respects, however, Heidegger departs from Husserl. In discussing the different ways an object can be intended, Heidegger uses the example of a chair in a manner that foreshadows his more developed account of how things are disclosed as equipment in worldly contexts through practical comportment. The chair, he says, can be taken as one kind of thing or another based upon different intentional orientations. For instance, the chair can be taken as an "environmental thing," as something to sit in, or it can be taken as a "natural thing" that is simply made of wood (GA 20, 49–50/ HCT, 37–8). The idea of intentional sense, that is, how or as what an object is intended, develops here in the direction of the hermeneutic "as," which plays such an important role in Heidegger's analysis of the reference and significance of equipment that shows up as something to be used for some purpose or another in the course of Dasein's activity (GA 2, 149, 157–8/BT, 144–5, 152–3). For instance, when in the kitchen making a cup of coffee, the kettle shows up as equipment for boiling water. Items of equipment ordinarily show up in terms of their usual meanings (e.g. that a kettle is for boiling water) because they are generally disclosed in relation to equipmental contexts that reflect established practices and the norms that govern them. However, Dasein's projection of a goal is also determinative of how an item of equipment is disclosed. So, for example, if no kettle for boiling water is available, a small pot might be disclosed for the purpose. Alternatively, if one needs to keep a cookbook open to a particular page, the kettle might show up as handy for use as a paperweight. Thus, how the object is taken is a function of one's comportment toward it based on one's project and one's background understanding of the situational context. Regardless of whether one takes the kettle as a utensil for boiling water or as a paperweight, one takes it as ready-to-hand in a sort of practical intentionality. For Heidegger, this "taking-as" is pre-predicative, and thus, in contrast to Husserl, the object as it is intended is given, not in judgment, but in a pre-judgmental intentionality upon which judgment can subsequently be based.

The second Husserlian notion that Heidegger discusses is categorial intuition, which as the term suggests refers to an intuition that apprehends the categorial structure of objects (GA 20, 64/HCT, 48). In introducing this idea, Husserl draws the distinction between empty intentions that merely signify their objects and intuitions that fulfill those intentions by giving the objects that were previously only emptily meant. For instance, if one says that the book is on the table, a state of affairs, namely the book's being on the table, is emptily intended. This same state of affairs can be given in an intuition that fulfills this intention, and such a fulfillment might occur in a perception in which one sees the book on the table. If the intuition fulfills the empty intention, then that means that the intentional object, in this case a state of affairs, is meant in the first case and given in the second. This raises the question of whether the state of affairs is given in simple perception strictly speaking. Husserl claims, and Heidegger agrees, that while certain elements of the state of affairs are given, for example, the book and the table, there are other elements that are not, such as the definite article, the preposition, and the copula "is." Yet, if the state of affairs is given in intuition, which it is, then these elements that are part of the state of affairs must also be given, and so Husserl concludes that there must be a categorial intuition.[7] One reason this is significant for both Husserl and Heidegger is that it challenges those readings of Kant that hold that categories are added by subjectivity to what is given in intuition (Hua XIX/2, 182–4; GA 20, 79/HCT 59). Here the view is that objects are given in intuition as already categorially formed.

For Heidegger categorial intuition has an additional significance, namely that it apprehends being. That is, it is owing to categorial intuition that we can apprehend the book's *being on the table* (GA 20, 71–81/ HCT, 53–60). Thus, it can be argued that categorial intuition is crucial to Heidegger's view that phenomenology is a method for ontology (GA 20, 98/HCT 72). Indeed, many years later in the Zähringen seminar in 1973, Heidegger refers to the importance of categorial intuition for his position (FS, 67). Husserl's abandoning of this important notion in *Ideas* may be one more reason why Heidegger, in his footnotes to *Being and Time*, tends to be rather more approving of *Logical Investigations*.

Because of categorial intuition and the access it gives us to being, Heidegger surmises that phenomenology provides us with a more original sense of the a priori than the one inherited from the tradition, which tends to conceive of it in Kantian terms as a structure of subjectivity that serves as a condition of the possibility of knowledge (GA 20, 99–103/HCT, 72–5). Against this, Heidegger thinks that there are a priori structures of the being of entities, and that these can be drawn out through categorial intuition. Here the differences between Husserl and Heidegger come into sharper relief. For Husserl, categorial intuition was important because it was a way to help us extract the categorial structure of objects with an eye toward identifying the a priori logical principles of their formation or constitution. For Heidegger, on the other hand, the goal is to disclose the structure of being by identifying ontological categories. Thus, for Heidegger phenomenology provides a method for arriving at a new sense of the ontological a priori.

Thus, Heidegger's discussion of the three fundamental contributions of phenomenology is not simply an account of its past accomplishments, but is instead a sketch of its future direction toward ontology. He writes: "We have thus determined that intentionality gives us the proper field of subject matter, the a priori gives us the regard under which the structures of intentionality are considered, and categorial intuition as the originary way of apprehending these structures represents the mode of treatment, the method of this research" (GA 20, 109/HCT, 80). That is, phenomenology is a method for analyzing being because being is given as the a priori element in intentional objects, and categorial intuition gives us a way of isolating this a priori element. The challenge will be to see how Heidegger intends to make good on this sketch of the direction for future phenomenological research.

To do that, it is necessary to consider what Heidegger takes to be the limitation of Husserl's phenomenology. There are two primary objections to mention, both of which are articulated in *History of the Concept of Time*. The first and more important objection is that Husserl fails to explore the being of intentionality because of his uncritical appropriation of the tradition's notion of consciousness, which Heidegger thinks is not drawn from "the things themselves" (GA 20, 140–2, 147/HCT, 102–3, 107). Thus, Husserl is not true to his own phenomenological method when it comes to consciousness, and the result is a distorted view of intentionality modeled on the theoretical attitude, namely, a detached stance wherein intentional objects are construed as presented to consciousness in judgments. Heidegger questions the priority that Husserl gives to the theoretical attitude in his theory of intentionality and claims that to understand the being of intentionality, it is necessary to understand the entity that is intentional. To accept the traditional

view that this entity is consciousness is, for Heidegger, to beg the question on this point.

Heidegger's second objection is to the phenomenological reduction, which he also thinks distorts the investigation of intentionality. Both moments of the reduction noted above are problematic. The first moment of the reduction involves suspending the natural attitude, which Husserl thought would bring the intentional into focus. But Heidegger thinks that the reduction brackets the reality of the intentional and thus takes us away from the phenomenon that should be investigated. He writes:

we start from the real consciousness in the factually existing human, but this takes place only in order finally to disregard it and to dismiss the reality of consciousness as such. In its methodological sense as a disregarding, then, the reduction is in principle inappropriate for determining the being of consciousness positively. The sense of the reduction involves precisely giving up the ground upon which alone the question of the being of the intentional could be based. (GA 20, 150/HCT, 109)

Heidegger also objects to the second moment of the reduction, in which the particularity of the ego is suspended in favor of the transcendental ego. This, too, transforms the character of intentionality from something that is necessarily individuated and mine to something that in principle belongs to anyone. Heidegger thinks that both moments of the reduction focus on the "what" of the intentional experience and ignore the "how" of that experience and thus fail to capture something important about intentionality. This leads Heidegger to conclude that "if the intentional is to be interrogated regarding its manner of being, then the entity which is intentional must be originally given, that is, it must be originally experienced in its manner of being" (GA 20, 152/HCT, 110). In other words, to explore intentionality, we need a phenomenological analysis of the being who is intentional.

That being is Dasein, and Heidegger develops extensive analyses of Dasein and its being in *Being and Time*. Where Husserl focuses on intentionality as a feature of consciousness that can be thought about in abstraction from its existence, Heidegger emphasizes that Dasein is an entity whose essence lies in its existence and whose existence is always individuated and personal (GA 2, 41–2/BT, 41–2). Intentionality, as Husserl claimed and Heidegger averred, is the structure of lived experience, but the structure of Dasein's lived experience is shown by Heidegger's analyses to consist in Being-in-the-world. Dasein's intentional relations are expressed in its practical comportment in the world, which is in turn possible on the basis of the disclosedness of the being of the world and of the entities within it. Thus, Dasein's dealings in the world are the site of its intentionality. But in the end, Dasein's being is not to be understood as coextensive with this comportment. By the end of Division I of *Being and Time*, Heidegger comes to the conclusion that Dasein's Being is care. In *History of the Concept of Time*, Heidegger writes that:

It could be shown from the phenomenon of care as the basic structure of Dasein that what phenomenology took to be intentionality and how it took it is fragmentary, a phenomenon regarded merely from the outside. But what is meant by intentionality—the bare and isolated directing-itself-towards—must still be set back into the unified basic structure of being-ahead-of-itself-in-already-being-involved-in [care]. (GA 20, 420/HCT, 303–4)

This suggests that Husserl's view of intentionality is partial and covers over some more primordial intentionality indicated by Dasein's Being as care. One might take this to mean that care represents a kind of practical intentionality that is more primordial than the intentionality exemplified by the theoretical attitude found in Husserl. However, in *Being and Time* Heidegger writes that "as a primordial structural totality, care lies 'before' every factical 'attitude' and 'position' of Dasein, that is, it is always already *in* them as an existential *a priori*. Thus this phenomenon by no means expresses a priority of 'practical' over theoretical behavior" (GA 2, 193/BT, 187). Thus, the priority of care does not amount to reversing the order of priority that Husserl gives to the theoretical over the practical. While it is true that Heidegger does want to focus more on practical comportment and that he does seem to think of it as a kind of intentionality, the point here is larger—it is that care is the ground of any intentionality at all. Care is not a comportment; it is what makes comportment possible. Dasein's Being as care opens up the world as a sphere of intelligibility that serves as a horizon for the encounter of entities and, through this prior disclosedness, makes comportment toward entities possible. The analysis of Dasein's being as care and Being-in-the-world is the analysis of the entity who is intentional that Heidegger thinks is missing from Husserl's phenomenology.

Husserl himself thought that Heidegger's work was unrecognizable as phenomenology and believed that Heidegger had misunderstood it in drawing it away from epistemology and toward ontology. However, one can readily see that Heidegger was deeply engaged not only with Husserl's work but with what he took to be the task of phenomenology. Heidegger arrives at the position that phenomenology is ontology and requires an analysis of Dasein in part by thinking *through* Husserl's work with the aim of extending and radicalizing it. There can be no doubt that Husserl's philosophy exerted a deep influence on the development of Heidegger's thought.

NOTES AND REFERENCES

1 For biographical information, see Hugo Ott, *Martin Heidegger: A Political Life* (London: Harper Collins, 1993).

2 See Steven Galt Crowell, "Husserl, Heidegger, and Transcendental Philosophy: Another Look at the *Encyclopedia Britannica Article*," in *Husserl, Heidegger, and the Space of Meaning* (Evanston, IL: Northwestern University Press, 2001), 167–81.

3 Edmund Husserl, *Logische Untersuchungen*, hrsg. Elmar Holenstein, *Husserliana: Band XVIII–XIX* (The Hague: Martinus Nijhoff, 1975, 1984); *Logical Investigations*, trans. J. N. Findlay (New York: Routledge, 1970). (Hua VIII, XIX/1, XIX/2).

4 Edmund Husserl, *Ideen zu einer reinen Phänomenologie und phänomenologischen Philosophie: Erster Teil*, hrsg. Karl Schuhmann, *Husserliana: Band III* (The Hague: Martinus Nijhoff, 1950; rev. edn 1976); *Ideas Pertaining to a Pure Phenomenology and a Phenomenological Philosophy*: Book One, trans. Fred Kersten (The Hague: Martinus Nijhoff, 1983).

5 See GA 2, 28–39/BT, 26–37, and GA 20, 110–21/HCT, 80–8.

6 Hua XIX/1, Investigation I.

7 Hua XIX/2, Investigation VI.

16

HEIDEGGER, NEO-KANTIANISM, AND CASSIRER

Peter E. Gordon

Of the many contemporary philosophical schools of the early twentieth century that aroused Heidegger's interest, the neo-Kantian school provoked greatest ambivalence. On the one hand, neo-Kantianism appears, especially in Heidegger's early work, as a paradigmatic philosophy of modernity: It is understood to be afflicted by some of the cardinal errors of the modern world—subjectivism, scientism, and the "forgetting of Being" (*Seinsvergessenheit*). On the other hand, Heidegger trained with the neo-Kantian Heinrich Rickert, and key themes of Kantian and neo-Kantian philosophy left their mark on Heidegger's early thought. Especially during the 1920s, Heidegger made frequent and largely negative reference to neo-Kantianism. His criticism of the philosopher Ernst Cassirer was particularly intense and culminated in the dramatic 1929 confrontation between the two philosophers in Davos, Switzerland.[1]

The neo-Kantian movement in Germany first arose in the later nineteenth century in opposition to dominant trends in both Hegelian and Schopenhauerian philosophy. Following Otto Liebmann's exhortation, "back to Kant," a diverse group of scholars united in the twofold effort of purging

philosophy of its metaphysical obscurities and restoring it to its proper task as a critique of knowledge. In his early work, *Kant's Theory of Experience* (1871), the German-Jewish philosopher Hermann Cohen laid down the movement's guiding insight that Kant was best understood as an epistemologist and a theorist of scientific method. During his tenure as Professor of Philosophy at the Philipps-Universität in Marburg, Cohen, in alliance with his colleague Paul Natorp, became a charismatic leader of the so-called Marburg school where many of the leading philosophers of the early twentieth century were to receive their training. Equally influential was the "Southwestern," or Baden School of neo-Kantianism at Heidelberg and Freiburg, which took shape under the guidance of Wilhelm Windelband, and later Emil Lask and Heinrich Rickert. Whereas the Marburg School focused chiefly on themes in Kantian epistemology, the Southwestern neo-Kantians paid greater attention to the philosophy of value and sought to theorize the epistemological distinction between the natural sciences and human sciences, including history.[2]

Building upon the Kantian idea of a strong divide between theoretical and practical reason, the Southwestern neo-Kantians argued that the law-like (or *nomothetic*) character of explanation in the natural sciences was ill-suited to the understanding of uniquely meaning-laden events in the human sciences. The human realm possessed its own *idiographic* method suitable for understanding unique occurrences rather than law-like regularities. Rickert's theories concerning the distinctive character of concept-formation in historical understanding (as presented in his 1902 book, *The Limits of Concept-Formation in Natural Science*) left a deep imprint on Heidegger's own theories of history. The early Heidegger saw the human understanding of history as grounded in a deeper phenomenon of human historical existence. He contrasted human historicity with what he called the "time-free" realm of nature (HCT, 230). This project comes most to the fore in *Being and Time* where Heidegger seeks to show how Dasein's own world owes its very intelligibility to an underlying temporal projection, or "historicity" (*Geschichtlichkeit*), without which our everyday understanding of historical events would not be possible. This strong view regarding the "primordial" or ontological constitution of historical experience reinforces Heidegger's view that situated cultural-historical understanding is prior to (and deeper than) natural-scientific understanding. The latter is demoted to a species of merely technological reason that requires a decontextualization or "deworlding" (*Entweltlichung*) of Dasein's care-laden world (SZ, 112/ BT, 147). This distinction contributed to Heidegger's well-known view that, due to the dominance of technology and the natural sciences, modernity is prone to misrecognize or forget its proper (*eigentlich*) manner of temporal being. What had been for the Southwestern neo-Kantians an essentially methodological distinction

between two ways of knowing, historical and natural-scientific, became in Heidegger's philosophy an ontological and normative distinction between authentic and inauthentic modes of existence.[3]

Heidegger's attitude toward the Marburg School was more conflicted. His ambivalence was due chiefly to an acknowledged affinity in philosophical doctrine, between transcendental idealism and Heidegger's own view of Dasein as the existential condition for the disclosure of the world. According to Kant, the world owes its order and fundamental intelligibility to the rules and forms (the "categories" and the "pure forms of intuition") that are an essential endowment of the human mind. Insofar as it is only in virtue of these rules and forms that things *appear* as a well-ordered world, we can say that the world of possible experience just *is* the world of appearances governed by the mind. This doctrine of transcendental idealism importantly resembles the doctrine of existential conditions Heidegger's lays down in *Being and Time*: Dasein, Heidegger argues, is the only being endowed with an understanding of Being (or *Seinsverständnis*). This understanding of Being is itself embedded in Dasein's very own manner of being-in-the-world, or existence, whose structure Heidegger anatomizes in the "existential analytic." This analysis reveals the basic modes of existence, or "existentials" that serve as the conditions for the possibility of Dasein's world. The noteworthy resemblance between transcendental idealism (Kant) and the existential analytic (Heidegger) is due to the fact that both doctrines aim to show that the only world of relevance to the human being is the world as it shows up in virtue of certain endowments that are peculiar to human understanding or existence. These endowments are therefore "transcendental conditions" in the Kantian sense. The strong dissimilarity is that, while Kant sees these conditions as grounded in the mind, Heidegger sees them as grounded in existence.

That Heidegger appreciated his philosophical debts to Kant's doctrine of transcendental idealism is obvious. In *Being and Time* he writes that Being is the "*transcendens* pure and simple.*" In a later chapter he suggests that Being is "in the consciousness," and he endorses the transcendental premises of Kant's critical turn: "If what the term 'idealism' says, amounts to the understanding that Being can never be explained by entities but is already that which is 'transcendental' for every entity, then idealism affords the only correct possibility for a philosophical problematic" (SZ, 3/ BT, 22; and SZ, 207–8/BT, 251). But notwithstanding the transcendental character of his project, Heidegger harbored fundamental objections to what he considered the metaphysical premises of Kant's philosophy.[4] Most of all, he rejected the intellectualist premise that the transcendental conditions for possible experience are primarily conceptual rather than intuitive and embedded in worldly existence. The attempt to overturn the priority of concepts in the constitution of a priori synthetic knowledge is among the major tasks of Heidegger's *Kant and the Problem of Metaphysics*.

The desire to overturn the priority of concepts over intuitions may also explain Heidegger's objection to the revisionist interpretation of Kantianism articulated by Hermann Cohen in *The Logic of Pure Knowledge* (1902). On Cohen's view Kant's adherence to the metaphysical independence of the thing-in-itself (*Ding an sich*) represented an embarrassing concession to the naïve empiricism of precritical philosophy. A properly critical perspective demanded that this metaphysical independence be abandoned: the Kantian faculty of sensibility (and space and time as the two pure forms of intuition) could no longer be seen as making an equal contribution, alongside the understanding, to the constitution of knowledge. Instead, Cohen saw space and time as conceptual in nature and he understood the thing-in-itself as an object having its origin in thought alone. Cohen modeled this idea, the "principle of origins" (or *Ursprungsprinzip*) after the calculus, where, on Cohen's interpretation, an infinitesimally small magnitude is generated from logical procedure. The principle of origins distinguishes Cohen's revisionist interpretation of Kantianism as strongly intellectualist and anti-metaphysical in character, and it is precisely this revision that Heidegger found most objectionable. In his Freiburg inaugural address, "What is Metaphysics," Heidegger went so far as to suggest that Cohen's principle of origins misunderstood the priority of thought to existence. The revelation of Dasein's nonfoundational condition was the primary phenomenon of the "nothing" out of which was born negation as a logical function: "The nothing is the origin of negation, not vice versa. If the power of the intellect in the field of inquiry into the nothing and into Being is thus shattered, then the fate of the reign of 'logic' in philosophy is thereby decided. The idea of 'logic' itself disintegrates in the turbulence of a more original questioning."[5]

Heidegger's largely negative assessment of the neo-Kantian legacy also extended Cohen's disciples. Ernst Cassirer (1874–1945) was a German philosopher of Jewish descent who taught at the University of Hamburg during the era of the Weimar Republic (1919–33). With the Nazi seizure of power he was forced into exile and spent the 1930s in transit (staying in Vienna, Oxford, and Sweden) before arriving in the United States in 1941. Early in his career Cassirer authored important studies on the history and philosophy of science, *Substance and Function*, *Einstein's Theory of Relativity*, and *The Problem of Knowledge*, works that reflect his neo-Kantian training at Marburg. In the 1920s Cassirer made a well-known shift—from the critique of reason to the critique of culture: Drawing inspiration from Aby Warburg's library in Hamburg, Cassirer laid out a broad theory of culture in a monumental three-volume study entitled *The Philosophy of Symbolic Forms*, the first volume on language (1923), the second on mythical thought (1925), and the third, entitled "The Phenomenology of Knowledge," on the rise of the natural sciences (1929). In his last years Cassirer authored a work in political theory entitled *The Myth of the State* (published posthumously in 1946), which concludes with critical remarks on Nazism and specifically mentions Heidegger as a philosopher who contributed to what Cassirer calls "the return of fatalism" in modern politics.

Heidegger's opinions of Cassirer were complex. Although Cassirer is not universally acknowledged today as a philosopher of the first rank, during the later 1920s his contemporaries ranked him among the most consequential philosophers in all of Germany. Indeed, Heidegger and Cassirer were often finalists for the most prestigious positions, including the Ernst Troeltsch Chair in philosophy at the University of Berlin (which was ultimately offered in 1930 to Heidegger, who declined it). Because Cassirer had moved beyond the Marburg neo-Kantian emphasis on the epistemology of the natural sciences to embrace the broader domain of human culture, it was plausible that at first Heidegger saw Cassirer as a potential ally for overcoming the science-focused and intellectualist tendencies of modern philosophy. In

a footnote to *Being and Time* Heidegger recalls that in 1923 he had met Cassirer at a Hamburg meeting of the Kant-Society and that "we agreed in demanding an existential analytic."[6]

By the later 1920s, however, Heidegger had come to believe that Cassirer exemplified the cardinal errors of modern philosophy. Heidegger's essential complaint is that Cassirer could not surrender the dogma of transcendental spontaneity, or unconditioned consciousness, that he had inherited from his Kantian antecedents. In *The Philosophy of Symbolic Forms*, volume two, Cassirer characterized primitive myth as a fabric of meaning generated by spontaneous acts of human consciousness. But in *Being and Time* Heidegger expresses skepticism regarding the Kantian principles supporting this characterization: "It remains an open question," Heidegger notes, "whether . . . the architectonics and . . . systematic content of Kant's *Critique of Pure Reason* can provide a possible design for such a task, or whether a new and more primordial approach may not here be needed."[7] In Heidegger's eyes this means that Cassirer had failed to grasp the true significance of myth as an instructive model for the way human beings always find themselves in thrall to rather than as the transcendental authors of cultural meaning. "Mythic Dasein," Heidegger argues, finds itself "delivered up to the world in such a way that it is *overwhelmed by that to which it is delivered up*."[8] Heidegger concludes that mythic Dasein was in this sense comparable to human existence per se insofar as "mythic Dasein is primarily determined by thrownness [*Geworfenheit*]."[9] Myth, in other words, is a welcome phenomenon for existential analysis insofar as it provided an illustration of Dasein in its mode of "average everydayness," where human existence finds itself always-already embedded in a context of engaged understanding and concern.

Heidegger's basic objection to Cassirer's neo-Kantian premise of mental spontaneity came to the fore in the spring of 1929 during their public conversation in Davos, Switzerland. Before their exchange, Heidegger offered a series of independent lectures on "Kant's *Critique of Pure Reason* as a Groundlaying for Metaphysics," a presentation that offered a preview of the argumentation of his book, *Kant and the Problem of Metaphysics*, published later that same year. To understand the stakes of the exchange with Cassirer it is helpful to recall the arguments of the book. Heidegger's reading of Kant was highly controversial and explicitly dissented from the then-dominant interpretation of the Marburg School. Against the Marburg reading of the first *Critique* as a theory of knowledge in service to the natural sciences, Heidegger saw the first *Critique* as a "groundlaying for metaphysics," that is, a preparatory inquiry into the ontological constitution of human being. In contrast to Cohen's emphatically intellectualist reading of synthetic a priori knowledge as conditioned primarily by the pure categories of the understanding, Heidegger insisted that the understanding could not be assigned the primary role in the constitution of experience. He claimed instead that both the understanding and sensibility (the two basic stems of human knowledge according to Kant) were grounded in the faculty of transcendental imagination as their common root. But according to Heidegger the imagination was itself grounded in "primordial temporality." Within Kant's own philosophy, in other words, there lay a hidden challenge to the supremacy of the rational mind. In his independent lectures at Davos Heidegger stated this conclusion in the

strongest terms: It implied "the destruction of the former foundation of Western metaphysics (spirit, logos, reason)." In the 1929 book on Kant, Heidegger added a further (and quite controversial) claim, that Kant first recognized the destructive implications of his own argument but "drew back in fear." Kant subsequently revised his argument for the *Critique*'s second edition so as to preserve reason's sovereignty. Heidegger's own interpretation brought to the surface the "unthought" thought in Kant's philosophy, that is, an understanding of the human being as a creature of insuperable *finitude* (*Endlichkeit*) whose innermost temporal constitution also determines the temporal character of all worldly knowledge.

In their debate at Davos Cassirer offered a series of challenges to this interpretation. Heidegger's antipathies to the neo-Kantian school were surprising, Cassirer said, since one might have thought Heidegger's philosophy itself bore the imprint of neo-Kantianism. Furthermore, Heidegger's interpretation of Kant's first *Critique* could not account for the mind's capacity to grasp forms of knowledge that were nonrelative to the finitude of the human being. Such objectivity was evident both in natural scientific knowledge and in the objectivity of moral truths as theorized in Kant's practical philosophy. Heidegger's philosophy disallowed this species of objectivity and thus implied that "truth is relative to Dasein." Cassirer further objected to Heidegger's portrait of the human being as a creature bound in its innermost constitution to anxiety. Cassirer confessed that he wished to remain faithful to Kant, and that his own philosophy of symbolic forms bore witness to the human capacity to transcend anxiety and to achieve a mode of objectivity through the medium of form. Cassirer's overall assessment of Heidegger's philosophy is summarized in two extensive footnotes that can be found in *The Phenomenology of Knowledge*, the third volume of *The Philosophy of Symbolic Forms*, where Cassirer expresses admiration for Heidegger's existential analytic but insists that its portrait of Dasein remains valid only for the world as it is grasped in the mode of the ready-to-hand. According to Cassirer, the difficulty is that Heidegger's analysis stops at the stage of existential spatiality and temporality and fails to appreciate the transition to a state of being that lies "beyond the existentiality of 'being-there.'"[10] For Cassirer, in other words, Heidegger remained an important theorist of Dasein in the mode of average everydayness but he could not appreciate the nonsubjective status of scientific and ethical knowledge.

Rumor and anecdote have left the impression that the Davos encounter represents a dramatic turning point in Continental philosophy. While the truth is more complex, Cassirer was clearly less charismatic than his interlocutor. Heidegger impressed many participants, especially students, as a thinker alert to philosophy's more urgent concerns. Cassirer's own criticism of Heidegger grew more pronounced in the years following their debate. In an extensive 1931 review of Heidegger's *Kant and the Problem of Metaphysics*, Cassirer offered a penetrating critique of Heidegger's work. According to Cassirer, Heidegger's desire to read Kant as a partisan for the renewal of metaphysics rather than a critic of metaphysics resulted in wilful distortion: "Heidegger speaks no longer as a commentator but as a usurper," Cassirer wrote, "who intrudes as it were on the Kantian system with force of arms to subject it and make it serve his [own] problematic." The key difficulty in Heidegger's interpretation on Cassirer's view was that it deployed (in Heidegger's words) a strategy of "violent"

interpretation to transform Kant's text beyond recognition. This was especially the case for Heidegger's highly original reading of the transcendental imagination as a "common root" beneath the understanding and sensibility, a reading that distorted Kant's own view of unconditioned mental spontaneity in the constitution of experience. Heidegger's emphasis on the essential finitude of human knowledge encouraged paradoxical-sounding language such as the characterization of our knowledge as a "purely receptive spontaneity" (a phrase Cassirer compared to "wooden iron"). Heidegger's interpretation of Kant as a theorist of unqualified finitude and anxiety belonged to "the world of Kierkegaard" and little to do with Kant himself, who remained in Cassirer's phrase "a thinker of the Enlightenment."[11]

Heidegger's critique of Cassirer's philosophy was equally sharp and occasionally verged on polemic. In his winter 1929–30 seminar on "The Fundamental Concepts of Metaphysics," Heidegger complained that "It is a widespread opinion today that both culture and man in culture can only be properly comprehended through the idea of expression or symbol. We have today a philosophy of culture concerned with expression, with symbol, with symbolic forms. [. . .] Yet we must as anew: Is this view of man an essential one?" The philosophy of symbolic forms was according to Heidegger not only incapable of grasping the fundamental condition of Dasein, it actually obstructed any understanding of this condition: "This philosophy of culture at most sets out what is contemporary about our situation, but it does not take hold of *us*," Heidegger explained. "What is more, not only does it not succeed in grasping us, but it unties us from ourselves [. . .] Our flight and disorientation, the illusion and lostness become more acute."[12] This negative verdict on Cassirer and neo-Kantianism is grounded in Heidegger's basic view that philosophy both reflects and reinforces broader facets of the human condition: The general neo-Kantian emphasis on the natural sciences was thus understood as symptomatic of technological modernity, while Cassirer's specific interest in the cultural sciences was deemed an evasion of the more "primordial" questions attending the human condition. Still more troubling was Heidegger's readiness to criticize the neo-Kantian school as a "leveling" philosophy that was "tailor-made for liberalism" whose influence could only be fought with "native-born" teachers.[13] Heidegger also warned a colleague that "we are faced with a choice, either to provide our *German* intellectual life once more with real talents and educations rooted in our own soil, or to hand over that intellectual life once and for all to the growing Jewification [*Verjudung*] in the broad and narrow sense."[14] Such remarks tend to validate Cassirer's complaint during the Davos debate that "Neo-Kantianism has become the scapegoat of the newer philosophy."[15] Whatever our ultimate verdict on the significance of Heidegger's political prejudices, it is clear that Heidegger saw in neo-Kantianism a philosophical school aligned with those features of the modern world for which he felt little sympathy.

NOTES AND REFERENCES

[1] On the Davos encounter, see Peter E. Gordon, *Continental Divide: Heidegger, Cassirer, Davos* (Cambridge, MA: Harvard University Press, 2010); also see Michael Friedman, *A Parting of the Ways: Carnap, Cassirer, and Heidegger* (Chicago: Open Court, 2000); and Dominic Kaegi and Enno

Rudolph (eds), *Cassirer-Heidegger. 70 Jahre Davoser Disputation*, Cassirer-Forschungen 9 (Hamburg: Felix Meiner, 2002).

[2] For an overall history of the neo-Kantian movement, see Klaus Köhnke, *The Rise of Neo-Kantianism: German Academic Philosophy between Idealism and Positivism*, trans. R. J. Hollingdale (Cambridge: Cambridge University Press, 1991); and also Thomas Willey, *Back to Kant: The Revival of Kantianism in German Social and Historical Thought, 1860–1914* (Detroit: Wayne State University Press, 1978).

[3] For a summary of Heidegger's views on Rickert and the Southwestern neo-Kantian school especially as regards the status of history, see Charles Bambach, *Heidegger, Dilthey, and the Crisis of Historicism* (Ithaca, NY: Cornell University Press, 1995).

[4] On this theme see Steven Crowell and Jeff Malpas (eds), *Transcendental Heidegger* (Stanford: Stanford University Press, 2007).

[5] "What is Metaphysics?" in PA, 92

[6] SZ, Div. I, chap. 1, n.xi/BT, Dvis. I, chap. 1, n.xi, 490.

[7] SZ, 51, n. 1/BT, ch. 1, 490, n. xi.

[8] Heidegger, "Review of Cassirer, *The Philosophy of Symbolic Forms*, Volume 2: *Mythic Thought*," in PT, 32–45; quote from 43.

[9] Heidegger, PT, 43.

[10] Ernst Cassirer, *The Philosophy of Symbolic Forms*, Volume III: *The Phenomenology of Knowledge* (New Haven, Yale University Press, 1957) 163, n. 2.

[11] Cassirer, Review of Heidegger, *Kant und das Problem der Metaphysik*, Kantstudien, 36 (1931), 1–26; quote from 24.

[12] FCM, 77.

[13] These remarks come from an official letter Heidegger wrote as rector at Freiburg: Heidegger, "Hönigswald aus der Schule des Neukantianismus" (June 25, 1933), in GA 16, 132–3.

[14] For an historical summary of this 1929 letter, see Ulrich Sieg, "Die Verjudung des deutschen Geistes," *Die Zeit*, December 22, 1989, "Feuilleton," 52.

[15] KPM, Appendix IV, 193–207; quote at 193, where the resonant term "scapegoat" (*Sündenbock*) is mistranslated as "whipping boy."

17

HEIDEGGER AND CARNAP: DISAGREEING ABOUT NOTHING?

Eric S. Nelson

OVERLAPPING ORIGINS

The differences between Heidegger and the prominent Vienna Circle logical positivist Rudolf Carnap (1891–1970) are frequently interpreted as an historical source of the division between a more speculatively and stylistically oriented "Continental philosophy" and a more scientific and logically oriented "Analytic philosophy." Nonetheless, Heidegger and Carnap shared a common intellectual context informed by the Southwest or Baden School of neo-Kantianism, Husserl's phenomenology, the life-philosophy of Dilthey and Nietzsche, the projects of experiential, linguistic and Gestalt-psychological holism, an antagonism toward traditional metaphysics as a reification of life and lived-experience, a suspicion of overly theoretical epistemological and abstract ethical discourses, and also the German youth movement of the years following the First World War.[1]

Because of Carnap's emphasis on applying the new formal logic pioneered by Gottlob Frege and Bertrand Russell to philosophical questions, his commitment to creating a new more logically rigorous form of empiricism, as well as his advocacy of the priority of the natural sciences and perhaps his progressive cultural ideas and social democratic politics, Carnap emerged as one of Heidegger's earliest critics. In "Overcoming Metaphysics through the Logical Analysis of Language," based on an earlier lecture (1929) and first published in *Erkenntnis*, 2, 1931/32, Carnap critiqued Heidegger's depiction of the nothing in "What is Metaphysics?" as a conceptually nonmeaningful confusion that involves the substantializing of the logical operation of negation that senselessly posits and reifies "nothing" as an object by taking it as a noun.

Metaphysical propositions, as well as utterances concerning moral and aesthetic values and norms, are neither false nor uncertain. They are also not hypotheses or conjectures that might be eventually empirically verified. According to Carnap's emotivist or non-cognitivist interpretation of such utterances, they are merely expressions of affective moods and emotional states disguised as theoretical and empirically verifiable propositions. If cognitively valid meaning rests in the possibility of empirical verification, then metaphysics consists of "pseudo-propositions" that are cognitively and epistemically, if not affectively or expressively, senseless.[2]

151

Accordingly, Carnap's and Heidegger's philosophy diverges over three central issues: the significance of nothing, the role of mood in disclosure and philosophical reflection, and the proper task of overcoming metaphysics in contemporary thought.

METAPHYSICS AND THE NOTHING

In his critique of Heidegger's thinking of the nothing as "the metaphysical question," Carnap argued that "the nothing" is derivative of the logical operation of negation. Negation is merely the reversal of an existential proposition, and thus cannot be treated as affirming existence, reality, or an object.[3] Negation immanently and derivatively denies the factual and logical propositions that it depends on for its significance. It is nothing but parasitical on positivity and has no further cognitive meaning. Carnap upholds that Heidegger's proposition that "nothing nothings" (*das Nichts nichtet*) has no genuine cognitive content that can be thematized and validated even as it elicits feelings akin to those evoked in poetry while senselessly ascribing conceptual validity, which consists of empirical verifiability and logical validity, to them.

In Heidegger's thinking, "*Nichts nichtet*" does not substantialize but brings out the verbal character (*nichtet*) of the nothing (*Nichts*). Nothing is neither the affirmation of existence nor a thing—and thus not the reification criticized by Carnap—nor is it a meaningless null. "Nothing" is not so much a substantive idea, as it is a formally indicative or hermeneutical concept for the early Heidegger. "Nothing" is a formal indication (*formale Anzeige*) that interpretively anticipates and opens up the experiential

and performative condition of the negativity that makes human thought—including logical negation and consequently all logic and science—possible.[4] Contrary to Carnap's argumentation, it is the encounter with elementary forms of negativity that makes the conceptual positivity of thought and the "positivism" of scientific inquiry thinkable.[5] Logical negation cannot be primary, since it is rooted in a more originary existential encounter with the negativity of the abyss and lack of ground of the nothingness disclosed in disorienting experiences such as those of radical anxiety, profound boredom, and the anticipation or premonition of one's own death. As dispositionally and affectively rooted in human existence, the apparent neutral and indifferent conceptualization of logical negation presupposes the interruptive encounter with our own groundlessness in lack, loss, frustration, denial, and suffering rather than, as Carnap maintained, the opposite. Rather than the nothing being meaningless, the disclosure of nothingness is in Heidegger's phenomenological analysis the very condition of meaning.

Carnap concluded from his critical linguistic analysis of Heidegger's interpretation of the nothing and of more traditional metaphysical thinkers that metaphysical utterances senselessly reify logical operations in making substantive assertions about being and nothing. Carnap contends that Heidegger's thinking of being exploits and hides the ambiguity of the verb "to be" as copula and the assertion of existence.[6]

The published version of "Overcoming Metaphysics" retains echoes of Carnap's earlier lectures in which metaphysics was critiqued through logical analysis and through a genealogical or genetic tracing of the history of words from meaningfulness to meaninglessness.[7] Primary examples of this transformation and loss of meaningfulness can be traced in words such as soul and God as well as ordinary words such as life, existence, and being when these are understood metaphysically.[8] Their continuing authority rests in their lingering earlier senses and in their affective aura. They have an ideological and obscurantist as opposed to a clarifying and enlightening function. Logical analysis is not purely theoretical in this lecture, as in Carnap's later analysis of language, since it serves an emancipatory function for scientific thought and practical life by therapeutically breaking the absorption in the magic and mania of reified words and the reified systems of thought they support. To this extent, Carnap's earlier project of overcoming metaphysics shares affinities with Heidegger's own early project of destructuring metaphysics and they could be said perhaps to offer two different strategies for returning to lived experience through the critical and emancipatory overcoming of its traditional reification.

LIFE, MOOD, AND MUSIC

In addition to skeptically applying argumentative strategies from the new formal logic to Heidegger's claims about nothingness, section seven of "Overcoming Metaphysics" illustrates Carnap's debt to the anti-metaphysical and interpretively-oriented life-philosophies of Nietzsche and Dilthey. Carnap deploys here Dilthey's argument that metaphysics is a transitional stage lacking both theoretical validity and contemporary practical necessity. Metaphysics is no longer myth and it is not yet art, even if it expresses an emotive state or mood without its non-cognitive character being acknowledged. Metaphysical

and speculative systems are consequently lost discourses alienated from the needs of genuine feeling and theory as well as the demands of practical life. They are at worst reactionary obscurantism and at best impoverished replacements for art, literature, and music in expressing "the feeling of life."[9]

Carnap concludes that "metaphysicians are musicians without musical ability."[10] They dress their lack of expressive talent in the garb of pseudo-theoretical language. He notes in the spirit of Schopenhauer, Nietzsche, and Dilthey that music is perhaps the purest expression of the feeling of life (*Lebensgefühl*); whereas the dogmatic and unverifiable systems of metaphysics confuse feelings with concepts, conflating affective life moods and practical situations and decisions with theoretically valid propositions.[11] This life-feeling or basic orienting mood is neither a mystical nor an elemental force, it is affective and expressive. Carnap, much like Dilthey, distinguishes the immanent articulation of the feeling and expressiveness of life from positing one metaphysical or vitalistic force that externally grounds or underlies life.

While Heidegger stresses the role of affective mood in the constitution of all cognition and experience, including the neutral objectivating or theoretical mood that he argues is the basis of the perspective of logic and science in "What is Metaphysics?" Carnap radically distinguishes and separates an emotivist realm encompassing expressions of mood and feeling in the context of artistic and practical situations from cognitively valid propositions. Propositions are either analytically valid, as in logic and mathematics, or empirically warranted. These latter nonlogical synthetic terms consist of observational empirical statements, nonobservational theoretical statements, and statements of their translation through the use of correspondence rules that contain both kinds of terms.

Despite this apparent duality between the subjective and the objective, Carnap recognized as much as Heidegger the affective grounds of the pursuit of science. He noted, in the context of the growing irrationalism and obscurantism of the late Weimar Republic, that the scientific spirit of dispassionate impartiality is also a mood and an *ethos*:

We too, have "emotional needs" [Bedürfnisse des Gemüts] in philosophy, but they are filled by clarity of concepts, precision of methods, responsible theses, achievement through cooperation in which each individual plays his part.[12]

A TALE OF TWO TURNS

Little would endure of Carnap's and Heidegger's early overlapping points of departure in their later thought. In contrast with Heidegger's shift to a more poetic discourse of being and a radicalized critique of modernity, science, and technology, Carnap's "turn" in the early 1930s involved a transition to a pragmatic-semantic approach to language governed by a "meta-theoretical" and pluralistic principle of tolerance in which metaphysical and ontological questions are bracketed in favour of questions of logical syntax.[13] At the same time, Carnap moved from the more phenomenological and phenomenalist explication of concrete Gestalt-like lived experience (*Erlebnis*) as the generative and reductive basis of scientific explanation in *The Logical Formation of the World* (*Der logische Aufbau der Welt*, 1928) to a more purely "physicalist" (i.e. a

strategically and methodologically justified materialist) interpretation (*Deutung*) of scientific inquiry.[14]

In Heidegger's "being-historical thinking" (*seinsgeschichtliches Denken*) of the 1930s, the logical positivist "overcoming" of metaphysics in "logistics" remains a tacit metaphysics that continues to supress the fundamental question of the meaning of being (*Sein*) and signals the fulfilment and culmination of the history of metaphysics in instrumental calculation.[15] It could be noted that Heidegger answered Carnap indirectly by modifying his approach to the nothing, including adjustments in his later additions to his criticized essay "What is Metaphysics?" and in polemical remarks expressed in 1935.

Heidegger linked the logical positivism of the Vienna Circle and the essay published in the circle's journal *Erkenntnis*, "Overcoming Metaphysics," whose author he does not explicitly name, with various symptoms of modernity such as Russian communism, Americanism, the uprooting and levelling of thinking in reductive instrumental calculation, and the technological destruction of nature.[16] The connection between these apparently unconnected and diverse phenomena is, Heidegger repeatedly states, "no accident."[17] They are unified through the seemingly merely linguistic question of the verb "is" and in being indications of the fateful forgetting of being that culminates in the pathologies of the rationalized and "profaned" world of modernity. Of course, Heidegger linked in this politically troubling passage the logical positivism of the Vienna Circle with modernist cultural and political developments that Carnap, and other members of the so-called "left-wing" of the Vienna Circle such as in particular Otto Neurath, stressed in the 1920s and 1930s. Heidegger diagnosed positivism as yet another symptom of the massification of humans, flight of the gods, darkening of the skies, and dominion of science and technology over nature characteristic of occidental modernity.[18]

NOTES AND REFERENCES

1   On the extensive range of cultural and philosophical influences on the early Carnap, see Gottfried Gabriel, "Introduction: Carnap Brought Home," in ed. S. Awodey and C. Klein, *Carnap Brought Home: The View from Jena* (Chicago: Open Court, 2004), 3–23, and Eric S. Nelson, "Dilthey and Carnap: Empiricism, Life-Philosophy, and Overcoming Metaphysics," *Pli: Warwick Journal of Philosophy*, 23 (2012), 20–49; on the significance of Husserl's phenomenology for the early Carnap, see Guillermo E. Rosado Haddock, *The young Carnap's unknown master: Husserl's influence on Der Raum and Der Logische Aufbau der Welt* (Aldershot: Ashgate, 2008).

2   Rudolf Carnap, "Überwindung der Metaphysik durch logische Analyse der Sprache," in *Scheinprobleme in der Philosophie und andere metaphysikkritische Schriften* (Hamburg: Meiner, 2004), 81, 103.

3   Ibid., 95.

4   I examine nothingness as disorienting interruption, existential enactment, formal indication, and fundamental openness in Eric S. Nelson, "Language and Emptiness in Chan Buddhism and the Early Heidegger," *Journal of Chinese Philosophy*, 37.3 (2010), 472–92; and Eric S. Nelson, "Demystifying Experience: Nothingness and Sacredness in Heidegger and Chan Buddhism," *Angelaki*, 17.3 (2012), 65–74.

5   GA 9, 116.

6   Carnap, "Überwindung der Metaphysik durch logische Analyse der Sprache," 99.

7   Ibid., 83, 88.

8   Ibid., 87, 89.

9   Ibid., 106–7.

10   Ibid., 107.

11   Carnap maintained this distinction between cognitive validity and emotively informed practice for the sake of both theory and practice in the context of the rise of National Socialism in his essay "Theoretische Fragen und praktische Entscheidungen," *Natur und Geist*, 9 (1934), 257–60.

12   Rudolf Carnap, *Der logische Aufbau der Welt* (Berlin: Weltkreis, 1928), xv; Rudolf Carnap, *The Logical Structure of the World*, trans. R. A. George (Berkeley, University of California Press, 1967), xvii. Compare Gabriel, "Introduction: Carnap Brought Home," 11.

13   Rudolf Carnap, *Logische Syntax der Sprache* (Wien: Springer, 1934).

14   On the relation between eliminating metaphysics and the principle of tolerance, see Gottfried Gabriel, "Carnap's 'Elimination of Metaphysics through Logical Analysis of Language'. A Retrospective Consideration of the Relationship between Continental and Analytic Philosophy," in ed. P. Parrini, W. C. Salmon, and M. H. Salmon, *Logical Empiricism: Historical and Contemporary Perspectives* (Pittsburgh: University of Pittsburgh Press, 2003), 37.

15   See ibid., 38.

16   GA 40, 227–8.

17   Ibid., 228; compare Michael Friedman's discussion of this passage in *A Parting of the Ways: Carnap, Cassirer, and Heidegger* (Chicago: Open Court, 2000), 22.

18   GA 40, 29, 34.

18

HEIDEGGER AND ARENDT: THE LAWFUL SPACE OF WORLDLY APPEARANCE

Peg Birmingham

When considering Heidegger's and Arendt's respective thought, all too often the familiar narrative is one of contrast. The story often told is one in which Heidegger is the thinker of mortality and being toward death, while Arendt is the thinker of natality and our capacity for beginning something new through speech and action. Yet, a note Arendt sends Heidegger on the occasion of the publication of *Vita Activa*, the German edition of *The Human Condition*, suggests that this often-repeated narrative is misleading and in need of retelling. Arendt writes:

> You will see that the book does not contain a dedication. Had things worked out properly between us—and I mean *between*, that is, neither you nor me—I would have asked you if I might dedicate it to you; it came directly out of the first Freiburg days and hence owes practically everything to you in every respect.[1]

Important here is Arendt's self-understanding that everything in her book devoted to the question of action "came directly out of the first Freiburg days and hence owes practically everything . . . in every respect" to Heidegger. This note is not Arendt's last word on the debt she owes Heidegger. In 1971, at the conclusion of the second volume of *Life of the Mind*, a book she now dedicates to Heidegger (we may conclude that there now exists a "between"), Arendt turns to Heidegger's "Anaximander Fragment" claiming that Heidegger's essay serves as the basis of her understanding of worldly appearance that for her is the condition for the public space and political action. In what follows, I first examine Heidegger's essay, "The Anaximander Fragment," focusing on his account of the "gathering" that constitutes lawful worldly appearance, which he names "the law of the possible." I then turn to Arendt's reading of Heidegger's essay, examining how it serves as the basis for her understanding of a common world, the world of the "between," which she claims is possible because it has as its condition worldly appearance as such. In conclusion, I argue that Heidegger's account of the lawful space of worldly appearing has significant importance for Arendt's political thought, specifically, providing the foundation for Arendt's claim of a "right to have rights."

HEIDEGGER'S "THE ANAXIMANDER FRAGMENT"

If there is a continuous preoccupation that marks Heidegger's thought from its earliest beginnings in *Being and Time* to the later essays on technology, it is the question of the will to power. Certainly this is the central focus of his essay, *The Anaximander Fragment*. Heidegger begins the essay by noting that he is following Nietzsche's translation of the fragment: "When things have their origin, there they must also pass away according to necessity; for they must pay penalty and be judged for their injustice, according to the ordinance of time" (GA 5, 296/EGT, 13). It is significant that Heidegger compares this earliest of Greek fragments to a "later" fragment in Western thinking, namely, Nietzsche's aphorism: "To *stamp* Becoming with the character of being—that is the *highest will to power*" (GA 5, 306/EGT, 22). Both Anaximander and Nietzsche speak of a fundamental power that comes to be. However, according to Heidegger, Nietzsche does not think the *being* of this power nor does he connect it to the question of justice and injustice. For Heidegger, this is precisely what the Anaximander fragment accomplishes. Heidegger states: "What is Greek is the dawn of that destiny in which Being illuminates itself in beings and so propounds a certain essence of man; that essence unfolds historically as something fateful, preserved in Being and dispensed by Being, without ever being separated from Being" (GA 5, 310/EGT, 25).

Thinking the original unfolding of Being, Heidegger is thinking the original power that allows for lawful worldly appearance. In *Letter on Humanism*, Heidegger names this original power the "enabling power of being." He states: "When I speak of the 'quiet power of the possible' . . . I mean Being which in its favoring presides over thinking and hence over the essence of humanity, and that means over its relation to Being. To enable something here means to preserve it is in its element, to maintain it in its element."[2] This enabling element is the "decisive essence of action [understood] as accomplishment,"[3] that is, that which enables something to unfold in its being. As just noted, Heidegger's focus in *The Anaximander Fragment* is to think the "decisive essence of action," which I suggest is the key reason why Arendt will turn to this essay when thinking the conditions for political action.

For Heidegger, the essence of action is rooted in the worldly appearance taking place between the arrival and departure of Being. In other words, the possibility of action is accomplished in beings appearing and lingering between two absences. Heidegger calls this lingering between two absences, "transiency." The worldly appearance of beings is transient, finite, and contingent. Heidegger states: "Accordingly . . . 'presently' means as much as 'having arrived to linger awhile in the expanse of unconcealment' . . . Such a coming is proper arrival, the presencing of what is properly present. . . ."[4] At the same time, Heidegger warns that the transiency off beings must not be set off from the permanence of Being. The unfolding power of Being never appears as one present being among others; instead, it remains concealed in its luminous letting-presence of beings. Thus, Being is *not* the "absolute actuality" of the unconditioned will. Instead, the power of Being is the "letting-presence" that holds itself back in its giving. Rather than "absolute actuality," Being is potentiality, as that which can never be taken up into actuality; it is that which escapes or refuses all unconditional will to power.

Going further, Heidegger argues that the giving of Being, "is not only giving-away; originally giving has the sense of acceding or giving-to. Such giving lets something belong to one another which properly belongs to it." Heidegger names this "belonging" the "jointure" (Dike) of being. The giving of Being allows for a fundamental belonging or "jointure" among beings. In other words, the common world has at its condition the giving of being that holds things together and allows being to belong together. Heidegger calls this jointure "order." At the same time, this "jointure" (*Dike*) can also be out of joint; this can also be because there is a disjunction between the giving of Being and the beings who linger in this givenness: "Everything that lingers awhile stands in disjunction. To the presencing of what is present, to the *eov* of *eovta*, *doika* belongs" (GA 5, 328/EGT, 42).

Heidegger then introduces another word to describe the giving of appearance: "*brauch*" or "*need.*" *Brauch*, he points out, comes from the Latin *frui*, meaning to brook or to "hand something over to its own essence and keep it in hand, preserving it as something present" (GA 5, 337/EGT, 52). Need or necessity does not mean scarcity, but abundance as the overflowing that needs (*frui*) to give. Heidegger goes on to name this abundance of giving, *Dike*. Dike is the law of belonging; it is that which "compels adaptation and compliance." Dike enjoins order and respect, demanding that beings linger, but not persist, in their appearance: "Enjoining order . . . [Being] delivers to each present being the while into which it is released. But accompanying this process is the constant danger that lingering will petrify into mere persistence" (GA 5, 339–40/EGT, 54). This persistence is another name for the unconditional will to power. Beings therefore appear within lawful bounds that cannot be transgressed without

paying the penalty of injustice (a-*Dike*). To commit injustice is to overstep the boundaries of one's finitude. I shall return to this momentarily.

To better understand how beings could commit injustice, we need to further grasp that for Heidegger the enabling power of being allows for the uniqueness of the self. Heidegger argues that necessity gives each being its own essence, while preserving it in a protective hold of belonging. The self therefore is both singular and plural, both unique and in a relation of belonging-together in being-with. Thus, in giving, *Dike* both gives and preserves the singularity or uniqueness of each individual being in its being-with others. Yet, the self, always conditioned and thrown into the overpowering order of *Dike* without any hope of autonomy, is absolutely accountable for that which happens in the worldly expanse of appearance. Human beings must respect this order: "If what is present grants order, it happens in this manner: as beings linger awhile they give reck [respect] to one another. The surmounting of disorder properly occurs through the letting-belong of reck [respect]" (GA 5, 333/EGT, 47). In respect for the lawful order of belonging-together, the self is given as a responsible and accountable self. Here Heidegger is challenging Kant. For Kant, freedom and responsibility are located in the autonomous subject who is both legislator and subject in a sovereign community of ends. Rather than the Kantian transcendent law that addresses the sovereign subject, Heidegger gives us "the law of the possible" that addresses a thrown and exposed self that finds itself belonging to and in a common world with others. This law, Heidegger claims, cannot be violated by a will to power that seeks to actualize possibility by imposing ultimate meanings or determinations upon it.

Recently, Giorgio Agamben has shown the problematic relation of possibility and actuality, particularly its relation to national identity and sovereignty:

Assuming my being-such, my manner of being, is not assuming this or that quality, this or that character, virtue or vice, wealth or poverty. My qualities and my being-thus are not qualifications of a substance (of a subject) that remains behind them and that I would truly be. I am never *this* or *that*, but always *such*, *thus*. *Eccum sic:* absolutely. Not possession but limit, not presupposition but exposure.[5]

Agamben learns from Heidegger that worldly appearance is first of all an unqualified exposure to the world; it is a limited and lawful exposure that can never be made fully actualized in terms of a sovereign will to power that seeks to understand the self as a set of qualifications or determinations, whether that be at the individual or political level.

ARENDT: ON THE GIVENNESS OF WORLDLY APPEARANCE

While Arendt never mentions Heidegger in *The Human Condition*, nevertheless she reveals her debt to him at the very beginning of her analysis of the *vita* activa by making a distinction between two senses of "publicity." Publicity, she argues, means first of all worldly appearance as such: "For us, appearance— something that is seen and heard by others as well as by ourselves—constitutes reality."[6] The second sense of publicity, she argues, denotes a common world: "Second, the term 'public' signifies the world itself, insofar as it is common to all of us and distinguished

from our privately owned place in it . . . It is related . . . to the human artifact, the fabrication of human hands, as well as to affairs which go on among those who inhabit the man-made world together."[7] Prior to and distinguished from the publicity of a "common world," there is worldly appearing *as such*, although not yet a common, political appearance, the latter being for Arendt constituted through the common interests, the *inter-esse*, of a plurality of human beings.

Although Arendt suggests that the second sense of publicity, the common world of making and acting, has as it condition the first sense of publicity, she spends no time in *The Human Condition* considering this first sense. Only in her reading of Heidegger's *The Anaximander Fragment* does she return to it, arguing that our activity in the common world with a plurality of others depends upon our belonging to the givenness of worldly appearance as such. Indeed, she makes explicit in her reading of Heidegger's essay that the givenness of worldly appearance is precisely what allows for the unpredictability of action as our capacity for beginning something new. In her reading of this fragment, she is particularly interested in Heidegger's understanding of *physis* as unconcealment:

. . . it belongs to the beings that they arrive from and depart into a hidden being. What can hardly have caused but certainly facilitated this reversal is the fact that the Greeks, especially the pre-Socratics, often thought of Being as *physis* (nature), whose original meaning is derived from *phyein* (to grow), that is, to come to light out of darkness. Anaximander, says Heidegger, thought of *genesis* [becoming] and *phthora* [passing away] in terms of *physis*, "as ways of luminous rising and declining."[8]

Physis is *genesis*, an unpredictable appearing. Indeed, she understands this genesis in terms of a "contingent causality" in which the *aitia* are the unpredictable causes of appearance. She then emphasizes the next sentence, "... *as it reveals itself in beings, Being withdraws.*" Arendt's emphasis here is on the original abandonment of appearing itself. More precisely, *physis* is abandonment. Here she is describing how the *aitia*, the constituting powers of appearing, is in an entirely different *ontological* relation to what appears. Or to put it more radically: there is no ontological relation between the potentializing power of being and its actual appearance. More precisely, the emergence of *physis* is not a relation of potentiality and actuality. Again following Heidegger, she argues "the coming and going, appearing and disappearing, of beings always begins with a disclosure that is an *ent-bergen*, the loss of the original shelter (*bergen*) that had been granted by Being."[9] This loss is *not* the suspension of Being, nor is it the abandonment of Being to itself. To think *physis* (coming-to-be of appearance) without any relation to Being in the form of potentiality that is then actualized is to think the letting-be of appearance as such. This is the radical sense of "givenness": there is no relation to Being—Being itself is the relation. Arendt cites Heidegger: "Presumably, Anaximander spoke of *genesis* and *phthora* [generation and decline] ... [that is] *genesis estin* (which is the way I should like to read it) and *phthora ginetai,* 'coming-to-be is,' and 'passing-away comes to be.'"[10] *Genesis estin:* which is the way both Arendt and Heidegger read it. *Physis* as *genesis estin* is the taking place of appearance as such.

Arendt then formulates a *law* of unqualified givenness: "... everything we know has become, has emerged from some previous darkness into the light of day, and this becoming remains its *law* while it lasts."[11] *Genesis estin* contains its own law; it is the law of becoming that holds sway over the abandonment of existence to itself. Following Heidegger on this point, Arendt argues that as finite, we are set adrift in the domain of coming-to-be: "In the beginning, Being discloses itself in being, and the disclosure starts two opposite movements: Being withdraws into itself, and beings are 'set adrift' to constitute the 'realm (in the sense of the prince's realm) of error.'"[12] Again, following Heidegger, Arendt argues that human existence is "irreparable" in the sense of being unjustifiable and without cause. Cut off and adrift from any sovereign constituting power or foundation, we are not, however, without law. The law of becoming (*physis*) is the law or rule of givenness.

To better understand this law, Arendt returns to an insight that inaugurates her reflections on appearance in the first volume of *Life of the Mind:* the instinct for self-preservation is not fundamental to our appearance. The law of becoming that holds sway in givenness is not the law of self-preservation with its accompanying desire for persistence, but instead, it is the law of givenness with its accompanying gratitude and sense of delight. Here she agrees with Heidegger's critique of the sovereign will, which in its desire for self-preservation and persistence breaks with the law of becoming: "The Will as destroyer appears here, too, though not by name; it is the 'craving to persist', 'to hang on', the inordinate appetite men have 'to cling to themselves.' In this way they do more than just err."[13] Following Heidegger, Arendt insists that to persist is "... an insurrection on behalf of sheer endurance." She understands this to mean that "... the insurrection is directed against 'order' (*dike*); it creates the 'disorder' (*adikia*) permeating the 'realm of errancy.'"[14] Disorder is the willful rebellion against the order of becoming in favor of some sort of sovereign endurance. *Adikia* is the rebellion against the lawful appearance of givenness in favor of an insurrectionary sovereign will that seeks to impose itself. Order or the lawfulness of worldly appearance is restored by our ability to say "Yes" to the *genesis estin*. Arendt argues that there is no higher affirmation than to say, "*Amo: volo ut sis*," "I love you, I want you to be"—and not "I want to have you" or "I want to rule you."[15] At the very heart of our capacity to act, therefore, is the unconditional affirmation of the given: *Amo—volo ut sis*.

HEIDEGGER AND ARENDT: A RIGHT TO BELONG OR A "RIGHT TO HAVE RIGHTS"

In the *Origins of Totalitarianism*, Arendt, reflecting on her status of a refugee fleeing Nazi Germany and for whom the universal declaration of human rights proved to be entirely illusory and without any political effect, states:

> The fundamental deprivation of human rights is manifested first and above all in the deprivation of a place in the world which makes opinion significant and actions effective. Something much more fundamental than freedom and justice, which are the rights of citizens, is at state when belonging to the community into which one is born is no longer a matter of course and not belonging no longer a matter of choice. . . .[16]

Arendt goes on to formulate a right more fundamental than the rights of citizens, namely, the right to belong to a political community or what she names "a right to have rights." She states, "We become aware of the existence of a right to have rights . . . and a right to belong to some kind of organized community, only when millions of people emerged who had lost and could not regain these rights because of the new global and political situation."[17] But on what basis do we have a right to have rights? What is the normative foundation for declaring that human beings have a right to belong?

I suggest that Heidegger's "law of the possible" provides this normative foundation. Recall that for Heidegger the law of the possible emerges through the givenness of appearance that allows for an originary belonging together of all beings. This originary belongingness constitutes what can be called "rightful appearance" as such. In other words, an "originary belonging" to worldly appearance as such provides the normative foundation for a right to belong to a political space. Still further, on the basis of the rightful appearance of the human being as such, the mutual recognition and granting of equal rights is a political imperative. While I cannot develop it here, Heidegger's understanding of the lawful givenness of being provides a way to rethink radically the modern problem of political sovereignty. We saw above that originary givenness thwarts any claim to sovereignty (particularly state sovereignty), because it is that which is always outside any identity (including national identity) that could argue for hegemony over unqualified existence. Thus, the basis of the "right to have rights" emerges: the right of givenness, unqualified mere existence, to appear and to belong to a political space.

The "right of givenness" is Arendt's debt to Heidegger. As she herself recognizes in the note she sends him on the publication of the *Vita Activa*, her political thought owes "almost everything in every respect" to Heidegger because he first made her aware of the lawful space of worldly appearance, an originary space of belonging that allows for the common world of political praxis. As Arendt's note and subsequent dedication tell us, while the common world of the "between" can at times be out of joint, it can be regained and built anew because it is sustained by the givenness of being-with and belonging-together, that is, the lawful space of worldly appearance as such.

NOTES AND REFERENCES

1 *Letters 1925–1975, Hannah Arendt and Martin Heidegger*, ed. Ursula Ludz. Translated from the German by Andrew Shields (New York: Harcourt, 2004), 124. (Translation modified). Letter dated October 28, 1960.

2 Martin Heidegger, "Brief uber den Humanismus" (1946) in *Wegmarken* (Frankfurt Am Main: Vittorio Klostermann, 1967), 314. English translation: Letter on Humanism, translated by Frank Capuzzi, in *Basic Writings*, ed. David Krell (New York: Harper and Row, 1977), 196–7.

3 Ibid., 311/193.

4 Martin Heidegger, «Der Sprauch das Anaxamander,» GA 5, 320/34.

5 Georgio Agamben, *The Coming Community*, trans. Michael Hardt (Minneapolis: University of Minnesota Press, 1993), 96.

6 Hannah Arendt, *The Human Condition* (Chicago: University of Chicago Press, 1958), 50.

7 Ibid., 52.

8 Hannah Arendt, *Life of the Mind*, vol. 2 (New York: Harcourt Brace Janovich, 1978), 190.

9 Ibid.

10 Ibid.

11 Ibid., 191, emphasis mine.

12 Ibid., 192.

13 Ibid., 193.

14 Ibid.

15 Ibid., 104.

16 Hannah Arendt, *Origins of Totalitarianism* (New York: HBJ, 1951), 296.

17 Ibid., 297.

19

HEIDEGGER AND GADAMER
Emilia Angelova

On Heidegger's invitation in 1960, Gadamer writes an indispensable text, the introduction for the *Reclam* edition of Heidegger's mid-1930s lectures on the work of art. In the same year the first edition of Gadamer's *Truth and Method* is published, with the last words in the introduction outlining the debt to Heidegger. Again, in 1965, in the foreword to the second edition of *Truth and Method*, Gadamer recognizes deep kinship and affinity with Heidegger, even as he notes several points of difference. This chronology is worth recounting for by 1960 close to 30 years of silence separate the two thinkers. With the silence broken in the 1960s, Gadamer, one of Heidegger's most outstanding students, will stay close to his teacher to the end of his life and beyond.

Gadamer's exposition of philosophical hermeneutics has roots in Heidegger's project of fundamental ontology and revolves on these points: (1) The objectives of knowledge (how far is modern science possible?) bring to the fore a difference that methodological dispute has long served to conceal and neglect dating back at least to Kant's philosophy of subjectivity. The task of hermeneutics exceeds a Kantian distinction based solely on method between human sciences (*Geisteswissenschaften*) and modern natural science. Unconcealment and revealment of

the prejudice of Kantian subjectivity, has a foundation rather in that which precedes and makes possible modern science, and does not limit itself to consciousness or method (including that of historicism of the *verstehende Geisteswissenschaften*) or a given mode of behaviour. (TM, xvii)[1] The term "hermeneutics" as used by Gadamer "denotes the basic being-in-motion of There-being which constitutes its finiteness and historicity, and hence includes the whole of its experience of the world." (2) In an ontological hermeneutics, then, Gadamer follows Heidegger that it is "the nature of the thing itself that makes the movement of understanding comprehensive and universal." This is based on Heidegger's temporal analytic of human existence (Dasein), which has "shown convincingly that understanding is not just one of the various possible behaviours of the subject, but the mode of being of There-being itself" (xviii). (3) Unifying ontological with historical hermeneutics, Gadamer claims that the "universality of the hermeneutic viewpoint" does not admit to an absolute validity arrived at by mere contrasting between historical and dogmatic method. Hermeneutical consciousness "exists only under specific historical conditions" (the principle of effective-history raised to general structural element of understanding) without

165

committing to historical relativity; this is so since "in all understanding of historical tradition 'effective-history' is itself operative (historical consciousness as living precisely involves a 'fundamental distance between the present and all historical transmission')" (xxi).[2] Against a certain "ambiguity" delineated in the received concept of historical consciousness (against claims about ineffability, and Droysen's historicism and Dilthey's conceptually weak conclusion about the culmination of all history in intellectual history), philosophical hermeneutics is hence to show itself in agreement with Heidegger's statement that "being that can be understood is language" (xxiii).

But Gadamer distances himself clearly where the question of the "end of metaphysics" as a science (the "cosmic night" and the "forgetfulness of being" (xxv)) is concerned. He distances himself from the later Heidegger (1) on the question that for Gadamer, the analyses of hermeneutic play (concealment and unconcealment) and of language are intended in a "purely phenomenological sense" (this puts language still in the realms of phenomenological demonstration since what is described is the experience of the subject) (xxiv); and as well, (2) on "assimilating the tradition" (against Heidegger, "I have emphasized the element of the assimilation of what is past and handed down" (xxv)). Gadamer claims proximity rather with Hegel's task of the "infinite relation" ("Hegel's speculative dialectic remains close to us" (xxiv)),[3] he insists that the task is one about maintaining hermeneutic consciousness of the continuity of the subject and the tradition, which "must be awakened and kept awake" (xxv).

Through the end of the 1960s, a period that is intensified as well by his debate with Habermas, Gadamer continues his efforts of thinking through the finitude of understanding, even if he risks becoming, as Habermas calls this, a "three way bridge-builder" between Heidegger and the discourse of the contemporaries.[4] "What is the secret of Heidegger's enduring presence?" asks Gadamer. To begin with, there is much at stake in this early word for secret, for Gadamer, as was mentioned, will not write on his teacher for decades; and Gadamer unambiguously defends Heidegger through both debates with Habermas. Today, Gadamer's own work in philosophical hermeneutics gains new momentum as the early lecture courses by Heidegger are made available and there is increasingly more scholarship engaging hermeneutics and the sciences.

In the 15 essays (written since 1960 and over 25 years) from *Heidegger's Ways*,[5] Gadamer breaks the silence that he had imposed upon himself during the intense debate and discussion that surrounded Heidegger in the period after the Second World War. As Dennis Schmidt notes, far from forgetting his teacher, Gadamer "found the requisite 'distance' needed if he was to write 'about' Heidegger" (HW, xvii). In formulating his own hermeneutics after receiving a philosophical impetus from Heidegger's early hermeneutics of facticity (since 1922, attending the first Freiburg lecture course[6]), and in carrying out his own philosophical project—thinking through the Greek texts, Aristotle, Plato, and beyond—Gadamer's own work is clearly driven by an ethical and political concern for history, and for the life of culture and peoples. Gadamer's distance from his teacher is creative, measured by history, and perhaps also "moral." Gadamer's philosophical hermeneutics preserves a deep fidelity to the project of thinking as interrogation, continually elaborating possibilities opened up by Heidegger. For Gadamer, it is unquestionable that Heidegger takes up with "radicality and boldness" the crisis of the "roots" of the inherited forms of thinking, in the age of closure that is occidental technological reason (193). Yet points of departure and disputation between the two thinkers remain, and this concerns mostly the later Heidegger, the thesis of the end of metaphysics and the "other" beginning.

Surely, Gadamer does not understand himself as a metaphysical thinker. But contra the thesis of the "end" of philosophy, his point of departure is thoroughly marked by commitment to the unity and continuity of the subject through history. This takes the shape of a decisive persistence on attending to the experience of the limits of language and of metaphysics, an attentiveness rather to the hermeneutic play of finite truth: in art (and its relation to truth); in language (and the claims of metaphysics and the positive sciences); and in history (and the open dialogue with the tradition and its texts). To this deep fidelity, yet difference, speaks the acknowledgment from the preface to *Truth and Method*: "Heidegger, like many of my critics, might see in this a lack of ultimate radicality in the drawing of conclusions" (TM, xxv). To this anticipated objection from the teacher, there is offered also the response that "[T]he finite nature of understanding is the manner in which reality, resistance, the absurd, and the unintelligible assert themselves. If one takes this finiteness seriously, then one must also take the reality of history seriously" (xxiii).

It remains essential to Gadamer's philosophical hermeneutics that a deep continuity with the unity of the subject must be preserved. Preserving this unity (recognition, and dialogue) is the task of thinking and interpretation. In this spirit Gadamer defends Heidegger (in 1981), giving important guidance to what the "French readers missed in Heidegger" (starting with Jean-Paul Sartre),

from the "Letter on Humanism": "the theme of ethics" (HW, 11). "What is alive and what is dead" in the thinking of Martin Heidegger, as Gadamer's phrasing runs, is a question decided by the "great thinkers' ability to overcome," "by virtue of what they have to say," "the stylistic resistance and stylistic distance that separates them from the present." By this measure alone Heidegger can proceed beyond and "overcome" the existentialist phase in philosophy, to be a "partner among philosophers included in a philosophical conversation that will continue through tomorrow" (13). Gadamer makes this point in recalling the opening lines of the letter: "For some time now we have not considered the nature of action decisively enough." This is a point worth reiterating for us also. That is, Heidegger's critique, unlike present day's "cultural criticism" (16) was "much more ambiguous"—and this holds of the earliest beginnings, of the "sharp and vehement critique of the 'they', of 'curiosity' and 'idle talk'" (ibid.). The same leveling and flattening with which the critiques of contemporary culture "accuse" the "technological culture" of repressing freedom, is also what takes hold of every aspect of our lives. Since *Being and Time* this "necessary concomitance" of "authenticity with inauthenticity, of the essential [*Wesen*] with the inessential [*Unwesen*], of truth with error [*Irre*]" (17)— defines Heidegger's task of revealment: not in any irrational way and "pathos of existence," but instead in that it "allows for understanding his work as posed to the present."

Gadamer's hermeneutics avoids a romantic criticism of both technology and logical positivism, much in debt to Heidegger's ways (not works) of thinking. Today for us Heidegger's question is posed by the manifestation in philosophy of a growing trend "toward logical clarity, exactness, and verifiability of all assertions," and once again, as Gadamer diagnosed, science is "adorned with unconditional faith." Renewed hermeneutic effort calls on the present, that today's situation has much to learn from Heidegger's "uniqueness" "among all of the philosophical teachers of our time"; for Heidegger's example lies in approaching the "same <thing> from the most diverse perspectives," thus giving the conceptual description the character of the "plastic arts, that is, the three-dimensionality of tangible reality" (ibid.). Today's philosopher, too, needs a warning that where "[t]he entire conceptual analysis is presented as an argued progression from one concept to another" (ibid.), one in turn "demands of philosophy a justification of its very existence" (16).

The last point sums up well the reasoning that Gadamer presents when he argues that there is room for holding off on Heidegger's late talk of the "end" of metaphysics. It is important to resist this talk, since "Heidegger's work" is not to be understood merely from a "historical perspective"; this latter would render it irrelevant to the present, "a slow movement of thinking from the recent past that grows ever more strange as it develops" (ibid.). For Gadamer, the shift claimed by Heidegger can be rendered in clear language: an "awareness of this shift [to talk of end of metaphysics] allows for an understanding" of his work: namely, a "visionary," a "thinker who sees" (17).

As we ponder this insistence on the powers of understanding and dialogue, we should remember that Gadamer's own early years as a student in Freiburg in 1921–2 and onwards were shaken by the "burning questions of a generation"—the horrors of the First World War. For he was no stranger to the sense of "distress" expressed in the lectures by the young Heidegger, a sense of

turbulence marking one "called to thinking as the mission of life": "In a whirl of radical questions—questions that Heidegger posed, that posed themselves to Heidegger, that he posed to himself—the chasm that had developed in the course of the last century between academic philosophy and the need for a world-view seems to close" (19). Gadamer says that after *Being and Time* (in which "a single question is posed and explored") none of Heidegger's later works "operate on a single, unified plane; they belong to different planes" (20). This diagnosis echoes rather the experience of radically bearing witness to a thinking in search of a new language, one better suited to new insights. Gadamer himself locates in Heidegger's own "preparatory" effort of thinking in the 1920s the justification for a continuity between the thinking of Being and the "so-called turn" (*Kehre*): "Heidegger does not so much pose the question of Being in *Being and Time* as prepare for it" (21):

What is happening there [da], what happens as a "Da," is what Heidegger later calls the *clearing of Being* [*Lichtung des Seins*]. A clearing is that which one enters after walking endlessly in the darkness of a forest when, suddenly, there is an opening in the trees letting in the light of the sun—until one has walked through the clearing as well and the darkness envelops one anew. (23)[7]

In short, Gadamer remains committed to that which unifies the various formulations of the question of the thinker, as "truly obsessed with his own affairs [*Sache*]" as Heidegger was. The unmistakable intensity and disclosive power of his encounters and identifications—including the interpretations of Hölderlin ("a type of freeing his tongue"), and concomitant with these interpretations,

Heidegger finding his own "new tone" in the lectures "The Origin of the Work of Art" (in 1936)—suggest only that the changes, far from inserting a break, showed but "stages": "The use of the word *earth* [in the 'Origin of Work of Art' lectures] gave the Being of the work of art a conceptual characterization that showed that Heidegger's Hölderlin interpretations (and these lectures) were stages on his own way of thinking" (22).[8]

NOTES AND REFERENCES

[1] Hans-Georg Gadamer, *Wahrheit und Methode* (Mohr: Tübingen, 1965)/*Truth and Method*, trans. Sheed and Ward Ltd. (1975), ed. Garrett Barden and John Cumming (New York: Crossroad, 1986). Hereafter cited as TM. See on this Robert Bernasconi, *Heidegger in Question* (New Jersey: Humanities Press, 1993), 170–90.

[2] The universality of the hermeneutic aspect and what is elicited in language "embraces the pre-hermeneutic consciousness as well as the modes of hermeneutic consciousness." But this is not relativism. "Even the naïve appropriation of tradition is a 'retelling', although it ought not to be described as a 'fusion of horizons'" (for the latter concept see TM, 486ff).

[3] For more see Hans-Georg Gadamer, *Hegel's Dialectic. Five Hermeneutical Studies*, trans.

P. Christopher Smith (New Haven and London: Yale University Press, 1976).

[4] See Habermas' *laudatio* for Gadamer in 1979 on the occasion of Gadamer's receipt of the Hegel-Prize titled "The Urbanization of the Heideggerian Province." For the debate see J. Habermas, "Zur Logik der Sozialwissenschaften," *Philosophische Rundschau* 14, Beiheft 5, 1966–67. Translation of the section on Gadamer is found in "A Review of Gadamer's *Truth and Method*," appearing in *Understanding and Social Inquiry*, ed. Fred Dallmayr and T. McCarthy (Notre Dame: University of Notre Dame Press, 1977), 335–63.

[5] Hans-Georg Gadamer, *Heidegger's Ways*, trans. John W. Stanley, intr. Dennis J. Schmidt (Albany: SUNY, 1994). Hereafter cited as HW.

[6] In HW 55–6; 126–7; 131–2. See also "Heidegger's One Path," trans. P. Christopher Smith, in ed. Theodore Kisiel and John van Buren, *Reading Heidegger from the Start*, (Albany: SUNY, 1994), 19–35.

[7] For a different reading of darkness, the clearing, and the experience of oblivion of being in Heidegger, see Robert Bernasconi, *Heidegger in Question* (New Jersey: Humanities Press, 1993), 8–9. Also see Eric S. Nelson, "History as Decision and Event in Heidegger," *Arhe*, IV.8 (2007), 97–114.

[8] Heidegger's series of the essay from the 1936 lectures in Frankfurt, which Gadamer attended, first appeared in German in 1950, in the collection *Holzwege*. See also commentary by David Farrell Krell, BW, 24 ff.

20

HEIDEGGER AND MARCUSE: ON REIFICATION AND CONCRETE PHILOSOPHY[1]

Andrew Feenberg

INTRODUCTION

Herbert Marcuse (1898–1979) completed his doctorate in 1922 but decided not to pursue the habilitation that would have qualified him for an academic career. Instead, he returned to Berlin where he established an antiquarian bookstore with a partner. When he read *Being and Time* shortly after its publication in 1927, he reconsidered his options. He believed that unlike the philosophy he had studied previously, Heidegger's philosophy was "concrete," relevant to life. He later said, "We saw in Heidegger what we had first seen in Husserl, a new beginning, the first radical attempt to put philosophy on really concrete foundations—philosophy concerned with human existence, the human condition, and not with merely abstract ideas and principles."[2]

In 1928 Marcuse became Heidegger's student and in 1930 he delivered a brilliant thesis entitled *Hegel's Ontology and the Theory of Historicity*. It is not clear whether Heidegger rejected the work but in any case it would soon be impossible for a Jew like Marcuse to find employment in a German university.[3]

Edmund Husserl, with whom Marcuse also studied, contacted Max Horkheimer on Marcuse's behalf. In 1933 Marcuse joined the Frankfurt Institute for Social Research Institute in exile.

Marcuse's most detailed discussion of his early relation to Heidegger is in a 1972 interview with Frederick Olafson. He observes that he and Heidegger's other students were surprised by their teacher's sudden adherence to Nazism. But he also claims that the gloominess of *Being and Time* already suggests a joyless, repressive concept of existence not incompatible with Nazism. There is one further comment in this interview that illustrates the unreliability of philosophers' self-interpretations. Marcuse says that he had few reservations about Heidegger's thought during this period, which implies that he was a loyal disciple. We will see that this is far from being the case.

In 1934 Marcuse settled accounts publicly with his Heideggerian past in an essay entitled "The Struggle against Liberalism in the Totalitarian State."[4] This essay argues that Heidegger and other Nazi sympathizers such as Carl Schmitt abandoned the fundamental

171

concepts and norms of the philosophical tradition. The "existentialists" attempted to concretize the abstract categories of philosophy but ended up producing new and still more empty abstractions that cancelled the ethical implications of the traditional ones and surrendered thought to power.

In 1947 Marcuse met Heidegger at his hut near Freiberg and came away dissatisfied: Heidegger apparently admitted his political errors but declined to make a public apology. In the following months, in an exchange of letters, Heidegger asserted the moral equivalence of Nazi crimes and the hardships suffered by Germans during and after the war. This was the last straw for Marcuse who denounced his former teacher in a final letter that broke off all relations.[5] Nevertheless, Heidegger's thought had a continuing influence on him.

Marcuse's appropriation of Heideggerian themes divides into two periods. The first phase has been called *Heidegger-Marxismus*. It focuses on the existential problematic of revolutionary action as a form of authentic existence. This phase is cut short not only by historical contingencies but by Marcuse's discovery in 1932 of Marx's *Economic-Philosophical Manuscripts*. The *Manuscripts* offered him a Marxist language and conceptual framework in which to pursue many of the themes of his Heideggerian phase. Much later, in the 1960s, Marcuse focuses on the critique of science and technology. In this period Heidegger again appears as a significant interlocutor, although there are few explicit references.

HEIDEGGER-MARXISMUS

Marcuse was a Marxist all his life. He participated in the soldier's councils in Berlin during the 1919 revolution that followed the First World War and remained true to the socialist ideal to the end. Thus his interest in Heidegger's philosophy may seem surprising. In fact he found in Heidegger the basis for a response to the crisis of Marxism.

With the defeat of the wave of revolutionary offensives that followed the First World War, the mechanistic and economistic Marxism of the prewar period was discredited theoretically. It could neither account for the one successful revolution in Russia—a backward country—nor the failed revolutions that occurred in advanced ones with low proletarian participation. Marxist theorists such as Georg Lukács argued for a theory of class consciousness to explain the actions of the proletariat, both its revolutionary enthusiasms and its disappointing acquiescence. Lukács introduced the concept of reification to describe the objectivistic and instrumentalist culture that blocked revolutionary aspirations in capitalist society.

This is where Heidegger comes in. One could read his theory of inauthenticity and authenticity as an implied critique of reification and a call to historical participation in a radical project of social transformation.[6] This was roughly how Heidegger himself understood his theory in 1933, with disastrous consequences. Marcuse appropriated the same theory for a diametrically opposed politics. Such different interpretations were possible because of what Marcuse would later call the "phony concreteness" of Heidegger's thought. However, at the time Marcuse believed Marxism could grant it truly concrete meaning.

Marcuse develops what I call a "meta-critique" of the Heideggerian concepts. On the one hand, he draws on Hegel and Marx to provide a social content to Heidegger's ontological claims. On the other hand, the Marxist concept of labor is onto-logically grounded in the Heideggerian con-cept of being-in-the-world. Heidegger's *Being and Time* was thus transformed into a politi-cal theory with a normative foundation.[7]

Marcuse argues that subject and object are related most fundamentally, *ontologically*, not through consciousness or knowledge but through labor. Being-in-the-world is now understood as the objectification of the self in the appropriation of thinghood. The relation between this rather forced interpretation and Heidegger's analysis of readiness-to-hand was apparent to Heidegger himself. In his only recorded comment on Marcuse, he says that Marcuse saw a parallel between Marx's claim that being has precedence over con-sciousness and his own rejection of the prior-ity of consciousness in *Being and Time*.[8]

Marcuse reinterpreted the concept of *Dasein* on these terms. Heidegger's concept already represents a concretization of the philosophical concept of the subject. He is influenced by Dilthey in identifying this concrete subject with the living individual as opposed to a pure cognitive function. Marcuse agrees with the general approach, but argues that the material needs of the individual are not merely an ontic complica-tion but belong to its essential nature. The temporality of *Dasein* is now concretized through the notion of labor. *Dasein* must "project" itself, not in the abstract but con-cretely through the transformation of nature. Its fundamental relation to the world, its "being-in" is now explained not just by the individual relationship to ready-to-hand tools, but by the social conditions of labor. This ties its ontologically fundamental rela-tion to the future to its social relations with the others alongside whom it labors.

This radical revision of Heidegger's con-cepts situates the individual in antagonistic relations. Class now enters the ontological domain described by Heidegger. Marcuse asks,

. . . is the world "the same" even for all forms of *Dasein* present within a con-crete historical situation? Obviously not. It is not only that the world of significance varies among particular contemporary cultural regions and groups, but also that, within any one of these, abysses of meaning may open up between different worlds. Precisely in the most existentially essential behaviour, no understanding exists between the world of the high-capitalist bourgeois and that of the small farmer or proletarian. Here the examination is forced to confront the question of the material constitu-tion of historicity, a breakthrough that Heidegger neither achieves nor even ges-tures toward.[9]

From a Heideggerian standpoint this seems a mere substitution of sociology for ontol-ogy. Is there not a more fundamental onto-logical level shared by all these various types of *Dasein*? Marcuse would agree, but he argues that that fundamental level can only be described starting out from the concrete human situation that is characterized by the struggle for the necessities of life.

Marcuse's politics then follow from his concretization of the concepts of inau-thenticity or "fallenness" and authenticity. Inauthenticity is no longer identified with absorption into the anonymity of "*das Man*" but is due to the reification or alienation of labor. Inauthentic objectivism is now iden-tified with the reduction of possibility to actuality in the reified world of the capitalist economy. Authentic action, which Heidegger describes as "precisely the disclosive projec-tion and determination of what is factually possible at the time," that is, the response called for by the situation, is now redescribed as the "revolutionary act" in which the situation—reification—calls for a transformation of the conditions of labor.[10] Marcuse writes, "Knowledge of one's own historicity and concrete historical existence becomes possible at the moment when existence itself breaks through reification."[11]

The existentiale Heidegger introduces appear arbitrary or excessively abstract in the light of Marcuse's meta-critique. But given the collapse of the idea of proletarian revolution, Marcuse's early attempts at concretization appear as arbitrary as Heidegger's. Nevertheless, the meta-critical structure of his Marxist argument will continue to rule his later much less orthodox writings. He will continue to transform philosophical abstractions into ontologized historical categories. The concept of reason is subjected to this treatment in the later critique of technology.

TECHNOLOGY AND RATIONALITY

In 1960 Marcuse published a short article entitled "De l'Ontologie à la Technologie: Les Tendances de la Societé Industrielle."[12] This article promises a forthcoming book that will be *One-Dimensional Man*. The article contains a significant reference to *Being and Time*. Once again Heidegger's text is meta-critically interpreted.

A machine, a technical instrument, can be considered as neutral, as pure matter. But the machine, the instrument, does not exist outside an ensemble, a technological totality; it exists only as an element of technicity. This form of technicity is a "state of the world," a way of existing between man and nature. Heidegger stressed that the "project" of an instrumental world precedes (and should precede) the creation of those technologies which serve as the instrument of this ensemble (technicity) before attempting to act upon it as a technician. In fact, such "transcendental" knowledge possesses a material base in the needs of society and in the incapacity of society to either satisfy or develop them. I would like to insist on the fact that the abolition of anxiety, the pacification of life, and enjoyment are the essential needs. From the beginning, the technical project contains the requirements of these needs. . . . If one considers the existential character of technicity, one can speak of a *final technological cause* and the repression of this cause through the social development of technology.[13]

This passage translates Heidegger's transcendental analysis of worldhood as a system of instrumentalities based on a generalized concept of "care" into the historically specific concept of "technicity" as the system of technology. Heidegger's "care" has become the orientation toward human needs that is intrinsic to instrumental action as such, including modern technology. But service to human needs has been blocked by capitalism. Thus what Heidegger thought of as an ontology of instrumental action unifying human being and world in terms of an unspecified possible end has become a normative account of the failure of technology to realize its quite definite proper end. Marcuse sets up the contrast between a truncated technological "a priori" aimed exclusively at domination and an alternative a priori that would fulfill the *telos* of technology in the creation of a harmonious society reconciled with nature. Technology is not neutral, but rather it is ambivalent, available for two different developmental paths.

In 1964 Marcuse finally published *One-Dimensional Man*. Chapters 5 and 6 can be seen as an implicit response to Heidegger's "The Question Concerning Technology." The problem Marcuse poses is how to explain the connection between capitalism as a system of domination and scientific-technical rationality. Chapter 5 corresponds to Heidegger's discussion of Aristotle and contrasts premodern ontology with modern science. Chapter 6 then explores the science-technology connection and concludes with a discussion of their political role under capitalism.

Marcuse's history of rationality can be read as an alternative to Heidegger's history of being. Marcuse explains that in its ancient Greek form, reason encountered a world of substantial things. For the Greeks, exemplified by Aristotle, things are not composed of functional units awaiting transformation and recombination, but rather they are "substances" with an essence that lays out their form and purpose. "Is" and "ought" are harmonized in the potentialities that belong to the essence. The Greek conception is realized practically in *technē*, the knowledge associated with craft production and artistic creation, which actualizes essence in a material.

This Greek conception of rationality is superseded in modern times by the scientific mode of experiencing and understanding the world. The new a priori has two essential features, quantification and instrumentalization. Science does not address experience in its immediacy but transforms everything it encounters into quantities. This stance eliminates purpose and hence also potentiality from the world. This is the basis of the value-neutrality of science, its indifference to the good and the beautiful in the interests of the true.

The world, now stripped of any valuative features and disaggregated, is exposed to unrestrained instrumental control. Within the framework of scientific research this instrumentalism is innocent enough. Science learns by manipulating its objects in experiments. But the innocence of science is lost when the possibilities of instrumental control opened by the a priori of science are exploited on a much larger scale by technology. This is the inner connection between science and technology. It reveals the inherently technological nature of science hidden in the cloister of the lab. Thus Marcuse writes, "The science of nature develops under the *technological a priori* which projects nature as potential instrumentality, stuff of control and organization."[14]

In support of this view Marcuse cites several passages from Heidegger's writings on science and technology. Heidegger explains that the "essence of technics"—Marcuse's a priori—is the basis of mechanization. "Modern man takes the entirety of Being as raw material for production and subjects the entirety of the object-world to the sweep and order of production." ". . . the use of machinery and the production of machines is not technics itself but merely an adequate instrument for the realization of the essence of technics in its objective raw materials."[15]

Marcuse diverges from Heidegger in arguing that the congruence of science, technology, and society is ultimately rooted in the social requirements of capitalism and the world it projects. As such science and technology cannot transcend that world. Rather, they are destined to reproduce it by their very structure. They are thus inherently conservative, not because they are ideological in the usual sense of the term, or because their understanding of nature is false. Marcuse never calls into question the cognitive value of science and technology. Rather, they are conservative because they are intrinsically adjusted to serving a social order that views being as the stuff of domination. Thus "Technology has become the great vehicle of reification."[16]

On this account capitalism is more than an economic system; it is a *world* in the phenomenological sense of the term. This world is the historical project of a specific historical subject, that is, it is only one possible world among those that have arisen in the course of time. The subject of this world, capitalism, can be displaced by another subject. The question of the future is thus raised.

The progressive alternative Marcuse imagines would have a different mode of experience, of "seeing," from the prevailing one. "The leap from the rationality of domination to the realm of freedom demands the concrete transcendence beyond this rationality, it demands new ways of seeing, hearing, feeling, touching things, a new mode of experience corresponding to the needs of men and women who can and must fight for a free society."[17]

Marcuse develops this idea in *An Essay on Liberation* with his theory of the "new sensibility."[18] The new sensibility projects an aesthetic lifeworld oriented toward needs rather than domination. It would be technological but in a different way, respectful of the potentialities of its objects, both human and natural. Is there a hint here of a response to Heidegger's suggestion that someday art might find the power to again shape worlds? Perhaps so, but by the time Marcuse writes this text Heidegger has disappeared as a reference.

NOTES AND REFERENCES

[1] This chapter is drawn from my book *Realizing Philosophy: Marx, Lukács and the Frankfurt School* (Verso Press, forthcoming 2014).

[2] Herbert Marcuse, *Heideggerian Marxism*, ed. R. Wolin and J. Abromeit (Lincoln and London: University Nebraska Press, 2005), 165–6.

[3] Douglas Kellner, *Herbert Marcuse and the Crisis of Marxism* (Berkeley: University of California Press, 1984), 406, n. 1.

[4] Herbert Marcuse, *Negations*, trans. J. Shapiro (Boston: Beacon, 1968).

[5] Richard Wolin, *The Heidegger Controversy: A Critical Reader* (Cambridge: MIT Press, 1993), 152–64.

[6] Lucien Goldmann, *Lukács et Heidegger* (Paris: Denoel/Gonthier, 1973).

[7] For a full account of these transformations, see Andrew Feenberg, *Heidegger and Marcuse: The Catastrophe and Redemption of History* (New York: Routledge, 2005).

[8] Martin Heidegger, *Four Seminars*, trans. A. Mitchell and F. Raffoul (Bloomington and Indianapolis: Indiana University Press, 2003), 52.

[9] Herbert Marcuse, *Heideggerian Marxism*, ed. R. Wolin and J. Abromeit, (Lincoln and London: University of Nebraska Press, 2005), 16.

[10] Martin Heidegger, *Being and Time*, trans. J. Macquarrie and E. Robinson (New York: Harper and Row, 1962), 345.

[11] Herbert Marcuse, *Heideggerian Marxism*, ed. R. Wolin and J. Abromeit (Lincoln and London: University of Nebraska Press, 2005), 32.

[12] Herbert Marcuse, "De l'Ontologie à la Technologie: Les Tendances de la Societé Industrielle," *Arguments*, 4.8 (1960)

[13] Herbert Marcuse, "From Ontology to Technology: Fundamental Tendencies of Industrial Society," in ed. D. Kellner and C. Pierce, *Herbert Marcuse: Philosophy, Psychoanalysis and Emancipation* (New York: Routledge, 2011), 136–7.

[14] Herbert Marcuse, *One-Dimensional Man* (Boston: Beacon Press, 1964), 153.

[15] Quoted in Ibid., 153–4.

[16] Ibid., 108.

[17] Herbert Marcuse, "Beyond One-Dimensional Man," ed. D. Kellner, *Herbert Marcuse: Towards a Critical theory of Society* (London and New York: Routledge, 2001), 117–18.

[18] Herbert Marcuse, *An Essay on Liberation* (Boston: Beacon, 1969).

PART III:
KEY WRITINGS

21

EARLY LECTURE COURSES
Scott M. Campbell

What are often referred to as "Heidegger's Early Lecture Courses" generally consist of those courses that span the period between 1919 and the publication of BT in 1927. He delivered these courses while he was Husserl's assistant at the University of Freiburg (1919–23) and then an associate professor at the University of Marburg (1923–8). Much of the scholarship on the early Heidegger has focused on how these courses and other texts from that time period develop into his *magnum opus*, BT, the text that established Heidegger's reputation around the world.

One who is familiar with BT will find many of the main ideas from that text sprinkled throughout the early lecture courses, but there are other, less familiar, ideas in these courses, and while Heidegger eventually abandons some of them, the early lecture courses are philosophically interesting in themselves. It is important to remember that these courses are not finished products written for publication but, indeed, lecture courses that were spoken out loud to students. In them, Heidegger is thinking through ideas and explicating philosophical texts, sometimes extemporaneously as many of the texts of these courses are drawn from student notes. Reading these courses, one often has the sense of being a student in them. Thus,

the early lecture courses are intellectually rich and exciting to read in their own right, not just because of the way in which they point toward BT.

It would be impossible to summarize all of Heidegger's early lecture courses in this brief synopsis. My goal here will be to isolate three key themes from those courses: (1) the meaningfulness of life, (2) religious experience, and (3) language and the Greeks. Early on, Heidegger was trying to develop an approach to philosophy that would grasp the immediacy of life-experience in its meaningfulness. Along the way, he engages in an analysis of life-experience in early Christian communities, an interpretation that is pivotal to his understanding of temporality. Once he goes to Marburg in 1923, he embarks upon a number of extraordinary analyses of Plato and Aristotle, with particular emphasis on Greek *logos*. In all of these early lecture courses, he wants to show how human beings understand themselves from within the contexts of their own lives, making his early project a hermeneutics of factical, everyday life. Looking at these themes, we will see that in his early lecture courses, Heidegger was trying to synthesize existential ideas about the contextual meaningfulness of life with ontological concerns about the nature of being.

THE MEANINGFULNESS OF LIFE

In the early lecture courses, one can see why Heidegger was initially thought to be an existentialist. In many of these courses, he is explicitly interested in exploring with his students the intensity of average, everyday life-experience and the philosophical import of that experience. Accordingly, Heidegger is developing a method of doing philosophy so as to grasp human life without turning it into a theoretical or objectified object, in other words, to investigate "The Being of life as its *facticity*" (GA 61, 114/PIA, 85). During these early years, the young Heidegger employed the method of phenomenology. In both GA 56/57 and GA 58, he examines the extent to which phenomenology is a primordial science, but in these and other courses he also questions whether any science can adequately interpret the phenomenon of life. Science, he says, is not able to gain access to the factical life-worlds in which we exist (GA 58, 77). He even says, "the idea of a science of life is an absurdity" (80). Thus, on the one hand, the young Heidegger recognizes that Husserl's phenomenological method advances beyond neo-Kantianism by showing things as they appear and not strictly according to the logical laws of thought. On the other hand, Heidegger does not think that Husserlian phenomenology can adequately grasp the meaningfulness of factical life. The object of phenomenology, for Husserl, was a domain of objects (GA 63, 71/OHF, 56). The "object" of phenomenology for Heidegger was factical life-experience in its meaningfulness.

In BT, Heidegger describes Dasein as being-in-the-world, where the world is understood as a context of meaningful relationships. One can trace this theme through the early lecture courses, starting with the War Emergency Semester of 1919, "The Idea of Philosophy and the Problem of Worldview" from TDP. In that lecture course, he discusses the historical-I, which is the human self understood not according to an arrangement of concepts (e.g. as rational animal, defined by a genus and a specific difference), but rather according to the increasing intensity of historical experience, what he calls "phenomenological life in its ever-growing self-intensification" (GA 56/57, 110/TDP, 84). This concept of the historical-I is the first incarnation of what will later become Dasein. Its explicit historicality, the sense of intensity that it maintains and its connectedness to factical life, conveys a sense of vitality that the more antiseptic term "Dasein" lacks. In GA 58, he explicitly distinguishes scientific experience (the way a botanist studies flowers, the way an art historian looks at Rembrandt paintings, the way that a theologian analyzes a liturgy) from factical life-experience (as one walks through a meadow enjoying the flowers, visits a museum to look at works of art, or attends a mass on Sunday) (GA 58, 65). Indeed, this lecture course in particular contains a variety of everyday examples, which show that factical life, even trivialities, are the stuff of philosophical analysis (104). We cannot take a theoretical or epistemological view of life, but rather view it factically in its meaningful character. He says:

Drinking tea, I take my cup in my hand. In conversation I have my cup standing before me. It is not the case that I grasp something colorful or even that in myself I grasp data of perception as a thing, and this thing as a cup, which is determined in time and space, something that gives itself in perceptual succession, something that could also eventually not exist. "My cup, out of which I drink"—its reality fulfills itself in meaningfulness, the cup is meaningfulness itself. I live factically always *caught in meaningfulness*, and every meaningfulness has its encirclement of new meaningfulnesses . . . I live in the factical as in a wholly particular *context* of meaningfulnesses, which are continually permeating one another, i.e. every meaningfulness is meaningfulness for and in a context of tendency and a context of expectation, which constructs itself ever anew in factical life. (104–5)

There is a particular concentration of worlds within the self-world, what he calls the intensifying concentration (*Zugespitztheit*) of the life-worlds in the self-world, and Heidegger describes here the layers of manifestation permeating each other that can be explicated from one's own self-life (54–5). Indeed, one must go further than brute experience and see that Heidegger is trying to grasp that primal, hidden domain that is the source or origin of the immediacy of life in its meaningfulness. In OHF from 1923, the last lecture course that Heidegger delivers in Freiburg as Husserl's assistant, he claims, emphatically, that "*Dasein [factical life] is being in a world*" (GA 63, 80/OHF, 62). Thus, in OHF, we see that it is being itself that underlies factical life and constitutes the primal source of life's engagement or encounter with the world.

In GA 61, Heidegger's notion of factical life changes to show that while human beings do live within rich and varied contexts of experience, they can also be so absorbed in the world that they misinterpret themselves. In this course, he outlines four categories of factical life: inclination, distance, blocking-off, and making things easy. These categories are based on how life manifests a temporal, caring movement into the self-world, the with-world, and the environing-world. They indicate the various ways in which life

identifies itself with these care-worlds so completely that it entirely loses a sense of itself. These categories are all modes of factical life's ruinance. Inclination shows factical life's self-sufficiency (*Selbstgenügsamkeit*) within those worlds. In its caring movement, life is inclined toward the world and bears its heaviness. The world and its distractions weigh life down. There is a distance between life and the world, but factical life destroys that distance or, rather, transposes that distance into the world itself, and then becomes a search for worldly measure: "rank, success, position in life (world), catching-up, advantage, calculation, bustle, noise, style . . ." (GA 61, 103/PIA, 77). The distance between life and world becomes exclusively a worldly phenomenon. Weighed down by the heaviness of the world and seeking after worldly success, factical life is still *there*, but it is blocking-off access to itself (GA 61, 107 /PIA, 80). There is an elliptical movement whereby life circles itself without ever finding itself. Heidegger develops these categories from Aristotle's claim in the *Nicomachean Ethics* that "virtue is difficult and vice is easy," and so the fourth and final category of factical life is effectively the ground for the other three. Human beings are always trying to make things easier for themselves such that life's caring movement into the world manifests as a kind of carelessness.

In these early lecture courses, we find Heidegger making a realistic portrayal of human life. We live within rich contexts of meaningful relationships, which consist of the connections and relations we have to other people, to objects, to the outside world, and to ourselves (the with-world, the environing-world, and the self-world). But the worlds in which we live can also be deceiving. We can be so taken in by them that we fail to see ourselves, identifying human life completely with the world in which we live. When Heidegger describes authenticity in BT, we find this same confluence of revelation and deception, so that Dasein is always both in the truth and in untruth (SZ, 222/ BT, 265). Note, too, that although Heidegger will not thematize the structure of *aletheia* as a simultaneous revelation and concealment/ errancy until much later, it is tacitly operative here in the early lecture courses.

RELIGIOUS EXPERIENCE

During the winter semester of 1920–1 and the summer semester of 1921, Heidegger presents a fascinating series of lecture courses on religious life. In the first of these courses, "Introduction to the Phenomenology of Religion," he is trying to grasp the intensity and immediacy of life-experience in the primal Christian communities. This is consistent with his approach to factical life during this period. His analysis in this course is of a particular community of people, and consequently it is less abstract than some of his analysis in BT. The course divides into two main parts. The first part is a general meditation on the method of formal indication. The second part uses the letters of St. Paul to capture the factical immediacy of life in the early Christian communities. Heidegger shows how categories of life can be applied to the factical lives of religious people.

His meditation on formal indication in this lecture course on religious life is particularly instructive. It is clear from this course that the primary goal of formal indication is to develop a method, grounded in phenomenology, which can sustain the temporal and historical movement of human life. He looks at three different approaches to

the historical here: the first is Platonic, the second is pragmatic, and third is based on life-philosophy. The Platonic approach, he says, renounces history. According to Heidegger, the approaches found in both pragmatism and life-philosophy are epistemological and objectify the historical, subjecting it to human manipulation. Thus, none of these approaches adequately captures the genuine historical movement of life.

It is possible that Heidegger would have spent the entire lecture course on these methodological ruminations, but at one point during the semester students in the course complained to the Dean of the University of Freiburg that this class actually contained no religious content. Immediately, Heidegger shifted gears and engaged upon a phenomenological analysis of the letters of Paul. In these interpretations Heidegger is trying to grasp the temporal immediacy of the lives of the early Christians, who believed that Jesus' return was imminent and so the world could end at any moment. There is a profound sense of urgency in Paul's letters as he exhorts them to become Christians (GA 60, 100/PRL, 70). Their factical lives as Christians are thus structured by faith, knowledge, and the *parousia* (the second coming of Christ), and these structures are grounded in the temporality of their own lives. When the early Christians asked Paul when Jesus will return, Paul turns the question back on them, forcing them to make a critical decision about who they are and what kind of life they want to lead. While they do not know exactly when Jesus will return, they are called upon to understand themselves as Christians: "it is essential that the word (*Verkündigung*) always remains there with you in a vital (*lebendig*) way" (GA 60, 117/PRL, 84). Heidegger's conclusion is that the early Christians lived time. As he says, "Christian experience lives time itself" (GA 60, 82/PRL, 57). Who they are (present) depends on having become a Christian (past) as they await the second coming of Christ (future).

LANGUAGE AND THE GREEKS

In 1923, Heidegger traveled to Marburg to become an assistant professor at the university. His lecture courses on the Greek thinkers during this time are extraordinary analyses of the texts of Plato and Aristotle, often line-by-line explications sustained throughout the semester. One marvels at how these close readings illuminate the facticity of Greek life. He does not focus on Aristotle's ontological system or on Plato's theory of forms. Instead, Heidegger was interested in bringing to life the Greek world from which the concepts of Plato and Aristotle developed, what we might call the factical conceptuality of ancient Greek philosophical concepts. For example, Heidegger accepts Aristotle's definition of the human being as a *zoon logon echon*. This is normally translated as "rational animal." Looking at the factical conceptuality of these concepts, however, Heidegger claims that in the Greek world, *zoon* did not just mean "animal," it meant "life," and *logos* did not just mean "reason" or "rationality," it meant "speaking." The human being thus is a *zoon logon echon*, but not a rational animal. The human, rather, is a living being in dialogical (speaking) relationships in a community with others, and this can be discerned within Aristotle's own definition when it is read from within the context of the factical world in which he lived.

One of the most extraordinary of Heidegger's early lecture courses is GA 18, in which he provides an analysis of Aristotle's *Rhetoric*. Many of the commentators on these early lecture courses have remarked that in the early courses Heidegger is more interested in Aristotle's practical works, the *Ethics* and the *Rhetoric*, than he is in the theoretical works, such as the *Physics* and *Metaphysics*. Indeed, he is attempting to interpret theoretical concepts out of the context of the factical life-world from which they derived. This is similar to his approach in the courses on religious life, where he tries to retrieve the factical life of the early Christian communities prior to the interpolation of philosophical concepts into religion and the subsequent development of theological dogma. His analysis of GA 18 is consistent with this approach. He uses Aristotle's analysis of the ordinary ways of speaking, arguing, refuting, debating, and discussing evident in the *Rhetoric* in order to grasp the basic orientation of human beings in the world. As he emphasizes, "*The Rhetoric is nothing other than the interpretation of concrete Dasein, the hermeneutic of Dasein itself*" (GA 18, 110/BCAR, 75). The main idea of this course is that *logos* or speaking is the fundamental way in which human beings orient themselves in the world (GA 18, 18/BCAR, 14–15). With this approach, he explores ideas of authentic speaking, being-in-the-*polis* (or city), and even ethical excellence.

In the winter semester of 1924–5, Heidegger continues his exploration of *logos* by analyzing Plato's *Sophist*. He actually begins with an extended treatment of Aristotle, following the hermeneutic principle that Aristotle understood Plato better than Plato understood himself. Although Heidegger is critical of Platonic dialectic because, he says, its goal is a pure seeing of the Ideas (which are beings and not being itself), he believes that Plato had a deeper and more original understanding of being and *logos* than modern thinkers. In a remarkable analysis at the end of this course, he connects *logos* to *deloun* to show that the primary way in which human beings are in the world is through a way of speaking that reveals or discloses phenomenal contexts through manifolds of words (GA 19, 594/PS, 411). In his interpretation of Greek Dasein, he presents *deloun* as a kind of nontheoretical disclosure that is operative in both speaking and attentive listening.

It is worthy of note that many of the basic ideas in Heidegger's reading of Greek *logos* from his Marburg period—about authentic language, speaking, and listening to others in a community, and revealing structural manifolds of words in discourse—either do not make their way into BT or are underdeveloped in that text. Reading the early lecture courses, we see that Heidegger was using the texts of Plato and Aristotle to develop ways of thinking about the complex relationships among speaking, being, and factical human life.

There are a variety of ways to interpret Heidegger's early lecture courses, but any approach would have to take account of the relationship between factical human existence and the meaning of being that he was exploring during this time period. Throughout all of these courses, Heidegger does not repeat himself. There are similar themes, but he does not rehash the same material over and over again or reuse his lecture notes from semester to semester. Each of the published courses contains new and original insights, and yet running through these courses is a restless quest to synthesize human existence with an understanding of who we are in our factical, everyday lives.

There are two primary vectors of experience that we find in these early courses. The first is contextual. We live within contexts of meaning structured by the various life-worlds:

the environing-world, the with-world, and the self-world, and there is a kind of intensifying concentration of permeating layers of meaning embedded within the self-world. The second vector of experience is temporal and historical. Heidegger often refers to ancient texts in order to retrieve original meanings, but there is simultaneously a propulsion forward, toward the future, into new ways of thinking. Taking up these two directions of experience, we try to make sense of our own lives. As he says in GA 58, "*We* are standing in *our* factical life, and we speak and understand in the circle of our understandability" (98). In other words, we try to become understandable to ourselves from within these various contexts as we look through the past and toward the future, which is why a hermeneutics of factical experience is running through these early lecture courses. In GA 63, he describes hermeneutics as pursuing our own self-alienation, but always within the contexts of our own unique and particular lives. From within our own life-contexts, our own experiences, our own historical epochs, and thus our own time, we try to understand who we *are*. Similar to Descartes, Heidegger starts philosophizing with the "I am," but whereas Descartes emphasizes the "I" or cogito, Heidegger emphasizes the "am," that is, the being of factical human life (GA 61, 174/PIA, 131).

It is interesting, yet perhaps somewhat puzzling, that the main topic of BT is neither being nor time but rather Dasein. BT attempts to lay bare hermeneutically the ontological structures of Dasein, which is the human being insofar as it is concerned about its own being. In this structure, we find the whole project of the early lecture courses coming together. The effort to synthesize ontological ideas about who the human being is with existential ideas about human life crystallizes in the notion of Dasein.

22

HEIDEGGER, PERSUASION, AND ARISTOTLE'S *RHETORIC*

P. Christopher Smith

In treating Heidegger's 1924 lectures, *Grundbegriffe der Aristotelischen Philosophie* (*Basic Concepts of Aristotelian Philosophy*, GA 18), this chapter explores the early Heidegger's revolutionary rehabilitation of rhetoric. We will be concerned with two issues here. First, we want to see how, in developing a "hermeneutics of facticity," Heidegger finds one of the most basic ways we "are" originally, "there" in the factual world to be precisely in our speaking to each other to take care of things. We want to see, in other words, how he considers human existence to be fundamentally rhetorical. Second, we wish to show how, more radically, within this rhetorical dimension of his "hermeneutics of facticity" Heidegger uses a strategy of *Destruktion* to overthrow our standard ideas about reasoning and display that at its *Grund* or ground any rhetorical communication is inextricably embedded in an affective setting and conditioned by it. This will clarify why Aristotle's treatment of *pathos* as a basic component of rhetorical persuasion receives Heidegger's particular attention.

It may well be, however, that in reading Heidegger's *Basic Concepts of Aristotelian Philosophy* as a rehabilitation of rhetoric, we are forcing this text in a very different direction from the one Heidegger had in mind.[1] As his 1927 *Sein und Zeit* (*Being and Time*) will make clear, Aristotle's exposition of the *pathê* or affects in the *Rhetoric* is of interest to Heidegger primarily because of the opening it provides for him to pursue the concomitance of human existence's thrusting of itself toward future possibilities (*Sich-Entwerfen*) and its inescapable experience of always having already been thrust (*geworfen*) into a certain mood, frame of mind or, literally, "way in which it finds itself feeling" (*sich befindet*).[2] The exposition of this concomitance in *Being and Time* paves the way for a discussion of *Angst* as the particular mood in which the meaningfulness of things is annihilated and in which, consequently, the self, having forfeited itself to the public world of what "everybody" thinks and does, is abruptly summoned back to its genuine being.[3] If one is seeking authenticity, as Heidegger is, the talk in the public realm, *die Öffentlichkeit*, the realm of rhetoric, is thus viewed as mere talk, *Gerede*, that not only falsifies the real nature of the things talked about but absorbs the self and hides it from itself. Accordingly, instead of countering the critique of rhetoric found in Plato's *Gorgias* and *Republic*, Heidegger is developing his

185

own version of it: the "everybody" that babbles on vacuously is Plato's *hoi polloi*, and the task is to "know yourself" by retrieving yourself from the received opinions (*endoxa*) being bantered about.

In the *Basic Concepts of Aristotelian Philosophy*, however, this trajectory has not yet been fully set and, remarkably, we still find there many rich and seminal passages on how communication originally takes place among human beings engaged in taking care of things in the everyday world. And for the purposes of a philosophical rehabilitation of rhetoric it is striking that quite unlike the Heidegger of *Being and Time* who condemns *die Öffentlichkeit* or the public realm of discourse as degenerate (see SZ, § 27), the Heidegger of the *Basic Concepts*, takes Aristotle's characterization of the human being in the *Politics* (1252b30) as the *zôion logon echon*, the live being having speech, to be proof that for Aristotle "there is contained in the very being of the human being the ground and basic existential possibility of being in the *polis*"; "Aristotle," he says, "takes being-in-the-*polis* to be the life proper to human beings (*das* eigentliche *Leben der Menschen*)" (GA 18, 46–7; my emphasis). Our speaking, he concludes, is the very essence of our "being together with each other," or as Aristotle puts this, our *koinô-nia*, our community (ibid., 47). Thus even if early on in the *Basic Concepts* we seem to be diverted from expositing a theory of how we speak and listen to each other publicly, rhetoricians can at least point out that Heidegger has argued here that "in this determination, *logon echon*, a fundamental characteristic of human existence becomes visible: "*being with one another*, and this, to be sure, not in the sense of merely being placed next to each other, but in the sense of *being involved in speaking to each other*—in communication,

refutation and disputation" (ibid.). Moreover, a validation of rhetoric is clearly evident in the three theses that Heidegger will make basic for his interpretation of Aristotle's *Rhetoric*: (1) "the being of the human being is being in a world," (2) "this being in a world is characterized by *logos*," (3) "this speaking itself is the way taking care of things [in the world] is carried out" (GA 18, 66). What is more Heidegger titles his chapter III "An exposition (*Auslegung*) of human existence (*Dasein*) in regard to the ground and basic possibility of speaking with one another, using the *Rhetoric* as a guide" (103). As he says there,

> The human being is a living thing that has its real existence in conversation and talk. . . . This constitutive ground (*Grundverfassung*) of Greek existence is where one should look for the soil (*Boden*) from which this [Greek] definition of the human being grows. (108)

Accordingly, the issue for a philosophy of rhetoric—and this is my concern here—is what one could achieve if one developed from Heidegger's revolutionary beginnings a rhetorical theory that stays with the priority of the being spoken to over speaking, and that consequently establishes, beneath all derivative abstractions, the ground and basis of human community in my hearing what is said to me by someone else. If this is so, my speaking to myself becomes entirely derivative.

Approaching the matter this way would have two advantages. First, it heads off Heidegger's turn inward and the residual Cartesianism that this turn implies. Listening to oneself, after all, is merely a modification of Descartes' *cogito me cogitare*, "I think myself thinking," from which he deduces his *cogito ergo sum*, "I think, therefore I am." The priority of hearing what another has said to me would force the restatement of this with something like *mihi loquoris ergo loquor*, "you speak to me, therefore I speak." In this way Aristotle's *koinônia* or community, with which Heidegger begins, would be recovered. And self-evidently I am not the "condition of the possibility" of the language I speak to others in my community, rather they are: I can only say things in response to what I have first heard from others. Second, in stressing the priority of what I have heard from another we could finally escape the mythology of "speech acts" as performances of some fictional agent "self."

This, of course is not the route Heidegger takes. To be sure, in treating Aristotle's three *pisteis*, or "persuaders," namely *logos*, *êthos*, and *pathos*, or the speakers' reasoning, their character, or the way they come across, and the feeling or disposition (*diathesis*) they wish to bring about in their audience, Heidegger's primary focus is on *pathos* and, with that, his attention shifts from what the speakers say to what is going on in their hearers. To be specific, Heidegger follows Aristotle in asserting that it is *pathos* that determines the *krisis* of the audience (see GA 18, 120 and *Rhet.* 1356a 14–16). The problem for us, however, those of us who might anticipate an account of their acoustical experience, is that Heidegger's translates *krisis*, not as *Entschluß*, or decision, but as "*Ansicht*," that is, a "view" or "opinion" that the audience comes to hold as a result of what the speaker has said to them. We have here a first indication of the overriding, ocular, rather than acoustical, concern that defines Heidegger's appropriation of Aristotle's *Rhetoric*: though *Entschloßenheit*, decisiveness or better, resolve, will figure prominently in *Being and Time*, here in the *Basic Concepts* Heidegger

at first takes even rhetorical speech as *disclosure of something we can see rather than as exhortation we either do or do not hear*. Indeed, he will argue that the rhetorical *logos* "has the basic, ground function of making plain (*dêloun*) that [world] which being-in-a-world resides in" (GA 18, 139). For him rhetorical speech brings something into view for onlookers who will see it in a certain way, and the *pathos* and frame of mind, *diathesis*, of these onlookers is of interest because it determines the view or *Ansicht* they will have of it.

If *krisis*, is taken as decision, however, the *pathos* and frame of mind of an audience determines whether they hear and obey (*hupakouein*) what the speaker is exhorting them to do. (If a parent says to a child, "Do you hear me?" "I see what you mean" is not the response expected!) To be sure, Aristotle himself has the very same ocular tendencies as Heidegger does, and *krisis*, as he uses the word, could often mean "judgment" and the related *krinein*, "to pass judgment"—but clearly not always. If, unlike Heidegger, we are to appropriate Aristotle's rhetoric for persuasion (*peithô*) rather than for exposition of a state of affairs, we would need a phenomenology of the experience of hearing, of what is done to us and with us when we are spoken to, such that we are changed, not in our *Ansichten* or views of things, but in what we are willed to do.

Despite his very different intent, however, there is much in Heidegger's interpretations that still can help us in this regard. That *krisis* is more than coming to an opinion or view about some subject matter (*Sache*; see 122), and more even than passing judgment as an impartial onlooker (*theôros*; see 124–5), is made clear in Heidegger's recounting of the double purpose of *sumbouleutikê* or deliberative rhetoric, which, as Heidegger puts it, "gives counsel" regarding a course of action. For as *protropê* or *apotropê*, this form of speech would literally either "turn someone toward" or "turn someone away from" an action (125). We are, in other words, talking about a visceral change in volition here and not just an intellectual change in opinion. And if, for the time being, Heidegger seems to overlook the physical, somatic basis for such a change in will, he does at least in passing call to our attention the word *thumos*, heart or breast, contained in the name for the rhetorical syllogism, the *enthumêma*, by saying that the rhetorical argument is meant be "taken to heart" (133).

As a matter of fact Heidegger will become more explicit on this visceral, volitional dimension of *krisis* via a detour through the *Ethics*' account of *prohairesis* or choice. For *krisis*, at least in *sumbouleutikê* or deliberative rhetoric, means, as it turns out, virtually the same thing as choice. In the *Basic Concepts*, 143 ff., Heidegger's immediate concern in treating *prohairesis* is precisely to differentiate between *doxa*, on the one hand, which Heidegger defines as the opinion or view (*Ansicht*) one has of something, and *prohairesis*, on the other, which he renders with the German *Entschlossensein*, meaning to have resolved or decided upon something. "A *prohairesis*," he says, "is concerned with the *prakton* [an action to be done], that which is decisive for taking care (*Besorgen*) of something at the moment" (145). "*Prohairesis*, committing oneself to, and deciding for something (*sich entschließen zu etwas*), aims at the *sumpheron*, namely something which, if undertaken, will be *to my advantage* in taking care, *Besorgen*, of some matter that I might take in hand" (147). *Doxa*, in contrast, is concerned with what is *alêthes* and *pseudes*, what is true or false: "With *doxa* the concern to comprehend what something

really is, about which there exists some opinion or view (*Ansicht*)" (ibid.).

What is *sumpheron* or the advantageous, as opposed to what is *blaberon* or harmful, is, of course, precisely the issue in *sumbeuleutikê* or deliberative rhetoric (see *Rhet.* 1358b 22). We note, accordingly, that what we have here, stated in an exposition of the *Ethics* and not the *Rhetoric*, is the very distinction we had been looking for between the purposes of argument in deliberative rhetoric and argument in demonstration: Unlike demonstrative argument, deliberative rhetoric—and this is rhetoric's most basic form—does *not* aim primarily at communicating an opinion or view (*Ansicht*) after all. Its concern, instead, is to bring its audience to a decision, an *Entschluß*, whether an action is to be undertaken or not. To be sure, this decision is not merely a matter of *epithumia* and *thumos*, desire and the heart or spirit, which lack the clarity of a "transparent decision (*Entschluß*)" (GA 18, 143). It will have an intellectual component, for, as the name *sumbeuleutikê* makes evident, it comes at the end of joint consultation and deliberation (*bouleuesthai*). Still, there is a lot more involved here than simply thinking things over. Since to decide on something is more a matter of volition rather than cognition, one must be made to *feel* like doing it. Not, "I see," but, "I hear you and I will," is the response sought, and no *logos* without *pathos* will bring this about.

For clarification that Heidegger sees the role of *pathos* in moving an audience to a decision, we can turn to a crucial passage in the *Rhetoric*, cited by Heidegger in the Greek (170):

ἔστι δὲ τὰ πάθη δι' ὅσα μεταβάλλοντες διαφέρουσι πρὸς τὰς κρίσεις. (*Rhet.* 1378a 20)

Piecing together the fragments of Heidegger's reading of this, we get something like the following translation:

> It is, however, the *pathê* by which, in our sudden conversion from one to another, we differ in the decisions [we make].[4]

Precisely in turning to the phenomenology of hearing that we have been looking for, Heidegger seizes upon the *di' hosa metaballontes* here, which he glosses as, "in regard to which 'a sudden conversion (*Umschlag*) occurs in ourselves'" (GA 18, 170), and with that, he moves to a most radical and astonishing break with philosophy's traditional emphasis on Socratic composure and self-control. He sees the *Umschlag* or sudden conversion as taking place in our, the listener's, *hexis*, which he renders as *Verfassung*, namely, the constitution, condition, state, habitude, we happen to find ourselves in. Such *Umschlagen in eine andere Verfassung*, or sudden conversion into another state can even take the form, he says, of being seized or being waylaid (*Ergriffenwerden, Überfallenwerden*) and, playing on the *Fassung* or "composure" stem of *Verfassung*, Heidegger adds that in this case the sudden conversion from one state to another amounts to *Aus-der-Fassung-Kommen*, meaning to "lose it" or "come unhinged" (171). Of course I can make myself "ready for this," (*Gefaßtsein dafür*); indeed, my *hexis* or state "determines the authenticity (*Eigentlichkeit*) of human existence in a moment of being ready for and accepting of something (*des Gefaßtseins für etwas*)," which takes the form of "Here I am come what may" (176). Still, I must acknowledge the possibility that within my being, something comes over me that "throws" me (*aus der Fassung bringt*) (ibid.).

The point for us, who are pursuing the implications for rhetoric of this *Destruktion* of the listener's self-possessed reason, is that Heidegger has uncovered the physiological, somatic ground and basis of supposedly rational thought in the conversion of the listener's *hexis* and *diathesis* brought on by a shift in the *pathê*. What takes place here is a sudden conversion in my whole psychosomatic being from one underlying state or habitude to another, and it is this conversion, not the *logos* or argument of what is said to me, that ultimately determines my *krisis* or decision. Remarkably, Heidegger argues that far from being firm, steady, unmoved, we are *metaballontes*, that is, in Heidegger's words, "we are reeling from one state and attitude (*Fassung*) into another," and, he continues, the defining feature of this transition is not the new state we arrive at, but our being in motion, "underway," between states, its peculiar "*Unruhe*," disquietude, unsettledness, perturbation. In the case of *phobos* or fear, this condition can even be characterized as *tarachê*, confusion, getting mixed up (*Verwirrung, Durcheinandergeraten*) (183) (so much for Epicurean *ataraxia* or imperturbability!).

This demolition of the listener's fictive disembodied, self-contained, rational detachment goes hand in hand with Heidegger's hermeneutics of facticity and its emphasis on our original being-*in*-the world. We are ec-static, "out there," so to speak, and thereby exposed physically, corporeally, to what comes over us even as we are overcome by it. The "states of mind" corresponding to these experiences are derivative epiphenomena that are grounded in what is happening to the body. It follows that *pathos*, from *paschein*, meaning literally to undergo, is to be understood as "*Mitgenommenwerden des menschlichen Daseins in seinem vollen leiblichen In-der-Welt-sein* (human existence being carried along in its complete bodily being-in-the-world)," and "For this reason," he explains, "the *pathê* are not 'psychological events,' not 'in consciousness'" (197). "The so called 'bodily conditions' (*Leibeszustände*) experienced with anxiety, joy and the like are no mere accompaniment to the phenomena, rather they belong to the characteristic being of the human being" (198).

The conclusion Heidegger draws from our ground in bodily feeling is stunning:

Insofar as the *pathê* (feelings) are not just an appendix of psychological events but the soil and ground from which speech grows and into which what has been said grows back, the *pathê*, for their part, provide the ground and basic range of affective possibilities that human existence is predisposed to feel, and within which it orients itself about itself. Its primary way of orienting itself, of clarifying its being in the world, is no form of knowing but a way one finds oneself feeling. . . . The possibility of speaking about things [authentically] is only given once these have been stripped of the appearance [of objectivity] they have when we first begin to deal with them and we grasp them within an affective predisposition or feeling characterized as such. (262)

The question for a philosophy of rhetoric, then, is just how speakers communicate on this ground and basic level, just how they can induce the prerequisite *metabolê*, the *Umschlag* or sudden conversion of affect in the inherently unstable psychosomatic unity that, beneath all fictions of pure reason, we

actually are. The self-evident answer is by voice and gesture, which is to say, music and dance. For the vibrations of voice with its variations in tone, volume, timbre, pitch as well as in tempo, rhythm, meter, and the correlative expressive motions of the body impact the audience immediately, and it is the bodily experience of these in the audience that invoke the reversed *hexis* or *diathesis*, the *Verfassung* or psychosomatic condition and disposition, that underlies not only our volitional decisions but in fact our cognitive views of things too. But Heidegger, of course, does not go so far as to say *this*.

NOTES AND REFERENCES

1   As the title of his lectures makes clear, *Basic Concepts of Aristotelian Philosophy*, Aristotle's *Rhetoric* per se is by no means the exclusive concern of Heidegger's investigations, and in his exploration of concepts basic to Aristotelian philosophy he will range over many other texts, among them, the *Metaphysics*, *On the Soul*, the *Nicomachean Ethics*, the *Politics*, the *Physics*, and *On Interpretation*.

2   See SZ, §§ 29, 31, 40 on the *gleichursprünglich* or equally basic *Entwurf* (one's thrust of oneself forward, or projection), *Geworfenheit* (the condition of having been thrust), and *Befindlichkeit* (the frame of mind that one always already finds oneself thrust into).

3   See SZ §§ 56–7 on *Angst* and the *Ruf des Gewissens* (call of conscience).

4   I would translate, "It is the *pathê* whose conversions from one to another alter the decisions [we make]." At issue is the subject of *metaballontes* and *diapherousi*. I take this to be *pathê*, but Heidegger takes it to be "we" (*wir*), reading the third person plural *diapherousi* as a first person plural in German. This is standard Greek usage, and right or wrong, it leads Heidegger in a most compelling direction.

23

BEING AND TIME
Dennis J. Schmidt

The philosophical project that unfolds in *Being and Time* resists any simple definition and any reduction to a position. None of the usual interpretive techniques seem to help one approach this unusual text, even the effort to situate it in the context of a larger tradition and other texts is difficult. At the outset however, one might get the impression that *Being and Time* can be located in a long and well-defined metaphysical tradition: it opens with its dedication to Heidegger's teacher, Husserl, moves to a citation from Plato's *Sophist*, and then, in the "Introduction," mention is made of a wide range of philosophers including Plato, Aristotle, Suarez, Aquinas, Descartes, Pascal, Kant, Hegel, Bergson, and Husserl. While it might seem that by doing this Heidegger locates his own work with reference to other works that have come to define a sort of orthodox philosophical canon, one soon learns that these references provide almost no help in situating the project of *Being and Time*. Adding to the sense that all of the markers that might orient the reader of this text offer no help whatsoever, one finds that the abundance of neologisms populating *Being and Time* constantly remind one that Heidegger finds the language of philosophy that he has inherited insufficient for "the business of philosophy [namely] to preserve the power of the most elemental words in which Dasein expresses itself" (GA 2, 220/ BT, 211). Even the key terms of Husserl's phenomenology—a philosopher and a methodology to which Heidegger pays explicit homage—are largely abandoned in *Being and Time*. So, in the "Introduction"—when one is searching for an orientation or context with which one might approach this text— one finds an unsettled and quite complicated sense of just how one is to enter into the philosophical project of *Being and Time*. From the beginning *Being and Time* seems determined to disorient its readers. In its efforts to set itself apart from philosophical traditions and languages, and to resist any easy appropriation into well-established contexts, *Being and Time* quietly announces the radicality of its own intentions.[1]

The first readers of *Being and Time* recognized this and so the first reviews spoke of the experience of reading this book as like "an electric shock" and a "lightning strike," and its young (37-year-old) author, Martin Heidegger, was described as "philosophically brilliant" and a "genius." Of course, not every reviewer was so positive and *Being and Time*, and its author, rapidly became the center of controversies that continue even into our time. It is now 85 years since the publication of *Being and Time* and during that period it seems as if *Being and Time* has become a work in the very same canon that it sought to disrupt. While the controversies surrounding Heidegger and his work have continued, what seems to have been lost today that the first readers of this remarkable text recognized is the sense of disorientation that comes as soon as one engages this book. However, to lose sight of this disorientation is to lose sight of the real access that opens up *Being and Time* since the first task it sets for itself is to reawaken a special perplexity, namely the perplexity that opens up the question of the meaning of being. Heidegger argues that the chief task of *Being and Time* is to unfold a question that must come to be understood as *inherently elusive*. In order to bring this question forward, it is necessary to begin with what is inherent to it: its difficulty, elusivity, resistance, and disorienting character. It is quite significant then that the first words of *Being and Time* note that the question of being "has today been forgotten" (GA 2, 2/BT, 1) and that the first aim of *Being and Time* is to "rekindle" and "explicitly retrieve" the question of being. It is this question of being, which is the fundamental ontological question, that guides the philosophical project of *Being and Time*. And yet, it is precisely this question that we have forgotten. From the outset, Heidegger makes clear that this forgetting of the question of being is not simply a "mistake" or an "error" that could be easily corrected: one does not forget the question of being the way one forgets one's keys, nor can one ask this question in the form that most questions take. Its obscurity and difficulty, its tendency to be forgotten, are not accidental, but belong intimately to the very question of being itself. It is a question that, initially at least, disorients.

In order to recover this question, Heidegger undertakes a phenomenological analysis of that being [*Seiende*] who asks the question of being [*Sein*]. This being who asks the question of what it means to be—and *not* to be—Heidegger calls "Dasein." The character of this being will only gradually become clear through analyses of how Dasein is "in" the world and it is important that the reader of *Being and Time* not quickly seek to find traditional philosophical notions—such as subject, human being, consciousness—that can serve as substitutes for the difficult task of understanding the being of Dasein, of the way being is in-the-world. If one needs to find a preliminary "definition" of Dasein, then it is best to say simply that it is that being who is defined and distinguished by always asking the question of being. Asking this question is the fundamental drive and preoccupation of Dasein—even when it is forgotten and even when it remains unthematized it remains definitive for the being and definition of Dasein—and the way Dasein is, is at each moment defined by this preoccupation with the question of what it means to be. Heidegger calls this way of being of Dasein in which it perpetually faces itself as a question "factical life" and he argues that the recovery of the question of being is first made possible by means of an analysis—more precisely, by the hermeneutics—of the factical life of Dasein: "Thus *fundamental ontology* . . . must be sought in the *existential analysis of Dasein*" (GA 2, 13/BT, 12).

In the final section of the "Introduction" Heidegger outlines the entire project of *Being and Time*. He announces that it will be divided into two parts and that each part will be divided into three divisions. Part one is to lay out the interpretation of Dasein and then the explication of time as the horizon for asking the question of being. Part two is to carry out a phenomenological destruction of the history of ontology in order to clear the way to a more radical formulation of the question of being. For reasons that have more to do with job security and the well-known publish or perish problem of the academic world (though he was, as his recently published lecture courses make clear, a powerful teacher of renown and originality, Heidegger had not published anything in the decade prior to publishing *Being and Time*), Heidegger elected to publish the first two completed divisions before the remaining four divisions were complete. And, for more complicated and philosophically very interesting reasons, Heidegger never published—at least as the continuation of *Being and Time*—the remaining four divisions.[2] It was not until the seventh edition of *Being and Time* (1953) that Heidegger would drop the designation "First Half" that had stood as a reminder that the published text of *Being and Time* was unfinished. With that edition Heidegger acknowledged that "the second half could no longer be added without the first being presented anew," unfortunately by removing the reminder that the published text is the torso of its own intentions, Heidegger quietly hides the best reminder that the book that we have does not carry out its own project. We never fully arrive at the question of *Being* (*and Time*), but remain largely concerned with the question of the analytic of Dasein that culminates in the presentation of Dasein and temporality. That some of the first interpreters of *Being and Time* mistook it as a work of existentialism (Sartre) or of philosophical anthropology (Husserl) can be accounted for by remembering what both of those commonplace interpretations forget: that the published text of *Being and Time* is unfinished. The best readings of *Being and Time* always bear in mind that this self-rewriting text is incomplete and that the question of being, the fundamental question of ontology

that drives and guides the project of *Being and Time*, is never fully broached in text that we have.

DIVISION ONE

The preliminary analysis of Dasein begins by asserting two key features of this being who asks the question of being: first, that "it is always mine" (GA 2, 41/BT, 41) and second that "the 'essence' of this being lies in its 'to be'. . . . its existence" (GA 2, 42/BT, 41). In other words, Dasein is inalienably singular and so must be understood in its concreteness, and it is always unfinished and underway, that is, it is always a matter of possibilities that it is to be or not to be and thus it is more than simply something actual.[3] In other words, from the outset Dasein is sharply distinguished from other kinds of beings that are defined by their actuality and simple presence. This is why Heidegger refers to the analytic of Dasein as an *existential* analytic, that is, as an inquiry into *how* Dasein comes to exist as it does rather than as seeking to define *what* Dasein is.[4] To this end, Heidegger's analysis seeks to expose the structures that make a being such as Dasein possible. Heidegger calls these structures "existentials."

It is not possible to even pretend to do justice to the careful and probing phenomenological analysis of Dasein that constitutes the bulk of division one of part one of *Being and Time* (strictly speaking, the preliminary analytic of Dasein is found in sections 12–42; GA 2, 52–200/BT, 53–193). One finds there discussions of the meaning of a world, of things and tools, of signs and significance, of meaning and intelligibility, of space and spatiality, of everydayness and the self, of mood, anxiety, and fear, of understanding, language, and propositions, of curiosity, gossip, of others, and of thrownness, of solicitude and care—among other themes. In the course of these analyses, we find a critique of Cartesian ontology (sections 19–21; GA 2, 89–101/BT, 87–99) that is introduced in order to provide a sharp contrast with the sense of a world and the being of Dasein Heidegger is presenting. After concluding the analytic of Dasein and before beginning its repetition in division two Heidegger provides another set of contrasts between what his analysis of Dasein has demonstrated and traditional, metaphysical assumptions. In these final sections of division one, Heidegger addresses the notions of reality and of truth (sections 43–4; GA 2, 220–30/BT, 193–220). Kant and Aristotle are frequently invoked in these sections, but it would be incorrect to suggest that Heidegger is providing a careful treatment of either figure in these sections; they serve more as foils for what Heidegger takes to be positions he is attempting to overcome.

In order to make sense of the analytic of Dasein two overarching points need to be kept in mind. First, that the existential structures exposed by this phenomenological analysis describe the various ways in which the factical life of Dasein unfolds in the world. They indicate the ways in which Dasein articulates itself, exists in the world, and so discloses itself to itself. It is important to emphasize that this self-disclosure of Dasein as it is in the world is *not* a cognitive matter, that is, it is not a form of self-knowledge or self-reflection as it has long been discussed in the history of philosophy.[5] Strictly speaking, Dasein exists *in and as* these structures, these existentials, and the way in which they unfold concretely thereby disclosing Dasein and the world in which it finds itself.

Heidegger puts the point this way: "*Dasein is its disclosedness*" (GA 2, 133/BT, 129). Second, although Heidegger examines these structures of Dasein's factical way of being as largely distinct matters, it must be stressed that Dasein is, and always understands itself, as a whole. Heidegger makes this clear when he says that all of the existential structures are "equiprimordial," that is, none of them has priority over any of the others. This means that the structures defining Dasein cannot be regarded as "grounds" upon which other structures rest; rather, the being of Dasein is much more appropriately characterized as the "event" in which all of these structures open Dasein to its world and thus to itself. This "wholeness"—this event—of Dasein is what Heidegger describes as "care" [Sorge]. Care names the structural wholeness of Dasein in which Dasein always finds itself already in a world, with others, and among things in such a way that Dasein must be understood as "ahead" of itself. Its being matters to Dasein because it remains always a question for itself, it exists as this question of the "to be": "a constant unfinished quality thus lies in the essence of the basic constitution of Dasein" (GA 2, 236/BT, 227).

The preliminary analysis of Dasein found in part one, division one exposes the equiprimordially fundamental structures that articulate and give shape to the way that Dasein is in the world and the way in which it finds itself there. This analysis is, as Heidegger reminds his reader, "preparatory" and "cannot lay claim to primordiality" (GA 2, 233/BT, 223) since the wholeness of the being of Dasein that is characterized there as care only shows Dasein as "still outstanding" and as "not yet" whole. The task of division two is to press upon this question of the authentic wholeness of Dasein by addressing the question of the "end" of Dasein. The analysis of

Dasein laid out in division one will then need to be rewritten in light of the real meaning of the wholeness of Dasein. Before turning to division two there is one further comment that should be made about the results of the analysis in division one.

One way of characterizing the largest result of this analysis is to say that the existential structures articulate the various ways that Dasein *discloses itself*. This disclosure is the way Dasein is "in" the world. Heidegger puts the point this way:

> Insofar as Dasein essentially *is* its disclosedness, and, as disclosed, it discloses and discovers, it is essentially "true." *Dasein is "in the truth."* This statement has an ontological meaning. It does not mean that Dasein is ontically always, or even only at times, inducted "into every truth," but that the disclosedness of its ownmost being belongs to its existential constitution. (GA 2, 221/BT, 212)

However, saying that Dasein is "in the truth" is only one way of speaking of the way it means to say that "Dasein is its disclosedness" (GA 2, 133/BT, 129). Since the factical being of Dasein, the existentials that structure its existence, include the ways in which Dasein hides from itself and loses itself in "the they" or becomes "entangled" in things and everydayness, it must also be said that Dasein is in "untruth." This means that "being closed off and covered over belong to the *facticity* of Dasein. The full existential and ontological meaning of the statement 'Dasein is in the truth' also says equiprimordially that 'Dasein is in untruth'" (GA 2, 222/BT, 213). In short, the same structures that open Dasein to its world and to the question that it is for itself—the question of having "to be"—equally and at the same time close Dasein off from its world and obscure

the question and character of its own being. In an earlier lecture course Heidegger had expressed this doubled situation of the factical life of Dasein by saying that "*Das Leben ist diesig, es nebelt sich immer wieder ein*" [life is misty, it always and again shrouds itself in fog]. Among the many important consequences of this insight into the doubled situation of Dasein as itself a movement of truth/untruth, one consequence needs to be mentioned as especially significant for the project of *Being and Time*. It is simply that in exposing this structural and constitutive tendency of Dasein to close itself off from the questions that define it, Heidegger gives an account of the forgetfulness that defines the question of being for us and that forms the opening remark of *Being and Time*. This forgetfulness is not an accident, not an error that could be evaded or avoided. It is rather the forgetfulness, the concealing of its own being, that belongs to the factical life of Dasein in the same way as that life articulates an opening and unfolding of its own being.

DIVISION TWO

Although these remarks on the doubled life of Dasein—the way that closure and disclosure that are woven together in the very structure of Dasein—are among the final comments in division one, Heidegger does not explicitly pursue this point. Rather, division two opens by asking once again the question of the wholeness of Dasein and by asserting that "the existential analytic of Dasein up to now cannot lay claim to primordiality. Its fore-having never included more than the *inauthentic* being of Dasein, of Dasein as *less than whole* (GA 2, 233/BT, 223). The problem is that "as long as Dasein is, something is always outstanding: what it can and will be" (GA 2, 233/BT, 224). This outstanding potential, this having to be, only ceases with the death of Dasein. In its death, Dasein reaches its wholeness. That is why division two opens with a discussion of "The possible being-a-whole of Dasein and Being-toward-death" (GA 2, 235–67/BT, 227–55).

Heidegger is quick to point out that strictly speaking no phenomenology of death is possible: I do not experience my own death and in experiencing the death of the other I never really experience death so much as the peculiar heartbreak of my own survival. Any "attestation" of death will necessarily need to be of a distinct character precisely because it eludes any and all direct experience. This paradox of death—that it is a possibility not to be evaded, that it is impossible to grasp phenomenally—can only be answered insofar as the existential meaning of death, that is the lived meaning of death as such a possibility, is unfolded. How, in other words, does death announce itself in advance of its actual appearance and what does this announcement mean for Dasein?

The most radical and penetrating announcement of the existential meaning of death, of its reality as a possibility that cannot be evaded, appears in what Heidegger refers to as the "call of conscience." Conscience is one of the central and most significant notions developed in *Being and Time*, but it is also one of the least understood and most misrepresented. Despite Heidegger's clear argument that conscience should not be interpreted as a moral phenomenon, the impulse toward such an interpretation is often not resisted. Conscience gives something to be understood, "it discloses" (GA 2, 269/BT, 259). It is a strange call that interrupts the flatness of everyday life and summons Dasein back to itself. Nonetheless, though it is a sort of

voice, the call of conscience does not reach words, but "speaks solely and constantly in the mode of silence" (GA 2, 273/BT, 263). It is in and as this silent call of conscience that Dasein reminds itself of its ownmost, inalienable possibility—death, as that which defines the mineness and wholeness of Dasein, and as that which defines the ultimate sense of what it means that Dasein has to be, that its being is futural. This is the point at which one begins to see how the analytic of Dasein begins to open up the question of being, the fundamental question of ontology.

The presentation of the notion of conscience, of this call of Dasein from itself to back to itself, marks a sort of summit of the phenomenological analysis of the existential constitution of Dasein. By means of unpacking the possibility of this call of conscience, Heidegger takes the next step in the project of *Being and Time*, that is, he moves from the analysis of Dasein in its wholeness to the "phenomenal exposition of temporality" (GA 2, 301/BT, 289). In other words, after the analysis of conscience *Being and Time* moves to the preliminary consideration of time as the horizon shaping the question of being. With this move begins the process that is to eventually lead to division three of part one in which Heidegger takes up the topic of "Time and Being." This new step begins with a "repetition" of the preliminary phenomenological analysis of Dasein in which the existential structures exposed by that analysis are now shown to be modes of temporality.

Demonstrating that the movement of time is the "ground" of the being of Dasein and thus makes possible the question of being the asking of which defines Dasein as the being that it is, is the final step in the published portion of *Being and Time*. To be sure, more themes do emerge in these final sections: for instance, the movement of time is shown as opening up the historical character of Dasein, its relationality beyond its immediate world and its present moment; likewise, Heidegger recognizes the conception of time that forms the real unity and ground of Dasein needs to be clearly distinguished from the traditional (Heidegger calls it "vulgar") sense of time as the linear movement of nows that succeed one another. The final sections of *Being and Time* are devoted to this task of contrasting the temporality that grounds Dasein with the metaphysical conception of time that has shaped philosophy from Aristotle's *Physics* up to Hegel.

It would be wrong to say that *Being and Time* has a clear conclusion. The final sections are devoted to highlighting the way in which the insights and project of *Being and Time* stands apart from traditional philosophy. The conclusion comes in the brief final section (GA 2, 436–7/BT, 413–15) in which Heidegger reminds his readers of the larger project that guides *Being and Time* and how it is that what has been achieved thus far in the first two of the six planned divisions still needs to be understood in that context of the largest question of being. To this end, the final words of *Being and Time* are more dedicated to raising questions than to offering conclusions. Almost one half of the final section is composed of questions that Heidegger reminds his reader remain open precisely as a result of the phenomenological analysis of Dasein completed thus far. Bearing these questions in mind, returning to the original plan of *Being and Time* that is laid out in the introduction but never completed, one is led to ask just how far the project of fundamental ontology that is developed in *Being and Time* can be carried out as it promises.

NOTES AND REFERENCES

[1] Of course, *Being and Time* did not suddenly appear *ab novo* and without any context or debts that can help one understand and interpret it. It was, however, only in the past two or three decades that we have had access to the most significant works that can shed light on *Being and Time* itself. Here I am referring to Heidegger's own lecture courses from the years immediately prior to the publication of *Being and Time*. Heidegger's students during these years— among them Hannah Arendt and Hans-Georg Gadamer—were able to follow the evolution of Heidegger's thought that would culminate in *Being and Time*. Many of the key issues that would be published in a more condensed form in that text were developed by Heidegger in lecture courses such as *Prolegomena zur Geschichte des Zeitbegriffs* (1925) and *Die Grundprobleme der Phänomenologie* (1927). In a similar fashion, later works—here one thinks above all of *Beiträge zur Philosophie* (1936–8)—offer insight into Heidegger's own self-critique and self-understanding of his achievement in *Being and Time*.

[2] One can argue, rightly, that several of the works of the late 1920s and early 1930s—for instance, *Kant and the Problem of Metaphysics* (1929), do represent at least sketches of those promised, but never published, sections of *Being and Time*.

[3] That is why Heidegger says that "higher than actuality stands possibility" (GA 2, 38/BT, 36).

[4] As examples of disciplines that seek this "what" and that are to be distinguished from the Dasein analytic, Heidegger refers to anthropology, psychology, and biology (GA 2, 45–50/BT, 44–9).

[5] In this regard, Section 14 (GA 2, 59–62/BT, 59–62) is especially significant. In that section Heidegger clearly distinguishes the forms of disclosure outlined by the existentials from any form of cognition. Knowing, in all of its forms, is he argues a "founded," not an original, way in which the world and the "self" is discovered: "in knowing, Dasein gains a new *perspective of being* toward the world always already discovered in Dasein. . . . Knowing is a mode of Dasein which is founded in being-in-the-world" (GA 2, 62/BT, 62).

24

THE ORIGIN OF THE WORK OF ART
Gregory Schufreider

Der Ursprung des Kunstwerkes designates both a topic and a text. And just as there are multiple versions of the text, there are a number of topics at issue, over and above the question of the origin of artwork. In fact, one might argue that Heidegger's aim in turning his attention to the work of art in the 1930s is to provide a new model of philosophy; although seeing this would require an appreciation of the precise way in which the topic of art is treated in a philosophical text that is designed to initiate a poetic thinking.

To complicate matters, there are at least a half a dozen versions of the essay, and more if we take into consideration the variations in the transcripts of the lectures taken by students who attended them. What has come to be designated as the "First Version" is the draft of a lecture that was never delivered. The text was published (in *Heidegger Studies*) in 1989, after an unauthorized version of a lecture that was first delivered in Freiburg in 1935 appeared in France (in 1987). These differ significantly from one another as well as from the official version of the essay that was published in *Holzwege* in 1950. That text was based on the typescript of three lectures delivered in Frankfort in 1936, although not without alteration in the later publication, including an Epilogue that was, at least in part, written later. An Addendum, written in

1956, was then added to the revised edition of the text that appeared in 1960. Finally, there is the *Gesamtausgabe* version, which includes Heidegger's marginal comments to the earlier editions, marking yet another incarnation of the text.

In what follows, we will be drawing our account primarily from this final version, noting differences from other versions only when unavoidable. In this respect, there are two worth mentioning from the start, namely, in connection with the First Version of the essay; for its stunning formulation that "truth is essentially earthy (*erdhaft*)" is omitted from later versions, as is its claim that *only* art "works." Given this distinctive emphasis, we begin with a discussion of work, before turning our attention to the Earth.

ORIGINATING ART

As necessarily as the artist is the origin of the work in a different way than the work is the origin of the artist, so it is equally certain that, in a still different way, art is the origin of both artist and work. (GA 5, 1/PLT, 17)

While modern thought may take it for granted that the artist is the origin of the work of art, on Heidegger's view, this cannot be true, at least not unambiguously. For the work is the origin of the artist, assuming that someone only becomes an artist by creating a successful work of art. The event that Heidegger calls "art" is not the work of a single individual but must be thought collectively: in terms of a community that is constituted historically in a complex dynamic between artists, works, and what he calls preservers. At the same time, while Heidegger undermines the modern emphasis on genius, he also rejects the ancient failure to distinguish art from craft, such that "*techne*" refers to a set of productive principles through which a work is created by following the rules; even if he would agree that art is a distinctive way of coming into being (*genesis*).

It may appear that what we have here are two opposed models of the origin of artwork: a production model, in which a product is produced by executing a set of procedural techniques, in contrast to a model of creation that emphasizes the free imagination of an artistic genius, which cannot be duplicated in its operation. Both, however, offer causal accounts—the first based on Aristotle's four causes, and the second by elevating what the classical account had relegated to the role of an efficient cause. In either case, art is thought in terms of metaphysical genesis: as an origin through which beings come into being in what Heidegger would regard as their ontical creation. By contrast, he would have us approach art ontologically, in a phenomenological ontology that thinks of "being" in terms of the different ways in which a being can appear. In that event, works of art are not simply ontical creations but involve an ontological determination; which is to say that "artwork" designates a specific way in which a being may appear, whether it is the

Pieta of Michelangelo or an inverted urinal signed "R. Mutt."

We mention Duchamp's *Fountain*, which Heidegger does not (although it was "created" in 1917), because it helps to raise the question of the origin of the work of art, neither in the predictable procedure of a technical production nor through the inexplicable genius of an artistic creation, at least not one that operates by generating new beings metaphysically. Instead, what would otherwise appear as an item of gear (when mounted on the wall in a washroom) or even as an object (on display at a plumbing showroom) presents itself as a work of art, virtually without ontical alteration, except in its signature presentation—unless we also count its change of location (to a gallery) and inversion, which renders it dysfunctional (as gear) but self-standing (as a work of art). Similarly, when it comes to the traditional art that is mimicked here, it should be clear that the "work" may appear as an "object" (in aesthetic appreciation) or as an item of "gear" (in interior decoration), not to mention as a "product" (of a creative operation) or even as a "commodity" (in an economic calculation). Assuming that these ontological categories designate different ways in which the same being can appear, the question remains: what constitutes the "workly" character of the work of art, if not the work that the artist does in making it? What work, in other words, does the work itself do, such that, when it works, it creates an artist? And under what conditions does a being appear (in its "being") as artwork, including the readymade, which (as its nickname indicates) abandons metaphysical creation in favor of an ontological originality that takes place right before our very eyes, in the event that what would otherwise appear as an item of gear presents itself as a work of art?

UNEARTHING A WORLD

*When a work is created, brought forth
out of this or that work-material—stone,
wood, metal, color, language, tone—we
say that it is made, set forth out of it.*
(GA 5, 31/PLT, 45)

In attending to the question of what makes
something art, we would, no doubt, have to
face the institutional determination of the
work, and not just in the museum (as an
institution in which it may be displayed—to
appeal to another ontological category—as
an "artifact") but insofar as a community is
involved in setting the historical conditions,
including for the advent of the readymade.
To oversimplify, we might say that the ontological dimension of the work of art will be
thought in terms of what Heidegger calls the
world, as an historical structure that is created collectively, while the insistence on its
ontical determination will involve a relation
to the Earth as a prehistoric base of operations. This oversimplification will have to be
corrected when we arrive at the most original thought in the essay on art, namely, of a
"rift-design" that is created through a conflict that is yet to be defined.

If we have appealed to the readymade, it is
not to suggest that Heidegger overlooks the
ontical aspect of artwork, given his insistence
on its relation to the Earth as the source of a
concrete creation. Even Duchamp's *Fountain*
presents itself with a certain ontical originality, not in a material creation but in its
presentation as an anomaly that isolates the
ontological dimension of the work, highlighting the question of what makes something
art. The answer, for Heidegger, is not that art
is whatever artists say it is. On the contrary,
his claim is that the successful work must
be thought in terms of what he dubs as "the

riddle of art," which entails an appreciation
of the way in which art "works" both ontically and ontologically. In that event, the task
(of philosophy), we are told, is not to solve
the riddle (of art) but to see it: to clarify how
an ontical creativity may be riddled with an
ontological originality, such that the origin
(*Ursprung*) of art is seen to operate in relation to a primal leap (*Ur-sprung*) that is suspended in a breach between world and Earth
that is created by the work itself.

In that case, we face a circle that may well
be puzzling, given that artwork must create its own origin: instigate a rift between
world and Earth whose resolution renders
the design of a veritable fault line as an
outline of truth in the making through the
struggle of creation. If what Heidegger calls
the world is an historical structure, then the
Earth is a prehistoric ground: an *Ur-* as well
as an *Ab-grund*; which is to say that, as both
a primal and abysmal ground, it is as likely
to undermine a world as to allow one to be
founded on it. For the ground is not a foundation but, in this case, an abysmal source on
which a world must be founded through the
work of art. This does not make the Earth a
"resource" (which is another way in which it
can appear, ontologically speaking, under the
auspices of modern technology), any more
than the work is to be thought of as an object
or an item of gear, let alone as a product or
commodity. Instead, a world must be created
and supported through work that has accom-
modated itself to both world and Earth: is set
between world and Earth or, to be precise,
sets up (*aufstellen*) a world by setting forth
(*herstellen*) the Earth through a settlement
of their inherent strife. In so doing, the work
is set back (*zurückstellen*) on an Earth that
secures (*feststellen*) a world, however tenu-
ously, given the struggle through which it
originates.

While it may to be obvious that, in art, an earth-material is worked into an historical structure, in Heidegger the result cannot be thought in terms of a static (let alone an eternal) form that dominates its matter, but in the configuration (*Gestalt*) of a framework (*Gestell*) that is clearly designated as a gathering of opposition in the linguistic operation of the above-mentioned set of "*stellens*." To appreciate the dynamic nature of the resolution of the conflict between world and Earth, we would have to add another piece to the puzzle by insisting that, for Heidegger, what is distinctive about such work is that, in setting up a world, the Earth is revealed as a self-concealing source: set forth in its concealment as an abysmal support that must be "unearthed" in a dual sense. Not only must the Earth be disclosed in a world, but if it is to be exposed in the integrity of its self-determination, it must be worked against itself: be literally "un-earthed" *as* the Earth in a world that does not violate its self-concealment. Instead, in the respect that is shown for it in its revelation, the Earth appears as the self-contained basis for a world to which it is indifferently opposed.

If the world of a people directs us to an historical dimension of phenomena, while the Earth marks the facticity of a prehistoric givenness, then artwork makes it clear that a world is not simply projected on but protected by the Earth insofar as it is created out of it. If the Earth is to be rendered suitable for historical habitation, it must be un-earthed, however ambiguously, even as a world is unearthed on the basis of it insofar as the configuration of the work is worked out in a conflict that stems from a profound indifference. While the Earth is disclosed in a world that must work with and against its inclination for concealment, the world is stabilized by being set back on an Earth that maintains its self-enclosure in a sublime seclusion. This is not a matter of isolation but of an integrity that keeps to itself in an indifference that must be thought in relation to a duality that is complicated by its simplicity, namely, that world and Earth are not two different things. For while there is an inherent asymmetry in their relation insofar as the Earth is indifferent to a world that depends upon it, there is a far more essential "in-difference" between them insofar as their difference is not ontical but ontological. The Earth is not just indifferent to the world but in-different from it insofar as the world "is" the Earth disclosed historically. In that event, the ontological (in)difference between world and Earth is not just instigated by and secured through but exhibited in the work of art as it displays its origin in its presentation.

In so doing, what art shows is that a world is not imposed upon beings (as the paradigm of the "object" may suggest) but unearthed in their midst through the creation (and installation) of specific beings, namely, "works" of art, that literally make a world out of the Earth. If we take art as our model, it is clear that a world "happens" as a concrete site for human habitation when the Earth appears within the confines of an historical structure. Moreover, if these works are to provide a foundation for the world, then they must be designed in and as a configuration of the conflict, such that, in the unearthing of a world through artwork, it becomes apparent that "truth is essentially earthy."

DESIGNING A RIFT

Truth establishes itself as a strife within a being that is to be brought forth only in such a way that the conflict opens up in this being, that is, this being is itself brought into the rift-design. (GA 5, 51/ PLT, 63)

If what Heidegger once referred to as our "being-in-the-world" must now be thought in relation to a being-on-the-Earth, then this is to insist that the world, as a meaningful whole, is founded on a massive insignificance that both precedes and exceeds wherever sense can be made of human existence. In that event, we must admit that all historical significance is instituted through and submitted to a formation that is "faulty," if we may take the term geologically: is full of faults, not as defects or mistakes but as cracks or breaks in the foundation. In this respect, it is the self-concealing operation of the Earth that keeps a world open: interrupts our inclination for totalization in an enclosure of sense as a framework of significance. Not only does the Earth inevitably disrupt our meaning, given its indifference, but a sublime insignificance may be glimpsed in the beauty of the breach that is created by works of art in the breakdowns as well as the breakthroughs that constitute a "continuous" history of creative struggle. For the Earth remains intact in its integrity throughout the fluctuations in "world-history," which is to say that there is only one "Earth" (which is why we capitalize it as a proper name) but many worlds.

While it should come as no surprise if the key term that unlocks the structure of the work of art has geological overtones, what is referred to as the "rift" (*Riß*) is designed to describe the structure of the strife between world and Earth as a breach in which each is related to the other in the concrete determination of a dynamic configuration. The crack or split between world and Earth creates a figurative fault line, which defines an opening between them that is configured in

the clash of their alignment. This dynamic "rift" is thought linguistically in terms of a complex "design": in relation to the sketch or layout (*Auf-riß*) of a ground plan or outline (*Grund-riß*), in this case, taken literally as a ripping open of the ground. Such a "rift-design," in other words, is rendered in a rent that rips through (*Durch-riß*) the ground, breaking it open in such a way that the breach defines the contour (*Um-riß*) of a concrete design. It is as if the ground must be ground down, if it is to take shape in a structure that is created as the configuration of a conflict between world and Earth that is etched into the work insofar as the work has been (sk)etched out of it. In this respect, the work of art is torn between the two, given its commitment to let the self-concealing Earth appear in a world that is clearly grounded on it.

If artwork is to found a world on the Earth, it must submit to both by creating a concrete relation between them: instigate a strife that is defined by the configuration of a rift-design in a dynamic event of uncon- cealment. Not only does the Earth appear in the unearthing of a world, but the work presents itself in its own originality: appears as an unprecedented revelation of the rela- tion between world and Earth, and in an origination that is apparent in the appear- ance of the work of art. In this respect, art involves an exhibition of truth in the beauty of the breach, assuming that what we see on display in the work is the creation of an historic opening between world and Earth: a time-space, to be exact, that arranges for the disclosure, not just of the work (as an onti- cal creation) but of all beings in the historical dimension of their appearance, thanks to the installation of art in their midst. This is to insist that art is in a position to set a standard for unconcealment, ontologically speaking:

THE ORIGIN OF THE WORK OF ART

to create a measure of "being" that the work brings with it in its own creation insofar as its appearance happens through a primal conflict that art is designed keep open, as if in the riptide of an historical momentum that does not subside in the meeting of its opposing currents. On the contrary, art accelerates history, setting its pace by intensifying the flow of time through the operation of a free creation that takes place spatially as well as temporally.

A MOVING BEAUTY

History is the transporting of a people into its appointed task as entrance into that people's endowment. (GA 5, 65/ PLT, 77)

If art involves an ontological determination, then this is to insist that a time-space of unconcealment is not only opened up in the conflict between world and Earth but that what Heidegger designates as "the truth of being" happens historically in ontical creations that are stationed in the midst of beings to set a standard for their appearance as phenomena. In facing what he dubs as the "clearing" (*Lichtung*), in the case in point, as an historical opening that takes place through creative "work," we come to the heart of Heidegger's thinking, and not only about the origin of art. On the contrary, it is his thought about the clearing of a time-space for the appearance of phenomena that gives to art a specifically Heideggerian look. As an historic event, what he calls "the open" is riddled with openings—which is what a work of art "is," and not only insofar as "great art" creates a breach in history, but in that the work generates a free and open space and

time in a clearing that is designed to keep the conflict between world and Earth happening by refining it in a dynamic design.

This refinement of the rift, as both a clarification and a condensation of conflict, takes place in the beauty of a concrete configuration that must be thought of not only as an open structure but as a structured openness. In structuring the strife, the work of art shows a certain restraint that displays the contention of the clearing in such a way as to keep its originality in play, working to disclose the struggle for beings in their historical being. Needless to say, the creation of what we might think of as a true beauty, given its relation to unconcealment, connects a world to the Earth more directly than a traditional sense of truth. In the end, it is the "earthy" dimension of truth that links it to the beauty of the work of art insofar as ontological truth must be installed (*einrichten*) or executed (*verrichten*) ontically in order to create a concrete opening for an historical existence. The disclosure of a free time-space must be arranged (*richten*) with an exactness (*Richtigkeit*) that is not a matter of correctness, or even of a mere precision, but of a literal accuracy in setting the directions from which a community may take its orientation (*Richtung*), in the case of art, through the erecting (*errichten*) of concrete sites of truth (*Wahrheit*) whose breakthroughs must be preserved (*verwahren*) collectively in order to sustain the momentum of a people's history.

Such a moving beauty will itself be thought in four movements, once again expressed in terms of a root that is pulled in different directions. This time the term "*rücken*" will be deployed to define a linguistic complex that is designed to track an elusive beauty in its dynamic operation. Through entrancement (*berücken*), engagement (*einrücken*), transport (*entrücken*), and derangement (*verrücken*), the work of art attracts an audience that is drawn to it thanks to a captivation that engages them in an historical movement insofar as they are transported to another world, as old standards are struck down and new ones are erected, which only take effect if preservers are willing to submit to them: are committed to protect the truth that is happening through the work as a standard-setting event of unconcealment. In submitting to an ontological derangement, not as the madness of the insane but in the ecstatic opening that is involved in resetting the range of the horizons of world-history, the audience participates in the beauty of art, whose origin, as we have insisted from the start, must be thought of as a collective creation.

In Heidegger's view, art takes part in the creation of a truth that is coming true historically, in work that sets the standards for the appearance of phenomena through its beauty. For beauty happens when ontological truth appears ontically: in its installation through the origination of specific beings that operate to set a standard of being in their own appearance. Such a measure-setting event, in the case of art, involves the self-evidence of its own creation, in which a being appears to set the standard for its own appearance, not to have one imposed upon it, and least of all by us insofar as we submit to it. Consequently, Heidegger will claim, following Hölderlin, that beauty is "the most apparent appearance," as an appearance in which appearance itself becomes apparent and, as such, strikes us with an amazement that is astonishing, if not awe-inspiring. In appreciating the unprecedented presence of the work of art in its originality, we are struck by the fact that it is at all—and not in the debilitation of anxiety but in the elation of a beauty that moves mountains into history insofar as it

displays the Earth in its entry into unconcealment, assuming that we agree not only with Heidegger's view of Cezanne's many renderings of Mont Sainte-Victoire, but appreciate that they are created out of paint.

POETIC THINKING

Does the clearing happen through language or does this appropriative event of clearing first grant articulation and renunciation and so language? Language and body (speech and writing). (GA 5, 62)

Given the word-play that we have seen on display, it should come as no surprise that a text on the origin of art would inevitably lead to the thought of linguistic work in its own originality as well as to a (re)consideration of philosophy as "a work of the word" in its "kinship" with poetry. This is not a matter of art yielding to philosophy, as in Hegel, and certainly not of poetry giving way to prose. On the contrary, the point, we would insist, is to recreate philosophy in the face of art; even if Heidegger will do so by insisting upon the priority of a poetic thinking.

While we cannot deny that the overall structure of "The Origin of the Work of Art" involves the plotting of what would appear to be a strategy of betrayal in its ultimate commitment to poetry, the tactics of the text would suggest otherwise. Admittedly, the movement of thinking begins by appealing to a model drawn from the plastic arts, in which the appearance of the Earth is evident, only to end by rendering them secondary to poetry, based on Heidegger's claims about the priority of language—which hardly seems to qualify as an "earth-material," even though he includes it in the list, along with stone and paint. And while he also includes a disclaimer, distinguishing poetry proper from the "poetic" nature of all art, his insistence on the centrality of linguistic creativity remains problematic.

It would appear, however, that sometime after 1960 Heidegger had second-thoughts, questioning the priority that he had attributed to language in the determination of the clearing, or at least wondering what it means to say that the other arts operate in an opening that "has already happened unnoticed in language." And without addressing this in detail, we would insist that the tactics of the text already suggest a different approach: not an eclipsing of the plastic by the poetic arts but the presentation of a linguistic creation as a plastic operation. Here we would have to appreciate the text not only in its configuration of opposing roots (*stellen, reissen, richten, rücken*) but in its rendering of each through a complex prefixing that operates through hyphenation: by inserting a rift in the word as a plastic act designed to break it open, and not just in the exposure of a root meaning but in a reconfiguration of the sight and sound of language insofar as a moment of silence has been inserted into the word through its punctuation. In so doing, words presents themselves with an unprecedented significance, such that we literally sense language as an original event, breaking the silence through which meaning comes into being.

25

INTRODUCTION TO METAPHYSICS
Gregory Fried

Since its publication in 1953, *Introduction to Metaphysics* has been one of Martin Heidegger's most widely read works, second perhaps only to *Being and Time* (1927). It was the first book by Heidegger to be translated into English, in 1959, before even *Being and Time* (1962). Heidegger himself signaled the book's importance in his Author's Preface to the seventh edition of *Being and Time*: "For the elucidation of this question [of Being] the reader may refer to my *Einführung in die Metaphysik*, which is appearing simultaneously with this reprinting" (SZ, viii/BTRM, 17). Based on lectures delivered in 1935, at the height of Heidegger's ardent embrace of National Socialism, it has also been one of his most controversial works, with debates breaking out from its first appearance in 1953.[1] We will return to the vexed question of Heidegger's politics, but it is also worth pointing out what has made this book attractive to readers: its accessibility, at least compared to some of Heidegger's more obscure works; the sweep of its themes, ranging across 2,500 years of Western philosophy; its powerful interpretation of classic works of literature, most prominently, the "Ode to Man" in Sophocles' *Antigone*. Developmentally, *Introduction to Metaphysics* occupies a transitional position in Heidegger's path, between the fundamental ontology and the analytic of

Dasein in *Being and Time* and the efforts in *Contributions to Philosophy* (1936–8) and later works to find language for a new kind of thinking. In this period Heidegger first begins exploring the poet Hölderlin, and we find here the same incipient attempt to engender a "poetizing thinking" (GA 40, 153/IM, 154) that would break past the nihilism of traditional metaphysics.

"INTRODUCING" METAPHYSICS

The first obstacle for a reader new to Heidegger is the deceptively ordinary title, *Introduction to Metaphysics*. This makes it sounds like a conventional primer on a shop-worn field in academic philosophy. At first, Heidegger seems close to the traditional understanding of metaphysics when he begins his course by asking, "Why are there beings at all rather than nothing?" This certainly does not seem like a question that a science like physics could answer. It reaches all the way back, then, to what Aristotle would have called *first philosophy*, which he treated in a body of works later referred to as his *meta ta phusika*, those texts that come "after the physics" and therefore inquire *beyond* the physical (see GA 36/37, 20–1/BAT, 17–19).

The most pressing metaphysical question asks why something, anything, should go to the bother of existing "at all." As Heidegger says, this metaphysical question *par excellence* "is not allowed to dwell on this or that domain of nature—inanimate bodies, plants, animals—but must go on beyond *ta physica*" (GA 40, 19/IM, 18). The question is not simply asking about what happens to be the substance and structure of this or that being or even of reality in general, but beyond this, why reality should have this substance and structure in the first place, what its most fundamental and essential cause is. Hence Heidegger writes: "The question we have identified as first in rank—'Why are there beings at all instead of nothing?'—is thus the fundamental question of metaphysics. Metaphysics stands as the name for the center and core that determines all philosophy" (GA 40, 19–20/IM, 19).

The novice reader might well misunderstand Heidegger to mean that he agrees that metaphysics should be central to philosophy. This would be a fatal mistake. Heidegger often spells out at great length a position he will ultimately bring to a dead end and declare inadequate, even if he might have seemed sympathetic to it along the way. Heidegger emphatically distinguishes between the ontological question about Being *as such* and the metaphysical question about beings (GA 40, 20/IM, 19). By asking exclusively about beings, their origin, and substance, Heidegger holds that metaphysics forgets the question of Being by treating it as another version of the question of beings. But as Heidegger has argued in *Being and Time* (SZ, 4/BTMR, 23), there is a difference between Being (*Sein*) and beings (*das Seiende*): Being is not itself a being, some metaphysical ground for everything that is, even if the metaphysical tradition interprets Being in this way (GA 40, 20/

IM, 19). But then what *is* Being? *That* is the question, and one Heidegger is in no hurry to answer.

Heidegger quite emphatically means his "introduction" to metaphysics in a literal sense as a *leading-in* of his listeners into what is at stake in how the history of metaphysics has obscured the question of Being:

"Introduction [*Einführung*] to metaphysics" accordingly means: leading into [*Hineinführung*] the asking of the fundamental question. . . . Leading [*Führung*] is a questioning going-ahead, a questioning-ahead. This is a leadership that essentially has no following. (GA 40, 22/IM, 21)

Heidegger seeks to awaken the *question* of Being by showing how metaphysics has resulted in a dead end in the two millennia after Plato. At the end of this long history of metaphysics, Nietzsche most prominently, but the West more broadly, has repudiated Being as something no longer worth asking about: "The word 'Being' is then finally just an empty word. It means nothing actual, tangible, real. Its meaning is an unreal vapor" (GA 40, 39/IM, 38). But precisely this experience of Being as an empty word, a mere vapor, is what Heidegger wants to question, and from there to reawaken a renewed understanding of Being, yet without simply slipping back into metaphysics.

It cannot be an accident for a thinker so careful about language to speak so deliberately of *Führung* in 1935. Here we have an example of Heidegger attempting to appropriate Nazi terminology for his own use and to construe leadership not as a blind following but as an incitement to one's own appropriation of what is essential. We see this when Heidegger rejects Nietzsche and asks,

"Is 'Being' a mere word and its meaning a vapor, or is it the spiritual fate of the West?" (GA 40, 40/IM, 40) For Heidegger, this question is a question about "our people," the Germans:

We lie in the pincers. Our people, as standing in the center, suffers the most intense pressure—our people, the people richest in neighbors and hence the most endangered people, and for all that, the metaphysical people. We are sure of this vocation; but this people will gain a fate from its vocation only when it creates *in itself* a resonance, a possibility of resonance for this vocation, and grasps its tradition creatively. (GA 40, 41/IM, 41)

It seems strange that Heidegger calls the Germans "the metaphysical people," given his attack on metaphysics, but this must be heard in the overall spirit of the lecture course: that confronting the historical meaning of metaphysics is an inescapable task, that doing this is the vocation of the Germans as part of the restoration of the question of Being. This is why Heidegger makes one of the most startling pronouncements in this course:

This Europe, in its unholy blindness always on the point of cutting its own throat, lies today in the great pincers between Russia on the one side and America on the other. Russia and America, seen metaphysically, are both the same: the same hopeless frenzy of unchained technology and of the rootless organization of the average man. (GA 40, 40–1/IM, 40)

For Heidegger, Germany lies "in the pincers" because the metaphysical understanding of the world underlies nations and political systems as diverse as Russia's communism and America's liberalism; they are "the same" not

because they are identical but because each in its way understands the world metaphysically. Both have forgotten the question of Being. So he proclaims, "To ask: how does it stand with Being?—this means nothing less than to *repeat and retrieve* the inception of our historical-spiritual Dasein, in order to transform it into the other inception" (GA 40, 42/IM, 41).

It would be hard to exaggerate the ambition couched in this declaration. Heidegger takes the reawakening of the question of Being as a decisive event in the "spiritual fate of the West," because how we understand what it means *to be* is the departure for the understanding of our entire existence. By "inception" (*Anfang*), Heidegger means not a mere chronological beginning point, but rather that which gives an historical epoch its trajectory. The inception to be reanimated, in this moment of national revolution, is the ancient Greek one, but not through rank imitation; Heidegger's notion of repetitive retrieval (*Wieder-holung*) does not mean duplicating facts or institutions; it means reawakening lost and neglected *possibilities* of Being inherent to that first, ancient inception—the one before the incipient nihilism of Plato's idealism took hold—and making it a fertile ground for bringing on this "other inception," a new departure for the West, led by Germany.

RETRIEVING THE GREEKS

Chapter 2, On the Grammar and Etymology of the Word "Being," engages in a Heideggerian "destruction" of the history of Western grammar in order to show how the meaning of Being, as a decisive *question*, has been obscured by developments in language and schools of grammar. Without going into the technical details,[2] Heidegger's point here is that the transition from the Greek to the Latin grammarians distorted the sense of what a verb is, so that what we now call the infinitive, from the Latin *modus infinitivus*, is taken to be the most abstract, least meaningful, and "emptiest" form of the verb (GA 40, 74/IM, 73). On this already attenuated basis of the infinitive, Indo-European languages have formed verbal substantives, such as *das Sein* from *sein*. While English constructs substantives from the gerund rather than from the infinitive, the result, such as "Being," is then an even further intensification of this generality. Furthermore, this making a substantive, a noun, out of the verb, leads to the most baleful distortion of all for Heidegger, namely, the confusion of Being with beings:

> The substantive *das Sein* [Being] implies that what is so named, itself "is." Being now itself becomes something that "is," whereas obviously only beings are, and it is not the case that Being also is. (GA 40, 73/IM, 73)

The way to understand the question of Being is to ask what it means *to be*, not what makes up the attributes of some noun-like, big-B "Being," a being like all other beings except that it somehow causes or explains all the rest of them. What it means *to be* is *verbal*, or temporal, and for this reason finite, historical, and situated in a context. This is why, when Heidegger looks at the conglomeration of Indo-European roots that make up the morphology of the verb "to be" (e.g. I am, you are, it is, they were, I have been, etc.), he discerns the unifying meaning of "living, emerging, abiding" (GA 40, 76–7/IM, 76). He understands this meaning even more primordially as "coming-to-presence" (*An-wesen*), or presencing (GA 40, 65–6/IM, 64), which does not mean Being is an object eternally present to us, but rather that Being unfolds a world of meaning in which beings come in and go out of presence for us. To use language not too alien to Heidegger, what is at issue in the question of Being is the temporal *whiling* of meaning that makes a historical world accessible.

Heidegger now introduces one of the Presocratic fragments that is of the greatest significance for him in this period, fragment 53 of Heraclitus about war (*polemos*), which he renders as follow: "Confrontation is indeed for all (that comes to presence) the sire (who lets emerge), but (also) for all the preserver that holds sway. For it lets some appear as gods, others as human beings, some it produces (sets forth) as slaves, but others as the free" (GA 40, 66/IM, 65).[3] *Polemos* as struggle (*Kampf*) or confrontation (*Auseinandersetzung*) is the process through which beings become meaningful to us, and so through which Being itself is manifested, by allowing things to take on clear boundaries as discernible, separate entities, each of which can take on a name in language: "Confrontation does not divide unity, much less destroy it. It builds unity; it is the gathering (*logos*). *Polemos* and *logos* are the same" (ibid.). Language is not a consequence of experience or a secondary feature of human understanding; language *assembles* the world as it *divides* it up into intelligible parts that can come into presence for us (GA 40, 93/IM, 91–2). "Where struggle ceases, beings indeed do not disappear, but world turns away" (GA 40, 67/IM, 65): a meaningful world requires the struggle over the interpretation of what things *are*.

BREAKING RESTRICTIONS

This emphasis on language as the heart of a hermeneutical struggle helps explain why Heidegger turns to Greek poetry and the Presocratics in this work. Here we see Heidegger attempting to develop a new vocabulary to articulate the recovered question of Being. Chapter 4, The Restriction of Being, encompasses the remaining and largest portion of the book. Heidegger examines four ways in which Western thought has sought to delimit Being: Being and becoming, Being and seeming, Being and thinking, and Being and the ought. The key is that Heidegger is attempting to deconstruct and reappropriate these formulaic oppositions so that they no longer serve as *restrictions* of Being (GA 40, 100–2/IM, 98–100). For example, in a conventional reading of Parmenides we are used to thinking of Being as "perdurance of the constant," as opposed to the Heraclitean *panta rhei* ("everything flows") of becoming (GA 40, 104/IM, 102), but Heidegger calls this conventional opposition into question. Similarly, we are used to thinking of Being as opposed to seeming, "the genuine versus the ungenuine" (GA 40, 105–6/IM, 103). But Heidegger insists that "Being essentially unfolds *as* appearing" (GA 40, 108/IM, 107). He argues that Being unfolds *as* what manifests itself, as what appears, as the phenomenon that emerges into the truth as unconcealment (*alêtheia*) (GA 40, 109/IM, 107). Truth as correctness is derivative to truth as appearing: only if beings are manifest to us as *somehow* meaningful can we then determine their "reality." But the history of the West has subsequently condemned seeming as *mere* seeming:

Only with the sophists and Plato was seeming explained as, and thus reduced

to, mere seeming. At the same time, Being as idea was elevated to a supersensory realm. The chasm, *khorismos*, was torn open between the merely apparent beings here below and the real Being somewhere up there. Christian doctrine then established itself in this chasm, while at the same time reinterpreting the Below as the created and the Above as the Creator, and with weapons thus reforged, it set itself against antiquity [as paganism] and distorted it. And so Nietzsche is right to say that Christianity is Platonism for the people. (GA 40, 113/IM, 111; Heidegger's brackets)

It is against this nihilistic metaphysics inherited from Plato that Heidegger seeks a revolutionary retrieval of the possibilities covered over in the pre-Socratic origins.

Heidegger devotes the most attention to Being and thinking. He starts with the modern understanding of thinking that *represents* Being as an object (GA 40, 124/IM, 123). But if *thinking* represents Being in its reality, then is not logic, "the science of thinking," what we are after here (GA 40, 128/IM, 126)? But Heidegger rejects logic as the final arbiter for thinking and the representation of reality, because "Being as unconcealment . . . is precisely what was lost due to 'logic'" (GA 40, 129/IM, 127). Logic assumes that the *assertion* is the locus of truth, but Heidegger holds that truth as *alêtheia*, as unconcealment, must transpire *prior* to any assertions and representations we make. Hence Heidegger's focus on *logos* in Greek not as language, discourse, or reason, but as something more primordial than all of these: *gathering* (GA 40, 132/IM, 131). Drawing on the fragments of Heraclitus, Heidegger argues that "*Logos* is constant gathering, the gatheredness of beings that stands in itself, that is, Being" (GA 40, 139/IM, 138). Given that "*polemos* and *logos* are the same," this means that the world as we think it is a world assembled in a meaningful way, with differentiations giving things the intelligibility that can be articulated in words and everyday discourse—and ultimately in logical assertions.

Now Heidegger turns to Parmenides to address what thinking itself means, other than the rules of logic that allows us, as subject, to make accurate sense of "Being" as an external object (GA 40, 144/IM, 144). Fragment 5 of Parmenides reads *to gar auto noein estin te kai einai*, conventionally rendered "but thinking and Being are the same" (GA 40, 145/ IM, 145). *Noein*, Heidegger insists, must be understood as *apprehension*, the way we *take in* the gathered meaning of the world (GA 40, 146–7/IM, 146–7). Heidegger asserts that Parmenides has been so obscured by the history that has made him seem self-evident that it would help to take a detour through the "Ode to Man" choral passage in Sophocles' *Antigone* (GA 40, 153–5/IM, 154–6). The passage begins "Manifold is the uncanny, yet nothing/uncannier than man bestirs itself . . ." (GA 40, 155/IM, 156). The key is the Greek *to deinon*, the uncanny, the terrible; human beings are the uncanniest, the most terrible, "because as those who do violence, they overstep the limits of the homely, precisely in the direction of the uncanny in the sense of the overwhelming" (GA 40, 160/ IM, 161). Only those whose daring (*tolma*; GA 40, 170/IM 172) undertakes the risk of this uncanny violence "rise high in historical Being as creators, as doers" (GA 40, 162/IM, 163). Against what Heidegger calls the overwhelming sway of Being itself, its capacity to unseat all human endeavors with mortality and finitude, the creators oppose the violence of their *technê*, their skillful knowing, in poetry, in statecraft, or in thought (GA 40/ IM, 169, 168; also GA 40, 66/IM, 65). The

deinon has two faces: the overwhelming sway of Being as *dikê*, the justice that constantly threatens to submerge us, and the violence of the creators, who strive to make something that will endure through their *technê* (GA 40, 169/IM, 171). Being *requires* the violence of these creative figures so that it may have a site in which to appear. This is Being's polemical necessity (GA 40, 171–2/IM, 173–4); otherwise, the world sinks into the self-evident, and all meaning gets taken for granted. "Therefore the violence–doer knows no kindness and conciliation (in the ordinary sense), no appeasement and mollification by success or prestige and by their confirmation" (GA 40, 172/IM, 174)—again we see Heidegger's rejection of anything resembling Christian norms or secular moralism.

Heidegger's claim now is that "the belonging–together of *noein* (apprehension) and *einai* (Being), which is said in the saying of Parmenides, is nothing but this reciprocal relation" of *dikê* and *technê* (GA 40, 174/ IM, 176). It cannot be exaggerated how far removed Heidegger's sense of justice (*dikê*) is from a moral–juridical one; he means it in a radically ontological sense as how Being gives the world its *fit*, its sense of an articulated, structured whole that nevertheless always threatens to exceed us and leave us destitute and at a loss for understanding. As such, *dikê* beckons human creative *technê* but also suspends these efforts over disaster "as the deepest and broadest Yes to the overwhelming" (GA 40, 172/IM, 174), for our works can never get out past Being and produce an everlasting dispensation that will bring the becoming of Being to an end. And so: "apprehension, in its belonging-together with Being (*dikê*), is such that it uses violence, and as doing violence is an urgency, and as an urgency is undergone only in the necessity of a struggle [in the sense of *polemos* and *eris*]"

(GA 40, 176/IM, 178; Heidegger's brackets). If thinking is *apprehension*, in this sense of engaging the meaning of Being in a creative *polemos*, an interpretive confrontation over the constitution of the world, then Being and thinking belong together in a manner prior to logic or to representational thinking. But through Plato emerged a form of thinking that reduces apprehension to the apprehension of an *idea* (GA 40, 189–90/IM, 192), and so the inception with Parmenides and Heraclitus collapses: "Consequently, what really is, is what always is, *aei on*. What is continuously coming to presence is what we must go back to, in advance, in all comprehending and producing of anything: the model, the *idea*" (GA 40, 201/IM, 206). Logic and representational thinking are grounded upon an interpretation of Being as what *is always* in the supersensory other–world.

We know the final opposition, Being and the ought, well enough: Being, what is, may well be opposed to what *ought* to be. Heidegger again sees the root of this in Plato's ideas: "As Being itself becomes fixed in its character as idea, it also tends to make up for the ensuing degradation of Being. But by now, this can occur only by setting something *above* Being that Being never yet is, but always *ought* to be" (GA 40, 206/IM, 211). Heidegger deems this a nihilism that manifests the oblivion of Being (GA 40, 211–12/ IM, 217), for it has laid the foundation for value-thinking: values become the ground for the ought as what *negate* Being and set something up in its stead as what ought to be. And

this is where Heidegger makes his infamous claim, when, condemning the theories of hack Nazi Party intellectuals, he writes that, "what is peddled about nowadays as the philosophy of National Socialism, but which has not the least to do with the inner truth and greatness of this movement [namely, the encounter between global technology and modern humanity] is fishing in these troubled waters of 'values' and 'totalities'" (GA 40, 208/IM, 213; Heidegger's brackets). At this point, the reader must decide how far to go with Heidegger in this *Introduction*: Is the question of Being more than an empty word-play, and if it is, does it really imply the intellectual and political deconstruction of the West that Heidegger demands? Or does the Western tradition retain resources that exceed Heidegger's apocalyptic confrontation?

NOTES AND REFERENCES

[1] See Herbert Marcuse and Martin Heidegger, "An Exchange of Letters" and Jürgen Habermas, "Martin Heidegger: On the Publication of the Letters of 1935," in ed. Richard Wolin, *The Heidegger Controversy* (Cambridge: MIT Press, 1993).

[2] See Gregory Fried, "What's in a Word? Heidegger's Grammar and Etymology of 'Being,'" in ed. R. Polt and G. Fried, *A Companion to Heidegger's* Introduction to Metaphysics (New Haven: Yale University Press, 2001).

[3] For more on this theme, see Gregory Fried, *Heidegger's* Polemos: *From Being to Politics* (New Haven: Yale University Press, 2000).

26

CONTRIBUTIONS TO PHILOSOPHY
Peter Trawny

When in 1989 the *Contributions to Philosophy (From Enowning)* was published, the academic community was surprised by a manuscript, a text, which was immediately compared and connected with *Being and Time.* Scholars spoke of a "first and a second master-piece,"[1] although in the history of philosophy there is hardly another philosopher who has written texts as different as these two books. Indeed the texts are not connected, except of course by the fact that Heidegger in the *Contributions* refers back to *Being and Time* and claims a dependency on the fundament of "the thing itself."

The diversity of Heidegger's texts exceeds the exemplar in the comparison of the *Contributions* with "Being and Time." Before the lecture courses, articles, and public lectures Heidegger had earlier written poems, and later intense meditations, which he himself called "What has been Thought" (*Gedachtes*). He wrote dialogues and a "three-way conversation," not to mention the very different correspondences with family members, friends, colleagues, and lovers. The *Contributions* are internally related to other "being-historical" manuscripts such as *Mindfulness* and *The History of Be-ing*, etc.

Such a plurality of ways of writing cannot be accidental for a philosopher. It must have a meaning. If it is the case that Heidegger transformed his "ways" of thinking into different "ways" of writing, then this decision presents a philosophical problem. What Heidegger's texts distinguished so uniquely can be characterized as the "*scriptuality*" (*Schriftlichkeit*) of his philosophy. This characterization is of course in itself problematic, because it suggests that there is a form for the thinking representing itself, that is, the writing, and the content, that is, the thinking itself. This difference is based on the idea that everything can be said in different ways. Following this idea we would fall into the crevasses of the metaphysical differentiation between form and matter.

But in the "Letter on Humanism" Heidegger speaks of the "now rare handicraft of writing" (GA 9, 174/PA, 262). This expression of course could refer only to handwriting, that is, to the fact that Heidegger wrote everything with a pen. This does not need to be wrong. But it is possible that the philosopher intends something else: The "handicraft of writing" is a knowledge, an intimacy with the different ways of writing. Thus the writing itself has importance and meaning. And the scripturality of Heidegger's philosophy then would be the significance of writing, and writings for and in this philosophy. The scripturality of this philosophy would have its own extension and abundance, its austereness and immense openness. From here on a new access to this philosophy would be possible.

In the *Contributions* Heidegger sublated the difference of form and matter. In his own words the *Contributions* are no "'work' of the style heretofore" (CP1, 3). The concept of "style" as stilus stems from the manual way of writing. Style is therefore a way to write. Where the concept actually adheres to the difference of form and matter (of medium and information—a banal difference), Heidegger uses it to overcome this difference. A letter to Ernst Jünger reads: "The question of style is in the same time a secret of workshop and profession (*Berufung*). It cannot be discussed in public. But it stays the most necessary and distressful for us. Style belongs to the thing itself." Style is not the thing itself, but it "belongs" to it. This means that the thing primarily becomes the thing itself, because the style renders it in this way.

The style plays not a minor role in the "Contributions." Heidegger speaks of "the will and the style of thinking" (CP1, 15), which as "style of inceptual thinking" (24) in "reservedness" is elucidated. Considered in this way the style is distanced from the form/matter-difference. The style, with and in which the *Contributions* are written, is basically the way, "inceptual thinking" is realizing itself. This style is given only in this thinking and this thinking only in this style. Thus a hint to interpret the style of the *Contributions* is indicated. For an "inceptual thinking" must necessarily distance itself from the thinking that follows or precedes it. Or it must generally be distinguished from all other kinds of thinking. If each thinking has its own style, then the "style of inceptual thinking" must be uniquely different.

This situation, namely that the *Contributions* are a beginning, is unfolded on the first pages of the text. The title "Contributions to Philosophy" gives the "impression," that they are concerned with the promotion of science. But this is only the appearance. For "philosophy cannot appear in public in any other way, since all fundamental words have been used up and the genuine relation to the word has been destroyed" (3). In other words: one who still wants to address a philosophical text to the public sphere has unavoidably to use trivial titles. For the public sphere is dominated by a discourse, which has lost the "genuine relation to the word."

In contrast the "proper heading" of the book is "From Enowning." It does not inform what is "reported" by the text, but rather the following is what is at stake: "[. . .] a thinking-saying which is en-owned by enowning and belongs to be-ing and to be-ing's word." The thinking of the *Contributions* is a correspondence or response to this, that which Heidegger calls "the enowning." If this thinking was able to inscribe itself in this text, it is assigned to "the enowning" itself. Only because the "enowning en-owns," that is, because it transfers thinking to a responsive relation to itself (to "enowning"), could the *Contributions* emerge.

With the distinction between a "public title" and a "proper heading" the *Contributions* immediately state a difference that determines the whole work and its thinking. This difference for Heidegger consists of that between a public discourse of science and the specific presuppositions of an original (more or less still missed) philosophic language unfolding itself from "enowning." This presumably is the difference, with which in different forms Heidegger's thinking is struggling everywhere.

A possible interpretation of this difference is one between an *exoteric discourse* of the public sphere (in which Heidegger himself participates, for instance, with lecture courses or public lectures, that is, with an academic mode of his philosophy) and an *esoteric philosophy*, which appears "For the Few and for the Rare" (9).[2] This difference can be explicated in many utterances of Heidegger. Thus, he claims of philosophy that "what is essential—after it, almost hidden, has gone to the fore—must retreat and become inaccessible (for the many), for this essential is unsurpassable and *therefore* must withdraw into the enabling of the beginning" (13). Or perhaps he illuminates the difference more acutely, when he argues that "making itself intelligible is the suicide for philosophy" (307).

In my eyes Heidegger does not inscribe himself in a conservative or pessimistic movement of European thinking, which is referring to a deep difference between the many (οἱ πολλοί) and the best (οἱ ἄριστοι). Rather he takes up the question: to what extent does philosophy need a language that cannot be subordinated to the general category of "publicity" (Kant). If we consider the "argument" as one of these criteria, Heidegger could only accept this as a form of one specific mode of thinking, but not as one of philosophy as a whole. And indeed, if taken as an essential criterion, the "argument" is effective as a selection and clean(s)ing. The majority of philosophy becomes mere literature.

THE HISTORICAL CONTEXT

The "Contributions to Philosophy" were generated between 1936 and 1938, whereas the "Preview" and the six following parts, named by Heidegger as "joinings," were written between 1936 and 1937, and the last part of the actual version of the text "The Be-ing" emerged in 1938. During the same period Heidegger worked at the first lecture course on Schelling in the summer of 1936, at both lecture courses on Nietzsche in the winter of 1936/37 and the summer of 1937. This was followed by a lecture course quite close to the *Contributions* about the "Basic Questions of Philosophy" in the winter seminar of 1937/38. Furthermore in 1936 Heidegger gave two public lectures in Rome, at first "Hölderlin and the Essence of Poetry," then "Europe and the German Philosophy."

Nor is this an exhaustive account of his work during this time. The editor of the *Contributions* Friedrich-Wilhelm von Herrmann calls attention to the fact that Heidegger was also working on other, as yet unpublished manuscripts such as "Current Comments on 'Being and Time'" (1936), "The ἀλήθεια. The Remembrance into the First Beginning" and "Disempowerment of the φύσις" (both 1937). It is assumed that the genesis of "Mindfulness" (1938/39) coincided with the accomplishment of the "Contributions." Such a confluence of the concurrent genesis of totally heterogeneous texts demonstrates in what dimension the question for the scriptuality of Heidegger's thinking is relevant.

In the middle of 1934 Heidegger declared his resignation from the rectorate of the university of Freiburg. This resignation sometimes has been interrelated to the resolution to write manuscripts apart from the public sphere. In this sense the specific character of the *Contributions* could be reduced to a political disappointment. This idea is not supported by Heidegger's continued assent during this period to defend the new state in seminars (for instance in the seminar on Hegel's "Philosophy of Right" in winter 1934/35), lecture courses, and public lectures. Furthermore, for quite some time before 1933 Heidegger wrote texts (for instance poems), which could not be understood as "academic."

When the work on the manuscript was completed in 1938, Fritz Heidegger, the brother of the philosopher, made a typewritten-copy, which in 1939 Martin Heidegger compared with the original. Well before the publication of the *Contributions* this typewritten-copy was distributed to certain students and friends of the philosopher. It is part of the history of the "Contributions," that a distinct circle of persons outside the public sphere knew the strange text.

The manuscript copy of the "Contributions to Philosophy" in the German Archive for Literature in Marbach contains a dedication, which was not carried over into the publication. For "Christmas 1957" Heidegger had dedicated the manuscript to Dory Vietta, the wife of Egon Vietta, who in 1950 published "The Question of Being by Martin Heidegger." The dedication consists of a handwritten copy of an ode of Pindar in the Greek original as well as in Hölderlin's translation. It includes erotic references. The question, whether the addition of this dedication to the manuscript has philosophical meaning, is debatable. But that the dedication belongs to its history, cannot be doubted.

THE STRUCTURE OF THE TEXT

Heidegger marks the structure of the *Contributions* as a *"jointure"* (*Fuge*) (CP1, 56, 81) of the "inceptual thinking." The word has many connotations. Certainly it brings to mind—in the sense of the Latin fuga— the musical principle of composing, which Johann Sebastian Bach in the first half of the eighteenth century brought to its acme. But

it is unlikely that Heidegger thought of this meaning of the word.

Rather he relied on two other meanings. At first the "jointure" is the gap of the space between two parts of a construction. In this sense Heidegger calls the structure of the *Contributions* also *Gefüge* (*jointure*), that is, an expedient adjustment. But, besides this the philosopher also refers to the meaning of "Fuge" as *Verfügung* (*conjointure*), that is, a binding, sometimes fateful decision.[3] "Both" are characterized as "an *endowment* (*Fügung*) of be-ing itself, of the hint and withdrawal of its truth."

An expedient adjustment is also a "system." But the "Fuge" is "something essentially different." For Heidegger the system is a form of metaphysics moving toward its end. It is "only possible as a consequence of the mastery of mathematical thinking (in its widest sense)" (45). Heidegger is thinking of the most geometrical prestructuring, the deductive organization of the system.

The six parts of the text, which are introduced by a "Preview," read: "Echo," "Playing-Forth," "Leap," "Grounding," "The Ones to Come," and "The Last God." They are called "the six joinings of the jointure," attempting "always to say the same of the same" (57). The "onefold of these 'joinings'" "can only be sustained from within the inabiding in Da-sein, which distinguishes the being of *those who are to come*." Thus the relation to *the* addressee is emphasized.

A special problem of the edition of the text represents its end, wherein the actual form of the book the "joining" "Be-ing" is to be found. Obviously Heidegger initially planned to integrate it as "Section II [Part II]" (365), but then he declared in handwriting that it was "not correctly arranged." This note led the editor to move that part to the end of the text. This resolution is clearly legitimate.

But it is also clear that Heidegger originally designed it as the second "joining." It is evident that reflections about "philosophy," the "ontological difference," and "language"—altogether contained by Be-ing"—could be placed at the beginning of the "Fuge." Finally a (dis-)closure of the book with the "Last God" would correspond to the character of "Gefüge" and "Verfügung."

THE "METHOD" OF THE CONTRIBUTIONS

For the understanding or interpretation of the "*Contributions to Philosophy*" the difference between a public and scientific discourse and a specifically philosophical or, better, a "being-historical" language is presupposed. Heidegger takes this difference as a fact. This is shown by the "Propositions about 'Science'" (100–10). In these propositions Heidegger refers to the academic innovation of "newspaper science" (106). This science was an ancestor of "communication science" along with "radio science" (*Rundfunkkunde*, see GA 78, 188–9) in possession of an institute at the university of Freiburg between 1922 and 1943. The "newspaper science," was absolutely not a mere polemical idea of Heidegger. It was in fact incorporated into academic study at a university, where "the objective and methodical difference between the natural and the human sciences [i.e. philosophy] will recede more and more" (CP1, 107).

The character of this academic institution for Heidegger consists in the event that the "present 'lived-experience' will continually be interpreted historically [historisch] and in this interpretation will be conveyed the *publication* for everyone" (ibid.). Hence it is the

dependency of the university addicted to a technically organized public sphere that lets Heidegger preserve a defined place for philosophy. In the *Contributions* the public sphere without a doubt is understood as an element of "machination." But already in *Being and Time* Heidegger interpreted the public sphere as the "real dictatorship of the 'they'" (BTMR, 164). In the "light of the public sphere" "everything gets obscured, and what has thus been covered up gets passed off as something familiar and accessible to everyone" (165). What is "what has been covered up" ("das Verdeckte")? It is what belongs to the phenomenon in the full sense; the phenomenon, which is always "*the clearing for self-sheltering-concealing*" (CP1, 237). The using up of the language Heidegger is speaking of at the beginning of the *Contributions* is realizing itself in a mass-media-instituted public sphere, which begins to provide the technical and economical and, that is, the discursive standards for the university.

Therefore philosophy has "no place" (108) in the university. It has "no such place at all, unless it be that place that philosophy itself grounds." But from an "established institution" there is "immediately" "no way" to philosophy. Hence seen in the authentic perspective of philosophy there is only the a-topic community of "those who *question*" (10) (*die Fragenden*), who cannot accept normative-discursive presuppositions, for there are primarily these presuppositions, which are called into question. An institution declaring it discourse for binding is, whatever it looks like, unphilosophical.

The language of philosophy cannot be taken from the scientific discourse. Indeed it cannot continue to emerge from the same area from which scientific discourse is emerging. This area for Heidegger is the language of metaphysics. In metaphysics language represents "the asserting of beings" (350). But is there "a new language for be-ing" (54)? Heidegger answers in the negative, even if this abnegation is not as evident as the philosopher declares (here and there he attempted to speak (or to *write*) such a language). This problem marks the place where Heidegger encounters the method of the "Contributions."

The "saying of be-ing" is happening in "words and namings which are understandable in the direction of everyday references to beings" (58). But if they are thought exclusively in this direction, they "are misconstruable as the utterance of be-ing." The "word itself" "discloses something (familiar) and thus hides that which has to be brought into the open through thinking-saying." This "difficulty" demands a specific "approach" (*Verfahren*).

This "approach" must "within certain limits extend to ordinary understanding and must go a certain stretch of the way *with* it," only "to exact a turning in thinking at the right moment, but only under the power of the same word." Heidegger names examples. One of these is the word "machination," which at first "means a way of human comportment." But "suddenly and properly" there emerges "the reverse: what is ownmost (or precisely *not* ownmost) to be-ing," from where primarily the possibility of this "comportment" is originating. This "reverse" is not a "trick to alter the meaning into mere words but rather *transformation of man himself*." In the "approach" of the *Contributions* the human being itself is determined to leave the space and the time of metaphysics.

This language of the *Contributions* is not the one of metaphysics or of science stemming from metaphysics, but "the most nobly formed language in its simplicity and essential force" (54). This is definitely not "ordinary language." More likely it is the language of poetry and in the *Contributions* the language of Hölderlin (297–8). However—Heidegger points this out several times (14, 42, but also 50)—it has to be a language of thinking as distinct from a language of poetry. Hence the demand for this language remains open.

The method of the *Contributions* consists of a decision for a certain usage of the word. This usage can be determined as an esoteric one, for it is preceded by a turning away from the language of metaphysics and science. The "approach" of the *Contributions* addresses itself ab initio only to those who are willing to approve or even to respect this turning away, or at least to understand its idea. To approve is the institutionalizing of a discourse, which with its criteria is inhibiting the possibility of philosophy. This turning away and the responding esoteric initiative characterizes the whole thinking of Heidegger since the 1930s. This thinking is refusing to subject itself to a discourse except its own. This is its freedom *and* its problem.

PROBLEMS OF RECEPTION

The reception of the works of Heidegger's thinking stands under particular conditions. If in art or in music it happens quite often that artists or composers provide comments or even interpretations of their works, in philosophy it is rare. This is not only because the concept of the "work" in philosophy cannot lay claim to the same (for instance aesthetic) meaning as in art. More than around *works* philosophy seems to circle around *arguments*. Nonetheless, perhaps like no other philosopher, Heidegger has criticized and interpreted his own works.

From the six remarks on the "Contributions to Philosophy" from the later text "Das Ereignis" (1941/42) only two are mentioned. In the *Contributions* the "question for being" is "still seized in the style of metaphysics, instead of thought in the way of the already conceived history of being" (4). Moreover the "idea of the last God is still unthinkable" (5).

If in the aesthetic context of the reception of artworks, the difference between the reflections of the artist and the artwork itself is so deep that the artist's reflection can be considered merely another interpretation of the artwork, the problem is more complex in philosophy. For a philosophical text does not define its limits and borders as strictly as an artwork. A text can be touched and sometimes seems to transform itself into its interpretations. Heidegger does not comment on that which is separate from him. Again and again he inscribes himself in his own works, or he even picks up the thread repeatedly. This is why Heidegger's critique of his own writings—rightly or not—claims a privileged meaning. But this is not the only problem of the reception of the "Contributions."

In general the text is considered as the "second major work" of Martin Heidegger (after *Being and Time*). Such an estimation seems to orientate toward Heidegger's own understanding of the work. Otherwise it is contrasted by the philosopher himself, when he chose the motto for the *Gesamtausgabe* "Ways—not works." This motto, if taken seriously, would open up a totally different access to the writings of this philosopher. The experimental character of Heidegger's scriptuality is yet to be discovered.

The reception of the *Contributions* has mostly ignored the difference between a public-scientific discourse and an authentic (Heideggerian) philosophical language (as was emphasized at the beginning). Thus the *Contributions* are integrated into academic Heidegger-research (as if they would be an "academic" text), realizing the addressee-related-writing of the text in a strange way. Just because there is no hermeneutic respect for Heidegger's denial of the academic and scientific way of writing, just because there is no mindfulness of the esoteric and always more esoteric gesture of Heidegger's thinking, a specific, and perhaps the whole research of Heidegger's philosophy is separated from an openness of thinking, that we can learn from Heidegger himself. Thus sects and cliques and groups are defining their territories and choking the philosophical dialogue. Only if we are critically aware of Heidegger's esoteric initiative, only if we are free enough to acknowledge the philosophical dimension of this initiative, which includes indeed the great majority of Heidegger's texts, and only if we are open-minded enough to see the possible failure of this initiative, will the reading of Heidegger take the necessary next step.

NOTES AND REFERENCES

[1] See Friedrich-Wilhelm von Herrmann, *Wege ins Ereignis. Zu Heideggers "Beiträgen zur Philosophie"* (Frankfurt am Main: Klostermann, 1994), 6. See also Emad and Maly in their Translator's Foreword, xv.

[2] See Peter Trawny, *Adyton. Heideggers esoterische Philosophie* (Berlin: Matthes & Seitz, 2011), or Richard F. Polt, *The Emergency of Being: On Heidegger's Contributions to Philosophy* (Ithaca, NY: Cornell University Press, 2006), 11–22. Also consider Hans Ruin, "Contributions to Philosophy," in, ed. Hubert L. Dreyfus and Mark A. Wrathall, *A Companion to Heidegger* (Malden, MA:

Blackwell Publishers, 2005), 358–73, and Daniela Vallega-Neu, *Heidegger's Contributions to Philosophy: An Introduction* (Bloomington: Indiana University Press, 2003), finally *Companion to Heidegger's Contributions to Philosophy*, ed. Charles E. Scott (Bloomington: Indiana University Press, 2001). As given in the translator's introduction of Rojcevicz and Vallega-Neu: "At issue in the *Contributions* are indeed private ponderings not composed for publication" (xv). Maybe the "publication" of the text was not in sight, but there is an important difference between Heidegger's esoteric initiative and "private ponderings." Philosophical thinking is never "private pondering." This is a real misunderstanding even of the style of the "Contributions."

3 Emad and Maly translate "*Verfügung*" with the neologistic "conjointure" and "access." One would have to find another solution.

27

THE HÖLDERLIN LECTURES
William McNeill

CONTEXTS

Heidegger scholarship generally has readily acknowledged that a decisive shift—the so-called turning—takes place in Heidegger's thought during the 1930s: a shift away from the hermeneutic phenomenological ontology of the *Being and Time* period (an ontology imbued with scientific and objectifying aspirations) and toward an overcoming of ontology (now viewed more historically as "metaphysics") that entails a turning of thought toward art and poetizing as well as a sustained critique of science and technicity, themselves outgrowths of occidental metaphysics. This shift in Heidegger's thinking during the 1930s is to this day not well understood, and this is due not only to the sheer volume of Heidegger's work during this period but also to its richness and complexity, not to mention the "politics" involved before, during, and after Heidegger's notorious assumption of the Rectorship of Freiburg university in 1933 and his failed attempt to engage National Socialism for his own political ends.

If one surveys Heidegger's work of the 1930s with a view to the multiple dimensions at stake in this shift in his thinking, then it is readily apparent that Heidegger has two main interlocutors during this time: Hölderlin

and Nietzsche. Of these two, it is Nietzsche who has received by far the greatest attention from scholars, and indeed for reasons that are quite understandable. Nietzsche's project of overcoming Platonism—that is, the fundamental structure of occidental metaphysics that institutes a difference between being and beings, between truth and appearances, positing a "true world" of ideas beyond and governing the realm of sensuous becoming—parallels Heidegger's own concern to overcome metaphysics and to recover an "other commencement" for Western-European thinking, one that might transform the human being's relation to being and to the Earth from a power-hungry relation of technological mastery to a more finite and responsive manner of dwelling with and upon the Earth, one mindful of the finitude of its own temporality and mortality. Heidegger's thoughtful yet critical encounters with Nietzsche in the mid- to late 1930s and early 1940s (essentially, up to 1941) indeed show a breadth and depth of engagement that appear second to none. That engagement begins with three major lecture courses: "The Will to Power as Art" (1936–7), "The Eternal Recurrence of the Same" (1937), and "The Will to Power as Knowledge" (1939), and continues with the essays and notes from 1939–41 (including the essay on "European

Nihilism" from 1940) that are collected in volume II of the original German edition of Heidegger's *Nietzsche*.

Nevertheless, the significance of this sustained and critical encounter with Nietzsche notwithstanding, it needs to be recognized that this encounter occurs within the greater context of a dialogue with Hölderlin.[1] The Nietzsche lectures are both preceded and followed by major lecture courses on Hölderlin, which also give rise to several published essays. In the winter semester of 1934–5, following his resignation from the Rectorship, Heidegger lectures on Hölderlin's hymns "Germania" and "The Rhine." In winter semester 1941–2, directly following his sustained engagement with Nietzsche, Heidegger returns to Hölderlin's poetry, presenting a second lecture course, this one on the hymn "Remembrance." In summer semester 1942 he gives the last of his lecture courses on Hölderlin, an interpretation (or more precisely, as he insists, a set of "remarks") focusing on the hymn "The Ister."[2] This return to Hölderlin's poetry was, it seems, entirely anticipated by Heidegger toward the end of the first Hölderlin course. There, speaking of Hölderlin's famous 1801 letter to his friend Böhlendorff, he remarked that:

What Hölderlin here sees as the essence of historical Dasein, the conflictual intimacy of endowment and task, was discovered again by Nietzsche under the titles of the Dionysian and the Apollonian, but not with such purity and simplicity as in Hölderlin; for in the meantime Nietzsche had to make his way through all those fateful steps signaled by the names Schopenhauer, Darwin, Wagner, *Gründerjahre*.[3] Not to mention the most fateful thing of all, namely, what subsequent and contemporary Nietzsche

interpretation has made of this in all its orientations. (GA 39, 293–4)

Heidegger's Nietzsche lectures would thus not only face the task of liberating Nietzsche's thought from all of these fateful entanglements and misguided interpretations, exposing the fundamental significance of Nietzsche's thinking as lying in its relation to the first commencement of occidental metaphysics and the light it sheds upon "the essence of historical Dasein," it would also free the path for a return to the "purity and simplicity" of Hölderlin's poetizing—a purity and simplicity that, admittedly, also demand the work of interpretation in order to be heard. In his lecture from the following semester, summer semester 1935, Heidegger again signals what, even prior to the Nietzsche lectures, appears to have already been decided: the superiority of Hölderlin over Nietzsche, the latter's greatness notwithstanding. Nietzsche's metaphysics, he remarks, "did not find its way to the decisive question, even though he understood the age of the great commencement of the entire Greek Dasein in a manner that was surpassed only by Hölderlin."[4]

The importance of Heidegger's Hölderlin lectures (and especially of the first lecture course) for understanding Heidegger's work of the mid- to late 1930s, and indeed all of his subsequent thought, can hardly be overstated. Here, we may recall briefly just a few external indications of this (there are many more that could be cited):

(1) The seminal essay on "The Origin of the Work of Art" was completed in its mature and final version in 1936. Yet Heidegger had already begun to work on the initial drafts of the essay in 1934–5, that is, during exactly the same period that he was delivering the first Hölderlin course. Not only does the

essay conclude by recalling the "infallible sign" of "Hölderlin, the poet, whose work still confronts the Germans as a test to be stood," and by citing lines from the hymn "The Journey" ("Reluctantly that which / Dwells near the origin abandons the locale"); it should be apparent to anyone familiar with Heidegger's work of this period that both the monumental theme of the "Earth"—a motif clearly adopted from Hölderlin—and the claim that all art, and indeed language itself, is in essence "poetizing" (*Dichtung*) cannot be adequately understood without an appreciation of the first Hölderlin course.

(2) The crucially important and roughly contemporaneous essay "Hölderlin and the Essence of Poetry," first delivered as a lecture in Rome in 1936 and subsequently to become the first published essay of Heidegger's on Hölderlin, is in all essential respects excerpted from the 1934–5 course. The much longer essay "Remembrance," published in 1943, is likewise essentially drawn from the 1941–2 lecture course on the same hymn. Both are contained in the volume of essays *Elucidations of Hölderlin's Poetry*.

(3) The 1935 lecture course *Introduction to Metaphysics*, in which we find the remark noted above concerning the superiority of Hölderlin's understanding of the first commencement over that of Nietzsche, is also conducted under the shadow of the 1934–5 Hölderlin course. Here, Heidegger attempts to retrieve the "poetizing thinking" of Greek tragedy, recalling Hölderlin's characterization of Oedipus as having "an eye too many," and venturing a first interpretation of the famous "ode to man" from Sophocles' *Antigone*—a choral ode that is absolutely central to Hölderlin's poetic thinking, and that Heidegger would return to in his later course on Hölderlin's "The Ister." The 1935 course ends with a quotation from Hölderlin's fragments for "The Titans" concerning the question of the "right time," the opportune moment (*Augenblick*) or *kairos*, now seen from the historical perspective of being setting itself to work.

(4) Heidegger's major manuscript of the 1930s, the *Contributions to Philosophy: Of Ereignis*, is suffused with Hölderlinian motifs and resonances, most prominently the theme of the Earth mentioned above, but also the question of the divine, of the "flight of the gods" poetized in the hymn "Germania" and the motif of "the last god." Hölderlin, Heidegger here announces, is the "most futural poet," as the one who experiences the flight of the gods of old and awaits the arrival of the gods to come, the one who stands within the time-space of this transition that, as the site of the historical moment of being's disclosure, opens the possibility of an "other commencement." The word *Ereignis* itself, referring to the appropriative event of being's happening, indeed may well be taken from Hölderlin.[5]

(5) The seminal essay "The Age of the World Picture" from 1938, Heidegger's first systematic critique of science and representation, likewise ends by raising the question of the "historical moment" and by citing Hölderlin's poem "To the Germans," concerning the untimely time into which the poet-thinker is transported.

(6) Heidegger's last lecture course, *What is Called Thinking?*, from 1951–2, draws heavily on Hölderlin, particularly in its opening phase, where Heidegger recalls the lines from the hymn "Mnemosyne" concerning man as a "sign that is not read," and also appeals to the lines from the poem "Socrates and Alcibiades" that run "He who has thought most deeply, loves what is most alive" in order to insist on thinking as a form of love.

(7) Finally, the roughly contemporaneous essay "The Question Concerning Technology," formulated between 1949 and 1953, notoriously ends with an appeal to Hölderlin's word ". . . where danger is, there / Grows the saving power also," and to Hölderlin's claim that ". . . poetically man dwells upon this Earth."[6]

THE FIRST HÖLDERLIN LECTURE COURSE: THE HYMNS "GERMANIA" AND "THE RHINE" (1934–5)

The first Hölderlin lecture course falls almost exactly into two halves, the first half devoted to articulating the initial approach to "Germania," and the second to an interpretation of "The Rhine" that then, in its closing stages, returns to "Germania" in order to display the inner unity of the two hymns and expose what Heidegger calls the "metaphysical locale" of Hölderlin's poetizing.

The first half of the lecture course is especially important, for Heidegger here devotes considerable effort to gaining a preliminary understanding of what poetizing (*Dichtung*) is, its essence and its linguistic character. The essence being sought, however, is not some universal essence of poetizing in general, but the essence of this, Hölderlin's, poetizing: the essence that is poetized in and through this singular poetizing. It is thus not to be imposed from the outside, as it were, through the philosophical application of a concept of poetizing to this particular instance. Rather, it must be gleaned by experiencing the power of the poetizing itself that is in question, through a "thoughtful encounter" with the "manifestation of beyng" that is achieved in this poetizing (GA 39, 6).[7] Hölderlin is "the poet of poets" (30),

one whose poetizing remains in proximity to thinking, to a supremely thoughtful saying of beyng in the poetic word. Thereby, thinking itself demands to be experienced differently, not as philosophical conceptuality, but as it is configured poetically, in and through the poetizing itself. Hölderlin is indeed, Heidegger insists, "our most futural *thinker*, because he is our greatest *poet*" (6), and by this formulation also signals that the issue of the manifestation of beyng in this poetizing will prove inseparable from the question of the "we," of the German people—a question to which he will shortly turn more explicitly. This claim, furthermore, points to the proximity and belonging together (though not the identity) of thinking and poetizing, where "thinking" is something other than traditional philosophy and is implicitly attuned to the poetic.

The phenomenon of attunement, indeed of what Heidegger terms a fundamental attunement, will prove crucial here. Our task in experiencing Hölderlin's poetizing is not to distill from it some spiritual content or symbolic meaning, some abstract truth, but rather, in resisting our everyday and commonplace view of poetry, to experience the power of the poetic word in exposing ourselves to its "saying" or "telling" (*Sagen*), to the overarching sweep and configuration of its resonance and oscillation, and to do so in letting ourselves be torn away by the poetic word in its very telling. For contrary to our everyday understanding, Heidegger explains, language is not reducible to a means of expression that articulates some spiritual meaning; it is not at all what it appears to be, something present at hand that we "have," just as we would have some piece of property. Rather, as he forcefully puts it, "It is not we who have language, rather language has us" (23).

As Hölderlin's poetizing itself articulates it, poetizing is, first, a telling in the manner of a making manifest that points. In the poem "As when on feast day . . .," Hölderlin writes:

Yet us it behooves, under God's
thunderstorms,
You poets! to stand with naked heads,
To grasp the Father's ray, itself
With our own hands and shrouded in
the song
To pass on to the people the heavenly
gift.

The poet, in Heidegger's words, thus "harnesses the lightning flashes of the God, compelling them into the word, and places this lightning-charged word into the language of his people" (30). In exposing himself to "the overwhelming power of beyng," the poet has the task of receiving the beckonings of the gods and passing them on to the people, and in so doing his poetizing is, in the words of the last line of the hymn "Remembrance," a "founding" (*Stiften*) of that which remains, a "founding of beyng," as Heidegger puts it, one that first grounds the historical Dasein of a people. Although from an everyday perspective it appears, in Hölderlin's words, to be "this most innocent of occupations" (33), poetizing is anything but one meritorious cultural activity among others. Rather, as Hölderlin elsewhere tells, it configures and founds the human being's dwelling upon this Earth:

Full of merit, yet poetically dwell
Human beings upon this Earth.

Following this initial situating of the language of Hölderlin's poetizing, Heidegger turns first to the question of the "we" of a historical people—a question he develops from the "turbulence" of the telling of the hymn

"Germania" itself—with particular attentiveness to the time of this "we"; and second, to unfolding the "fundamental attunement" of the hymn "Germania," which proves to be that of a "holy mourning 'with' the waters of the homeland." The "homeland," Heidegger insists, does not here mean a mere birthplace or geographical region, but rather "the power of the Earth" upon which the human being, in his or her historical Dasein, poetically dwells (88). The mourning is "holy": not just any mourning, but a mourning arising out of the experience of the "flight of the gods" enunciated in the opening lines of "Germania." As such, however, this mourning, as a "plaint" and "distress" arising from the necessity of renouncing the gods of old, is not merely a preserving of the gods that have been, but simultaneously a readiness and awaiting of the future and of that which is to come. The poetic attunement unfolds precisely as this "power of temporality" in which we are "torn" in these two directions, and it is in inhabiting this "time that tears," to use Hölderlin's words, that the time of a historical people is first temporalized in and as a poetic attunement (109). This time of the "we," of a historical people, is, however, uncertain and unknown; it remains concealed from us, Heidegger insists, and may at most be intimated by the poet whose soul, in the words of Hölderlin's poem "To the Germans," is transported "beyond its own time." Seeking the "true time" for his own time, remarks Heidegger, the poet is necessarily removed from the time of the present day (50); he must inhabit the "peaks of time" (52), and his dwelling on the peaks of time, as a creator, is "a persistent waiting and awaiting *the event* [Ereignis]," "a making ready for the true that shall once come to pass [*sich ereignen*]" (56). The word *Ereignis*, which becomes the keyword of

Heidegger's thinking from the mid-1930s on, is here appropriated from Hölderlin's hymn "Mnemosyne," which speaks of the *sich ereignen*, the "coming to pass," of the true:

> ... Lang ist
> Die Zeit, es ereignet sich aber
>
> Das Wahre.
> ... Long is
>
> The time, yet what is true
> Comes to pass.

In the second half of the lecture course, Heidegger turns his attention to one of the aforementioned "waters" of the homeland, specifically the river poetized in Hölderlin's hymn "The Rhine." Keeping in mind a remark from one of Hölderlin's fragments on Pindar, that the river is that which "violently creates paths and limits upon the originarily pathless Earth" (92–3), Heidegger identifies as the "pivot" of the entire hymn the first line of strophe X, "Demigods now I think." The river Rhine itself is poetized as a demigod, that is, as something that is at once more than the human and yet less than the gods. It does not merely occupy an existing space between humans and gods, however, but first creates and opens up this very space in which the essence of both humans and gods can be asked about. The poet thinks the demigods when, as the opening line of the hymn puts it, he is sitting "at the portal of the woods," that is, at the threshold of the poet's homeland. The poet, Heidegger comments, "sits at the threshold of the Earth of the homeland, 'there' he thinks the demigods" (169–70); and this thinking is, according to the first strophe, an "unsuspecting" apprehending of a destiny: the poet is, "from out of his pondering that which is distant and has been, unsuspectingly torn

out and around into the thinking of his own homeland" (171). The "destiny" (*Schicksal*) that comes toward him in this pondering is indeed "the key word of his poetizing," it is "the name for the beyng of the demigods" (172).

In the poetizing of the Rhine as a destiny, "destiny" does not mean any kind of fatalism or predestination. It names, rather, the being and becoming of the river itself in its very flow. "The river Rhine *is* a destiny, and destiny comes to be only in the history of this river" (196). This flowing of the river, however, is determined by its relation to its origin. In the remaining part of the course, Heidegger ponders above all what is at stake in the "enigma" of this relation, for it is that enigma that is poetized in and as the hymn itself, according to lines 46f.:

> Enigma is that which has purely sprung
>   forth. Even
> The song may scarcely unveil it.

The poet dwells close to the origin (*Ursprung*). According to the second strophe, he hears the river in its origin, "in the coldest abyss," as yet to spring forth; mere mortals, by contrast, have "fled the locale." Yet the task of this poetizing is not to unveil the origin as such, but the river in its "having purely sprung forth" (*Entsprungensein*), and to do so in a "veiled saying" that scarcely unveils the entire enigma. And this can be accomplished only through a poetic thinking of the entire course of the river, as determined by its relation to the origin, a relation that will prove to be intrinsically discordant. Whereas mortals flee from the origin and attend only to what has already sprung forth, without giving thought to its having sprung forth (or, if they think the origin, they think it only in terms of what has already sprung forth, that is, metaphysically), the task of Hölderlin's poetizing is different:

> Yet just as the origin that has merely sprung forth is not the origin, neither is the merely fettered origin. Rather, the entire essence of the origin is the fettered origin in its springing forth. Yet the springing forth itself first comes to be what it is as the river runs its entire course; it is not limited to the beginning of its course. The entire course of the river itself belongs to the origin. The origin is fully apprehended only as the fettered origin in its springing forth as having sprung forth. (202)

Yet something decisive happens in the course of the Rhine's flowing. Although originally driven toward Asia—which Heidegger, drawing on another hymn, takes to include Greece—this original directionality is suddenly broken off, and the river turns north, toward Germany, a turning indicative of a "counter-will" to the original will of the origin. We cannot here convey the entire detail and subtlety of Heidegger's ensuing analysis, and we shall have to come back to "The Rhine" in our remarks on "The Ister." It must suffice here to indicate that Heidegger proceeds to interpret this counter-will as a strife and "blessed enmity" within beyng, a counter-turning that is still a unity ("blessedness"), and to unfold this enigma in terms of what Hölderlin names "intimacy," *Innigkeit*. "Intimacy" does not, for Hölderlin, mean any kind of human relationship: it is his word for "that originary unity of the enmity of the powers of what has purely sprung forth. It is the mystery belonging to such beyng" (250). *Innigkeit* is Hölderlin's word for the being of nature itself, a being that, in the poem "As when on feast day . . .," is said to be "intimative" (*ahnend*)—as are the poets themselves.

The poetizing of this poet is thus nothing other than nature coming into being—telling of itself and founding its being in such telling:

> Because the poets are not directed toward nature as an object, for instance; because, rather, "nature" as beyng founds itself in saying, the saying of the poets as the self-saying of nature is of the same essence as the latter. This is why it is said of the poets: they "intimate always." (258)

"Nature" here is thus not an entity, but a word for beyng itself. Yet the nature or beyng in question here is not indeterminate, for the poet's task is to found, through his poetizing, the historical dwelling of a people upon this Earth, to found "the land as land and as homeland of the people" (259). The question of this people—of the "we" and of the historical time of the "we," the historical moment—is, as we have indicated, central to Heidegger's concern here. The question of the "we" is the question of the Germans; Hölderlin is not only the "poet of poets and of poetizing," he is "the poet of the Germans," one who must become a power or force in "the history of our people." The issue concerns "'politics' in the highest and authentic sense, so much so that whoever accomplishes something here has no need to talk about the 'political'" (214). For the "political" in the narrower sense of the affairs of state first arises from poetizing: "[. . .] the historical Dasein of the peoples . . . springs from poetizing, and from the latter springs authentic knowing in the sense of philosophy, and from both the effecting of the Dasein of a people as a people through the state—politics" (51). Toward the end of the lectures on "The Rhine" Heidegger returns to this question of the historical moment, of the moment named in "Germania" as "the middle of time," as "that historical Dasein in which and as which the essence of this land finds itself and completes itself" (289). This middle of time, however, first arises from having-been (the flight of the gods) and future (to be founded in poetizing), and as such, is nothing given, but an identity that must first be attained in and through struggle. Heidegger here appeals, in closing, to Hölderlin's letter to Böhlendorff from 1801 (the same year as the two hymns were written), which insists that the struggle of historical existence is always to transform what is given one as an endowment ("one's own," the "national") into what is given one as a task (the "free use of the national"). For the Germans, endowed with the gift of conceptual clarity, ordering, and planning, this means learning "to be struck by beyng," and this is the opposite of the situation faced by the Greeks, who were struck by the "fire from the heavens" (the "violence of beyng," as Heidegger translates it) and had to harness this excess in bringing it to a stand in the work. This reversal of historical predicament is also, for Heidegger, indicative of the special relationship between the German and the Greek: "In fighting the battle of the Greeks, but on the reverse front, we become not Greeks, but Germans" (293).[8]

HÖLDERLIN REVISITED: THE LECTURES ON "REMEMBRANCE" (1941–2)

In the winter semester of 1941–2, following a seven year hiatus marked by his critical encounters with Nietzsche, Heidegger returned to lecture on Hölderlin. At the beginning of the lecture course he announced that the course would be concerned with five different poems: "Remembrance," "The Ister,"

"The Titans," "Mnemosyne," and "Ripe, bathed in fire . . ."; of these, however, only the first two received extensive attention: "Remembrance" in winter semester 1941–2, and "The Ister" the following semester.

The interpretation of "Remembrance" is remarkable with regard to a number of themes, which we can only indicate briefly here. First, the interpretation of "greeting," which Heidegger at once links to the phenomenon of remembrance and, by way of anticipation, to the flow of the river poetized in "The Ister." The hymn opens with the lines:

The Northeasterly blows,
Most beloved of the winds to me
For it promises fiery spirit
And good voyage to those at sea.
But go now, and greet
The beautiful Garonne,
And the gardens of Bordeaux
. . .

The single line "But go now, and greet," Heidegger insists, conceals the entire mystery of what is called remembrance (GA 52, 49; 55). Remembrance, *Andenken*, is poetized as a greeting; as a greeting, it is a thoughtful turning toward that which is greeted. Heidegger unfolds the structure of greeting from a meditation on the opening lines that poetize the blowing of the wind, in an intricate analysis that we cannot reproduce here.[9] Genuine greeting, as an address (*Zuspruch*) turned toward the one greeted, is recognition: the recognition that recognizes the one greeted in "the nobility of their essence" and through such recognition lets them be what they are. Greeting is thus "a letting be of things and of human beings" (50). In the structure of greeting poetized in "Remembrance," that which is to be greeted, however, itself inclines toward the poet, approaches him in his very thinking—something the poet poetizes in the striking line "Still it seems to think of me" (*Noch denket das mir wohl*), which opens the second strophe—and this mysterious turning or reversal of direction indeed characterizes the very structure of remembrance, and perhaps of thought itself. It is as though, Heidegger remarks, "a river that runs out and goes into the sea suddenly flowed backward in the opposite direction, toward the source," here alluding already to the hymn "The Ister," in which the river is said "almost" to flow backward (54).

A second major theme of the 1941–2 course, one that takes up and develops the structure of greeting and that subsequently dominates the entire course, is the question of festival and festivity. While we must again forego a detailed interpretation here, we may simply note the striking claims made by Heidegger, first, that festival (which for Hölderlin means the "bridal festival" of humans and gods, poetized in "The Rhine") comprises the "incipient greeting" in which humans and gods are greeted by "the holy," and that this originary greeting is "the concealed essence of history." It is, says Heidegger, "*the* Ereignis, *the* commencement" (70). Correspondingly, "the holy" comprises "an attunement more incipient and more originary" than every other human attunement.[10]

Third, Heidegger returns in this lecture course to the question of "the free use of one's own," the question with which he had concluded the first Hölderlin course. The poet of "Remembrance," composed after Hölderlin's return from Bordeaux in France, of course sends his greeting from his homeland, from "Germania." Yet it is arguably the least convincing, most reductive move in Heidegger's entire interpretation when he essentially translates Bordeaux into Greece and the ancient Greek world: the "brown women"

of the south of France (line 18) represent, he insists, "the Greek world" and the festival of humans and gods once celebrated there (80); the "golden dreams" (line 23) likewise refer to the Greeks and to the Greek world (113, 122); the land of southern France depicted in the poem "stands poetically for Greece" (184); indeed, the hymn "Remembrance," ostensibly about France, is in fact, by virtue of its poetizing of the relation of Greece to Germany, claimed to be the "most German of all German poems" (119). Heidegger's interpretive move here is aware of appearing arbitrary, but justifies itself by appeal, on the one hand, to a second letter of Hölderlin's to Böhlendorff, from 1802, following his return from Bordeaux, where the poet writes explicitly of experiencing "the fire from the heavens" there—attributed to the Greeks in the earlier, 1801 letter—and of being "struck by Apollo" (22–4; 184); and on the other hand, to the lines in "Remembrance" that read "But now to Indians / The men have gone," that is, as Heidegger reads it, beyond France (which allegedly stands for Greece) and to Asia, to the Indus, from which, according to the poem "The Eagle," the German ancestors once arrived. The sweep of Hölderlin's poetic vision would thus exceed the more proximate remembrance of Bordeaux in relating the origins of the Germania to the more distant and remote lands of Greece and Asia. Still, the sidelining of Bordeaux and the heavy emphasis on "the German" cannot but appear troubling.[11]

THE LAST HÖLDERLIN LECTURE COURSE: "THE ISTER" (1942)

The course on "Remembrance," in its concluding phase, already situated its interpretation of that hymn with a view to the hymn "The Ister" (the Greek name for the lower Danube[12]), which poetizes a return from the Indus to the homeland on the part of those in search of "what is fitting" (i.e. "one's own," which Heidegger interprets as "the holy"). It thus explicitly anticipated and prepared the ground for the course of the following semester on "The Ister," identifying the latter as "the authentic river of the homeland of this poet" (GA 52, 185). The final Hölderlin lecture course is indeed entirely articulated around the question of the homeland, more precisely: of what it means to come to be "at home" or "homely" (*heimisch*) in "one's own." The course is remarkable not only for the way in which it seeks to integrate these later courses on "Remembrance" and "The Ister" with the earlier interpretations of "Germania" and "The Rhine," poems to which it returns in its concluding phase, but also for the extensive interpretation of the first choral ode from Sophocles's *Antigone*, an interpretation that—quite unexpectedly—occupies almost half the entire lecture course.[13]

The 1942 course falls into three parts: an initial, introductory part, rejecting a metaphysical or symbolic reading of Hölderlin's poetry and reflecting on the essence of the river hymns; the second, intermediary part containing the lengthy commentary on the *Antigone* chorus; and the third, concluding part, reflecting on the essence of the poet as sign, and on the divergent relation to the origin poetized in the "Ister" and "Rhine" hymns.

Antigone, admittedly, attunes the entire 1942 lecture course. Heidegger indeed opens the course by prefacing his reading of "The Ister" with some remarks on the meaning of "hymn," in which he appeals to the words of Antigone at lines 806f. and interprets the meaning of *humnos* as a celebratory song

that prepares for the festival—the festival that, in the case of Hölderlin's river hymns, will prove to be the bridal festival of humans and gods. Yet the course is no less attuned by the first line of the hymn, "Now come, fire!," a call enunciated by those who are already called upon, who are of a calling, "eager . . . to see the day," as the hymn continues. The emphatic "Now" with which hymn opens, though seeming to speak from the present into a future to come, speaks in the first instance into what has already happened; as such, it "names an appropriative event [*Ereignis*]" (9), one that has appropriated those who have been called upon, brought them into this moment of poetic saying. This emphatic "Now," Heidegger insists, "gives the entire poem its proper and singular tone" (8). Yet the Ister, as a river, is not just a "Now," a moment of time, but, as Hölderlin indicates in the poem "Voice of the People," the rivers simultaneously intimate what is to come and vanish into what has been: they are "intimative" and "vanishing," and as such, "are themselves time," remarks Heidegger. While they do not take the path of human beings, according to the same poem, there is nevertheless a love of them, a belonging to them, a going along with the rivers on the part of human beings.

Yet the first strophe of "The Ister" names not only a "now" but also a "here": "Here, however, we wish to build" (line 15). Although in its flowing or "journeying" the river always occupies another "here," it marks the site of dwelling for human beings, which Heidegger goes on to call the "locality" for human dwelling upon the Earth, the site where they can come into their own (*das Eigene*) and be "at home" (*heimisch*). Yet precisely this, dwelling within one's own, "is that which comes last, and is seldom successful, and always remains what is most difficult" (24). Humans thus have the task of first coming to be at home, of coming to be at home in and through the poetizing that the river itself is, through the journeying of the locality of human dwelling, a journeying that is historical: "The river is the journeying of the coming to be at home of historical human beings upon this Earth" (37–8).

That human beings must first come to be at home in what is their own, however, entails that they are "at first and for a long time, and sometimes forever, not at home"; coming to be at home thus entails "a passage through the foreign" (60). For Hölderlin, "one's own" names the fatherland of the Germans; the finding of this "forbidden fruit"[14] must entail a passing through and encounter with the foreign. Yet "the foreign" is not any arbitrary foreign, but one that is intrinsically related to one's own, "the foreign of one's own," the foreign that is already within one's own: for the poet Hölderlin, the Greek poets Pindar and above all, Sophocles. The foreign in question thus belongs to one's own: it is "the *provenance* of the return home," for the Germans, the Greek world (67). Heidegger's claim that throughout Hölderlin's poetic telling of the human being's coming to be at home "there repeatedly resonates a singular poetic work of a singular poet," namely the first choral ode of Sophocles's *Antigone*, now becomes the occasion for an extended interpretation of the ode (63). This interpretation is not only much more extensive than that offered previously in Heidegger's 1935 course *Introduction to Metaphysics*; it also differs in significant respects. Heidegger now not only integrates his commentary into the context of Hölderlin's poetizing and the question of translation (both his own translation of the choral ode, and Hölderlin's translations of Pindar and Sophocles) but also largely retracts the entire discourse of violence (*Gewalt* and

Gewalttätigkeit) in which the earlier interpretation was couched. The human being, in the word of the chorus, is *to deinon*, which Heidegger again renders as "the uncanny" *das Unheimliche*, in the sense of not being at home among beings. Uncanniness marks the very being of the human being: it is not a state or predicament to be overcome, nor does it first arise as a consequence of human existence. Humankind, rather "emerges from uncanniness and remains within it—looms out of it and stirs within it" (89). Far from being something to be overcome, such not being at home is something that has to be taken on, assumed as the very essence, the abode or dwelling place of the human being, an abode that prevails amid change and becoming, journeying and flowing. And precisely this, according to Heidegger's interpretation, is, in her own words, the essence of Antigone: *pathein to deinon touto*, "to take up into my own essence the uncanny that here and now appears" (127). Coming to be at home thus means, not overcoming our not being at home, but appropriating it as our essence, coming to dwell within it, "coming to be at home in not being at home." Antigone herself, Heidegger writes, "*is* the poem of coming to be at home in not being at home" (151).

When Heidegger returns to Hölderlin in the extremely rich and compressed closing part of the lecture course, it is on the one hand to contrast the different relation to the origin that is poetized in the "Ister" and "Rhine" hymns. Whereas "The Rhine" tells of a violent relation to the origin, in which the river attempts to rush "with violence" to the heart of the mother, to the Earth of the homeland, and is rejected into an unknown destiny (201),[15] "The Ister," in its seeming "almost to flow backward," comes from the encounter with the foreign back to a more intimative dwelling close to the source. Yet the foreign is not thereby abandoned or left behind, but remains determinative for the journeying and flow of the river. The Ister has invited the Greek demigod Hercules from the land of the heavenly fire as a guest, as "the presence of the unhomely in the homely"; the return to the home is never a simple appropriation of one's own, insists Heidegger: "The appropriation of one's own *is* only as the encounter and guest-like dialogue with the foreign. [. . .] The relation to the foreign is never a mere taking over of the Other" (177, 179). The "source" that is poetized in Hölderlin's hymn is thus not a metaphysical source or pure origin, but must be thought in terms of the destining of a historical vocation that occurs as the unfolding of a dialogue with the foreign: "The Ister *is* that river in which the foreign is already present as a guest at its source, that river in whose flowing there constantly speaks the dialogue between one's own and the foreign" (182). Heidegger's own remarks break off, not with an assured conclusion as to the historical vocation of the Germans in relation to the Greeks, but with an insistence on the need to think through the "as yet concealed law" at work in the relations between "The Rhine," "The Ister," and "Germania." Indeed, the Ister hymn itself "breaks off," as a sign that "makes manifest, yet in such a way that it simultaneously conceals" (202)—as a sign that, in the words of "Mnemosyne," with which Heidegger concludes the course, "is not read," of a "we" who "have almost lost our tongue in foreign parts."

CONCLUDING REMARKS

One can readily make the case that Hölderlin is Heidegger's most important and persistent interlocutor from the mid-1930s on.

Heidegger's encounters with Hölderlin are crucial for understanding the turn to language that characterizes his later work, as well as his meditations on art, technicity, and poetic dwelling. They are also crucially interwoven with issues of politics and history, interpretation and translation, attunement and memory. In particular, they offer rich resources for pursuing questions of national identity, linguistic identity, and the historical constitution of traditions, questions that today appear more pressing than ever.

NOTES AND REFERENCES

[1] Furthermore, Heidegger's dialogue with Hölderlin needs to be understood in the context of existing Hölderlin scholarship at the time. For an overview, with particular reference to the hymn "Remembrance," see Robert Bernasconi, "Poets as Prophets and as Painters: Heidegger's Turn to Language and the Hölderlinian Turn in Context," in ed. Jeffrey Powell, *Heidegger and Language*, (Bloomington: Indiana University Press, 2013).

[2] In addition to the three major lecture courses on Hölderlin (published as GA 39, GA 52, and GA 53), and to the collection of essays published by Heidegger (GA 4), we also possess a substantial collection of notes and drafts (GA 75). Audio recordings of Heidegger reading Hölderlin are also available (*Martin Heidegger Liest Hölderlin*, ISBN-10: 3608910484), as is a recording of his 1960 lecture "Hölderlin's Earth and Heaven" (*Hölderlins Erde und Himmel*, ISBN-10: 3608910492). The present essay confines itself to providing an overview of the three lecture courses.

[3] The term *Gründerjahre*, "founders' years," refers to the period of rapid industrial expansion in Germany from 1871–3, following the Franco-Prussian war of 1870.

[4] *Einführung in die Metaphysik* (Tübingen: Niemeyer, 1987), 97. On Nietzsche and Hölderlin, see also Heidegger's later remarks in the 1941–2 course on "Remembrance," GA 52, 78–9.

5 See the remarks below on the first Hölderlin course.

6 See also Heidegger's essay of the same title, ". . . Poetically Man Dwells . . .," delivered as a lecture in 1951 (GA 7, 189–208/PLT, 211–29).

7 Heidegger in this lecture course generally uses the German *Seyn*, an archaic form of *Sein* ("being") that was used by Hölderlin, although his appropriation of this archaic spelling is not completely consistent and Heidegger occasionally reverts to *Sein*. *Seyn* has here been rendered as *beyng*, which happens to be an archaic form of the English *being*.

8 It is on account of this special relationship that Heidegger earlier refers to "the Greek-German dispensation," *der griechisch-deutschen Sendung*, out of which thinking must enter its originary dialogue with poetizing (GA 39, 151). On the centrality of the Böhlendorff letter of December 4, 1801 for all three lecture courses on Hölderlin, see Julia A. Ireland, "Learning in Dialogue: The Letter to Böhlendorff and Hölderlin's Conception of History." Paper presented at the 2010 meeting of the Heidegger Circle, Stony Brook University, Manhattan, New York. Available to members in the conference *Proceedings* via www.heideggercircle.org.

9 For more details see my remarks in "Buried Treasure: Greeting and the Temporality of Remembrance in Heidegger's Lectures on 'Andenken.'" Paper delivered at the 2010 meeting of the Heidegger Circle, Stony Brook University, Manhattan, New York. Available to members in the conference *Proceedings* via www.heideggercircle.org.

10 For more on this, see my remarks in "An Attunement More Primordial Than Every Other Human Attunement: Inaugural Time in Heidegger and Hölderlin." Paper delivered at the 2004 meeting of the Heidegger Circle, hosted by The University of New Orleans and Louisiana State University. Available to members in the conference *Proceedings* via www. heideggercircle.org.

11 Heidegger goes so far as to situate "the brown women" of "Remembrance" in relation to "the German women" referred to in Hölderlin's "Song to the Germans" (GA 52, 79–80). An outraged Adorno complains that Heidegger drags the German women in by the hair. For a commentary, see David Farrell Krell, "The Swaying Skiff of Sea: A Note on Heidegger's—and Hölderlin's—Andenken." Paper delivered at the 2010 meeting of the Heidegger Circle, Stony Brook University, Manhattan, New York. Available to members in the conference *Proceedings* via www.heideggercircle.org.

12 Heidegger notes that Hölderlin uses the Greco-Roman name for the lower Danube (in German, the *Donau*) to designate the upper course of the river, "as if the lower Donau had returned to the upper, and thus turned back to its source" (GA 53, 10).

13 Heidegger's course on "The Ister" has, moreover, inspired a film under the same title, produced and directed by David Barison and Daniel Ross. Details can be found at www. theister.com.

14 Hölderlin's words from a late fragment, cited by Heidegger at the outset of the first Hölderlin course (GA 39, 4).

15 Heidegger here refers to lines 94ff. of the hymn "The Journey" ("Die Wanderung").

28

THE "LETTER ON HUMANISM": EK-SISTENCE, BEING, AND LANGUAGE

Andrew J. Mitchell

The famed "Letter on 'Humanism'" was a response to French philosopher Jean Beaufret, who wrote to Heidegger on November 10, 1946 posing a number of questions relating to the issue of humanism and asking what role, if any, remains for humanism in Heidegger's thinking. The response, initially entitled "On 'Humanism': Letter to Jean Beaufret, Paris," was Heidegger's first publication after the Second World War.[1] Given that its author was under a teaching ban imposed by the French Denazification committee at this time, it could be said to be the first public appearance of the man Heidegger as well. As such, the "Letter" provides Heidegger with a forum for presenting himself and his thinking anew, something of which Heidegger takes full advantage. The letter is at great pains to read Heidegger's current thoughts as continuous with what has gone before. As such, it is a central document in what has been called Heidegger's "self-interpretation."[2] It also provides a forum for him to publicly demonstrate his ties with French philosophy and his lack of animosity in this regard.[3] The topic of humanism likewise allows him surreptitiously to distance himself from a Nazi regime that was roundly condemned as barbarous and inhuman.[4] Along with these personal and political contexts, the letter has provided new avenues for appreciating Heidegger's thinking, whether by connecting it back to the Renaissance (as per the work of Grassi) or running ahead to deconstruction (where it figures in Derrida's essay "The Ends of Man"). It is likewise noteworthy for the relation it articulates between ethics and ontology, for its considerations of animality, and for its provocative remarks on the holy and the divine.

Granting the importance of these moments of context and consequence in and for the "Letter," at its heart it is a thorough statement of the interrelation between the human, being, and language, and it is to this interrelation that the following will attend. Indeed, the three are brought together on the very first page, where Heidegger tells us: "Language is the house of being. In its accommodation dwells the human" (GA 9, 313/239, tm). Only by thinking through this constellation of human, being, and language can any questions concerning humanism be addressed.

The letter begins by reflecting on thinking and its inextricable connection to language (GA 9, 313–19/PA, 239–44). As thinking and language have been considered distinctive of the human, the "Letter" then turns to the issue of humanism, tracing its history through the

237

Renaissance adoption of the Roman appropriation of the late-Greek concept of παιδεία. This history is complemented by consideration of humanisms prevailing at the time, specifically, those of Marxism, existentialism, and Christianity (GA 9, 319–23/PA, 244–7). As all of these address the nature of human existence, whether wittingly or not, the next section of the letter turns to Heidegger's own notion of existence (GA 9, 323–9/PA, 247–51). Since this notion of existence relates to being—is, in fact, a relation to being—what follows is a presentation of Heidegger's current understanding of being (GA 9, 329–37/PA, 251–7), including discussion of the "forgetting" of being and the homelessness that this entails (GA 9, 337–44/PA, 257–62). After this treatment of human existence and being, the letter returns to the question of humanism, responding to possible objections to the view (GA 9, 344–52/PA, 262–8), expounding some of the ethical consequences of the position reached (GA 9, 352–61/PA, 268–74), and concluding as it began with further reflections on the nature of thinking (GA 9, 361–4/PA, 274–6). What comes into focus across all of this is a new interrelation between human existence, being, and language.

For Heidegger, humanism has always been a concern that the human should remain human, that is to say, that it keep to its humanity and not become inhuman. Humanism is thus a matter of the human retaining its humanity, or rather, its essence: "in what does the humanity of the human being consist? It lies in his essence" (GA 9, 319/PA, 244). And yet precisely this essence is what has been distorted by the history of metaphysics, for, according to Heidegger, the "essence" of the human, "lies in its ek-sistence [Ek-sistenz]" (GA 9, 325/PA, 247) and this "ek-sistence" has been mischaracterized traditionally as existentia, or the "actuality" of a subtending essentia,

or "possibility." As Heidegger explains, "The statement: 'The human ek-sists' is not an answer to the question of whether the human actually is or not; rather, it responds to the question concerning the 'essence' of the human" (GA 9, 327/PA, 249, tm). To address Beaufret's question concerning humanism thus requires thinking further into the essence of the human, that is, ek-sistence.

The term itself, ek-sistence, is hyphenated so as to emphasize the prefix ek-, and the exteriorization that it entails. Ek-sistence is outside of itself. It is ecstatic, as Heidegger had already observed in *Being and Time*. And as that text shows, Dasein has its being to be, it is always already ahead of itself, always futural. This futural nature of Dasein is coincident with its own "thrownness." Dasein is thrown into the world, with its being "to be," and in the midst of its thrownness projects its existence. This way of being is a way of being "outside" of itself, no longer one condemned to the prison house of the ego. It is an ecstatic existence.

What the "Letter" proposes, however, is that we understand this ecstatic ek-sistence now in terms of a standing "in." As Heidegger makes plain in the letter, "Such standing in the clearing of being I call the ek-sistence of the human" (GA 9, 323–4/PA, 247, tm). The human is outside of itself, but this does not place it in some kind of void. Instead, the human that stands out (ek-stasis) is standing in (in-herence) the "truth" of being: "the way that the human in his proper essence presences to being is ecstatic inherence [Innestehen] in the truth of being" (GA 9, 330/PA, 251, tm). We will return to this notion of a "truth" of being presently, for now, let us simply note that to be "out" is to be "in." Indeed, that only by being outside of oneself, that is, by being no longer encapsulated in an ego, can one really be exposed to anything at all. Only when the refuge of the ego shell is abandoned, can our ecstatic, exposed existence be permeated by being and stand *in* it: "Ek-sisting, he [the human] stands in [*steht . . . in*] the dispensation [*Geschick*] of being" (GA 9, 336/PA, 256, tm). "Inherence" is another name for exposure.

But Dasein would not ecstatically stand in anything at all, if being were not receptive to that stance. Dasein has its being "outside" of itself, it is "inherently" ecstatic. But all this is so much as to say that the "outside" in question is nothing empty. There is a "there" there (*Da*-sein). It is the there *of* being. The ecstatic existence of Dasein is an entrance into being. For lack of a better word, being is the "medium" for this ecstatic appearance. And to be sure, one of the most intriguing aspects of the "Letter" is the variety of ways in which it presents this medial nature of being itself. Being is thought here expansively. Heidegger alternately speaks of the "house of being," the "nearness of being," the "clearing of being," the "light of being," the "open of being," and "being as the element" (in the sense of one's fitting environs). In all these senses, what is at stake is not something contained, but instead a realm, an arena, a field of appearance. In what follows, I will refer to being in this sense as a "medium" for appearing, though the term will require some elaboration to defend against understanding it as simply a space between otherwise present entities.

Given this expansive, medial character, Heidegger can write, "being is essentially broader [*weiter*] than all beings and is equally nearer to the human than any being" (GA 9, 331/PA, 252, tm), adding later "so is being essentially broader [*weiter*] than all beings, because it is the clearing itself" (GA 9, 337/ PA, 256). The breadth of being is its expansive character. Being is not a being. But it is also not without relation to beings. Being is an expanse for appearance, a medium.

Heidegger identifies being in the text as this *openness*, "he [the human] stands out in the open of being, which is being itself" (GA 9, 350/PA, 266, tm), or, again, as *clearing*, "the clearing itself is being" (GA 9, 332/PA, 253). Being is the open and the clearing. In this context, "truth" is equally a term of expansion, that is, the "truth of being" is the breadth of being, hence locutions such as the "dimension of the truth of being," the "house of the truth of being," and "the element of the truth of being," merely to name a few.

We might take what Heidegger says at the outset of the letter in regards to "the element" as bearing on this entire list of expansive names for being. Heidegger explains that, "the element is authentically that which enables: the enabling" (GA 9, 316/PA, 241, tm). Being as element enables beings. It makes them "possible" (*möglich*). But the relation here must be more carefully understood, instead of a "making" crudely construed, it is more of a letting be, it lets beings "essence," using the word as a verb. Being as element is what lets beings be what they are and lets them be this essentially. This sense of "essence" is a way of being of these beings. It is a way of being that "affiliates" (*mögen*) them to the medium, to being. In so doing, beings exhibit a certain relationality. When beings are construed as objects situated in a void and standing apart from a subject, there is no relation, only encapsulation. Heidegger notes in the text how "the dominance of subjectivity" leads to "the metaphysically conditioned establishment and authorization of the openness of beings in the unconditional objectification of everything" (GA 9, 317/PA, 242). And nevertheless, "what something is in its being is not exhausted by its being an object" (GA 9, 349/ PA, 265, tm). There is "more" to the being of things than objectivity. This surplus is its relation or affiliation to being, its belonging to its element. This relationality is prior to objecti-fication. It occurs within "the openness [die Offenheit] of being," within "the open region [Offene] that first clears the 'between' within which a 'relation' of subject to object can 'be'" (GA 9, 350/PA, 266, tm).

In this thinking of the element of being, the element that makes beings possible, Heidegger recasts the notion of a "condition of possibil-ity" in terms of a letting be whereby the par-ticular being is "affiliated" to the medium in which it appears. Such a "condition" of possi-bility is not indifferent to that which appears within it. Being and beings are affiliated and held in a relation to one another (this is the importance of the etymological connection between medium as enabling, vermögen, the possible, das Mögliche, and affiliation, mögen). Ek-sistence does not stand in a void, but participates in a medium. That medium is being. But it is not a medium in the sense of an independent, indifferent third thing (or void) that would intervene between two oth-erwise present entities. Instead, the medium "likes" what appears in it, lets it essence.

But it is not enough to construe being as a "medium" in this way. Being might still seem a container for ek-sistence. Indeed, for the ecstaticity of ek-sistence, being can be no void, but it can likewise be no plenum either. If ek-sistence is exposed and permeated by being, then that being cannot be stagnant, it must be always arriving. Heidegger thinks this in terms of a sending, whereby being is given or sent to us, not so as to have already arrived in full, but as being underway, arriv-ing at us. His term for this is Geschick, which is typically rendered "fate" or "destiny," both fitting terms, but terms that tend to obscure the connection with sending (schicken). Thus, in what follows, Geschick shall be ren-dered "dispensation" with the understanding that one's fate lies in an accommodation to

the dispensed. What is dispensed, however, is being. Now every giving, every dispensa-tion, is a testament to the distance traversed. We are reached by what is given both despite and on account of that distance. Thus every giving requires that something be held back, such that this distance may be marked. In the words of the letter: "Being comes to its dispensation in that It, being, gives itself. But this says, thought dispensationally: It gives itself and refuses itself simultaneously" (GA 9, 335/PA, 255, tm). Only through such a refusal can it reach us at all. It reaches us without ever becoming entirely present. It comes extended in this way, spaced from us. It comes, in short, as a clearing: "This dispen-sation takes place as the clearing of being" (GA 9, 337/PA, 257, tm). Put more elabo-rately: "only so long as the clearing of being takes place does being convey itself to human beings. But the fact that the Da, the clearing as the truth of being itself, takes place is the sending [Schickung] of being itself. This is the dispensation [Geschick] of the clearing" (GA 9, 336/PA, 257, tm).

The dispensation is also thought by Heidegger in terms of a "claim" (Anspruch), something that metaphysics in its objectifying tendencies is unable to hear: "Metaphysics excludes the simple essential condition that the human only essences in its essence in that it is addressed [angesprochen] by being. Only from out of this claim [Anspruch] 'has' he found that wherein his essence resides" (GA 9, 323/PA, 247, tm). Ecstatic Ek-sistence resides in a medium always addressing it, encroaching on it, pouring in on it. Ek-sistence is immersion, properly understood. The coming of being can like-wise be cast in terms of an arriving (being as das Ankommende), with Heidegger observ-ing that "thinking is related to being as to what arrives (l'avenant)" (GA 9, 363/PA,

275). Indeed, thinking is nothing other than exposing oneself to this arrival and letting oneself be marked (claimed) by it. The mark of the claim is attested in language.

Language names the interface between ek-sistence and the coming of being. Heidegger's concern in the "Letter" with thinking is ultimately a concern with language. Thinking, the metaphysical privilege of the human, is an exposing of oneself to the dispensation, claim, and arriving of being such that this advent be brought to language. Heidegger could not be more clear: "To bring to language ever and again this arriving of being [*Ankunft des Seins*] . . . is the sole matter of thinking" (GA 9, 363/PA, 275, tm). Indeed, for being to arrive at all, for there to be a sending, it must be remarked. Otherwise there would be oblivion. Language is thus more than an *ex post facto* testament to the arrival of being, *it is that arriving itself*: "Language is the clearing-concealing arriving [*Ankunft*] of being itself" (GA 9, 326/PA, 249, tm).

If language is the efflorescence of this contact between ecstatic ek-sistence and the dispensation of being, the effulgence of the interface between these two movements, all language becomes testimony. Language is the preservation of this event. As such, it entails a sheltering function, as in the famous claim from the very first page of the letter: "Language is the house [*Haus*] of being. In its accommodation [*Behausung*] dwells the human" (GA 9, 313/PA, 239, tm).

But what language preserves of this event must itself be protected. For under the reign of subjectivity, language "falls into the service of expediting communication along routes where objectification—the uniform accessibility of everything to everyone—branches out and disregards all limits" (GA 9, 317/PA, 242). Thinkers and poets are the ones who attend to language in a way that breaks with its

traditional construal as language of a subject (understood on the basis of the *animal rationale*, see GA 9, 333/PA, 254). They do not insist on language as means of expediting information transfer, but allow it to trace the contour of eksistence and being, to be shaped by that juncture and announce that contact. They are the "guardians" of the house, as Heidegger explains, "Those who think and poetize are the guardians [*Wächter*] of this accommodation. Their guardianship [*Wachen*] accomplishes [*Vollbringen*] the openness of being, insofar as they bring this to language through their saying and preserve it [*aufbewahren*] in language" (GA 9, 313/PA, 239, tm).

By guarding (*wahren*) and preserving (*aufbewahren*), a protected space (a house and accommodation) is created. Within the space of this protection—otherwise known as "truth" (*Wahrheit*)—what appears does so as protected. The true (*das Wahre*) is protected (*bewahrt*). The claim of being that reaches the human, the call of being, is a call to participate in such protection, the truth of being. The question of "humanism" and "human dignity" must be reoriented around this fact. The human becomes shepherd: "The human is the shepherd of being . . . whose dignity consists in being called by being itself into the guardianship of its truth [*Wahrnis seiner Wahrheit*]" (GA 9, 342/PA, 260, tm). To hear the call is to let oneself be addressed by the claim of being and thus to attest to the ecstaticity of ek-sistence. To hear the call is to be struck by it and as a human this means to bring it into language.

In all we have said, being has marked itself in language. At the close of the letter, however, Heidegger suggests a reciprocal movement whereby thinking sets its mark in language, too: "With its saying, thinking lays inconspicuous furrows in language. They are still more inconspicuous than the furrows that the farmer, slow of step, draws through the field" (GA 9, 364/PA, 276). Language attests to the belonging together of the human and being. Any humanism must begin from this.

NOTES AND REFERENCES

[1] It was first published in the 1947 volume *Plato's Doctrine of Truth* (Bern: Verlag A. Francke, 1947), as something of an appendix behind a reprinting of the title essay on Plato from 1942. A headnote to the volume states: "The attached letter is to Jean Beaufret (Paris) as a response to questions posed in his letter of November 10, 1946. The questions arose from the French translation of the lecture [Plato's Doctrine of Truth] prepared by Josef Rovan" (*Platons Lehre*, 4). Beaufret's letter to Heidegger is printed in François Fédier, *L'Humanisme en Question: Pour aborder la lecture de la "Lettre sur l'humanisme" de Martin Heidegger* (Paris: Les Éditions du Cerf, 2012), 14–15. *Plato's Doctrine of Truth* was a volume in the series "Überlieferung und Auftrag" (Tradition and Mission) edited by Ernesto Grassi and Wilhelm Szilasi. Grassi had previously published the Plato essay in the second issue of his journal *Geistige Überlieferung* (*Spiritual Tradition*). Nevertheless, due to the circumstances of the war, a reprinting of the essay was in order. Heidegger himself pointed to the treatment of this essay as evidence of the antagonism between him and the National Socialist party. In a November 11, 1945 letter to the rectoral committee of his university, Heidegger cites a National Socialist directive that states: "The essay by Martin Heidegger, 'Plato's Doctrine of Truth,' in the *Journal for Spiritual Tradition*, shortly to appear with Helmut Küpper Publishers, Berlin, shall be neither reviewed nor named. Heidegger's participation in this second volume of the journal, which otherwise can be thoroughly discussed, is not to be mentioned" (GA 16, 403). The headnote to the 1947 volume repeats these claims, "mention in the press and review was forbidden, publication as a separate printing was likewise denied" (*Platons Lehre*, 4). Grassi thus had some reason to see to a second publication of the essay five years after its first appearance. The letter, despite its second billing in the volume (the title page identifies the volume as *Plato's Doctrine of Truth with a Letter on "Humanism"*), is actually much longer than the essay it follows (66 pages for the letter vs. 47 for the essay).

[2] The "Letter" is a strongly retrospective affair, with Heidegger referencing all of his published works from *Being and Time* to date. Indeed, he cites *Being and Time* no less than 30 times in the course of the essay, along with *Kant and the Problem of Metaphysics*, "What Is Metaphysics?" "On the Essence of Reason," and "On the Essence of Truth." On equal footing with these works he also cites all four of the Hölderlin essays he had published up to this point. Indeed, the only major publication that is not cited is the infamous Rectoral address, "The Self-Assertion of the German University," though critical reference is made in the letter to collectivism as completing "the unconditional self-assertion [*Selbstbehauptung*]" of individualism (GA 9, 341–2). On Heidegger's self-interpretation as a whole, see Friedrich Wilhelm von Herrmann, *Die Selbstinterpretation Martin Heideggers* (Meisenheim am Glan: Anton Hain, 1964).

[3] The French connection is well documented. The seminal work in this is Dominique Janicaud, *Heidegger en France*, 2 vols. (Paris: Hachette Littératures, 2005). A key text is also Frédéric de Towarnicki, *À la rencontre de Heidegger: Souvenirs d'un messager de la Forêt-Noire* (Paris: Gallimard, 1993). Details surrounding the "Letter" can also be found in Fédier, *L'humanisme en question*.

[4] There is not much to be directly gleaned about his relation to National Socialism in the "Letter." He makes critical comment of the "self-assertion" (*Selbstbehauptung*) of individualism, which could be seen as a retort to his own Rectoral Address, "The Self-Assertion of the German University" (see GA 9, 341–2/PA, 260), and he closes the letter with words that could apply to his own silence regarding the events of the war. The "fittingness of thoughtful saying," he writes, requires that we "ponder *whether* what is to be thought is to be said—to what extent, at what moment of the history of being, in what sort of dialogue with this history, and on the basis of what claim, it ought to be said" (GA 9, 363/PA, 276).

29

THE BREMEN LECTURES
Andrew J. Mitchell

Heidegger's 1949 Bremen lecture cycle, *Insight into That Which Is*, stands alongside the early *Being and Time* (1927), and the mid-period *Contributions to Philosophy* (1936–8), as a third, decisive milestone along Heidegger's path of thought. Comprised of four lectures—"The Thing," "Positionality," "The Danger," and "The Turn"—*Insight into That Which Is* combines provocative flair with an unflinching assessment of the times. While situating *Insight into That Which Is* alongside *Being and Time* and the *Contributions to Philosophy* might first appear hyperbolic, Heidegger himself puts great stock in these lectures.[1] Indeed, as Heidegger's first public appearance after the war, the Bremen lectures inaugurate his later thinking.

In saying that the Bremen lectures are the inauguration of Heidegger's "late" thought, I have a rough tripartite periodization of Heidegger's work in mind: early (1912–32, culminating in *Being and Time*, 1927), middle (1933–44, centering around the *Contributions to Philosophy*, 1936–8), and late or "postwar" (1945–76, taking its orientation from *Insight Into That Which Is*, 1949). While these are not arbitrary categorizations, their bounds are not rigidly fixed either. Indeed, good cases could be made for further dividing each of these periods:

separating the juvenilia from the works of fundamental ontology, for example, or the rectoral texts from the esoteric notebooks and the exoteric lecture courses of the late 1930s and early1940s, or, lastly, distinguishing the work of the 1960s, that is, the homeland speeches and aesthetic investigations (signally, of sculpture) from the immediately postwar period of the fourfold running through the 1950s. Nevertheless, the heuristic benefits of such a rough division warrants this simplified, tripartitioned approach to Heidegger's remarkable path of thought.

The Bremen lectures are Heidegger's first lecture appearance after the Second World War, held while he was under a teaching ban imposed by the French authorities in the wake of the war. As such, they were held at no university, but instead at the private Club zu Bremen, which, as one contemporary put it, was "made up of big businessmen, specialists in overseas commerce, and directors of shipping lines and dockyards."[2] To this audience, then, Heidegger delivered what an attending reviewer called "the boldest statement of his thinking."[3] To be sure, while Heidegger already had published something after the war, the "Letter on 'Humanism'" of 1947, this text was largely retrospective (see the entry on the "Letter" elsewhere in this volume) and, as Heidegger himself says in an opening note to the letter, "the letter contin- ues to speak in the language of metaphysics, and does so knowingly" (GA 9, 313 n. a/P 239 n. a). As we have seen, with "The Thing" (and the Bremen lectures more generally), Heidegger announces his thinking "on its own terms." It is also worth noting that the "Letter" makes no overt mention of the war, whereas the Bremen lectures address the war at its most horrifying, with Heidegger infa- mously discussing the concentration camps themselves. Despite the (merely) chrono- logical precedence of the "Letter," then, it is *Insight into That Which Is* that stands as the inauguration of Heidegger's "postwar" or "late" thinking.

In the Bremen lectures, Heidegger offers a concrete "ontology" of existence within a world given over to contemporary technol- ogy. It is here, in the opening lecture "The Thing" that Heidegger first introduces the term "fourfold" (*das Geviert*), which is the key to his new understanding of the thing (see the entry under "fourfold" in this volume). Understanding the thing as arising from a "gathering" of the fourfold means understanding the thing as noth- ing self-enclosed or encapsulated. Rather, the thing is now understood as opened and spilling over into relations with what lies beyond it. Things are defined relationally and in sustaining these relations and being sustained by them in turn; things are singu- lar, unique. What makes a thing the unique thing it is, is its place within this network of mutually supportive relations. The thing is nothing self-same and self-present but essentially defined by what lies outside of it. Things are contextual, open. But this same openness that singularizes the thing and by which the thing relates to what lies beyond it also entails that what lies beyond the thing, the world, now relates back to it. And for

Heidegger this world is one that has been claimed by technology.

The second lecture in the cycle, "Positionality," details the nature of a world so claimed. He first coins the term "position- ality" (*das Ge-Stell*) in this lecture as naming the very essence of technology. Positionality institutes the regime of "requisitioning" (*das Bestellen*), whereby all that is becomes trans- formed into so much "standing reserve" (*das Bestand*), replaceable commodities utterly available for ordering and delivery along supply routes of unending circulation. The standing reserve is the mode of presence for all that exists under the dominance of contemporary technology and it is the only permissible mode: "In positionality, the pres- encing of all that presences becomes standing reserve" (GA 79, 32/BF 31). What circulates under the aegis of positionality is no longer the object, but instead the "standing reserve." Heidegger could not be more clear on this point: "Nature is no longer even an object [*Gegen-stand*]" (GA 79, 44/BF 41). The object, as *Gegenstand*, requires an "over and against" (a "gegen") in which to stand. This space of the *gegen*, for its part, names a dis- tance between subject and object, the space of representation. But it is precisely this dis- tance that is put in question by positionality. Instead of a space between subject and object, there is now a suffusion into that space and a smothering of the difference between subject and object in the general transformation into standing reserve. No space is unclaimed or off limits. Nearly 25 years later in the 1973 seminar in Zähringen, Heidegger remains true to this insight, describing how the human "has gone from the epoch of objectivity [*Gegenständlichkeit*] to that of orderability [*Bestellbarkeit*]. . . . Strictly speaking, there are no longer objects" (GA 15, 388/FS, 74). In the words of the Bremen lectures where the idea is first forged: "Where the standing reserve comes into power, even the object crumbles as characteristic of what presences" (GA 79, 26/BF, 25).

That the fourfold would be thought in conjunction with technology is nothing accidental. Indeed, for Heidegger it is the fourfold that grants the thing its relational character, a relationality that likewise singularizes the thing. When each thing is opened to the world around it, stands in contextualizing relations with this world, and when those relations are essential to the thing itself, then the place of the thing within this world becomes irreplaceable. Or rather, the relational thing is specified and singularized through these relations. Things are unique. But Heidegger now sees the essence of technology to lie in the circulation of "standing reserve" (*das Bestand*), wherein one piece of standing reserve is replaceable by another. And it is the essence of technology to drive for its own expansion. Thus an essential tension exists between the singularity of the thing and the replaceability of the standing reserve.

The third lecture, "The Danger," locates this tension within beyng itself. The conflict of singularity and replacement is no accidental misfortune that has befallen our world. Rather, the technological challenge to things is effected by being itself. Along with requisitioning (*Bestellen*), then, Heidegger identifies pursuit (*Nachstellen*) as determinative of contemporary existence, the pursuit whereby beyng pursues itself with its own forgetting. This forgetting is a mistaking of the thing as something immediately available, as without the medium through which its relations might stream, as apart from the medium of truth (*Wahrheit*), as suffering an ontological kind of neglect or "unguarding" (*Verwahrlosung*). Heidegger can thus make the provocative

claim that "beyng is unqualifiedly in itself, from itself, for itself, the danger" (GA 79, 54/BF, 51). This self-diremption within being has been broached by Heidegger before. It was the "most secretive" thing that Hölderlin could say in the first Hölderlin lecture course of 1934, "the innermost contrariety in beings as a whole . . . the highest questionability in the essence of beyng" (GA 39, 269). In the 1946 essay on Anaximander, it was cast in terms of an "insurrection" on the part of beings themselves (GA 5, 356/OBT, 268, tm). Despite these precursors, however, nothing could prepare the listener for the grizzly reckoning with the times that Heidegger would now detail:

Hundreds of thousands die in masses. Do they die? They perish. They are put down. Do they die? They become pieces of inventory of a standing reserve for the fabrication of corpses. Do they die? They are unobtrusively liquidated in annihilation camps. And even apart from such as these—millions now in China abjectly end in starvation. (GA 79, 56/BF, 53)

These stand as Heidegger's first words on the aftermath of the war, startling words that have garnered Heidegger condemnation since long before their first publication in German in 1994. When it is even acknowledged that Heidegger is here drawing out the full consequences of the self-pursuit of being, of a world given over to technological commodification, Heidegger's claim is taken as cold and indifferent. The careful phrasing and rhetorical force of the passage says otherwise. These are not the words of a business report, they are shocking and unsettling and are so intended. An insight into that which is demands it.

The last lecture, "The Turn," shows that the source of the technological danger in being means that a relation to technology is a relation to being. The turn is from a false belief in the annihilation of being by technology to an understanding of existence as never so pinioned between the false alternatives of presence or absence. The turn effects a thinking of nonpresence, of the trace, we might say (to take up a vocabulary Heidegger employs in the 1946 text "What Are Poets For?" as well as his earlier Hölderlin readings). It is in these pages that Heidegger first brings Hölderlin into conversation with contemporary technology, famously citing the couplet: "But where the danger is, there grows/ also what saves" (cited at GA 79, 72/BF, 68). The insight proclaimed in the lecture cycle's title is this very insight into the transitional, relational, and endangered existence of all that is. Where an appendix to "The Thing" informed us that things "have never yet been as things" (GA 79, 23/BF, 22), we now see the reason for this. The thing is nothing apart from the threat of its replacement. Singularity demands this. Relationality cannot remove itself from the world, but must engage with it at its most essential level. Only in so doing can there be things at all, things that are nothing present and self-evident, but things that are always ever "not yet" things. The "insight into that which is" is an insight into that which is "not yet." Heidegger thinks the belonging together of technology and the fourfold, standing reserve and thing.

What this means is that the thing is always endangered, always further commodifiable and assailable. But it also entails that this process can never be completed. Were it to be so we would be relieved of all responsibility. Heidegger's refusal to think in such black and white alternatives means we always remain a part of the world, open to its appeal. Were the thing simply "to thing," it would be a new order, a new beginning,

a fresh start. It would leave metaphysics behind. There would be a new fully present order separated by a gap of pure absence from a now outdated order that is completely left behind. That is to say, this thinking of sequentiality reiterates the very motifs of metaphysics, specifically the oppositional thinking of presence and absence, that it seeks to escape. Heidegger's name for this failed and ultimately metaphysical project is "overcoming" (Überwindung). He contrasts it with "converting" (Verwindung), a term that likewise makes its first public appearance in Heidegger's work with the Bremen lecture "The Turn." Through "conversion" metaphysics is not left behind, but instead taken to its limit, shown that it has a limit, that all supposed closure is really an exposure, that the same line that encloses likewise exposes, that closure is impossible, that we dwell in this between.

To understand how this configuration of singularity and replacement marks the Bremen lectures as inaugurating Heidegger's "later" thought, a brief look at the situation in his middle period is revealing. We will take the Contributions to Philosophy (Of the Event) and the essay "The Age of the World Picture" as representative here. Simply stated, Heidegger's middle period is a thinking of, and worry over, "modernist" objectification. With the Bremen lectures, Heidegger achieves a position of "postmodern" commodification (replaceability).

In this middle period of the mid- to late 1930s, Heidegger first comes to understand being (beyng) as essentially defined by withdrawal. Beings, for their part, are understood as concomitantly abandoned, where "abandonment" names a way of essencing that is not entirely present (what is abandoned maintains a relation to something outside of it that it essentially does not possess, its abandoner, we might provisionally say). Against this understanding of a withdrawn and abandoning beyng, however, against this strange and newly framed essencing of beyng, Heidegger poses the object, objectification. The "antagonist" of the middle period, in other words, the great danger facing us, is that of objectification. For this reason the *Contributions* can be said to remain within a "modernist" framework.

In the *Contributions*, Heidegger observes that beings are abandoned to the world, and this means they are abandoned into machination, which many would see as a proto form of Heidegger's thinking of technology. Nothing could be further from the truth. In regard to abandoned beings, the *Contributions* make clear that, as so abandoned, "the being then appears thus, it shows itself *as object and present-at-hand*, as if beyng did not essence" (GA 65, 115/CP, 91, tm, emphasis modified). Machination thus names the constellation of forces that struggle for the objectification and presence of the world at the time of the *Contributions*. Beings are representationally objective in that text, as per Heidegger's understanding of machination there as "machination, that interpretation of beings as re-presentable and re-presented [*Vor-stellbaren und Vor-Gestellten*]" (GA 65, 108–9/CP, 86). The essay "The Age of the World Picture" makes the connection explicit: "This objectification of beings is accomplished in a setting-before, a representing [*Vor-stellen*], aimed at bringing each being before it in such a way that the person who calculates can be sure, and that means be certain, of the being" (GA 5, 87/OBT, 66, tm). Indeed, representation so dominates the age that only what is represented is admitted as true or extant, "so construed, only what becomes an object *is*, that is, counts as extant" (GA 5, 87/OBT, 66, tm).

The danger for the human in this is accordingly that of understanding oneself in terms of objectified "lived experience" (*Erlebnis*). Under the reign of machination, experience itself is objectified. The human is delivered over to a sham world of objectified experiences that may be hoarded and possessed. They are available for the taking by the intrepid adventurer. As he notes, "The being counts first as extant, insofar as and to the extent that it is included in and related back to this life, i.e., is experienced in life [*er-lebt*] and becomes lived experience [*Erlebnis*]" (GA 5, 94/OBT, 71, tm). Heidegger's vitriol in the *Contributions* over "movies and trips to the beach" should be understood in this regard (GA 65, 139/CP, 109). The *Contributions* is a thinking of objectification.

With the Bremen lectures, all this changes. The Second World War provided Heidegger with insight into the consumption of all beings in the service of what Ernst Jünger termed a "total mobilization." The human, too, was now enrolled in cycles of consumption like any other "raw material," as the war made gruesomely clear. This experience undergirds Heidegger's later writing, starting with the Bremen lectures. It is in these that the war is first registered in his lectures or publications.[4] The insight that "agriculture is now a mechanized food industry, in essence the same as the production of corpses in the gas chambers and extermination camps" is light years away from a worry over people visiting the beach (GA 79, 27/BF, 27). The Bremen lectures consequently inaugurate Heidegger's "late" work as explicitly "postwar," and the thinking of replacement that he undertakes in these, as opposed to modernist objectification, makes them "postmodern" as well.

Heidegger's genius in the Bremen lectures is to refuse to separate the two economies of singularity (the thing) and replacement (the standing reserve) as two separate orders of being. The thing does not come after the standing reserve. There is no epoch of the thing that would follow upon that of techno-logical positionality and in which we would finally be "at-home." Instead, Heidegger insists on the tension between the two, between the thing and the standing reserve, positionality and the fourfold, *Gestell und Geviert*, the danger and what saves. In sum, it is not that there is something salvatory somewhere apart from an external danger that we happen to have fallen into. Rather Heidegger thinks the danger and the saving together. A proper appreciation of this means thinking from the between, thinking in terms of traces. This is the way of thinking that is truly postmodern for Heidegger, a thinking of the between (and not simply the simulta-neity of oppositions, each internally coherent in itself, in a kind of duck-rabbit coupling). It is neither an either/or nor a both/and as there are no longer present-at-hand relata standing outside the relation to be brought together or separated apart in a manner that never compromises their self-identity. There is instead relationality. The Bremen lectures present Heidegger's fullest account of such an existence and one that remains determi-native for the rest of the way along his path of thought.

NOTES AND REFERENCES

[1] See the letter to Sinn, cited in the entry to "The Fourfold" elsewhere in this volume, where Heidegger notes that "The Thing" is the only time he published his thinking as expressed "on its own terms." As "The Thing" opens the cycle *Insight into That Which Is* and indeed depicts the necessary counter force to technological replaceability as detailed in the second and third lectures of the cycle, it would seem that the Bremen lectures as a whole would most fully express Heidegger's thinking "on its own terms."

[2] The businessman F. W. Oezle, cited in Heinrich Wiegand Petzet, *Auf einen Stern zugehen: Begegnungen mit Martin Heidegger 1929 bis 1976* (Frankfurt am Main: Societäts Verlag, 1983), 59. English translation: *Encounters & Dialogues with Martin Heidegger*, trans. Parvis Emad and Kenneth Maly (Chicago: The University of Chicago Press, 1993), 53.

[3] Egon Vietta, cited in Petzet, *Auf einen Stern zugehen*, 62/56.

[4] To be sure, the war plays a role in the "Evening Conversation" of 1945 in the *Country Path Conversations*, but this text remained unpublished until its appearance in the *Gesamtausgabe* in 1995. Another 1945 text, "Poverty," also addresses the war, but this was an extremely private lecture spoken before a handful of people in no official context. The Bremen lectures are the first public declaration. The first mention in print will be in his contri-bution to the exhibition catalog of the sculptor Ernst Barlach in 1951 (subsequently included as section 24 of "Overcoming Metaphysics" in the 1954 volume *Vorträge und Aufsätze*).

30

LATER ESSAYS AND SEMINARS
Lee Braver

Heidegger changed his mind; that is why we speak of a "later" Heidegger. The simple division between an early and a later phase—the arrangement that initially structured Heidegger studies—is now generally seen as too stark. For one thing, over his 80 years of thinking Heidegger changed his mind a lot, not just once. Almost every decade of his career a new topic surfaces as the central idea that gets retrospectively read back into not just his own previous work but into the history of Western civilization. However, the "turning" that took place around 1930 is sharper and deeper than the later transitions.

Nor need we exaggerate this change into a complete break that repudiates his early work. Of course there are continuities. Later and early Heidegger are both recognizably, indeed unmistakably, Heidegger. But these continuities are incomplete. *Being and Time* contains an important discussion of truth, for example, which already makes the crucial move of defining it as unconcealment. But these 20-odd pages are a far cry from the extensive, complex, historically informed discussions of the topic in the 1930s, and throughout the rest of his career.

Of course, the primary continuity—the primary fact about Heidegger's thought in general—is the question of being. He never strays far from this home key, even when he modulates it into other keys or even crosses it out in favor of other terms. But that is one of the strange things about *Being and Time*—there is far more time in it than being. He tells us from the outset that he wants to reawaken the *question* of being rather than provide an answer, to revive a long-dormant puzzlement rather than settle it, and in this aim he has surely succeeded. The part that was to have dealt directly with being—division III of part one—was never published, making it impossible to construct a substantive continuity between his early and late work on his views about being.

While the continuities are vague and sketchy, we find ideas in the later work that are either absent from or that even directly conflict with the early. I want to lay out here, as clearly and directly as I can—as becomes a good companion—the main topics of Heidegger's later work and, more briefly, how they differ from his earlier views.

STYLE

Perhaps the first thing that strikes the reader about the later works is how hard they are. This may be the second and third thing too and, all too often, the last thing as well.

249

"Hard" does not do them justice—more than impenetrable, they seem to actively resist comprehension, like a hermeneutically repulsive magnetic field. *Being and Time* is difficult—you have to master a whole vocabulary in order to read it—but it is recognizably philosophical in form and content. With the proper background, the book becomes a bit of an Easter egg hunt for ideas plucked from predecessors: one spies a bit of Kierkegaard here mixed in with a splash of Hegel there, with a sprinkle of Aristotle over the lot—and that is just one chapter!

When one reads the later work, on the other hand, it is hard to know where to begin—or to middle or end. Here too, mastering the vocabulary helps immensely although his favorite words keep evolving. Perhaps the single best advice to reading Heidegger is to take him at his word, that being is the skeleton key to all philosophy, especially his. Unlike *Being and Time*, which the reader can get quite a bit out of without paying much attention to being, it is hard to advance a single step in the later volumes without a solid grasp of it. With a grasp—well, it is still tough going, but progress can be had, so let us turn to being.

BEING

Being and Time teaches us the ontological distinction between beings and being, which is more straightforward than it sounds. Beings are just what you think they are—the various entities that populate our lives—and being means the kind of entities that they are. It is quite close to the traditional notion of essence, though more dynamic: things actively *are* or, in a sense, behave in certain ways that determine what is appropriate to do with

them. People, for example, have a very different way of being than chairs, which is why we talk to and ask permission of the former but sit on the latter (Kant made this distinction between persons and objects central to his ethics). Perhaps the main point of the book as we have it is that we inappropriately tend to interpret both of these kinds of beings in the manner of a third type—bare inert objects.

Now Heidegger maintains this framework in his later work, although he adds more modes of being: artworks and technology, for example, and what he calls "things," which are very different from objects. But he also adds to the ontological difference a third layer that barely appears in *Being and Time*, which he sometimes calls being itself or the truth of being. This means the manifestation of beings to us, the fact that we can become aware at all. This "clearing" was the defining feature of Dasein in the early work, but there he explains our awareness by appealing to our nature, the way philosophers like Kant and Husserl do. It is because we are the kinds of creatures that we are and because we do the kinds of things that we do that beings show up for us at all, and in the specific ways that they do. The later work turns this formulation around: it is because beings show up for us and in the specific ways that they do that we are the kinds of creatures that we are and do the kinds of things that we do. Being is something that happens to us rather than something we do, even autonomically. This, along with the dynamic connotation, is why he comes to use the term *Ereignis*: being manifesting itself is an event in which we are caught up rather than an act we perform.

This changes everything. *Being and Time* works out "fundamental ontology," which founds the study of being on a grasp of ourselves since being, in a Kantian way, is a projection of our nature. It is our use of tools that structures them as ready-to-hand; they change over to presence-at-hand when we stop to study them. The later work reverses "fundamental ontology" into an ontological foundation: everything must be understood in light of the fact and way that being appears to us. The later work as a whole can be described as working out the consequences of this one insight, which is why he says that, "the primal mystery for all thinking is concealed in" Parmenides' phrase, "for there is Being" (BW, 238). Heidegger patiently, doggedly, takes up one topic after another and works out new understandings of them in light of this idea. Let us examine a few of the most important.

THE WILL, NIETZSCHE, AND TECHNOLOGY

There are debates about how to read Heidegger's early view of authenticity and the will, as there are debates about most of his positions, but I read him as basically an existentialist voluntarist. This means that, largely inspired by Kierkegaard, he believed that we passively drift through our lives, acquiescing unquestioningly in our society's values until something shakes us from this complacency. This interruption can be a mid-life crisis, a bout of depression, or just the vivid dawning of one's mortality, but afterwards one can explicitly decide upon how to live one's life rather than just doing "what one does."

This ethics obviously places great emphasis on the making of explicit decisions. While Heidegger rejects the possibility of a transcendent perspective that could validate particular ways of living as objectively or absolutely right, he does praise "choosing to choose" (GA 2, 270/BT, 314) as the right way to approach the problem. Much of his later work, however,

dismantles this emphasis, even its coherence, as he comes to see it as a symptom of our age that he associates with Nietzsche and technology.

Heidegger studies many thinkers extensively, but Nietzsche ranks as one of the most important. Heidegger spent four years teaching him and left 1,200 pages of surprisingly readable lecture notes. He argues that after the pre-Socratics, for whom he has a great affinity, Plato instituted a fundamental distinction between appearing and being, between how we experience reality and what it is really like. This distinction instigates metaphysics as the search for true reality beyond mere appearance, and while this project has gone through many forms, it has always remained true to this basic approach. What counts as appearance and what counts as real and how we distinguish the two has fluctuated considerably, but the formal distinction and the goal have stayed the same throughout.

Nietzsche represents the other bookend to the history of metaphysics, bringing it to a close by ringing the final variation on Plato's appearance-being duality. His is the final variation because it directly reverses Plato, making the empirical, changing world the one that is really real and the intellectual, eternally stable Ideas mere whiffs of smoke, dreamed up to render the mob more governable. This reversal draws metaphysics to a close, allowing us to pursue fundamentally different forms of thought while keeping Nietzsche himself stuck within it, insofar as just reversing appearance and reality still retains the distinction.

Nietzsche believes that traditional values have been supported by superstition, religion, and metaphysics (among which he sees little difference) and, with their demise, the old values are fading as well. We can no longer believe in objective values; we project them onto the world much the way Kant has us injecting categories like time or causality into experience.

Nietzsche thinks we have always been the creators of meaning but now that we realize it, we can take control of this process and deliberately forge more life-affirming values.

This is to treat values as a kind of technology, broadly understood. Heidegger's analysis of technology is more concerned with an attitude or mentality than the proliferation of gadgets. These are just a symptom of a deeper underlying mindset that treats all inconveniences or obstacles as things to be taken care of. If something keeps us from getting what we want, then we should roll up our sleeves and come up with a way to remove it. Fixing problems often involves making devices, which is why electronic tools share the name, but the essence of technology goes much deeper and pervades virtually all aspects of our lives. Descartes, for example, was an arch-technologist even though he lived before modern devices. He saw that Medieval ways of thinking were not getting the job, were not getting us good medicine or machinery, so he set about constructing a new way of thinking. He correctly intuited that before we could start making new inventions we needed new rules for the direction of the mind, a new instruction manual for the brain. Nietzsche similarly urges us to erect axiological structures that will enhance our well-being. Ultimately, these ideas all circle around autonomy, the attempt to decide our own fate, which is the organizing ideal of the Enlightenment. In epistemology, we do not rely on authorities but find out the truth for ourselves; in ethics, we do not accept any tablet of values handed down but give ones to ourselves; in gadgetry, we do not rest with the limitations evolution has saddled us with, but create our own tools and habitat.

Heidegger sees a paradox at the heart of this quest for autonomy that has structured much of the intellectual history of the last 400 years. Absolute control over the world and ourselves is incoherent. Thought for Heidegger is essentially a response to what solicits it.[1] We think about what attracts our attention, what "calls out" for thought—a different translation of the title usually rendered as *What Is Called Thinking*. We dream of self-creation. Descartes complained bitterly of the way he had unquestioningly accepted beliefs as a child. He never really thought about them so, in a way, *he* did not believe them; he just ran across them in his head as he rummaged around. He must empty his head of these merely found elements in order to reconstitute his belief system under his control, with his express consent, and *those* beliefs will truly be his. The self that is made of them will truly be him. Nietzsche seeks an *amor fati* that will reconcile himself to the fact that he did not will his own past.

But what beliefs does Descartes accept into that epistemologically sterile operating room? Those that he finds so persuasive that he simply cannot doubt. Clear and distinct perceptions are those whose siren song he cannot resist, those he cannot help but believe (the attempt to prove them via divine veracity, of course, argues in a circle by employing ideas legitimated through clear and distinct perception). Heidegger does not criticize Descartes for this, but for thinking that he could do anything else. No matter what kind of test Descartes uses on his beliefs, it ultimately comes down to his passively finding which beliefs pass it. Moreover, the choice of the test itself cannot be tested on pain of circularity or infinite regress, so that selection is made on the basis of which one appears best to him. Nietzsche wants to decide which values are best without relying on those he has been socialized into accepting, but he needs some basis on which to judge, a basis that itself cannot have been chosen. Choices can only occur on the basis of something that has not been chosen. "Every decision, however, bases itself on something not mastered . . . else it would never be a decision" (BW, 180). This does not make them not our choices, however, because there is no other way to act. A being with no previous preferences whatsoever would be impotent, not free, unable to select from among options that made no appeal to him.

Although this analysis applies to all actions, it has particularly devastating consequences when applied to the technological attitude. We moderns organize the world around us so that it serves our needs and desires with maximum efficiency, making everything serve us from the sun and wind to the ways we think and value. We seek more and more control, but we did not in fact decide to see the world as to-be-controlled; rather, problems simply appear to us as to-be-solved-by-our-efforts, the way chocolate ice cream shows up as should-be-eaten. "Technological activity . . . always merely responds to the challenge of enframing, but it never comprises enframing itself or brings it about" (326). Thus if we fully understand our drive to control, we realize that we are not in control of it. This is how Heidegger reads Hölderlin's lines: "precisely the essence of technology must harbor in itself the growth of the saving power. But in that case, might not an adequate look into what enframing is, as a destining of revealing, bring the upsurgence of the saving power into appearance?" (334). Properly understanding the nature of the essence of technology limits this essence by showing us that we neither created nor control it.

NIHILISM AND GELASSENHEIT

In fact, it is worse than simply a paradox; feeding the will this way prevents a good life.

Nietzsche thinks that we face nihilism or the loss of all values because the death of God—their former support—pulls them down with Him. Nietzsche's solution is to invent new values to pump meaning back into our rapidly deflating lives. Heidegger argues that this "solution" actually poses a greater danger. Besides being conceptually impossible, as described above, the attempt to throw off the ballast of tradition leaves the individual naked and alone. The kinds of standards or principles we come up with on our own are paltry things, lacking the authority to command assent and the gravitas to order a life. "No one dies for mere values" (OBT, 77). Instead, "according to our human experience and history, everything essential and great has arisen solely out of the fact that humans had a home and were rooted in a tradition" (HR, 325). Nietzsche argues that because we live in an unprecedentedly godless time, we lack values and so must create them for ourselves. Heidegger believes that we live in a time of nihilism or cosmic homelessness precisely *because* we are trying to create values for ourselves. Refusing "external" authority robs us of the sense of worthiness, "the unity of those paths and relations in which birth and death, disaster and blessing, victory and disgrace, endurance and decline acquire the shape of destiny for human being" (BW, 167), that orient the kind of world that makes a home for a people.

The question as to what we ought to do about this situation is tricky, in that trying to *do* anything perpetuates the technological attitude by implying that it is up to us to take control of our fate. Instead, "everything depends on our inhering in this clearing that is propriated by Being itself—never made or conjured by ourselves. We must overcome the compulsion to lay our hands on everything" (NIII, 181). As opposed to his early notion of resoluteness, we do not choose our lives, even after soul-shattering moments; we are thrown into them, given the particular tastes and traditions that guide all decisions. We do not so much make decisions, as much as we are made by them, as we respond to the call of the world.

The right attitude is not to resent this as a foreign imposition upon our natural integrity, for there is nothing to be imposed upon prior to this formation. Rather, we should be immensely grateful for the fact that we can be aware of anything at all. As far as we know, we are the lone flickering of consciousness in all of existence. In this vast universe, all takes place in darkness, unknown and unexperienced, except in this clearing where things are lit up. Here there is a spark, the halo of a small, fragile light in which reality comes to know itself through us.

This is the tremendous adventure of consciousness. We, perhaps alone in all of existence, have been given the ability to see and know and think and feel. What Hegel called a highway of despair Heidegger considers the blessing of destiny. We are absurdly, ridiculously fortunate, and yet what do we do with this *ur*-gift that enables all presence? We who can know, ignore 99 percent of the world; we can become aware but we let all fade into inconspicuous background, drifting through "the oblivious passing of our lives" (BP, 297) on auto-pilot. We can express this awareness in words, but rely on easy clichés.

A grateful life would be one lived in appreciation of this cosmic gift, this extraordinary chance that has somehow been granted to us. Heidegger encourages the attitude of *Gelassenheit*, a releasement or letting-be that dwells with and on our experience, a patient attending to the way things show themselves to us the way one cares for and nurtures a plant. A paradigm of this attitude would be, I think, Zen *satori*, but also what happens

when one is struck by a work of art. All sense of control over the situation ebbs away, leaving one "captivated," part of an experience that is not the grasping of an idea. The artwork unfolds as the eye or ear attends to it, showing more depth and detail, ultimately making one alive to the simple fact of seeing and hearing. Artworks "make unconcealment as such happen in regard to beings as a whole. . . . That is how self-concealing Being is cleared" (BW, 181).

This happens in thinking when we think about the fact that experience is given to us. We did not create it, we do not control it, and we should be tremendously grateful for the gift. Thanking, Heidegger writes in a rare wordplay that comes through in English, is thinking. We should truly use this capacity to think, and we should think about the fact that we can think. Whereas the poet is the one who truly hears words instead of passing them back and forth like coins with their faces worn off by over-use; "it is necessary for thinking to become explicitly aware of the matter here called clearing" (442). This is, for Heidegger, the logical culmination of phenomenology, phenomenology squared if you will, as the study of awareness becomes the awareness of awareness itself. The phenomenological attitude is not limited to a specialized activity one does in one's study but should infuse one's entire life with a higher attentiveness, a more sensitive attunedness to the luminosity of the world.

NOTES AND REFERENCES

[1] For more on this topic, see my "Never Mind: Thinking of Subjectivity in the Dreyfus-McDowell Debate," in ed. Julian Schear, *Mind, Reason and Being-in-the-World: The McDowell-Dreyfus Debate* (New York: Routledge, 2013), and chapter four of *Groundless Grounds: A Study of Wittgenstein and Heidegger* (Cambridge: MIT Press, 2012).

PART IV:
THEMES AND TOPICS

31

ART
Andrew Bowie

Heidegger's assessment of specific works of art is largely based on quite traditional assumptions. He sometimes pays significant attention, for example, to not particularly outstanding poetry, such as that of Conrad Ferdinand Meyer, and his criticisms of Wagner are largely copied from the later Nietzsche's pseudo-classicist rejection of the supposed excesses in Wagner's music. Heidegger is also famously mistaken in "The Origin of the Work of Art" about Van Gogh's painting of shoes, which he sees as those of a peasant woman, but which seem to have been Van Gogh's own. Like Kant, who was famously limited in his awareness of significant art, Heidegger's relationship to art tends generally not to be important for what he says about major works of art. However, again like Kant, Heidegger also helps to open up a whole new way of thinking about the significance of art both for modern philosophy and in more general terms, whose implications are still being understood. This mismatch between engagement with works of art in the manner of critics and other artists, and philosophical insight into art might suggest that Kant and Heidegger are imposing on art ways of thinking that are actually alien to it. Indeed, this kind of imposition is easy to show in many versions of the philosophy of art in the analytical tradition, where

the concern is too often with tedious, and largely vacuous classificatory ontology. In such cases what matters about art disappears because of the concern to analyze the object "art" in conceptual terms. The importance of Heidegger's approaches to art lies, in contrast, in how they help us to see why philosophy may sometimes have more to learn from art than vice versa.

Heidegger's earlier philosophy, before the essay "The Origin of the Work of Art" (1935), does not address art in any substantial way, so why does art become a crucial point of orientation for his work from this time onwards? *Being and Time*, as Mark Okrent, Charles Taylor, Richard Rorty, and others have suggested, has an essentially pragmatist dimension, in which the understanding of being is dependent on the ways in which *Dasein* responds in practical terms. The hammer that changes status from *zuhanden* to *vorhanden* when it breaks shows up its significance in terms of a world of practical action that is determined by the needs and desires of *Dasein*. This version of the understanding of being can, though, seem to depend on an idealist projection of significance onto the world by the subject. There is much more to Heidegger's phenomenological ontology than this, but ways in which understanding of the world must also derive from the world itself can be inadequately articulated in certain kinds of pragmatist perspective. If, as Heidegger seeks to do, one wishes to get out of a subject/object philosophical model that separates two aspects and then has to account for the fact that they cannot be wholly separate, one needs ways of doing this that do not reproduce the original problem despite themselves. It is this situation that leads Heidegger toward art.

Is art, then, the "object" that shows how the subject/object model can be circumvented? The point, of course, is that art is not an object: the object Beethoven's Ninth Symphony or Van Gogh's painting of shoes consists of what can be said about them that is subsumable within objective conceptual terms: a mass of frequencies and durations, in the case of the Beethoven (or a pile of printed paper, a digitally encoded set of sounds, etc.), and a chemical and physical object "displaying colored properties," or whatever, in the case of Van Gogh. If one begins with their status as objects, the fact that these are works of art would then appear to consist either in their supposedly possessing a further property not possessed by objects that are not art, or in the fact that they are taken to be art by their listeners and viewers, which is a further example of the projection of significance by the subject. It is this approach that Heidegger rejects as failing to grasp what is at issue in art, and this rejection has considerable philosophical consequences.

Heidegger's alternative is, as Manfred Frank has suggested, encapsulated by Paul Klee's remark that art "renders reality visible," rather than representing it. In Heidegger's terms, then, art has to do with "unconcealment," "world-disclosure," and the question is why this becomes so significant both for Heidegger's philosophical project and for decisive issues in modern philosophy. Such

an approach goes counter to the apparently obvious view that what philosophy needs to do in relation to art is to explain how nonaesthetic objects become works of art. This view starts with the assumption of an objective world of physics and chemistry as the foundational reality, which leads to the puzzle of what makes physical and chemical objects be able to be art. In contrast, what happens in art is seen by Heidegger as prior to the objectifications that enable the explanatory and predictive success of the sciences.

Art has to do with how the world makes sense at all, where the fact that it can be explained in terms of natural laws is, however important that undoubtedly is, a derivative way of relating to being (see "The Age of the World Picture"). In the contemporary world the assumption has increasingly come to dominate that, in the long run, everything will ultimately become explicable via the growing reach of explanations derived from physics, chemistry, and biology. Recent books using evolutionary psychology to account for art are a characteristic offshoot of this metaphysical assumption. Heidegger, and the hermeneutic, phenomenological, and Critical Theory traditions deriving from Kant and German Idealism, show that the idea that all other forms of understanding will eventually be explained by scientific objectification is unsustainable. A challenge to the objectifying model that dominates much Western philosophy already formed the core of *Being and Time*, and Heidegger's move to focusing on art relates to other changes associated with the "turn." In the "turn" the role of *Dasein* becomes less dominant because of what is encapsulated in the idea of language as the "house of being," in which things make sense by the way in which they are expressed in language. There is a connection here between the way language is understood and the way art is understood. In both cases, it is not subjective projection that makes sense of things, but rather the existence of forms of articulation and expression that are prior to individual subjects, and which those subjects come to "inhabit." Whether this obscures the role of subjective initiative in both language use and the creation of art is a complex subject. In the present context what matters, though, is how Heidegger shows that art is not something that can be adequately understood either just from the side of the subject, or just from the side of the world as described in objective terms.

The importance of these issues is evident in the contrast between the role of art in the analytical, and in the European traditions of philosophy. The former is often critical of an apparent overestimation of the significance of art in the latter, which they rightly observe does not play a determining role for many people in many areas of modern life. Ernst Tugendhat suggests the reasons for this kind of objection as follows, in relation to his interpretation of the tradition to which Heidegger belongs: "it may be correct that art has something to do with truth, but this can hardly be demonstrated by pointing out that a work of art has the function of showing something."[1] Tugendhat assumes that truth has to be analyzed in semantic terms before one can begin to argue about the truth conveyed by art, but the question he does not adequately address is what makes the semantic approach itself possible at all, which is what Heidegger tries to understand in terms of unconcealment.[2] A further objection here is that if the importance of art in the European tradition were just based on contemporary artistic production and reception, the emphasis art receives might well be said to be based on a misapprehension. Hegel's judgment that art no longer plays the central social role it did, for example, in the Athenian polis is clearly true. Hegel infers from this that: "The *science* of art is thus in our time much more necessary than in times in which art for itself as art provided complete satisfaction."[3] However, he means by this that philosophy takes the central role, which is just as unconvincing today as the idea that art plays a central role in contemporary society. The counter to the Hegelian understanding of art that Heidegger helps to articulate becomes apparent if one questions the scope of the notion of "art."

Much debate in discussion of modern art in particular concerns the criteria for deciding whether something is art or not. The obvious lack of agreed criteria is itself the clue to how to respond to the question. If we see art in terms of ways in which sense is made, there can be no general criteria for deciding whether something is art or not, in the same way as there are no universal criteria for deciding on all cases of what makes sense. Clearly much depends here on how one understands the notion of "making sense." Within an established discipline or practice, criteria of sense will often be norms that have become regarded as legitimate by those involved in the discipline or practice: playing too many notes outside diatonic harmony in certain kinds of diatonic music makes no sense, for example. However, it is easy to think of contexts in which playing "wrong notes" would make sense, and the development of Western music has often involved just this. It is precisely the way in which, by stepping outside of some of the norms that constitute a practice, new sense can be made that is philosophically crucial, because this is part of what follows from Heidegger's idea of unconcealment. Schleiermacher already saw "art" as "that for which there admittedly are rules, but the combinatory application of these rules cannot in turn be rule-bound," on pain of a regress of rules for rules, which would make making sense impossible.[4] Language involves this art, as understanding another's utterances cannot be achieved just in terms of pregiven norms: the awareness of which norms should be relevant in a context cannot be generated by another norm. As such, sense depends on contexts of understanding and action that cannot be wholly established in advance, and which can be changed by new articulations. This idea relates to what Heidegger discusses in terms of the idea of "world" in the "Origin of the Work of Art."

Heidegger's questioning of what becomes the dominant analytical perspective lies, then, in the fact that any objectifying form of explanation depends on the constitution of a context of inquiry. This constitution depends in turn on the emergence of sense in ways that Heidegger comes to think are to be understood by what happens in art, and cannot themselves all be objectively explained. What we have said so far should enable us to grasp the sometimes rather cryptic way Heidegger talks about art's importance for philosophy. In "On the Essence of Truth" the hiddenness of being as a whole, Heidegger claims, "never results after the fact as a consequence of the always piecemeal cognition of entities. The hiddenness of being as a whole, the real un-truth, is older than every openness of this and that entity."[5] The alternative model to the analytical perspective is summarized by the claim in the art essay that "science is not an original happening of truth but in each case the extension of a realm of truth which is already open."[6] The question is how to think about the way realms of truth become open, and this is what the artwork is supposed to enable us to grasp. This does not happen via an explanation, but instead by a transformation of the world: "the work in no way affects

what there is up to now via causal contexts of interaction. The effect of the work does not consist in an effecting. It resides in a transformation, which happens from out of the work, of the un-hiddenness of beings and that means: of being" (GA 5, 58). What this means becomes clearer from Heidegger's examples.

Even though Heidegger's Van Gogh example is factually probably mistaken, what it suggests can still be used as a model of how art is world-disclosing. The painting is not essentially a representation of shoes, which can be better achieved with a photograph, it is rather "the opening up of that which the material, the pair of peasant shoes is in truth. This entity steps out into the unhiddenness of its being" so that there is a "happening of truth at work" in the painting (21). The crucial idea is that the world of which the "material" is an integral part emerges via the way the shoes make sense of their context, even though the context itself is not what is represented. Similarly, Beethoven's Eroica Symphony can be described, for example, in terms of melodic, rhythmic, and harmonic ideas. The happening of truth through the symphony lies, though, in the specific sense that the music makes by evoking a world that combines a new expansive freedom with new forms of order. The happening of truth cannot be without the work, but it is the way that the world is made manifest in new ways that constitutes the work's truth.

Heidegger's example of the Greek temple is particularly resonant, and has had significant effects on how some architects regard what they are doing. Once again, there is an inversion of the received way of thinking about what is at issue. The assumption would normally be that first there is nature, then there is the temple. In one sense this is obviously true, but the point of Heidegger's idea of unconcealment is that what is manifest is what is brought to light by the work, not something that is always already "present":

In standing there the building ["*Bauwerk*," which contains the sense of "work" as in "art work"] stands up to the storm which rages over it and in this way first shows the storm in its power. The splendor and the glowing of the stone, apparently itself dependent on the blessing of the sun, first renders the lightness of the day, the breadth of the sky, the darkness of the night manifest. (27)

It is the making manifest of something that otherwise remains hidden by establishing a context of significance that is decisive in this conception. The philosophical importance of this approach lies precisely in the reminder that however much we expand our explanatory cognitive reach, what enables the world to make sense is not exhausted by this. Indeed, such expansion can itself lead to things being hidden. Sense here consists in what connects us to the world, makes us devote ourselves to it, rather than making it an object of manipulation. The historically shifting line between knowing about the world and the world making sense became a vital philosophical issue via what Max Weber termed the "disenchantment" of the world in modern science and bureaucracy, and Heidegger offers resources for responding to disenchantment that do not rely on an illusory reenchantment.

The inversion from a perspective that seeks to ground itself on what can be objectively known is characterized in the Heidegger's essay in terms of the relationship between "earth" and "world." Heidegger derives this contrast (with no real acknowledgment) from the work of Schelling, which he was studying at the time he wrote the essay on art. Schelling thinks in terms of the relationship between "ground" and "existence," which he

also sees in terms of contractive and expansive forces. If the former dominates, there can be no world, but a world of pure expansion would just dissipate into formlessness. There is therefore a constant tension in how the world is manifest, between the need for some kind of ground to make it intelligible at all and the realization that seeking to make the ground totally intelligible renders it devoid of sense. Sense in Schelling's "On the Essence of Human Freedom" and his later philosophy therefore depends on freedom, and freedom demands that from which we liberate ourselves, upon how we transcend the ground without seeking completely to overcome it.[7]

With respect to art, one can get an understanding of what this implies via the idea that great music is grounded in what can destroy sense: transience, loss, longing, and pain are essential aspects of the ground of the greatest music, which makes a world out of this ground that at least temporarily makes sense. In a related manner, Heidegger sees the "earth" via the example of a stone, whose weight "rejects . . . any penetration into it. If we try to do this by breaking up the cliff, then it never shows an inside, something revealed, in its pieces" (GA 5, 32). The earth constitutively involves hiddenness, but at the same time, it is the ground of what can become manifest: the sculptor who uses the stone can liberate significance that the attempt to penetrate and analyze the stone can destroy. The "creation of the work" also destroys some aspect of the earth: "But this use does not use up and abuse the earth as a material (*Stoff*) but rather first frees it to itself," by "constituting the truth in the form (*Gestalt*)" (50). World and earth are "essentially different and yet never separated. . . . The opposition of world and earth is a conflict" (34) via which the truth of being arises in a manner that is both revealing and concealing.[8]

261

Heidegger's approach in the essay is in some respects weighed down by his traditionalism, and by a rhetoric that echoes the *Rektoratsrede*. He talks of *"Dichtung"*—which has the sense of "Poesie," "creative making" in Romantic thought—now becoming a "saying" [*Sage*, with the implications of "saga"], so that: "In such a saying the concepts of the essence of a historical *Volk* are pre-formed for it, i.e. its belonging to world-history ['*Welt-Geschichte*,' which implies the sense of history as 'being sent']" (60). It is therefore important to separate the interpretative issue of how "The Origin of the Work of Art" relates to the philosophical and other history of which it is a questionable part, from the philosophical question of the text's own bringing to light of truth about art in contemporary discussion. The focus on the notion of "work" can, for example, hide the fact that the happening of art is not dependent on art being in the form of a "work": revelatory jazz performances, of the kind that helped constitute the world of Civil Rights by establishing new forms of cultural identity, are not best seen as "works" of the kind Heidegger uses as examples. Indeed, Martin Luther King's "I have a dream" speech can be seen in this context as a happening of truth of the kind Heidegger is concerned with: it does not succeed predominantly on the basis of propositional claims, but rather by helping form a new world vision with rhythms of language derived from the tradition of gospel singing. When Heidegger says "language first brings the entity as an entity into the open (*ins Offene*)" (59), we can extend the conception beyond the kind of "medium size dry goods" to which he refers, to anything that becomes unconcealed by language that makes truth happen. This can, for instance, be a therapist using an apparently banal locution to a patient, which unlocks a truth for the person that enables them to cope with what has been tormenting them for years.

The core philosophical issue with respect to Heidegger and art is, then, what can be developed from his best ideas for a reorientation of philosophy toward the question of making sense of the world,[9] rather than continuing to seek a ground for epistemology, of the kind that history shows is not what actually results from philosophical reflection. If we are concerned about the future of philosophy as part of modern culture, it will be as a resource for making sense, rather than as an adjunct for the natural sciences, that philosophy will prosper.[10]

NOTES AND REFERENCES

1 E. Tugendhat, *Philosophische Aufsätze* (Frankfurt: Suhrkamp, 1992), 430.
2 See M. Wrathall, *Heidegger and Unconcealment* (Cambridge: Cambridge University Press, 2011) for a convincing rejection of Tugendhat's critique of Heidegger on truth and world-disclosure.
3 G. W. F. Hegel, *Ästhetik*, Vols 1 and 2, ed. Bassenge (Berlin, Weimar: Aufbau, 1965), Vol. 1, 21.
4 F. D. E. Schleiermacher, *Hermeneutics and Criticism*, trans. A. Bowie (Cambridge: Cambridge University Press, 1998), 229.
5 GA 9, 191.
6 GA 5, 48.
7 See A. Bowie, *Schelling and Modern European Philosophy* (London: Routledge, 1993).
8 For more on this, see A. Bowie, *From Romanticism to Critical Theory. The Philosophy of German Literary Theory* (London: Routledge, 1997).
9 On this see the outstanding A. W. Moore, *The Evolution of Modern Metaphysics. Making Sense of Things* (Cambridge: Cambridge University Press, 2012).
10 See A. Bowie, *Adorno and the Ends of Philosophy* (Cambridge: Polity, 2013).

32

BIRTH AND DEATH
Anne O'Byrne

Even if Dasein is "assured" in its belief about its "whither," or if, in rational enlightenment, it supposes itself to know about its "whence," all this counts for nothing as against the phenomenal facts of the case: for the mood brings Dasein before the "that it is" of its "there," which, as such, stares it in the face with the inexorability of an enigma. (BTMR, H. 136)

Death is everywhere in *Being and Time*, and it would be difficult to understand Heidegger's work or make any claim about his thinking without having undergone that text and its unrelenting confrontation with our mortal finitude. Our being is being-toward-death, and our mode of being in time is essentially futural as we project ourselves on the certainty of our own deaths. For Heidegger, famously, death is our ownmost, nonrelational possibility that is certain and not to be outstripped (BTMR, H. 264). Much has been written about this and anything that has been written about birth in Heidegger's work has had to take this overwhelming emphasis into account.[1] Yet what happens if, now, we take birth and death together, and take seriously the *and* that holds them in relation and that requires us to talk of coming to be *and* passing away, of emergence into the world *and*

leaving it, and, moreover, to talk of them in the same breath? After all, this is the condition of finitude. We are finite by virtue of having an end *and* a beginning.

What interested Heidegger was never the phenomenon of death or of birth but, rather, what death and eventually birth had to do with the sort of beings we are. That is to say, death and birth happen, and they are the object of empirical study by biologists and anthropologists who assign them meaning in specific physical and cultural contexts, but they have no being and are not beings. Neither ever *is*. From the point of view of ontology, birth and death are relevant only as the concrete instantiation of our natal and mortal mode of being. In *Being and Time*'s existential analytic, the being under consideration is "each time mine" and mortality or being-toward-death shows the futural character of *my* temporal being. Yet I have argued elsewhere that natality or being-toward-birth complicates that temporality and also points to our being-with others, making the being in question essentially plural.[2] It is a matter of *our* being. Then, when we turn to thinking mortality and natality together, the *and* shows us stretching along between birth and death, not as though strung between discrete points that mark the ends of our finite existence, but as actively stretching along, making us open to the most intimate extremities of existence. It is not a matter of adopting an open stance or attitude, or of deliberately taking up a more or less open mode of living; rather, Dasein *is* being-open. Thomas Sheehan has argued that Heidegger's theme, late and early, is "our finitude as opening up the world/clearing/open that we essentially are."[3] If so, our birth, growth, and death show *how* we are essentially open beings.

Pursuing this thought through and beyond *Being and Time* means following a series of displacements. *Jemeinigkeit*—the mine-ness of the being that is at the center of the investigation of Being—is set in place in the opening lines of S.9 of *Being and Time*: "We are ourselves the entities to be analyzed. The being of any such entity is *each time mine*" (H. 41). The initial aim of the work is to make us perplexed about Being, and the seat of that perplexity will be the being that is a question for itself, the being we have long thought that we know best of all. The first task is to displace that familiarity, and pushing aside the terms *subject, self, human, rational animal,* etc. in favor of *Dasein* is Heidegger's opening move. In the course of division one of *Being and Time* he goes on to reorder our understanding of time such that we may no longer think of ourselves as moving through a series of presents away from the past into the future, from birth to death. He writes: "[t]he non-relational character of death understood in anticipation individualizes Dasein down to itself" (H. 263); "when Dasein exists, it is already *thrown* into this possibility" (H. 251); authentic being-toward-death is a project in that Dasein projects itself upon it as an eminent possibility of its own (S, 53); "the authentic future is the toward-oneself . . . existing as the possibility of a nullity not-to-be-bypassed" (BTMR, H. 330). Indeed, he argues that Dasein's temporality

is predominantly futural as we project ourselves upon our possibilities of being. This is how—very briefly put—death permeates our existence. The future orients our existence; death, mortality, and futuricity dominate the work.

Yet, throughout division one, the place of birth and natality is held open by the thought of thrownness. Heidegger writes: "Thrownness is neither a fact-that-is-finished nor a Fact that is settled" (H. 179). Far from it. We are thrown into the world and this—not death—is the source of our constantly disruptive existential anxiety. "Anxiety is anxious about naked Dasein as something that has been thrown into uncanniness [*Unheimlichkeit*]. It brings one back to the pure 'that-it-is' of one's ownmost individualized thrownness" (H. 343). Reading this in natal terms allows us to make concrete and explicit what otherwise remains hidden in the folds of the text. First, in our natal thrownness we come face to face with the fact that we once were-not-yet, and with the contingency of our having come to be at all. There is every reason to be anxious about naked, thrown Dasein because there is no reason for its having been thrown. We could very easily have never come to be. Second, we arrive new into a world that is already old, and our arrival is a moment of possibility and renewal but also, inevitably, disruption.[4] Thus, third, making the world *our* world is a task, and it will turn out to be a shared task. Put another way, we receive the historical task of making the past our past despite its being irrevocably gone and thoroughly inappropriable.[5]

How does this come to be a shared task? What does birth have to do with opening Dasein to plural being? For most of *Being and Time* Heidegger holds off the first person plural. Dasein is singular, and both its death and birth are presented as above all having to do with its individuality. While he does attend to *Mitsein* [being-with] and even acknowledges that Dasein and *Mitsein* are co-originary, the problem of plural Dasein emerges fully only once birth is explicitly addressed for the first time in division two. The context is Heidegger's approach to the historical (and eventually political) character of our being.[6] He writes in Section 72:

> The question [of the wholeness of Dasein] itself may ... have been answered with regard to being-toward-the-end. However, death is, after all, only the "end" of Dasein and formally speaking, it is just *one* of the ends that embraces the totality of Dasein. But the other "end" is the "beginning," "birth." Only the being "between" birth and death presents the whole we are looking for. (H. 373)

The wholeness of Dasein will continue to elude Heidegger precisely because of the unpredictable, disruptive newness that he can no longer ignore once he opens up the question of birth. Birth cannot be accounted for using terms borrowed from the characterizations of death, nor even thrownness. Thus Heidegger's own schema is displaced. Rather than nonrelational, birth is *ur*-relational, since no one is born alone. Birth is not our ownmost, since it is an event and an experience for others—notably our mothers—before we can call it our own. It does not mark us as futural so much as subject to a syncopated temporality where we can only catch up with our birth after the fact. We only ever encounter ourselves as having always already been born, and we are always already with others.

Such displacements are inevitable once we grasp the dynamic character of Dasein's lived existence. According to the metaphysical opposition between the finite and the infinite,

to be finite is to lack perfection and find oneself subject to limitations. If we follow Heidegger's lead in setting aside this opposition, finite being emerges instead as being in the mode of openness and dis-closure. Death and birth are limits toward which we are. Concretely, natal, mortal being means we encounter ourselves in specific contexts at specific points in lives that are marked by growth, development, and deep transformation.[7] This is what is signaled by the *and* of *birth and death*.

At this point in his opus, in the late sections of *Being and Time* where the pursuit of a complete account of Dasein is once again derailed, Heidegger does not pursue these indications and the account of historicity famously passes from individual Dasein to the being of a people [*Volk*]. Yet there are signs that he understood it early on. In his lectures of the War Emergency Semester of 1919 *Towards the Definition of Philosophy* (TDP, GA 56/57, 63–76 (German), 53–64 (English)) he urged his students to take up formal indication as a means of philosophizing in a way grounded in life, specifically one's own life. In 1926, life and change become explicit concerns as he broaches the ontology of life and Dasein in terms of the Aristotelian concepts of dunamis and energeia (BCAP, GA 22). Yet in the period of *Being and Time* he broadly sets aside the concern by distancing himself from anthropology and the tradition of life philosophy, and by establishing the ontological difference. Not only that, but soon after *Being and Time* both these strategies begin to break down. The 1928/29 lectures *Einleitung in der Philosophie* show him sketching a phenomenology of childhood and human development (GA 27, 123–49) and thinking through Dasein's disclosedness [*Erschlossenheit*] alongside Dasein's being-with [*Mitsein*]. In the 1928 lecture course *The Metaphysical Foundations of Logic*, he acknowledges that the struggle to prevent ontological enquiry slipping back into the realm of merely ontic observations has become difficult to sustain, indeed, so difficult that he suggests abandoning the ontological difference in favor of what he names *metontology*. He writes:

> [W]e need a special problematic which has for its proper theme beings as a whole. This new investigation resides in the essence of ontology itself and is the result of its overturning, its μεταβολή [metabole]. I designate this set of questions *metontology*. And here also, in the domain of metontological-existentiell questioning, is the domain of the metaphysics of existence (here the question of an ethics may properly be raised for the first time). (MFL, 157; GA 26, 199)[8]

Metontology disappears from Heidegger's work after this lecture course, but it marks a stage on his way to a transformed philosophy that comes together in the mid-1930s and comes most clearly to light in the publication of "The Origin of the Work of Art" in 1950. By this point, any metaphysics of existence seems to have been definitively left behind, and Dasein, mineness, ourness, and birth and death are displaced. He writes in the same period, in *Contributions to Philosophy (from Enowning)*, that the shift in his vocabulary from *Sein* [being] to *Seyn* [be-ing] is meant to indicate that *Sein* is no longer thought metaphysically.

Yet, as I mentioned earlier, Heidegger's concern was never with the phenomena of birth and death but, at least for a period, with the natal, mortal, living mode of being. Studying birth *and* death has led us to finitude and the openness of finite being, and there are good reasons to think that this remains

central to his later thinking, whether or not we agree with Heidegger's own assessment of that thinking as post-metaphysical. Thomas Sheehan makes one version of this argument based on *Contributions to Philosophy: From Enowning*, where he sees Heidegger's deepest interest in dehypostasized being emerge as an interest in our being open, together. He writes:

> Human openness is always co-openness (*Mitdasein*). Our sociality—co-extensive with finitude, and its first gift—is what makes it possible and necessary to take-as and to understand "is." Our sociality is *die Sache selbst*. (Sheehan, 199)

Peter Sloterdijk makes another version based on the "Letter on Humanism" (1949) and in his essay "Domestikation des Seins: die Verdeutlichung der Lichtung" [The Domestication of Being: The Clearing up of Clearing].[9] Focusing on the use of *Lichtung* (which could be translated as clearing, lighting, or lightening), he avoids the interpretation that understands it as a clearing into which a being might step and instead argues in frankly anthropological and biological terms for an natal understanding of *Lichtung* as an open-ended *Menschenwerdung* [becoming-human]. The dwelling is the place of becoming-human; our bodies are the site of *Lichtung* and; brains are the *Lichtungsorgane* par excellence (*Nicht gerettet: Versuche nach Heidegger*, 195–6). Thanks to our neotenie—the fact that we are born prematurely and in need of years of care—our becoming-human happens in a plural context.[10]

Birth and death, then, can show us a new version of Heidegger, but it is one that part of us may find disappointing. Is everything that is radical about Heidegger's work now in danger of being domesticated? Will all the shattering insights of fundamental ontology and beyond be retrieved not as metaphysics but as anthropology? This is a real worry only if we insist on an opposition between domesticity and radicality. If we regret the radicality of Heidegger's work it may be that what we miss is the high loneliness and existential courage that comes with broaching Being, or the feeling of purity that is the reward for resolutely pursuing the question past all theological, scientific, and quotidian distractions.[11] When it turns out that the root of us all and of each one of us is in the *domos*, the *oikos* that is the scene of our first coming to be and that is our first world, we fear that existential courage might look less like standing out into the gathering storm and more like standing up to one's parents. Yet there is high art there—perhaps less Caspar David Friedrich and more Jan Vermeer—and poetry, and philosophy too.

NOTES AND REFERENCES

1 On birth in Heidegger, see Artur Boelderl, *Von Geburts wegen: unterwegs zu einer philosophischen Natologie* (Wurzburg: Koenigshausen and Neumann, 2007); Lisa Guenther, "Being-from-others: Reading Heidegger after Cavarero," *Hypatia* 23.1 (Winter 2008), 99–118; Leslie MacAvoy, "The Heideggerian Bias Toward Death: A Critique of the Role of Being-Towards-Death in the Disclosure of Human Finitude," *Metaphilosophy* 27.1–2 (January 1996), 63–77; Anne O'Byrne, *Natality and Finitude* (Bloomington: Indiana University Press, 2011); Christina Schües, *Philosophie des Geborenseins* (Freiburg: Alber, 2008).

2 See O'Byrne, *Natality and Finitude*.

3 Thomas Sheehan, "A Paradigm Shift in Heidegger Research," *Continental Philosophy Review* 34.2 (2001), 183–202.

4 See Felix Ó Murchadha, "Future or Future Past: Temporality between Praxis and Poiesis in Heidegger's *Being and Time*," *Philosophy Today* 42.3 (October 1998), 262–9.

5 See Françoise Dastur, *Death: An Essay on Finitude*, trans. John Llewelyn (London: Athlone Press, 1996).

6 Karl Löwith is reported to have once asked Heidegger about the link between his philosophy and his politics and was told in reply that the link was historicity.

7 See David Wood, "Reading Heidegger Responsibly: Glimpses of Being in Dasein's Development," in ed. François Raffoul and David Pettigrew, *Heidegger and Practical Philosophy* (Albany: SUNY Press, 2002), 219–36.

8 As both William McNeill and Steven Galt Crowell argue, metontology does not ever happen, but is a provocative, revealing attempt. See William McNeill, "Metaphysics, Fundamental Ontology, Metontology, 1925–35," *Heidegger Studies* 8 (1992), 63–81 and Steven Galt Crowell, "Metaphysics, Metontology, and the End of *Being and Time*," *Philosophy and Phenomenological Research*, 60.2 (March 2000), 307–31.

9 Peter Sloterdijk, "Domestication des Seins: die Verdeutlichung der Lichtung," in *Nicht gerettet: Versuche nach Heidegger* (Berlin: Suhrkamp, 2001), 142–234. My thanks to Nathan Van Camp for this reference.

10 A third version, less focused on a specific text of Heidegger's, is Jean-Luc Nancy's *Being Singular Plural*, trans. Robert Richardson and Anne O'Byrne (Stanford: Stanford University Press, 2000).

11 See Sheehan, "A Paradigm Shift in Heidegger Research."

33

THE BODY
Kevin Aho

One of the most significant contributions of Heidegger's *Being and Time* (1927) is the dismantling of an embedded assumption in the Western philosophical tradition that privileges the cognizing mind and the standpoint of theoretical detachment. On this view, it is only by means of adopting a disinterested and disembodied attitude that the philosopher can be genuinely objective and acquire clear and distinct knowledge about various aspects of reality. As Plato says in the *Phaedo*, "If we are ever to have pure knowledge of anything, we must escape from the body, and contemplate things by themselves with the soul itself" (66e). In *Being and Time*, Heidegger famously reverses this position, arguing that the standpoint of theoretical detachment is actually derivative and parasitic on the embodied and situated practices of everyday life. According to Heidegger, humans already embody a kind of tacit understanding or familiarity with things that has nothing to do with mental processes. As we go about our daily lives—handling equipment and engaging in various social practices—the things that we encounter already make sense to us in ways that can never be made theoretically explicit. Heidegger calls this vague, precognitive familiarity with things "the understanding of Being" (GA 2, 5/BT, 25), and he will refer to the practical way in which human

beings live or embody this understanding as *Dasein*, a colloquial German expression that can mean "ordinary human existence."

Dasein is not to be understood as a thing or substance, an autonomous mind, a casually determined body, or some combination of the two. (GA 2/BT, §§9–10) Dasein, rather, refers to the situated activity of being human, where "human" is understood not as *a* being but as a self-interpreting, self-understanding *way of being*. The word is meant to capture the way that human beings are already "there" (*Da*), that is, bound up and involved in a context of sociohistorical meanings that they already vaguely understand. Thus, "to *exist*," says Heidegger, "is essentially . . . to *understand*" (GA 24, 391/BP, 276, my emphasis), and understanding is not mental or cognitive. It is informed, rather, by how we are situated or "thrown" (*geworfen*) into the world, and our "situatedness" (*Befindlichkeit*) is revealed to us in terms of particular moods that make it possible for things—like our jobs, relationships, possessions, and personal identities—to emotionally "matter" to us in the ways that they do. (GA 2, 137/BT, 176) But if it is true that Dasein already embodies this noncognitive, affective understanding of Being, critics have long been puzzled as to why *Being and Time* offers no account of the body's role in this understanding. Is it not my body after all that represents the situated site of this understanding?[1]

To address this criticism we have to first get clear about what we mean by "the body." Edmund Husserl's work in *Ideas II* and, later, in *The Crisis of European Sciences and Transcendental Philosophy* is especially important because he articulates the crucial distinction between two senses of the body in the German language, the quantifiable "physical body" (*Körper*) and the "lived-body" (*Leib*).[2] The conception of *Körper* is largely informed by Cartesian and Newtonian science where bodies are defined in terms of first, having a material composition that is measurable; second, having determinate boundaries and causal interaction; third, occupying a specific spatiotemporal location; and finally, being configured as an "object" that is separate from and represented by the cognizing "subject." In this sense, any physical object—a rock, tree, cultural artifact, or human being—is an instance of *Körper*, but this definition does not help us understand the body as it is lived, felt, or experienced. Related to the words for "life" (*Leben*) and "experience" (*Erlebnis*), the "lived-body" (*Leib*) is not an object or thing that we "have" and that can be viewed from a standpoint of theoretical detachment. It is, rather, a reference to the experience of *my own body*, and this experience is not encapsulated or self-contained; it is fundamentally bound up and entwined in the "life-world" (*Lebenswelt*) that I am involved in. This sensual intertwining makes it impossible for me to perceive my body as a discrete object because I am already perceptually situated and oriented in the world on the basis of my body. Husserl explains: "I do not have the possibility of distancing myself from my body (*Leib*), or my body from me." This is because "The same body

that serves me as a means of all perception stands in my way in the perception of itself and is a remarkably incompletely constituted thing."[3] Indeed, in the seamless flow of my everyday life, I am altogether unaware of my body because I am already *existing* or *living* through it. As Merleau-Ponty will later write, "I am not in front of my body. I am in it or rather *I am it*."[4]

But a systematic treatment of the sensing, orienting, and kinesthetic aspects of the "lived-body" is precisely what is missing in Heidegger's account of everyday existence in *Being and Time*. As French critic Alphonse de Waelhens famously quipped, "[Heidegger] already presupposes that the subject of daily existence raises his arm, since he hammers and builds; that he orients himself, since he drives an automobile . . . In *Being and Time* one does not find thirty lines concerning the problem of perception; one does not find ten concerning that of the body."[5] What are we to make of this omission?

First, critics have to recognize that *Being and Time* is by no means a complete manuscript. Heidegger only completed the first two divisions of part one of the book. The third division of part one, entitled "time and Being" and the whole of part two, which was also to consist of three divisions, were never completed (GA 2, 39–40/BT, 64). Thus, the fact that Heidegger does not treat the body in *Being and Time* has to be understood within the context of a fundamentally unfinished manuscript. And if we look at the lectures immediately preceding and following the publication of *Being and Time* we see Heidegger already addressing a number of different aspects of embodiment. For instance, his early Freiburg lecture courses offer extensive critical treatments of the phenomena of "life" (*Leben*) and "lived-experience" (*Erlebnis*) (e.g. GA 56–7/TDP, §20; GA 60/

PRL, §§12, 17; GA 61/PIA, §3; GA 63/OHF, §§5–6). In his 1928 lecture course on Leibniz, Heidegger acknowledges that "Dasein is among other things in each case dispersed in a body" and goes on to discuss the problem of a sexed or gendered incarnation of Dasein (GA 26, 173/MFL, 137), a theme he returns to in the winter semester course of 1928/29 (GA 27, §20).[6] And, in his 1929/30 course *The Fundamental Concepts of Metaphysics*, Heidegger offers a lengthy treatment of sense organs, moods, and of Dasein as a unique "world-forming" (*weltbildend*) animal that is fundamentally different from the "impoverished" or "world-poor" (*weltarm*) nature of nonhuman animals (GA 29–30/ FCM, §§46, 49–63). Heidegger will go on to address aspects of Dasein's animal-nature in a number of other writings and lectures from his middle and later period (e.g. GA 7/BW; GA 8/WCT; GA 5/BW; GA 12/OWL).

Second, we need to acknowledge that Heidegger appeared to be genuinely perplexed about how to interpret Dasein from the perspective of embodiment. In *Being and Time* (§23), for example, he recognizes that Dasein's "bodily-nature" (*Leiblichkeit*) plays a significant role in spatially orienting us in the world in terms of our experiences of distance and directionality, but does not explain how the body does this. Indeed, he appears to dismiss the problem altogether when he writes in a parenthetical remark that Dasein's "'bodily nature' hides a whole problematic of its own though we shall not treat it here" (GA 2, 108/BT, 143).[7] Later, in his 1966–7 Heraclitus seminar, he will refer to Dasein's bodily nature as "the most difficult problem" (GA 15/HS, 147), and in 1972 he admits that he was unable to respond to earlier criticisms of *Being and Time* regarding his neglect of the body because "the bodily [*das Leibliche*] is the most difficult [problem to understand]

and I was unable to say more at the time" (GA 89, 292/ZS, 231).[8] These remarks seem to indicate that a thematic treatment of the body would have been important in fleshing out the account of Dasein in *Being and Time* but that Heidegger may have been unsure about how to go about it.

Finally, critics have to recognize that Heidegger does, in fact, offer an analysis of Dasein from the perspective of the *Körper/Leib* distinction. Although there are some indications in earlier texts and lectures (e.g. GA 20/HCT, §18; GA 24/BP, §13; GA 2/BT, §§9–10), one of the clearest articulations is found in his 1936/37 winter semester course on Nietzsche, *The Will to Power as Art*, when Heidegger writes, "We do not 'have' a body in the way we carry a knife in sheath. Neither is the body a natural body that merely accompanies us and which we can establish, expressly or not, as being also 'at hand'. We do not 'have' a body; rather, we 'are' bodily . . . we are somebody who is alive" (GA 6.1/N1, 99). This description sets the stage for Heidegger's most sustained and systematic treatment of the body in a series of seminars with psychiatrists and medical students that took place in Zollikon, Switzerland from 1959–69.

In the *Zollikon Seminars* Heidegger successfully fills out the account of embodiment that is missing in *Being and Time*, and this helps to clarify why Dasein should not be understood as a bounded, biochemical thing that is "physically present" (*körperhaft*). In these seminars, Heidegger makes it clear that prior to any scientific or naturalistic account that explains "what" I am as a corporeal object, I am already existing or "bodying forth" (*Leiben*) as a situated, affective, and motile way of being-in-the-world. The body, from this perspective, "is in each case *my body*," and it is not "here," like a table or chair, occupying a determinate time and place (GA 89, 113/ZS, 86). Unlike *Körper*, my body is not a self-contained thing; it does not "stop with the skin" because it is already "out there," stretching beyond the corporeal into a shared world as it moves through its environment, handles equipment, and engages with others (GA 89, 112/ZS, 86). My body, in this regard, already orients me in the world, constituting a perceptual "range" or "horizon" within which things can be encountered.

Echoing the earlier accounts of Husserl and Merleau-Ponty, Heidegger refers to the body in terms of the spontaneous mediating activity that I cannot get behind or objectify because it is already opening up the perceptual "horizon" that I exist in. "The limit of bodying forth," says Heidegger, "is the horizon of being within which I sojourn" (GA 89, 113/ZS, 87). This mediating activity reveals the extent to which my body already possesses a kind of unitary, sensory grip on its surroundings. It is already perceptually directed toward things and understands how to move through its environment; it already encounters things in terms of directions of right and left and front and back, and tacitly senses where things are in terms of distance and location (GA 89, 293–4/ZS, 232). Here, direction, distance, and location are not grasped thematically in terms of objects in geometric space. I do not, for instance, initially experience my cell phone as an object that is five meters from the couch. The phone is already understood in terms of my embodied familiarity with a particular living space as something "handy," "close by," or "too far away." This familiarity reveals the seamless kinesthetic bond between my body and the world and it also helps us to get clear about the body's role in Heidegger's account of emotions or moods.

For Heidegger, moods are not to be understood as discrete sensations or "states of mind" that take place "inside" of us (GA 2, 136–7/BT, 176). As an embodied way of being-in-the-world, there is no distinction between "inner" or "outer" because our emotional lives are already bound up in the world, already situated and entwined in public contexts of meaning. In fact, it is this embodied intertwining that makes it possible for us to be in a mood in the first place, that is, to be in situations where things meaningfully affect as dull, frightening, embarrassing, or confusing. This means moods are always working behind our backs prior to any mental intentions, already providing a background sense of what "counts" and "matters" to us in particular situations.[9] When, for instance, Heidegger notices "Dr. K" rubbing his temples at the seminar table, he immediately senses the meaning of this act because he is already attuned to the situated mannerisms and gestures that are unique to the academic world. This particular gesture reveals that Dr. K. was puzzled and "was thinking of something difficult" (GA 89, 115/ZS, 88). Heidegger's example reveals that in bodying-forth, we are affectively open and responsive to specific contexts of meaning, and this receptivity or "world-openness" to the significance of things suggests that we are always already in a mood (GA 89, 292/ZS, 231). In this sense, says Heidegger, moods are "like an *atmosphere* in which we first immerse ourselves in each case and which then attunes us through and through" (GA 29–30, 100/FCM, 67).

In giving an account of how Dasein's bodily nature situates and orients us in the world, the *Zollikon Seminars* provide a critical supplement to *Being and Time* and help to explain why Heidegger says that "all existing, our comportment, is necessarily a bodily (*leiblich*) comportment . . ." (GA 89, 258/ZS, 206) and that "bodying-forth as such belongs to being-in-the-world" (GA 89, 248/ZS, 200). But it is also important to note that the primary aim of Heidegger's project is not simply to critique the tradition of disembodied theorizing as parasitic on the situated and embodied practices of everyday life. Heidegger's aim, rather, is to address the "question of the meaning of Being" in general. In this regard, the analysis of "everydayness" (*Alltäglichkeit*) in *Being and Time* is merely provisional or "preparatory" (GA 2, 17/BT, 38). Heidegger's core concern is giving an account of how we are appropriated by and belong to the unfolding historical "event" (*Ereignis*) of meaning itself, an impersonal event that opens up a disclosive space or "there" (*Da*) prior to my own bodily emergence on the scene. This space constitutes all of the possible ways that I, as an embodied way of being, can understand and make sense of things, including myself. This is why Heidegger says that the concept of Dasein in *Being and Time* is often misunderstood as a reference to *one's own* individual existence. The emphasis, for Heidegger, is not on the individual but on the *Da*, on the open region or space of meaning that is already "there." "The *Da* in *Being and Time* does not mean the statement of a place for a being but rather it should designate the openness where beings can be present for the human being, and the human being also for himself" (GA 89, 156/ZS, 120).

NOTES AND REFERENCES

1. There have been a number of commentaries in recent years that engage Heidegger's thought from the perspective of embodiment as well as his failure to address the body in *Being and*

Time. See, for instance, K. Aho, *Heidegger's Neglect of the Body* (Albany, NY: SUNY Press, 2009); R. Askay, "Heidegger, the Body, and the French Philosophers," *Continental Philosophy Review*, 32 (1999), 29–35; D. Cerbone, "Heidegger and Dasein's Bodily-Nature: What is the Hidden Problematic?" *International Journal of Philosophical Studies* 33 (2000), 209–30; M. Haar, *The Song of the Earth: Heidegger and the Grounds of the History of Being*, trans. R. Lilly. (Bloomington, IN: Indiana University Press, 1993); T. Kessel, *Phänomenologie des Lebendigen: Heideggers Kritik an den Leitbegriffen der neuzeitlichen Biologie* (Freiburg und München: Karl Alber, 2011); D. F. Krell, *Daimon Life: Heidegger and Life-Philosophy* (Bloomington, IN: Indiana University Press, 1992); D. M. Levin, *The Body's Recollection of Being: Phenomenological Psychology and the Deconstruction of Nihilism* (New York: Routledge, 1990); F. Schalow, *The Incarnality of Being: The Earth, Animals, and the Body in Heidegger's Thought* (Albany, NY: SUNY Press, 2006); D. Vallega-Neu, *The Bodily Dimension in Thinking* (Albany, NY: SUNY Press, 2005).

2. For an analysis of the distinction between *Körper* and *Leib* in Husserl see §§35–42 of *Ideen zu einer reinen Phänomenologie und phänomenologischen Philosophie. Zweites Buch: Phänomenologische Untersuchungen zur Konstitution*, ed. M. Biemel (The Hague: Martinus Nijhoff, 1952). English translation: *Ideas Pertaining to a Pure Phenomenology and to Phenomenological Philosophy, Second Book*, trans. R. Rojcewicz and A. Schuwer (Dordrecht, The Netherlands: Kluwer, 1989). Also see §28 and §62 of *Die Krisis der europäischen Wissenschaften und die transzendentale Phänomenologie: Eine Einleitung in die phänomenologische Philosophie*, ed. W. Biemel (The Hague: Martinus Nijhoff, 1954). English translation: *The Crisis of European Sciences and Transcendental Philosophy*, trans. D. Caar (Evanston, IL: Northwestern University Press, 1970).

3. Husserl, *Ideas Pertaining to a Pure Phenomenology, Second Book*, 167.

4. Maurice Merleau-Ponty, *Phenomenology of Perception*, trans. C. Smith (London: Routledge, 1962), 150, my emphasis. The

influence of Husserl's account of the body on Merleau-Ponty's philosophy is well known. Merleau-Ponty described his studies of Husserl's manuscripts at the Archives in Leuven as "*une expérience presque voluptueuse*." See R. Rojcewicz and A. Schuwer, "Translator's Introduction" to Husserl's *Ideas II*, xvi. For an excellent comparative analysis of the conceptions of embodiment in Edmund Husserl and Maurice Merleau-Ponty, see T. Carman, "The Body in Husserl and Merleau-Ponty," *Philosophical Topics*, 27.2 (1999), 205–26.

5 Alphonse de Waelhens, "The Philosophy of the Ambiguous," in Maurice Merleau-Ponty, *The Structure of Behavior*, trans. A. Fisher (Boston: Beacon Press, 1963), xix. David Krell offers a much more accurate accounting of all the places that Heidegger uses the terms *Leib* and *Körper* and their various cognates in *Being and Time*. See Krell's *Daimon Life*, 33–63, esp. 325, n. 17.

6 As of this writing, *GA 27, Introduction to Philosophy (Einleitung in die Philosophie)* has yet to be translated.

7 Heidegger should have been aware of Husserl's reflections on the body in *Ideas II* as he was writing *Being and Time*. Husserl sent a copy of the manuscript to Heidegger in 1925 while he was lecturing at Marburg, and one cannot help but notice certain similarities regarding their accounts of spatial orientation. See *Ideas II*, §§41–2 and *Being and Time*, §23.

8 See K. Aho, *Heidegger's Neglect of the Body*, 4.

9 See C. Guignon, "Moods in Heidegger's *Being and Time*," in eds C. Calhoun and R. Solomon, *What is an Emotion: Classical Readings in Philosophical Psychology* (Oxford, UK: Oxford University Press, 1984), 229–39.

34

DASEIN
François Raffoul

When Heidegger introduced the term Dasein, as a terminological choice, in *Being and Time*, it was in the perspective of providing an *access* (*Zugang*) to the question of the meaning of being. An analysis of the being of Dasein (the very task of *Being and Time*) must, in the final analysis, allow for the interpretation of that which is *asked about* (*das Gefragte*) in the questioning, namely the *meaning of being*, and in fact presupposes it. The analysis of Dasein is ultimately subordinated to the elaboration of the question of being, Heidegger speaking of the "provisional" (*vorbereitenden*) character of the analysis of Dasein. At the same time, the term "Dasein," which ordinarily means "existence" in German, is said to designate "the being of human being" (SZ, 25/BT, 24) and the "being which we ourselves in each case are" (SZ, 7/BT, 7). Thus, from the outset, the problematic of Dasein combines the question of the meaning of being with the most extreme individuation. "The question of the meaning of being is the most universal and the emptiest. But at the same time the possibility inheres of its most acute individualization in each particular Dasein" (SZ, 39/BT, 37).

In the early writings, Dasein arises out of the opening of being *in and as a question*. The question of being is such that, once its

questionableness (*Fraglichkeit*) is unfolded, it includes us in an essential way. Heidegger presents this implication in "What is Metaphysics?" in the following way: "First, every metaphysical question always encompasses the whole range of metaphysical problems. Each question is itself always the whole [*das Ganze*]. Therefore, second, every metaphysical question can be asked only in such a way that the questioner as such is also there within the question, that is, is placed in question" (GA 9, 103/PA, 82). This betrays that the human being must essentially remain a question, that our essence is questionable. As Heidegger writes in *Introduction to Metaphysics*, "The determination of the essence of the human being is *never* an answer, but is essentially a question" (GA 40, 107/IM, 149). To that extent, it is a matter of rendering the essence of the human being uncanny, if not "dangerous," if it is the case that, "The human being is *to deinotaton*, the uncanniest of the uncanny" (GA 40, 114/IM, 159). Here one glimpses the intimate relation between the questionableness (*Fraglichkeit*) of Dasein in *Being and Time* with the dangerousness (*Gefährlichkeit*) of the human being in the *Contributions*. Just as Dasein was accessed in *Being and Time* in terms of the questionableness of being, later the dangerousness of the question "who are we?" is "the only way for us to come to ourselves" (GA 65, 54/CP2, 44).

At the time of *Being and Time*, Dasein's implication in the general question of the meaning of being is analyzed as Dasein's privilege or priority (*Vorrang*). Dasein has a privilege in the ontological inquiry because it has—and is—an understanding of being. Dasein emerges as what is "interrogated" (*das Befragte*) in the question on the meaning of being because it is that being who can *understand* the question of what it *means* to be. Further, Dasein does not "simply occur among other beings," but rather "is concerned *about* its very being" (SZ, 12/BT, 10). Only a being that can have a relationship to other beings and who at the same time has the possibility of questioning, that is, a being that does not simply appear "among" other beings, but whose constitution of being is to have "in its very being, a relation of being to this being" (SZ, 12/BT, 10), should be *interrogated* in its being. Dasein has thus "proven itself to be that which, before all other beings, is ontologically the primary being to be interrogated" (SZ, 13/BT, 12).

The problematic of an analysis of Dasein must therefore be situated in the *Seinsverständnis*, which Heidegger presents, quite simply, as a "fact" (*Faktum*) (SZ, 5/BT, 4). Such understanding is *not* a "human" determination, but a *characteristic of being*. This is why the privilege of Dasein is not ontic or anthropological, but ultimately *ontological*. "*Understanding of being is itself a determination of being of Dasein [Seinsverständnis is selbst eine Seinsbestimmtheit des Daseins]*. The ontic distinction of Dasein lies in the fact that it *is* ontological" (SZ, 12/BT, 11). Dasein is thus the ontological name of the human being, and constitutes a radical break with the traditions of anthropology and subjectivity, a break that Sartre and the early existentialists missed in their mistranslation of Dasein as "*réalité humaine*," or human reality. In fact, the very terminological choice inherent in the notion of Dasein was motivated by the project "to liberate the determination of the human essence from subjectivity, but also from the definition of *animal rationale*" (GA 9, 368/PA, 282–3). Heidegger indeed stressed in *Being and Time* that the thinking of Dasein—that is, "the beings that we ourselves are"—must avoid terms such as subject, soul, consciousness, spirit, person, and even life [*Leben*] and man [*Mensch*]" (SZ, 46/BT, 45).

With the term Dasein, Heidegger undertook an ontological questioning on the human being, interrogated solely in terms of its *being*, that is to say, in terms of being itself. This is what Heidegger clarified in *Der europäische Nihilismus*, explaining that in *Being and Time*, on the basis of the question no longer concerning the truth of beings but the truth of being itself, "an attempt is made to determine the essence of man solely in terms of his relationship to Being (*aus seinem Bezug zum Sein*). That essence was described in a firmly delineated sense as *Da-sein*" (GA 6.2, 194/NIII, 141). The term Dasein then became oftentimes hyphenated as Da-sein, in order to stress this sheer relatedness to being. The term Da-sein, as Heidegger specified in his 1949 introduction added to *What is Metaphysics?* designates in the *same* stroke the human being's relation (opening) to being and being's relation to the human being: "To characterize with a *single* term both the relation of Being to the essence of the human being and the essential relation of the human being to the openness ('there,' ['*Da*']) of Being [*Sein*] as such, the name of 'Dasein' [there-being] was chosen for the essential realm in which humans stand as humans" (GA 9, 372/PA, 283, tr. modified).

DASEIN IN THE TURN

As we saw, the understanding of being is not a property of humans among others, but that which defines the human being. Humans are made possible by the understanding of being and not the inverse. "*Accordingly, the understanding of being is the ground of the possibility of the essence of the human being*" (GA 31, 125/EHF, 87, tr. modified). To this extent, it is not posited by us, but is an event in which we find ourselves among all other beings. "With the existence of human beings there occurs an irruption into the totality of beings, so that now the being in itself first becomes manifest" (GA 3, 228/KPM, 160). One moves from a thematic of the understanding of being to that of a happening of being. Dasein has its origin in the event [*Ereignis*]. Therein lies the turn (*Kehre*) in Heidegger's work, from a thinking centered on Dasein's openness to being to a thinking that meditates the openness of being to Dasein:

> The thinking that proceeds from *Being and Time*, in that it gives up the word "meaning of being" in favor of "truth of being," henceforth emphasizes the openness of being itself, rather than the openness of Dasein in regard to this openness of being. This signifies 'the turn,' in which thinking always more decisively turns to being as being. (FS, 41)

Heidegger returned to the significance of the turn in his letter to William Richardson (1962), to explain that the problematic of Dasein corresponded to a moving away from the language of subjectivity,

> One need only observe the simple fact that in *Being and Time* the problem is set up outside the sphere of subjectivism—that

the entire anthropological problematic is kept at a distance, that the normative issue is emphatically and solely the experience of Da-sein with a constant eye to the Being-question—for it to become strikingly clear that the "Being" into which *Being and Time* inquired cannot long remain something that the human subject posits.

The turn was thus already present in *Being and Time*, insofar as the thinking of Dasein already exceeded the problematic of subjectivity: "It is rather Being, stamped as Presence by its time-character, [that] makes the approach to Da-sein. As a result, even in the initial steps of the Being-question in *Being and Time* thought is called upon to undergo a change whose movement corresponds with the reversal [*Kehre*]."[1]

Heidegger's thinking thus increasingly turned toward the truth of be-ing as such (and no longer beingness), and inquired into the truth of be-ing out of be-ing *itself*. Heidegger considers that his earlier work was still too attached—reactively or "defensively"—to the metaphysical subjectivistic way of thinking, and attempts to think the truth of be-ing out of itself. "The very first task, however, is precisely to discontinue postulating the human being as a subject and to grasp this being primarily and exclusively on the basis of the question of being, and only in this way" (GA 65, 489/CP2, 385). Heidegger explained further the shift in his thinking by stressing that, "In *Being and Time*, Da-sein still has an appearance that is 'anthropological,' 'subjectivistic,' 'individualistic,' etc." (GA 65, 295/CP2, 233). But, Da-sein, as "the overcoming (*überwindung*) of all subjectivity, itself arises out of the essential occurrence of being [*Wesung des Seyns*]" (GA 65, 303/CP2, 240), and is now approached from the key word in his thought, *Ereignis*, that is, from the happening of the truth of be-ing. Heidegger explains that the "relation" between Da-sein and beyng was first grasped in *Being and Time* as "an 'understanding of being,' where 'understanding' is meant in the sense of projection and that in turn as *thrown*, i.e., as belonging to appropriation by beyng itself" (GA 65, 252/CP2, 199, tr. slightly modified).

FROM DASEIN TO DA-SEIN: THE BETWEEN

Thinking from the truth of being itself does not mean that the reference to the human being is abandoned, but rather that there is a sort of dislodging of humans into a dimension, which Heidegger calls the "between," from which they become for the first time *themselves*. "In the history of the truth of being, Da-sein is the essential *intervening incidence*, i.e., the in-cident of that 'between' into which humans must be dis-lodged in order to first be *themselves* again" (GA 65, 317/CP2, 251). If the human being is to become Da-sein, this implies a transformation, "*the transformation of human beings themselves*" (GA 65, 84/CP2, 67), from the anthropological enclosure to the belonging to the truth of be-ing (Da-sein). Through this displacing, humans will "come to stand in the event and remain steadfast there in the truth of beyng" (GA 65, 26/CP2, 23). What this situation reveals is that Dasein is necessarily "in play" in the event of be-ing, and that "the human being, and then again not the human being, and indeed in each case in a reaching out and a dislodging, is somehow in play in the grounding of the truth of beyng. Precisely what is thus question-worthy is what I call Da-sein" (GA 65, 313/CP2, 314).

Heidegger grasps this implication in terms of a certain *need*: Dasein is required, implicated in, *needed*, in the event of be-ing: "Beyng needs humans [*Das Seyn braucht den Menschen*] in order to occur essentially"; and *in turn*, humans "belong to Beyng [*der Mensch gehort dem Seyn*] so that they might fulfill their ultimate destiny as Da-sein" (GA 65, 251/CP2, 198). Further, Heidegger clarifies that, "Beyng is nothing 'human' in the sense of a human dominion, and yet the essential occurrence of beyng needs [*braucht*] Da-sein and hence also needs the steadfastness of the human being" (GA 65, 265/CP2, 209, tr. slightly modified). One could not emphasize enough the importance of such a neediness for a redefinition of the human being as Dasein, *as well as for the determination of the essence of be-ing itself*, Heidegger going so far as to state that needing (*Brauchen*) constitutes the essence of be-ing: being needs Dasein for its manifestation, and Dasein is needy due to its thrownness. This need reveals the co-belonging between humans and be-ing. Be-ing needs us because "only on the ground of Da-sein . . . does being enter into truth" (GA 65, 293/CP2, 231). To that extent, "the essential occurrence of beyng requires the grounding of the *truth* of be-ing and that this grounding must be carried out as *Da-sein*" (GA 65, 176/CP2, 138).

As such, this represents what Heidegger calls the "counter-resonance" (*Gegenschwung*) of needing and belonging, or the "counterplay between call and belonging" (GA 65, 311/CP2, 246), a "between" approached in the *Contributions* under the expression of "domain of the proper" (das *Eigentum*). It is in this perspective that Heidegger insists that Da-sein is to be thought as the *between*, a "between" clearly marked in the new writing of Dasein with a hyphen, as Da-sein. That "between," explicitly contrasted with his earlier vocabulary of transcendence, is the play between the enowning throwing call of be-ing and the belonging of Dasein as standing in. Being only holds sway where and when there is Dasein, and *in turn* Da-sein "is" only where and when there is be-ing. Da-sein is itself by standing in be-ing and is exhausted in such a between. Dasein now designates the *belonging-together of the human being and Being.* Who are we? We are the ones called by be-ing, needed by be-ing to sustain its essential sway.

WHO ARE WE?

A clarification is needed concerning the sense and role of that "we," which might be misconstrued, superficially, as the collective form of the people as opposed to the individual I or singular "mine" of *Being and Time.* In fact, Heidegger clarifies from the outset that neither the I nor the we—understood within the opposition of the individual to the collective—are adequate to determine Dasein. In *Introduction to Metaphysics*, Heidegger explained that the selfhood of humanity "does not mean that humanity is primarily an 'I' and an individual. Humanity is not this any more than it is a We and a community" (GA 40, 152/IM, 153). One therefore needs to be careful when attempting too quickly to interpret the presence of the "we" as the sign of the passage from an individualistic problematic to a communal one. Both the individualistic and the communal orientations are for Heidegger nothing but two variants of the traditional metaphysics of subjectivity, and this is why "there is no room at all here for the interpretation of the human being as 'subject,' whether in the sense of the egological or communal subject" (GA 65, 488/CP2,

384). The problematic is therefore neither restricted to nor aimed at the figure of the people, here relegated to both subjectivism and biologism.

One might ask, then, how is the question, "who are we," to be taken? And what does "we" mean, or, as Heidegger puts it: "*which ones* do we mean in speaking of 'we'?" (GA 65, 48/CP2, 39). First, Heidegger clarifies, the "we" is not some given present people, for the question remains of how what is ownmost to a people is to be determined. "*Only on the basis of Da-sein is it possible to grasp the essence of a people,* which means at the same time to know that a people can never be a goal and a purpose." (GA 65, 319/CP2, 252). The "we" thus does not refer to an ontic presence or to an actual people or community, but must be aligned with beyng itself: "the question of who are we must remain purely and fully incorporated into the asking of the basic question: how does beyng essentially occur?" (GA 65, 54/CP2, 44). In the question "who are we," what is inquired about is not some given "us" but rather what is proper to *being* ourselves, that is, to being a self. This is why any question concerning the "we" presupposes the question of the who. In the question "who are we?" the emphasis is on the "who": asking about who *we* are "already contains a decision about the Who" (GA 65, 48/CP2, 34). Heidegger sees in this circle of the we and the who the very reverberation of the turning (*Widerschein der Kehre*). The question "who are we?" aims at a dimension that is said to be more originary than any I or we. "*Selfhood is more originary (ursprünglicher)* than any I and you and we. These are as such first gathered as such in the *self* and thereby become each respective 'self'" (GA 65, 320/CP2, 253). Dasein names original selfhood, "in whose domain 'we,' you and I, in each case come to our *selves*" (GA 65, 67/CP2, 54).

DASEIN AS EK-STATIC STANDING-IN BEING

In late writings and seminars, Heidegger continued to posit the distinctive role of the human being in the event of being. And how could it be otherwise, if, as he explains in the Zollikon seminars, "there cannot be the being of beings at all *without* the human being" (Z, 221/ZS, 176)? For the manifestedness of being, Heidegger stresses, "what is needed is the [ecstatic] standing-in [*Innestehen*] of the human being in the Da [there]" (Z, 221/ZS, 176). Now, as we have seen, Dasein's being does not lie in subjectivity but indeed in the dimension of being itself, especially since "in the determination of the humanity of the human being as ek-sistence what is essential is not the human being but being—as the dimension of the *ecstasis* of ek-sistence" (GA 9, 333-4/PA, 254). This means that ecstasis is related to being, and not simply to the reversal of immanent subjectivity. "The ecstatic essence of existence is therefore still understood inadequately as long as one thinks of it as merely a 'standing out,' while interpreting the 'out' as meaning 'away from' the interior of an immanence of consciousness or spirit" (GA 9, 374/PA, 284). The "out" should be taken instead as the openness of being itself, Heidegger proposing the term *Inständigkeit* to designate this standing in the Da of being.[2] "Today, Heidegger adds, I would formulate this relation differently. I would no longer speak simply of ek-stasis, but of instancy in clearing [*Inständigkeit in der Lichtung*]" (FS, 71). Da-sein is rethought as standing-in the truth of being.

Ek-statis is ultimately to be taken as *openness*. As Heidegger clarified in the Zollikon seminars, "In *Being and Time*, being-*open* (*Da*-sein) means *being*-open (Da-*sein*). The 'Da' [of Da-sein] is determined here

as 'the open'" (Z, 282/ZS, 225). This is why he explained that: "This being-in-an-open-expanse is what *Being and Time* called (Heidegger even adds: 'very awkwardly and in an unhelpful way') Dasein" (FS, 69).[3] Dasein itself comes to designates openness. "Dasein must be understood as being-the-clearing. The *Da* is namely the word for the open expanse" (ibid.). The very notion of an understanding of being, which had defined Dasein in the early writings, is reinterpreted as openness: "But since the human being can only be human by understanding being—that is, insofar as he is standing in the openness of being—being human, as such, is distinguished by the fact that to be, in its own unique way, is to be in this openness" (Z, 157/ZS, 121).

CONCLUSION: DASEIN AS TOPOLOGICAL REVOLUTION

Heidegger often states that a leap is needed to access our proper being, a leap from the subject to Da-sein. Heidegger's thinking of Dasein leads us to a *topological* revolution through which the human being is dis-placed from the ego cogito and resituated within the event of the truth of be-ing. Here lies the *topological* revolution of the understanding of the human being, now conceived of as the ek-static place for being's coming to presence. In his 1949 introduction to *What is Metaphysics?* Heidegger rejected the interpretation that considered that "in place of" the term *Bewusstsein* he substituted Dasein. "Any attempt at thoughtfulness is therefore thwarted as long as one is satisfied that in *Being and Time* the term 'Dasein' is used in place of 'consciousness.' As if this were simply a matter of using different words!" (GA

9, 373/PA, 283). With the choice of the term Dasein, it was not a question of a simple substitution of terms that would leave the place assigned to the human being undisturbed, but a revolution in the place of the essence of the human being. This is why

> the term "Dasein" neither takes the place of the term "consciousness," nor does the "matter" designated as "Dasein" take the place of what we represent to ourselves when we speak of "consciousness." Rather, "Dasein" names that which is first of all to be experienced, and subsequently thought of accordingly, as a place (*Stelle*)—namely, as the locality of the truth of Being (*die Ortschaft der Wahreit des Seins*). (GA 9, 373/PA, 283)[4]

It is in this sense that Dasein is the index of a topological revolution of the original being of humans. It is to such a revolution that Heidegger's thinking of Dasein invites us.

NOTES AND REFERENCES

[1] Martin Heidegger, Preface to William J. Richardson, *Heidegger. Through Phenomenology to Thought* (New York, NY: Fordham University Press, 2003), xviii, modified.

[2] "What is meant by 'existence' in the context of a thinking that is prompted by, and directed toward, the truth of Being, could be most felicitously designated by the word 'instancy' [*Inständigkeit*]" (GA 9, 374/PA, 284, modified).

[3] In a letter to Roger Munier from 1973, Heidegger also explains that his thinking "places the very one who is questioning, and thus the Da-sein of the human, into question." He then adds: "It is important to experience Da-sein in the sense that man himself *is* the '*Da*,' i.e., the openness of being for him, in that he undertakes to preserve this and, in preserving it, to unfold it" (FS, 88).

[4] As Heidegger also wrote in *Nietzsche II*: "The locale of the place of being as such is being itself . . . This locale, however, is the essence of man" (*Die Ortschaft des Ortes des Seins als solchen ist das Sein selber. Diese Ortschaft aber ist das Wesen des Menschen*) (GA 6.2, 357/ NIII, 217).

35

EREIGNIS

Daniela Vallega-Neu

Since 1936, the year Heidegger began to write *Contributions to Philosophy (Of the Event)*, *Ereignis* names the very core of how Heidegger attempts to think the truth of being in its historicality.[1] *Contributions to Philosophy* is the work in which Heidegger lays out his thought of *Ereignis* for the first time, but Heidegger develops it further in volumes following *Contributions*[2] and also in the last period of his writings.

Heidegger's thought of the truth of being in terms of *Ereignis* begins with the abandonment of the transcendental-horizontal approach to the question of being (which marked his earlier fundamental ontology of *Being and Time*) in the attempt to speak more inceptually, more originally, *from within* an authentic experience of being. In the project of *Being and Time* being as such is questioned through Dasein's transcendence. Dasein always already transcends particular beings (*Seiendes*) such that in Dasein's being-in-the-world the being (*Sein*) of other beings also and thus being as such is disclosed. The itinerary of *Being and Time* leads toward the discovery of a temporal horizon out of which being discloses as presence; however the path of questioning still goes "toward" the temporal horizon of being. In *Contributions*, the task is to think *out of* the temporal horizon of being as such, a temporal horizon that since the 1930s Heidegger calls the "truth of beyng."

EREIGNIS (APPROPRIATING EVENT) AND THE TURNING (KEHRE) IN THE EVENT

To think and speak *out of* the truth of beyng is possible only if thinking attempts to stay attuned to an authentic mode of being in which the thinker finds himself/herself displaced (Heidegger speaks of a "leap") from both everyday and theoretical modes of being and thrown into the groundless openness of being as such. The truth of beyng needs to be sustained in order to occur as truth, and this is why thinking needs to *be* (-sein) "there" (da-) in that groundless openness. It is then that thinking may find itself *ereignet*, "appropriated" by beyng and beyng in its truth may be experienced and thought as *Ereignis*, as "appropriating event."[3] In other words, out of the experience of being thrown into being, we experience a disclosing event in which we first find also our own being; we experience our being as *er-eignet*, "appropriated" in the event that—in turn—first discloses in this appropriation.[4]

The appropriating event cannot be represented in terms of a linear process such that some "being" appropriates another "being," namely Da-sein, but instead oscillates *between* the truth of beyng and Da-sein, such that both occur simultaneously. Heidegger speaks in this context of the *Kehre im Ereignis*,

283

the *turning in the appropriating event.*[5] He articulates this turning as well in terms of an oscillation between the appropriating call (*Zuruf*) and a belonging (*zugehören*).[6] The truth of beyng as event discloses only *in* Da-sein, in the moment of appropriation and belonging. Furthermore, Da-sein (now written with a hyphen) does no longer designate a human entity at all, nor does it designate simply human being, although it does require humans as the ones who *are* (-*sein*) the *there* (*Da*), the open site of a historical time-space.

EREIGNIS, ATTUNEMENT, AND HISTORY

The appropriating event (*Ereignis*) is not something one may willfully engage, but there are fundamental attunements or dispositions (*Grundstimmungen*, like *Angst* in *Being and Time*) that dispose thinking such that it undergoes the experience of the event. In *Contributions*, the basic dispositions that transpose into the event of the truth of beyng are those of an epoch rather than those of a singular human being. Heidegger mentions especially "shock" (*Erschrecken*), "restraint" (*Verhaltenheit*), and "diffidence" (*Scheu*). Disposed by shock, one realizes that in our epoch being does not occur as an appropriating event but rather as a withdrawal (*Verweigerung* or *Versagung*).[7] This relates to the realization that the way beings appear is determined by machination (*Machenschaft*, the dominion of the makeability) and lived experience (*Erlebnis*) such that beings are abandoned by beyng and beyng in its truth remains completely forgotten. Restraint (which comprises shock and diffidence) disposes thinking to remain turned toward the withdrawal of beyng, toward the lack that

marks our era, such that this lack is sustained in Da-sein.[8] Thus the truth of beyng finds an open site. This truth occurs as "hesitant withdrawal" such that in this hesitation, unconcealment of the concealment occurs. The preservation of this unconcealed concealment becomes more and more important in Heidegger's thinking of the event in the volumes following *Contributions*. The concealment belonging to beyng is precisely what remains concealed and thus forgotten in metaphysics ("the first beginning").[9] Thinking, as it finds itself appropriated and responds to the appropriating call, is dis-lodged into an untimely situation. It enters a realm "in-between" where it is no longer forgetful of the truth of beyng, and yet, in the sense of the history of a people, the event of appropriation does not occur, and people remain disposed by machination and lived experience. The moment in which *Ereignis* would hold sway historically, would mark an "other beginning" of history. In *Contributions*, we need, then, to distinguish *Ereignis* in an epochal sense from *Ereignis* in so far as it is intimated "by the few future ones" and sustained in the thinking and saying of a single thinker or poet. This single thinkers and poets are transposed (appropriated) into the *transition* into the other beginning and in this transition their thinking and saying is inceptive (*anfänglich*).[10]

ENT-EIGNUNG (DIS-APPROPRIATION) AND ENT-EIGNIS (EX-PROPRIATION)

In our epoch of the utmost abandonment of beings by beyng, beyng at first is experienced as withdrawal, that is, not as appropriation but as "dis-appropriation," as *Ent-eignung*.[11] *Ent-eignung* in this sense has a "negative" connotation; it indicates that in our epoch

Er-eignis does not (yet) occur and the truth of beyng (especially the concealment belonging to it) remains concealed. This is not due to a human fault but rather is rooted in the way beyng itself unfolds in the first beginning, namely as presence.

Later, in "The Thing" (1950), Heidegger speaks of *enteignen* in a positive sense as a "letting go in to the proper" and in *Time and Being* (1962), Heidegger speaks of *Ent-eignis*—again "positively"—in terms of the originary concealment that belongs to the truth of beyng even when it occurs as *Er-eignis*.[12]

EREIGNIS AS INCEPTION

In *Über den Anfang* and *Das Ereignis* (1941–2) Heidegger's thinking of the event moves further into the concealed dimension belonging to Ereignis while venturing to be more inceptive. Even with previous acquaintance with Heidegger's *Contributions*, the volume *Das Ereignis* remains extremely difficult to access because of an even more radical attempt to speak *out of* an experiencing of the event. Heidegger now characterizes the movement of thinking as "departure" and "downgoing" into the beginning. "*Downgoing* is inception of the beginning in its inceptiveness [Der Untergang *ist Anfängnis the Anfangs in seiner Anfänglichkeit*]."[13] "*The event* [now] names the inception of the beginning that properly clears itself."[14] In *Über den Anfang* he writes: "Beginning is the taking into safe keeping of the departure [*Abschied*] into the abyss."[15] Heidegger begins to articulate the relation between the inceptive thinking and the epochal dis-appropriation of beings in terms of "the passing [*Vorbeigang*] by each other of the abandonment of beings

by being and the twisting free of being into the beginning."[16] One may interpret this as a preliminary form of the differentiation he makes in *Time and Being* (1962) between, on the one hand, the appropriating event as the "giving" of historical determinations of being (such that this giving is not itself a form of history), and, on the other hand, the historically determined epochs.

THE FULL EXPANSE OF EREIGNIS: *DA-SEIN, GODS AND HUMANS (ZUEIGNUNG AND ÜBEREIGNUNG), WORLD AND EARTH, BEINGS*

In *Contributions*, besides the relation between the truth of beyng, being-t/here (*Da-sein*), and humans, *Ereignis* has other essential dimensions belonging to it. The full expanse of the appropriating event comprises gods and humans, world and earth, as well as beings; and Heidegger thinks Da-sein (being-there) as the "in-between" of these multiple dimensions.[17]

In Da-sein—when the appropriating event occurs—our being is appropriated in relation to the gods such that we are assigned (*Zueignung*) to the gods and the gods are consigned (*Übereignung*) to us. For Heidegger, the gods lack being; they *are* not and need humans as the ones who sustain the open site of truth such that a grounding of Da-sein occurs.[18] This moment would mark the other beginning of history; Heidegger calls it a moment of decision; it comprises "the passing of the last god." This moment does not result in a presencing of gods (as if they were beings); rather the gods remain tied to the essential concealment belonging to the event. This is why gods and humans emerge in the event both in their separation (*Geschiedenheit*) as well as in their assigned/appropriated encounter.

It is *within* this encounter between gods and humans that the strife of world and earth as well as the relation to beings are situated in the thought of *Contributions*.[19] With the appropriation of Da-sein is disclosed the "strife of world and earth"[20] that is related to what Heidegger calls the "sheltering" (*Bergung*) of the truth of beyng into beings. The truth of beyng occurs as *Ereignis* only when world and earth find an open site by virtue of beings, that is, works of art, deeds, things, and above all and first of all—words.[21] (Otherwise beings remain *ent-eignet*, that is, "dis-appropriated" by beyng, as said above.) Thus *Ereignis*, as the moment of an other beginning of history, occurs only in the assignment of the gods to humans and the consignment of humans to gods, in which Da-sein is grounded such that in Da-sein, the strife of world and earth is sheltered in a being. This would also be the moment of the passing by of the last god.

In the grounding of the truth of beyng, beyng and beings are transformed into their simultaneity.[22] Yet this simultaneity does not abolish all difference between beyng and beings. According to what Heidegger thinks during the time he is writing *Contributions*, the strife of world and earth functions as a form of medium between the truth of beyng and beings. He says that the truth of beyng cannot be "directly" sheltered in beings but first needs to be transformed into the strife of world and earth.[23]

EREIGNIS AS THE MIRROR PLAY OF THE FOURFOLD (ENTEIGNENDE VEREIGNUNG)

The relation between "gods and humans" and "world and earth" in *Contributions*, foreshadows Heidegger's thinking of the fourfold (*Geviert*) of gods and humans, sky and earth. Viewed from the horizon of *Contributions*, essays like "The Thing" (1950) and "Building, Dwelling, Thinking" (1951) think ahead into an occurrence of *Ereignis* such that a sheltering of truth in beings takes places and thus beings "gather" the event of appropriation. Yet whereas in *Contributions* Heidegger speaks of the strife of world and earth, in the later writings he speaks of the relation between sky and earth; all four elements of the fourfold are said to constitute the "worlding" (*Welten*) of the world. When speaking of the fourfold in the essay "The Thing," Heidegger thinks that *Ereignis* occurs through the appropriating mirror-play of the fourfold such that "each of the four mirrors in its own way the presence of the other. Each therewith reflects itself in its own way into its own, within the unity of the four."[24] In this context, Heidegger uses the term *Vereignung*: "The mirroring appropriates [*ereignet*]—by clearing each of the four—their own essence into the simple appropriation [*Vereignung*] to each other."[25] The prefix "ver" has (in this context) the sense of an achievement; we may thus translate *Vereignung* as "achieving appropriation." The essay "The Thing" also contains a different use of the term "*enteignen*" than in *Contributions*. When speaking of the fourfold, Heidegger will play with a more positive meaning of the prefix "*ent*"; this time, he stresses the sense of "letting go" or "letting free" that the term contains (whereas in *Contributions* he emphasized the sense of privation). He writes: "Each is expropriated [*enteignet*], within their mutual appropriation [*Vereignung*], into its own being." Heidegger sums up: "This expropriative appropriating [*dieses enteignende Ereignen*] is the mirror-play of the fourfold."[26]

GE-STELL AS A PRELIMINARY FORM OF EREIGNIS

Heidegger's meditations on the mirror play of the fourfold are one way into thinking the event of appropriation. Another one is his meditations on *Ge-stell*, ("framework" or "enframing").[27] Through the notion of *Ge-stell*, Heidegger reflects further on what in *Contributions* he calls the domination of machination, calculation, and lived experience. An experience of the truth of beyng as appropriating event first requires that we experience and acknowledge the abandonment of beings by beyng. This abandonment is rooted in beyng's withdrawal that, in metaphysics, issues a "technological" disclosure of beings, which covers over the essential concealment belonging to the truth of beyng. A meditation on the essence of technology leads precisely to this essential concealment of beyng out of which may arise an intimation of the truth of beyng as *Ereignis*. It is thus that Heidegger can speak of *Ge-stell* as a preliminary form of *Ereignis*.[28]

In *Identity and Difference* (1957) Heidegger writes that we need to pay attention to the claim that speaks in the essence of technology: "Our whole being everywhere finds itself challenged [. . .] to devote itself to planning and calculating everything. [. . .] The name for the gathering of this challenge which places man and being towards each other [*einander zu-stellt*] in such a way that they challenge each other is 'the framework' [*das Ge-stell*]"[29] The belonging together of man and beyng through this mutual challenging reveals "that and how man is appropriated over [*vereignet*] to being, and being is appropriated [*zugeeignet*] to human being."[30] Thus, realizing how we are challenged into the planning and calculating of everything reveals our relation to beyng as occurring

through the event of appropriation—if we explicitly enter into this relation.

EREIGNIS AND GESCHICK (THE SENDING OF HISTORY)

In *Contributions* it remains somewhat ambiguous whether *Ereignis* only names how beyng occurs initially, in the moment of decision of the other beginning, or whether Heidegger thinks of the possibility of a whole epoch in which appropriation occurs more fully. Later, in *Time and Being*, Heidegger makes a clearer differentiation between *Ereignis* and the history of being in its epochal forms.[31] Here, Heidegger thinks of *Ereignis* in terms of the sending of epochs and calls the history of being that is sent in the sending *Geschick* (destiny):

> In the sending of the destiny of Being, in the extending of time, there becomes manifest a dedication [*Zueignen*], a delivering over [*Übereignen*] into what is their own [*Eigenes*], namely of being as presence and of time as the realm of the open. What determines both, time and being, in their own, that is, in their belonging together, we shall call: *Ereignis*, the event of appropriation.[32]

The event of appropriation is nothing "behind" being and time but rather names their appropriation, the event of their coming into their own and in relation to each other. Heidegger points out that the appropriating conceals itself as "it gives" time and "it gives" being. In the German sentence "*Es gibt Zeit*" (it gives time) the "*es*" has a similar function as in the sentence "it rains." There is no thing that rains. Similarly, there is no thing that gives time or gives being; appropriation occurs as the giving, but in such a way that as "it" gives, "it" conceals itself.

As the sending of time and being, the event of appropriation is not itself a form of being; it is unhistorical while it determines the history (or histories) of being. Accordingly, for a thinking that turns into the event of appropriation as a sending that withdraws or conceals itself (here is where Heidegger speaks of *die Enteignis* or "expropriation" in the more original sense) "the history of Being as what is to be thought is at an end."[33] In one of the seminars held in Le Thor in 1969 Heidegger again draws the differentiation between *Ereignis* and the history of being: "There is no destinal epoch of enowning [*Ereignen*]."[34] Heidegger also specifies "in enowning, the history of being has not so much reached its end, as that it now appears *as* history of being." In summary, in his later thought, Heidegger understood *Ereignis* to be the event of appropriation out of which epochs of being occur.[35] The event of appropriation itself remains concealed in the way being discloses in each epoch, unless thinking enters the event of appropriation and finds itself as appropriated thinking "of" the event.

NOTES AND REFERENCES

[1] See Heidegger's indication of this in ZSD, 46/ TB, 43. For earlier uses of the term *Ereignis* by Heidegger, see William Koch, "Richard Capobianco: Engaging Heidegger," *Human Studies* 34 (2011), 231–6; and Daniela Vallega-Neu, "*Ereignis*: the event of appropriation," in ed. Bret Davis, *Martin Heidegger (Key Concepts)* (Durham: Acumen, 2010), 141f.

[2] All these volumes attempt to think being in its historicality out of an experience of being as event. They comprise GA 65 (1936–8), GA 66 (1938–9), GA 69 (1938–40), GA 70 (1941), GA 71 (1941–2), GA 72 (1944), and GA 73 Only a few texts (lectures) published

during Heidegger's lifetime explicitly deal with *Ereignis*. In *On Time and Being* Heidegger names the "Letter on Humanism," four lectures given in 1949 to which belong "The Thing," "Enframing," "Danger," and "The Turn," the lecture on technology, and "Identity and Difference." (TB, 36) We should add to these texts the said lecture and seminar on "Time on Being" as well as "Four Seminars" (FS).

[3] *Ereignis* in German usually means "event," but, like in many other instances, Heidegger likes to play with a wider semantic field that opens up once we hear the word more literally by breaking it up into its two semantic components "*er-*" and "*-eignis*." The prefix "*er-*" carries the sense of a beginning motion or of an achievement, whereas "*-eignis*" refers to the word "*eigen*," which in German usually means "own," but which is also at play in a word that is familiar to us from Heidegger's *Being and Time*, namely "*eigentlich*," in English "proper" or "authentic." This has lead scholars to translate *Ereignis* not simply with "event" but also with the neologism "enowning," or with "appropriation," or, "the event of appropriation."

[4] See GA 65, 239/CP2, 188, section 122. Compare also sections 133–6.

[5] See GA 65/CP2, sections 140, 141, and 191; in section 217, for instance, this turning is articulated as oscillation between appropriating call and belonging.

[6] GA 65/CP2, section 217. "*Zugehören*" contains the root meaning "*hören*," to hear.

[7] See *Contributions*, the "fugue" titled *Anklang* (translated as "Resonating," or "Echo") section 50 and following (GA 65, 107ff./CP2, 85ff.).

[8] This relates to being-towards-death as Heidegger elaborates it in *Being and Time*. Only in resolute anticipation of the possibility of the impossibility of being does being as such disclose out of its temporal horizon.

[9] Compare "The Essence of Truth." BW, 130f.

[10] See the sections on the future ones in *Contributions*.

[11] GA 65, 120/CP2, 95. Heidegger does not use the substantive *Ent-eignis* in *Contributions* but uses the verbal form: beings remain dis-appropriated (*ent-eignet*) by beyng.

[12] "Expropriation [*Ent-eignis*] belongs to appropriation as such. By this expropriation,

appropriation does not abandon itself—
rather, it preserves what is its proper [*sein Eigentum*]," ZSD, 23/TB: 22f.

13 GA 70, 142.

14 GA 71, 147.

15 GA 70, 11.

16 GA 71, 84.

17 GA 65, 310f./CP2, 146f.; sections 190 and 191.

18 GA 65, 470.

19 See section 190 of *Contributions* (GA 65, 310/ CP2, 246) where Heidegger even diagrams this relation.

20 Compare Heidegger's essay "The Origin of the Work if Art." BW, 143–212.

21 See *The Origin of the Work of Art*, where Heidegger speaks of poetry in a larger sense as encompassing all creation and preserving of a work (BW, 199). For the relation between language and *Ereignis* see Vallega-Neu, "Poetic Saying," in *Companion to Heidegger's* Contributions to Philosophy; and Dastur, "Language and *Ereignis*," in *Reading Heidegger*, 355–69.

22 GA 65, 14/CP2, 14.

23 GA 65, 391/CP2, 308.

24 VA, 172/PLT, 177.

25 VA, 172. My translation.

26 VA, 172/PLT, 177. For the relation between the *Ereignis* as the mirror-play of the fourfold and Heidegger's thought of *Gelassenheit* see Bret Davis, *Heidegger and the Will* (Evanston, IL: Northwestern University Press, 2007) 231–8.

27 ZSD, 38f/TB, 36.

28 TB, 53/ZSD, 57.

29 Martin Heidegger, ID, 22f/34f. Translation slightly altered.

30 ID, 24/36.

31 Heidegger's meditations especially in *Über den Anfang* (GA 70) and *Das Ereignis* (GA 71) pave the way toward that differentiation.

32 TB, 19/ZSD, 20.

33 TB, 41/ZSD, 44.

34 FS, 61.

35 These epochs are usually equated with the epochs of Western thought, namely the Greeks, the Middle Ages, Modern Though, and the current epoch of technology. But all these epochs belong to metaphysics and metaphysics may be seen as one large epoch in relation to which Heidegger thinks the possibility of another beginning of history.

36

ETHICS
François Raffoul

INTRODUCTION

Heidegger's thought of ethics needs to be approached, from the outset, in terms of what he called, in the "Letter on Humanism," an "originary ethics" (*ursprüngliche Ethik*). The first significant aspect of such an expression is that it seeks to capture ethics in relation to being itself, for it is precisely the thinking of being that is defined as an originary ethics. Heidegger explains that the "thinking which thinks the truth of being as the primordial element of the human being ... is in itself the originary ethics" (GA 9, 356/PA, 271). This already indicates that Heidegger's understanding of ethics unfolds in terms of being itself, the adjective "originary" also indicative that it will not be an issue of ethics as an applied discipline, or even normative, which would then be applied, but of an originary phenomenon.

Nonetheless, Heidegger has often been reproached for his alleged *neglect* of ethical issues, specifically his inability to provide or articulate an ethics, or even a perspective for practical engagement in the world. The simple fact that he never wrote an ethics, as he himself admits in his "Letter on Humanism," seems an eloquent fact in this regard. One also thinks here of the famed *Spiegel* interview, and Heidegger's persistent

and stubborn refusal, despite the increasingly desperate attempts by his interlocutor, to state how philosophy can be a guide for concrete affairs in the world. For, as he explains, "only a God can save us," and humans can only ready themselves ... to be ready for such an arrival, something that might take, we are told, "at least 300 years."[1] Whatever the reasons advanced, Heidegger's thought, it has been concluded, cannot contribute to ethics.

It is true that Heidegger did not propose a system of morality, a body of prescriptive norms or values. It is also well-known that he took issue with ethics as a discipline (GA 9, 354/PA 269). Rather, he attempted to rethink the very site of ethics, what Derrida, following Levinas, called the "ethicality of ethics." This ethicality lies, as we mentioned, in relation to the very event of being. Heidegger brackets out the metaphysical understanding of ethics as a system of moral norms and instead conceives of the ethical in terms of our relation to being: not some theoretical principles to apply, but as the very unfolding of human existence. For instance, when Heidegger takes issue with ethics as a metaphysical discipline, it is with the intent of uncovering a more originary sense of ethics as "authentic dwelling" and "standing-in" the truth of being. When in *Being and Time* he took issue with the distinction between good and evil, characterized as ontic and derivative, it was in order to retrieve an original guilt (*Schuldigsein*) that is said to be more originary than good-and-evil morality and that provides an ontological foundation for morality (SZ, 286/BT, 264). When Heidegger criticized the theme of empathy (SZ, 124–5/ BT, 117), it was not in order to condemn an ethical motif as such but to show how the problematics of empathy are still too dependent on Cartesianism and ego-based philosophies. Instead, Heidegger provides an ontological analysis of "being-with," that is, the originary being-with-others of Dasein that renders moot the question of accessing another mind through empathy.

Ultimately, for Heidegger, as he states in the "Letter on Humanism," the thinking of being is an originary ethics because being is not some substantial ground but an event that calls for a responsible engagement.

DASEIN AS AN ETHICAL NOTION

It could be argued that the concern for ethics has been constant in Heidegger's thought, to the extent that being displays its own ethicality. This appears clearly in the very notion of Dasein, which as concern, care, and responsibility, is defined in ethical terms. Dasein is delivered over to its being, "entrusted" with being or charged with the responsibility for its being: "We are ourselves the entities to be analyzed. The being of any such entity is each time mine. These entities, in their being, comport themselves towards their Being. As beings with such being, they are charged with the responsibility [*überantwortet*] for their own Being" (SZ, 41–2/BT, 41, tr. modified).

This ontological ethicality of Dasein is factical through and through. Heidegger's critique of traditional ethics was, first, a critique of its *abstract* character. As early as 1921–2, during the winter semester course at the University of Freiburg on *Phenomenological Interpretations of Aristotle*, Heidegger opposed the belief in "an *absolute system of morality*, a system of ethical value and value-relations that are valid in themselves." Instead, he writes of a concrete factical ethics, which he refers to as a "living morality" (GA 61, 164/PIA, 124). Dasein has no predicates but in each case it *is* its possibilities. Because Dasein is a *way* of being, a "how" and not a "what," it can *modify* or *modalize* itself into authentic and inauthentic modes. The ethical for Heidegger is situated in factical existence itself, in its specific motion and oscillation between the proper and the improper. Now, in the authentic mode of existing, we do not go off to some other plane distinct from factical existence. Authenticity has no other *content* than that of everyday existance; it is but a modified form of it. "Authenticity is only a *modification* but *not a total obliteration* of inauthenticity" (GA 24, 243/BPP, 171). Heidegger clarified that no "values," no "ideal norms," float above factical existence. When one considers the *Eigentlichkeit/Uneigentlichkeit* alternative in *Being and Time*, one sees that it is a matter of an existence coming into its own, the immanent movement of a radically finite and open event, and not the "application" of rules, from above, to a previously an-ethical realm. Existence thus displays its own ethicality, is ethical through and through, and for that reason does not need to be "ethicized" from above. In a sense, for Heidegger, ethics is ontology itself; there is no need to "add" an ethics to an ontology that would have been presupposed as unethical. This is why, as J-L. Nancy writes, "'*Original ethics*' *is the more appropriate name for* '*funda-mental ontology.*' *Ethics properly is what is fundamental in fundamental ontology.*"[2]

ETHICS AND THE USELESS

Heidegger points to this originary dimen-sion of ethics when he takes issue with the motif of application. For instance, in *Introduction to Metaphysics*, Heidegger stresses the untimely nature of philosophy (GA 40, 10/IM, 9), as he would still do in the *Spiegel* interview, and claims that philos-ophy is in a certain essential sense "useless" (*Nutzlos*) (ibid.). Indeed, philosophy "is not a kind of knowledge which one could acquire directly, like vocational and tech-nical expertise, and which, like economic and professional knowledge in general, one could apply directly and evaluate accord-ing to its usefulness in each case" (GA 40, 10/IM, 9). It is due to its originary dimen-sion that philosophy is not an applied dis-cipline, that it cannot be instrumentalized. We might add that it is foreign to ethics as well, for as we saw above, ethics is not the application to an an-ethical realm of theo-retical principles, but the very motion of an existence coming into its own. According to Heidegger, asking for philosophy to have a result or a use is actually a demand of tech-nological thinking, of what he calls "machi-nation," *Machenschaft*.

Originary ethics cannot be measured in terms of results, or production of effects. The useless opens the space of ethics, while instru-mentality closes it. The essence of thinking as originary ethics, Heidegger writes in the very first lines of "Letter on Humanism,"

is not that which causes an effect, nor is it governed by the value of utility. In fact, in the *Beiträge*, Heidegger makes the claim that genuine thinking is "powerless," in the sense that the "inventive thinking" [*Er-denken*] of the truth of be-ing "tolerates no immedi-ate determination and evaluation, especially since this power must transpose thinking into being and bring into play the whole strangeness of beyng. Accordingly, the power of thinking can never depend on its having objective results in beings" (GA 65, 47/CP2, 39). This is all the more the case since as we know any calculation of effects produced quickly proves incalculable. Hence the site of originary ethics is not a subjective agency but instead "requires the most radical loss of self, and it is in this madness that, properly attuned, one is drawn toward, opened to, the gift of Being" (VP, 147).

DESUBJECTIVIZING ETHICS: ON DECISION

Another key feature of this original ethics, apart from its "uselessness," is thus its radi-cally nonsubjective nature. Ethics is no longer tied to the subject, but to the event of being: it is not the active manipulation of entities, but the enactment of being itself. Such an enact-ment is not the act of a subjectivity, because, as Heidegger says of projection (*Entwurf*), it is always thrown (*Geworfen*), and therefore *before the subject*. This radically nonsub-jectivistic approach appears in the motif of decision.

Decision is traditionally assigned to a willful subject and an agent who decides, to such an extent that decision in the end becomes only about such a subject. The stress is always on *who* decides, *who* has the *power* to decide, *who* leads and *who* the "deciders" are. In such a context, decision is identified with subjectivity, and the power of such subjectivity. In contrast, Heidegger attempts to remove decision from the horizon of subjectivity. In the *Contributions*, he states clearly that ordinarily, when we speak "of de-cision (*Ent-scheidung*), we think of a human act, something carried out, a procedure." However, decision is not a power or a human faculty: "What is essential here, however, is neither the humanness of the act nor the procedural quality" (GA 65, 87/CP2, 69). Rather, "decision is related to the truth of being, not only related to it but rather determined by it alone" (GA 65, 100/CP2, 79, my emphasis). Decision is no longer about the glorified subject, displaced from a subject-based thinking to a thinking that is concerned with what the decision is about, the "decisive."

Emphasizing the "decisive" and the "decidedness" (*Entschiedenheit*) in decision (*Entscheidung*) suggests that in decision the matter is not already settled, not already decided. Rather, the matter is *to be decided*. This undecidedness points toward the decidedness of any decision, and is its proper site. As Heidegger puts it, decision (*Entscheidung*) "thereby is already *decidedness* (*Entschiendenheit*)" (GA 65, 102/CP2, 80). De-cision is not a choice between given ontic possibilities, but is *the essence of being itself*, and in fact "*truth* itself is already that which is *to be decided per se*" (GA 65, 102/CP2, 81). Heidegger speaks of a decision for be-ing (*Entscheidung für das Seyn*) (GA 65, 91/CP2, 93, tr. slightly modified). Being is what is at issue or to be decided in the decision, and decision is about nothing but being. Being as the decisive, being as the matter of decision, away

from the enclosure of subjectivity, this would be one of the main features of the ethicality of being.

ETHICS AS RESPONSIBILITY FOR BEING

Being is thus a matter of a decision, of what we might call a responsible decision. For as there is a decision for being, there also is a responsibility for being.[3] In fact, Heidegger defined Dasein in terms of responsibility in at least three respects: responsibility defines the essence of Dasein as a care and concern for being; Dasein comes to itself in a responsiveness to a call; responsibility names the human being's relationship to being, that is, the cobelonging of being and the human being.

First, the very concept of Dasein means: to be a responsibility of and for oneself, as Dasein designates that entity in which being is at issue. Being is given in such a way that I have to take it over and be responsible for it. Care, concern, solicitude, anxiety, authenticity, being-guilty, all are different names for such originary responsibility: Dasein is concerned about its own being, or about being as each time its own. This determination of Dasein from the outset defines it as a responsibility of being.

Second, Dasein is not a pre-given subject, but is instead approached in terms of a response to an event that is also a call, thematized in *Being and Time* as the call of conscience and in later writings as the call or address (*Anspruch*) of being. Responsibility is not based on subjectness (accountability) but constitutes Dasein as the called one (responsiveness). There lies the hidden source and resource of responsibility: to be responsible means, before anything else, to respond, *respondere*. Playing on the proximity between *Verantwortung* and *Antwort*, Heidegger explains in the 1934 summer semester course on *Logik als die Frage nach dem Wesen der Sprache* that the decision for being alluded to above is about a kind of answering (*Antworten*) in which we take over an answering . . . it is about an *answering for* (*Verantworten*). Responsibility (*Verantwortung*) should thus not be understood in its moral or religious sense, as responsibility before the moral law or before God, but "is to be understood philosophically as a distinctive kind of answering" (GA 38, 121/ LEL, 101). This "response" or attunement to the call of being is an original responsibility.

Thirdly, after *Being and Time*, Dasein was referred to more and more as the "called one," *der Gerufene*, having to answer for the very openness and givenness of being and be its "guardian." To be responsible here means to have been struck, always already, by the event of being. Responsibility refers to that event by which being "enowns" humans, and represents human beings' very belonging to being as well as their essence as humans. The response to the call becomes rethought as belonging to the call, and ultimately as correspondence to being.

The event of being thus engages an original responsibility, a responsibility for being. One notes such original responsibility in what is called in the *Beiträge* the taking-over (*über-nahme*) by Dasein of its belonging to the truth of be-ing in which it is *thrown* (thrown, that is to say—once rethought from be-ing-historical thinking— appropriated). In paragraph 198 of the *Beiträge*, Heidegger would speak of the *über-nahme der Er-eignung*, a sort of original

responsibility in *Ereignis*, the taking-over of a being-appropriated as the way in which Dasein in its being-with-itself essentially occurs. Heidegger writes of the "taking over of the belonging to the truth of being, leaping into the there (*Übernahme der Zugehörigkeit in die Wahrheit des Seins, Einsprung in das Da*)" (GA 65, 320/CP2, 253, tr. modified). Responsibility then means: appropriated by the truth of be-ing, and owning up to such appropriation by sustaining it, enduring and taking-over the exposure to it.

Heidegger is very careful to stress that "the projection of the essence of beying is merely an answer to the call" (GA 65, 56/ CP2, 45), and one sees here how the realm of the ethical—of originary ethics—is located in the space of a certain call, a call to which a response always corresponds. Such an original responsibility cannot even be characterized as *human*, following Heidegger's claim that "in the determination of the humanity of the human being as ek-sistence what is essential is not the human being but being" (GA 9, 333–4/PA, 254). In fact, for Heidegger responsibility is not a human characteristic, but instead a phenomenon that *belongs to being itself*. It is not "I" who is the subject of the event of being: on the contrary, I am thrown into it—that is, "appropriated—by be-ing, in be-ing, and for the sake of be-ing, insofar as be-ing is my ownmost," Heidegger insisting that care is uniquely a care "*for the sake of beyng*—not of the beyng of the human being but of the beyng of beings as a whole" (GA 65, 16/CP2, 15, modified). In his thinking of ethics and responsibility, Heidegger thus breaks with a subject-based thinking, breaks from the tradition of autonomous subject, and with an anthropological way of thinking. The entirety of ethics is to be recast in terms of being itself, and no longer based on the human subject. Responsibility names the cobelonging of being and Dasein (a cobelonging not posited by the human being but rather one in which the human is thrown). It is in that dimension that we are to situate the thinking of ethics, or original ethics, in Heidegger's work. As he put it in the Zollikon seminars, "To stand under the claim of presence is the greatest claim made upon the human being. It is 'ethics'" (Z, 273/ ZS, 217).

NOTES AND REFERENCES

[1] "Only a God Can Save Us" in T. Sheehan (ed.), *Heidegger: The Man and the Thinker* (Chicago, IL: Precedent Publishing, 1981), 60.

[2] Jean-Luc Nancy, "Heidegger's Original Ethics," in eds François Raffoul and David Pettigrew, *Heidegger and Practical Philosophy* (Albany, NY: SUNY Press, 2002), 78.

[3] See my *The Origins of Responsibility* (Bloomington, IN: Indiana University Press, 2010), chapter 7.

37

THE FOURFOLD
Andrew J. Mitchell

Heidegger's thinking of the fourfold (*das Geviert*) is a thinking of the relationality of things. It names the "gathering" of earth, sky, divinities, and mortals that Heidegger views as constitutive of the thing. The thing so constituted, however, is one that is resolutely finite and opened to the world beyond it. As such, the thing can no longer be considered an "object" in the sense of a self-contained, encapsulated, discrete entity that would stand ever only over and against a subject. Instead, the thing exists relationally, in engagement with the world, and the fourfold is what makes this relational existence possible.

The term "fourfold" first emerges in the 1949 lecture cycle *Insight into That Which Is* held at the private Club zu Bremen while Heidegger was under a teaching ban from the French authorities in the wake of the Second World War. This lecture cycle—comprised of the lectures "The Thing," "Positionality," "The Danger," and "The Turn"—is Heidegger's first lecture appearance after the war and it marks the debut of a new configuration of his thinking, one centered on "things." It is thus a major step along his path of thought. Indeed, in a 1964 letter, Heidegger states in no uncertain terms that, "*Apart from the thing lecture, I have never once presented my own thinking purely on its own terms in publications, however far it has come in the meantime, but* rather have presented it always only in such a manner whereby, as a first attempt, I have sought to make my thinking understandable in terms of the tradition."[1] The fourfold is Heidegger's thinking "on its own terms."

THE FOURFOLD

Given this remark of Heidegger's, it should come as no surprise that the presentation of the fourfold found in "The Thing" is not stated in the staid language of traditional philosophy, but veers toward the poetic (the same holds for the subsequent presentation of the fourfold in the 1951 lecture "Building Dwelling Thinking"). We read:

The earth is the building bearer, what nourishingly fructifies, tending waters and stones, plants and animals. [. . .]

The sky is the path of the sun, the course of the moon, the gleam of the stars, the seasons of the year, the light and twilight of day, the dark and bright of the night, the favor and inclemency of the weather, drifting clouds, and blue depths of the ether. [. . .]

The divinities are the hinting messengers of godhood. From the concealed reign of these there appears the god in his essence, withdrawing him from every comparison with what is present. [. . .]

The mortals are the humans. They are called the mortals because they are able to die. Dying means: to be capable of death as death. (GA 79, 17/BFL, 16–17)

These four elements of the fourfold are what join together to constitute the relational thing. Each warrants comment in turn.

The Earth

The earth is perhaps the most familiar of the four components of the fourfold. The earth is materiality. The earth is the material out of which things are composed. But we go wrong to think this material quality of the earth as anything substantial or stable. To understand this earth, we must rid ourselves of such substantialist prejudices. This is just what Heidegger's emphasis on the earth as a "bearer" (Tragende) is meant to do. In the fourfold the earth names the way that things exist as sensuously and materially apparent. Heidegger's name for this is "bearing."

Bearing is not to be confused with "ground" (Grund) or grounding. In the typical grounding scenario, that which is grounded, the object, is traced back to a substantive, eternal basis, its essence, for example. What is grounded is dependent upon the ground and follows from it. With bearing, Heidegger indicates instead a cobelonging. What is borne (das Getragene) requires its bearer (der Träger), but it likewise constitutes that bearer through the state of being borne. In a similar sense, we might say that a parent is only a parent thanks to the child. While the parent bears the child, it is only through the child that the adult first becomes a parent.

What this means is that there ultimately is no ground, or no ultimate ground. The only traction that we find in this world is through a reciprocal relation of holding each other afloat. We bear each other, we bear the world, but those same others and that same world bears us up in turn.

With such a flimsy support of thingly existence, it is no wonder that the earth can be nothing substantive. Instead what the earth bears is called a "fructifying" (Fruchtende). What the earth bears comes to fruition, it blossoms into appearance. The earth bears the sensuous appearance of things. And it is only in this sense that it can be the "material" of things. The earth as sensuous gleam (Glanz) is what things are composed of. Things do not exist materially, they exist phenomenally. They are composed not of inert, dead matter, but of shining, phenomenal radiance. They make up a world that reaches out to us, radiates to us.

The nature that Heidegger lists in his depiction of the earth—stone, water, plants, and animals—all make appearances in his work of the late 1940s and 1950s. Each is rethought in terms of just this manner of existing, a nonsubstantive bearing relation. Nothing is simply inert, stones speak, rivers poetize, and both plants and animals move past any presumed encapsulation in an environment (Umwelt) or "disinhibiting ring" (Enthemmungsring).

The Sky

If the earth is the phenomenal appearance of things, then it needs some space in which to appear. The sky is this space. The ungrounded earthly appearing that gleams in an untethered radiance can only do so through a medium capable of receiving it. The sky is that medium. Without the sky, there would be no earth. The two together form the "dimension," are united in a "marriage" (GA 7, 198/PLT, 218; GA 79, 11/BFL, 10). For the sky to be able to do this, however, it cannot be a mere void. A void would be the correlate to the modern object, the absence correlate to objective full presence. With the abandonment of a thinking of objective presence, however, we likewise abandon the thought of sheer absence; we abandon the thought of a void. And the sky is no void. Instead, it is a complex and varied medium, an "ether," as Heidegger says.

The sky is a space of movement and change. The change of the sky yields a particular kind of time, the "natural" time of heavenly alteration. Day passes into night, the sun recedes before the moon and stars. These changes of the day are part of a larger cycle of changes of the year. The seasons change. These temporal shifts are accompanied by changes of the light. Thanks to the sky, things appear under different lightings, show themselves differently at different times. The color of the sky is "blue," that is to say, neither pitch black nor bright white, but a color between these two, the color of the between and mediation.

No void, the sky is a textured space. As an "ether," there is a viscosity to it. The density of the sky varies and it undulates in accordance with the things and relations that run through it. This nonhomogeneity of the sky is amplified by passing patches of opacity (clouds) that appear throughout it. Still more, large swaths of the medium are subject to occasional seizures of great violence (storms), releasing untold destructive powers. But that same sky is capable of matching our mood, of cheering us up (*Aufheitern*) and elating us. It provides a space of relief from our mundane preoccupations, where we might look up from our labor (*Aufschauen*) and open ourselves to change.

To think the relationality of things, this notion of medium is crucial. If things are to be understood as relational, they are outside of themselves. This means they must enter a space that is capable of receiving them, a space suited to them. The sky is this space. And what appears under the sky is affected by appearing there. Because the sky is not empty space or a void, it has an effect upon all that appears within it. What appears is weathered by the sky. What exists blanches and wears away. Whatever appears cannot last for long.

DIVINITIES

The divinities are messengers, "hinting messengers of godhood" and each of these terms is crucial for understanding their function in the constitution of a relational thing. By writing this messengerial role into the "thinging" of the thing, Heidegger moves into a new paradigm of meaning for his later work. As the researcher in the "Dialogue on Language" (1953) remarks, "it would scarcely have escaped you that in my later writings the names 'hermeneutics' and 'hermeneutical' are no longer employed" (GA 12, 94/OWL, 12, tm). In place of this, we find a thinking of the message. The divinities are the inaugural moment of this new (nonhermeneutical) thematic of the message.

Since Heidegger's first Hölderlin reading, the hint (*Wink*) has named the way of presencing of that which is not simply present. Hölderlin's notion of a "flight" of the gods is understood as itself a hint. The hint names the presence of what is no longer present, it announces an absence. But in announcing an absence, it is no longer utterly absent. It is remarked. The hint thus troubles the very opposition between presence and absence.

Even more, the hint is understood in terms of the trace. Heidegger's thinking of "godhood" here (first broached in two texts from 1946, the "Letter on 'Humanism'" and "What Are Poets For?") makes this abundantly clear. Godhood is the medium of the godly (of the gods), but only insofar as the element of this godhood is found in the "holy" (*das Heilige*), itself the medium for the appearance of the "hale" (*das Heile*). The hale for its part is a mode of presencing that resists the total availability of the standing reserve. Technology would make everything unconcealed, yet the hale (*das Heile*) keeps a concealment. But it would appear that today all is standing reserve (*Bestand*), that there is nothing hale. As Heidegger explains, today "not only does the holy remain hidden as the trace of godhood, but even what is hale, the trace of the holy, appears to be extinguished" (GA 5, 295/OBT, 221; tm). But it only appears to be extinguished, it is "not yet" so. There still remains a glimmer of concealment and this is what the divinities signal to us, why there is meaning, and why they can only hint at it.

The divinities are messengers of this, between origin and destination and defined by a meaning they do not possess as their own. They ensure that we remain between presence and absence, that metaphysical closure yet entails an "outside," and that the exposure to this outside is meaningful. They promise a space of meaning, the space of a message. The things themselves are "messaged" to us, that is, are meaningful. And this without the imposition of a meaning structure on the part of the human, a hermeneutic circle in which only Dasein is meaningful. Heidegger's later thinking of meaning begins from this.

MORTALS

Death is constitutive for the mortals. In *Being and Time*, Heidegger explored the strange nonpresence of death. On the one hand, death is most our own in that no one can die our deaths for us, but on the other, death is nothing we possess, when it is here, we are gone, and when we are here, it is not. Existence was thus defined by this nonpossession of one's own. What is most our own is no possession and this frustrates the attempts of the ego to seclude itself in isolation, to have itself. To be mortal is to be defined by dispossession, by a death we can never have. What is most my own remains outside of me, and this fact cracks me open, and is thus my fundamental opening to world.

In his later thinking, Heidegger takes this notion of death a step further. Now death is understood as something of which the mortals are "capable" (*vermögen*). But this is a technical term for Heidegger. The "Letter on 'Humanism'" explained what is most enabling in this regard as an "element," that is, a medium: "The element is what properly enables [*das Vermögende*]: it is the enabling [*das Vermögen*]" (GA 9, 316/PA, 241). The death that the mortal does not possess, but which enables the mortal to be mortal, is a death that opens them to the outside. Mortals are outside *in* their death. Death is the medium of mortality.

Consequently, "mortals" names those beings defined by exposure and openness to the world. The essential plurality of the name points to their communal nature. As "Building Dwelling Thinking" explains, "mortals dwell insofar as, by their own essence, namely, that they are capable of death as death, they accompany [others] in the use of this capability so that there may be a good death" (GA 7, 152/PLT, 148; tm). This is dwelling, an exposed, relational existence upon the earth, under the sky, before the divinities, and with others, with the things. Mortals are no longer world-building Dasein, but so thoroughly members of a community as to forego such privilege by participating in the fourfold's play of thing and world.

The presence of mortals within the thinging of the thing does not entail that things only exist for the mortal or that the mortal is somehow the source of things. Rather, if things are understood to be relational, then those relations must be ones that reach out to us. There could not be a relational world of things that remained indifferent to us. Relationality must be absolute or it is nothing. And this means that we are always already claimed by the world, appealed to by things. This responsibility is the gift of mortality. It lets there be a good death.

THE MIRROR-PLAY OF THINGS

Earth, sky, divinities, and mortals join together in creating the finite, relational thing. But it is not enough to arrange the four alongside each other. As Heidegger notes, "the united four are already suffocated in their essence when one represents them only as individuated actualities that are grounded through one another and are to be explained in terms of each other" (GA 79, 19/BFL, 18). Instead, we must understand them in their "fouring" (*Vierung*), in their belonging together.

The thing is a "gathering" of the fourfold and this concentration of the four enables the "thinging" of the thing. Without this gathering, there would be no things. So let us make no mistake, when Heidegger speaks of the coming together of the four, he is speaking of the very "core" or "heart" of things. He is telling us what transpires in the very make up of a thing at its most basic level. Thus it should come as no surprise that his

depiction of this relationship is somewhat obscure, but this obscurity should not belie the profundity that is at stake. Heidegger presents the thinging of the thing, the gathering of the fourfold, as a kind of play, more particularly, a "mirror-play" (*Spiegel-Spiel*; GA 79, 19/BFL, 18).

Each of the four in its way mirrors the essence of the remaining others again. Each is thus reflected in its way back into what is its own within the single fold [*Einfalt*] of the four. This mirroring is no presentation of an image. Lighting up each of the four, this mirroring appropriates the essence of each to the others in a simple bringing into ownership [*einfältige Vereignung*]. In this appropriating-lighting way, each of the four reflectively plays with each of the remaining others. (GA 79, 18/BFL, 17)

Here Heidegger is thinking of the way in which the four belong together. We have proposed understanding the four as constituting the finite thing. The earth composed of its phenomenal radiance. This required a medium through which to move, the sky. That mediated appearing was inherently meaningful, constituted as a message sent to us via the divinities, and directly appealed to us as exposed mortals. The four mirror each other in that none of them is anything stable or self-identical, but instead are ungrounded, shifting, sent, and dying. The same structure of mediated appearance appears in each of them. Each of the four can thus be said to "mirror" the others.

But Heidegger goes further than this. To understand the thing as relational, the core itself must be nothing self-same. As Heidegger explains it, each of the four belongs to the others. Mirroring "appropriates the essence of each to the others." Each is sent out to the others, reflected over to them, but only in order to be reflected back to itself. Indeed, what it "itself" is, is nothing other than this originary reflection. Otherwise put, the four do not have distinct identities that can be aligned alongside each other. Each is so intricately involved with the others that each receives whatever identity it has from that relationship. To think the four as mirroring is to think them as bouncing past their own limits. It is to think the identity of the thing as nothing present. The language of appropriation here should not lead us astray. What is appropriated is only the constitution of a self that partakes in this fourfold, and does so from out of a prior reflection, a prior "expropriation" (Enteignung) as Heidegger explains:

> None of the four insists on its separate particularity. Each of the four within this bringing into ownership [Vereignung] is much more expropriated [enteignet] to what is its own. This expropriative bringing into ownership [enteignende Vereignen] is the mirror-play of the four-fold. From it is entrusted the single fold of the four. (GA 79, 18/BFL, 17–18)

Mirroring thinks the expropriation at the heart of appropriation and belonging. At the center of the thing is no thing. Or better, at the center of the thing is the middle or medium (Mitte) through which the radiance of the four passes. The members of the fourfold at the middle of the thing each give themselves to and receive themselves from each other. They appropriate their existence from out of an original expropriation. In this relation, no member of the four remains within itself. The mirror play takes place beyond the plane of the "mirror." The play does not take place within any of these mirrors. Rather the play occurs outside all of them, between them, in the middle (Mitte) of them. This is the expropriative heart of finitude.

The fourfold is thus Heidegger's attempt to think the utter relationality of things. To do so requires breaking with all objectivist presuppositions and prejudices. It requires that we no longer see the thing as constrained from without or even self-contained from within. We think things now relationally and this means contextually, appearing at a place and being affected by that placement. Because of this, we would go wrong to think of the fourfold and the thing as a new order of being or as opening up a world beyond our current one. Instead the utter relationality of the thing entails that it is completely given over to our world, the world dominated by contemporary technology. The singular relational structure of the thing is essentially threatened by technological replacement and a transformation into standing reserve (Bestand). The thing can never abolish this and still remain the relational thing that it is. Heidegger will ultimately insist that we think these two together, thing and standing reserve. And for this reason he can write, "things have not yet ever been able to appear as things at all" (GA 79, 9/BFL, 9). Such is the condition of finite relationality that the fourfold presents, to be between, not yet one thing, no longer another.

NOTES AND REFERENCES

1 Letter to Dieter Sinn of August 24, 1964, cited in Dieter Sinn, Ereignis und Nirwana: Heidegger—Buddhismus—Mythos—Mystik. Zur Archäotypik des Denkens (Bonn: Bouvier Verlag, 1991), 172, emphasis modified.

38

LANGUAGE
John McCumber

Martin Heidegger's views on language are not only important in themselves, but the changes in them provide an index to his philosophical developments and provide a pathway for relating it to other approaches in philosophy, particularly the "linguistic turn" in twentieth-century analytical philosophy. The main landmarks for charting Heidegger's views on language are *Being and Time* (1927), "The Origin of the Work of Art" (1935), and "Remembrance" (1943), all of which were published during his lifetime.

EARLY VIEWS: BEING AND TIME

In his 1929 fragment "On Heidegger," Ludwig Wittgenstein makes an observation about the early Heidegger:

> I can understand quite well (*ich kann mir wohl denken*) what Heidegger means by "Being" and "Angst." The human being has the drive to run up against the limits of language. Consider for example the astonishment that anything exists. This astonishment cannot be expressed in the form of a question, and there is also no answer to it at all. Everything which we might want to say can a priori only be

senseless. But in spite of that we do run up against the limits of language.[1]

It is not clear whether Wittgenstein is referring to *Being and Time* itself or to the lecture "Introduction to Metaphysics," both of which had appeared by this time. In either case, however, Wittgenstein's remark is acute, because at this time Heidegger himself had not seen the intimate connection between his reawakening of the question of being and the topic of language. Only in 1936, with "The Origin of the Work of Art," does language begin to assume fundamental significance for Heidegger—a significance that it retains throughout his later thought.

In § 7 of *Being and Time* (BT, 27–39), Heidegger approaches language in terms of the phenomenological "philosophy of consciousness" he has inherited from Husserl and reinterpreted via Greek thought (primarily Aristotle). Thus, in allegiance to Husserl, Heidegger conceives language in relation to appearances, not facts or states of affairs; but he develops this understanding via a reflection on the Greek word *logos*, which he understands in terms of the Greek *dêloun*, to make clear. *Logos* is thus primarily a way of making appearances clear. It provides a direct "showing" of phenomena, rather than the conveyance of thoughts or beliefs residing in the mind of a speaker to the mind of a hearer:

> communication is never anything like a conveying of experiences, for example opinions or wishes, from the inside of one subject to the inside of another. . . . Being-with is "explicitly" *shared* in discourse: that is to say, it already *is*, only unshared as something not grasped and appropriated. (152)

The sentence "Martin Heidegger was a philosopher," for example, does not function to express a speaker's belief about Heidegger; it brings us to an encounter with Heidegger himself. Nor, however, does it express a "fact" about Heidegger: in contrast to logic-based approaches to language, Heidegger does not accord priority to propositions. The primary "units" of language are not truth-bearers correlated to facts, such as sentences of propositions, but can include anything that helps someone get a clearer view of a phenomenon.

This flexibility is in turn derived from Heidegger's Husserlian view of truth. For Husserl, "truth" is a matter of the fulfillment of intentions over time: an intentional object (i.e. object of awareness) is "true" if it confirms, or fills in, what was only vaguely present in previous experiences.[2] To be true is thus to be part of a temporal process: if, in Heidegger's example (217) I stand with my back to the wall and say that "the picture is hanging askew," to say that this sentence is true means, among other things, that if I turn around I will see that the picture is indeed askew. If I turn around and see it hanging straight, the sentence was false: as Husserl puts it, "instead of the [originally] intended itself a *different thing* comes forth, at which the [original] positing of the intended fails and it takes on the character of nothingness."[3]

Language is thus introduced, at *Being and Time* § 7, as a phenomenological tool for making appearances clear. When Heidegger extends his analysis of language beyond this, language remains a tool: it is seen in terms of how language helps us Be-in-the-world (150). In such Being, we primarily relate to things by using them (62–72). In order to use something, I must have what Heidegger calls a "context of signification," or what I will call a "script," for dealing with it. Such "scripts" can be quite simple: in the case of a knife, for example, they include holding it by the handle rather than the blade, bringing it into contact with something I want to cut, and so on. Also part of the script is the point of the whole endeavor: I am cutting cloth to make a dress, or cutting a steak in order to eat it, and so on. Our "everyday" life, for Heidegger, amounts to a movement through such preestablished contexts or scripts.

Words clearly play important roles in this. I am able to identify something as belonging to a particular script, for example, when I have a word for that thing: if I could not call something a knife, I would not be able to recognize it as a knife and could not use it. This identity-providing function of language is thus a condition of my use of tools—and my use of words as well. It is for Heidegger a deeper level of language than spoken speech, one that he calls "discourse" (*Rede*).[4] Discourse, the "existential-ontological foundation of language" (150) is thus language insofar as it is viewed, not as a vehicle of communication, but as the medium in which a human being makes sense of the world. As such, it is the articulation of being-in-the-world itself, and is the field of encounter of Dasein's other two basic "properties" or *Existenziale*: understanding, which articulates our current situation with respect to the future, and state-of-mind, which articulates with respect to the past (320–1).

Not all languages, however, have the same repertoire of names; we have already seen Heidegger allude to this when he recurred to the Greek *dêloun* to clarify the nature of language. German does not have that word, and so is unable to articulate its own nature as language. The words available in a language thus limit the scripts that speakers of that language can follow, and so the "understandings" they can have. My understanding of something is inevitably conditioned by the words available to me, and so is always interpretive or "hermeneutical." This means that predication is a sort of illusion: "S is P," which suggests that entity S simply has the property P, is really a matter of "x as y": here is how we, given our current language, should take this entity. The traditional view of predication results from an artificially "theoretical" frame of mind (139–40).

The availability of words, finally, is a function of the world. This is because scripts, to begin with, are not freestanding: one script can be an ingredient in a more complex script, and can have simpler scripts as its own ingredients. The scripts available to Dasein, and so the words available to it, are thus interwoven; and the totality of interwoven scripts for a particular Dasein constitutes its world. World is thus the enabling horizon of particular scripts, or contexts of signification, and the words we actually use grow up to these: "words accrue to significations" (151).

The account of language in this reputedly "existential" work thus exhibits none of the individualism so often associated with existentialism. Rather, language itself is grounded on the preestablished significations of the world. It is the homogenized product of previous speakers, and is inadequate to express my own "authentic" individuality. Thus the "call of conscience," which summons Dasein to its "ownmost possibility," death, is a wordless *Schweigen*, a keeping-silent, which is "indefinite" and outside the worldly articulations of both discourse and understanding (252–3, 273, 296).

THE ORIGIN OF THE WORK OF ART

Language moves to center stage for Heidegger in the 1936 "Origin of the Work of Art" (1935), and it does so at the same time world is demoted from its primordial status as the source of all meaning. Seeking to understand the nature of "things" in general via an understanding of the nature of works of art, Heidegger argues that to every work of art there belongs a "material," not in the traditional Aristotelian sense of a quiescent matter into which the artistic form is projected (see OBT, 9–10), but in the sense of something that is dynamic and configuring. Heidegger calls this "earth" (BT, 21–2, 23–7).

We can begin to understand the role of earth in the constitution of a thing by recurring to an example that Heidegger himself mentions (OBT, 43): Albrecht Dürer's claim that he did not "put" the forms of his woodcuts into the wood from which they were made, but "wrested" them—out of the grains, stress lines, and fractures of that particular piece of wood. From this we can see, first, that earth is pre-human, so that the term conveys the dynamism of the "natural" world: the work of art thus originates from the natural significance of the earth (24–5). Second, earth needs to be made clearer, its shifting "grains" brought out into the open where we can experience them. It is then inherently undisclosed, and as such is "self-secluding" (25).

The opening-up of earth so that its dynamic traits can be experienced is accomplished by

305

humans (whom Heidegger now calls "mortals") in many ways, but language occupies a major place in all of them. Consider water. Water can obviously be "present" to a stone lying on the bottom of a stream: the water touches the stone, moves it along downriver, gradually grinds it into an ellipsoid, and so forth. But the water is not present to the stone *as water*, for there are many other dimensions to water as we encounter it: it runs in other streams, falls from the sky, and nourishes plants; it can be drunk or bathed in, used in religious ceremonies, and so on. These different occurrences of water constitute it as the "phenomenon" that it is for human beings; but they remain unknown to the stone.

They also remain hidden from essentialist philosophical accounts of water, such as Saul Kripke's, according to which water necessarily is H_2O.[5] The first Heideggerean response to Kripke is not that he is wrong, that things have no necessary features (that point would come later), but that this account of water is oversimplified: it subtracts from water all the ways in which we interact with it, relegating them to the status of mere "appearances." As Husserl taught, appearances are important.

The "watery" phenomena listed above are very different from one another. There is no reason why what runs through rivers must fall out of the sky, or that it should also nourish plants and humans. It is quite possible, in a Wittgensteinian spirit, to imagine a tribe who thought that those phenomena in fact had nothing to do with one another. One thing we can see immediately about that tribe is that it would have no word for "water": no word that covers the disparate phenomena that our word covers. The reason we have that word is that our linguistic forebears not only recognized the role of H_2O in those disparate contexts, but thought that role was important

enough to be marked. Only when it is marked in that way does H_2O become "water."

Prior to something's being named, then, it exists in an "earthly," dispersed state: its various modes and roles are not explicitly brought together so it can be experienced as what unifies them. It is via a thing's name that, in Heidegger's term, it is first "projected" onto the various scripts or contexts of signification in which it can subsequently recur. Speech that does this originary projecting is what Heidegger calls "poetic": poetic naming places an "earthly," and so natural, being into a new set of contexts of signification, and so into a new world (OBT, 45–6). Language, as poetic, no longer is conditioned by world; it opens it up (22–4).

LATER HEIDEGGER: POETS AND THINKERS

It is perhaps past time to question the premise of this article: does not an article on "Heidegger and Language" presuppose that there is such a thing as language? And is such a presupposition consonant with Heidegger's thought?

If the fundamental vehicle of language is the poetic name, and if the poetic name functions as a work of art, then it would appear that overall discussions of "language" are beside the point. For "work of art" is not a universal essence that could be understood apart from encounters with individual works of art; each such work is unique, and its uniqueness is essential to its character as an artwork (37, 39–40). True to this, Heidegger's later writings on language are generally keyed to concrete cases of poetic naming—that is, to actual poems or statements of "great" philosophers.

His later procedure is illustrated by his 1943 essay on Hölderlin's poem "Andenken,"—an essay, which, tellingly, carries the exact same title as the poem. Heidegger begins from a traditional view of what a poem is: a bounded whole of words structured by a single theme, that of remembrance; produced by an author, Hölderlin, out of certain circumstances in his life, and aimed at being clearly understood by the reader. He begins, in other words, with the poem understood in terms of Aristotle's material, formal, efficient, and final causes. This traditional view of the poem begins to fail, however, when Heidegger points out that the poem's original title (*Der Ister*) names the Danube and alludes to the Rhine. These are the two rivers that flow through Hölderlin's native Swabia, nourishing it and relating it to the rest of the world (EHP, 106). The "origin" of the poem is thus displaced from the poet to the Swabian earth and its two rivers.

Another problem with the ordinary understanding of the poem concerns its title. *Andenken* in German usually means remembrance or souvenir. But the poem, in its crucial center (the first line of the third stanza) asks a question: where are [the poet's] friends? (*Wo aber sind die Freunde?*) This question is about their present location, and so cannot be answered by memory. And the last line of the poem refers to poets as "founding" something—an act that clearly bears reference, not to the past, but to the future. The "remembrance" of the title is then uncanny indeed: it is a "remembrance" of something that is not in the past but (perhaps) in the future; the rest of the poem, Heidegger says, expands on the meanings of such remembrance (107–9).

True to Heidegger's later emphasis on concreteness, the bulk of his essay presents a close reading of the poem: "Even the most inconspicuous word and every 'image'

which seems fit only for poetic decoration," Heidegger declares, "is an [essentially disclosing] word . . ." (124). In the course of his essay, as Emil Staiger notes with some wonderment, Heidegger actually does discuss every single word of Hölderlin's 59-line poem.[6]

As Heidegger views it, the path of the poem is the following. The first five lines introduce the basic relationship between Hölderlin, Being (the "Northeaster" that blows), and the "future poets of Germania," the "seafarers" (109–11). The rest of the first stanza and the second stanza describe the poet's own trip to France (107). The third stanza shows the poet back in his native land, engaged in dialogue with others there; the fourth begins to poetize his solitude in his native country, and does so by showing how his dwelling in his native land is a nearness to "the source" (which, presumably, is Being; 159–60). The fifth and final stanza continues these themes, restating the necessity for travel to foreign lands and the nature of the voyage, culminating in two different visions of "Andenken." One of these, a wandering over the sea, is a constant running-toward-the-foreign that awakens, and consistently forgets again, what is one's own. The other is the steady loving gaze backwards to the Source. Neither of these, Heidegger argues, is the primordial type of "Andenken," (163–5). There is thus a third type of "Andenken," the truest form of remembrance for Heidegger, which in dwelling by the Source does not simply leave the sea voyage behind but rather makes it into its own authentically disclosed object:

Remembrance thinks of the location of the place of origin in thinking of the journey of the voyage through the foreign. Remembrance thinks of the source because of its reflecting on the sea that was traversed, into which the source flowed out as the river. (171)

Through all of this, Heidegger's basic procedure is simple. He takes each word or phrase of the poem and thinks it through in terms of its significance to poetry as *Andenken*, in the three senses of that word. The seafarers thus become the poets themselves. The *braune Frauen* of Bordeaux become participants at the "wedding festival" of mortals and immortals that gives birth to poetry (125–31). The "dark light" of the wineglass becomes the mortal thoughts through which is expressed what the poet has seen, and so on (141–3). The poem thus is read as unified, not by a determinate theme or "message," but by the equiprimordial interplay of the different meanings of the word *Andenken*.

The essay "Andenken" thus continues the dimension of language first explored in the Husserlian framework of *Being and Time*: it does not present, but *is* the gradual coming-to-clarity of a single word, *Andenken*. In contrast to the graduality of Husserlian versions of intentional fulfillment, however, the essay does not progress by establishing and moving along syntactic or semantic connections among the poem's component terms. Rather, it interprets the poem's movement as one of "jerks" and contrasts. Thus, Heidegger's final statement on Hölderlin's poem is that it is a single articulated structure of *aber*—"but" or "however" (172). The German *aber*, which on Heidegger's analysis is the key on which the poem is structured, serves to indicate not a smooth development from what has gone before and still less a logical inference, but precisely the introduction of something new and unexpected. And indeed, on Heidegger's treatment of the poem, both the poem itself and his own discussion of it contain abrupt changes of theme

and perspective—changes along thematics that are as different from one another as the "watery" phenomena mentioned above, but which are ultimately unified by the irreducible ambiguity of the poem's title.

The three meanings of *Andenken*, again, have no clear relationship to one another: wandering and retrieval, leading back to a source, and founding something still futural cannot be derived either from one of their number or from some more general concept. Heidegger's main gesture in this essay is thus to highlight irreducible ambiguities in the meanings of this and its other terms, and to show how such ambiguity is itself the basic unifying force in the poem. This confronts the ordinary way of understanding the poem with its own limits. For if we are going to approach words in the usual Western way, as sensible signs of supersensible meanings, each single word should have a unique meaning. Heidegger can shatter that usual understanding by pointing out that the meanings of some of the words employed by Hölderlin, or another poet or philosopher, have, rather than a single general meaning, an irreducible plurality of specific ones.

In all this the word *Andenken* functions for Heidegger not only in but as a work of art. The "earth" on which it is grounded is first its own previous existence on the German language (as remembrance of things past), against which it must fight in the poem; a second dimension to its earthiness is the diverse phenomena that come together in is final ambiguity. The "open" clarity into which these mobile elements are brought is furnished by the whole of words that is the poem itself, structured on the single word "aber." The result is that each word on the poem is put together with the other words in ways that have not happened before, so that every word meaning in the poem is a new one. In this way, language itself founds new words; and when we take them to heart, we can found new ways of life and new worlds.

NOTES AND REFERENCES

1 B. F. McGuinness (ed.), *Luqwig Wittgenstein und der Wiener Kreis* (Oxford: Blackwell, 1967), 68. This remark is discussed in detail by Michael Murray in his *Heidegger and Modern Philosophy* (New Haven, CT: Yale Uiversity Press, 1977), 80–3.

2 Edmund Husserl *Cartesian Meditations*, trans. Dorion Cairns (The Hague: Nijhoff, 1970), 93–4.

3 Ibid., 93.

4 See John Sallis, "Language and Reversal," *Southern Journal of Philosophy*, 8 (1970), 381–98.

5 Saul Kripke, *Naming and Necessity* (Cambridge, MA: Harvard University Press, 1980), 116.

6 Emil Staiger, "Hölderlin-Forschung Während des Krieges," *Trivium*, IV (1946), 215. Also see on this Beda Alleman, *Hölderlin et Heidegger*, trans. Francois Fedier (Paris: Presses Universitaires de France, 1959), 151–5.

39

THE NOTHING
Gregory Schufreider

. . . is it so obvious that every "not" signifies something negative in the sense of a lack? (SZ, 285–6/BTMR, 331–2)

The thought of nothing spans virtually the entirety of Heidegger's career, not to mention the history of Western philosophy. Rather than attempting to provide a survey of either, let alone of both, we would like to take advantage of a text that is expanded across Heidegger career. For the 1929 lecture "What Is Metaphysics?," (in)famous for its pronouncement that "nothing nothings," had a "Postscript" added to it in 1943 and an "Introduction" in 1949, entitled "The Way Back into the Ground of Metaphysics." Following these developments in Heidegger's thinking will allow us to see his view of nothing in relation to the tradition of metaphysics while, at the same time, emphasizing the revisions of his own approach, and not only insofar as he (re)sets the original text between an introduction and a postscript but in that we intend to place all three between the bookends of SZ (1927) and a letter that was eventually published under the title *Zur Seinsfrage* (1955). In this respect, we will be prefacing our own remarks to "What is Metaphysics?" with a discussion of nothing in *Being and Time* and following them with an epigraph designed to make it clear that

the question of being can only be properly addressed by thinking nothing.

It goes without saying that nothing is an elusive topic. Rather than try to pin it down, we propose to approach the question from different directions, in effect, distinguishing five different ways of thinking nothing, which are not mutually exclusive. On the contrary, we would hope to see the first four movements, if not converging then at least verging on the fifth.

THINKING NOTHING EXISTENTIALLY

The "nothing" with which anxiety brings us face to face, unveils the nullity by which Dasein, in its very basis, is defined . . . as thrownness into death. (SZ, 308/ BTMR, 356)

"What Is Metaphysics?" is designed to continue a discussion that is pivotal in *Being and Time*, even if the later will approach the topic of anxiety—as a way to get at nothing—from a different direction. If the aim of SZ is to reawaken the question of being, its strategy is to revitalize our sense of being existentially: through an analysis of human existence that is designed to strike questioners directly by raising the question of their own being as a concrete being. In that case, "nothing" will not be thought as an abstract concept (any more than "being" will) but in terms of what the text will designate as the "facticity" of an individual(ized) *Dasein*.

Ironically, the "fact" of *Dasein*'s being determines it to be a being whose being is pervaded by a negativity that is woven into the complexity of its open structure. Not only in its "being-towards-death" is *Dasein* shown to be a being that is bound to and for nothing, but its self-determination requires it to become the basis of a nullity insofar as it must assume responsibility for what it is not, namely, its thrown facticity. And it must do so on the basis of a self that it is not (yet): through the appeal of a call (of conscience) that issues from what amounts to the silent voice of a missing person.

More importantly, when it comes to a structural negativity, and in direct connection to SZ's scenario of selfhood, death is the ultimate in thrown facticity. This is not just a matter of the fact that my life will end but of the facticity of a concrete existence that is pervaded by nothing. In thematizing a "thrownness into death," it must be clear that *Dasein*'s "being-towards-death" is not a matter of externalities but designates a structural determination. What we might dub as an immanent death is not the coincidence of my eventual demise but is meant to suggest a relation to (my own) nothing(ness) that pervades my being existentially. To claim that death is immanent is not to say that it can happen at any time, ontically speaking, but to insist that an ontological relation to nothing pertains to the temporal structure of my being as *Dasein*.

In that event, the existential character of being-towards-death, as a distinguishing feature of human being, does not exhaust its relation to nothing. On the contrary, that *Dasein* can be invaded by a sense of its own nothingness in the experience of anxiety shows an openness to nothing that directs us to "the *ontological source* of negativity." Anxiety over death not only individuates *Dasein* but discloses it as the being that it is: a being not only pervaded by a sense of its own nothingness but one that, to be such, must be exposed to nullity—which is to say that *Dasein* must be free to relate both to what is and to what is not, and not just with respect to its own being.

THINKING NOTHING PHENOMENOLOGICALLY

The nothing itself nihilates. (GA 9, 114/ PA, 90)

While SZ had raised the question of the source of negativity, its analysis of "the not" itself is postponed in favor of an approach to nothing that stresses the facticity of *Dasein*'s being-towards-death as an existential structure of its being. By contrast, in "What Is Metaphysics?" death will not be mentioned insofar as its account of anxiety is developed along the trajectory of *Dasein*'s transcendence, in its freedom to project beyond beings into nothing.

The account of nothing in the 1929 lecture begins from what one might think of as the traditional metaphysical approach, which interprets "nothing" as "not-something." This, of course, is to think of nothing in terms of negation; which is to say that such an approach aims to show that nothing cannot be thought in itself but strictly in terms of the negation of something. On the one hand, this is consistent with the most ancient ontology, which claims that nothing cannot be thought, while, on the other hand, it supports the metaphysical aim of showing that when we are thinking nothing, we are not thinking about something but, on the contrary, thinking "not-something."

Taken to its extreme, however, this "not-something" can be thought more generally in terms of the negation of all beings: of a metaphysical nothingness that may be regarded as the annihilation of what is. In that case, "nothing" is thought to designate what Heidegger characterizes as "the negation of beings as a whole." In his view, this will constitute an ontical approach to nothing, not one that understands it ontologically; even if it operates more universally: not just in terms of the negation of a specific being but as the total annihilation of what is.

In contrast to this metaphysical sense of nothing, arrived at through the theoretical operation of a universal negation, Heidegger will propose a phenomenological approach based on a "nihilation" of beings that takes place in anxiety as an experience of nothing and that is captured in his claim that "nothing nothings." Instead, that is, of thinking of nothing as a noun that refers to a universal state of nonbeing, he verbalizes the term, suggesting that we would have to think nothing in its operation as the source of negation, not the other way around. In this respect, it is not just a question of nothing as "no-thing" but of a "noth-ing" that must be thought of as an original event.

In anxiety, *Dasein* experiences an ontological nullification in relation to beings, not as their ontical annihilation but in relation to a "nothing" that appears "at one with" them in this key mood: in a neutralization that renders our ordinary relation to beings null and void, given our inability to engage with them, either theoretically or practically.

Instead, beings withdraw into a whole that can neither be grasped intellectually nor instrumentally. In this respect, *Dasein* may be said to face the void that is left insofar as beings have slipped away in(to) a profound meaninglessness: present themselves with a pervasive sense of utter insignificance, in what amounts to a dysfunctional indifference, given the dis-integration, dis-orientation, and dis-sociation that *Dasein* experiences in anxiety. In the nihilation of these existential structures—disrupting our integration into the midst of beings and the spatial orientation that goes with it by neutralizing social relations—*Dasein* is faced with nothing, not with any particular being; which is to say that nothing appears "along with" beings insofar as they are withdrawing as a whole. As Heidegger would put it: nothing is there (*da*) with (*mit*) beings, not in the nothingness of my being-towards-death but insofar as they appear neither as items of gear nor as objects but as "beings" pure and simple.

While withdrawing as a whole, beings nonetheless press in on us in anxiety: oppress as well as impress us insofar as we are overwhelmed by the fact that they "are." We are, in other words, struck by the wonder of their being, and precisely in the face of the fact that they are not nothing—which is to say that "what is" appears insofar as it is, and is not nothing. In that event, nothing is thought ontologically: not as if it were a being (or, for that matter, a "non-being") but as making an appearance in a specific way in which beings appear. Moreover, this experience makes it clear that all appearances (of beings as phenomena) are possible only on the basis of nothing: insofar as *Dasein* must be free from an ontical captivity if it is to relate to beings in different ways, ontologically speaking. In this respect, the experience of anxiety demonstrates that we are free not only to relate to beings but to transcend them in a projection into nothing, disclosing an ontological condition that reveals *Dasein* in its freedom to relate to their "being."

THINKING NOTHING METAPHYSICALLY

[N]othing . . . is the veil of being. (GA 9, 312/PA, 238)

In its way, the 1929 lecture on anxiety still thinks of nothing in relation to *Dasein*, albeit in stressing its transcendence (projecting beyond beings) instead of its facticity (being-towards-death). The approach will be different in 1943, when Heidegger appends a postscript to the text that links the thought of nothing to the history of Western metaphysics.

What must be clear from the start, namely, from the title of the lecture, is that the point of "What Is Metaphysics?" is not to conceive of nothing metaphysically but, on the contrary, to see how thinking nothing phenomenologically may direct our response to the question of the essence of Western metaphysics. In contrast to a traditionally metaphysical approach to nothing, the claim that "nothing nothings" is designed to describe an event that happens in a key mood and is thought to unlock the essence of metaphysics in its relation to nothing, although not in its interpretation as "not-something." Unlike fear, not only is anxiety an experience without an object—and therefore over nothing—but *Dasein* experiences a "nihilation" of beings insofar as they slip away as a whole into insignificance, given that we are not taken up by their practical utility (instrumentality) or their theoretical intelligibility (objectivity)

but struck by the wonder that they are. And it is in response to this ontological experience that metaphysics is said to formulate its central question, as the "why" is "forced to our lips" insofar as *Dasein* is exposed to the "nihilation" of what is: such that nothing is revealed as a void into which beings as a whole are "dis-appearing" phenomenologically and through which the mystery of their being is disclosed.

In this respect, Heidegger is subjecting metaphysics to a phenomenological de(con) struction, tracing the (metaphysical) thought of "nothing" back to its (phenomenological) roots in the "clear night" of anxiety, in which beings are cleared out of the way in order to make room for nothing as a "veil" through which we may catch a glimpse of "being." In his view, traditional metaphysics remains in thrall to beings (as does modern science) insofar as it thinks of being in terms of beings: of beings "as such" and, therefore, not of being itself; just as, in limiting its thinking to beings, it is bound to interpret nothing as "not-something," if not as a "non-being." At the same time, while being has been repressed in the tradition, a trace of it is nonetheless expressed in the formal structure of the fundamental question of Western metaphysics: "Why are there beings and not rather nothing?" For while the question here is clearly about beings, a veiled reference to being may be detected in what would appear to be a supplementary addition, in the concluding mention of "nothing," albeit in its own negation.

While metaphysics concentrates on the question of why beings are, Heidegger would have us face the question of how nothing operates in relation to being, in the case of metaphysics, as a veil or mask that inevitably reveals what has been concealed in its history. In effect, "nothing" holds the place of "being" insofar as it has been forgotten, if not forsaken by Western metaphysics: it operates as a memento of what is missing in the abandonment of being in the history of philosophy. This historic oversight will be emphasized in the "Postscript" to "What Is Metaphysics?." By that time, Heidegger will be thinking in terms of a "history of being" and the need to overcome metaphysics, if we are, once again, and along the lines of yet another strategy, to feel the force (this time historically) of ontological questioning. Here it will be critical that, while our sense of being has gotten lost in the tradition in its reduction to a question about beings, a trace of being remains in a reference to nothing from which we would presumably need to take our lead, if Western philosophy is to get back on track. While the 1929 lecture ends (quoting Plato) by claiming that metaphysics belongs to the nature of human being, its 1943 Postscript will be emphasizing the need to overcome it, just as Heidegger's view of nothing will have undergone further refinement in what amounts to the Introduction to his *Introduction to Metaphysics*.

As if to indicate (if only formally) that this "difference" is not the same as other differences, that 1935 lecture course will explicitly set the discussion of the relation between being and nothing apart from the other "delimitations" of being in Greek philosophy, namely, in its determination through the distinctions between being and appearing, being and becoming, being and thinking, and being and valuing. It is the latter relation (between being and the good) that Heidegger will find most problematic, as it is introduced in the work of later Greek philosophy, specifically, in Plato, and is said to run through the history of metaphysics, right up to its final "victim," namely, Nietzsche. For while raising the specter of nihilism, Nietzsche will make

the mistake of taking it to be a problem of value and, as such, fail to see it in relation to the question of being. Put, perhaps, too simplistically, if nothing must be thought ontologically, then being must be thought nihilistically: in terms of a true nihilism, which thinks through the relation between being and nothing such that philosophy is in a position to part the veil that has been covering being, and precisely in an opening to nothing. In this respect, addressing the question of being historically will require the formulation of a nihilistic ontology, in contrast to what Heidegger would have us think of as an "onto-theo-logical" metaphysics.

THINKING NOTHING ONTOLOGICALLY

How does it come about that beings take precedence everywhere and lay claim to every "is," while that which is not a being—namely, the nothing thus understood as being itself—remains forgotten? (GA 9, 382/PA, 290)

In 1949, Heidegger will expand the text of "What Is Metaphysics?" by adding an "Introduction" to the lecture and its Postscript. There he will indicate that, to regroup historically, we need to find "The Way Back into the Ground of Metaphysics," in a text that takes its directions from a reconsideration of the Cartesian image of the tree of knowledge, whose trunk is physics, and branches the various sciences, but whose roots are metaphysics. And while Heidegger would like to extend the metaphor by attending to the soil in which the tree is rooted, namely, being, a nihilistic ontology would also have to expose the hole in the ground through which the roots are free to take root, and which would be obvious were the proverbial tree to fall, roots and all. For if metaphysics is rooted in ontology, then the tree of philosophy would have to be uprooted if we are to face the opening in which Western thought originates.

In overcoming metaphysics, and its subsequent forgetfulness, a history of "being" would take us back to its original "naming" in Greek philosophy. In so doing, however, we would face an equally original nihilation, not just of beings but of being itself insofar as it is thought in relation to nothing. Needless to say, the question of the relation between being and nothing is not only decided in the founding of ontology in Parmenides but their association is clear in Heidegger's thinking of the ontological difference. The distinction between being and beings is not an ontical difference, like the difference between different beings, but is designed to indicate the different ways in which the same being can appear ontologically: as an item of "gear" or an "object," a "work" of art or a "being" pure and simple. In that case, the failure to think through the ontological difference in metaphysics leads to its confusion about nothing, just as its failure to think of nothing properly has led to a confusion about being. If beings are all that is, then being will not only be thought of as a being but, at best, as the supreme being insofar as it is thought to be the causal ground of other beings.

The onto-theo-logical confusion (of being with a being) that riddles metaphysics is presumably corrected in Heidegger's phenomenological ontology, in which being is associated with a "clearing" that takes place in the midst of beings: a time-space opening for the appearance of phenomena, which is said to be "more like the nothing that we scarcely know." And while, in the mid-1930s, he tried to separate an ontological from a metaphysical tradition in Western philosophy, hoping to distinguish the branch that runs from Plato to Nietzsche from its roots in early Greek thinking, especially, Heraclitus and Parmenides, by the late 1940s Heidegger is having his doubts about ontology, which we take to be indicated by his development of a "mythopoetic" alternative to the traditional vocabulary of philosophy.

As insightful as the thought of the ontological difference may be, it requires a priority of being that obstructs a proper access to nothing; for while it may not literally bar the way (as in Parmenides), ontology represses nothing (in its captivation with being) as surely as metaphysics forgets being (in its captivity to beings). Not only, then, would we have to trace the roots of metaphysics to the ontological soil in which it thrives, but we would have to step back into the opening in which the ground of being is prepared. While metaphysics may well think of beings with respect to their being, such that being is thought in relation to beings (not as "being itself"), not even the ontological difference will allow us to think of being without beings, even if it is not thought theologically. Instead, we would have to appeal to a pre-ontological difference, in which being is thought in relation to nothing: a nihilistic difference that, from the start, was seen to be different from all other differences—as if nothing makes no difference at all and, as such, makes all the difference.

Insofar as the original distinctiveness of being is determined in its difference from nothing, it is based on the claim that, unlike other differences, being does not have an opposite, so long as we are clear that nothing is nothing. In that case, while this may set ontology in motion and initiate the singular priority of being in Western philosophy, it is actually nothing that makes the difference here, albeit in its nihilation: makes the difference between being and nothing different from those differences in which different elements are opposed to one another (hot to cold, moist to dry, etc.). If nothing cannot be thought of as the opposite of being, it is because nothing nihilates itself and, in so doing, creates an opening in which being is determined, seemingly without opposition. In that event, what we face in the creation of ontology is the original nihilation of nothing in the name of being: in a difference that nihilates itself insofar as it is drawn through its denial as a difference.

If ontology represses nothing as surely as metaphysics forgets being, then how are we to retrace nothing in a nihilation that takes place in the face of being: in its self-effacement, given that we would expect nothing less of nothing? If "nothing" holds the place of "being" as a sign that stands (in) for it, ironically (even if appropriately) designating what is missing in the metaphysical tradition, then how are we, at the end of philosophy, to mark what has been repressed in the name of being from the start, assuming that the founding of Western ontology entails an original exploitation of nothing's nihilation?

THINKING NOTHING EPIGRAPHICALLY

[T]he essence of nihilism points us toward a realm that demands a different vocabulary . . . Accordingly, a thoughtful look ahead into this realm can write "being" only in the following way: ̶b̶e̶i̶n̶g̶. (GA 9, 401–11/PA, 310)

In the end, we must think of nothing not just as an opening to being (when the veil is parted) or even as an opening in it (as a hole in the ground) but as an opening through which being happens (as an event) in an original nihilation. The nihilistic operation that is at work in the naming of "being" in Western philosophy is graphically marked in the marginal comments that Heidegger will later make to the Introduction to "What Is Metaphysics?," presumably included after his writing of a letter addressed "To the Question of Being" and published in 1955. As infamous as the claim that "nothing nothings," Heidegger's revolutionary crossing out of "being" is directed to an abysmal connection that is opened up through the ×, in what amounts to a graphic description of the relation between being and nothing. As an editorial indication of the "nihilation" of a word, the × is to be read as an epigraph of nothing, marked by what would otherwise operate as a self-deleting sign. In this case, however, the × is left in the text, and not simply as a sign of deletion but in a nihilation of "being" that is performed in the act of writing. In that (historic) event, nothing is not thought verbally but through an inscription that "de-scribes" being in a nihilistic epigraphy that marks the withdrawal of what Heidegger has taken to be the key word of Western philosophy.

In the graphic depiction of ̶b̶e̶i̶n̶g̶, the ×ing out of "being" is not a mere negation, even if it brings the history of both metaphysics and ontology to an end. Instead, the × is designed to operate as the sign of a crossing (over and out) that points the way to Heidegger's Fourfold of earth, sky, divinities, and mortals. As such, it marks an opening between ontological and mythopoetic vocabularies in what has become a bi-textual corpus. Consequently, if the depletion of being completes its history through an inscription of nothing that points to its departing into the *Geviert*, then the reference to "mortals" should remind us that, even in the Fourfold, death will operate as "the shrine of nothing." In the end, then, we might return to the beginning of SZ, executing its promise for "a destruction of the history of ontology" by remarking on the way in which nothing might be (re)inscribed into the text. For by ×ing out every sign of being in a radical revision of SZ, we would inevitably have to describe our own ~~being~~ as *Da~~sein~~* in a signature act of nihilation.

40

ONTOTHEOLOGY
Iain Thomson

Understanding "ontotheology," I have long argued, provides a skeleton key to Heidegger's later thinking, unlocking the door to that work in a way that shows it to be much more unified, coherent, and defensible than previously recognized.[1] Simplifying that story here, I briefly explain how Heidegger's understanding of Western metaphysics as ontotheology emerges as one of the deepest lessons of his longstanding deconstruction of the history of being (section 1) and how it justifies his ontological critique of the nihilistic spread of our late-modern technological understanding of being (section 2). I then show how this critical understanding of ontotheology as the dual core of the tradition of Western metaphysics in general—and as the basis of our own nihilistic epoch of late-modern technologization in particular—motivates Heidegger's own positive vision of a genuinely meaningful postmodernity (section 3), and conclude by addressing a cluster of common misunderstandings of his view (section 4).

ONTOTHEOLOGY AS THE DUAL CORE OF WESTERN METAPHYSICS

The later Heidegger's famous "history of being" focuses on the way Western humanity's

understanding of being—that is, our most basic sense of what it means for anything to be—gets disclosed, focused, transmitted, and transformed over time. The history of being thus presupposes the (initially vertigo and so resistance inducing) thesis I call ontological historicity. Ontological historicity is simply the insight that humanity's basic sense of "reality" changes with time. As Heidegger puts it, "what one takes to be 'the real' is something that comes to be only on the basis of the essential history of being itself" (NII, 376/NIV, 232). Heidegger takes this insight into historicity over from Hegel (who similarly sought to chart humanity's unfolding "shapes of spirit"), but purges the idea of Hegel's implicit teleology and refocuses it to fit his own understanding of Western philosophy as concerned centrally (albeit unknowingly) to understand what it means to be.

The fundamental historical changes in humanity's "understanding of being" are accomplished by the metaphysical tradition.[2] Heidegger's critique of the "nihilism" (or meaninglessness) that Western metaphysics increasingly generates, however, tends to obscure the pride of place he in fact assigns to metaphysics in establishing and transforming our basic sense of being: "Metaphysics grounds an age in that, through a specific interpretation of what is . . ., it gives the age the ground of its essential form" (GA 5, 75/QCT, 115/OBT, 57). Here Heidegger advances the thesis I call *ontological holism*: Because everything intelligible *is* in some way, if you change our historical conception of what "isness" itself is, you thereby set in motion a transformation in our sense of everything. Hence: "Western humanity, in all its comportment toward entities, and that means also toward itself, is in every respect sustained and guided by metaphysics" (GA 6.2, 309/NIV, 205). By focusing Western humanity's historically unfolding understanding of what "is-ness" is, metaphysics plays a foundational role in establishing and transforming our very sense of the intelligibility of all things, ourselves included. How exactly does Western metaphysics accomplish this task?

In a word, *ontotheologies* are what focus and disseminate Western humanity's basic sense of what it means to be. What, then, is an "ontotheology," and how does it allow metaphysics to focus and transform our historically shifting understanding of being? An ontotheology is basically a *double* answer to the question, what (and how) *is* an entity? To put it as simply as possible, if you think of reality as a beach ball (like Parmenides' "well-rounded sphere"), then an ontotheology is an attempt to grasp the beach ball from the inside-out and the outside-in at the same time. Ontotheologies doubly "ground" the entire intelligible order by uncovering both its innermost "ontological" core and its outermost "theological" expression, linking these antipodal perspectives together so as to ground an historical age's sense of reality from the inside-out and the outside-in simultaneously. In this way, our changing understanding of "the being of entities" (i.e. of what and how all entities *are*) get shaped

and reshaped by the ontotheological tradition running from Plato to Nietzsche.

The best way to see this is to reconstruct the historical emergence of the ontotheological core of metaphysics (a task we can only briefly summarize here).[3] The ontological and theological paths of Western metaphysics begin when Thales and Anaximander understand the same question—namely, What is the final "ground" (*archê*) of reality?—in diametrically different ways by seeking this ground in reality's innermost core and outermost horizon, respectively. By understanding the ground of reality as "water," Thales is the West's first *ontologist*. Thales teaches us to look within what-is in order to discover, at its deepest core, that final ground out of which everything else is composed, and so to understand being in terms of this final underlying ground (the method our physicists still pursue). Taking the opposite approach (which we might now call "cosmological"), Anaximander seeks to grasp the ground of all things by getting outside them to that ultimate source from which they finally derive. Taking up this God's eye perspective, Anaximander seeks to vindicate the meaningfulness of the cosmic order as a whole—which he does, but only by denying that finite existence is intrinsically meaningful (to exist as a discrete entity is to violate the undifferentiated source of all individual things, to which we thus justly return by ceasing to be). Proclaiming his nihilistic cosmodicy from the God's eye perspective, Anaximander becomes, in Heidegger's terms, the first *theologian*.

It took a thinker as great as Plato, Heidegger's "first metaphysician," to give us the first unified *ontotheology*. Plato implicitly combines Thales' and Anaximander's opposite ways of grasping the "ground" of what-is in his own doctrine of the forms, which explains both the underlying unity of all entities and their highest fulfillment outside the finite world. The form of beauty in the *Symposium*, for example, explains what unifies all the different kinds of beautiful things; they are all imperfect instantiations of the perfect form of beauty. As this suggests, it also explains the highest fulfillment of beauty: the perfect form of beauty itself, an eternal form compared to which nothing in this imperfect, temporal world can ever measure up. By again condemning the finite world of human experience by comparing it to a standard unrealizable in this life, Plato deeply embeds Anaximander's "otherworldly nihilism" into the theological perspective (Christianity later takes over Plato's transcendence-valorizing, finitude-denigrating perspective—for example, by condemning this world as a "vale of tears" compared to the heavenly afterlife—thereby becoming "Platonism for 'the people,'" as Nietzsche famously observed. Yet, even Nietzsche himself inadvertently falls victim to this nihilism of otherworldliness when he suggests that existence cannot be affirmed without the "unknowable" doctrine of eternal recurrence).[4]

The ontotheological duality implicit in Plato's forms becomes explicit when Aristotle makes it into his conception of primary and secondary substance, or "thatness" and "whatness" (influentially reversing the priority Plato assigned the rational idea over its empirical embodiment). The medieval scholastics transform Aristotle's conception into *existentia* and *essentia*, thereby inscribing this fundamental ontotheological distinction between the "existence" and the "essence" of entities into the very core of the metaphysical tradition of conceiving being. This basic metaphysical duality then continues all the way until Nietzsche. In Heidegger's controversial reading (which is undeniably reductive but also, I have argued, deeply revealing), Nietzsche both completes and destroys the metaphysical tradition of ontotheological foundationalism when he conceives "the totality of entities as such" as essentially "will-to-power" existing in an endless cycle of "eternal recurrence."[5] As Heidegger writes:

> The mode in which entities (whose *essentia* is the will to power) in their entirety exist, their *existentia*, is "the eternal return of the same." The two fundamental terms of Nietzsche's metaphysics, "will to power" and "eternal return of the same," determine entities in their being in accordance with the perspective that has led metaphysics since antiquity, the *ens qua ens* in the sense of *essentia* and *existentia*. (GA 5, 237–8/OBT, 177)

In sum, metaphysics understands being (*ens qua ens*, being as being) in terms of the being *of entities* (and thereby misses "being as such," a crucial point to which we will return), and it understands the being of entities *ontotheologically* by grasping entities in terms of *both* their essence *and* their existence, that is, both ontologically (from the inside-out) and theologically (from the outside-in). In this way, metaphysics grasps reality floor-to-ceiling, microscopically and telescopically, or, in a word, *ontotheologically*.

Ontotheologies "determine entities in their being" (as Heidegger puts it in the passage above) when they doubly anchor an epoch's historical understanding of being. Ontotheologies do this only when they *succeed* in grasping reality from both extremes at once, temporarily establishing both the microscopic depths and ultimate telescopic expression of what-is. Successful ontotheologies uncover and link the deepest and broadest ways of understanding what and how entities *are*, thereby *doubly grounding* the understanding of being that an age finds itself unable to get beneath or beyond for a time (the time of an "epoch"). Ontotheologies thus supply neither the unshakeable and so unchanging foundation (*Grund*) they seek, nor merely offer us the endless flux of a groundless abyss (*Ab-grund*); instead, they yield a "perhaps necessary appearance [*Schein*] of ground" (*Un-grund*) (GA 40, 5/ IM, 3) for each historical age.

As a result, historical intelligibility takes shape neither as a chaotic Heraclitean flux (*pace* Derrida) nor as an unbroken Parmenidean unity (*pace* Rorty).[6] Instead, according to Heidegger's punctuated equilibrium view of historicity (a view I call *ontological epochality*), our changing understanding of being takes shape as a series of three drastically different but internally unified and relatively coherent, overlapping historical "epochs": the ancient, the medieval, and the modern. (In the end, Heidegger subdivides the ancient epoch into the Presocratic and the Platonic, and the modern into the early modern and the late modern, for a total of five ages in the Western "history of being," five overlapping historical *constellations of intelligibility*.) In each of these "epochs," the overwhelming floodwaters of being are temporarily dammed ("epoch," as readers of Husserl know, comes from the Greek word for "to hold back"—or, as Derrida liked to say, "to put in parentheses") so that an island of historical intelligibility can arise out of the river of historicity. Ontotheologies are what build, undermine, and rebuild these dams, or (if you prefer) what put the parentheses around an epoch, temporarily shielding its unifying sense of being from the corrosive sands of time.

OUR LATE-MODERN ONTOTHEOLOGY AS THE ENGINE OF NIHILISTIC TECHNOLOGIZATION

With this background sketch in place, we can now understand the most pressing problem to which the metaphysical tradition has led us, namely, the growing nihilism of our current, "technological" understanding of being. One of Heidegger's deepest but most often overlooked insights is that our late-modern, Nietzschean ontotheology generates the nihilistic technologization in whose currents we remain caught.

Our late-modern age is what Heidegger calls "enframing" (*Gestell*), and (like all other ages in the history of being) it is unified by its underlying understanding of being. Our "technological" understanding of being follows directly from our Nietzschean ontotheology; we tend to understand the being of all entities as eternally recurring will to power— that is, as an unending disaggregation and reaggregation of forces with no end beyond the perpetuation of force itself. (If I press you on what this table is, for example, you will probably end up saying that it is an arrangement of subatomic particles moving so fast that the table appears solid, when in fact it is just a rather temporary and empty form that these underlying forces have taken.) Insofar as we implicitly understand what-is through this ontotheological framework, not only do we dissolve being into becoming, but we tend to relate to and so transform all entities into mere "resources" (*Bestand*), intrinsically meaningless stuff standing by to be optimized, ordered, and enhanced with maximal efficiency.

As this Nietzschean, technological ontotheology becomes more entrenched, this historical transformation of beings into mere resources becomes more pervasive, and so

322

(according to the first law of phenomenology, the distance of the near) it increasingly eludes our critical notice. Indeed, we late-moderns come to treat ourselves in the very same terms that underlie our technological reframing of the world. No longer modern subjects seeking to master an objective world, we are turning the techniques developed for controlling the objective world back on ourselves, and this objectification of the subject is transforming us into just another intrinsically meaningless resource to be optimized, ordered, and enhanced with maximal efficiency—whether cosmetically, psychopharmacologically, genetically, aesthetically, educationally, or otherwise "technologically."[7] The deepest problem with this "technologization" of reality is the nihilistic understanding of being that underlies and drives it: Nietzsche's ontotheology dissolves being into *nothing* but "sovereign becoming," an endless circulation of forces, and in so doing, it denies that things have any inherent nature, any genuine meaning capable of resisting this slide into nihilism (any qualitative *worth*, for example, that cannot be quantified and represented in terms of mere "values").

BEYOND ONTOTHEOLOGY: A GENUINELY MEANINGFUL POSTMODERNITY

Every previous historical understanding of being understands being reductively as only "the being of entities," and thereby forgets "being as such," a dynamic *ontological excess* that both informs and partly escapes all the ontotheologies (indeed, all the concepts) that attempt to fix it in place once and for all. I have argued that this insight into "being as such"—that is, the recognition that

there is something—which is not a thing, not an entity—that lends itself to and yet also exceeds every metaphysical conception of "the being of entities"—constitutes the sine qua non of the "later" Heidegger (and the core of the so-called turn). Heidegger struggled throughout his life to clarify this crucial phenomenological insight, continually seeking new names with which to attune us to this dynamic and never finally circumscribable ontological excessiveness, this inexhaustible "abundance" that, as he nicely put it, "gives itself and refuses itself simultaneously" (GA 9, 335/PA, 255).[8]

What, then, is the difference between our late-modern technological understanding of being and the genuinely *post*modern understanding of being for which Heidegger calls? A truly *postmodern* understanding of being needs to push through and beyond the late-modern understanding of entities as *nothing* but forces caught in an endless process of becoming. For Heidegger, we do that when we come to see this "nothing" not as nothing at all but, instead, as the "*noth-ing* of the nothing"—that is, as the way in which we post-Nietzscheans first encounter that inherently pluralistic phenomenological excess that makes intelligibility possible. The crucial difference—indeed, the very difference between the "danger" of nihilistic technologization and the "promise" of a meaningful postmodernity—is that, whereas Nietzsche dissolves being into *nothing* but becoming, Heidegger sees this "nothing" not as empty of meaning but as the not-yet-a-thing, the phenomenological "noth-ing" whereby the abundance of being offers us its inchoate hints of meaningful possibilities. Rather than preconceiving reality as an inherently meaningless conglomeration of forces ready to be reshaped to fit our preconceived ideas or to receive whatever values we project onto it,

Heidegger thought that we need instead to learn to recognize and begin to do justice to the ways "be-ing" continues to offer these meaningful possibilities to us.

In other words, a truly postmodern understanding requires us to recognize that, when approached with a poetic openness and respect, things push back against us, making subtle but undeniable claims on us. We need to acknowledge and respond creatively and responsibly to these claims if we do not want to deny the source of genuine meaning in the world. For, only meanings that are at least partly independent of us and so not entirely within our control—meanings not simply up to us to bestow and rescind at will—can provide us with the kind of touchstones around which we can build meaningful lives and loves. Heidegger sometimes describes our encounter with such genuine meanings as an "event of enowning" (*Ereignis*), a significant event in which we come into our own as world-disclosers by creatively enabling things come into their own, just as Michelangelo came into his own as a sculptor by creatively responding to the veins and fissures in a particularly rich piece of marble in order to bring forth his "David," just as a woodworker comes into her own as a woodworker by learning to respond to the subtle weight and grain of an individual piece of wood, or as teachers comes into their own as teachers by learning to recognize, cultivate, and so help develop the particular talents and capacities of individual students.

This poetic openness to that which pushes back in reality is what we could call a sensitivity to *the texture of the text*, which is "all around us" (GA 77, 227/CPC, 147). (This is the seditious way I would like to re-Heideggerize Derrida's famous aperçu, "there is nothing outside the text.") The current of technologization tend to sweep right past the texture of the texts all around us (and can even threaten to render us oblivious to it-most plausibly, if genetic enhancement inadvertently eliminates our defining capacity for creative world-disclosure).[9] But Heidegger is clear that once we recognize this technological current, we can learn to resist it, and so develop a "free relation to technology" in which it becomes possible to thoughtfully use technologies against nihilistic technologization, as we do when we use a camera, microscope, telescope, or even glasses in order to creatively help bring out something there in the world that we might not otherwise have seen, a synthesizer or computer to make a new kind of music that helps us develop our sense of what genuinely matters to us, or when we use a word processor to bring out our sense of what is really there in the issues and texts that most concern us, and so on.

GOD AND POSTMODERNITY BEYOND THE FATALISTIC MISREADING

Let me briefly address a common misunderstanding of the view outlined here. That Heidegger thinks metaphysics *pervasively* shapes historical intelligibility does not mean that he thinks there is no way to get beyond metaphysics (or that nothing escapes its reach), so that we are doomed to be its helpless victims and unwitting perpetrators.[10] On the contrary, once we learn to discern the specific metaphysical currents in which our late-modern age remains caught (by recognizing the ontotheology that continues to drive these currents), it becomes possible to attend to the crucial phenomena that resist the nihilistic metaphysics of late-modernity,

324

phenomena that can thus help lead us into a genuinely meaningful postmodernity.[11]

According to Heidegger's history of being, our basic understanding of the being of entities changes drastically over time and yet is neither a constantly shifting medium we can alter at will nor an unchanging monolith over which we exert no influence. The role human beings play in the disclosure and transformation of our basic sense of reality occupies a middle ground between these poles of voluntaristic constructivism and quietistic fatalism. Heidegger is primarily concerned to combat the former, "subjectivistic" error—that is, the error of thinking that human subjects are the sole source of intelligibility and so can reshape our understanding of being at will—because that is the dangerous error toward which our modern and late-modern ways of understanding being increasingly incline us. As a result, his rhetorical exaggerations often lead readers mistakenly to conclude that he makes the converse error of fatalistic "quietism" himself (and thus that he thinks humanity is completely passive with respect to our "fundamental metaphysical positions" concerning "the truth of entities as such and as a whole," at best able to prepare for some vague postmodern understanding of being whose contours we cannot yet anticipate). That, however, is a superficial misreading of his view.

Indeed, Heidegger's oft-quoted line from his famous *Der Spiegel* interview, "Only another God can save us," is probably the most widely misunderstood sentence in his entire work. By another "God," Heidegger does not mean some otherworldly creator or transcendental agent but, instead, another *understanding of being*.[12] He means, quite specifically, a post-metaphysical, post-epochal understanding of "the being of entities" in terms of "being as such," to use

his philosophical terms of art. Heidegger himself equates the last God with a postmodern understanding of being, for example, when he poses the question "as to whether being will once more be capable of a God, [that is,] as to whether the essence of the truth of being will make a more primordial claim upon the essence of humanity" (GA 5, 112/ OBT, 85).[13] Here Heidegger asks whether our current understanding of being is capable of being led beyond itself, by giving rise to other world-disclosive events that would allow human beings to understand the being of entities neither as modern "objects" to be mastered and controlled nor as late-modern, inherently meaningless "resources" standing by for optimization but, instead, as things that always mean more than we are capable of expressing conceptually (and so fixing once and for all in an ontotheology).[14]

Such exemplary disclosive events are what Heidegger calls an *Ereignis* or "event of enowning." In such events, entities, the being of entities, and Dasein all come into their own by disclosing being as such. For example, Van Gogh's painting of "A Pair of Shoes" (1886) allows Van Gogh to come into his own as a painter by bringing painting into its own (as Derrida saw, Heidegger's Van Gogh paints the truth of painting itself by painting the *a-lêtheiac* or earth-worlding disclosure that painting *is*), and the artwork also discloses the being of entities in its ownmost by allowing us to understand being not simply as "equipmentality" (as in division 1 of *Being and Time*) but, instead, to recognize even the understanding of being as equipment as a partial understanding of being made possible by a deeper phenomenon it does not exhaust, namely, being as such.[15] In other words, Heidegger thinks that only an understanding of being as both informing and exceeding (yielding and overflowing, lending itself to and withdrawing from) all those efforts, practical and theoretical, by which we disclose our historical worlds can move us beyond the nihilism of modern "subjectivism" and late-modern "enframing" into a genuinely meaningful postmodernity.

Rather than despairing of the possibility of such an inherently pluralistic, postmodern understanding of being ever arriving, moreover, Heidegger thought it was *already* here (as suggested earlier, historical ages *overlap*), embodied in the "futural" artwork of artists like Hölderlin and Van Gogh, simply needing to be cultivated and disseminated in myriad forms (clearly not limited to the domain of art, *pace* Badiou) in order to "save" the ontologically abundant "earth" (with its inexhaustible plurality of enduringly meaningful possibilities) from the devastation of technological obliviousness, thereby leading us beyond many of the deepest problems we now face. When Heidegger stresses that thinking is at best "preparatory" (*Vorbereiten*), what he means is that great thinkers and poets "go ahead and make ready" (*im Voraus bereiten*), that is, that they are ambassadors, emissaries, or envoys of the future, first postmodern arrivals who, like Van Gogh, disseminate and so prepare for this postmodern future with "the unobtrusive sowing of sowers" (GA 5, 210–11/OBT, 158).[16]

NOTES AND REFERENCES

[1] Space constraints require this chapter to simplify views developed in Iain Thomson, *Heidegger on Ontotheology: Technology and the Politics of Education* (Cambridge: Cambridge University Press, 2005) and Iain Thomson, *Heidegger, Art, and Postmodernity* (Cambridge: Cambridge University Press,

2011), so I refer to the relevant chapters of those books below.

[2] Heidegger thinks great poetry and other world-disclosive artworks first embody the understanding of being than a metaphysician universalizes in a successful, epoch-grounding ontotheology (see Thomson, *Heidegger, Art, and Postmodernity*, chs 1–2).

[3] On the historical emergence of metaphysics as ontotheology, see Thomson, *Heidegger on Ontotheology*, ch. 1. On the links that join ontology and theology, see Thomson, *Heidegger, Art, and Postmodernity*, ch. 1.

[4] See Friedrich Nietzsche, *Beyond Good and Evil*, trans. W. Kaufmann (New York: Vintage, 1966), 3. On how Nietzsche falls victim to the very otherworldly nihilism he diagnosed (and for a partial defense of Heidegger's controversial interpretation of Nietzsche), see Thomson, *Heidegger, Art, and Postmodernity*, ch. 1; and Iain Thomson, "Transcendence and the Problem of Otherworldly Nihilism: Taylor, Heidegger, Nietzsche," *Inquiry*, 54.2 (2011), 140–59.

[5] Nietzsche ended the dual foundationalism of ontotheology by postulating that reality is nothing but forces struggling against other forces so as to maximally perpetuate force itself, and that reality exists (seen from the God's eye view) as an endless cycle of cosmic becoming. That Nietzsche thus cuts the strings of foundationalism does not stop his ontotheology from becoming the groundless ground for our own late-modern age.

[6] See, for example, Jacques Derrida, *Who's Afraid of Philosophy? Right to Philosophy 1*, trans. J. Plug (Stanford: Stanford University Press, 2002), 123. Whereas Derrida was skeptical of Heideggerian *epochality* because he thought the unity it claims to read off history was in fact a distorting philosophical projection, Rorty made it clear (in a personal conversation) that he was skeptical of *historicity*, since he did not believe human beings had changed much in the last 2,700 years. Rorty said that if you time-travelled back to ancient Greece and could speak the language, everyone would be pretty much like us. By contrast, Derrida sometimes suggests that even among contemporaries, individual idiolects are so pervasive that genuine

understanding, if it occurs, is an amazing accomplishment. See, for example, Jacques Derrida, *Monolingualism of the Other; or, The Prosthesis of Origin*, trans. P. Mensah (Stanford: Stanford University Press, 1998).

7 On this crucial difference between modernity and late-modernity and its *dangerous* technological consequences, see Thomson, *Heidegger on Ontotheology*, ch. 2 and Thomson, *Heidegger, Art, and Postmodernity*, chs 2 and 7.

8 The later Heidegger's search for names with which to convey "being as such" yielded a long succession of different terms of art for this "be-ing" that gives itself to intelligibility ("the nothing," "earth," "be-ing," "being written under a "cross-wise striking-through," the "it" of "there is/it gives [*es gibt*]") as well as for the *way* "it" gives itself (the "noth-ing" of the nothing, "*alêtheia*" or "dis-closedness," "the *presencing* of presence," the "difference," the "fourfold," even the "event of enowning [*Ereignis*]"). With such poetic names Heidegger tries to neither separate nor hypostatize this be-ing and its giving (by privileging presence over presencing, for example, or by treating intelligibility as the gift of a given entity, such as an ontotheological creator God). In so doing, he seeks to get behind the ontotheological tradition to recover an encounter with that inexhaustibly pluralistic "non-identical same" that metaphysics sought to bifurcate and determine once and for all (see Thomson, *Heidegger on Ontotheology*, ch. 1).

9 See note 10.

10 My ambiguous parenthetical might be a bit misleading because Heidegger thinks that *the nothing*—that is, the active "nothing" of the nothing, the subtle and inconspicuous hints of that which is not (yet) a thing—*does* escape the reach of modern metaphysics and so can help lead us beyond it. That the reach of our late-modern ontotheology could become total is what Heidegger calls the greatest danger, and it is likely to happen only if, in our ongoing quest for genetic optimization, we unintentionally engineer away our essential capacity for world-disclosure. (Heidegger's dystopian vision is lent some support by the recent spate of reports suggesting that intellectual performance enhancing drugs diminish

creative thinking.) Yet, Heidegger also though that as this danger grows, so does the promise of a postmodern understanding of being. On the "noth-ing," see Thomson, *Heidegger, Art, and Postmodernity*, ch. 3, and see ch. 7 for the relation of this nothing to the greatest danger and the saving power. On Heidegger's critique of technologization, see Thomson, *Heidegger on Ontotheology*, ch. 2. See the fatalistic misreading in, for example, Dana Belu and Andrew Feenberg, "Heidegger's Aporetic Ontology of Technology," *Inquiry*, 53.1 (2010), 1–19.

11 See Thomson, *Heidegger, Art, and Postmodernity*, chs 3 and 7.

12 Heidegger writes: "The Last God: Wholly other than the past ones and especially other than the Christian one" (GA 65, 403/CP2, 319).

13 Here the "truth of being" is shorthand for the way an understanding of "the being of entities" (i.e. a metaphysical understanding of "the truth concerning entities as such and as a whole" or, in a word, an *ontotheology*) works to anchor and shape the unfolding of an historical constellation of intelligibility. Its "essence" is that inexhaustible source of historical intelligibility the later Heidegger calls "being as such," an actively *a-lêtheiac* (i.e. ontologically "dis-closive") Ur-phenomenon metaphysics eclipses with its ontotheological fixation on finally determining "the being of entities." (That "being as such" lends itself to a series of different historical understandings of "the being of entities" rightly suggests that it *exceeds* every ontotheological understanding of the being of entities.) The "essence of humanity" refers to *Dasein*'s definitive world-disclosive ability to give being as such a place to "be" (to happen or take place); it refers, that is, to the *poietic* and maieutic activities by which human beings creatively disclose the inconspicuous and inchoate hints offered us by "the earth" and so help bring genuine meanings into the light of the world.

14 That the "God" needed to "save us" is a postmodern understanding of being is one of the central theses of Thomson, *Heidegger, Art, and Postmodernity* (see esp. chs 1, 3, 6, 7, and 8). On Heidegger's view of God and religion, see also Thomson, "Transcendence and the Problem of Otherworldly Nihilism."

15 See Jacques Derrida, *The Truth in Painting* (Chicago: University of Chicago Press, 1987), discussed in Thomson, *Heidegger, Art, and Postmodernity*, ch. 3.

16 As this suggests, historical ages are not simply dispensed by some superhuman agent to a passively awaiting humanity. Rather, actively vigilant artists and particularly receptive thinkers pick up on broader tendencies happening independently of their own wills (in the world around them or at the margins of their cultures, for example) and then make these insights central through their artworks and philosophies (see Thomson, *Heidegger, Art, and Postmodernity*, chs 1–3).

41

RELIGION AND THEOLOGY
Ben Vedder

During his whole live Heidegger has been in discussion with religion and theology. But the way he did it is not easy to make understandable from a classic philosophical point of view, because Heidegger criticizes the classic metaphysical philosophy, as we all know. A dominant tendency of a philosophical understanding of religion is to make religion itself into a part of philosophy. This is particularly apparent where all forms of religion get absorbed into an ontotheological philosophy. In such cases religion is understood from a concept of God, which is, as a philosophical idea, the beginning and the end of philosophical rationality. Hegel's philosophy is perhaps the clearest example of this tendency. When ontotheology is taken up in this way, however, certain possibilities for understanding religion are foreclosed. But regarding Heidegger it is a question whether he speaks as a philosopher or as a theologian. This problem is most clear in Heidegger's exclamation: "Only a God can save us!"[1]

How can a philosopher exclaim that only a God can save us? It is my view that Heidegger's thinking on religion occupies a place between the forms of poetic and philosophical speaking. To understand the poetic aspect of Heidegger's language, one must turn to his interpretations of Hölderlin (EHP). And to give his philosophical expression its proper context one must refer to his "Letter on 'Humanism,'" wherein religion is located in the neighborhood of the thinking of being (PA, 239–76). Yet religion maintains its own tension with regard to both sides: if we grasp religion completely from a (ontotheological) philosophical point of view we tend to neutralize it; on the other hand, if we conceive it simply as poetic expression, we tend to be philosophically indifferent to it. These tensions urge us to take up the question of Heidegger's position. It turns out that Heidegger's thinking is, in the end, a theological thinking of a specific kind. It is a theology in which he avoids every connection to an ontotheological concept of God. His thinking of being tends toward a poetic theology of naming the gods, which is both a praising and an invocation of them. According to Heidegger the thinking of being is a movement no longer in accordance with the thinking of faith or of divinity (*Gottheit*). Each of these is heterogeneous in relation to the other. The experience of the thinking of being manifests itself rather as a topological disposition, that is, as an indication of a place characterized by availability. It is a topological disposition for waiting for, though not expecting, the reception of being, as a place for the happening of being. Therefore Heidegger states that he does not know God; he can only describe

God's absence. His atheistic philosophy (in the sense of an ontotheology) maintains an openness toward the possible reception of religious gods.

The young Heidegger grew up as a seminarian in a ahistorical neoscholasticism. Only later, after he stopped studying theology, he became more interested in the historicity of religion through his reading of Friedrich Schleiermacher. He started to reject a theoretical approach to religion while nevertheless endeavoring to preserve the piety of philosophy—including the piety of the philosophy of religion. In a certain sense one could call this the prehistorical Heidegger.[2] The term prehistorical refers to the timeless character of scholastic and neo-scholastic Catholicism, the intellectual environment out of which Heidegger emerged, and the period prior to his adoption of a historical perspective. But at the same time he develops a persistent questioning toward the ontological and temporal as the "earlier" and "prior." This persistent questioning he understands as piety.

After Heidegger had finished his studies in theology and philosophy he became more interested in phenomenology. Where the object of phenomenology is concerned, he attempts to remain radically atheistic, yet on the other hand, he seeks to be pious and devoted when it comes to this same object. The pious person here is the devoted ascetic who understands his object as it demands to be understood, that is, from out of its factical character. Only when philosophy has become fundamentally atheistic can it decisively choose life in its very facticity, and thereby make this an object for itself. Because philosophy is concerned with the facticity of life, the philosophy of religion must be understood from that same perspective. For Heidegger the very idea of philosophy of

religion (especially if it makes no reference to the facticity of the human being) is pure nonsense.[3] Such nonsense evolves out of a lack of piety, that is, a merely theoretical approach that fails to attune itself to the facticity of life. Thus, Heidegger's endeavors to destruct ontotheology have their roots in his experience that theistic and theoretical conceptuality is not appropriate to understand the facticity of life.

Through his explication of the notion of historicity, Heidegger was able to find a path leading out of the closed religious world in which he was raised. This rupture takes place with his encounter with Schleiermacher. Through Schleiermacher's thinking, Heidegger was offered the possibility of isolating the religious as the absolute; and in so doing, he was led away from both theology and theoretical philosophy in his thinking. Out of this engagement, Heidegger was able to conclude that the religious is none other than the historical, due to the fact that the radicality of a personal position is only to be uncovered within history.

Heidegger directed his philosophy toward the facticity of human being, which will be developed as the historicality of Dasein. The attempt to think facticity was his guiding interest during this early period, and it is from the standpoint of this interest that his approach to religion must be understood. As the winter semester approached in 1920, Heidegger announced his upcoming lecture course, entitled "Introduction to the Phenomenology of Religion" (PRL). Heidegger asks whether the kairological moment, which is important in early Christianity, can be preserved within the history of the actualization of life and the unpredictability of the *eschaton*. It could potentially be understood as a possibility that we ourselves have or something that is under our control, so that the future that withdraws from us becomes part of our own planning. Yet, if it were to be understood thus, the specific character of the *kairos* would then be lost in a totalizing form of calculation. The future would then be conceived in the end as a horizon of consciousness out of which experiences evolve in a certain order. For what takes place with regard to the content in the moment of the *kairos* can itself never be deduced.

Heidegger's interpretation of Saint Paul and of Augustine is an elucidation of this. Heidegger's quest for truth is no longer devoted to the highest being, as was the case during his early studies in Freiburg. Rather, Christian religion has to be understood out of its own situation and out of the presuppositions contained within it. It should not be taken up from a philosophical framework, as if from the standpoint of some highest being, precisely because the philosophical idea of a highest being hinders our understanding of facticity, and with this, religion as an expression of facticity. In Heidegger's thinking, the orientation toward the highest is instead reformulated as a historical orientation. We see this change actualized in Heidegger's earliest writings, and it involves as well the philosophical paradigm with which he approaches religion. What we are left with, then, is a religion that is an expression of historicity.

Heidegger looks for a better philosophy, but not for a new faith that would be a faith without philosophy. In his complete devotion to philosophy, he distances himself from religious philosophical approaches, in which a religious a priori is supposed. He distances himself as well from a conciliation of faith and reason that would reduce faith to reason, as in the philosophies of Kant and Hegel. Nor does he assume the harmony of faith and reason at which Thomistic philosophy aims. Instead, the metaphysical paradigm is put into perspective, where one can see how it opposes the understanding of facticity. Heidegger seeks an atheistic philosophy, or at the very least, a philosophy without an a priori concept of God.

Heidegger understands faith as the natural enemy of philosophy (PA, 53).

Faith appears as a possibility of existence, yet one that implies death for the possibility of the existence of philosophy. The fundamental opposition of two possibilities of existence cannot be realized by one person in one and the same moment. Yet neither excludes a factical and existentiell taking seriously of the other. This does not mean that the scientists in each respective field must behave like enemies. The existentiell opposition between faith, on the one hand, and philosophical self-understanding, on the other, must be effective in its scientific design and in its explications. And this must be done in such a way that each meets the other with mutual respect. This can be undertaken more easily where one sees more sharply the different points of departure. Christian philosophy, therefore, is in Heidegger's view a "square circle."

Nevertheless, one can thoughtfully question and work through the world of Christian experience, the world of faith. This would be, then, theology. Heidegger sees in theology's dependence on philosophy a lack of greatness in theology itself. Only ages that really no longer believe in the true greatness of the task of theology arrive at the pernicious opinion that, through a supposed refurbishment with the help of philosophy, a theology can be gained or even replaced, and can be made more palatable to the need of the age. Philosophy for originally Christian faith is foolishness (IM, 8). If Heidegger rejects the philosophical paradigm with which religion is usually approached, the question of from where stems the ontotheological philosophical approach of religion arises. This ontotheological approach is at work even today. Heidegger sees its origin in Aristotle's philosophy. For Heidegger, Greek philosophy reaches its climax in Aristotle and is decisive for the whole of Western philosophy. Therefore, Aristotle's thinking is a normative point from which the philosophical tradition can be determined more precisely. The well-thought-out way in which Aristotle follows the motive of philosophy marks at the same time the limit of the whole tradition, which becomes visible now as a finite possibility for thinking and as a temporary answer to the question of being.

Already, in his earliest writings, Heidegger emphasizes the relation between ontology and theology in Aristotle's first philosophy. Heidegger sees the metaphysical tradition as an ontotheological tradition that follows from the tendency for philosophy to forget its original motive. This tendency is due to the fact that understanding has its concrete possibility for being actualized in being free from daily concerns, which places the possibility of theorizing against the background of the facticity of life. *Theorein* is the purest movement that life has available to it. Because of this, it is something "God-like." But for Aristotle the idea of the divine did not arise in the explication of something objective that was made accessible in a basic religious experience; the *theion* is rather the expression for the highest being-character that arises in the ontological radicalization of the idea of being.

Being is understood from a normative perspective, from the perspective of the highest way of being. Connected with this is the highest way of moving, which is pure thinking. This also determines the way Christianity speaks about the highest being of God. The question of whether there is ontology without a theology for Heidegger is, however, no longer a question within the domain of philosophy and metaphysics. He determines metaphysical philosophy as ontotheology. The question of being as a question is forgotten in philosophy. Rather, it is within what he calls the domain of "thinking." The motive of philosophy, strictly speaking, has disappeared from philosophy, but it has been preserved in the thinking of being. This domain of thinking is, in a sense, a counter paradigm to philosophy in which the question of being is not answered with an entity that represents the highest way of being, the whole of being and the cause of being.[4]

Heidegger's criticism with regard to the metaphysical concept of God is especially directed toward the concept of God as cause. In the wake of Aristotle, being is understood as *actualitas*. The highest representation of *actualitas* is an entity, which as a determining characteristic has this *actualitas* in the purest way. This means that it is *actus purus*. Being in the first and the purest way is proper to God. Such a metaphysics does not transcend the level of entities, because it does not understand the difference between being and entity (ontological difference). On the one hand, it speaks about being as a characteristic of entities and is only understood as this characteristic (*actualitas* as determination of the dominant understanding of an entity). On the other hand, it sets as the ground of entities another entity, which possesses the criterion for being an entity in the most perfect way. In a certain sense, God is an exemplary instance of being as *actualitas*, of something that actualizes completely. This idea of actualization is also present in the modern ideal of the self-actualization of the human being.

But Heidegger does not understand human being from the perspective of self-actualization. The quest for meaning is a quest for the whole space in which man can exist. This whole cannot become a fixed property. In the end, we are not that which makes us possible, for it is earlier than and prior to us. Man is understood by Heidegger as an entity that cannot appropriate the whole of his conditions of possibility, because he cannot appropriate his temporality that is always earlier.

The implications of the ontotheological structure of metaphysics are worked out on the basis of Heidegger's interpretation of Nietzsche. Heidegger considers Nietzsche, just like all great thinkers in philosophy since Plato, to be an ontotheological philosopher. Entities are only entities out of the unifying principle of the Will to Power according to Nietzsche. Therefore, Nietzsche's metaphysics is, as ontology, at the same time a theology. This metaphysical theology is a specific kind of negative theology, its negativity shown in the pronouncement "God is dead." (QCT, 53–112). Nevertheless it remains metaphysics, be the God living or dead.

Where God is dead, he is absent. This is something different from the denial of God in atheism, which remains tributary to ontotheology. The loss of God, however, is not thought within metaphysics, that is, as ontotheology. Heidegger thinks this experience of the absence of God as an experience of the poets. Metaphysics cannot experience the loss of God because it is theologically structured. For the poet, on the other hand, the absence of God is not a lack; it is not an empty space that needs completion. Nor is it necessary to appeal to the God that one is used to. It is about presenting and holding out the absence of God. The poet can live in a domain of decision where ontology is not necessarily theologically structured, since in poetry the poet has to seek, but not into the divine. In poetry there is no a priori divine entity. It is the poet's care to face up to the lack of God without

fear. With the appearance of godlessness, he must remain near to the God's absence.

In Heidegger's view, what happens in our time is that the ontotheological temple of metaphysics is crumbling; the death of God is a symptom if this crumbling of metaphysics. According to Heidegger and Nietzsche, the death of God is a historical event, which means a history (*Geschichte*), a story. It is an event that makes history. The nature of this history can be continued, be it the history of a God or a hero, but it is a history next to other histories. This history is the history of the bereavement of a God. This does not mean that this history itself has a God, for God is also subjected to the destinies of history (*Geschick*). It is a history that makes history. In Heidegger's view, historicity is connected with the historicality of Dasein. This historicality is still there when God is dead, and even when the human being, as *causa sui*, is dead.

As a counter-paradigm to the metaphysical idea of God, Heidegger introduces the difficult notion of a last God (CP1, 285–93). The last God is totally other to the Christian God, it is a passing God. This presupposes that this God is not explicable from the perspective of entities, whether the entity be anthropological or ontological. Understanding the divine from a perspective or framework in which God is the fulfillment of a maladjusted human need for certainty goes against the possibility of experiencing the last God. The last God is without a reference or presupposition of "something" eternal and unchangeable. This points to a "theology" that is completely historical, because its subject is historical: a passing God. But Heidegger would never call this "theology," because all (metaphysical) theology presupposes the *theos*, the God as an eternally present entity; and it does this so certainly that everywhere where (metaphysical) theology arises, the God already flies.

It is not sufficient to say in the era of nihilism that God is dead or that transcendental values pass away; rather, one must learn to think a God's being, as well as its truth, as passing-by. It is no longer the God of metaphysics or the theistic God of Christianity. It is the metaphysical conceptuality that hinders to think the passing-by God.

As said before the "Letter on 'Humanism'" plays a crucial role with regard to Heidegger's position toward the way he considers notions like the gods and the holy. Here he asks how the thinking of being makes possible the thinking of the divine. It is no accident that Heidegger rejects the reproach of atheism with regard to his thinking. With the existential determination of the essence of the human being, nothing is decided about the "existence of God" or his "non-being" any more than about the possibility or impossibility of gods. He does not speak out about the existence of a God or godhead, but this is because he thinks about the possibility and framework within which something like a God has to be thought.

With regard to the framework of the highest entity and the self-actualized human being, the subjectivistic and anthropological interpretation of humanity is most radically rejected in Heidegger's notion of the fourfold (*Geviert*). The fourfold indicates the unity of earth and sky, divinities and mortals. The divinities are the beckoning messengers of the godhead. Out of the hidden sway of the divinities, the God emerges as what he is, which removes him from any comparison with beings that are present. The mortals are the human beings. But human beings are not mortal because of the finitude of life; they are mortals because they can die. To die means to be capable of death as death. And this means to experience death as the shrine of Nothing. As the shrine of Nothing, death harbors within itself the presencing of Being. But this is something of which man as *causa sui* is not capable.

From the perspective of man in the nearness of the fourfold, Heidegger prefers to keep silent with regard to theology insofar as it is dominated by a subjectivistic anthropology. Someone who has experienced theology in his own roots, both the theology of the Christian faith and that of philosophy, would today rather remain silent about God when he is speaking in the realm of thinking (ID, 54–5). With these words, Heidegger points out that when one keeps silent it is not only due to a lack of knowledge but to dissociate oneself from ontotheology and its fusion with Christian theology. Whether there is a place here for negative theology is very doubtful, because negative theology remains paradigmatically connected with ontotheology.

It is also important to ask which role the holy plays in Heidegger's view of the divine. It seems that there is no direct connection between naming the holy and thinking of being. In the postscript to "What is Metaphysics?" Heidegger writes that thinking, obedient to the voice of being, seeks from being the word through which the truth of being comes to language. Of like provenance is the naming of the poet (PA, 237).[5] Because poetizing and thinking are most purely alike in their care of the word, they are at the same time farthest separated in their essence. The thinker says being. The poet names the holy. This kinship and difference make further examination of the relation between being and the holy more urgent.

Heidegger links the experience of the holy to the experience of being as wholesomeness. Ontotheology is an understanding of being in which God and the gods do not have a place. As long as there is a forgottenness of being in ontotheology, there is also a forgottenness of the historicality of the gods.

It is important in understanding religions and their gods to understand them historically. Such a time needs the poets to get an entrance to the holy.

The holy has to appear as that in which human being can find its wholeness. The holy is not God, the godhead, the highest entity of metaphysics, or the divine grace. It is an ontological phenomenon, expressed in the thinking of being, that can be the entrance to the religious. Without understanding the holy, we behave with respect to it like tourists and visitors to a museum. Therefore an understanding of it from the perspective of the historicality of being is an entrance to understanding religion and the religions, God and the gods.

It is important to see that Heidegger approaches gods and religion as historical. Theology, as part of metaphysics, is not something that has a place in the historicity of the event of being, according to Heidegger. Counter to this, Heidegger develops the paradigm of the fourfold. The counter-paradigm of the fourfold no longer implies a subjectivistic or ontotheological relation to the divine and the holy. However, this does not mean that mortals or human beings, as understood from within the fourfold, have no relation with the gods. In a certain sense, they have a theology when they sing and praise the gods. We can see this especially in what Heidegger says about the poet, particularly Hölderlin. In Heidegger's view it is the poet who can wait and long for the coming; he is, based on this longing, capable of naming the holy. In naming the holy, the poet creates a holy place to prepare an abode for gods and mortals. Mortals dwell in that they await the divinities as divinities. In hope they hold up to the divinities what is unhoped for.

Heidegger's interpretation of the poetic word has a theological element in it. He places the theological element of thinking in the poetical work of the poet. Heidegger's philosophy thus has its own theology within the thinking of being. *Theologos, theologia* mean at this point the mytho-poetic utterance about the gods (ID, 54). The saying of the poet is only possible when he listens to the word. The poet knows that he or she is called by the gods in order to praise their name. This implies that the poet at first has to be a listener, to know how to receive and to get the word like a gift and an endowment. *Theologia* in this respect is at first instance a praising that springs from the experience that it is called, without a connection to a dogma or a church. This poetical *theologia* does not ask for the first cause or the totality of entities. This *theologia* is the song that is sung by the poet.

NOTES AND REFERENCES

1 M. Heidegger, "'Only a God Can Save Us': *Der Spiegel*'s Interview with Martin Heidegger," *Philosophy Today*, 20 (1976), 267–84.
2 See for this and other parts of this article: B. Vedder, *Heidegger's Philosophy of Religion, From God to the Gods* (Pittsburgh: Duquesne University Press, 2000), 11–33; B. Vedder, "A Philosophical Understanding of Heidegger's Notion of the Holy," *Epoche, a journal for the history of philosophy*, 10 (2005), 141–54; B. Vedder, "Heidegger's Explication of Religious Phenomena in the Letters of Saint Paul," *Bijdragen, International Journal in Philosophy and Theology*, 70 (2009), 152–67.
3 M. Heidegger, "Phenomenological Interpretations with Respect to Aristotle," trans. Michael Baur, *Man and World*, 25 (1992), 393.
4 B. Vedder, *Heidegger's Philosophy of Religion, From God to the Gods* (Pittsburgh: Duquesne University Press, 2007), 93–112.
5 About the difference between the poetic and the thinking experience, see OWL, 69–70.

42

SCIENCE
Trish Glazebrook

The first generation of Heidegger schol-ars in North America was quite clear that Heidegger "never developed a systematic philosophy of science."[1] Nonetheless, his engagement with science begins as early as 1912 and continues until his death in 1976. In the earliest text, *Das Realitätsproblem in der Modernen Philosophie* (GA 1, 1–15), he articulates what is later call "instrumental realism": scientists (unlike philosophers) are not plagued by metaphysical doubt; "daz-zling results" (3) encourage scientists to take for granted the reality of objects of research. From that beginning, his thinking can be understood as ongoing development of the thesis that science is the mathematical pro-jection of nature. Accordingly, his analysis of science is the lynchpin for a lifelong engage-ment with the question of how understand-ing can be projective without thereby being hermeneutically violent.

His answer is a call for a new beginning that is precisely alternative to the modern, scientific, representational, and calculat-ing thinking that overruns the earth as the essence of technology through the exploita-tion of nature. This movement in Heidegger's thinking can be traced through three themes. First, reflection on disciplinary specializa-tion reveals that sciences have no access to their own essence. Secondly, phenomenology

leads Heidegger to the conclusion that sci-ence necessarily entails nihilism. Finally, Heidegger's long-standing engagement with Aristotle opens the possibility of a new dwelling that does not reduce thinking to representation and being to objectivity. This is not to say that there would no longer be science. Rather, the mathematical projection of nature would no longer one-sidedly deter-mine the human experience of modernity as global conquest.

SPECIALIZATION

R. Crease calls for analyses of specialized sci-ences and scientific practice in Heideggerian philosophy of science.[2] Applications of Heidegger's critique of science to specific scientific disciplines have indeed burgeoned in recent years. Sciences addressed include quantum physics,[3] biology,[4] psychology and psychoanalysis,[5] and artificial intelligence and cognitive science.[6] Babich argues, how-ever, that the real significance of Heidegger's analysis is his call for rigorous, critical analy-sis of science.[7] Such analysis reveals that sci-ence determines modernity, yet the sciences are incapable of self-critique concerning this historical role.

Until Heidegger stops doing fundamental ontology, his account of science is entangled with his claim that philosophy is a science.[8] At first, he holds merely that projection functions in knowledge to determine disciplinary specialization. In *Der Zeitbegriff in der Geschichtswissenschaft* in 1916, he distinguishes history from physics by means of projection of their time concept. In *Basic Problems of Phenomenology*, he grounds the regional ontologies of the sciences in philosophy as fundamental ontology. That is, the sciences carve off some realm of being to take as their object, while ontology is the science of being. Thus he says in the *Beiträge* that there is no "science," but rather "science" is "only a formal title whose essential understanding requires that the breakdown into disciplines, into individual and separate sciences, be thought along" (GA 65, 145/CP1, 101). In *Being and Time*, he claims that sciences specialize through projection of basic concepts and suffer crisis when these concepts undergo revision (SZ, 9/BTMR, 29).

In 1929, in the *Antrittsrede*, Heidegger explicitly argues that "Our existence—in the community of researchers, teachers, and students—is determined by science" (GA 9, 103/BW, 94), and he poses the question of metaphysics as the question of "What happens to us essentially, in the grounds of our existence, when science becomes our passion?" (idem.). He comments on the division of the sciences into specialized disciplines and their consolidation into the university, and argues that "the rootedness of the sciences in their essential ground has atrophied [*abgestorben*]" (GA 9, 104/BW, 94). That is, fundamental ontology can no longer ground the sciences because the relation between beings and being is *abgestorben*, which in medicine means necrotized and, keeping with the root metaphor, in botany means

died back. Heidegger argues that the only meaningful source of unity for the sciences is provided by "the practical establishment of goals by each discipline" (GA 9, 104/ BW, 94), and in the *Rektoratsrede* some four years later, he argues that questioning understood as the highest form of knowing "shatters the division of the sciences into rigidly separated specialties . . . and exposes science once again to the fertility and the blessing bestowed by all the world-shaping powers of human-historical Dasein."[9] Some 20 years later, he emphasizes "the inconspicuous state of affairs" (VA, 63/QCT, 179) concealed in the sciences "as the river lies in its source" (idem.). Around the same time, in *What Is Called Thinking?*, he argues that the "sciences come out of philosophy . . . [and] they can never again, by their own power as sciences, make the leap back into the source from which they have sprung" (GA 8, 52/ WCT, 18). He never gives up the claim that the reflection necessary for such critical analysis of science cannot itself be scientific.

The latter lecture course, *What Is Called Thinking?*, is notorious for its claim throughout that "Science does not think" (GA 8, 4/ WCT, 8), but Heidegger also asserts throughout the lectures that "most thought-provoking of all is that we are still not thinking" (GA 8, 2/WCT, 4). The lectures are aimed at showing how representational thinking is impoverished philosophically as it gains access to beings but cannot ask the question of being. The "sciences do in fact decide what of the tree in bloom may or may not be considered valid reality" (GA 8, 18/WHD, 43), Heidegger notes, but the sciences themselves cannot question this decision. Accordingly, the relation between philosophy and science is now clear. Philosophy must be unscientific precisely to make possible thinking of the question of the relation between being and beings, the thinking Heidegger later calls in the 1950s *Besinnung*, translated in "Science and Reflection" as "reflection," and in GA 66 as "mindfulness."

Philosophical reflection on the sciences reveals that modernity is determined by an extremely narrow conception of reality derived from the sciences. Heidegger's critique of technology has received much more attention than his critique of science; but it is science, not technology, that for Heidegger is "the theory of the real" (VA, 42/QCT, 157; et passim). By the time Heidegger argues this point, he holds the sciences no longer capable of self-transparency—the crisis of science is that the sciences cannot see their own essence (VA, 62/QCT, 179).

The issue of specialization thus disrupts Heidegger's commitment to philosophy as science. Only from outside science can the thinking pose the question at the root of the sciences that Heidegger articulates in a lecture to the Faculty of Medicine at the University of Freiberg in 1937 of what is worth knowing.[10] Thus it is less surprising than it initially seems that Heidegger chooses the question of the essence of science in "The Age of the World Picture" to lay bare "the entire essence of the modern age" (GA 5, 76/QCT, 117).[11] Philosophy cannot ground the sciences, but anyone thinking philosophically, including scientists, can question the role of science in human experience.

PHENOMENOLOGY[12]

That science is the mathematical projection of nature is a central thesis in Heidegger's phenomenology. In §7(c), he borrows Husserl's maxim, "To the things themselves!" to delimit his preliminary conception of phenomenology. In §69(b), this conception is "developed for the first time" (SZ, 357/BTMR, 357) in the search for the existential conception of science. Heidegger cannot provide "a fully adequate existential Interpretation of science" (idem.) until he has clarified "the meaning of Being and the 'connection' between Being and truth ... in terms of the temporality of existence" (idem.), that is, the central problem of *Being and Time*. His subsequent deliberations on science are, he says, preparatory to that central issue. Science is thus more fundamental to *Being and Time* than has been typically thought.[13]

Yet the inquiry in §69 does not show that the sciences are phenomenological in the sense of getting at the things themselves. In the theoretical attitude, the circumspective concern of the natural attitude is not just stripped away; rather, the "understanding of Being ... has changed over" (SZ, 361/BTMR, 412). Readiness-to-hand, is replaced by another interpretive projection, presence-at-hand. The sciences are thus hermeneutic.[14] What is decisive for them is "the way in which Nature herself (sic) is mathematically projected" (SZ, 362/BTMR, 413–4). This is the first indication of the mathematical projection of nature that Heidegger traces in *Die Frage nach dem Ding* to the grounding function of transcendental subjectivity in Cartesian and Kantian idealism.

In *Being and Time*, he notes that "this projection discloses something a priori" (SZ, 362/BTMR, 414), and in *Die Frage nach dem Ding* he defines the mathematical exactly as what is a priori rather than being found in experience, of which the numerical is the most obvious example (GA 41, 73–7/BW, 275–8). Hence the sciences may not describe anything beyond the imaginative projections of transcendental subjectivity. Heidegger remains caught in the problem he articulated in 1912 that in modern philosophy "even the mere positing of an external world independent of consciousness is inadmissible and impossible" (GA 1, 3), yet scientists take it for granted that they have access to reality. In *Being and Time*, he is thus caught in the seemingly contradictory claims that "entities *are*, quite independently of the experience by which they are disclosed" while "Being 'is' only in [Dasein's] understanding" (SZ, 183/BTMR, 228), repeated in 1928 in *The Metaphysical Foundation of Logic* (GA 26, 194–5 and 216/MFL, 153 and 169). So how is it possible for sciences to gain knowledge of independent entities rather than just synthesizing imagined objects? There must be something onto which to project.

In "What is Metaphysics?" in 1929, he argues that "That with which the scientific confrontation . . . occurs are beings themselves—and beyond that nothing" (GA 9, 105/BW, 95). Moreover, the sciences are only possible because Dasein is transcendent, that is, "holding itself out into the nothing" (GA 9, 115/BW, 103), yet science "wants to know nothing of the nothing" (GA 9, 106/BW, 96). *Introduction to Metaphysics* picks up where *What Is Metaphysics?* leaves off, with the question, "Why are there beings at all, and not rather nothing?" (GA 9, 122/BW, 110). Heidegger argues that "'physics' determines the essence and the history of metaphysics from the inception onward" and "metaphysics steadfastly remains 'physics'" (GA 40, 20/IM, 19). This is because, as he noted in 1930, when human beings first asked what beings are, that is, at the origin of philosophy in ancient Greece, "being as a whole reveals itself as *physis*, 'nature,' which here does not yet mean a particular sphere of beings but rather beings as such as a whole, specifically in the sense of upsurgent presence [*aufgehendes Anwesens*]" (GA 9, 189–90/BW, 126).[15] Nature is more than the objects of science; it is what presences of its own accord.

Thus "*physis* is indeed *poiêsis* in the highest sense" (VA, 15/QCT, 10) in the technology essay, and in the *Beiträge*, *physis* is "the measure and is 'earlier than,' source, origin. The earliest, what comes to presence first, presencing is *physis* itself" (GA 65, 222/CP1, 155), immediately covered over by Plato's idea. Accordingly, the a priori, what is first, is no longer upsurgent presence, but the idea that in modernity belongs to the *ego cogitans* and is projected onto beings as the meaning of being. Hence modern science, as the mathematical projection of nature rather than mindful attentiveness, is a bastardized form of what Aristotle called *technê*, the projection of form onto matter, and modern science can never, in Heidegger's analysis, simply let beings be. Thus in the last text Heidegger composed prior to his death, he simply asks:

Is modern natural science the foundation of technology—as is supposed—or is it for its part, already the basic form of technological thinking, the determining fore-conception and incessant incursion of technological representation into the realized and organized machinations of technology?[16]

Technology can conquer nature as standing-reserve because modern science already projects nature mathematically as object.

That narrow conception, essential to science, is objectivity, articulated clearly in "The Question Concerning Technology" as the projection of nature as "a coherence of forces calculable in advance" (VA, 25/QCT, 21). At issue there, however, is not the essence of science but the essence of technology: *Ge-stell*, translated as "Enframing." In fact, in Heidegger's analysis, Enframing as "standing-reserve [*Bestand*]" is only possible because prior to domination of the essence of technology, the essence of modern science holds sway as objectivity. Heidegger argues in *What Is Called Thinking?* that "Modern science is grounded in the nature [*Wesen*] of technology" (GA 8, 155/WCT, 135), implying that the essence of technology is prior. But a short time later, in the technology essay, he argues instead that the "modern physical theory of nature prepares the way first not simply for technology but for the essence of modern technology" (VA, 25/QCT, 23). That is, the essence of technology drives "the organized global conquest of the earth" (GA 6.2, 358/NIV, 248) because science determines modernity but has at its core what for Aristotle belonged to *technê*: representational thinking. The relation between the essence of science and the essence of technology began historically, in Heidegger's view, with Aristotle; and it is only by going back to that originary account of *physis* that *physis* can be the "counter-ground [*Gegengrund*]" by which to understand the "transformation [*Umbildung*]" of *technê* into "'technicity' [*Technik*]" (GA 66, 368).

DWELLING

In 1939, Heidegger lectures on Aristotle's *Physics* B, 1. He has already considered Aristotle's account of *technê* in "The Origin of the Work of Art" where he resisted understanding art as the imposition of form onto matter. This resistance is a long-standing thinking that goes back to Brentano's reading of Aristotle's analogy of being by way of the categories, that is, that being can be understood first and foremost as substance

in which accidents inhere. Heidegger had been given a copy of Brentano's *On the Several Senses of Being in Aristotle* for his eighteenth birthday, and later said this book drove him to write *Being and Time*.[17] In 1921–2, Heidegger's lecture provides a phenomenological reading of Aristotle that is preoccupied with making sense of the givenness of world in factical life, and the accepted reading of the analogy of being by way of the categories is not put into question. In the analogy, however, Aristotle details at *Metaphysics* 5.7 that being can also be understood as accidental, true or false, and by way of actuality (*entelecheia*) or potentiality (*dunamis*). In 1931, Heidegger gives a lecture course on Aristotle's *Metaphysics* 9, 1–3 in which he treats actuality and potentiality in detail. He suggests that Brentano has a tendency to recognize actuality and potentiality as categories (GA 33, 45) but does not himself articulate fully a different reading until the 1939 lectures on the *Physics*, where he reads the analogy of being by way of actuality and potentiality in their own right rather than reducing them to categories.

In those lectures, Heidegger details the distinction between production (*technê*) and nature (*physis*) for Aristotle: production entails a conception of what is to be produced in the mind of the artist prior to production. If nature required such a paradigm, says Heidegger, "an animal could not reproduce itself without mastering the science of its own zoology" (GA 9, 290/PA, 222). In art, then, form is imposed onto matter by the artist—exactly the account of art Heidegger rejected in the 1935 lecture, "The Origin of the Work of Art" where he argued instead that art is itself world-opening origin. In 1939, he argues that nature cannot be understood by analogy to artifacts, as if natural entities are matter on which form has been imposed by, for example, a divine craftsperson in the Judeo-Christian account. Such an analogy, he argues, fails "from every conceivable point of view. This means: we must understand the essence of *physis* entirely from out of itself" (GA 9, 292/PA, 223). That is to say, the sciences, if they are to understand nature, must be phenomenological. Rather than coming to natural entities with an a priori conception, that is, a projected representation under the model that Aristotle noted best belongs to production, sciences gain knowledge by letting being be.

In 1930, Heidegger argued in the truth essay that freedom is not a property of human being, but "reveals itself as letting beings be [*das Seinlassen von Seiendem*] . . . to engage oneself with the open region and its openness in which every being comes to stand, bringing that openness, as it were, along with itself" (GA 9, 188/BW, 125). Likewise, the 1955 lecture, *Gelassenheit*, retains this notion of letting (*lassen*) as a releasement toward beings that is attentive and meditative, in contrast precisely to the "calculative thinking [*rechnende Denken*]"[18] that characterizes the sciences. The calculative function of the sciences is explicit in the 1935–6 lectures, *Die Frage nach dem Ding*, where Heidegger argues that calculation is the most familiar form of the mathematical, but that *ta mathemata* meant more broadly for the Greeks, "things insofar as we take cognizance of them as what we already know them to be in advance, the body as bodily, the plant-like of the plant, the animal-like of the animal, the thingness of the thing, and so on" (GA 41, 73/BW, 275). Modern science cannot, however, let beings be in order to experience the Greek sense of "self-unfolding presencing [*sich entfaltende (öffnende) Anwesung*]" (GA 66, 87). Modern human being is thus alienated from nature in science.

In §40 in *Being and Time*, Heidegger connects anxiety (*Angst*) with *Unheimlichkeit*, usually translated as "uncanniness" but meaning literally un-home-iness. He implies, since it "is a basic kind of Being-in-the-World" (SZ, 188/BTMR, 233), that it pervades the human condition. He does not connect this homelessness to the sciences in *Being and Time*, but soon thereafter, however, Heidegger understands that such homelessness is distinctively modern and a consequence of the scientific projection of nature. By the mid-1930s, for example, he argues that "Anxiety [*Angst*] in the face of be-ing has never been greater than today" (GA 65, 139/CP1, 97), and that nihilism is an "abandonment of being" (GA 65, §52 et passim) that "is essentially co-decided by modern science . . . insofar as modern science claims to be one or even *the* decisive knowing" (GA 65, 141/CP1, 98) such that any attempt to find the echo of be-ing in the abandonment of being "cannot avoid being mindful of modern science" (idem.). For only through reflection, thinking that is not the representation and calculative thinking of the sciences, can human being be at home in nature in the dwelling alluded to in the 1951 lectures "Building, Dwelling, Thinking" and ". . . Poetically Man Dwells. . . ."

NOTES AND REFERENCES

1 J. J. Kockelmans "The Era of the World-as-Picture" in eds J. J. Kockelmans and T. J. Kisiel, *Phenomenology and the Natural Sciences* (Evanston, IL: Northwestern University Press, 1970), 184–201, 184. See also W. J. Richardson, "Heidegger's Critique of Science," *New Scholasticism*, 42.4 (1968), 511–36, 511. See P. Heelan's response to this paper, "Heidegger's Longest Day: Twenty-Five Years Later" in B. E. Babich (ed.), *From Phenomenology to Thought, Errancy, and Desire: Essays In Honor of*

William J. Richardson (Dordrecht: Kluwer, 1995), 579–87. See T. Glazebrook, *Heidegger's Philosophy of Science* (New York: Fordham University Press, 2000) for arguments that Heidegger did in fact have a philosophy of science.

2 R. Crease, "Heidegger and the Empirical Turn in Continental Philosophy of Science" in ed. T. Glazebrook, *Heidegger on Science* (Albany, NY: SUNY Press, 2012), 225–37, uses formal indication as an example of a Heideggerian concept that can be adapted for understanding scientific practice; he gave a related paper on formal indicators in Heidegger at the forty-third Annual Meeting of the Heidegger Circle in Cincinnati in 2009.

3 See J. R. Watson and E. Richter on quantum physics in T. Glazebrook, *Heidegger on Science* (Albany, NY: SUNY Press, 2012), 47–65 and 67–90.

4 See L. Hatab on biology in Glazebrook, *Heidegger on Science*, 93–111.

5 Contributions on psychology and psychoanalysis have been emerging since Heidegger's exchanges with Medard Boss that began in 1947 (M. Boss (ed.) *Zollikoner Seminare, Protokolle—Gespräche—Briefe* (Frankfurt am Main: Vittorio Klostermann, 1987)). H. Dreyfus has written on Heidegger and psychology since his 1980 "Dasein's Revenge: Methodological Solipsism as Unsuccessful Escape Strategy in Psychology" (*Behavioral and Brain Sciences*, 3.1, 78–9).

6 Dreyfus has also written on cybernetics and artificial intelligence (e.g. "Why Heideggerian AI Failed and How Fixing It Would Require Making it More Heideggerian," *Philosophical Psychology*, 20.2 (2007), 247–68). Both analyses have their conceptual origins of his reading of being-in-the-world as "coping" (H. Dreyfus, *Being-in-the-World: A Commentary on Heidegger's* Being and Time, Division I (Cambridge, MA: MIT Press, 1991), and see his responses to his critics in M. Wrathall and J. Malpas (eds), *Heidegger, Coping and Cognitive Science: Essays in Honor of Hubert L. Dreyfus*, Vol. 2 (Cambridge, MA: MIT Press, 2000). On October 7, 2010, the University of Edinburgh hosted a workshop on Heidegger and cognitive science; M. Wheeler defended and

M. Ratcliffe rejected Heideggerian cognitive science (www.philosophy.ed.ac.uk/events/heideggerworkshop.html).

7 B. Babich "'The Problem of Science' in Nietzsche and Heidegger," *Research Resources*. Paper 7. http://fordham.bepress.com/phil_research/7 (Accessed May 12, 2012).

8 See J. J. Kockelmans, "Heidegger on the Essential Difference and Necessary Relationship between Philosophy and Science," in J. J. Kockelmans and T. J. Kisiel (eds), *Phenomenology and the Natural Sciences* (Evanston, IL: Northwestern University Press, 1970), 147–66 and T. J. Kisiel, "Science, Phenomenology, and the Thinking of Being," 167–83, in the same volume, on the relation between philosophy and science.

9 Martin Heidegger, *Die Selbstbehauptung der Deutschen Universität* (Frankfurt am Main: Vittorio Klostermann, 1983), 13; Martin Heidegger, "The Self-Assertion of the German University: Address Delivered on the Solemn Assumption of the Rectorate of the University of Freiberg; The Rectorate 1933/34: Facts and Thoughts," trans. Kirsten Harries, *Review of Metaphysics*, 38 (1985), 467–52, 474.

10 Martin Heidegger, "Die Bedrohung der Wissenschaft," *Zur philosophischen Aktualität Heideggers, Band 1*, ed. Dietrich Papenfuss und Otto Pöggler (Frankfurt: Vittorio Klostermann, 1991), 5–27; see T. Glazebrook, *Heidegger's Philosophy of Science* (Albany, NY: State University of New York Press, 2000), 148–52.

11 See J. J. Kockelmans, "The Era of the World-as-Picture," in eds Kockelmans and Kisiel, *Phenomenology and the Natural Sciences* (Evanston, IL: Northwestern University Press, 1970), 184–201 for a detailed reading of this lecture concerning science.

12 See J. J. Kockelmans, *Heidegger and Science* (Washington, DC: University Press of America, 1985) for a thorough reading of the influence of the phenomenological tradition on Heidegger's critique of science.

13 J. D. Caputo, "Heidegger's Philosophy of Science: The Two Essences of Science," in eds J. Margolis, M. Krausz, and R. M. Burian, *Rationality, Relativism and the Human Sciences* (Dordrecht: Martinus Nijhoff, 1986), 43–60, 43 argues in fact that even "the later

Heidegger himself neglected his own earlier reflections" on science.

14 P. Heelan, who began as a physicist, has been providing critical analyses of science as hermeneutic practice since the 1970s. He engages Heidegger throughout, but also explicitly states at the After Postmodernism Conference at the University of Chicago, November 14–16, 1997 that "Hermeneutic philosophy refers mostly to M. Heidegger's" (www.focusing.org/apm_papers/heelan.html (Accessed July 17, 2012)).

15 See W. Marx, *Heidegger and the Tradition*, trans. T. Kisiel and M. Greene (Evanston, IL: Northwestern University Press, 1971), 139–43 on *physis* and *Anwesen*.

16 M. Heidegger, "*Neuzeitliche Naturwissenschaft und moderne Technik*," Research in

Phenomenology 7 (1977), 1–4, with translation by J. Sallis.

17 F. Brentano, *On the Several Sense of Being in Aristotle*, trans. R. George (Berkeley: University of California Press, 1975). Heidegger confirms that this text drove him to write *Being and Time* in M. Heidegger, "The Understanding of Time in Phenomenology and in the Thinking of the Being-Question," trans. T. Sheehan and F. Elliston, *Southwest Journal of Philosophy*, 10.2 (1979), 199–201, 201, and in his inaugural address to the Heidelberg Academy of Science, noted in H. Siegfried, "Martin Heidegger: A Recollection," *Man and World*, 3.1 (1970), 3–4, 4.

18 M. Heidegger, *Gelassenheit* (Pfullingen: Verlag Günther Neske, 1992), 12 et passim.

43

SPACE: THE OPEN IN WHICH WE SOJOURN

John Russon and Kirsten Jacobson

We have a basic experience of "there." "There" is opposed to "here," to be sure, but more basically "there" is "somewhere," a primordial situating that precedes, makes possible and contains the opposition of "here" and "there": "there is" reality, it "takes place." This "taking place" has the dual sense of "happening" and "occupying a determinate location vis-à-vis others in the universal arena of appearing": "there" is both the singular fact of the global happening of reality, and it is the always local specificity of things situated with respect to other things and to ourselves. This "there" is the *"Da"* with which Heidegger's investigations throughout his career are preoccupied. We are intrinsically engaged with that *Da*: we are *Dasein*, "there-being."

The *Da*, the "there," is space, but saying the word "space" does not suddenly make transparent the sense of the *Da*; on the contrary, reflecting on the phenomenon of "there" draws our attention to the fundamental enigma of space, the enigmatic way that we find ourselves in the midst of things, thrown into a world that presents itself simultaneously as embracing us and as spread away from us into the distance. Late in his career (1969), in his Zollikon seminars, Heidegger remarks:

> In *Being and Time*, being-*open* (*Da*-sein) means *being*-open (Da-*sein*). The "Da" is determined here as "the open." This openness has the character of space. Spatiality belongs to the clearing [*Lichtung*]. It belongs to the open in which we sojourn as existing beings. (GA 89, 283/ZS, 225)[1]

We are *Da-sein*, which is to say we are open to a reality that is open to us, and that is a reality in which things open onto other things. Before engaging in any technical reflections on "space," we must first push ourselves to notice—and notice the mysterious wonder of—*this fact of the open*: we should notice that there is a "there is" for us. We live as the witnessing of a clearing in which it is given to us to notice, it is given to us that there is something to notice.

Heidegger's philosophy is fundamentally a phenomenology, that is, it is a description of experience as it is lived. To respond meaningfully to his philosophy—to understand it—we must first engage ourselves in the project of reflecting upon the character of our own experience: we must begin by reflecting on this, our fundamental experience of "being there." Having attuned ourselves to the mysterious character of the happening of our experience, we can follow Heidegger's ever-deepening reflections on the nature of space—the nature of the *Da*—throughout his writing.

LIVED-SPACE

Heidegger's first and most revolutionary contribution, and the one that provides the context for all his subsequent reflections on space, is the emphasis in *Being and Time* on the primacy of the "ready" [*zuhanden*] character of the world.[2] Though we are intelligently, meaningfully, and discriminatingly related to the very specific features of our surrounding environment, in our everyday experience we integrate ourselves with them without making them the explicit objects of our attention. While one is walking, reaching into a pocket or grabbing for the telephone, one will typically be talking with a friend about the plans for the evening or some other topic. The explicit, "conspicuous" object of attention is the evening's events, while the surrounding world of ground, limbs, pocket, and telephone whose support we gather up in our behavior is "inconspicuous"—nonthematic in, though utterly essential to, our experience.

This nonthematic involvement with the determinacies of our environment is not an optional or secondary aspect of our experience, but is our primary way of existing. First and foremost, we "dwell" in the world, which means we always experience *from* a network of "involvements," a lived inhabitation of the world, and thus this *world* that provides the context and background for our lives is the most basic phenomenon of our experience: it is what most basically appears, what is "there."[3] We are *Dasein*—"being there"— first in this sense that *our very existence* is this being stretched out into the things that make our "home."[4]

This "existing as stretched out into things" is our *spatiality*, our *being* spatial. Space is not first a characteristic of the object of our experience but is the very character of *how we exist*.[5] The close and the distant are not primarily matters of the quantity of separation between objects, but are matters of our comfortable absorption in or our alienated unfamiliarity with our world. What is near is near because we have turned ourselves toward it and taken the thing up into our care. What is far is far because we are not focusing our attention on it or because it lies out of reach of a project we undertake. Space, first, is the proximity to or distance from our world that we *live*.

It is this "lived spatiality" that Heidegger studies in *Being and Time*.[6] "In accordance with its Being-in-the-world," Heidegger writes, "Dasein always has space presented as already discovered, though not thematically" (GA 2, 112/BT, 147): even when space as such has not yet become an explicit object of focal concern for us, we already "know" space in that we are oriented in our irremovable involvement with the world in terms of our felt proximities and the ways in which we are oriented *from* this home *to* what is distant. Heidegger studies these characteristics of our spatiality under the headings "de-severance" [*Ent-fernung*] and "directionality" [*Ausrichtung*].[7]

"De-severance" is the way in which our being is always characterized by finding things at a distance, by having things presented to us in their separation from us.[8] As I launch upon a project of writing, the things not connected with this writing slip away and I bring near those that enable my writing. The pencil, for example, emerges as a relevant option and takes its place in the heterogeneous network of papers, surfaces, lights, and limbs that, in their separation from me, *are* the possibility of my writing. In engaging with the "region" of writing, these differentiated options become simultaneously close and distant: as de-severing, we are always doing away with the "farness" between things and us precisely in allowing them to exist for us as relevant differences/distances.[9] This "making close" that is de-severing is not reducing of the quantity of bodily separation between my body and some thing, but is rather letting "any entity be encountered close by *as the entity which it is*" (GA 2, 105/BT, 139). De-severance is the way in which things are only ever far from us on the basis of their being close to us.

In this description of de-severance, we see as well our "directionality." "Every bringing-close," Heidegger writes, "has already taken in advance a direction towards a region out of which what is de-severed brings itself close" (GA 2, 143/BT, 108). We exist as directional insofar as we are always bringing things close to us *from out of a region* to which these things belong, which is to say, we do not indifferently relate to the things of the world, but we are instead always *oriented* toward the world in some meaningful way or other. We experience the world *as* regional, as having locations—the relevant, oriented domains of our involvement—in which certain things are gathered together through our projects and, more generally, our care, and we experience things as *belonging to* regions, as coming out of a place to which they belong.[10]

The world of our experience is not at root an alienated assemblage of isolated things set off against each other and against an isolated knowing subject in space as a uniform and empty "container," but is, rather, the heterogeneous fabric of availability upon which we draw to carry out our practices of everyday life, a fabric meaningfully articulated in determinate regions that provide the context to which things themselves belong. The subject as an isolated consciousness, things as isolated individuals and the "empty" space in which we imagine them to be contained are derivative realities that emerge from within this primordial, lived spatiality, rather than being the original terms of reality.[11]

EARTH AND TIME-SPACE

The phenomenological descriptions of "world" in *Being and Time* challenged our typical understanding of the world by compelling us to notice a realm of lived space, "beneath," so to speak, the objective reality of discrete objects situated in empty space. In "The Origin of the Work of Art," Heidegger compels us to shift our attention from the "world" of availability to the "earth" that is the originary matrix that is the very possibility of world. Heidegger describes phenomenologically the experience of an ancient Greek temple, noting how the temple, rather than presenting itself as an object, in fact articulates a world, shaping for us a perspective on ourselves and nature: "the temple, in its standing there, first gives to things their look and to men their outlook on themselves" (GA 7, 28/PLT, 42). The artwork is the gesture by which a community carves out for itself a *Weltanschauung*—a "worldview"—but this world is itself the taking up of possibility that, *qua* possibility, does not "itself" have the form of "world." This possibility of world is the "earth."

Whatever appears "co-arises" with a perspective upon it, and, as thus inherently "for" a perspective, is meaningful: it has *Sinn*— "sense" or "direction"—as we saw already in our discussion of *Dasein*'s directionality. The basic phenomenon of meaningful appearance, *Being and Time* argued, is the world, that is, we do not first encounter discrete things and discrete other subjects and then gradually "build up" to an experience of reality as a whole but, on the contrary, we begin with an experience of a meaningful world as a whole, within which or out of which discrete figures emerge. *Qua* perspectival, however, any situation of appearing—any being-in-the-world—is always selective and one-sided. The world is always a culturally and historically specific way of apprehending the possibilities of appearing, of apprehending what it is "to be," of encountering the "there." Other ways of being-in-the-world— other *worlds*—however, are also possible. A world, as a specific way of appearing, shows *itself*, but *through* itself it is also manifesting the *possibility* of appearing. The possible, always failing to appear *as such*—as possible—nonetheless always appears *as* the actual. This *possibility of* world, realized in and as the world, but not reducible to it, is "earth."

If we now return to our initial phenomenological project of describing experience and thus ask, "What is appearing?" or "What is there?" we can advance beyond our earlier answer. Earlier, we recognized that, through the temple, for example, a world appears. Now we can deepen our description further and say that, through the temple, *earth* is appearing *as world*. Indeed, earth is appearing *as appearance*. All *appearing*, hence

all being-in-the-world, is earth showing itself—or, more exactly, earth *as such withdrawing from* appearance such that a world might appear.[12] With earth we have the very possibility of the "there is," that which in its withdrawal gives there to be the meaningful space of our lives.

Heidegger's discussion of "earth" thus draws our attention to the "enabling power" that precedes our experience of the meaningful articulation of space.[13] This notion is further developed in the concept of "time-space," [*Zeit-Raum*] in *Contributions to Philosophy* (1938). Heidegger writes:

> One must first generally attempt to think what is ownmost to time so originarily (in time's "ecstasis") that time becomes graspable as the possible truth for be-ing [*Seyn*] as such. But already thinking time through in this way brings time, in its relatedness to the *Da* of *Da-sein*, into an essential relationship with the spatiality of *Da-sein* and thus with space. . . . But measured against their ordinary representations, time and space are here more originary; and ultimately, they are time-space [*Zeit-Raum*], which is not a coupling of time and space but what is more originary in their belonging together. (GA 65, 189/CP1, 132)

Being and Time took temporality as its clue for investigating the nature of being: the articulation and realization of our care in the experience of lived time is our fundamental hold on the relationship of what is, what was, and what will be, and is thus the fundamental fabric of the meaningfulness— the *Sinn*—of our experience.[14] Yet, *Being and Time* revealed, this, our meaningful grasp of the world, is not a matter of intellectual representation, but is a matter, as we saw above, of lived spatiality, an inhabitation of

SPACE

a world.[15] This inseparability of time and space—of "meaning" and "extension," so to speak—invites us to recognize a source for each that precedes their apparent separability. This is the "time-space" [*Zeit-Raum*] of *Contributions to Philosophy*.

As earth is that of which world is the realization, *Zeit-Raum* is that of which the space and the time that we live are realizations. As what makes possible space and time, *Zeit-Raum* is not properly graspable in the terms *of* space and time. Such terms, however, are the terms of meaning for us. *Zeit-Raum*, then, as the "ground" of meaning, is itself outside the domain of meaning: it is precisely meaningless. In this sense, *Zeit-Raum* is "ground" in the sense of "*Abgrund*"— abyss.[16] The recognition of *Zeit-Raum* is the recognition that meaning *as such* cannot be "the last word," so to speak, but *as meaning* precisely points to its own rootedness in a kind of absence of meaning.

Recognizing this absence of meaning is neither a theoretical matter, nor a matter of "nihilism," but is, as Heidegger already anticipated in his study of anxiety in *Being and Time*, precisely a lived realization of one's own exposure to an "outside" that, as such, can never be brought within the confines of comfortable experience: an outside in which we can never be at home.[17] The experience of space is always the experience of being exposed to our limits, and here, in this engagement with the deepest sense (or absence of sense) of space, we similarly engage this exposure at it most extreme level.[18] *Dasein* understood as our lived spatiality of being-at-home itself depends on *Da-sein* understood as an originary homelessness that is our relation to space as *Zeit-Raum*.[19]

Da-sein, the site of our homeless exposure to *Zeit-Raum*, is not simply other than *Dasein*, our being-at-home in the world.

Zeit-Raum, the possibility of meaningful space and meaningful time, is neither a spatially separate existent nor a temporally antecedent reality; indeed, it does not exist in any way other than *as* space and time. "There is" only the *event* [*Ereignis*] that is the appropriating of the possibility of being in the happening of a meaningful world.[20] The event is the co-occurrence of *Zeit-Raum* and of space and time, but it is precisely the event of their separation from each other: they each exist only in and as this constitutive "strife."[21] Similarly, in our inhabitation of a familiar world— our existence as *Dasein*—there always lurks *Da-sein*, our constitutive homelessness that carries within it a call to recognize that we are thus exposed to the abyss; and, equally, our homeless *Da-sein* can exist in no way other than as making a home in being, appropriating being in one way or another. What is ultimately at stake in our spatiality is the "how" of our appropriation: specifically, what is at stake is whether we live our *Dasein* in a way that acknowledges this, its inherent *Da-sein*.

MACHINATION AND DWELLING

Da-sein, according to *Contributions to Philosophy*, is the "site for the moment of the grounding of the truth of be-ing" (GA 65, 323/CP1, 227).[22] We exist as the site as which the event of being as the strife of earth and world is enacted, and recognizing this is recognizing the fundamental responsibility that defines us. Indeed, our spatiality is ultimately a grappling with what matters most deeply and originally.

Contributions to Philosophy emphasizes the contemporary political and social problem of what Heidegger there calls "machination" [*Machenschaft*]. We saw in our initial study of lived space the problem of confusing the mathematically measurable empty space of our objective relation to the world with the original spatiality of our dwelling. "Machination" is the carrying out at a global level of this misapprehension of our inherent spatiality: with machination, we inhabit space in a way that denies the nature of spatial inhabitation—we *dwell* in a way that betrays dwelling—and the *res extensa* as which space appears when we confront the world as an object becomes an exploitative inhabiting of the world that actively transforms the world into a desert.[23] Hence the concern of *Contributions to Philosophy*: "We need to show how it happens that space and time become framing representation . . . for 'mathematical' calculation and why these concepts of space and time dominate all thinking" (GA 65, 373/CP1, 260). The reorientation in our understanding of space that Heidegger's philosophy offers is itself crucial to resisting the inherently destructive way in which we currently inhabit our world.

The analysis of "dwelling" [*Wohnen*] in "Building, Dwelling, Thinking" (1951) offers resources for a significantly different approach to our inhabitation of our places from that enacted in machination. The description of the Greek temple in "The Origin of the Work of Art," revealed that how we build is how we articulate space, which, indeed, is how we open a world. Space is not a given empty container and building is not merely instrumental; rather, how we build our architectural spaces is how we disclose space as a place for dwelling. Our building simultaneously releases to us how the world can be inhabited and, correlatively, is expressive of how we are:

The way in which you are and I am, the manner in which we humans *are* on the

earth, is *Buan*, dwelling. . . . The old word *bauen*, which says that man *is* insofar as he *dwells*, this word *bauen* however *also* means at the same time to cherish and protect, to preserve and care for. (GA 7, 149/PLT, 147)

How we establish our habitation—how we "build"—is how we "shelter" [*bergen*] what Heidegger in "Building, Dwelling, Thinking" calls "the fourfold," which he there identifies as the essential character of being: "Dwelling, as preserving [*als Shonen*], keeps the fourfold in that with which mortals stay: in things" (GA 7, 153/PLT, 151).[24] What this means, in short, is that building is not simply instrumental shelter for us from the natural elements; it is, on the contrary, how we shelter all that is of value in the world, how we shelter the possibilities for being. Though our study of space recognized the priority of *Zeit-Raum*, the weight of this recognition is the acknowledgment that it is only in our actual dwelling that this enabling power is housed. As "the site for the moment of the grounding of the truth of be-ing," our existence inherently puts upon us the capacity to shape how the possibilities of being will be realized, a capacity that involves the danger that we will live in destructive denial of the very fabric of meaning but a capacity that is equally the possibility of sheltering the giving power.[25]

This emphasis on the concreteness and existential intimacy of space is brought to a powerful conclusion in Heidegger's studies of sculpture from the 1960s. "Art and Space," (1969), is a meditation on how the sculptural work releases the nature of space to our experience. It is only in our actual dwelling that the possibility of space exists, and sculpture brings to appearance this dependence of space upon the places of which it is the possibility: "Place is not located in a pre-given space, after the manner of physical-technological space. The latter unfolds itself only through the reigning of places of a region" ("Art and Space" 11). And, just as space is not an indifferent container of indifferent places, so is place not an indifferent container for an indifferent thing: "We would have to learn to recognize that things themselves are places and do not merely belong to a place" (ibid.). This line of thinking is completed in the closely related "Remarks on Art-Sculpture-Space," where Heidegger identifies the crucial role of the body in relation to space:

> The human has no body and is no body, but rather it lives its body [*Leib*]. The human lives in that it bodies [*leibt*], and thus is it admitted into the open of space, and through this self-admittance it holds itself already from the outset in a relation to its fellow humans and things.[26]

We began by noting that our being is Da-sein, which is "*being*-open." Sculpture reveals that this being-open is enacting only as our "bodying." It is ultimately in and as the concreteness of our bodily engagement with things that "there is."[27]

CONCLUSION

What is "there"? We will never exhaust the description of this, and so we will never exhaust our account of space, the enigmatic possibility and actuality of the world that constitutes the context and fabric of our lives. Space is where we live in the comfortable familiarity of being-at-home, and also where we encounter the call to shelter the

very possibility of meaning in an acknowledgment of our homelessness. How we heed this call will be decisive in this technological world that is premised upon the denial of our essential reality.

NOTES AND REFERENCES

[1] See Thomas Sheehan, "A Paradigm Shift in Heidegger Research," *Continental Philosophy Review*, 32 (2001), 1–20.

[2] GA 2, 63–113/BT 91–148, division 1, chapter 3, "The Worldhood of the World." The concept of "world" is also discussed extensively in the 1927 lecture course, *Die Grundprobleme der Phänomenologie*, GA 24, 230–41 and 412–29/BP, 162–70 and 291–302, and in earlier courses such as the 1925 course, *Prolegomena zur Geschichte des Zeitbegriffs*, GA 20 210–325/HCT 156–236, division 1, chapter 3, sections 19–25. For the idea that Heidegger's later philosophy of space represents a fundamental shift in position, see Andrew J. Mitchell, *Heidegger among the Sculptors: Body, Space and the Art of Dwelling* (Stanford: Stanford University Press, 2010); for a powerful criticism of this position, see François Raffoul, "The Event of Space," *Gatherings: The Heidegger Circle Annual*, 2 (2012), 89–106.

[3] For "dwelling," see GA 2, 54/BT, 79–80; for "involvements," see section 18, GA 2, 84/BT, 116, and to compare the notion of "equipmental totality," see GA 2, 68/BT, 97.

[4] See GA 2, 11–15 and 52–9/BT, 32–5 and 78–86. See Kirsten Jacobson, "A Developed Nature: A Phenomenological Account of the Experience of Home," *Continental Philosophy Review*, 42 (2009), 355–73. Initially, Heidegger presented "*Dasein*" as a word without hyphenation; later, he hyphenated the word "*Da-sein*." In discussing *Being and Time*, we use the term without hyphenation; the relation between the earlier and later uses is considered in the second section of this chapter.

[5] GA 2, 138/BT, 104: "To encounter the ready-to-hand in its environmental space remains ontically possible only because Dasein itself is 'spatial' with regard to its Being-in-the-world."

6   Sections 22–4, "The Spatiality [*Räumlichkeit*] of Dasein." See Yoko Arisaka, "On Heidegger's Theory of Space: A Critique of Dreyfus," *Inquiry* 38 (1995), 455–67; Jing Long, "The Body and the Worldhood of the World," *Journal of Philosophical Research*, 31 (2006), 295–308.

7   See also GA 20 306–25/HCT 223–36, section 25.

8   See Hubert Dreyfus, *Being-in-the-World: A Commentary on Heidegger's Being and Time, Division I* (Cambridge: MIT Press, 1991), 132; Jeffrey Malpas, *Heidegger's Topology*, (Cambridge: MIT Press, 2006), 91, 376; Peg Birmingham, "Heidegger and Arendt: The Birth of Political Action and Speech," in eds François Raffoul and David Pettigrew, *Heidegger's Practical Philosophy* (Albany: SUNY Press, 2002), chapter 12, 197.

9   For "regions," see GA 2, 103/BT, 136–7.

10 See Edward S. Casey, *The Fate of Place: A Philosophical History* (Berkeley: University of California Press, 1997), 247–56.

11 Heidegger's phenomenological description of lived experience also challenges the mutual isolation that we typically presume to exist between subjects; see *Being and Time*, division 1, chapter 4.

12 Compare Heidegger's remarks on a "phenomenology of the inapparent," GA 15, 135/FS, 80.

13 See Thomas Sheehan, "*Kehre* and *Ereignis*: A Prolegomenon to *Introduction to Metaphysics*," in eds Richard Polt and Gregory Fried, *A Companion to Heidegger's Introduction to Metaphysics* (New Haven and London: Yale University Press, 2000), 3–16, 263–74, especially 7.

14 "The meaning [*Sinn*] of *Dasein* is temporality," GA 2, 331/BT, 380.

15 See GA 2, 367–9/BT, 418–21 for Heidegger's discussion of the relation of space and time in *Being and Time*.

16 GA 65, 371–88/CP1, 259–71: "Der Zeit-Raum als der Ab-grund." On this theme, see Friedrich-Wilhelm von Herrmann, "Wahrheit-Zeit-Raum," in ed. Ewald Richter, *Die Frage Nach der Wahrheit* (Frankfurt am Main: Klostermann, 1997). Compare Heidegger, *Der Kunst und der Raum* (St. Gallen, Switzerland: Erker Verlag, 1969), translated by Charles H. Siebert as "Art and Space," *Man and World*, 6 (1973), 3–8, 7: "Space—does it belong to the primal phenomena at the awareness of which men are overcome, as Goethe says, by an awe to the point of anxiety? . . . For behind space, so it will appear, nothing more is given to which it could be traced back. Before space there is no retreat to something else." See Stuart Elden, "Contributions to Geography? The Spaces of Heidegger's *Beiträge*," *Environment and Planning D: Society and Space*, 23 (2005), 811–27.

17 See especially GA 2, 186/BT, 180.

18 See Mitchell, *Heidegger among the Sculptors*, 52.

19 Heidegger takes up our "homeless" or "unhomely" character in *Being and Time* (e.g. GA 2, 189/BT, 183). It is a central theme of the 1942 lecture course, *Hölderlin's Hymne "der Ister,"* GA 53.

20 *Zeit-Raum* is "originally the site for the moment of enowning [*Augenblicks-Stätte des Ereignisses*]." (GA 65, 30/CP1, 22)

21 See GA 65, 29/CP1, 21: "Time-space [is] the *site for the moment* of strife. . . . Strife [is] the strife of *earth and world*, because truth of be-ing [takes place] only in sheltering, sheltering as grounding the 'between' in beings: the tug of earth and world."

22 See John Sallis, "Grounders of the Abyss," in eds Charles Scott, Susan Schoenbohm, Daniela Vallega-Neu, and Allejandro Vallega, *Companion to Heidegger's "Contributions to Philosophy"* (Bloomington: Indiana University Press, 2001), 181–97.

23 See Elden, "Contributions to Geography?" 819.

24 In *Contributions to Philosophy*, similarly, Heidegger identifies the "hidden essence" of *Zeit-Raum* as "nearness and remoteness, emptiness and gifting, fervor and dawdling," in contrast to quantitative measurability we commonly take to be definitive of objective space and time (GA 65, 372/CP1, 260).

25 Compare GA 7, 29–36/BW, 333–41.

26 *Bemerkungen zu Kunst—Plastik—Raum*, ed. Hermann Heidegger (St. Gallen, Switzerland: Erker Verlag, 1996), 13; quoted in Mitchell, *Heidegger among the Sculptors*, 40.

27 On the concreteness of space see Jeffrey Malpas, *Heidegger and the Thinking of Place: Explorations in the Topology of Being* (Cambridge MA: MIT Press, 2012) and the review of this book by François Raffoul, *Notre Dame Philosophical Reviews*, July 19, 2012.

44

TECHNOLOGY
Hans Ruin

Up until the mid-nineteenth century, the question and problem of technology was not seen as an issue of great philosophical interest. It is in the social philosophy of Marx and other left Hegelians that one can first see a genuine shift among philosophers in this respect. The modes of production and thus the very technical means of life are now seen as cultural forces in their own right, and thus as influencing the thoughts, experiences, and self-understanding of a society. In 1877 Ernst Kapp, a philosopher and a contemporary of Marx, publishes the first book with the title "Outline for a Philosophy of technology" (*Grundlinien einer Philosophie der Technik*), where he launches the idea of the tool as an "organ-extension" of man.

With the First World War the question takes on another urgency. The war was not only a human and cultural disaster of previously unseen dimensions. It was also an experience of how the machinery of war somehow seemed to have taken over the lives of men, and made them into its servants rather than its masters. Together with the rapid and convulsive industrialization of the West it contributed to bringing the question of technology to the forefront of the cultural and philosophical debates in postwar Europe.

In the 1920s many European philosophers and intellectuals turn their interest toward technology as the defining issue of our time. Ortega y Gasset in Spain, Nikolai Berdjajev in Russia (and France), Oswald Spengler, Ernst Jünger, and Ernst Cassirer in Germany, and many others take part in the discussion of the meaning and consequences of the technologizing of culture. The culmination of the Second World War brought the whole matter to yet another level. The atomic bomb marked a new step in both the technological and the spiritual evolution of humankind. It now had the ability to abolish life on earth as such. With the parallel discovery of the human genome, humanity appeared to have fulfilled the ancient phantasies of a demiurge that in his hands had the power and the *techne* to create and destroy life.

The first phase of this discussion takes place when Heidegger is developing his own version of phenomenology as existential ontology. Yet, in his early published works, including *Being and Time*, the question of technology does not stand forth as a fundamental concern. It is not until the early 1950s that he explicitly and publicly takes on the question of technology as a philosophical theme in its own right. He then gives several public lectures on this theme, which are then edited into the immensely influential essay "The Question Concerning Technology" in 1954. Here he describes the essence of

353

technology as "enframing" (*Ge-stell*) and as the defining characteristic of our age. *Techne* in its double legacy, as both technology and as art, is here presented as the source of the greatest danger but also as a potentially saving power, as both *Gefahr* and *Rettung*. To contemplate (*besinnen*) this situation is a crucial task for philosophy, perhaps even its greatest responsibility in the present. In his last words to his colleagues and friends in America in 1976, the year of his death, he writes that contemplating technology is the most important task if we are to counter the forgetfulness of being.

For a long time it was believed that the problem of technology was something that belonged only to Heidegger's later work. But with the publication of his lectures from the 1920s onward it has become clear that his interest in and perspective on this problem must be seen in a new light. First of all, he was greatly influenced by the earlier cultural and philosophical debate about the role and meaning of technology, in particular by the writings of Ernst Jünger. Also, the problem of the technical and its effect on language and thinking is something that guides his critical assessment of the history of metaphysics from the very earliest writings onward.

Heidegger's essay on the question of technology is today the single most quoted paper in the field of Science and Technology Studies. One reason that it has become so influential is that it seeks to capture the problem of the technical on such an extremely general level, both philosophically and historically, connecting it with the meaning and development of the metaphysical and philosophical tradition as such. Yet, because of how intricately it is folded into his overall philosophical problematic, it is often poorly understood. It is only by locating its analyses and conclusions in the broader context of the emergence

and development of his phenomenological ontology and its inner tensions that one can make better sense of it, and also that one can formulate relevant criticisms.

As a short historical background it is helpful to rehearse a few basic points from Aristotle, who remained the main reference for Heidegger on this issue throughout his life. In book six of *Nicomachean Ethics*, Aristotle provides the first known philosophical definition of *techne*: "A *techne* is a rational quality concerned with making, that reasons truly" (1140a). The translation of *techne* is here a philosophical problem in itself. The standard Latin translation of *techne* was always *ars*, and following this it was rendered in the modern Latinized European languages as *art*, and in the Germanic languages as *Kunst* (where the etymology points back toward a verb for knowledge and ability, *kunna*). In some translations of Aristotle we find the extended translation "art or technical skill," to mark the difference from art in the more modern aesthetic sense. But it is important to note that Aristotle and the Greeks did not clearly distinguish between what we think of as technology on the one hand and the fine arts on the other. *Techne* was essentially the name for a creative and productive form of knowledge, an intellectual virtue comparable to other intellectual virtues, notably scientific knowledge and wisdom. As such it also had something to do with *truth*. In another famous and somewhat enigmatic passage from the same text, Aristotle writes: "There are five ways in which the soul achieves truth (*aletheuein*), namely through *techne*, scientific knowledge, prudence, wisdom, and intelligence" (1139b).

The meaning of this statement has been the source of much debate. Whatever Aristotle meant, its importance for Heidegger's understanding of technology can hardly be overestimated. The relation between *techne* and truth and the disclosure of being is a question that guides his attempts to think technology philosophically from the very earliest lectures. Throughout this trajectory, the double legacy of *techne*, as both art and technology, will also generate shifting constellations. We will come back to it as we proceed, but with this background in mind I now turn to how the problem of technology first appears in his work.

In 1922, Heidegger composed a survey article to summarize the interpretations of Aristotle on which he had been working for several years (PIA). The dense text can be read as a condensed outline of *Being and Time* five years before its publication. It also contains some very important remarks on the technical that anticipates his later thinking. He stresses here the importance of analyzing how the vocabulary of early Greek metaphysics is created, and what its guiding models and motives are. As an example he turns to how Aristotle conceptualizes *substance*, Greek *ousia*. When designating the most fundamental nature of being by this term, Aristotle has been guided, Heidegger argues, by an understanding of being as something created in *poiesis*, as a *Hergestelltsein*, a "being-fabricated." The German word is important here, for it marks the first in a long sequence of concepts forged around the root verb *stellen*, to place or put, at the extension of which he eventually coins that of *Ge-stell*.

In Greek metaphysics being is thought in its general essence as something produced that is then grasped in language through its *eidos*, its visibility. This way of making being appear and stand forth, and thus to be true, Heidegger continues, is the way of *techne* or technics. So the technological understanding of being is in fact what we could call the basic model of understanding being, and the

one according to which Greek metaphysics built its fundamental conceptual structure. Only by becoming critically aware of what we could thus call a certain *technical bias* in the very construction of metaphysical language, can we also engage in an exploration directed toward other, complementary, and supposedly also more fundamental senses of being.

This conclusion is not simply a descriptive hypothesis that concerns the first emergence of a metaphysical conceptuality. It also holds a critical potential. For in questioning the validity of the original conceptual configuration it also opens up a space for critical reflection on the inherited understanding and meaning of being that will continue to direct his critical questioning of inherited metaphysics.

When Heidegger publishes *Being and Time* five years later, the core of its argument is the critique of a substance metaphysics, which understands being along the line of what is present-at-hand (*Vorhandenheit*). The connection to the earlier analysis of the "technical" roots of metaphysics is not, however, obvious at first glance. In *Being and Time*, the explicit theme of technology and *techne* is hardly mentioned. It is clear from some remarks in passing that he attaches a somewhat negative sense to *the technical*. When discussing the phenomenological method, he emphasizes, for example, that it should not be understood along the lines of a "technical device" (GA 2, 27/BT, 26). And in a later passage from the book he makes a distinction between what he calls a "genuine reflection on method" from "empty discussions of technology" (GA 2, 303/BT, 290). In order to ground this vaguely negative conception of the technical we need to see it in the context of the larger project in BT, its criticism of modern Cartesian substance ontology, and how it carries on the basic connection between a technical approach to being and metaphysical language.

In *Being and Time* the critique of substance ontology does not, unlike the earlier draft, take its starting point in a Greek "technical" sense of being. Instead it points to Cartesian metaphysics as the root of seeing being as a pure extension in space. Heidegger uses Descartes' famous example of a piece of wax to demonstrate his point. By reducing the object to its pure extension in space, Descartes has abstracted it from its immediate surroundings, in order to visualize it only as a calculable material extension.

In order to "destruct" this understanding of thingness, Heidegger turns to the Greek word for "thing," which is *pragmata*, signifying etymologically "that with which we are concerned." These entities are not meaningless extensions in space, but always contextually meaningful in terms of a surrounding world of concerns. They are, he says, "readiness-to-hand," *Zuhandenheit*. Their understanding and meaningfulness presupposes precisely that they are not objectified, but rather lived in their spontaneous referential context. From this perspective it is possible for him to develop his analysis of "world" as something more than simply a constellation of material entities. The primary phenomenon of world is a lived, meaningful referential context, into which we are always already thrown.

From the viewpoint of the earlier critique of substance metaphysics this is a bit confusing. Through his interpretations of Aristotle he had reached the conclusion that Greek instrumental and technical understanding of being accounts for a kind of elementary forgetfulness in the history of metaphysics. But now the artifact, tool or equipment, as in Greek *pragmata*, is instead presented as a critical contrast in relation to a more

distanced and objectifying modern Cartesian understanding of nature in modernity. This is what permits him to speak of readiness-to-hand, *Zuhandenheit*, as a more original manifestation of being than present-at-hand, *Vorhandenheit*.

From one perspective the ontology developed in *Being and Time* could thus be described as a pragmatist ontology of the artifact and the tool, since the being of readiness-to-hand is argued to be more fundamental than the secondary and theoretically mediated present-at-hand of the simply contemplated object of nature. It has also been interpreted in this way, especially by some of Heidegger's American readers.

Even though the rationale behind his analysis was to critically reflect on the form of objectification of nature that emerges with modern science and its metaphysics, its implications nevertheless remain problematic, not least for Heidegger himself. For if nature is understood along the model of a useful thing or readiness-to-hand, then the phenomenological analysis would seem to reinstall a subjectivist and anthropocentric determination of the world that it sought to transcend. If we read *Being and Time* from this angle we can also sense why he subsequently adopted a critical distance toward its analyses.

This is the case in particular in the essay "Origin of the Work of Art" from 1935. This is his most important statement on Art, but as such it is also an important statement on the *technical*, since art or *Kunst* goes back to the same Greek word *techne*. Readers often fail to fully appreciate the interconnectedness of the question of art and technology in Heidegger's work. But here, in the artwork essay, he literally builds his argument by pitting the two senses of ancient *techne* against one another. In seeking to expand his earlier critique of substance ontology, he states that the true being of an artwork cannot be grasped along the model of objective present-at-hand entities, as *Vorhandenheit*. However, neither can it be understood along the model of the useful tool or readiness-to-hand, as *Zuhandenheit*. Nor indeed can nature be understood along any of these models. For natural being is rather characterized by an elusive way of self-containment (*Eigenwuchsig*), a kind of auto-emergence.

When we turn to the artwork, however, it turns out that it in fact differs from all of these three types of being. Instead it is a special way of bringing together and letting appear the being of nature, not *consuming* it as a raw material for the purpose of its own utility, but rather by *letting it appear* and come to presence. It is in this sense that the artwork can be a "happening of truth."

In contrast to the analysis in *Being and Time*, the mode of equipment or usefulness is thus here what lies in the way of grasping the genuine phenomenon of nature. On the other hand, this truth can be discerned through the event of the artwork. As a work of truth, the artwork is what reveals the deeper meaning of nature that is concealed as long as nature is interpreted only through the traditional—technologically oriented— matrix of matter and form. So in the place of *techne* as artifact, the essay opts for *techne* as artwork. From the viewpoint of the Artwork essay, there is thus also a positive possibility emanating from the Greek *techne*, not as the instrument of immediate life concerns, but as the poetic bringing forth of something into its presence.

At this stage in Heidegger's thinking the two conflicting modes of *techne* thus begin to structure his thinking in a cross-wise, chiastic way. *Techne* in the sense of the fabricated artifact functions from the inception of

metaphysics as the matrix for thinking being as a disconnected entity, in a way that comes to the fore in modernity, where the truth or event of being is covered over and domesticated in a representational and objectifying (technical) understanding. At the same time, *techne* as art emerges as a unique avenue toward thinking the event of truth, in a way that does not objectify being, but rather permits it to prevail in its own essence, in its dual nature as presence and absence at once. As we shall see shortly, the 1953 essay on technology brings this confrontation between the two forms of *techne* to an even higher level.

In the years that follow upon the Artwork essay, from the mid-1930s onward, Heidegger embarks on a huge undertaking, to reassess the entire movement and inner motivation of German idealism and its legacy, including Nietzsche. From an initial positive appreciation of both Schelling and Nietzsche as attempts to escape from the confines of metaphysics in its traditional form, he gradually reaches the conclusion that not only all of German idealism, but also Nietzsche himself, are ultimately symptoms of a more encompassing metaphysical development. The true legacy of metaphysics is a will to power and domination that brings everything under its yoke, and that finds its concretization in modern technology, especially in its relation to nature.

His own radicalized attempt to abandon the confines of Western thinking is manifested most dramatically in his writings from the mid-1930s onward, notably in *Contributions to Philosophy* and *Besinnung* (GA 65 and GA 66). In these posthumously published works we find the first steps in his critical assessment of technology as a world shaping power, a power that is about to transform the sense of nature, leading to a forgetfulness of being (GA 65, 277). Here he also tries to develop new modes of thought, as well as a series of new concepts. Central for the former attempt is to shape a mode of thinking that avoids the objectification of conceptual thought, by including its own "belonging" to that which is thought. In these experimental works, written mostly under the years of dictatorship, Heidegger elaborates many of the thoughts that will eventually surface in his postwar lectures and writings. It is a question of saying things so as to call forth the attention of the listener to how she has already been claimed by what she is trying to think.

In the 1953 lecture on technology this strategy and therapy is at the heart of its argument and style. Unlike the common approach to the philosophical question of technology, Heidegger holds that the *essence* of something is not simply the answer to its fundamental *what*. In the case of technology the standard answer is that technology is a means to an end, an instrument for action, or as in the earlier theorists an "organ-projection." But against this standard response, he suggests that we look instead for *how* technology brings about its truth. Then we do not only ask for the truth *about* technology, but rather for the truth *of* and *through* technology.

At this stage he also recalls the passage from the *Nicomachean Ethics* referred to above, according to which "*techne* is a way of making true." He uses it to convey the point that *techne* has to do with bringing about the true, in the sense of letting something come into its appearance, and thus of disclosing it. The primary way in which technology discloses nature is as "exploitation," or a "commanding," as *Herausfordern*. It discloses nature as that which can and should be commanded. But not only that, it also discloses man to himself as "commanded to

command nature," *herausgefordert die Natur herauszufördern* (VA, 21/BW, 320). This is the concentrated formulation behind the idea of *Ge-stell* as the essence of technology. It manifests itself as a *demand* inherent in man himself and as a consequence of his freedom, in and through which he takes control over nature and over himself. It is a "destiny," but not in the sense of being ordained by a superior power, but as a way in which humans encounter nature and themselves.

As such a destiny it is not given once and for all, but rather as something toward which we can seek to establish a more free relation. By *listening* to its claim or its demand (*Anspruch*), and by permitting it to resonate as such, it can also become a "freeing claim" (VA, 29/BW, 331). For this reason the *Ge-stell* constitutes a fundamentally ambiguous situation. From a superficial perspective the concept and diagnosis itself may appear only as an anti-modernist and even reactionary assessment of the present. But Heidegger's point is that it also contains new possibilities of experiencing this very modernity, if we are able to listen to the way that it speaks in and through us.

The danger inherent in the *Ge-stell* also holds a saving potential. In his later writings, Heidegger would often quote the lines from Hölderlin's Patmos, "But where danger is, grows the saving power also." In the essay on technology this quotation holds a very special place, for it summarizes the way in which he wants the *Ge-stell* to be understood, namely as an "ambiguous" situation of danger and saving at once. The latter possibility rests, however, on the condition that man can reach a thoughtful and reflective relation to that which is, as it is disclosed in the *Ge-stell*.

At the very end of the essay he explicitly takes up this ambiguity in terms of the aforementioned double inheritance of the Greek *techne*. Once, he says, *techne* also meant the "bringing forth of the true into the beautiful" (VA, 38/BW, 339). To the hope of technology belongs this possibility of bringing it back to a sense of a poietic disclosure, first carried and made possible in the arts, which were known by the Greeks also as *techne*. But this is only possible on the condition that philosophy thinks the technological condition to its end. So at the end of it all it is as if *techne* comes forward to reveal a liberating perspective on that which is, liberating it, as it were, from itself.

45

TRUTH
Daniel O. Dahlstrom

When someone protests that a certain depiction of events is not "a true picture of what happened," the expression "a true picture" is typically metaphorical. Yet the metaphor captures a common enough experience. Accounts and representations of things, relations, or events often leave out or significantly distort what is, within a particular context, essential to them and to the recognition of them. Obviously even a picture (from snapshots to computed tomography scans or MRIs) can be less than accurate, and moving pictures no less so. Nevertheless, we frequently picture things to facilitate our ways of talking about things and getting closer to the truth of a matter.[1] And the reverse is also true. Consider the animated discussions of the Zapruder film capturing Kennedy's assassination or of the images of the recently discovered streaks on Martian slopes.

In a sense, recourse to the interaction between picturing and discussing, far from boosting our confidence in them, may seem to underscore their feebleness. A picture may be worth a thousand words but at a time when a thousand is hardly enough. If a pictorial representation contributes to a linguistic representation or vice versa, the fact remains that they are representations and, as such, a skeptic may insist, always fall short of the things themselves. Yet the feebleness of these

forms of representation is no reason to give up on them. They call for interpretation and revision, but their very possibility turns on a capacity at least to approximate the truth. Nor do we have any other access to the truth than that provided by them. Even if the skeptical claim (representation) that representations generally fall short of the things themselves is not self-refuting (though perhaps regressive), the claim gets any traction it possesses from the presumption of the disclosiveness of at least some representations.

Yet the skeptic is on to something on which Heidegger repeatedly insists, namely, the fact that access to the truth is not the same as the truth itself. Truth is the disclosure of the presence (being) of beings to us. The difference between disclosure and presence here is slight, underscoring the metonymy of "truth" and "being" for Heidegger. However, while we can conceive a presence not present to someone or perhaps anyone, the same does not hold for a disclosure. Moreover, in order for the presence of something to be disclosed to us, we have to represent it. That is to say, there is no truth without our representation as an ingredient part of the truth.[2] But that representation, while necessary, is by no means sufficient for the disclosure of the presence of beings to us. Nor can we directly represent that disclosure itself in the ordinary ways that we discursively represent objects (though we can indirectly represent, that is, think it).[3]

Tarski's rendition of the correspondence theory of truth can be read as illustrating Heidegger's point. "The snow is white" is true if and only if the snow is white. The clause predicated as true is equivalent to the unquoted clause because the latter refers to snow presenting itself as white. On some interpretations, the equivalence implies that the truth-predicate is redundant, superfluous, or perhaps merely an expression of assertive force. This implication reinforces Heidegger's point that truth as correspondence cannot be the end of the story. It presupposes the disclosure of that to which the true assertion corresponds.

Meanwhile, neither the predicate "true" nor the unquoted statement in the Tarskian formula directly represent that disclosure in the way that we take terms like "snow" and "white" to represent an object and its properties respectively. The disclosure of the presence of white snow is neither white nor snowy. The correspondence theory of truth—in classical terms, the conformity of the understanding to the thing (*adaequatio intellectus ad rem*)—necessarily supposes that things present themselves of themselves in accordance with the way they are understood. Not unlike skeptics such as Hume and Kant in this regard, Heidegger stresses that the proposition or understanding (*intellectus*) involved is not by itself sufficient to demonstrate as much. What it supposes, in other words, is the disclosure of the presence (being) of things to the understanding. Heidegger—with Husserl and in contrast to his skeptical predecessors—accordingly understands this disclosure as the primordial phenomenon of truth.

It is a long-standing logical prejudice that truth is a property of a proposition, assertion,

or judgment.[4] The prejudice is logical in the sense that logic, as the study of inference, presupposes the possibility of properly formulated propositions that are thus capable of being true or false and of being premises or conclusions of inferences. The components of propositions are not true or false themselves. Thus, "the sun"—like "shines sun the"—is neither true nor false, but "the sun shines" can be. Inference is a relation between propositions that need not be true. However, adherence to the rules of inference guarantees that if the premises of the inference are true, so is the conclusion. If it is true that "the sun shines" and that "whatever shines, shines on something," then it is true that "the sun shines on something." Hence, it is the assertions or statements making up the premises and conclusion that are the bearers of truth. These "truth-bearers" are thus allegedly the site of truth.

Heidegger explicitly exposes and reverses this logical prejudice. The assertion is not the site (place, *Ort*) of truth but rather truth is the site of the assertion (SZ, 214/BT, 206). That is to say, we make assertions and they have their distinctive referential, predicative, and communicative functions because they can be truthful, that is, they can be helpful and, in some cases, are even necessary for disclosing how things are (the presence of things to us).[5] But we do not disclose how things are for the purpose of making assertions.[6]

Mention was made earlier of the fact that talk of truth can only be indirect and metaphorical, at least relative to ordinary ways of speaking in a seemingly straightforward and literal manner. What passes for straightforward and literal, however, is relative to a world defined by human concerns and interests. Contemporary science is a techno-science that marshals those ordinary ways of speaking into ever more canonical forms that define the universe of discourse. In these contexts of everyday common sense and scientific research, there is accordingly no place—there are no words—for the truth as the disclosure of the presence of things. What passes for "truth" in common sense and science is what the world presents to confirm human mastery of it.

Truth in Heidegger's sense is both supposed by yet hidden from standard ways of relativizing truth to the representation of it. It is supposed since the way the world presents itself (e.g. as capable of being mastered) is not itself the doing of human beings. Once again this basic point cuts across the everyday world and the world of science. If I go into the woods searching for edible mushrooms, I am only able to find them if they present themselves as such. If someone asks me how to tell the nonpoisonous from the poisonous mushrooms, I may describe some identifying feature or even show them a picture. But the description or picture are true only if the mushrooms present themselves as so described or pictured—and that is not something that follows automatically from the description or picture. So, too, whatever is true about the discovery and harnessing of electricity is not the product of the discovery and harnessing itself. At the same time, what the discovery and the harnessing in question represent is electricity, not the disclosure of its presence, that is, the very disclosure that makes the discovery and harnessing possible. Insofar as everyday and scientific representations are confined to beings (mushrooms, electricity), truth as that fundamental, underlying disclosure of their being remains hidden.

In terms of Heidegger's intellectual biography, his appreciation of the hiddenness of truth stems in part from his understanding of Husserl's theory of categorial intuition. Categorial intuitions are discernments of what correspond to logical structures and judgments but are not reducible to the latter. The objects of categorial intuitions include states of affairs (corresponding to the logical structure "Fx" or "S is P"), ideas (corresponding to universals, such as "whiteness"), and, notably, being (corresponding in today's terms to existential quantification, "$\exists x(Fx)$"). The categorial objects of these intuitions do not correspond to those of straightforward, sensory perceptions, though categorial intuitions build upon the latter. For example, in a straightforward sense I see the snow, I may even see in a way the white of the snow, but in neither of these ways do I see the being of the snow (i.e. that it exists). Still, I see categorially, as it were, that the snow is there, thanks in no small part to the sensory perception. Similarly, the truth of the representation of the snow as existing is not the same as the snow itself or the white of the snow. Yet I see categorially the truth of the assertion that the snow exists. In relation to any straightforward, sensory perception, what corresponds to "being" or to "truth" is hidden.

Perhaps more important to Heidegger's understanding of truth as the hidden disclosing of the presence of beings to us is his interpretation of the Greek word traditionally translated as truth, namely, *aletheia*. The emphasis that Heidegger places on this interpretation for the history of philosophy and, indeed, the state of the contemporary world in the grip of technology can scarcely be underestimated. Key to Heidegger's interpretation is the fact that the Greek word is built from a root (*lethe*) meaning hiddenness and from its privation in the form of the prefix (the alpha "*a*"). In other words, *a-letheia* means, quite literally, un-hiddenness. The early Greeks (Anaximander, Heraclitus, and Parmenides) appreciated the hiddenness of beings generally—albeit without fully thinking it through

(GA 54, 95/P, 64). As Heraclitus in particular recognized, nature (*physis*) loves to hide and *a-letheia* is a restless gathering (*logos*) and conflict (*polemos*) of hiddenness and un-hiddenness as the primordial opposites. As the disclosure (unhiddenness) of the presence (being) of things, truth presupposes their foregoing closure (hiddenness). At the same time un-hiddenness is something wondrous that happens, a movement of dis-closing and emergence into presence, that is the fundamental sense of *physis*, the term that captures the most basic Greek understanding of being. This unhiddenness is captivating and human beings are themselves caught up in the natural process—and uncanny violence—of wresting this unhiddenness from the primordial hiddenness of things.[7]

With the beginnings of metaphysics (i.e. the work of Plato and Aristotle), the notion of hiddenness is increasingly submerged in favor of a concern with the unhiddenness of beings. So taken were these thinkers by the wonder of the sheer unhiddenness of things that they equated *aletheia*, conceived simply as unhiddenness, with being. The truth (*aletheia*) is understood as the unhidden look of things (Plato's *ideas*) or what is always already unhidden and finished in things (Aristotle's *to ti en einai* and *energeia*). In a controversial interpretation of the Cave Allegory of Book VI of the *Republic*, Heidegger contends that Plato's yoking (*sugon*) of *aletheia* to the manifest way things *look* in the light marks a key moment in the devolution of truth as unhiddenness into truth as correctness and correspondence.[8]

Neither Plato nor Aristotle construed truth (*aletheia*) as something fabricated or derivative of human representation and production. Yet they set the stage for this modern development. In their preoccupation with the unhiddenness of things (an unhiddenness that not incidentally abets the use and production of things), they disregard the sense of hiddenness that underlies truth as unhiddenness. This disregard brings in its wake a progressive obliviousness to the root significance of *aletheia*, that is, that struggle between hiddenness and unhiddenness that also sustains them and their relationship. As a result, in modernity, not only the hiddenness of things is forgotten; so, too, is the unhiddenness itself, as the focus shifts from things insofar as they are unhidden to objects insofar as they can be represented, produced, and managed.[9]

The center of gravity of Heidegger's account of truth in the 1920s shifts after 1930. Yet echoes of the medieval doctrine of the convertibility of being and truth (as transcendentals) reverberate in both accounts. Before 1930 Heidegger pursues fundamental ontology, a clarification of the sense of being that is presupposed for ontology generally, through existential analysis, that is, analysis of the sense of being of those who exist. What distinguishes existence or being-here (*Da-sein*) is the fact that it is—of itself—the "clearing" in terms of which what is at hand is accessible in the light and hidden in the dark. In other words, "*Dasein is its disclosedness*" and, as such, the most basic sense in which truth *is* (SZ, 133/BT, 129). "Truth in the most primordial sense is the disclosedness of being-here, to which the un-coveredness of inner-worldly entities belongs" (SZ, 223/BT, 214). In other words, our being-here fundamentally coincides—is fundamentally convertible, as it were,—with our truthfulness, that is, the way we disclose the presence of beings. As Heidegger himself puts it, "being and truth >>are<< equiprimordially" (SZ, 230/BT, 220). At the same time the dis-closedness (truth) of being-here (*genitivus appositivus*) presupposes being closed-off from things as well, in the sense that they are hidden from us, distorted, or disguised, sometimes even by their own doing (think of chameleons). Hence, "being-here is equiprimordially in the truth and un-truth" (SZ, 223/BT, 214). This un-truth, it bears emphasizing, is not in the first instance falsehood. It corresponds instead to the fact that beings are never fully present to us and, indeed, not primarily because of us, but because of the character of their presence itself.[10] Just as truth entails un-truth, so being as presence entails absence.

In the course of the 1930s, historical being (*Seyn*) replaces being-here as the locus of truth.[11] The notion of truth as a clearing continues to hold center stage but Heidegger no longer identifies it with being-here. Instead being-here is a necessary part of the event (*Ereignis*) of that clearing or disclosure of historical being (*Seyn*) that conceals itself in the process. As noted above, it is not only the presence (being) of beings and thus the disclosure (truth) of that presence that are incomplete and fraught with absence. The very disclosure of that presence conceals itself as well. This self-concealing—being's withdrawal or *epoche*—is the event that underlies the ways in which beings historically are present to us. Sometimes Heidegger employs "being" (*Sein*)—in contrast to "historical being" to signify the way beings are conceived metaphysically within a particular historical epoch. Historical being is the groundless, grounding event in terms of which beings are rendered present to being-here, allowing beings and being-here alike to come into their own. Against this backdrop Heidegger characterizes truth as "the clearing for the self-concealing," the self-concealing of historical being "in the clearing of the here [*da*]," where the "truth-bearer" is the appropriating event (GA 65, 344, 346/CP1, 240, 242). "The clearing of the concealment does

not mean the superseding [*Aufhebung*] of the hidden and setting it free and transforming it into something unhidden but precisely the grounding of the abyssal ground for the *concealing*" (GA 65, 352/CP1, 246).

One form of this grounding is art. "In the work [of art] the happening of truth is at work" (GA 5, 45, 59, 65/BW, 183, 196, 202). Truth happens as an openness in the midst of beings that is characterized by the strife between earth and world, at once inseparable and essentially different from one another (GA 5, 35/BW, 174). The earth constantly closes itself off from the familiar world that affords things their proximity and distance, the same world where decision, measure, and a people's fate hang historically in the balance—on earth. The truth that places itself in the artwork is "the strife between clearing and concealment in the opposition of world and earth to one another" (GA 5, 50/BW, 187).

In 1964 Heidegger makes some significant qualifications, if not retractions regarding his previous handling of the question of truth in terms of *aletheia*. He acknowledges that "the natural concept of truth" does not signify un-hiddenness and that the "question of *aletheia*, un-hiddenness, is thus not the question of truth as such." He also concedes that the claim that an essential change took place in regard to truth, namely, from un-hiddenness to correctness, is "untenable." Such a claim leaves the false impression that the early Greeks did not already use *aletheia* in the sense of correspondence or agreement (*homoiosis*). Moreover, the identification of *aletheia* with truth naively overlooks the weight of the traditional understanding of truth as *veritas*, a major historical obstacle to appreciating the full significance of un-hiddenness. Construing *aletheia* as truth also confuses the possibility of truth with any sort of actual verification (GA 14, 85ff./ID, 69–72).

However, whatever the weight of these qualifications, they do not constitute a retraction of Heidegger's basic contentions: that there is no un-hiddenness (truth in the primordial sense as *a-letheia*) and thus no truth in any sense, without hiddenness; that what it means "to be" (or, equivalently, the truth of historical being as the appropriating event) coincides with the struggle by which the un-hiddenness of things is wrested from their hiddenness; that the meaning, future, and liberation of human existence consist fundamentally in resolutely owning up to this struggle over all others.[12]

NOTES AND REFERENCES

[1] Aristotle, *De anima*, III (431a16): "the soul never thinks without an image"; see, too, ibid., 432a8–9.

[2] SZ, 226/BT, 217: "Newton's laws, the law of contradiction, and any truth whatsoever, are true only as long as Dasein *is*"; GA 65, 356/CP1, 249: "§ 229. Truth and Being-here [*Da-sein*]. The clearing for the self-concealing illumines itself in the projection. The throwing of the projection occurs as Da-sein . . ." (see, too, GA 65, 329/CP1, 231). To put the point more prosaically, truth supposes the very opposite of inactivity on our part even though it is not the product simply of anything we do.

[3] At this juncture the mill-run skeptic and Heidegger probably part ways. If the skeptic insists on the direct representation of things, the assertion that truth cannot be directly represented appears to the skeptic as a confirmation of the skeptical contention. For Heidegger, by contrast, it signals the limits of representational thinking in this sense.

[4] Longstanding debates about the truth-bearers often turn on differences between propositions and sentences, statements and judgments, and the like. While not eschewing such differences, Heidegger's criticism of the logical prejudice does not discriminate accordingly. So, sometimes he speaks of the prejudice of construing

the assertion or statement (*Aussage*) as the site of truth, other times the judgment (*Urteil*) or even the proposition or sentence (*Satz*); see SZ, 214/BT, 206.

[5] Heidegger elaborates these three functions of assertions (that they are about or refer to something by way of determining it through predication and that they are means of communication) in § 33 of SZ.

[6] Heidegger notably defends Aristotle from the charge of buying into the logical prejudice. Aristotle defines assertions in terms of truth rather than vice versa and he plainly recognizes a nonpropositional access to truth; see SZ, 226/BT, 216f.

[7] Heidegger finds a telling account of the Greek understanding of the violence of this wresting in the song of the chorus in Sophocles' *Antigone*; see GA 40, 120–32/IM, 167–83.

[8] GA 9, 223–4/PA, 171–80; GA 34, 21–112/ET, 17–81; GA 65, 331–5/CP1, 232–5.

[9] Crucial to the eventual loss of the primordial senses of hiddenness and un-hiddenness entailed by *aletheia* is its Latin translation as *veritas*. Instead of being itself a privative term, supposing an underlying hiddenness as something positive, *veritas* in the sense of imperial Roman and Ecclesial rightness or correctness becomes basic and its privation is no longer hiddenness, but something negative, namely, *falsitas*. For an extended account of this development, culminating in truth as the "judiciousness" (*Gerechtigkeit*) of the will to power, see GA 54, 42–86/P, 28–58.

[10] On the various modes of hiddenness, see GA 54, 86–130/P, 58–87.

[11] In "§ 35. Ein Hinweis auf die Wahrheitsfrage" in *Besinnung*, Heidegger lists nine key places between 1930 and 1940 where he explicitly addresses the question of truth (GA 66, 107/M, 89f.). This list supports his retrospective in 1969 where he charts the course of his thinking as proceeding from the question of the *sense* of being to that of the *truth* of being and, finally, that of the *place* of being. Notably he emphasizes that he understands truth in the second question not as the correctness of an assertion but as "unhiddenness" or "clearing" (GA 15, 344f./FS, 46f.).

[12] On resoluteness as the authentic truth, see GA 5, 55/BW, 192; GA 13, 63f.; GA 65, 87/CP1, 60f.

PART V:
RECEPTION AND INFLUENCE

46

HEIDEGGER AND SARTRE: HISTORICITY, DESTINY, AND POLITICS

Robert Bernasconi

In 1946 in *Letter on Humanism* Heidegger presented what is sometimes thought of as a devastating critique of Sartre, but only a year earlier in a note to himself he endorsed Sartre's reading of *Being and Time*. Heidegger wrote in relation to Corbin's translation of "What is Metaphysics?": "Decisive effect on Sartre: from there *Being and Time* understood for the first time" (GA 3, 251/KPM, 176). Indeed on October 28, 1945 Heidegger wrote to Sartre, not only acknowledging that in *Being and Nothingness* Sartre had shown a level of understanding of *Being and Time* that he had not found elsewhere, but also recognizing him as an independent thinker in his own right.[1] Acting completely out of character, Heidegger told Sartre that he accepted Sartre's critique of the account of *Mitsein* in *Being and Time* and he acknowledged the legitimacy of Sartre's insistence on being-for-others. At the same time Heidegger told Sartre that he himself had meanwhile moved on and that what was most important to him now was establishing an original relation with the beginning of Western history. It was a remarkably conciliatory letter, even if one cannot avoid the suspicion that Heidegger was soliciting Sartre's help during what after Germany's defeat was a difficult

time for him. But in *Letter on Humanism* Heidegger gave no hint that he had read any of *Being and Nothingness*. He focused only on *Existentialism is a Humanism*, the transcript of an occasional lecture delivered late in 1945 and intended for the general public rather than an academic audience. Sartre's lecture was itself more conciliatory in tone toward Heidegger than *Being and Nothingness* had been, but Heidegger would not have appreciated this work of popularization in which Sartre seemed to present the two of them as if they were members of the same branch of atheistic existentialism.[2] They did not meet until 1952 after which Heidegger spoke more favorably of their 90-minute conversation than did Sartre.[3]

In *Existentialism is a Humanism* Sartre had little to say about Heidegger in the essay but he did attribute to atheistic existentialism the conviction that the human being first "materializes in the world, encounters himself, and only afterward defines himself."[4] This is how Sartre explained the formulation "existence precedes essence." In *Letter on Humanism* Heidegger sought to distance himself from this formula by objecting that Sartre was still using the terms existence and essence according to their metaphysical meaning and that by merely reversing the terms he remained within Western metaphysics: "The differentiation of *essentia* (essentiality) and *existentia* (actuality) completely dominates the destiny of Western history and of all history determined by Europe" (GA 9, 329/P, 250). For Heidegger it was not as a result of a simple failure of human thinking that Western metaphysics had failed to ask the question about the destiny of being, but it belonged to that destiny itself. This notion of destiny is one of the keys to understanding what separated Sartre from Heidegger.

Sartre's specific criticisms of Heidegger in *Being and Nothingness* are now no longer generally considered to be as incisive as Heidegger suggested in his letter. Sartre himself went back on some of them as his own thinking developed and his appreciation of Heidegger's early thinking deepened as a result. Sartre had bought a copy of *Being and Time* at the end of 1933, but he did not begin to read it seriously until the summer of 1939. He explained the delay in terms of his fondness for Husserl and when he wrote *Being and Nothingness* he was still closer to Husserl than Heidegger. Nevertheless, in his *War Diaries* for February 1940, at a time when he was teaching Heidegger's philosophy to his fellow inmates in a prison of war camp, he judged his discovery of Heidegger to be "providential" because it taught him the meaning of authenticity and historicity at the very time when the war had made these notions indispensable to him.[5] In order to understand how this external influence on him could be made sense of within his philosophy of freedom, Sartre wrote "I can rediscover Heidegger's assumption of his destiny as a German, in that wretched Germany of the postwar years, in order to help assume my destiny as a Frenchman in the France of '40."[6] Sartre never lost his sense that there was a difference between these two destinies, Heidegger's and his own, but, as I shall show, the precise sense he gave them changed.

Heidegger's polemic against Sartre did not constitute a major part of the *Letter on Humanism*. This essay's philosophical significance lies rather in seeing how Heidegger, after being largely silent, chose to introduce his readers to his thinking of the history of being. But it was also a somewhat cynical attempt on his part to rehabilitate his damaged reputation after the war.[7] In addition to dismissing nationalism, Heidegger presented his thought as open to "a productive dialogue with Marxism" in a way that he alleged that Sartre was not (GA 9, 340/P, 259). Heidegger seems to have been playing it safe given the proximity of the Soviet army, but the philosophical basis of this claim was that, according to what he had read of him, Sartre did not recognize "the essential importance of the historical in being" (ibid.).

Heidegger scholars have formulated the criticisms that they believe Heidegger should have leveled against Sartre's *Being and Nothingness*. Most notably, Michel Harr accused Sartre of preserving "the fundamental structures of metaphysics," when, for example, he described the presence of consciousness to itself as "an act of self-foundation and the origin of all meaning."[8] Even when Sartre tried to follow Heidegger, as when he took up section 13 of *Being and Time* and attempted to break with Husserl by treating knowledge as a founded mode of being in the world, he allegedly ended up reaffirming the preeminence of knowledge by linking understanding with consciousness.[9] One might respond that Sartre insisted that already in *Being and Nothingness* "Consciousness is not knowledge but existence."[10] But ultimately for a Heideggerian it is Sartre's retention of the language of consciousness that assigns him irretrievably to the Western metaphysical tradition.

Whether *Being and Nothingness* is as Cartesian as is usually maintained should be questioned. It is true that Sartre insists on the *cogito* as his point of departure but he adds "that it leads us only on condition that we get out of it."[11] Heideggerian critics of Sartre who accuse him of dualism seem to be as mesmerized by—to use Simone de Beauvoir's phrase—a "pseudo-Sartrianism," just as Merleau-Ponty was.[12] They treat Sartre's for-itself and in-itself as if they had the ontological status of subject and object, whereas even in *Being and Nothingness* Sartre recognized them as abstractions. Against dualism he wrote: "the For-Itself and the In-itself are reunited by a synthetic connection which is nothing other than the For-itself itself."[13] To be sure, Sartre's reading of Heidegger in *Being and Nothingness* is inadequate by today's standards.[14] But increasingly it is the *Critique of Dialectical Reason* from 1960 that is recognized as Sartre's masterpiece and it is to this work, which has inspired philosophers from the Third World who recognized its powerful resources for identifying systemic oppression as a prelude to resisting it, that we should now turn.[15]

In *Letter on Humanism,* Heidegger reinterpreted his earlier thinking in the light of what came later, and this enabled him to exaggerate Sartre's misunderstanding of *Being and Time.* By contrast, Sartre's inclination was often to be dismissive of his own earlier ideas. This was especially true of some of his more brazen pronouncements about human freedom. They are significant in this context because they can be understood as having arisen from overemphasizing the project within Heidegger's account of the thrown project.[16] Arguably this is also what went wrong with the formulation "essence precedes existence" if one understands it, as Sartre did, in terms of the human being's encounter with the world. In any event, to correct this Sartre introduced into *Critique of Dialectical Reason* the notion of the practico-inert. The practico-inert is "Simply the activity of others in so far as it is sustained and diverted by inorganic inertia."[17] That is to say, it is the level where alienated praxis and worked inertia are equivalent.[18] Whereas the upshot of the discussion of freedom in *Being and Nothingness* was that even a slave is free because the slave can choose him- or herself on the ground of slavery, in the *Critique* Sartre protested that it is not the case that all men are free in all situations, "I mean the exact opposite: all men are slaves in so far as their life unfolds in the practico-inert field and in so far as this field is always conditioned by scarcity."[19]

The justification of this notion of scarcity lies in concrete history, but the idea is absent from *Being and Nothingness* and there is some indication that it finds its way into Sartre's philosophy as he tried to explore more deeply the basis of his distance from Heidegger. Sartre never responded publicly to Heidegger's *Letter on Humanism*, and with the possible exception of a remark in *Notebooks for an Ethics*, where he dismissed both Husserl and Heidegger as "small-time philosophers" in contrast with Hegel and even Marx, there is no indication that Sartre was offended by Heidegger's criticisms.[20] However, in the unpublished manuscript *Truth and Existence*, written only one year after the "Letter" appeared, and more focused on Heidegger's essay "Essence of Truth" that had only recently appeared in French translation, there was not a point by point rebuttal, but at least some clear indications of how Sartre would have responded to *Letter on Humanism*. One sees this, for example, in his comments on the idea of historical complacency that arises from the acceptance of destiny, Sartre writes: "As for this Being itself, it is conceived in the inauthentic (happiness or the harmonious society), because it is first of all posited by needs (hunger, revolt against slavery, etc.)."[21] Indeed, he already anticipates in this text what he says in the *Critique*, that need is concretized in scarcity and that scarcity is the material condition of antagonism.[22]

When Haar reads how Sartre in *Search for a Method* dismissed the philosophy of Karl Jaspers but judged the case of Heidegger "too complex" to discuss, he concluded that this was an evasion of the philosophical problems.[23] In my account, by contrast, these lines reflect Sartre's new appreciation for the philosophy of *Being and Time*. This interpretation is supported by Pietro Chiodi who argued that "the *Critique* is a straightforward return to the Heideggerian position after the attack on it in *Being and Nothingness*."[24] The basis for this claim is the recognition that by the time he wrote *Critique of Dialectical Reason* Sartre had come to a richer understanding of what Heidegger had meant by the thrown project. The *rapprochement* does not extend to all other aspects of the book, such as the so-called phenomenological destruction, nor to the late Heidegger. Furthermore, one has to differentiate how Heidegger seems to have understood the thrown project in *Being and Time* and how Heidegger had reinterpreted it in *Letter on Humanism* where the thrown project is no longer thrown by Dasein but by being itself (GA 9, 337/P, 257). Sartre had no reason to accept Heidegger's attempt to tie the thrown project to the thinking of destiny such that "Da-sein . . . unfolds essentially in the throw of being as a destinal sending" (GA 9, 327/P, 249).

Nevertheless, we can recognize the thrown project of *Being and Time* in the *Critique* in

Sartre's definition of praxis as "an organising project which transcends material conditions towards an end and inscribes itself, though labor, in organic matter as a rearrangement of the practical field and a reunification of means in the light of the end."[25] And the proximity to Heidegger is even clearer when Sartre insists on knowing as a moment of praxis.[26] But what gives new depth to this account is the extent to which it is tied to a new appreciation of material circumstances. As one commentator describes it, in the *Critique* Sartre renders the *cogito* dialectical and thus acknowledges that consciousness and materiality are indissolubly connected.[27] Sartre liked to borrow a phrase from Engels to make the same point: "Men themselves make their history but in a given environment that conditions them."[28]

Sartre was clearly well aware of his proximity to Heidegger and the evidence is in the text. The evidence for this emerges when we juxtapose the accusations leveled against Sartre by the Heideggerians that he did not understand Heidegger, with Sartre's comment in *Search for a Method* that "Lukács has the instruments to understand Heidegger, but he will not understand him."[29] Lukács had attacked not only Sartre in *Existentialisme ou Marxisme?* but also albeit to a lesser extent Heidegger, Jaspers, and Merleau-Ponty.[30] In the course of defending himself, Sartre chose also to come to Heidegger's defense. After saying that Lukács does not understand Heidegger, Sartre added: "And there is no longer any Marxist, to my knowledge, who is still capable of doing so."[31] By implication, Sartre was saying that he alone among Marxists understood Heidegger, and anyone who wants to understand Sartre also needs to understand Heidegger. It was hardly the most tactful way to introduce a volume designed to convince Marxists of Marxism's compatibility with existentialism, but it shows the depth of his appreciation of his debt to the early Heidegger.

Sartre's relation to the late Heidegger is very different. Although most of the references to Heidegger in *Critique of Dialectical Reason* are to the early Heidegger and, moreover, are in *Search for a Method* and so are outside the main body of the book, one passage in the *Critique* proper develops a powerful rejection of the "late Heidegger" for not being faithful to *Being and Time* and in ways that return to the themes raised by *Letter on Humanism*. Sartre writes: "The reason why Heidegger payed tribute to Marxism is that he saw Marxist philosophy as a way of showing, as Waelhens says (speaking of Heideggerian existentialism), 'that Being is Other in me . . . (and that) man . . . is himself only through Being, which is not him.'"[32] Sartre is clearly referencing the passage in *Letter on Humanism* where Heidegger alleged that Sartre was without the means to enter into a productive dialogue with Marxism. Furthermore, in referencing Heidegger's existentialism he was also reiterating the characterization to which Heidegger in the same essay had objected. Sartre continued: "But any philosophy which subordinates the human to what is Other than man, whether it be an existentialist or Marxist idealism has hatred of man as both its basis and its consequence: History has proved this in both cases."[33] That is to say, history has given us National Socialism and Stalinism and the former is reflected in Heidegger's decision to conceive of the human being as "the bearer of the opening of Being" as the latter is reflected in the external materialist dialectic. Both Heidegger and the Marxist idealists oppose the human to what is Other than man. Sartre in his inimitable way insisted that what underlies both

of them is hatred of man in the sense that they are not only victims of alienation but its accomplices too.[34]

This does not end the harsh things Sartre was willing to say about those aspects of Heidegger's philosophy from which he wanted to distance himself. In an interview in May 1975, when told that some students wondered if they could take a philosopher seriously who at one point was a Nazi, Sartre sided with them, but not because of his Nazism. "I would reproach him, but rather for a lack of seriousness. His attitude showed a compliance with the regime in power in order to continue teaching his courses more than an awareness of any value that Nazism claimed to have."[35] Sartre was willing to condemn Heidegger for his Nazism, but he was equally willing to condemn him in the face of any attempt to excuse him on the grounds that politics was of no importance to him. According to Sartre, there was a time when philosophy could be separated from politics, but that time had passed. It is on that question, rather than the issue of whether Heidegger had understood Sartre, or Sartre had understood Heidegger, that the destiny of the proper names Heidegger and Sartre will ultimately be decided. It will be determined not by the circumstances that Sartre evoked when he referred to their different nationalities, but by whether one believes one can separate philosophy from politics, which since 1933 has been the overriding question no reader of Heidegger can afford to ignore.

NOTES AND REFERENCES

[1] The letter is published in French in Frédéric de Towarnicki, *À la rencontre de Heidegger* (Paris: Gallimard, 1993), 83–5.

2 Jean-Paul Sartre, *L'existentialisme est un humanisme* (Paris: Nagel, 1946), 17; trans. Carol Macomber, *Existentialism is a Humanism* (New Haven: Yale University Press, 2007), 20.

3 Towarnicki, *À la rencontre*, 85–6.

4 Sartre, *L'existentialisme est un humanisme*, 21; trans. Macomber, *Existentialism is a Humanism*, 22.

5 Jean-Paul Sartre, *Carnets de la drôle de guerre* (Paris: Gallimard, 1995), 403; trans. Quintin Hoare, *War Diaries* (London: Verso, 1984), 182.

6 Sartre, *Carnets*, 408–9; trans. Hoare, *War Diaries*, 187.

7 See Ethan Kleinberg, "The 'Letter on Humanism.' Reading Heidegger in France," in eds Jonathan Judaken and Robert Bernasconi, *Situating Existentialism* (New York: Columbia University Press, 2012), 386–413.

8 Michel Haar, "Sartre and Heidegger," in eds Hugh J. Silverman and Frederick A. Elliston, *Jean-Paul Sartre. Contemporary Approaches to his Philosophy* (Pittsburgh: Duquesne University Press, 1980), 168.

9 Haar, "Sartre and Heidegger," 170–1.

10 Jean-Paul Sartre, *Vérité et existence* (Paris: Gallimard, 1989), 18; trans. Adrian van den Hoven, *Truth and Existence* (Chicago: University of Chicago Press, 1992), 4.

11 Jean-Paul Sartre, *L'être et le néant* (Paris: Gallimard, 1943), 116; trans. Hazel E. Barnes, *Being and Nothingness* (London: Methuen, 1957), 73–4.

12 Robert Bernasconi, "Sartre's Response to Merleau-Ponty's Charge of Subjectivism," *Philosophy Today*, 50 (Supplement 2006), 113–25.

13 Sartre, *L'être et le néant*, 711; trans. Barnes, *Being and Nothingness*, 617.

14 Nevertheless, for an example of how Sartre might still be defended, see Steve Martinot, "Sartre's being-for-Heidegger; Heidegger's being-for-Sartre," *Man and World*, 24.1 (1991), 63–74.

15 For example, Frantz Fanon, *Les damnés de la terre* (Paris: Maspero, 1961); trans. Richard Philcox, *The Wretched of the Earth* (New York: Grove Press, 2004). See Robert Bernasconi, "Racism is a System: How Existentialism became Dialectial in Fanon

and Sartre," in ed. Steven Crowell, *Cambridge Companion to Existentialism* (Cambridge: Cambridge University Press, 2012), 342–60.

16 See Robert Bernasconi, *How to Read Sartre* (London: Granta, 2006), 43–52.

17 Jean-Paul Sartre, *Critique de la raison dialectique* (Paris: Gallimard, 1960), 547; trans. Alan Sheridan-Smith, *Critique of Dialectical Reason* (London: New Left Books, 1976), 556.

18 Sartre, *Critique de la raison dialectique*, 154; trans. Sheridan-Smith, *Critique of Dialectical Reason*, 67.

19 Sartre, *L'être et le néant*, 635; trans. Barnes, *Being and Nothingness*, 550. Sartre, *Critique de la raison dialectique*, 369; trans. Sheridan-Smith, *Critique of Dialectical Reason*, 331. To be sure, on closer examination there is a passage already in *Being and Nothingness* that comes closer to what he says in the *Critique* than some commentators are willing to concede. The difference is that in *Being and Nothingness* the Other limits my freedom, whereas in the *Critique* it is the material conditions. Sartre, *L'être et le néant*, 326; trans. Barnes, *Being and Nothingness*, 267.

20 Jean-Paul Sartre, *Cahiers pour une morale* (Paris: Gaillimard, 1983), 67; trans. David Pellauer, *Notebooks for an Ethics* (Chicago: University of Chicago Press, 1992), 61.

21 Sartre, *Vérité et existence*, 12; trans. Hoven, *Truth and Existence*, 1–2.

22 Sartre, *Critique de la raison dialectique*, 192; trans. Sheridan-Smith, *Critique of Dialectical Reason*, 113. Compare Sartre, *Vérité et existence*, 84; trans. Hoven, *Truth and Existence*, 44n.

23 Haar, "Sartre and Heidegger," 169. Jean-Paul Sartre, *Critique de la raison dialectique*, 21n; trans. Hazel E. Barnes, *Search for a Method* (New York: Alfred A. Knopf, 1963), 15n.

24 Pietro Chiodi, *Sartre and Marxism*, trans. Kate Soper (Hassocks: Harvester Press, 1976), 8.

25 Sartre, *Critique de la raison dialectique*, 687; trans. Sheridan-Smith, *Critique of Dialectical Reason*, 734.

26 Sartre, *Critique de la raison dialectique*, 63; trans. Barnes, *Search for a Method*, 91.

27 Leo Fretz, "Individuality in Sartre's Philosophy," in ed. Christina Howells, *The Cambridge Companion to Sartre* (Cambridge: Cambridge University Press, 1992), 80, 89.

28 Friedrich Engels to Borgius, January 25, 1894. In Karl Marx and Friedrich Engels, *Werke*, vol. 39 (Berlin: Dietz, 1984), 206. Quoted Sartre, *Critique de la raison dialectique*, 60; trans. Barnes, *Search for a Method*, 85.

29 Sartre, *Critique de la raison dialectique*, 34–5; trans. Barnes, *Search for a Method*, 38.

30 Georg Lukacs, *Existentialisme ou Marxisme?* (Paris: Nagel, 1948).

31 Sartre, *Critique de la raison dialectique*, 34–5; trans. Barnes, *Search for a Method*, 38.

32 Sartre, *Critique de la raison dialectique*, 248; trans. Sheridan-Smith, *Critique of Dialectical Reason*, 181. The quotation is from Alphonse de Waelhens, *Phénoménologie et Vérité. Essai sur l'évolution de l'idée de verité chez Husserl et Heidegger* (Paris: PUF, 1953), 160. It should be noted that this book and specifically this passage concerns the early Heidegger. Sartre also cites Walter Biemel's book, which has more to say about the later Heidegger: *Le concept de monde chez Heidegger* (Paris: Vrin, 1950).

33 Sartre, *Critique de la raison dialectique*, 248; trans. Sheridan-Smith, *Critique of Dialectical Reason*, 181.

34 Ibid.

35 Jean-Paul Sartre, "An Interview with Jean-Paul Sartre," in ed. Paul Arthur Schilpp, *The Philosophy of Jean-Paul Sartre* (La Salle, IL: Open Court, 1981), 32. It should also be recalled that in Occupied France after the publication of *Being and Nothingness* Sartre was criticized for his interest in a Nazi philosopher like Heidegger. Kenneth and Margaret Thompson, *Sartre. Life and Works* (New York: Facts on File, 1984), 50.

47

HEIDEGGER AND MERLEAU-PONTY: THOUGHT IN THE OPEN

Wayne J. Froman

Merleau-Ponty's *Notes de Cours 1959–1961*,[1] from his lectures at the Collège de France, published in 1996, provide background for the significant appearance in his *The Visible and the Invisible: Followed by Working Notes*,[2] unfinished at the time of his death and published posthumously in 1964, of Heideggerian terminology.[3] The publication of Heidegger's early lectures, including, from the summer of 1920, *Phenomenology of Intuition and Expression* (GA 59/PIE), which will be particularly helpful here, provide important background for *Being and Time* (GA 2/BTMR, BT), and at the same time are of help in understanding the pertinence of Merleau-Ponty's thought to Heidegger's. The issue in these lectures is facticity, and along with it, historicity. Facticity, the very fact that we are and must be, tends to obscure itself and this marks movement away or distancing from facticity. This is a historicizing intrinsic to lived experience and it opens us to cultural and historical factors. In that facticity is the fact that we are and must be, in one way or another, there is a movement of return. This movement amounts to our living out, what Heidegger calls a "*vollziehen*," an enactment, a carrying out, or perhaps, execution, of what Heidegger here calls a

"sense-complex" that comes about by way of the historicizing of our lived experience. Philosophy's task, as Heidegger understands it here, is the primordial carrying out of this movement, and with this sense of primordiality, Heidegger takes up the issue of "constitution," which figures in phenomenology as, so to speak, an ultimate dynamic. The coming about of this "sense-complex" by way of the initial self-obscuring or movement away that pertains to facticity marks the occurrence or the event of world, and along with that, as Heidegger will accentuate in *Being and Time*, how we are always already in-the-world by way of a structure where the unity is Care (*Sorge*).

Importantly, the falling away of facticity, its self-obscuring, always comes first. It is not after the fact. Thus, there is no initial coincidence, and this is the significance of the word "complex" in reference to facticity. We are always already in-the-world. In *Being and Time*, Heidegger will characterize facticity as a "thrown projection." The point to the effect that there is no initial coincidence is what makes Heidegger's phenomenological analysis here a "de-struction" of both "intuition" and "expression." "Intuition," associated by Husserl with an end-point of phenomenological reduction, where the content of awareness is apprehended apodictically in its self-givenness or self-evidence, would amount to an immediate and direct apprehension of what is there to be apprehended, but by virtue of the fact that the obscuring of facticity and the movement away comes first, there is no such coincidence in the first place to be recovered or regained. The sense of a direct and immediate apprehension of what is there to be apprehended is bound up with the Cartesian Cogito, the "I think," which is characterized by direct and immediate access to its content, providing a certainty that would have to be included, somehow, in any knowing.

When Heidegger then examines two competing philosophical trajectories at the time, that of Paul Natorp and that of Wilhelm Dilthey, he finds them both lacking, in different ways, and to different degrees, with regard to the issue of facticity. Natorp advocated a methodological "reconstruction" of Platonic truths and in doing so took as a starting point a vantage point already sufficiently distanced from the fact that we are and must be as to preclude the sense of facticity and a return to the context of lived experience. Dilthey, in understanding the subject matter of the historical sciences as self-expressions of life that can be understood by means of hermeneutics, rather than by means of the explanatory methodology of the natural sciences that is bound up with a Cartesian sense of the Cogito, was surely closer to facticity and historicity. But Dilthey's far-reaching insights notwithstanding, what Heidegger finds is: "Dilthey did not see that only a radicalism that makes all concepts questionable can lead further. The entire conceptual material must be newly determined in primordial apprehension. That is the particular tendency of phenomenology" (PIE, 129).

In *Being and Time*, Heidegger proceeds with phenomenological analysis of that entity we are, *Dasein*, that is, the entity characterized by ex-istence, by our always already being-in-the-world, which is the mark of our facticity. *Dasein* is characterized, in effect, by a running ahead of itself (*vorlaufen*). In Division I, "Preparatory Fundamental Analysis of *Dasein*," of Part I, the only part to ever see the light of day, Heidegger specifies three "*existentialia*," structural features of the "existential constitution of the 'there'" (the *da*) of *Dasein* whereby *Dasein* gets disclosed: *Befindlichkeit*, mood (or attunement, or disposition), *Verstehen*, understanding, and *Rede*, discourse. Mood, which Heidegger analyzes first, is disclosive of being-in-the-world as a whole (BTMR, 176). Mood always involves a moving away and a moving toward. For example, fear involves that of which one is fearful, and it involves that for which one is fearful. What distinguishes the mood of anxiety, which Heidegger characterizes as a rare mood that can precede an individual's being in the Moment (*Augenblick*), is that what one is anxious about and that for the sake of which one is anxious are the same, namely, one's very being-in-the-world.

After the analyses of the three structural features of our being-in-the-world, no one of which lies deeper than or accounts for the others, which is to say that they are "equi-primordial," and after the specification that the unity of these features lies in Care (*Sorge*), Heidegger asks about the possibility of bringing *Dasein* as a whole within our grasp. This would guard against the possibility of an undermining of the analysis. Heidegger finds possible means for bringing *Dasein* as a whole within our grasp, which is to say, in effect, thinking *Dasein* from one end to the other, in *Dasein*'s being toward a distinctive "end," namely, death or mortality. This suggests the possibility of an "authentic" mode of existence that amounts to the "how" of being in the Moment (*Augenblick*), which is to say, the authentic present. This authentic present lies in the alignment of extremities of future and past, where the former is understood in terms of *Dasein*'s running ahead of itself unto death or mortality, and the latter is understood in terms of a resolute return, in effect, to facticity, a return that is prompted by the call of conscience. The analysis of the possibility of an "authentic" mode of existence then becomes the point of departure for a preliminary reinterpretation of *Dasein*'s existential structure in terms of the temporalizing of *Dasein*.

After that preliminary reinterpretation of *Dasein*'s existential structure, Heidegger observes that a deeper rethinking of the character of *Dasein* would have to take into account the other "end" of *Dasein*, in addition to death or mortality, namely, birth. Now, in the next to last chapter of what was to be part I of a two-part *Being and Time*, Heidegger explicitly brings up the issue of history. Here Heidegger characterizes his thinking as hermeneutical in a manner that takes up the work of Count Von Yorck in the service of Dilthey's insights. Count Von Yorck had emphasized the historicity of the practitioner of hermeneutics, so to speak, in distinction from the historicity of the hermeneutical subject matter, so to speak. What Heidegger specifies here is that the possibility for understanding historicity lies in understanding the temporalizing of *Dasein*. While Heidegger's discussion here of historicizing is brief, it is clear from his earlier lectures, and in particular from his *Phenomenology of Intuition and Expression*, that this is hardly a tacked-on afterthought. It is, in fact, the destination of his thinking here.

From the initial characterization of our facticity in terms of *Dasein*'s running ahead of itself, the sense in which *Dasein* is always already in-the-world, to the appearance late in the text of the question of history, what is undermined is the direct and immediate access to its own content of the Cartesian *Cogito*. This direct and immediate access to its own content is indicative of the classical sense of *substance* that goes back to the manner in which Aristotle takes the culmination of Greek philosophy in Plato's thought to its farthest reaches. What is at stake in that culmination of Greek philosophy is the identification of Being with presentness, which means with ongoing presence. That identification will define philosophical thought since the Greeks. Descartes unquestioningly adopts the sense of substance. In modern thinking, Kant's transcendental philosophizing, for all its radicality, will nonetheless sustain that sense of substance in its analysis of reflection. In Heidegger's understanding, the longstanding model, in effect, for what becomes the standard ontology, is found in the conception of perception as a bringing together of a concept with a sensory manifold, a "making present" that amounts, in effect, to a subjectivizing of perception in a manner consistent with a tendency in Greek thought, and which reinforces an unquestioned identification of Being with ongoing presence. What drops out is any sense of facticity's self-obscuring and the movement away or forgetting that precedes a living out, in one way or another, an enactment of the sense-complex that takes shape with this historicizing. In Heidegger's *The Basic Problems of Phenomenology*, a lecture course from the same year as the publication of *Being and Time*, 1927, he writes:

When Kant says, therefore, that existence—that is, for us, extantness, being on or at hand—is perception, this thesis is extremely rough and misleading; all the same it points to the correct direction of the problem. On our interpretation, 'being is perception' now means: being is an intentional comportment of a peculiar sort, namely, enpresenting; it is an ecstasis in the unity of temporality with a schema of its own, praesens. 'Being equals perception,' when interpreted in original phenomenological terms, means: being equals presence, praesens. At the same time, it thus turns out that Kant interprets being and being-existent exactly as ancient philosophy does, for which that which *is* is the hupokeimenon, which has the character of ousia (substance). In Aristotle's time ousia in its everyday, pre-philosophical sense is still equivalent to property, estate, but as a philosophical term it signifies presence. (BP, 315)

In *Phenomenology of Perception*, published in 1945, Merleau-Ponty carries out a "de-struction" of perception.[4] He first distinguishes theoretical accounts of perception that are empiricist in character from theoretical accounts of perception that are intellectualist in character. According to the former, perception's content comes about basically by way of an automatic physiological process. According to the latter, perceptual content comes about by way of an intervention, such as attention or judgment, by the intellect. Merleau-Ponty then points out that both types of theoretical accounts employ the notion of sense data or bare units of sensation. Furthermore, we never encounter such units in our awareness. These are purely constructs employed in contrived theoretical depictions of perception. At one point, Merleau-Ponty characterizes perception as just that act that creates its data at

a stroke. The point here is that there can be no "data" until the perception takes place.[5] Merleau-Ponty next distinguishes between our body as objectivistically conceived, which is to say conceived subjectivistically, and our body as lived, the phenomenal body, or one's own body (*le corps propre*), or the lived body (*le corps vécu*). Here Merleau-Ponty explores the spatiality of the body and motility, the synthesis of the body understood as ec-static by way of the living of the body, the sexual schema of the body, and the body as expression and speech. All of this is prior to our body as objectivisitically conceived, which is to say, conceived subjectivistically. None of this can be understood by way of an objectivistic analysis, which relies on a subjectivistic point of departure.

In part II of the text, Merleau-Ponty explores "the world as perceived." He proceeds by way of "sensory experience" where the synthesis is again prior to objectification by a subjectivity. Having begun from the lived body, and proceeding by way of "sensory experience," Merleau-Ponty reaches the other pole, so to speak, of this trajectory, "the world as perceived," which includes "the things" and the natural world as well as "others" and the human world. Along the way, there are indications of how all this may actually be perceived in a manner that is not bound up with objectification.

In part III of the text, the final part, Merleau-Ponty addresses the Cogito, temporality and freedom. Importantly, with each step into a "subjectivity," Merleau-Ponty discovers our being-in-the-world. In the chapter devoted to the Cogito, Merleau-Ponty suggests a "tacit cogito" that is prior to Descartes's articulated Cogito and that lies in the context of existence, the context of our being-in-the-world. Importantly, by the time Merleau-Ponty begins work on *The Visible* and the Invisible, we find in the Working Notes for the text published along with it that he had found the "tacit cogito" untenable insofar as it would imply an adequation at the level of existence or being-in-the-world. He also indicates in a Working Note that the analysis of the Cogito should have been related explicitly to the analysis, earlier in *Phenomenology of Perception*, of the body as expression and speech. That analysis is, in effect, the high point of Merleau-Ponty's exploration of the body as lived where he finds that speech, despite all the complexities of language as spoken, comes about by means of a gesture, which is to say, on the basis of the living of the body. If we take into account the fact that the subject matter of history has long and for the most part been specified as *res gestae*, in distinction from the Cartesian domains of *res cogitans* and *res extensa*, we find, despite what may seem to be the case at first sight, that we are not that far from Heidegger's crucial concern with historicizing in his work up through and including *Being and Time*, and which he would eventually understand in its pertinence to the character of aletheia.

In one of the Working Notes for *The Visible and the Invisible*, Merleau-Ponty observes that while his analyses in *Phenomenology of Perception* may be taken as psychological in character, his findings there must be understood in terms of their ontological import. In *The Visible and the Invisible*, which was to have been the next major text, Merleau-Ponty takes up those findings in a more primordial manner. What he does first is to analyze three primary modes of philosophizing: philosophy that proceeds in terms of reflection, philosophy that proceeds in terms of dialectic, and philosophy that proceeds in terms of intuition. With regard to philosophies of reflection, the initial step that takes

one to the context of reflection remains itself unjustified and facticity is simply lost from sight. With regard to dialectical philosophizing, which reaches its culmination in Hegel's work, an ultimately "auto-critical" dimension would be needed in order that facticity not drop out in the course of the dialectical ascent. This is not provided by Sartre's "truncated dialectic" in *Being and Nothingness* insofar as the theoretical diremption between Being and Nothingness with which it begins disallows any sense of the precedence of a movement away as it pertains to facticity. Finally, with regard to philosophies of intuition, Merleau-Ponty first addresses Husserl's appeal to intuition, and in particular, the so-called *Wesenschau*, or intuition of an essence. Merleau-Ponty observes that the question of Being remains an issue behind any attempt to determine an essence, as it does where questions of fact are concerned, and along these lines, he finds that there is a certain interchangeability between the two questions. Merleau-Ponty also observes that Husserl never reached a presumed intuition of an essence that he did not find it necessary to reexamine. Where all this leads, Merleau-Ponty concludes, is in the direction of Heidegger's eventual understanding of the verbal sense of the German word "*das Wesen*," essence. Merleau-Ponty writes:

There is no emplacement of space and time that would not be a variant of the others, as they are of it; there is no individual that would not be representative of a species or of a family of beings, would not have, would not be a certain style, a certain manner of managing the domain, of radiating about a wholly virtual center—in short, a certain manner of being, in the active sense, a certain *Wesen*, in the sense that, says Heidegger, this word has when it is used as a verb.[6]

In a footnote to this passage, Merleau-Ponty cites Heidegger: "The high school building, for us who return to it, thirty years later, as for those who occupy it today, is not so much an object which it would be useful or possible to describe by its characteristics, as it is a certain odor, a certain affective texture which holds sway over a certain vicinity of space."[7]

After this, Merleau-Ponty turns, more briefly, to Bergson's appeal to intuition. While affirming Bergson's sense of the type of language required of the philosopher,[8] Merleau-Ponty finds, nevertheless, that "what Bergson lacks is the double reference, the identity of the retiring into oneself with the leaving of oneself, of the lived through with this distance."[9] This *écart*, this "divergence," this "reversal," this "differentiation" that Merleau-Ponty finds at the heart of "intuition" decisively rules out the adequation of the Cogito (although Merleau-Ponty allows for a possibility that Descartes must have been aware of what precedes a theoretical diremption of the empirical and reflection's context) and it returns us directly to Heidegger's crucial concern with historicizing as this shows up early on in the course of his de-struction of intuition, and then again, near the close of *Being and Time*. The importance of this finding for Merleau-Ponty can be gauged in terms of the following two passages. The first is from a Working Note: "The true philosophy = apprehend what makes the leaving of oneself be a retiring into oneself, and vice versa. Grasp this chiasm, this reversal. That is the mind."[10] In other words, it marks what is distinctive to who we are. The other passage is found in the chapter "Interrogation and Intuition":

As my body, which is one of the visibles, sees itself also and thereby makes itself the natural light opening its own interior to the visible, in order for the visible there to become my own landscape, realizing (as it is said) the miraculous promotion of Being to "consciousness," or (as we prefer to say) the segregation of the "within" and the "without"; so also. . . .[11]

In the chapter "Interrogation and Intuition" we find the following: ". . . the world and I are within one another, and there is no anteriority of the *percipere* to the *percipi*, there is simultaneity or even retardation."[12] It is on the basis of this "simultaneity," or this "retardation" (which accounts for a sense that the *percipere* is anterior), or this deferral (to adopt a term of Derridian provenance), that we might understand better why Merleau-Ponty observes in one of the Working Notes that it is by understanding perception that we will be able to respond to the questions that pertain to history.[13]

Another term whereby Merleau-Ponty refers to the *écart*, the divergence, the differentiation, the reversal, is "openness," or simply, "the open." It is here where exteriority and interiority reverse into one another, here where "the world worlds," that Heidegger's thought seeks a dwelling. His discussion of the time-space of the Moment (*der Zeitraum des Augenblicks*) in the mid-1930s unfinished text *Beiträge zur Philosophie: Vom Ereignis* (first published in 1989) (GA 65, CP2), where the themes of his later thought come into view, points in this direction. Prompted by Hölderlin, Heidegger would address "the open" in later texts in terms of a gathering of the Fourfold or the Quadrate (*Geviert*) of earth, heavens, mortals, and divinity, which separates while bringing together. Where Heidegger takes up this thought of the "nearing" of the Fourfold at the close of his lecture "The Turning," (*die Kehre*) from 1949, we find what may well be the one point in

Heidegger's writings where what he says takes the form of prayer: "May world in its world-ing be the nearest of all nearing that nears, as it brings the truth of Being near to man's essence, and so gives man to belong to the dis-closing bringing-to-pass that is a bringing into its own" (QCT, 49). By way of a philosophi-cal gesture of interrogation prompted by the enigma that perception gives us access to the things even while it removes us to a margin of the world, a gesture of eliciting a response from that "mute or reticent interlocutor" that is Being, Merleau-Ponty, in the last chapter he wrote for *The Visible and the Invisible*, begins to take his bearings in the Open, and he observes here how having entered it, "one does not see how there could be any ques-tion of *leaving* it."[14] This is a mark of the primordial or the originary character of what Merleau-Ponty calls "this strange domain."[15] This primordiality is a first indication of *das Ereignis*, the event of world, as addressed by Heidegger in his later work, an event that is not epochal and that cannot be recaptured by the Greek metaphysics of presence. Both Merleau-Ponty and Heidegger caught sight of this in the strange precedence of the move-ment away, the forgetting, or the withdrawal that characterizes our being-in-the-world.

NOTES AND REFERENCES

1 Maurice Merleau-Ponty, *Notes de cours: 1959–1961* (Paris: Gallimard, 1996).

2 Maurice Merleau-Ponty, *Le Visible et l'invisible* ed. Claude Lefort (Paris: Gallimard, 1964); *The Visible and the Invisible: Followed by Working Notes*, trans. Alphonso Lingus (Evanston, IL: Northwestern University Press, 1968).

3 For a reading of the pertinent *Notes de cours* lectures, see my "Merleau-Ponty's 1959 Heidegger Lectures: The Task of Thinking and the Possibility of Philosophy Today," in ed. David Pettigrew and François Raffoul, *French Interpretations of Heidegger: An Exceptional Reception* (Albany, NY: SUNY Press, 2008).

4 Maurice Merleau-Ponty, *Phénoménologie de la perception* (Paris: Gallimard, 1945); *Phenomenology of Perception*, trans. Colin Smith (London: Routledge & Kegan Paul, 1962); 2nd edn, 2002.

5 This parallels Merleau-Ponty's finding in his previous book, *La structure du comporte-ment* (Paris: Gallimard, 1942); 2nd edn, 2006; *The Structure of Behavior*, trans. Alden Fisher (Boston: Beacon Press, 1963), where he observes that the linear model of the arc of stimulus-response breaks down once one real-izes that there can be no "stimulus" until the response takes place.

6 Merleau-Ponty, *The Visible and the Invisible*, 114–15.

7 Martin Heidegger, *Introduction to Metaphysics*, trans. Ralph Manheim (Garden City, NY: Anchor Books, 1961), 27–8 cited in Merleau-Ponty, *The Visible and the Invisible*, 115.

8 See Merleau-Ponty, *The Visible and the Invisible*, 125.

9 Ibid., 124.

10 Ibid., 199.

11 Ibid., 118.

12 Ibid., 123.

13 Ibid., 196.

14 Ibid., 152.

15 Ibid.

48

HEIDEGGER AND ADORNO
Iain Macdonald

A random sampling of Adorno's many references to Heidegger will likely leave the reader with a strong impression of his view. Yet it would be wrong to infer from the severity and unrelenting nature of his objections that his opposition to Heidegger is thoughtless or malicious. On the contrary, although it is harsh and persistent, it is philosophical at its core.

The critique of Heidegger spans the entirety of Adorno's career, beginning in 1931 with his inaugural address, "The Actuality of Philosophy," and returning in numerous texts, right up until his death in 1969. The core theses of the critique are laid out in detail in *Jargon of Authenticity* (1964) and in part one of *Negative Dialectics* (1966). The lecture course entitled *Ontologie und Dialektik* [*Ontology and Dialectics*], from 1960–1, is also of direct relevance. Other texts contain material of interest as well, such as the 1932 lecture on "The Idea of Natural-History" and the lecture course entitled *Philosophische Terminologie* [*Philosophical Terminology*], from 1962–3. There are scattered remarks in many other works.

LAYERS OF CRITIQUE

Part of the difficulty of getting at the heart of Adorno's critique of Heidegger is that it is quite varied in tone and substance. In general, three layers of criticism may be discerned in his writings. His position becomes clearer as we peel back these layers.

The first layer provides the rhetorical shell of the critique. Here, we find the remarks that openly mock or pour scorn on Heidegger's language and approach. Adorno refers, for example, to Heidegger's agrarianism[1] and his "homely murmuring," calling attention to a resemblance of some of his writings to "trusty folk art."[2] Adorno also compares Heidegger's attempts "to think being without beings" (GA 14, 29/TB, 24) to the behavior of the obsessive compulsive, who must constantly wash his hands to keep from getting them dirty (OD, 102–3).[3] We should also include under this heading the particular derision that Adorno reserves for Heideggerians who mimic their master's way of speaking and thereby lapse into performative contradiction. This is the "jargon of authenticity" at its most pernicious and the critique is correspondingly unforgiving: "the stereotypes of the jargon seem to guarantee that one is not doing what, in fact, one is doing, namely, bleating with the herd; they seem to guarantee that one has achieved it all oneself as an unmistakably free person. The formal gesture of autonomy replaces the content of autonomy" (GS 6, 425/JA, 18). In other words, the question of whether or not one is free and "authentic" cannot be decided by the use of catchwords. This, however, is merely the first layer of criticism.

The second layer concerns fascism and Nazism. Adorno was well aware of Heidegger's involvement with the Nazi party and cites Karl Löwith in this connection.[4] Moreover, he suggests that Heidegger's philosophy promotes emotional investment in something like the "National Socialist *Volk*-community" (GS 6, 463/JA, 76). Likewise, Adorno refers to Heidegger as belonging to a group of "*Blubo* friends" (i.e. "*Blut und Boden*" or "blood and soil" comrades) and Heideggerian jargon is said to be the philosophical continuation of "blood and soil" rhetoric (GS 6, 449, 480/JA, 55, 100). Elsewhere, he refers to Heidegger as an *alter Kämpfer*, or member of the old guard, a phrase that implies a commitment to National Socialism prior to 1933 (OD, 74). Perhaps most damningly, Adorno claims that Heidegger's "philosophy is fascist to its innermost cells" (GS 19, 638). Some commentators take such references to be determining, subsuming Adorno's critique of Heidegger under his critique of fascism.[5] But this would be to stop short of the real substance of Adorno's view, not least because such remarks are relatively marginal in the context of the overall critique.

THE CRITIQUE OF ABSTRACTION

The third and final layer of Adorno's critique of Heidegger is composed of more substantial philosophical challenges to the thinking of being. Among these, the critique of abstraction is perhaps the most important because it is tied to two other essential components of

Adorno's reading of Heidegger: the legitimate need to which Heidegger's thought responds, and the kind of thinking that should arise from the disappointment of that need.

It may seem strange at first that abstraction should be one of Adorno's central criticisms. After all, in *Being and Time*, Heidegger argues explicitly that *Dasein* must be analyzed in its concreteness, that is, in its everydayness and according to its facticity and *Jemeinigkeit*—its concrete mineness. It was this approach that more or less briefly impressed Adorno's future colleagues, Herbert Marcuse and, astonishingly, Max Horkheimer.[6] As Adorno puts it in *Jargon of Authenticity*: around 1925 there was a perceptible need for a philosophy that responded to the "concretion of experience, thought, and comportment in the midst of a total situation that served an abstraction: exchange" (GS 6, 475/JA, 92). This "ontological need," as he calls it, was quite real and valid: the new ontology's enthusiastic reception "would be unintelligible if it did not meet an emphatic need, if it were not a sign of something missed" (GS 6, 69/ND, 61). Heidegger seemed to meet that need by offering, for example, a critique of inauthentic and impersonal social relations, as well as a philosophical approach, apparently interested in historicality, that might serve to ground social philosophy. However, for Adorno, Heidegger's "treatment of relevant things relapsed into abstraction" (GS 6, 71/ND, 63).

This relapse is perhaps most evident in Heidegger's approach to history and the philosophical tradition, as outlined, for example, in his so-called deconstructive readings of Western metaphysics. In the 1920s, Heidegger at first called for a "recursion" (*Rückgang*) to the tradition that would appropriate the relation to being concealed within it (GA 24, 31/BP, 23). In later years, this recursion undergoes a transformation into the "step back" (*der Schritt zurück*), by which the engagement with the tradition aims not at something that has already been thought but rather at "something that has not been thought, from which thought receives its essential space" (GA 11, 57/ID, 48). As Heidegger puts it, "the step back goes from what is unthought [*vom Ungedachten*], from the difference [between being and beings], into what remains to be thought [*in das zu-Denkende*]" (GA 11, 59/ID, 50).

The step back is therefore not merely a critical-interpretive gesture. At root, it is a step *away* from any thinking that primarily treats of beings or of being in terms of beings. But it is also a step *toward* a new way of thinking, one that addresses being itself as event (*Ereignis*). Of course, thought must "prepare" for the step back "in view of" beings as they are *now*, that is, as technologically determined and reduced to mere functionality (GA 11, 60/ID, 51). Nevertheless, the step back is most essentially a "step out of technology and technological description and interpretation of the age, into the *essence* of modern technology, which remains to be thought" (GA 11, 61/ID, 52). Hence, for Heidegger, the step back cannot be directly critical of social and scientific etiolations of experience, which are at best mere symptoms and incitements. It is the openness of being in its relation to the human being that must be grasped—not the sociohistorical arrangements of beings that occur within that openness.

Consequently, the task of thinking being cannot surrender to "the dialectical mediation of the movement of absolute spirit and of the historical process of production" (GA 14, 70/TB, 56), that is, Hegel, Marx, and the sociohistorical interests motivating their philosophies. Indeed, Heidegger will even say

that Marx's call to transform the world tacitly depends upon the possibility of an adequate interpretation *not* of existing actuality, but of what a world is in general—the hidden possibility of world, as opposed to social relations among things in the world.[7]

If Heidegger's thought was appealing in the 1920s because it seemed concrete and developed a critique of inauthenticity that was rooted in *Dasein*'s everydayness, then increasingly it shed the appearance of this concretion and everydayness for a history of being that openly rejected as insufficiently thoughtful the social and practical problems of alienation and the historical relations of production—whence the relapse into abstraction. For Heidegger the only history that philosophy can legitimately concern itself with is one that "does not consist in the happenings and deeds of the world," nor "in the cultural achievements of human beings" (GA 13, 61–2/DT, 79), all of which take place only as a mere mode of ἀληθεύειν, of "rendering beings manifest" (GA 9, 340/PA, 259). Strictly speaking, thinking must penetrate beyond history, into historicality and its temporal conditions, that is, into the very possibility of metaphysical questioning—and ultimately into ἀλήθεια, that is, the play of concealment and unconcealment itself.

Thus, in Adorno's view, Heidegger is more concerned with primordial possibility than with the real possibility of emancipation, which is suppressed by existing conditions. Moreover, it seems clear that for Heidegger the possibility of an other beginning for thinking remains indefinitely blocked by metaphysical prejudices that we cannot seem to escape: "The age of the 'systems' has past. The age that would elaborate the essential form of beings from out of the truth of beyng [*Seyn*] has not yet come" (GA 65, 5/CP2, 6). Consequently, the retreat into primordiality entails a projection of the corrective to metaphysical prejudice onto a distant future, effectively detached from the present. For Heidegger, we can only strive to awaken "a readiness in man for a possibility whose contour remains obscure, whose coming remains uncertain," all the while living in equal uncertainty about "whether world civilization will soon be abruptly destroyed or whether it will be stabilized for a long time [in a monotonous sequence of changing fashions]" (GA 14, 75/TB, 60).

To this sort of talk, Adorno responds with a charge of willful indifference to existing suffering: "A new beginning [*Neubeginn*] at an alleged zero point is the mask of intense forgetting—sympathy with barbarism is not extrinsic to it" (GS 6, 79/ND, 71). The question is this: is the uncertain promise of a transition to a new age not tantamount to allowing the existing world to follow its wicked course untrammeled, perhaps to catastrophe? The more we look to the primordial origin or to the uncertain future, the more we turn a blind eye to contemporary barbarism. But what is this intense forgetting of which Adorno speaks? This question can be answered in two parts.

First, Adorno acknowledges—even appreciates, to some extent—that being (*Sein*) refers to an insufficiency of beings, that is, that the current organization of beings is false, and that another way of thinking is not only logically possible, but indicated by the existing order, however faintly or negatively. Indeed, Adorno will even say that the being of beings "reminds us" of an essential fact: that "any being whatever is more than it is" (GS 6, 109/ND, 102), and that it is the proper task of language to name this nonidentical "more" or hidden potentiality in things. But for Adorno this potentiality is precisely *in things*, which means: in the way things are

socially determined (e.g. Marx names surplus value as the hidden origin of exploitation and the objective impetus to emancipation). By contrast, Heidegger "blurs the distinction between the 'more' for which language gropes and the being-in-itself of this more" (GS 6, 421/JA, 12). In other words, Heidegger treats this "more" not as a contextually determined social problem—whereby an emancipatory potential is suppressed by existing material and historical relations—but rather as inherent to being itself beyond any particular historical organization of things (e.g. the refusal, withdrawal, etc. proper to being). Thus for Adorno, emancipatory potential requires the rigorous determination of existing conditions and, ultimately, a refinement of the entwinement of subject and object in concrete society, whereas "Heidegger seeks to hold on to the pointing-beyond-itself, and to leave behind, as rubble, that beyond which it points [i.e. beings]" (GS 6, 109/ND, 102). Essentially, what Heidegger forgets is the fact that all "thinking is bound to beings" (GS 6, 110n/ND, 103n). To the extent that the concreteness of the "more" is "forgotten" in the thinking of being, the world is left to its vices—while awaiting, perhaps forever, a reorganization of beings from out of the truth of beyng.

Second, the accusation of an "intense forgetting" of beings is reinforced by Adorno in the claim that Heidegger "ontologizes the ontic" and thereby reifies states of affairs that cannot be reified. For example, he castigates Heidegger for normalizing anxiety (*Angst*): "categories such as anxiety—of which, at the very least, we cannot stipulate that they must be everlasting—are transfigured into constituents of being" (GS 6, 125/ND, 119). Similarly, thrownness (*Geworfenheit*) and the structures of *Dasein* more generally "drown out intimations of objective negativity [i.e. of an emancipatory 'more'] through the message of an implicit and essential order of things [*Ordnung an sich*], up to the most abstract order, that of the structures of being" (GS 6, 96/ND, 89). The problem, put succinctly, is that "the categories of the jargon [i.e. primarily the existentiales of *Being and Time*] are happily put on display, as though they were not abstracted from generated and transitory situations, but rather belonged to the essence of the human being as inalienable possibility. The human being is the ideology of dehumanization" (GS 6, 452/JA, 59). That is, what is socially constructed and ought to be surmountable is instead presented as fundamental and ineluctable (e.g. anxiety, curiosity, idle talk, and even death, insofar as one is defined by such terms). As such, "suffering, evil, and death are to be accepted, not to be changed. The public is being made to rehearse a balancing act: they are being prepared to see their nothingness as being; to revere avoidable or at least corrigible distress as what is most human in the image of the human; to respect authority on the basis of innate human insufficiency" (GS 6, 456–7/ JA, 67). Here again, the criticism is that Heidegger has gone to great lengths to forget beings and the suffering of the human being in particular. He renders fixed that which is fluid, and natural that which is social—and thereby robs us of the possibility of changing our sorry lot by projecting this possibility onto an uncertain and unclear other beginning beyond metaphysical prejudices, from which, for the foreseeable future, we can only "prepare" to break free.

Thus the main line of the critique of Heidegger amounts to this: the jargon "wants to be immediately concrete without sliding into mere facticity and is thereby forced into secret abstraction" (GS 6, 475/ JA, 92–3). The ontological need to speak of relevant things beyond the academicism and formalism of traditional metaphysics, while quite legitimate, is disappointed by Heidegger's thought, which demands of us that we look away from the specific problems that assail us, toward the general possibility of the openness of being. The charge of abstraction thereby rests on four interrelated points: history is eclipsed by historicality and temporality; the talk of hidden origins and of overcoming metaphysics disregards the pressing problems of today; the "more" of the being of beings is hypostatized; and the structures of *Dasein* unduly fix and normalize aspects of existence.

By contrast, for Adorno, the ontological need is to be met by determining and naming the "more" that is implied by the systematic, socially constructed features of wrong life. It is in this sense that "dialectics is the ontology of the wrong state of things" (GS 6, 22/ND, 11): the only true ontology would be one that describes *not* what is, but rather what *ought not to be* and the real possibility of its overcoming.

HEIDEGGER'S RESPONSE

Heidegger never responded directly to Adorno's critiques. However, in a 1969 interview with Richard Wisser (just a few weeks after Adorno's death), he answers the charge that his thought was unconcerned with "concrete society and all its various responsibilities and worries, troubles and hopes" (MHIG, 69). He must certainly have had Adorno in mind. His response, which is very brief, is that such critiques are simple *misunderstandings:* "the openness of being *needs* human beings and, inversely, . . . the human being is human only insofar as he stands in the openness of being" (ibid.). The social aspect of Wisser's question is passed over in silence. But in off-the-record remarks to Wisser, Heidegger was more direct—and severe. To the question whether philosophy has a social mission, he replied, somewhat curtly: "No! I see none!"[8] Further prompting by Wisser was met with great reserve. In the same informal discussion, he also wondered aloud about "the kind of man" who would seek to "bring him down" as he thought Adorno had (FI, 283).[9]

Heidegger's correspondence with Ernst Jünger shows that Adorno's name and views were known to him at least as early as 1966 and quite possibly long before.[10] As to whether he had read Adorno or whether the critique had merely been reported to him, there is one crystal clear indication, again recorded by Wisser in 1969: "I have read nothing by him. Hermann Mörchen once tried to talk me into reading him. I never did" (283–4). Nevertheless, Heidegger questions Adorno's credentials and suggests to Wisser that he was merely a sociologist, not a philosopher (284).

and substantially modified his approach after *Being and Time*. However, he does note the shifts from *Dasein* to being (*Sein*), and from being to beyng (*Seyn*) and to the typographical crossing out of the word being (OD, 71–2).

Second, Adorno fails to follow up on specific points of intersection between his thought and Heidegger's, even to dispel the illusion of compatibility; rather, he flatly denies all compatibility (GS 19, 638). Nevertheless, certain points of intersection do suggest themselves: for example, their special appreciation of the poet Paul Celan and their interest in defending the priority of possibility over actuality (against a longstanding metaphysical tradition). More generally, it is a pity that Adorno did not pursue reflections such as the following, from a 1949 letter to Horkheimer: "I've been thinking a lot about Heidegger and will send you . . . a few more notes. In the meantime, his *Holzwege* [*Off the Beaten Track*] has appeared (he is *in favor* of occasional paths [*Holzwege*] in a way that's not very different from our own), but I've not quite got around to it, am too deep into Kant and Aristotle."[11]

LIMITATIONS OF ADORNO'S CRITIQUE

Although Adorno's critique of Heidegger takes on many aspects of his thought, at least two important limitations should be mentioned here.

First, Adorno's critique nearly always focuses on *Being and Time* or the stakes of fundamental ontology (he had a first edition of *Being and Time* that he annotated quite heavily in places). He does not pay careful attention to the fact that Heidegger dropped the term "fundamental ontology"

NOTES AND REFERENCES

[1] For example, see Theodor W. Adorno, *Philosophische Terminologie*, 2 vols (Frankfurt am Main: Suhrkamp Verlag, 1973), 1, 154–64.
[2] Theodor W. Adorno, *Gesammelte Schriften*, ed. Rolf Tiedemann, 20 vols (Frankfurt am Main: Suhrkamp Verlag, 1997), 6, 44, hereafter cited as GS/Theodor W. Adorno, *The Jargon of Authenticity*, trans. Knut Tarnowski and Frederic Will (London/Evanston: Routledge and Kegan Paul/Northwestern University Press, 1973), 53, hereafter cited as JA. Please note that translations from the German have been tacitly emended where necessary throughout this article.

3 I sometimes quote writings of Heidegger's that Adorno may not or could not have known when these contain succinct formulations of the themes that are the objects of his criticisms. In any case, any reconstruction of the main line of the critique requires reference to passages and contexts other than those Adorno cites directly.

4 Adorno, GS 6, 135–136n/Theodor W. Adorno, *Negative Dialectics*, trans. E. B. Ashton (London: Routledge, 1973), 130n, hereafter cited as ND.

5 See Fredric Jameson, *Late Marxism: Adorno, or the Persistence of the Dialectic* (London: Verso, 1990), 9.

6 Horkheimer met Heidegger while on a study trip to Freiburg in 1921, when Heidegger was still Edmund Husserl's assistant. Marcuse went to Freiburg in 1928 in order to study with Heidegger, but abandoned this plan in 1932 due to a lack of support from Heidegger and the darkening political context. See Rolf Wiggershaus, *The Frankfurt School*, trans. Michael Robertson (Cambridge: Polity Press, 1994), 102–4 and 45, respectively.

7 Richard Wisser (ed.), *Martin Heidegger im Gespräch* (Freiburg und München: Verlag Karl Alber,1970), 68–9, herafter cited as MHIG.

8 Richard Wisser, "Das Fernseh-Interview," in ed. Günther Neske, *Erinnerung an Martin Heidegger* (Pfullingen: Verlag Günther Neske, 1977), 260, hereafter cited as FI.

9 Worthy of note is that Heidegger openly laid claim to Siegfried Landshut, editor of the first German edition of Marx's early writings, as a pupil of his (FI, 276). The evidence suggests that Heidegger knew these writings very well.

10 Ernst Jünger and Martin Heidegger, *Briefe 1949–1975*, ed. Günter Figal and Simone Maier (Stuttgart/Frankfurt am Main: Klett-Cotta/Vittorio Klostermann, 2008), 58.

11 Theodor W. Adorno and Max Horkheimer, *Briefwechsel*, 4 vols (Frankfurt am Main: Suhrkamp Verlag, 2003–6), 3, 351.

49

HEIDEGGER AND LEVINAS
Jill Stauffer

These lines, and those that follow, owe much to Heidegger. Deformed and ill-understood? Perhaps. At least this deformation will not have been a way of denying the debt. Nor this debt a reason to forget. . . .[1]—Emmanuel Levinas

Perhaps most readers of Levinas are not looking to him for a balanced reading of Heidegger—and that is fortunate, since they will not find it in Levinas' works. For that reason, perhaps most readers of Heidegger, when they venture into Levinas' pages, are confused by the version of Heidegger they find there. Levinas is not known for his faithful readings of other philosophers' works: Sartre, Hegel, Husserl, and Bergson are also interpreted creatively. Of course, "creative" reading of the philosophical tradition is a skill (or liberty) one could as easily learn from Heidegger as Levinas. But that should not absolve us of the need to puzzle out some of the lines of influence and resistance in the relation of Levinas' thought to Heidegger's.

In the 1920s, Levinas studied with both Heidegger and Husserl. In 1932 Levinas published the essay "Martin Heidegger and Ontology," wherein he wrote:

For once, Fame has picked one who deserves it. . . . Anyone who has studied philosophy cannot, when confronted by Heidegger's work, fail to recognize how the originality and force of his achievements . . . are combined with an attentive, painstaking, and close working-out of the argument.[2]

Levinas omitted that passage when he revised the essay for publication in 1949.[3] In *Existence and Existents*, published in 1947 but written largely while he was in held in a forced labor camp during the Second World War, Levinas wrote:

If at the beginning our reflections are in large measure inspired by the philosophy of Martin Heidegger, where we find the concept of ontology and of the relationship which man sustains with Being, they are also governed by a profound need to leave the climate of that philosophy, and by the conviction that we cannot leave it for a philosophy that would be pre-Heideggerian.[4]

Levinas reconsidered Heidegger's thought in the wake of the calamity of the Second World War. That explains this essay's epigraphical quote from Levinas: he owes much to Heidegger's thinking; his reading of Heidegger is "deformed" but does not deny its debt to that work; but the debt and the work do not override the responsibility Levinas felt to distance himself from that philosophy—to leave its climate.

Heidegger modified Husserl's phenomenological method to suit his own choice of focus—which he described as Western metaphysics' neglect of the question of Being, emphasizing the ontological difference between Being and beings. For Heidegger that means, put roughly, that the Being of beings is not a being—that there is something beyond the existence of an existent. However, in Levinas' reading, Heidegger sets out to recover Being from a tradition that has obscured it, and in doing so plants Western philosophy more squarely than ever in a tradition that subordinates—and always has subordinated—the relation of human beings to other human beings to the relation between Dasein and Being.[5] Heidegger worries about beings' forgetfulness of Being. Levinas worries about human beings' forgetfulness of other human beings.

One might on first glance suspect that Levinas aims to reverse the order of Heidegger's thought. But the relation is not so straightforward. When Levinas says he wants to escape the "climate" of Heidegger's philosophy or get "beyond being," he means he seeks to get outside of ontology, for the sake of ethics—but not in an "ontic" direction. Heidegger describes to us a temporalized subject for whom much is always yet to be decided; he offers an analysis of authentic and inauthentic ways of dwelling for that creature, where all hangs on the relation of beings to Being. Levinas, like Heidegger, gives us a temporalized subject for whom dwelling alongside others is a necessity rather than a choice, but emphasizes human passivity in relation to other human beings over the capacity for resolute choosing of one's own fate. Levinas' subject is passive in important

ways with regard to its relation to others, the passing of time, and formation of its self. One could say the same of Heidegger's subject: Dasein's thrownness stands for its position in a world that predates it, etc. Later concepts such as *Gelassenheit*, *Lichtung*, and *Ereignis* also describe a subject's passivity with regard to world (though Levinas seems to limit his thinking about Heidegger to *Being and Time*). But passivity ends up placing different constraints on the existence of an existent in the two thinkers' thoughts—and that changes how we define the kind of being a human being is. In a larger work it would be possible to trace more explicitly the limits of the overlap between the two thinkers. But if it is true that Levinas left "the climate" of Heidegger's thought, the more interesting question may be what *that* means. It comes down to a difference of emphasis rather than a reversal or outright refusal of Heidegger's phenomenology.

Heidegger considers himself to have reversed the philosophical tradition's priority of epistemology over ontology by situating knowledge within a being always already in a world and defined by moods or modes of comportment toward that world, while Levinas takes Heidegger to be involved in reducing everything that is "other" to what is the same, which amounts to a violence against the other—a forgetting of the other. In arguing that, Levinas seems to forget that Heidegger defines Dasein as *Mitsein*, being-with:

Da-sein is essentially being-with. The phenomenological statement that *Da-sein* is essentially being-with has an existential-ontological meaning. It does not intend to ascertain ontically that I am factually not objectively present alone, rather that others of my kind also are.[6]

It is a structure of Dasein's being that it exists alongside others—and not just in an empirical (or ontic) sense. *Mitsein* is a condition prior to any freedom. Dasein just is the kind of being that lives in a world with others.

Here is where Levinas wants more information. Is Dasein responsible for those others? Are there limits on what Dasein may do with other Daseins? (Is Dasein ever plural?) But those are not Heidegger's questions,[7] and that bothered Levinas, especially in the wake of Heidegger's membership in the Nazi party. This is the nodal point of the difference in emphasis. Heidegger chooses Being. Levinas chooses human beings.

The divergence comes to the fore when we consider the role death plays in their respective philosophies.[8] For Heidegger being-toward-death is how Dasein grasps the potentiality of its own ability to be:

> Care is Being-towards-death. We have defined "anticipatory resoluteness" as authentic Being towards the possibility which we have characterized as Dasein's utter impossibility. In such Being-towards-its-end, Dasein exists in a way which is authentically whole as that entity which it can be when "thrown into death."[9]

It is easy enough to exist lightly, to float on the surface of things, and deny one's own finitude. But if one is to grasp one's own potential, Heidegger suggests, one needs a sense of that finitude, and its relation to temporality.[10] Just as *Mitsein* does not mean that one empirically stands next to others in the world, being-toward-death does not mean that one simply needs to know that one will die:

> [Dasein's] finitude does not amount primarily to a stopping, but is characteristic of

temporalization itself. The primordial and authentic future is the "towards-oneself" (to oneself!), existing as the possibility of nullity, the possibility which is not to be outstripped.[11]

It is not only that someday one will cease to exist, and one knows this because one observes that death happens. The reminder of life's finitude turns Dasein back on itself, calling on it to take up its own life authentically rather than falling into "the they," living inauthentically, never taking the trouble to be its own basis. The possibility of impossibility—nullity, death—individualizes Dasein if Dasein heeds it as a call to authenticity.

Levinas might want to argue that the emphasis on authenticity assumes a form of freedom or volition blind to the subject's passivity. But, as we have seen, that would ignore the passivity inherent in the structure of care that Heidegger identifies with Being-toward-death, where "the phenomenon of care in its totality is essentially something that cannot be torn asunder; so any attempts to trace it back to special acts or drives like willing or wishing or urge or addiction, or to construct it out of these, will be unsuccessful."[12] Instead, the key factor differentiating Heidegger from Levinas on death is its singularity, that "death is in every case mine."[13] If Dasein as care is always ahead of itself (projecting itself forward even in inauthenticity) because there is always something still outstanding that has not yet become actual for Dasein, then one can never experience one's life as a whole. Only death makes of life a whole, and death is not an event that Dasein can experience. Dasein does experience being left behind by those who die and thus comes to understand something of death. But that is an empirical concern, sometimes a psychological reality, but not the existential meaning of death. Death is "in every case mine" because "no one can take the Other's dying away from him."[14] One can die for another, but that is a concrete sacrifice that does not take away the Other's death, even if it prolongs her life.

Levinas gives that truth a different sense. According to Levinas, death is, for Heidegger, "the most proper, the most untransferable, and the most inalienable possibility of Dasein"[15]—it is the meaning of *jemeinigkeit*. But Levinas argues:

Sympathy and compassion, to suffer for the other or to "die a thousand deaths" for the other, have as their condition of possibility a more radical substitution for an other. This would be a responsibility for another in bearing his misfortune or his end *as if one were guilty of causing it.*[16]

That one can die for another is more than an empirical truth. The "as if" of guilt is important here: responsibility is not tied to acts and intentions but rather is constitutive of human subjectivity as a form of responsiveness against which no one is free to choose. That might echo Heidegger's "thrownness," but the overlap is not perfect. To bear the misfortune of an other as if one were guilty of it is to remain indifferent to a discourse of authenticity:

In this sense, the sacrifice for another would create an other relation with the death of the other: a responsibility that would perhaps answer the question of why we can die. . . . The death of the other is not only a moment of the mineness of my ontological function.[17]

Rather than the self's own death individualizing the self as properly its own, the death of others individualizes the self as responsible, such that the necessity of being in the world with others carries a different meaning.

Not only the *death* but the life of others individualizes me. For Levinas, a self is formed responsively, in a ceaseless oscillation between the self's innate capacity to enjoy its own life—its conatus—and its prevolitional responsiveness to other human beings, who have always already invaded the self, placing its conatus in question.[18] Individuation comes not from anticipatory resoluteness but from being called by an other as irreplaceable. It is "I" who am called and not someone else.[19] I cannot shrug off the responsibility by generalizing the call in accord with an idea of formal equality.

Of course, the Levinasian idea of guilt in some ways parallels Heidegger's reminder that the ontological guilt Dasein bears—when conscience calls on it to be responsible for its Being—is not to be understood as "information" about the self, is not ontic.[20] Rather, it is existential, a call directed only to Dasein, a summons to take up its own potential. As Heidegger puts it:

The "summons to Being-guilty" signifies a calling-forth to that potentiality-for-Being which in each case I as Dasein am already. Dasein need not first load a "guilt" upon itself through its failures or omissions; it must only *be* "guilty" *authentically*—"guilty" in the way in which it is.[21]

If you hear the call to conscience in the right way, you will be able both to embrace the potentiality of your own being and to free yourself to hear the call. You will have chosen your authentic self.

Both descriptions assign to human beings forms of passivity and guilt that are not empirical.[22] The "why?" attached to death is, for Levinas, about what we owe to others whereas for Heidegger it is about the self's resolute attention to its own authenticity. It is possible to make an ethical judgment about which approach is "better," but it is not absolutely necessary that we do so. We gain important, and importantly different, insight from each.

A related difference of emphasis emerges in the two thinkers' discussions of the problem of evil. For Heidegger evil is an ontological category, interesting only insomuch as it helps clarify the self's existential status. Similarly the Good "does not have any moral meaning."[23] Heidegger's conception of evil comes largely from Schelling. What Heidegger likes about Schelling's description of evil is that it moves beyond questions of morality into the ground of freedom, which includes freedom for good or evil.[24] That insight allows Heidegger to compare, structurally, the relation of Being and beings to that of evil and good. Both are about choices one might make against a backdrop of what is unchosen.[25]

For Heidegger, evil at times describes something that Dasein fears ("We do not first ascertain a future evil and then fear it" but rather we feel fear because we have already discovered something fearsome[26]); it can also describe death (as something we do not desire, and probably fear).[27] When Dasein fears, it fears for itself ("That which fear fears about is that very entity which is afraid—Dasein. Only an entity for which in its Being this very Being is an issue, can be afraid."[28]). For Heidegger, evil is something that fear fears, and fear opens up anxiety about nothingness, forestalling Dasein's embrace of its own authenticity. There is no mention of evil inflicted on others, nor concern about whether evil calls on us to respond, to protect lives beyond our own. Those are not his questions.

For Levinas, evil is tied to suffering. Those who suffer are overwhelmed by an evil that rends their humanity in a way that transcends the active/passive distinction. They are overcome "otherwise than by non-freedom," in a manner more cruel than the negation that characterizes being rendered unable to act freely.[29] As such, what matters for Levinas about evil is not chiefly whether or not one acts freely or authentically, as it is not "through passivity that evil is described, but through evil that suffering is understood."[30] We may be free to do good or evil, but that does not capture all of what matters about evil. According to Levinas, suffering is useless. It is "for nothing." The pain of cancer, of torture, abuse or oppression, of chronic disease—these are evils and none of them "do" anything useful, nor are they easily modified by the body's consciousness, its anxiety, or its psychological states. Even the most resolute decision is hard-pressed to evade severe suffering's invasion of consciousness. Nor would we *want* to find pain useful, as that might amount to a theodicy, where we use redemptive narratives to explain pain by finding it justified or beneficial. It is never right to justify another human being's pain. The only useful thing pain may do is open up the interhuman channel of communication, whereby another's groan or a call for aid brings out in me a duty to help.[31]

For Heidegger evil is part of a story about freedom and authenticity. For Levinas it is tied to the exigency of human responsibility for other human beings. This passage from Levinas illuminates much of the substance of the difference:

There is a radical difference between suffering in the other ... and suffering in me, my own experience of suffering whose constitutional or congenital uselessness can take on meaning, the only one of which suffering is capable, in becoming a suffering for the suffering (inexorable though it may be) of someone else. This attention [to the suffering of others] and this action [to alleviate it] are so imperiously and directly incumbent on human beings that it makes awaiting them from an all-powerful God impossible without lowering ourselves.[32]

Here Levinas seems to suggest that, in the face of twentieth-century experiments in cruelty, one cannot say that "only a god can save us now" and retain one's humanity.[33] Evil is implicated in suffering, and suffering is useless—unless it is my own suffering on behalf of someone else. Heidegger would likely say that such sacrifice does not take away another's death—and that is surely true. For Levinas, it misses the point. He asks:

But is it so certain, after all, that the essence of death, which is fulfilled in anxiety, must be thought, according to the description of *Sein und Zeit*, as nothingness? Is the secret about death not phenomenologically inherent in death and the anxiety of dying? Is it not a modality, or the anticipated sharpness, of suffering—and not the solution of the dilemma: to be or not to be?[34]

Death is about more than one's own existence; it is a modality of suffering, part of the interhuman relationship. It calls on me to be responsible.

It might be tempting to say that Levinas, discontented with Heidegger's philosophy or even with his political choices, aimed to reverse Heidegger's phenomenology, choosing beings over Being. But the relation between the two lines of thought is more complex.

Reversal would preserve the underlying logic. Levinas' goal was to range beyond it. He takes up various of the themes Heidegger explored and uses them, even deforms them, in order to advance a rival theory of the subject, one concerned with the self but centered on the other "despite itself," in such a way that authenticity and death—"to be or not to be"—are not the main questions animating the kind of being a human being is. When Levinas chooses to "leave the climate" of Heidegger's philosophy, but not "for a philosophy that would be pre-Heideggerian," he is both giving credit where it is due and asserting the need he felt to make a decisively different philosophical move.

NOTES AND REFERENCES

1 Emmanuel Levinas, *Otherwise than Being or Beyond Essence*, (OB) tr. by Alphonso Lingis (Pittsburg, PA: Duquesne University Press, 1998), 189, n. 28.
2 Emmanuel Levinas, "Martin Heidegger and Ontology," *Diacritics*, 26.1 (Spring 1996), 11, as quoted in Michael Smith, *Toward the Outside: Concepts and Themes in Emmanuel Levinas* (Pittsburg, PA: Duquesne University Press, 2005), 127.
3 Michael Smith points this out in *Toward the Outside*, 127.
4 Emmanuel Levinas, *Existence and Existents*, trans. Alphonso Lingis (Pittsburg, PA: Duquesne University Press, 2001), 4.
5 Emmanuel Levinas, *Totality and Infinity: An Essay on Exteriority*, trans. Alphonso Lingis (Pittsburg, PA: Duquesne University Press, 1969), 46.
6 BT, 120.
7 But see, for instance, Lawrence Vogel, *The Fragile "We": Ethical Implications of Heidegger's* Being and Time (Evanston, Il: Northwestern University Press, 1994). One could also read the work of Arendt, Sartre, Beauvoir, Lacan, Taylor, Derrida, Vattimo, Agamben, and others as framing ethical (and other) questions in a Heideggerian vein.

8. See Tina Chanter, *Time, Death and the Feminine: Levinas with Heidegger* (Stanford, CA: Stanford University Press, 2001) for an in-depth consideration of Levinas and Heidegger on death, time, and responsibility.
9. BT, 329–30.
10. See Peter Gratton, "Heidegger and Levinas on the Question of Temporality," *Journal of Philosophical Research*, 30 (2005), 157–68 for a deeper analysis of how the two thinkers conceptualize temporality.
11. BT, 330.
12. BT, 193–4.
13. BT, 240.
14. Ibid.
15. Emmanuel Levinas, *God, Death and Time*, (GDT) trans. Bettina Bergo (Stanford, CA: Stanford University Press, 2000), 39–40.
16. GDT, 39.
17. Ibid.
18. See Levinas OB, "Substitution," 99–129.
19. See OB, 144ff.
20. BT, 287.
21. Ibid.
22. Wayne Froman argues, along these lines, that the two thinkers are at cross-purposes in "Levinas and Heidegger: A Strange Conversation" in ed. Daniel Dahlstrom, *Interpreting Heidegger: Critical Essays*, (New York: Cambridge University Press, 2011), 256–72.

23. ET, 77.
24. See STEHF, 98f.
25. See STEHF. See also Drew Dalton, "Otherwise than Nothing: Heidegger, Levinas and the Phenomenology of Evil," *Philosophy and Theology*, 21.1–2, 105–28, 2009.
26. BT, 141.
27. Ibid., 248.
28. Ibid., 141.
29. Emmanuel Levinas, "Useless Suffering," (US) in trans. Michael Smith and Barbara Harshaw, *Entre Nous: Thinking of the Other* (New York: Columbia University Press, 1998), 92.
30. Ibid.
31. See Levinas, US.
32. Levinas, US, 92.
33. See "'Only a God Can Save Us Now': *Der Spiegel*'s Interview with Martin Heidegger on September 23, 1966," trans. Maria P. Alter and John D. Caputo, *Philosophy Today* 20 (1976), pp. 267–85. A related point: Levinas argues that technology is not only will to power, but rather is also "perhaps only the price that must sometimes be paid by the high-mindedness of a civilization called upon to feed human beings and lighten their sufferings" (Levinas, US, 94).
34. Emmanuel Levinas, "Transcendence and Evil," in trans. Bettina Bergo, *Of God Who Comes to Mind* (Stanford, CA: Stanford University Press, 1998), 129, translation modified.

50

HEIDEGGER AND DERRIDA

François Raffoul

Derrida's relation to Heidegger can be described as marked by a deep ambivalence. While he has always recognized his debt toward Heidegger, although he went so far as to state that, "What I have attempted to do would not have been possible without the opening of Heidegger's questions,"[1] Derrida has also nevertheless consistently expressed reservations or differences with that thought.[2] In a late interview from 1999 with Dominique Janicaud, he described his ambivalence toward Heidegger in this way: "In any case, it is [a relation] of admiration, respect, recognition, and at the same time a relation of profound allergy and of irony."[3] Derrida further elaborated on this "profound allergy" toward Heidegger—an allergy that is not without recalling Levinas' famed remark on the "profound need to leave the climate of Heidegger's philosophy"[4]—by comparing Heidegger to a sort of severe father, a kind of suspicious superego that constantly has Derrida under surveillance: "For me, he is something like a watchman [veilleur], a thinking that always keeps watch over me—an overseer [surveillant] who is always watching over me, a thinking through which I constantly feel that I am under surveillance" (HF, 103). Nonetheless, Derrida presents his relation to Heidegger as unique, if not incomparable: "I know of no

other thinker, neither in this century nor in general, with whom I have had, with whom I still have a relationship of admiration that is as contradictory and as uneasy" (ibid.). The reader is often faced with this ambivalence in Derrida's writings, which offer, on the one hand, uncannily precise and insightful, and indeed faithful readings of Heidegger's text with, on the other hand, less than generous interpretations. This situation accounts in any case for how Derrida perceived his own position, which he described thusly: "I found myself, I still find myself, with others, in the situation of a non-devotee who, at the same time, cannot stand the anti-Heideggerians. We are caught in the cross-fire. I am as allergic to the Heidegger devotees as I am to the run-of-the-mill anti-Heideggerians."[5]

With respect to the debt that Derrida recognized toward Heidegger, we could mention here what Derrida said in a 1987 interview, "Heidegger, the Philosophers' Hell," regarding the importance of Heidegger's thought: "For more than a half century, no rigorous philosopher has been able to avoid a debate with [explication avec] Heidegger," a thinking that "is also multiple and that, for a long time to come, will remain provocative, enigmatic, still to be read."[6] Even through the criticisms, reservations, and "explications," Derrida still refers to Heidegger as an indispensable resource for future thought. Indeed, "from the moment one is having it out with [*s'explique avec*] Heidegger in a critical or deconstructive fashion, must one not continue to recognize a certain necessity of his thinking, its character, which is inaugural in so many respects, and especially what remains to come for us in its deciphering?" (*Points*, 183–4). In any case, he explains, "an endless *Auseinandersetzung* with Heidegger was engaged and set forth in all my texts" (HF II, 101).

What is at stake in this "*Auseinandersetzung*"? Derrida considered that for all of its advances, Heidegger's thought remained in several key moments caught in the very metaphysics it attempted to overcome: "despite this debt to Heidegger's thought, or rather because of it, I attempt to locate in Heidegger's text . . . the signs of belonging to metaphysics, or to what he calls onto-theology" (*Positions*, 8). In particular, Heidegger's determination of difference as ontological difference "seems to me still held back in a strange way within metaphysics." In contrast, Derrida seeks to open a thought of differance that "is no longer determined, in the language of the West, as the difference between Being and beings" (*Positions*, 9–10). Derrida thus marks a distance with Heidegger around this motif of presence, going so far as to state that, "I sometimes have the feeling that the Heideggerian problematic is the most 'profound' and 'powerful' defense of what I attempt to put into question under the rubric of the *thought of presence*" (55). This question of presence is without a doubt the veritable knot between Derrida and Heidegger,[7] as Derrida recognized in his interview with Janicaud. With respect to the question of presence, "indeed, I found a knot there, which at bottom I always thought was there, whether rightly or

not" (HF, 101). For Derrida, deconstruction is above all the deconstruction of presence, whereas for Heidegger *Destruktion* seeks to unveil the original meaning of being as presence (*Anwesenheit*).[8]

Some biographical information that may not be widely known about Derrida's first exposure to Heidegger's thought, and how he forged his own problematic of deconstruction, might be useful here. In his interview with Janicaud, Derrida returned to his intellectual formation, stressing how prominently Heidegger already figures. He mentions having first heard of the name Heidegger as early as *hypokhâgne*, in the year 1948–9; he recalls having read, in the University of Algiers library, texts by Sartre containing numerous references to Heidegger, as well as the texts from Heidegger that were collected and translated by Henry Corbin, namely, fragments from *Sein und Zeit*, and *Was ist Metaphysik?* As early as 1948–9, then, Derrida recounts, "I was also very aware of him, because of classes and because of the role that I saw him play in the French intellectual landscape—with Sartre notably, and more distantly Merleau-Ponty" (HF, 89). Significantly, Derrida describes how he felt so much closer to Heidegger than to Husserl (he insists on the fact that he studied Husserl only *after* he had been working on Heidegger) and how he "resonated" with the "pathos" of Heidegger's questions. "The question of anxiety, of the experience of nothingness before negation, corresponded well to my personal pathos, much more so than the cold Husserlian discipline, to which I came only later" (HF, 90). Then, in the early 1950s, after having entered the École Normale Supérieure, Derrida attended the lectures of Jean Beaufret, the recipient of "The Letter on Humanism." One must also mention here the several courses that Derrida devoted to Heidegger in the early 1960s when he was teaching as an assistant at the Sorbonne: for instance in 1960–1 in a course on the present; in 1961–2 on the notion of world in Heidegger; in 1963–4 on error and errancy in Heidegger; in 1964–5 on the question of being and history in Heidegger.[9]

The debate around the senses to give to deconstruction constitutes the very core of Derrida's relation to Heidegger: "my endless debate with Heidegger concerns the meaning to be given to deconstruction, the usage of this word. What concept corresponds to this word? This is an endless explication" (HF, 105). Let us stress from the outset that the very word *déconstruction* originated in a translation of Heidegger's own text, as Derrida recognized in the 1983 "Letter to a Japanese Friend." In that essay, Derrida begins by recalling how even in the French language, the word *déconstruction* mobilizes the question of translation within one's language: the term *déconstruction* is not a master-word or a transcendental signified but always already caught in a "context" and in a metonymic chain of signifiers, enjoying no particular privilege there. "The word 'deconstruction,' like all other words, acquires its value only from its inscription in a chain of possible substitutions, in what is too blithely called a 'context.'"[10] Derrida then narrates how that term, *déconstruction*, was chosen as a rendering of Heidegger's *Destruktion*: "When I chose this word, or when it imposed itself upon me—I think it was in *Of Grammatology*—I little thought it would be credited with such a central role in the discourse that interested me at the time. *Among other things I wished to translate and adopt to my own ends the Heideggerian word Destruktion or Abbau.*"[11] Heidegger had attempted (among other places, in the 1955 essay, "On the Question of Being"[12])

to articulate the positive intent of the term *Destruktion* by appealing to the word *Ab-bau* (Derrida explained also that he chose the word "*déconstruction*" in order to avoid the negative connotation of the term "destruction" to render *Destruktion*). In 1968, the French translator of that essay, Gérard Granel, a close friend of Derrida since their years together at the École Normale Supérieure, rendered *Abbau* (described as a dismantling, a sort of taking things apart, senses that would become central in Derrida's understanding of deconstruction as the opening of a difference, a gap or a spacing) as Dé-*construction*.[13] The term appeared in Derrida's writings at the same time, and it is highly probable that Derrida discovered or rediscovered the term in his friend's translation.[14] That term thus first entered the intellectual world in France as a translation of Heidegger. Curiously, although he recognized that debt in the passage just cited from "Letter to a Japanese Friend" (1983), in his late interview with Janicaud, Derrida no longer recalled exactly when he heard the term:

It makes me sad, but I am not able to reconstitute this evolution and this transformation for myself, in other words, the moment I arrived at the schema of deconstruction (the word *Destruktion*, for example, I don't remember—but is my memory reliable?—having paid attention to it thematically during those years). I think it is later. I wouldn't swear to it. (HF, 95)

The term *déconstruction* was is any case taken up by Derrida in his own thought of *différance*, and if deconstruction has become identified with the name and the thought of Jacques Derrida, its provenance was decidedly Heideggerian.

As we saw above, for Heidegger *Destruktion* seeks to unveil the original meaning of being as *Anwesenheit*. This is where Derrida seeks to introduce a break with Heidegger. For what does deconstruction give access to? Not to some original givenness of being, as Derrida believes Heidegger may have "hoped," not to some transcendental signified escaping the play of *différance*, but rather to an unsubstantial gap or spacing, to the *a* of differance, that is, to a *nothing* with no substantiality of its own. It is not the access to another domain, but simply the *differential gap of the construction*. In this sense, Derrida clarifies, the "undoing, decomposing, and desedimenting of structures . . . was not a negative operation. Rather than destroying, it was also necessary to understand how an 'ensemble' was constituted and to reconstruct it to this end."[15] Any construction supposes a gap within it, and that gap draws the contours of the construction, while marking its limits, its exposure to the void, and already its self-deconstruction. And we know that for Derrida deconstruction must be understood first and foremost as a self-deconstruction. In the "Letter to a Japanese Friend," he thus explained: "Deconstruction takes place, it is an event that does not await the deliberation, consciousness, or organization of a subject, or even of modernity. *It deconstructs itself* [*ça se déconstruit*]."[16] It deconstructs itself because, "Deconstruction is something which happens and which happens inside; there is a deconstruction at work within Plato's work, for instance."[17] It deconstructs itself because the construction harbors a fault or an aporia within it. Deconstruction for Derrida will not be the return to and appropriation of some original element of being. This is why, for Derrida, is not a question of reappropriating the proper of human existence, but of

manifesting the impossibility of the proper, leading us to an aporia or impossible.

Thus, although Derrida certainly shares with Heidegger the conviction that deconstruction has a positive or "affirmative" sense,[18] it nonetheless remains an "experience of the impossible." To the extent that deconstruction reveals the faults of the system, the places where the system does not work, this affirmative sense of deconstruction as openness must always be associated with, as Derrida put it, "the privilege I constantly grant to aporetic thought."[19] Deconstruction as such, Derrida tells us, needs to be understood as aporetic thinking, and he still evoked in a late text "all the aporias or the 'impossibles' with which deconstruction is concerned (*toutes les apories ou les 'im-possibles' qui occupent la 'deconstruction'*)."[20] In a later text on the secret, Derrida writes that "the system *is impossible*."[21] With deconstruction, he continues, "it has been a question of showing that the system *does not work*" (TS, 4, my emphasis). Deconstruction thus will not lead to the reappropriation of the proper, but to the impropriety of the proper, to the im-possible.

Derrida takes issue with Heidegger's alleged privileging of the proper. Indeed, Derrida seeks to break with the very distinction between the proper (*eigentlich*) and the improper (*uneigentlich*), a distinction that for Derrida is metaphysical.[22] In "*Ousia and Grammē*," Derrida claimed that for Heidegger, "the Primordial, the authentic are determined as the *proper* (*eigentlich*), that is, as the *near* (proper, *proprius*), the present in the proximity of self-presence" (*Margins*, 64, n. 39). This can be seen for Derrida at the very beginning of *Being and Time*, namely "in the decision to ask the question of the meaning of Being on the basis of an existential analytic of Dasein" (ibid.). That privilege given to the propriety and proximity of self-presence "can propagate its movement to include all the concepts implying the value of the 'proper,'" Derrida adding in a parenthesis a list (not included in the English translation) that includes all derivations of the motif of the proper in Heidegger's thought: "(*Eigen, eigens, ereignen, Ereignis, eigentümlich, Eignen,* etc.)" (ibid.). The dominance of the motif of the proper in Heidegger's thinking can then be found in the relation established between being and the human Dasein, Derrida associating "the proper" (*le propre*) with "the near" (*le proche*): "The near is the proper; the proper is the nearest (*prope, proprius*). Man is the proper of Being, which right near to him whispers in his ear; Being is the proper of man, such is the truth that speaks, such is the proposition that gives the *there* of the truth of Being and the truth of man" (*Margins*, 133). Gesturing to an outside that would come to threaten this circularity, Derrida suggests that it is that very "security of the near" that "is trembling" today, and it is that privilege of the proper that he seeks to destabilize and undo.

For Derrida seeks to claim the impossibility of appropriation and the primacy of expropriation. In *On Touching—Jean-Luc Nancy*, Derrida cites a passage from *The Gravity of Thought* where Nancy wrote that existence "*is* the appropriation of the inappropriable."[23] Derrida reads that expression by insisting on the expropriation of the proper, which he calls "exappropriation." Ex-appropriation designates that "interminable appropriation of an irreducible nonproper" that limits "every and any appropriation process at the same time."[24] From this thinking of the inappropriable in existence, Derrida introduces the motif of the impossible: "Another way of saying that

'existence,' 'is,' 'Being' . . . *are all names of the impossible* and of self-incompatibility."[25]

Now, we should note that with respect to this charge of a privilege of the proper in Heidegger, Derrida has wavered somewhat. In *Philosophy in a Time of Terror*, for instance, Derrida states that the Heideggerian thought of being as event, as *Ereignis*, involves a certain *expropriation*. Going against the grain of his previous interpretations, Derrida claims that "the thought of *Ereignis* in Heidegger would be turned not only toward the *appropriation* of the proper [*eigen*] but toward a certain expropriation that Heidegger himself names [*Enteignis*]."[26] He thus explicitly links the Heideggerian thought of the event to the inappropriable and the impossible: "The undergoing [*l'épreuve*] of the event, that which in the undergoing or in the ordeal at once opens itself up to and resists experience, is, it seems to me, a certain inappropriability of what comes or happens [*ce qui arrive*]."[27] There is thus inappropriable in the very happening of the event, and Derrida recognizes the presence of an inappropriable in Heidegger's thought of being as event.

This appears in fact in Heidegger's understanding of the phenomenological method. For the very concept of phenomenology, insofar as it is defined as a "letting something be seen" (*sehen lassen*), a *legein*, a bringing to light, necessarily implies the withdrawal of the phenomenon. The original phenomenon, precisely as that which is to be made phenomenologically visible, does not *show itself*:

What is it that phenomenology is to "let be seen"? What is it that is to be called a "phenomenon" in a distinctive sense? What is it that by its very essence becomes the necessary theme when we indicate something *explicitly*? Manifestly, it is something that does *not* show itself initially and for the most part, something that is *concealed* [*verborgen*] in contrast to what initially and for the most part does show itself. (SZ, 35/BT, 33)

Phenomenology, in its very essence, is thus a *phenomenology of what does not appear*, a phenomenology of the inapparent, as Heidegger described it in the 1973 Zähringen seminar (FS, 80). *Destruktion* in Heidegger's sense thus manifests a struggle with the concealment of phenomena, engaging what he called in his course on *Plato's Sophist* "a constant struggle against the tendency to cover over residing at the heart of Dasein" (GA 19, 52/PS, 36–7). This betrays that Heidegger's *Destruktion* has to do with a certain experience of or negotiation with the secret, the inappropriable, and indeed perhaps is an "experience of the impossible," as Derrida attempted to think it in his own "aporetic thinking."

In fact, as Derrida had to admit, there is in Heidegger's thinking of being the presence of an irreducible expropriation. Being is the withdrawal, and it calls us from this withdrawing. One notes the presence of such inappropriable in all stages of Heidegger's thought: in the "ruinance" of factical life in the early writings and lecture courses; in the *Uneigentlichkeit* of existence and the *Schuldigsein* of conscience in *Being and Time*; in the thrownness and facticity felt in moods, in the weight of a responsibility assigned to an inappropriable finitude; in an untruth co-primordial with truth; in the concealment that not only accompanies but is indeed harbored in unconcealment; in the withdrawal in the sendings of being; and finally in the presence of *Enteignis* within *Ereignis*. Each time and throughout, one finds in Heidegger this motif of an exposure

to an inappropriable. Indeed, the event of appropriation that *Ereignis* is said to designate includes eminently the expropriation of *Enteignis*. As Heidegger explained in *On Time and Being*:

Appropriating makes manifest what is proper to it, that Appropriation withdraws what is most fully its own from boundless unconcealment. Thought in terms of Appropriating, this means: in that sense it expropriates itself of itself. Expropriation [*Enteignis*] belongs to Appropriation [*Ereignis*] as such. By this expropriation, Appropriation does not abandon itself—rather it preserves what is its own. (GA 14, 27–8/TB, 22–3, translation slightly modified)

And it may well be around this motif of the inappropriable at the heart of appropriation, that is, ex-appropriation, that Derrida may be closest to Heidegger, closer than it would seem, that is, than Derrida would have liked.

NOTES AND REFERENCES

[1] Jacques Derrida, *Positions*, trans. Alan Bass (Chicago: University of Chicago Press, 1981), 9.
[2] The reverse is not the case: in his interview with Dominique Janicaud (In *Heidegger in France, II. Interviews* [Paris: Albin Michel, 2001, hereafter cited as HF II]41), Walter Biemel indicates that Heidegger did in fact "follow" Derrida's work, and, still according to Biemel, that he looked upon it favorably, as we can also gather from two letters that Heidegger wrote to Lucien Braun (the first from September 29, 1967 and the other from May 16, 1973), regarding the possibility of a meeting with Derrida, which Derrida had suggested. See Lucien Braun's report in *Penser à Strasbourg* (Paris: Galilée, 2004), 21–6.
[3] In HF, II, 103.
[4] Emmanuel Levinas, *Existence and Existents*, trans. Alphonso Lingis (Pittsburg, PA: Duquesne University Press, 2001), 4.

⁵ HS. Interestingly, this late statement echoes, almost word for word, a passage one finds in a footnote from "*Ousia and Grammē*," in which Derrida already denounced "the complicity which gathers together, in the same refusal to read, in the same denegation of the question, of the text, and of the question of the text, in the same repetitions [*redite*], or in the same blind silence, the camp of Heideggerian devotion and the camp of anti-Heideggerianism." Jacques Derrida. *Margins of Philosophy*, trans. Alan Bass (Chicago, IL: Chicago University Press, 1982), 62, n. 37, translation modified.

⁶ Jacques Derrida, *Points . . . Interviews, 1974–1995*, trans. Peggy Kamuf and Others (Stanford, CA: Stanford University Press, 1992), 182–3, translation modified.

⁷ Although by no means the only *difference or disagreement* between them. In that same 1987 interview, Derrida gives a long list of his disagreements with Heidegger. They include: the "questions of the proper, the near [*proche*], and the fatherland (*Heimat*) [*patrie*], the point of departure of *Being and Time*, technics and science, animality, or sexual difference, the voice, the hand, language, the 'epoch,' and especially, this is the subtitle of my book [*Of Spirit. Heidegger and the Question*], the question of the question, which is almost constantly privileged by Heidegger as 'the piety of thinking'" (*Points*, 182). As readers of Derrida reading Heidegger, we could add to that list: Derrida's critique of Heidegger's alleged anthropomorphism, from "The Ends of Man" to *The Animal that Therefore I Am* and beyond, the hierarchies of *Being and Time* (such as the subordination of regional ontologies to fundamental ontology or the distinction between existential analytic and biology and anthropology, between existence and life), the motif of the "as such" in the existential analytic, the prioritization of death as some transcendental ground of existence, the critique of a certain solipsism of the existential analysis excluding the death of the other from its domain, the notions of "truth of being" and "ontological difference," the privileging of the gathering (*Versammlung*), which suppresses otherness, the problematic of truth and truth-keeping, the unity of the history of being, etc.

⁸ In *Four Seminars*, in the 1969 Thor seminar (FS, 42), we thus read: "The previous session concluded with a recollection upon how the question of being was first raised in *Being and Time*. . . . [Heidegger] begins by naming the authentic name of the method followed: "destruction"—this must be understood in the strong sense as *de-struere*, "dis-mantling" [*ab-bauen*], and not as devastation . . . But what is dismantled? Answer: that which covers over the meaning of being, the structures amassed upon one another that make the meaning of being unrecognizable . . . Further, destruction strives to free the original meaning of being (*Anwesenheit*)."

⁹ Regarding these courses, see the list established in the *Derrida Seminars Translation Project*'s website: http://derridaseminars.org/seminars.html

¹⁰ "Letter to a Japanese Friend," in *Derrida and Differance*, eds David Wood and Robert Bernasconi (Evanston, IL: Northwestern University Press, 1988), 4.

¹¹ "Letter to a Japanese Friend," in *Derrida and Differance*, 1. My emphasis.

¹² Martin Heidegger, "On the Question of Being," in ed. William McNeill, *Pathmarks* (New York: Cambridge University Press, 1998), 315.

¹³ Martin Heidegger, "*Contribution à la question de l'être (1955)*," in *Questions I* (Paris: Gallimard, 1968), 240.

¹⁴ As Francoise Dastur observes, "if in *Being and Time* it is a question of *Destruktion*, the term *abbau*, "deconstruction," which is also present in Husserl, appears on page 315 in Martin Heidegger, "On the Question of Being" . . . *where Derrida probably found it*." "The Reception and Nonreception of Heidegger in France," in eds David Pettigrew and François Raffoul, *French Interpretations of Heidegger* (Albany, NY: SUNY Press, 2008), 288, n.26, my emphasis.

¹⁵ "Letter to a Japanese Friend," in *Derrida and Differance*, 3.

¹⁶ "Letter to a Japanese Friend," in *Derrida and Differance*, 4, translation slightly modified.

¹⁷ *Deconstruction in a Nutshell: A Conversation with Jacques Derrida* (NY: Fordham University Press, 1997), 9.

¹⁸ Derrida clarified this affirmative sense in the 2004 *Humanité* interview, in terms of

an openness toward what comes: "A slogan, nonetheless, of deconstruction: being open to what comes, to the to-come, to the other."

19 Jacques Derrida, *Rogues. Two Essays on Reason*, trans. Pascale-Anne Brault and Michael Naas (Stanford, CA: Stanford University Press, 2005), 174, n. 3.

20 Jacques Derrida and Elisabeth Roudinesco, *For What Tomorrow . . .*, trans. Jeff Fort (Stanford, CA: Stanford University Press, 2004), 48, translation modified

21 Jacques Derrida and Maurizio Ferraris, *A Taste for the Secret*, ed. G. Donis and D. Webb (Malden, MA: Polity Press, 2001), 4, my emphasis. Hereafter cited as TS, followed by page number.

22 "Now, is not the opposition of the primordial to the derivative still metaphysical? Is not the quest for an *archia* in general, no matter with what precautions one surrounds the concept, still the 'essential' operation of metaphysics?" asks Derrida (*Margins*, 63).

23 Jacques Derrida, *On Touching—Jean-Luc Nancy*, trans. Christine Irizzary (Stanford, CA: Stanford University Press, 2000), 299. See also Jean-Luc Nancy, *The Gravity of Thought*, trans. François Raffoul and Gregory Recco (Atlantic Highlands, NJ: Humanities Press, 1997).

24 Derrida, *On Touching—Jean-Luc Nancy*, 181–2.

25 Ibid.

26 Giovanna Borradori, *Philosophy in a Time of Terror: Dialogues with Jürgen Habermas and Jacques Derrida* (Chicago: University of Chicago Press, 2003), 90.

27 Ibid, translation modified.

51

HEIDEGGER AND FOUCAULT
Leonard Lawlor

In his final interview, Foucault famously says, "For me, Heidegger has always been the essential philosopher. My whole philosophical development was determined by my reading of Heidegger."[1] There is no question that this quotation means that Heidegger had a tremendous influence on Foucault's thinking. One is hard-pressed, however, to understand the nature and scope of the influence since Foucault never wrote a text devoted to Heidegger. Lacking a book or even an article on Heidegger, one ends up searching for comments by Foucault that seem to allude to Heidegger.[2] For example and most obviously, it seems impossible not to think of Heidegger when one sees the title of Foucault's last published book, *The Care of the Self*. Yet, the situation is really worse. Not only do we not have a book or article written by Foucault on Heidegger, Heidegger's name does not even appear in the books Foucault published during his lifetime—except once.[3] The only occurrence of Heidegger's name appears in chapter nine, "Man and his Doubles"—in a section called "The Retreat and Return of the Origin"—in Foucault's 1966 *The Order of Things*. Here is the occurrence:

This is why modern thought is devoted, from top to bottom, to its great preoccupation with return, to its concern with recommencement, to that strange, stationary disquietude which forces upon it the duty of repeating repetition. Thus from Hegel to Marx and Spengler we find the developing theme of a thought which, through the movement in which it accomplishes itself . . ., curves over upon itself . . . [and] achieves its circle. In opposition to this return . . ., we find the experience of Hölderlin, Nietzsche, and Heidegger, in which the return is given only in the extreme retreat of the origin.[4]

This single occurrence of the name "Heidegger" indicates that Foucault's relation to Heidegger centers on the task or even the duty of repetition or retrieval ("répétition" in French, "Wiederholung," in German).[5] Although Foucault forms an opposition between the two conceptions of return—Heidegger in the company of Hölderlin and Nietzsche, and opposed to Hegel, Marx, and Spengler—both, he says, "prescribe something like the 'Same'" (OT, 334). As we know from the title of the chapter, "Man and his Doubles," it seems that Foucault thinks that Heidegger's task of a retrieval of the question of being retrieves only what is the same as man's being. Therefore, if Foucault's thought goes beyond Heidegger's—at least beyond the Heidegger that this comment implies—then

Foucault's task of retrieval seems to concern whether there is a repetition that is not restricted to the same, whether there is a repetition or retrieval of something other than the being of man. As we shall see, Foucault's task lies in the retrieval of the question of the being of language.

This claim about the retrieval of language defining Foucault's thinking might seem controversial since, after *The Order of Things* and after *The Archeology of Knowledge*, Foucault's thinking takes up the problem of power. Yet, we must not forget that at a crucial juncture in *The Archeology of Knowledge* (he has just referred to *The Order of Things* through the phrase "les mots et les choses," the actual French title of *The Order of Things*), Foucault insists that he is interested, not in the sign, but in what he calls the "more" of discourse.[6] It is this "more" that leads Foucault, at the end of his career, on the other side of his power studies such as *Discipline and Punish* and *The History of Sexuality 1*, to consider the ancient notion of *parrēsia* (*franc-parler*, fearless speech, outspokenness). The "more" of discourse allows one to speak out and speak freely, and in this way discourse is able to intervene in arrangements of power. Therefore, it is possible to say that the task of "the retrieval" (*la répétition*) of the being of language determines the entire trajectory of Foucault's work in general. We can make this claim in another way if we recognize, as Heidegger did, that there can be no thought without language. Then the repetition of the being of language determines the most general task of Foucault's thinking—even when it concerns power—since his thinking aims to produce histories of thought. Of course, characterizing Foucault's work as the history of thought reinforces the importance of the one occurrence of Heidegger's name.[7] So, let

us examine "Man and his Doubles" in order to determine more fully this one occurrence and thereby understand the trajectory of Foucault's thought in general.

It is well known that, like all of Foucault's histories (up until the 1984 *Use of Pleasure*, which concerns the ancient Greeks), *The Order of Things* examines a discontinuity between the Classical Age (the seventeenth and eigteenth centuries) and the Modern Age (the nineteenth and twentieth centuries). The discontinuity occurs at the moment of the Enlightenment and the French Revolution. Prior to the Enlightenment, in the Classical Age, words or language in general had a function of representing things. Thanks to this function, humans were able to characterize and classify, make equivalencies and exchanges, establish identities and differences among things. The function of language then—in the Classical Age, words are thought to be transparent—allowed humans to set up a "table," as Foucault says, of representations, by means of which one was able to understand the world. Importantly, this grid of representations, made possible by language in its transparency, was an order *external* to the things themselves (OT, 311). Now, at the threshold of the nineteenth century, according to Foucault, the Classical order of words and things dissolves. During the time of the French Revolution and after, certain thinkers (Cuvier, for example) working in the areas of knowledge called natural history, exchange, and grammar "demand" that life, labor, and language "define themselves" (312). In other words, they demanded that life, labor, and language be understood in terms of conditions of possibility *internal* to life, labor, and language themselves. Although Foucault will alternate among these three areas throughout "Man and his Doubles," he privileges language since the unmaking of the Classical order was due to language losing its transparency function. When things "withdraw" into themselves, language acquires its own being.

The end of the Classical order, for Foucault, is not merely negative or destructive. When this withdrawal of things into themselves occurs, life, labour, and language become "phenomena." Here we can see the impact of Enlightenment thinking and in particular Kant. As phenomena, things are "given." As given, they take up an "external relation" not with an order—the order is internal to the things, in the noumena behind the phenomena—but with the human being, who has the power of representation and self-representation. When this shift occurs in the human being, when we start to think of ourselves no longer as having a human nature (which is opposed "term by term" to nature (309)), when we start to think of ourselves as spectators of phenomena, then, for Foucault, "man" is invented. In other words, "man" is required when things become phenomena since he is the one to whom the phenomena are given. Moreover, since man is the one who lives, who labours, and who speaks, he seems to have a privileged position among other animals who live, do things, and express themselves in sounds, a privileged position in these areas of knowledge, called in the Modern Age, "biology," "economics," and "philology." However, as Foucault says, "this imperious designation is ambiguous" (313). On the one hand, the positive content of biology, economics, and philology tells man that he is finite; the "givens" or "phenomena" of man's being are corporeality, desires, and language. On the other hand, the knowledge of life, labor, and language is itself determined as finite, since man knows through his body, in relation to his desires, and in the language that

he speaks. Using Kantian terminology, we can say that man does not have intellectual intuition. Thus, man's being is ambiguously doubled between a finitude that is the same as itself since the same body, the same desire, the same language are known and conditions knowledge, and a finitude that is "radically other," since the finite conditions of knowledge indicate a "fundamental finitude" that seems not to depend on man having a history or a language. The fundamental finitude depends only on "its own fact" (315).

Foucault's introduction of "man" in this way in *The Order of Things* is well-known. It refers not to a shift in our physical make-up, but in the way we think of ourselves. Undoubtedly, Heidegger's publication of *Being and Time* had a transformative effect on how we think about our existence. Thanks to Heidegger (and probably thanks to the popularization of his ideas by the French Existentialists), we think of ourselves as finite. And, if we want to be precise about our finitude, we must think of ourselves as finite in the double way in which Foucault describes it: a positive finitude and a fundamental finitude. Thus, due to this Heideggerian inheritance, Foucault speaks of an "obligation to ascend or descend to an analytic of finitude" (ibid.). The allusion to Heidegger's "Dasein analytic" in *Being and Time* is obvious. But, the phrase "the analytic of finitude" especially resembles certain phrases Heidegger uses in *Kant and the Problem of Metaphysics*, where Heidegger's project consists in a "retrieval" of human finitude.[8] For Foucault, as for Heidegger, the analytic of finitude concerns "man's mode of being." Most importantly, however, Foucault states that "man's primary characteristic is entirely that of repetition" (ibid.). Defining the primary characteristic of man's being as repetition means, for Foucault, that man's

411

being is defined as the "same"; the death that gnaws at man's life and the death that is fundamental are the same. As Foucault says, "From one end of experience to the other, finitude answers itself; it is the identity and difference of the positivities, and of their foundation, within the figure of the *Same*" (ibid.; Foucault's emphasis and upper-casing). In the Modern Age, human finitude comes to be thought no longer in a negative relation to the infinite (as a "fallen" existence); it is defined entirely in terms of itself (316).

Having defined "man's primary characteristic" as repetition (the repetition of the positive and the fundamental), Foucault then extends the analytic of finitude into three other "doubles" that define man: "the transcendental repeats the empirical, the *cogito* repeats the unthought, the return of the origin repeats its retreat" (317). The repetition of the same in the transcendental and the empirical alludes to phenomenology since Foucault speaks of the discourse of "lived-experience" (*vécu*), lived-experience being a central phenomenological concept (321).[9] The repetition of the same in the *cogito* and the unthought alludes more clearly to Heidegger. In fact, the repetition of "The *Cogito* and the Unthought" seems to allude to Heidegger's idea of an "originary ethics," since Foucault speaks of an "imperative" of thought, an imperative on the basis of which thought "must" think man's other, thereby making it the same as himself (328). However, as we have already noted, it is in this fourth and last repetition, the retreat and return of the origin, that Foucault mentions Heidegger by name.

Foucault calls the fourth repetition that defines man's mode of being "the relation to the origin" (ibid.). He distinguishes this origin from the ideal genesis imagined in Classical thought, but he also distinguishes

it from the historicity of things as it is conceived in the Modern Age. In the Modern Age, the historicity of things seems to resemble a cone, whose summit is a point of identity; then history seems to evolve from that identity, resulting in dispersion and diversity, in becoming other (329–30). In contrast, the origin, for man in Modern thought, is a kind of otherness since his origin is a past on which man cannot locate himself: the "already begun" (330). Man always finds himself alive against the background of life that began long ago, his labor finds itself within institutions already established, and he speaks from a language he did not invent. Foucault calls man's relation to this "already begun" "the originary" (ibid.). Foucault's introduction of this word alludes to Heidegger, since the French "originaire" translates Heidegger's German "Ursprünglichkeit," as it is found, for example, in *Being and Time* and in *Kant and the Problem of Metaphysics*.[10] As in Heidegger, Foucault describes the originary as that which is "closest" to man since he lives, labours, and speaks, and yet it is what is "distant" since life, labour, and language "belong to a time that has neither the same standards of measurement nor the same foundations as him" (ibid.). The originary is what connects man to what is "not contemporaneous with him" (331). Because of this non-contemporaneity, it is not possible to attribute, according to Foucault, an origin to man. Yet, because man seems to have no origin, to be virtually outside of time, he also appears to be that being from which all the chronologies of life, labour, and language have derived. Therefore, Foucault concludes that there is a double retreat of the origin: the origin of things always withdraws to a beginning earlier than man, while man withdraws from things as that from which all the durations of things can begin.

This double retreat, however, makes possible, according to Foucault, a "third retreat" (332). Because man seems to be the source for all the chronologies, a task arises for thought in the Modern Age (ibid.). Thought calls into question everything that pertains to time. It contests the origin of things in order to discover the "origin without either origin or beginning." Foucault calls this "originless origin" the "rip" (the French word is "déchirure," which probably is intended to render Heidegger's idea of a "Riss") from which, itself having no chronology or history, time has issued forth (ibid.). Time then would be, as it were, "suspended" in thought—in the sense that making this timeless origin be visible thought would seem to have made time stand still. And yet, thought itself would not be able to escape from time because it is not contemporary with the originless origin of time. In the Modern Age, thought can never be contemporary with the origin. However, as Foucault stresses, the suspension of time in thought is able to make the relation of thought and origin "flip over." Previously, the origin withdrew from thought into the past; now, however, it withdraws from thought going out into the future. In other words, after finding itself coming too late for the origin, thought now projects the origin out in front as what is still to be thought (ibid.). It is at this moment in "Man and his Doubles" that Foucault mentions Heidegger's name. Although Foucault does not say this, the task for thinking that aims at suspending time amounts to Heidegger's task of a retrieval of the meaning of being as time.

According to Foucault, however, this retrieval (*Wiederholung*), as we saw at the beginning, is a retrieval of the same. Why is the Heideggerian task a retrieval of the same? Foucault does not really answer this question anywhere, not in "Man and his

Doubles" or in *The Order of Things*, nor anywhere in his corpus.[11] A clue seems to appear, however, when he says in "Man and his Doubles" that "[the origin] is promised to [man] in an imminence that will perhaps be forever snatched from him" (334–5, see also 332). The clue seems to be this: it is difficult to conceive promising in any other way than as something to be kept; as something to be kept, a promise must be fulfilled. Then as something to be fulfilled, it seems that promising must always be based in a lack. The same dominates this retrieval or return or repetition because the promising, to which Foucault seems to be referring, is conceived as a deficiency (342). The withdrawal of the origin produces a deficiency, but the deficiency, it seems, produces something like an outline or a figure in relief that the future fills in. In other words, what is to come is determined as what is going to fill in this lack. The still coming future will be the same as what was outlined with the withdrawal of the origin into the past. There seems, however, for Foucault, another and stronger step in this argument, if we understand it correctly. Foucault speaks of "the insurmountable relation of man's being to time" (335). Thus it seems that the lack is a lack in "man's own being" (ibid.), which means that the return of the origin—promised and not yet fulfilled—is a fulfilment of *man's being*. Man is the figure in relief made by the withdrawal. The return of the origin therefore is a return of the same being as us. The circle of withdrawal and return closes and encloses us.

Is there a way to break out of this circle of man, this eschatological return? In "Man and his Doubles," Foucault suggests that we must ask this question: "Does man truly *exist*" (322, my emphasis)? This question, with the emphasis on the "exist," makes us question beyond man's being. What lies beyond man's being? At least at the time of *The Order of Things*, the answer to the question of what lies beyond man's being is the being of language. In *The Order of Things*, the being of language seems for be, for Foucault, opposed to the being of man. What is the being of language for Foucault? We recall that, according to Foucault, language in the Classical Age had a function. It transparently represented things, which allowed the things to be ordered in a table of representations. In other words, through this function, it occupied the middle between things and order. This conception of language also implies that language stands in the middle as a transparent medium between a speaker who intends to say something and a hearer who understands the transported meaning. Language in this conception has no other being than transitivity. Language as transitivity dissolves at the time of the Enlightenment. As in Mallarmé's poetry—Mallarmé is Foucault's example, along with Nietzsche—language then takes on a new density since it no longer occupies the middle. Therefore it no longer functions transitively. It no longer has a destination, an end or *telos* or *eschaton*. Then language no longer folds back over itself into a circle. The being of language in Foucault is "radical intransitivity." Through radical intransitivity, language is liberated from its finitude, allowing it to take on an indefinite potentiality (300).

Of course, the later Heidegger of *On the Way to Language* defines the being of language no longer in terms of its communicative function. Indeed, he seeks the being of language within poetry, just as Foucault seems to do in *The Order of Things*. Yet, in the "Language" essay in particular, Heidegger conceives language as a promise, which seems to restrict the potentiality of language to a circular return, even to a return of man.[12] We know that Foucault does not

conceive language in terms of promising—and in this way we confirm our opening thesis about the most general task of Foucault's thinking—because Foucault argues late in his career, in *The Government of Self and Others* that *parrēsia* is not a performative utterance. *Parrēsia* is always something *more* than a performative. As examples of performative utterances, Foucault speaks of "I baptize you" and "I apologize," but he could just as well have spoken of "I promise." In contrast to performative utterances such as "I promise," "there is," Foucault says, "*parrēsia* at the moment when the statement of [the] of truth constitutes an irruptive event opening up an undefined or poorly defined risk for the subject who speaks."[13] Involving a nondefined or badly defined, indeed an unforeseeable risk for the speaker, this kind of event—perhaps this event is really what Heidegger has in mind with the *Ereignis?*—is not promising. With *parrēsia*, there is no outline of what is coming. In fact, we do not know what is coming, and thereby the circle of man is unwound. Indeed, it seems for Foucault that only the event of *parrēsia* opens up what he calls early in his career "the play of masks," and late in his career "the indefinite work of freedom."[14] Or, we could say, echoing Heidegger, that *parrēsia* answers the question of what calls for thinking.

NOTES AND REFERENCES

[1] Michel Foucault, "Le retour de la morale," in *Dits et écrits, IV, 1980–1988*, édition établie sous la direction de Daniel Defert et François Ewald (Paris: NRF Gallimard, 1994), 703; English translation by Thomas Levin and Isabelle Lorenz as "The Return of Morality," in ed. Lawrence D. Kritzman, *Michel Foucault. Politics, Philosophy, Culture:*

Interview and other Writings, 1977–1984 (New York: Routledge, 1988), 250, translation modified. For Foucault's early studies, see Didier Eribon, *Michel Foucault*, trans. Betsy Wing (Cambridge, MA: Harvard University Press, 1991), 30–1. David Macey, *The Lives of Michel Foucault* (New York: Vintage, 1993), 34. The quotation with which I began is often cited. See Alan Milchman and Alan Rosenberg, *Foucault and Heidegger: Critical Encounters* (Minneapolis: University of Minnesota Press, 2003). Béatrice Han's essay in this volume is particularly interesting. Béatrice Han, "Foucault and Heidegger on Kant and Finitude," in *Foucault and Heidegger*, 127–62. See also Jean Zoungrana, *Michel Foucault. Un parcours croisé: Lévi-Strauss, Heidegger* (Paris: L'Harmattan, 1998).

2   Heidegger's name appears often in Foucault's interviews and occasionally in his courses. Michel Foucault, "Méthodologie pour une connaissance du monde: comment se débarrasser du marxisme," in *Dits et écrits, III, 1976–1979*, édition établie sous la direction de Daniel Defert et François Ewald (Paris: NRF Gallimard, 1994), 604–5. Michel Foucault, *Leçon sur la volonté de savoir. Cour au Collége de France. 1970–1971. Suivi de Le savoir d'Œdipe* (Paris: Hautes Études Gallimard Seuil, 2011), 206. Finally, see Paul Veyne, "The Final Foucault and his Ethics," in ed. Arnold I. Davidson, *Foucault and his Interlocutors*, (Chicago: University of Chicago Press, 1997), 231n.1.

3   This claim is not quite correct since Foucault mentions Heidegger by name in his 1954 introduction to Binswanger's *Le rêve et l'existence*. Yet, here, Foucault seems merely to brush any concern with Heidegger aside. See Ludwig Binswanger, *Le rêve et l'existence* (Paris: Desclée de Brouwer, 1954), 13–14; English edited by Keith Holler as *Dream and Existence* (Atlantic Highlands, NJ: Humanities Press, 1993), 32–3.

4   Michel Foucault, *Les mots et les choses* (Paris: Tel Gallimard, 1966), 345; English translation by A. M. Sheridan Smith as *The Order of Things* (New York: Vintage, 1970), 334. Hereafter cited with the abbreviation OT. I have frequently modified the English translation.

5   "Wiederholung" is a fundamental feature of Heidegger's thinking at the time of *Being and Time*. See GA 2, 2/BT, 1 and GA 2, 385/BT, 367. It organizes as well Heidegger's 1929 *Kant and the Problem of Metaphysics*. See GA 3, 204/KPM, 143.

6   Michel Foucault, *L'archéologie du savoir* (Paris: NRF Gallimard, 1969), 67; English translation by A. M. Sheridan Smith as *The Archeology of Knowledge* (New York: Pantheon, 1972), 49.

7   Deleuze claims that Heidegger's question of what calls for thinking "haunts" all of Foucault's thinking. Gilles Deleuze, *Foucault* (Paris: Minuit, 1986), 124; English translation by Seán Hand as *Foucault* (Minneapolis: University of Minnesota Press, 1988), 116.

8   See, in particular, GA 3, 88/KPM, 62: "the task of an analytic of transcendence, i.e., of a pure phenomenology of the subjectivity of the subject, namely, as a finite subject."

9   The English translation renders "vécu" as "actual experience." "Vécu" however is the standard French translation for the German "Erlebnis," which is usually rendered into English as "lived-experience." Here Foucault seems to allude to Husserl and probably early Merleau-Ponty.

10   See GA 2, 151/BT, 146 and GA 3, 126/KPM, 89. "Ursprünglichkeit" is also rendered into English as "primordiality." The originary is a primary concern of Foucault's *Introduction to Kant's Anthropology*. And later in 1971, he expresses suspicion of the concept of origin. See Michel Foucault, "Nietzsche, la génealogie, l'histoire," in *Dits et écrits. Volume I 1954–1975*, édition établie sous la direction de Daniel Defert et François Ewald, avec la collaboration de Jacques Lagrange(Paris: Quarto Gallimard, 2001), 1008; English translation by Donald F. Brouchard and Sherry Simon as "Nietzsche, Genealogy, History," in ed. James D. Faubion, *Essential Works of Foucault. Volume 2: Aesthetics, Method and Epistemology* (New York: New Press, 1998), 373.

11   In "Ariane s'est pendue," Foucault says that "[To think intensity] is to reject finally the great figure of the Same, which, from Plato to Heidegger, has not stopped locking Western metaphysics into its circle" (my translation). But here too, Foucault provides no

explanation. See Michel Foucault, "Ariane s'est pendue," in *Dits et écrits. Volume I 1954–1975*, édition établie sous la direction de Daniel Defert et François Ewald, avec la collaboration de Jacques Lagrange (Paris: Quarto Gallimard, 2001), 798.

12 Heidegger, GA 12, 12/PLT, 190: "Language brings about and produces [*er-gibt*] man, and so thought, man would be one promise [*ein Versprechen*] of language." Heidegger hyphenates "er-gibt" here so that it indicates that language has given man over, as if he were a gift, instead of man producing language. Instead of language being one of man's activities, man is one of language's "products" or even "promises" (*Versprechen*). For Heidegger, it seems that humans keep the promise—come into their own—by co-responding to the call that defines language (see GA 12, 170/OWL, 76).

13 Michel Foucault, *Le gouvernement de soi et des autres. Cours au Collége de France. 1982–1983* (Paris: Seuil, 2008), 61; English translation by Graham Burchell as *The Government of Self and Others. Lectures at the Collége de France, 1982–1983* (London: Palgrave MacMillan, 2010), 63.

14 For masks, see OT, 385, and Sheridan, *The Archeology of Knowledge*, 131, and Brouchard and Simon, "Nietzsche, Genealogy, History," 386. For "the indefinite work of freedom," see Michel Foucault, "What is Enlightenment? ('Qu'est-ce que les Lumières?')," in *Dits et écrits, IV. 1980–1988*, édition établie sous la direction de Daniel Defert et François Ewald (Paris: NRF Gallimard, 1994), 574; English translation by Catherine Porter as "What is Enlightenment?" in *The Essential Works of Foucault, Volume I: Ethics, Subjectivity and Truth* (New York: New Press, 1997), 315–16.

52

HEIDEGGER AND DELEUZE[1]
Andrea Janae Sholtz and Leonard Lawlor

It is difficult to determine the exact relation Deleuze has with Heidegger's work since Deleuze never wrote an extensive text on Heidegger.[2] Nevertheless, on the basis of Deleuze's numerous mentions of and allusions to Heidegger,[3] we are able to determine two points of intersection.[4] First and most importantly, there is the issue of difference or even *the* difference, that is, the difference between being and beings (between *Sein* and *Seiende*, in German; between *l'être* and *l'étant*, in French), but also the difference between thinking and being, between subject and object, between words and things, between things said and things seen, and between statements and visibilities. Here the issue is how to conceive the "between" of these doubles. Both Deleuze and Heidegger recognize one fundamental requirement for conceiving the "between": the "between" must not be conceived as a separation; there must be no dualism. Therefore, both Deleuze and Heidegger make use of the image of the fold. This image suggests no separation, since folding one sheet of paper over itself does not tear the sheet into two separate pieces. Yet, what Deleuze sees in the Heideggerian fold is a sameness between being and the beings, between all the doubles. So what distinguishes Deleuze from Heidegger is a second requirement for conceiving the "between": the "between" must

not be conceived as a middle; there must be no continuity. For Deleuze, the "between" must be conceived through an image that differs from the neat alignment of the fold: it must be conceived as a struggle or even as chaos that breaks, stretches, or unhinges the fold, the asymmetry of a zigzag.[5] The second issue in which Deleuze and Heidegger intersect is thinking. The second issue flows out of the first since for both Deleuze and Heidegger the problem is once again that of the "between," the "between" of thinking and what is to be thought. Heidegger seems to conceive this relation on the basis of a repetition of the original sense of philosophy, as *philia*, while Deleuze conceives this relation—transforming philosophy into misosophy—as violence. Only the violence of an encounter makes thinking be creative. As we can see already, the problem in both of these issues is that of the foundation: sameness and original sense function as the foundation, while struggle and violence are the nonfoundational.[6] Now we can see these two points of intersection most clearly in one of Deleuze most sustained discussions of Heidegger, his "Note on Heidegger's Philosophy of Difference" found in chapter one of his 1968 *Difference and Repetition* (DR, 89–91/64–6).

Chapter one of *Difference and Repetition* brings us directly to the issue of difference (and the "between") since it is called "Difference in itself." Here, Deleuze brings to light the various ways in which the Western metaphysical tradition has made difference come to be reconciled with the demands of "the concept in general." The concept in general demands that difference be represented. Converted to a representation (a mental representation in the human subject), difference becomes a difference between two determinable things. As a "between" two, it comes to be defined as resemblance, and then resemblance is able to be transformed into the identity of an abstract or general concept. The concept is the third or middle term through which the two determinable objects are compared and made equal, in a word, mediated. As representation, difference is subordinated to identity and mediation, it is subordinated to dialectic in either its ancient or modern form (44–5/29). Thus difference comes to be conceived only for or in relation to something that serves as its foundation or ground. Indeed, difference becomes nothing but the negation of the foundation, a negation that, when it is itself negated, returns difference to the foundation from which it derived (we shall turn to this idea of "return" in a moment, but we can see already that in the representational concept of difference, difference is nothing but a bare repetition of the foundation; the dialectic is always circular). Clearly, in this conception—difference (or differences) relates negatively back to a foundation, which is the abstract identity of the concept (the third term of mediation)— difference is no longer conceived in terms of itself or "in itself." Although he analyzes Aristotle (ancient dialectic) and Hegel (modern dialectic), Deleuze orients the entire chapter toward one overarching movement in Western metaphysics: Platonism (91/66). As is well-known, in this chapter, Deleuze defines the task of contemporary philosophy as "the

reversal of Platonism" (82/59). However, and not so well-known, echoing Heidegger, Deleuze also calls for a "destruction" of Platonism (91/66). Indeed, it is precisely in the center of this "destruction" that we find Deleuze's five-point summary of "Heidegger's Philosophy of Difference" (89–91/64–6).

Here are the five points. Since Platonism defines difference as the negation of the foundation, Deleuze starts with the "not" in Heidegger.[7] More specifically, he starts here because Hegelian dialectic, as we just suggested and as Deleuze had shown earlier in the chapter, had tried to explain negation in propositions by putting nonbeing right into being; this nonbeing within being would be the negative; but the negative would have no other function, according to Deleuze, than to be itself negated, and therefore difference, as in Platonism, would be returned to identity (64/45, 78/55, 88–9/63). So, in the *first point*, Deleuze says that, in Heidegger, the "not" does not express the negative—Heidegger is not Hegel—rather the "not" expresses the difference between being and beings. In the *second point*, Deleuze says that the difference between being and beings is not the "between" in the ordinary sense.[8] Instead, it must be understood as the fold, the "Zwiefalt." For Deleuze, the fold image means that being constitutes the being in the double movement of unconcealment (or "clearing") and concealment. Difference understood as the fold is constitutive of being. In other words, being, in Heidegger, differentiates the being off from a sort of background of obscurity. In this way, Deleuze gives a new sense to Heidegger's expression "ontological difference": being is the active "differenciator" of beings (90/65; see also 154/117).[9] Like the first two points, the *third* takes up a well-known aspect of Heidegger's thought: "the question of being."[10] Deleuze says that "ontological difference corresponds to the question." In other words, through the "correspondence," Deleuze makes an equivalency between being and questioning. He makes this equivalency not only because it seems to be faithful to Heidegger's thinking but also because Deleuze had already suggested that Plato (not Platonism) had transformed being itself into questions and problems by means of his mythological accounts of origins. For instance, the oracular saying at Delphi explains Socrates' origin, but the saying itself raises problems and questions for Socrates (88/63). Through this paradoxical origin, Deleuze is arguing, one is able to insert nonbeing into being but not in a way that nonbeing exists simply to be itself negated and thereby returned (as in a circle, again) to the identity of being. As equivalent to a question, being actively constitutes beings as differences, as if they were so many different answers to a question that remains open and consequently unanswerable. As a kind of nonbeing, difference (or the question)—*fourth point*—"is *not*," as Deleuze says (our emphasis of "not"), "an object of representation."[11] The "turn beyond metaphysics," in Deleuze's interpretation of Heidegger, amounts to insisting that metaphysics cannot think "difference in itself." The Heideggerian "turn," for Deleuze, is a resistance to conceiving difference as a third term "between" being and beings, it is a "stubborn" resistance to mediation. Finally, the *fifth point*: "Difference cannot, therefore, be subordinated to the Identical or the Equal, but must be thought as the Same, in the Same" (Deleuze's capitalizations). Through the Same ("le Même" in French, "die Selbe" in German), Heidegger is trying to think a "gathering" that is not reducible to empty indifferent oneness.

Deleuze intends these five point to show how certain readings of the later Heidegger (Deleuze probably has Sartre in mind) are really misunderstandings. In particular,

Deleuze's five points aim to outline a more accurate reading of the Heideggerian "not: "the Heideggerian NOT refers not to the negative in being, but to being as difference; it refers not to negation but to the question" (Deleuze's capitalization of "not"). Deleuze's defense of Heidegger is so strong here that he says that he considers the Heideggerian "correspondence" between difference and the question, between the ontological difference and the being of the question, "fundamental." Despite this attachment to Heidegger's thought, Deleuze suggests that Heidegger's own formulas for the "not" might be to blame for the misunderstandings of his later work. Indeed, through a series of questions, Deleuze distances himself from Heidegger's thinking. In particular, Deleuze is not certain that speaking of the Same (gathering), rather than Identity, is really enough to think original difference (see also 154/117).[12] Deleuze asks, "Is Sameness enough to disconnect difference from all mediation?" This question implies, as we shall see, that the fold, for Deleuze, must not be a "homology" between being and beings. The distance, however, that Deleuze takes from Heidegger's thought really comes down to the status of the being (*Seiende* or *l'étant*), not the status of being (not *Sein* or *l'être*). The question for Deleuze is the following: "Does Heidegger make the conversion by means of which being [*l'être*] must be said only of difference and in this way being [*l'être*] revolves around the being [*l'étant*]?" (translation modified). In other words, "Does Heidegger conceive the being [*l'étant*] in such a manner that the being [*l'étant*] is removed from all subordination in relation to the identity of representation?" Deleuze concludes, "It seems not, given [Heidegger's] interpretation of Nietzsche's eternal return" (91/66).[13]

Whether or not Deleuze's claim about Heidegger's interpretation of Nietzsche's eternal return doctrine—in *Difference and Repetition* (but already in the 1962 *Nietzsche and Philosophy* [see NP, 211n1/220n31]), it is clear that Deleuze thinks that Heidegger does not understand the eternal return doctrine—is correct, it tells us a lot about how Deleuze conceives his own thinking in relation to that of Heidegger. When Heidegger interprets the eternal return doctrine as being "metaphysical," Deleuze thinks that Heidegger is claiming that the return of the eternal return is a founded repetition. That is, it is the repetition of an identity that predetermines all the answers to the question, as if for Nietzsche the repetition was a repetition of permanence, as if for Nietzsche repetition did not produce a multiplicity of new answers, as if for Nietzsche therefore there was no true becoming. In contrast, what Deleuze sees in the eternal return doctrine is a very specific kind of repetition, one that, as he says, "makes a difference" (DR, 85/60). The repetition to which the eternal return refers, in Deleuze's interpretation of Nietzsche, is a repetition that repeats no identity. It is a foundationless repetition. It is foundationless insofar as it repeats the being (*l'étant*), but the being—an individual thing—is not conceived as copy of an original or of a model. The being is conceived as a singularity or as an event. A singular event, for Deleuze, is a true "commencement" so that the repetition of the eternal return is a "recommencement." Being based in a commencement, in an event, the recommencement is not determined. Therefore the recommencement—the return of the eternal return—has the potential to produce more differences, more events, more novelties, more answers to the question (258–61/200–2). The repetition is creative. This formula seems to be contradictory since repetitions repeat and therefore cannot be creative. Yet, one can understand the formula if one thinks of the artwork. An

event such as the writing of *Hamlet* was based in no determinate model, no exact foundation, and no self-identical origin; therefore its subsequent theatre productions, while repetitions, all are able to be different. Undoubtedly, with this description of recommencement (creative repetition[14]), Deleuze seems to be very close to Heidegger's own reflections on the artwork, on the *Abgrund* (the foundationless), on the *Ereignis* (the event of propriation), and on another beginning. Indeed, the French word "recommencement" could be rendered in English as "another beginning." Yet, insofar as Deleuze thinks that Heidegger does not understand Nietzsche's eternal return doctrine, he thinks the real issue between his own thinking and that of Heidegger is the idea of foundation: founded repetition versus unfounded repetition. It is a question, as Deleuze would say in his later works, of becoming and deterritorialization.[15]

The question of foundation is at work as well in the issue of thinking. In *Difference and Repetition*, Deleuze refers several times to Heidegger's famous question of what calls for thinking (in particular, 188/144; but also 252–3/195–6, 259/200, 353/275).[16] Of course, Deleuze recognizes that this question means that it is possible for humans to think. But, he also recognizes that for Heidegger that possibility does not mean that we are thinking or even capable of thinking. In short, for Heidegger—and Deleuze completely agrees with Heidegger—thought thinks only in the presence of what is to be thought. And what is to be thought is not only what gives food for thought but also and especially the unthinkable or the nonthought, that is, the fact that "we are not yet thinking" (188; here Deleuze is quoting Heidegger's *What is called Thinking?*; the passage from *Difference and Repetition* that we are paraphrasing here from 188/144 is untranslated in the English translation). Yet, for Deleuze what is at issue is how Heidegger conceives the relation between thought and what is to be thought. Deleuze claims (in a footnote, which reinforces what we saw in "The Five Points") that the later Heidegger (the Heidegger of *What is Called Thinking?*) remains attached to "the primacy of Same" (Deleuze's capitalization of the word "the Same," "le Même"). The primacy of the same means that Heidegger, according to Deleuze, conceives the relation between thought and what is to be thought as a "homology" (188n1/321n11). Thus, the homology between thought and what is to be thought, according to Deleuze, turns the Heideggerian fold into a kind of benevolent desire; it bears a strong resemblance to the *philia* of philo-sophy. In short, Heidegger seems to conceive the fold as an interlacing, or even a chiasm. For Deleuze, however, the fold must be understood as a fold between two kinds of forms, as if being and beings, thought and the object of thought, and between things said and things seen, as if all of the doubles are formalized. These two forms are not homologous but hetero-geneous and different from one another; the fold is in fact a "non-relation" (F, 117/109).[17] Yet, although different, they encounter one another across an element that is not the form of either of the doubles. The element must be conceived as formless or informal. This negation—in-formal—implies that prior to the fold, there is an "unfold."[18] The "unfold" is not an interlacing but a "strangle-hold" (119/112). For Deleuze, therefore, and unlike for Heidegger, the fold between being and beings, between things seen and things said, between words and things, subject and object, etc., the "between" of all of these dif-ferences is conceived as violence or a struggle. Indeed, without the violent relation, without "an encounter," it is not clear why humans would ever start to think. As Deleuze says,

"everything begins with misosophy" (DR, 182/139).

The question of philosophy is the one that Deleuze asks in his last book (coauthored with Félix Guattari): *What is Philosophy?* In fact, this question brings us to what must count as a third point of intersection between Deleuze and Heidegger: the fact that philoso-phy historically begins in Greece. Of course, it is not controversial to claim that Heidegger's philosophy revolves around some sort of retrieval of the original Greek inspiration for philosophy. Deleuze, however, explains Heidegger's impulse to retrieve the Greeks as a particularly modern (nineteenth and twenti-eth century) endeavor, and, even more, a par-ticularly German endeavor (QPh, 97/101). Generally, according to Deleuze, German phi-losophy (Deleuze mentions Kant, Hegel, and Heidegger) wants to "reconquer" the Greek philosophical territory (that seemingly has been given over to barbarians, nomads, and anarchy [100/104[19]]). In order to reconquer the Greek territory, German philosophy "must constantly clear and consolidate the soil, that is, it must found [*fonder*]" (ibid.). Once again, we see how the issue of foundation organizes all of Deleuze's reflections on Heidegger's thought. But more specifically, Heidegger, according to Deleuze, conceives the Greeks as the Autochthon: philosophy arises naturally out of the Greek soil. It is not imported from elsewhere; it does not come from another ter-ritory. Thus, according to Deleuze, Greece is for Heidegger an origin (91/95). As the word "autochthonous" suggests, origin means something like an internal necessity between the Greeks and philosophy (89/93), as if phi-losophy could not have appeared elsewhere, as if from this origin the history of philosophy, which Heidegger calls "the history of being," develops according to a kind of "analytic and necessary principle" (90/94). Because the

Greeks are the origin, and despite the fact that the Greeks do not articulate their relation to being, "in Heidegger," Deleuze says, "there is no question of going farther than the Greeks; it is enough to resume their movement in an initiating, recommencing repetition" (91/95, translation modified). Deleuze is arguing that since the history of being is necessarily connected to a repetition of the Greek origin, Heidegger's idea of "another beginning"—"the initiating, recommencing repetition"—is a founded repetition. Heidegger's repetition congeals at and around the Greek origin as if what the Greeks did "is valid once and for all" (92/96).

The congealed repetition of the Greeks brings Deleuze to Heidegger's so-called political mistake, his association with Nazism in 1933. In fact, what Deleuze is doing here is providing an explanation of the so-called mistake. Deleuze says, "Heidegger wanted to rejoin the Greeks through the Germans at the worst moment of their history" (104/108). "At the worst moment of their history": this occurred when the Germans conceived themselves as a pure race. The "mistake" is that Heidegger takes the Germans, the pure race, for the Greeks, the origin of philosophy. Although Deleuze wonders if Heidegger's philosophical concepts are therefore not "intrinsically sullied," he admits that Heidegger may have just been confused, that he lost his way, that his eyes got tired. Nevertheless, it seems that, for Deleuze, Heidegger's confusion had its source in the concept of the Greeks as an autochthonous origin—a virtually *pure* origin of virtually *pure* philosophy could *only* call forth a *pure* people. In contrast, for Deleuze, the Greeks were not an origin and they were not pure: philosophy was "brought [to Greece] by immigrants" (89/93). If Heidegger had understood philosophy on the basis of this migratory event, he would

have known that the people called forth by philosophy (and art) is "not one that claims to be pure, but rather an oppressed, bastard, lower, anarchical, nomadic, and irremediably minor race" (104–5/109). Earlier we said that for Deleuze everything begins with misosophy. Now we can see that, for Deleuze, everything begins with nonphilosophy, with the nonphilosophers, the artists, the barbarians, the anarchists, the nomads, with the ones who contaminate us, who make the violence of the encounter. They are the ones who make us think; they are the ones who call for thinking. Yet, Deleuze knows that we would not have the question of what calls for thinking without Heidegger. This is why he says, "We must not refuse to take Heidegger seriously" (F, 118/111).

NOTES AND REFERENCES

[1] The following abbreviations are used here to refer to Deleuze's works: DR: *Différence et répétition* (Paris: Presses Universitaires de France, 1968). English: Paul Patton, *Difference and Repetition* (New York: Columbia University Press, 1994); NP: *Nietzsche et la philosophie* (Paris: Presses Universitaires de France, 1962). English: Hugh Tomlinson, *Nietzsche and Philosophy* (New York: Columbia University Press, 1983); F: *Foucault* (Paris: Éditions de Minuit, 1986). English: Seán Hand, *Foucault* (Minneapolis: University of Minnesota Press, 1988); QPh: with Félix Guattari: *Qu'est-ce que la philosophie?* (Paris: Éditions de Minuit, 1991). English: Hugh Tomlinson and Graham Burchell, *What is Philosophy?* (New York: Columbia University Press, 1994).

[2] There is evidence that early in his career, during the 1950s, Deleuze studied Heidegger. See Gilles Deleuze, "Qu'est-ce que fonder?," accessed on December 6, 2011, www.webdeleuze.com. This text is the transcription of Deleuze's 1956–7 "cours hypokhâgne," at Lycée Louis le Grand. In the context of a discussion of foundation in Kant, he refers several times to Heidegger's *Kant*

and the Problem of Metaphysics. Also, in 1953 he wrote book reviews on Régis Jolivet's *Le problème de la mort chez M. Heidegger et J.-P. Sartre* and K. E. Lögstrup's *Kierkegaard und Heideggers Existenzanalyse und ihr Verhältnis zur Verkündigung*.

3 For references to Heidegger, see: NP 44–5/39, 123/108, 174/151, 194/169, 194n4/203n30, 174n/215n3, 211n1/220n31; DR xvi–xvii, 1/xix, 52/35, 89–91/64–6, 154/117, 169/129, 188/144, 252–3/195–6, 260/200–1, 353/275, 384/301 and 333n11, 188n1/321n.11, 391/334; ID: *L'île déserte et autres texts*. David Lapoujade (ed.) (Paris: Editions de Minuit, 2002). English: Mike Taormina, *Desert Islands: and Other Texts*, 1953–74, David Lapoujade (ed.) (New York: Semiotext(e), 2004), 106/75, 110/77, 112/79, 219/157, 222/159, 225/161, 363/260, 156/301n14; D (*Dialogues*) 18–19/12–13; MP (*A Thousand Plateaus*) 156/125, 501–2n78/561n.85; C1 (*Cinema 1*) 20n1/219n15; C2 (*Cinema 2*) 204/156, 218/167, 218n23/310n23; F (*Foucault*) 57–8/50, 66/59, 95–9/89–93, 102/95, 115–121/107–13, 121–8/114–20, 107n16/146n16, 115n33/148n33, 118n36/148n36, 119n38/149n38, 121n41/149n41; TF (*The Fold. Leibniz and the Baroque*)16/10, 36/26, 42/30, 50–51/35–36, 71, 36n27/154n14; QPh 43/40, 55/55, 56/56, 89–100/93–104, 104–5/108–9, 88n5/223n5, 140n10/228n10, 169n17/231n17; N (*Negotiations*) 47/31, 130–3/95–7, 144–5/107, 152–3/112–13; TRM (*Two Regimes of Madness*) 129/141, 226/241, 239/256, 356/380; CDG (seminars at the Université Paris VIII Vincennes and Vincennes St. Denis 1971–87, accessed on February 3, 2012, www.webdeleuze.com) IMAGE MOUVEMENT IMAGE TEMPS: Vincennes—St Denis—00/00/1982, 01/00/1982; KANT: Vincennes—March 21, 1978, March 28, 1978, April 4, 1978; LEIBNIZ: Vincennes— May 20, 1980, 00/00/1987, Vincennes—St Denis—20/01/1987.

4 Alain Badiou argues for their proximity based on the univocity of Being (*The Clamor of Being* (Minneapolis: University of Minnesota Press, 2000) (orig. pub. 1997)); Constantin Boundas views Deleuze's *Difference and Repetition* as a response to Heidegger's *Being and Time* but claims the lines of divergence ultimately outweigh those of proximity ("Martin Heidegger,"

Graham Jones and Jon Roffe (eds) *Deleuze's Philosophical Lineage* (Edinburgh: Edinburgh University Press, 2009), 321–38); Miguel de Beistegui draws them together as thinkers of different sides of Being, ultimately irreconcilable (*Truth and Genesis: Philosophy as Differential Ontology* (Bloomington: Indiana University Press, 2004). Claire Parnet identifies a correlation in their occupation with the nonthought within thought, yet admits in her conversation with Deleuze that "You [Deleuze] are not a Heideggerian" in Gilles Deleuze and Claire Parnet, *Dialogues* (Paris: Flammarion, 1976). English: *Dialogues II* (New York: Columbia University Press, 1977), 31/23. Janae Sholtz claims Deleuze radicalizes the Heideggerian relation between the aesthetic and a people-to-come (*The Transformative Potential of Art: Creating a People in Heidegger and Deleuze*. Dissertation (University of Memphis, 2009)). Also see: Dronsfield, Jonathan "Between Deleuze and Heidegger There Never is Any Difference," in David Pettigrew and François Raffoul (eds), *French Interpretations of Heidegger: An Exceptional Reception*. Suny Series in Contemporary French Thought (New York: SUNY Press, 2008), 151–66; Keith Robinson, "Towards a Political Ontology of the Fold: Deleuze, Heidegger, Whitehead and the 'Fourfold' Event" in Sjoerd van Tuinen and Niamh McDonnell (eds.) *Deleuze and the Fold: A Critical Reader* (New York: Palgrave Macmillan, 2009), 184–202.

5 The zigzag is imaged repeatedly by Deleuze: as undermining totality, a crack, asymmetrical (MP, 263/216, 341/278); "an extremely sinuous fold . . . a primal tie that cannot be located" (TF, 162/120); "something which passes or happens between two as though under a potential difference" and a "broken line . . . that slips between" (*Dialogues*, 13/6, 41/32); ". . . c'est ptêt' le mouvement élémentaire, c'est ptêt' le mouvement qui a présidé à la création du monde . . ." (*L'Abécédaire de Gilles Deleuze*, filmed by Pierre-André Boutang in 1988–9).

6 We have simplified Deleuze's distinction between foundation and nonfoundation. In fact, in *Difference and Repetition*, what is at issue is to found or ground (*fonder*) and begin (*commencer*). Yet, for Deleuze a genuine founding must "metamorphose"; however to have a genuine founding what is founded must

be related to a "without ground" (*sans-fond*)
(DR, 200/154). Thus to ground in Deleuze is
never a repetition of the same.

7   Deleuze cites Heidegger's "On the Essence of
Ground," and "What is Metaphysics," both
in Martin Heidegger. *Pathmarks* edited by
William McNeil (USA: Cambridge University
Press, 1998), 97–135 and 82–96.

8   Deleuze cites Heidegger's "Overcoming
Metaphysics," in trans. Joan Stambaugh, *The
End of Philosophy* (USA: Harper & Row,
1973).

9   See also TF where Deleuze late in his career
(1988) takes up again Heidegger's language of
the *Zwiefalt* (TF 42/30).

10 Deleuze cites again "On the Essence of Ground."

11 Deleuze cites again "Overcoming
Metaphysics." But here in the fourth point, he
also cites Jean Beaufret's *Introduction à une
lecture du Poème de Parménide* (Paris: Presses
Universitaires de France, 1955), and Beda
Alleman, *Hölderlin et Heidegger* (Paris: Presses
Universitaires de France, 1954).

12 By focusing on the same (gathering), Deleuze's
criticism of Heidegger is virtually identical
to that of Foucault and that of Derrida. See
Michel Foucault, *Les mots et les choses* (Paris:
Tel Gallimard, 1966), 345; anonymous English
translation as *The Order of Things* (New York:
Vintage, 1970), 334. See Jacques Derrida,
Mémoires pour Paul de Man (Paris: Galilée,
1988), 136; English translation by Cecile
Lindsay, Jonathan Culler, and Eduardo Cadava
as *Memoires for Paul de Man* (New York:
Columbia University Press, 1986), 141–2.

13 Here Deleuze cites Heidegger's interpretation
of Nietzsche in *What is Called Thinking?*

14 In *Difference and Repetition*, Deleuze calls
what we are calling a "creative repetition" a
"clothed" or disguised" repetition. See DR,
114/84.

15 Deleuze develops the concepts of becoming and deterritorialization in MP. See MP,
305/249 for becoming; see MP, 211/172.

16 See also F, 124/116: "In truth, one thing haunts
Foucault—thought. The question 'what does
thinking mean? What do we call thinking?'
is the arrow first fired by Heidegger . . . the
arrow par excellence" (translation modified).

17 The fold in Deleuze is equivalent to what
he calls a "plane of immanence." The most
important definition of the plane of immanence appears in *What is Philosophy?* See
QPh, 50/48–9.

18 Deleuze speaks of the "unfold" (*dépli*) in TF
(P, 50–1/35–6). The word "unfold," however,
really comes from Foucault. See Foucault,
Les mots et les choses, 353; *The Order of
Things*, 342. In our discussion of the fold in
Deleuze, we have inserted some comments
from Deleuze's *Foucault*. Near the end of
this book, Deleuze compares Foucault's
thought to that of Heidegger (and to that of
Merleau-Ponty) (F, 115–20/108–13). This is
an important and truly illuminating comparison. Indeed, there can be no question that
Deleuze's *Foucault* is one of the best books
ever written on Foucault's thinking. Yet, as
some have claimed, *Foucault* appears to be as
much a book about Deleuze's thinking itself
as is it about Foucault's. See Thomas Flynn,
*Sartre, Foucault, and Historical Reason,
Volume Two* (Chicago: University of Chicago
Press, 2005), 350n22: ". . . [Deleuze's] important book on Foucault . . . is an original
attempt to think his own thought through
that of Foucault." It is possible therefore that
Deleuze is presenting his own thinking under
the proper name "Foucault." Yet, Deleuze
does not put the name "Foucault" between
scare quotes and he claims unequivocally
that he is presenting Foucault's thinking as
such in his book. The possibility, however,
that "Foucault" is actually Deleuze presents
a serious interpretative problem for anyone
who wants to incorporate *Foucault* into
an exposition of Deleuze's thinking. This
problem explains why we have used *Foucault*
sparingly in our exposition. No matter what,
however, we think *Foucault* is one of the
most important philosophy books written
in the twentieth century. For instance, what
Deleuze says about dualism in Foucault
specifically and about dualism generally is
extraordinarily illuminating (F, 89/83).

19 In this comment, Deleuze cites the Preface to
the First Edition of Kant's *Critique of Pure
Reason* (see Allen W. Wood, editor, *Basic
Writings of Kant* (New York: The Modern
Library, 2001), 3–6), where Kant speaks of
the land of metaphysics being given over to
barbarians, nomads, and anarchy.

53

HEIDEGGER'S ANGLO-AMERICAN RECEPTION
Leslie MacAvoy

Heidegger's work has been best received within Anglo-American philosophy by philosophers interested in pragmatism, and, indeed, reference is often made to the "pragmatist reading" at least when discussing texts like *Being and Time*. This essay shall explore three prominent "pragmatist" interpretations of Heidegger. All of them share as a common theme a critique of representationalism, but each elaborates this critique in very different ways. For this reason, it makes sense to think of "pragmatism" as functioning as a kind of family resemblance concept.

The three positions to be explored here are put forward by Hubert Dreyfus, Mark Okrent, and Richard Rorty. Dreyfus offers a pragmatist reading of Heidegger, particularly of *Being and Time*, insofar as he emphasizes the place of practices in Heidegger's philosophy and the priority given to the practical over the theoretical. He is particularly interested in using Heidegger's phenomenological account of subjectivity to challenge positions within the philosophy of mind that give priority to mental representations. Okrent focuses less on practices as such and more on purposive, practical activity itself and how epistemic conditions may be articulated in connection with this more pragmatic

context. He characterizes Heidegger's position as a "transcendental pragmatism." While Okrent does not directly address representationalism, the verificationist thesis for which he argues has anti-representationalist consequences. Finally, Rorty sees affinities between Heidegger's position and pragmatist approaches in the philosophy of language insofar as both are critical of metaphysics and representationalism. His position could be considered pragmatist in the further sense that he is more concerned with a philosophy's usefulness than he is with its truth, and this informs his appropriation of Heidegger's thought.

The *locus classicus* for pragmatist readings of Heidegger is the analysis of Dasein's everyday Being-in-the-world in *Being and Time*. Heidegger indicates that his project is to arrive at some philosophical understanding of being and thus to do fundamental ontology. But, as he also says in the introduction, the point of access for investigating this question is an analysis of Dasein because Dasein is that entity that has an understanding of being (GA 2, 12–13/BT, 11–12). Though this understanding of being is not explicitly grasped, it operates in the background in everything that Dasein does, so to bring it to philosophical awareness, an analysis of Dasein in its way of being is required. That way of being is existence, or Being-in-the-world, and the objective of much of the first division of *Being and Time* is to offer a phenomenological analysis of it.

In developing this position, Heidegger directly opposes the more traditional Cartesian view that a relation to the world is extrinsic to what it is to be a subject. The first important point, then, is that the subject, Dasein, is necessarily related to the world. Furthermore, Heidegger explicitly rejects the notion that to be "in" the world can be understood in terms of contingent, external, spatial, or locative relations such as are indicated by expressions such as the water is "in" the glass (GA 2, 54/BT, 54–5). By contrast, the sense of Being "in" that he seeks concerns dwelling within or inhabiting the world. Thus, as Heidegger begins his investigation into Being-in-the-world, he focuses on practical activity and practical comportment, which he calls "dealings" (*Umgang*) (GA 2, 66/BT, 66). The second important point, then, is that the relation to the world is one of practical involvement. This move challenges the priority typically given to the theoretical attitude over the practical attitude as a perspective from which to grasp what things are.

A significant feature of Heidegger's analysis pertains to the way practical understanding operates by situating particular objects or items of equipment within broader equipmental contexts or totalities of significance that function as horizons in relation to which something becomes intelligible. Thus, Dasein demonstrates not only an understanding of an item of equipment by using it but a familiarity with a whole range of equipment to which this particular item belongs and a grasp of how all of it might be mobilized toward the completion of a project. So, for

instance, the writer uses the pen to write, but to understand the pen as something to be used for writing indicates a more general familiarity with the practice of writing, the other items of equipment that are bound up with the pen in such activities, etc. These equipmental contexts are bound together for Heidegger by a set of references through which each item in the context points to and thus signifies the others. Thus, the understanding operative in practical comportment is holistic, and the things we encounter make sense and are intelligible because they are disclosed to us as situated within worlds. Such worlds are to be conceived as structured spaces of meaning.

Heidegger's rich analysis of Being-in-the-world has provided many resources to supply various pragmatist accounts. Dreyfus, in his well-known book *Being-in-the-World* highlights the role of the practical in *Being and Time*.[1] He argues that the practical comportment Heidegger describes in chapter 3 of Division I of *Being and Time* depends upon a familiarity with meanings that are tied to practices, and that practices by their very nature must be shared and social. This interpretation emphasizes the role of the "they" and *Mitsein* in Dasein's Being-in-the-world. That is, for Dasein the world is always a world that it shares with others, and which it discloses on the basis of structures of intelligibility that are also shared.[2]

Dreyfus's reading of Heidegger is dominated by a focus on the critique of two related forms of Cartesianism. The first form is an epistemological Cartesianism according to which subjects are characterized primarily as knowers who come to know objects by contemplating them. This view construes the relation between subject and object in terms of detachment, and Dreyfus associates it with the theoretical attitude. The second form is an ontological Cartesianism according to which objects to be known are conceived of as "present-at-hand" or "occurrent" [*vorhanden*]. Against the theoretical attitude and the ontological priority given to presence-at-hand connected with it, Dreyfus argues that Heidegger gives priority to the practical attitude. He glosses Heidegger's account of dealings with equipment as "skilled coping," and he emphasizes Heidegger's point that things show up for Dasein as ready-to-hand in this sort of comportment.

This theme of the priority of the practical attitude over the theoretical attitude, and in general the view that the theoretical attitude is somehow derivative of the practical attitude and achieved through a kind of disengagement from it, runs throughout Dreyfus's interpretation and underlies his characterization of Heidegger's account of understanding as a *knowing how* to be contrasted with the *knowing that* associated with the theoretical attitude.[3] It is further reinforced by Heidegger's claim that assertion is a derivative form of interpretation. For Heidegger, interpretation is a development of understanding that involves an articulation of what the understanding understands, and there is an argument to be made that this interpretation occurs in practical activity itself. That is, when Dasein deals with equipment, it takes each item *as* something or other, that is, *as* a table or a door (GA 2, 149/BT, 144–5). Heidegger calls this the hermeneutic "as." In discussing assertions, Heidegger notes that it too contains an "as-structure," but the "as" in this case is an apophantic "as," which is bound up with the structure of predication (GA 2, 154–5/BT, 149–50). Thus, in the assertion "the paper is white," the paper is asserted *as* being white. For Heidegger the transformation of the hermeneutic to the apophantic "as" involves a subtracting of the reference relations in virtue of which, in practical contexts, something can be taken as something or other (GA 2, 158/BT, 153). Thus, the apophantic "as" is derivative of the hermeneutic "as," and assertion is derivative of interpretation.

Heidegger's position here lends support to Dreyfus's view regarding the priority of the practical, and also serves as the basis for his claim that the *knowing how* associated with understanding and interpretation is nonpropositional and nonconceptual. Dreyfus holds that propositional form is introduced into meaning in the move from interpretation to assertion. He claims that while assertions clearly have propositional form and involve concepts, interpretation, which occurs purely in practical activity, has no such form and thus *knowing how* entails an understanding of nonpropositional, nonconceptual meaning. Dreyfus's commitment to this position comes clearly into view in his debate with McDowell about whether there is any sort of experience that is nonconceptual but nonetheless meaningful or whether, as McDowell maintains, experience must be conceptual "all the way out."[4] This sheds important light on Dreyfus's interest in Heidegger's critique of Cartesianism, namely that what is perhaps most important about it for him is that it entails a critique of representationalism because practical comportment represents a kind of intentionality that is not directed at mental representations.[5]

Dreyfus's reading of Heidegger might be considered pragmatist in several ways. First, he emphasizes the theme of practical comportment in Heidegger, and stresses that the source of meaning that makes up the world as a structure of significance is shared social practices. Second, Dreyfus not only gives priority to the practical over the theoretical, he renders the practical in some degree ineffable in relation to the theoretical. In his view, theoretical understanding, bound up as it is with what can be represented conceptually and propositionally, is impoverished relative to what is understood in practical understanding, which cannot be fully or adequately "translated" into this theoretical idiom. This leads to a philosophical stance in opposition to representationalism.

Okrent also characterizes Heidegger's position in pragmatist terms and, at least for a significant portion of his book *Heidegger's Pragmatism*, shares Dreyfus's focus on Heidegger's work during the period of *Being and Time*.[6] Okrent considers Heidegger's philosophy to be pragmatist for several reasons. First, it is anti-essentialist. Second, his entire account is about the primacy of a kind of practical understanding that is rooted in shared practices about how to do things to achieve some end. Third, this focus leads to a kind of "pragmatist metaphysics" insofar as Heidegger ends up holding the view that the meaning of being is a function of Dasein's understanding of being.

Okrent is primarily interested in the epistemological consequences of this pragmatism and in bringing Heidegger into conversation with the Anglo-American tradition of epistemology. He argues that Heidegger's position amounts to a kind of pragmatist recasting of a more standard verificationist position. Verificationism holds that the meaning of a sentence is a function of what would count as evidence for its truth. Heidegger's position is not primarily about the meaning of sentences, but about the meaning of acts, given the priority granted the practical sphere. Okrent argues that the form of verificationism found in Heidegger's work is the view that "the meaning of any act, intention, or assertion is a function of the evidence that

would count in favor of its truth or success."[7] An act is successful if it brings about the state of affairs intended by the action, and so we can verify whether an act counts as being an act of a certain kind (or having a certain meaning) by judging whether it is successful, or has a reasonable chance of success, with regard to its goal. For instance, something counts as an act of hammering if it succeeds in achieving the goal that acts of hammering have, that is, of pounding nails into boards. Someone who uses a shoe to perform this action might be said to be performing an act of hammering just as much as someone who uses a hammer, provided that there is success or a reasonable chance thereof. On the other hand, someone who picks up a wet noodle to perform the same action could not be said to be performing an act of hammering because the aimed for state of affairs will never be achieved through this act. So Okrent says that "the specific meaning of an act of interpretation, then, is fixed by the conditions which the act is to bring about, and this in turn is the state of affairs which the agent of the act would take as evidence for the 'truth' of the act."[8] Okrent continues: "for Heidegger, the fundamental notion of evidence is tied to the way in which purposeful, practical activity must be recognizable as successful or unsuccessful if the activity is to count as purposeful at all."[9]

This amounts to an extension of pragmatist considerations to a verificationist account insofar as verificationism is extended from sentences to acts. Acts can have meaning, and that meaning is determined relative to what would count as evidence of the action's success. But for Okrent, Heidegger's pragmatism goes even further because he holds that the meaning of the being of something is tied to Dasein's understanding of being. This claim is particularly important for Okrent's view that Heidegger is a transcendental pragmatist. To be a transcendentalist in Okrent's sense is to be concerned with the necessary conditions for something, in this case, for intentionality. In this view, then, Heidegger's philosophy is transcendental in that it is concerned with the necessary conditions for intentionality, and Heidegger finds those conditions to be rooted in Dasein's being, which for Okrent has to do with purposive, practical activity. So, the transcendental ground for intentionality turns out to be practical, and so Heidegger is a pragmatist on transcendental grounds, which makes him a transcendental pragmatist.[10] Although Okrent does not address representationalism directly, as Dreyfus does, the verificationist position that he emphasizes is anti-representationalist. Representationalist theories are typically conceptually related to correspondence notions of truth, that is, that for some idea or proposition to be true, it must accurately represent reality. Verificationism focuses instead on the evidence that justifies a belief, claim, or action where that evidence might be coherence with other beliefs or actions, and so, by contrast, is often associated with a coherentist theory of truth.

Rorty's approach to pragmatism and consequently to Heidegger is somewhat different. Rorty's pragmatism entails the view that truth is a function of the coherence of discourses and the usefulness of those discourses for accomplishing certain ends. Since philosophical discourse is just another discourse, there can be no sense in which it is true except in the pragmatic sense, so a philosophical discourse will only be true to the extent that it is useful for accomplishing some end. This stance leads Rorty to conclude that the pragmatist should also be an ironist toward philosophical discourse, and his writing conveys the general sense that he

is not too bothered about whether he gets the thinkers he reads right. He simply uses them for accomplishing a purpose, and this contributes to the sort of playfulness one finds in his reading of Heidegger and other philosophers. This playfulness is decidedly not a feature of the other pragmatist interpretations considered here.

Rorty is motivated to adopt a pragmatist position mainly by a critique of representationalism. His objection to representationalism is that it purports to make the truth of sentences depend upon their correspondence to the world. Such a view holds that there is a truth to the world, and that sentences, or language, are only derivatively true in relation to the degree to which they "copy" this truth. Rorty rejects this. He claims that there is no truth to the world; truth is only a property of sentences, and sentences are descriptions of the world.[11] He suggests that however plausible the notion that language represents the world may seem to be, it is much less tenable when we shift our consideration from sentences to vocabularies in general, where it seems fairly clear that the criteria that determine which words one should use are actually set by language games, not correspondence relations with the world. To a large degree this aspect of Rorty's pragmatism is rooted in a Wittgensteinian view about language, namely that language is based on language games that are essentially practices. In this regard, signs are just linguistic tools for achieving certain ends, and how they are to be used is set by the norms that function as rules within some particular language game. Language games and all practices are, in the end, contingent, meaning that although we have a set of words that we use to talk about the world, we might have had a different set of words.[12] This realization should lead us to oppose essentialism as well as representationalism, and thus one can see that Rorty's pragmatism does indeed draw attention to the primacy of practices.

It is also clear that this view contributes to the ironist stance. Rorty thinks that beliefs and desires are related to one another in the sense that a belief can be said to be true or false partly because of how useful it is for helping us achieve our desires. This leads to the view already mentioned that philosophy should be viewed as a tool, as something that is useful for something, and the use to which Rorty thinks philosophy should be put is overcoming representationalism and the idea that there are any things in themselves that we can know with certainty.[13] He associates this way of thinking with the Cartesian-Kantian tradition, which has generated all sorts of philosophical problems that are in fact pseudo-problems. Following Wittgenstein, Rorty thinks we need to show the fly the way out of the bottle, and he looks to a wide variety of philosophers to assist with this project.

Rorty's reading of Heidegger is motivated by this interest, and he thinks that Heidegger's philosophy can be useful for his anti-representationalist goals. On the one hand, Rorty agrees with Dreyfus, Okrent, and others and for the same reasons that Heidegger is a pragmatist in *Being and Time*. Dasein discloses the world in relation to its projects, and these are contingent, fragile, and could have been otherwise. Thus, Rorty sees Heidegger as sharing the pragmatist view about contingency. On the other hand, Rorty claims that by the 1930s Heidegger moves away from this pragmatism as he undertakes the history of being in the Nietzsche lectures. Interestingly enough, however, it is this period of Heidegger's philosophy upon which Rorty himself seems far more interested in drawing because of its more overt

critique of the metaphysical tradition. Thus, Rorty appropriates Heidegger for his purposes because he thinks he is useful, but also because he thinks that Heidegger's critique of metaphysics overlaps in important ways with the pragmatist critique as one finds it in a figure such as Dewey. First, both Heidegger and the pragmatist identify "pseudo-problems" that arise from a sort of sedimented way of thinking inherited from the tradition, and second, both distrust the theoretical attitude as a kind of "view from nowhere" that can be used for apprehending truth.[14]

In conclusion, one can see that the "pragmatist" approach to Heidegger encompasses a fairly wide variety of interpretations, and though they may all be loosely grouped together as concerned with a critique of representationalism, the way this critique is elaborated varies quite a bit. Dreyfus is mainly interested to engage positions in philosophy of mind, Okrent in epistemology, Rorty in philosophy of language and metaphysics. All share an interest in illustrating the relevance of Heidegger's thought to a wider philosophical audience, and in this regard these philosophers have done much to help close the perceived gap between continental and analytic philosophy.

NOTES AND REFERENCES

[1] Hubert L. Dreyfus, *Being-in-the-World: A Commentary on Heidegger's "Being and Time," Division I* (Cambridge, MA: MIT Press, 1991).

[2] This view is also put forward by Robert Brandom in his influential essay, "Heidegger's Categories in *Being and Time*," *The Monist*, 66 (1983), 387–409.

[3] Dreyfus, *Being-in-the-World*, 184. In various places, Heidegger seems to suggest that the opposition between the theoretical and the practical might not be a straightforward as Dreyfus suggests. See GA 2, 357–8/BT, 340–1.

4 See John McDowell, *Mind and World* (Cambridge: Harvard University Press, 1996). For Dreyfus's critique of McDowell, see Hubert L. Dreyfus, "Overcoming the Myth of the Mental: How Philosophers Can Profit from the Phenomenology of Everyday Expertise," *Proceedings and Addresses of the American Philosophical Association*, 79.2 (November 2005), 47–65; Hubert L. Dreyfus, "Overcoming the Myth of the Mental," *Topoi*, 25.1–2 (2006), 43–9. For the debate that ensues between McDowell and Dreyfus, see "Hubert L. Dreyfus, "The Return of the Myth of the Mental," *Inquiry*, 50.4 (August 2007), 352–65, and John McDowell, "What Myth?" *Inquiry*, 50.4 (August 2007), 338–51.

5 That Dreyfus is critical of this view is evident throughout his commentary on Heidegger, especially as he formulates the opposition between Husserl and Heidegger. It also surfaces repeatedly in his debates with Searle.

6 Mark Okrent, *Heidegger's Pragmatism: Understanding, Being, and the Critique of Metaphysics* (Ithaca: Cornell University Press, 1988).

7 Ibid., 5.

8 Ibid., 127.

9 Ibid., 128.

10 Continuing in the same vein, Okrent holds that Heidegger is also a kind of metaphysical pragmatist because he turns to a pragmatic account to address metaphysical questions, and Okrent says that "any position asserting that all *metaphysical* questions can legitimately be answered only pragmatically is pragmatic" (ibid., 10).

11 Richard Rorty, *Contingency, Irony, Solidarity* (New York: Cambridge University Press, 1989).

12 Rorty, *Contingency, Irony, Solidarity*, 9f.

13 Richard Rorty, *Essays on Heidegger and Others: Philosophical Papers Volume 2* (New York: Cambridge University Press, 1991), 4–5.

14 Rorty, *Essays on Heidegger and Others*, 10–11.

54

HEIDEGGER AND ENVIRONMENTAL PHILOSOPHY

Trish Glazebrook

Heidegger never had an environmental philosophy as such. Environmental philosophy was only just emerging when he passed away in 1976.[1] Nonetheless, he had a robust philosophy of nature. Hwa Yol and Petee Jung made the first contribution to Heideggerian ecophenomenology in 1975 with "To Save the Earth" that they alternatively called "To Dwell Rightly on Earth," and described as "a phenomenological reflection on the ecologic conscience . . . following Heidegger's path."[2] They argue that what Heidegger calls care (*Sorge*), when misconstrued individualistically, becomes "*careless* thought in man's domination or will to power over nature and the earth" (Jung and Jung, "To Save the Earth," 111). As an alternative, they explore Heidegger's later work on poetic dwelling and letting beings be. This interpretation of him was radically novel for its time and its central theme remains throughout Heideggerian ecophenomenology: the intellectual history of the West began with the Greek interpretation of nature and culminates in the essence of technology. Equally novel, Seidel (1979) mined Heidegger for resources for ecologists, a direction explored ten years later by Padrutt at the conference noted below, and again ten years later by Holland.[3]

It took some time, however, for environmentalism to gain ground in Heideggerian scholarship. The 1980s saw a disparate collection of almost entirely unrelated papers. In 1982, Cave used Heidegger's notion of care (*Sorge*) to argue against utilitarian arithmetic and for a "higher qualitative good" that justifies animals' right to life.[4] Zimmerman was the most influential of Heidegger's environmentalist interpreters. He argued in 1983 that Heidegger's thinking supports radical environmentalism.[5] In 1984, Foltz used Heidegger's historical analysis of Western metaphysics to locate the conceptual roots of contemporary environmental crisis in "the very texture of Western thinking."[6] In 1985, Westra, quoting Zimmerman (1983), used care in support of intergenerational environmental justice by arguing that leaving beings free to be what they are does not exploit them instrumentally for their value in the future.[7] In 1986, Zimmerman argued further that Heidegger's thinking has much in common with deep ecology.[8] Deep ecologists Devall and Sessions were influenced by Zimmerman's reading of Heidegger to support their arguments that the intellectual history of the West is anthropocentric, that Heideggerian "letting beings be" provides an

Eastern alternative, and that authentic dwelling is possible on its basis.[9]

The decade culminated in 1989 with a conference at Truman State University, "Heidegger and the Earth," that resulted in a collection of essays on earth, world, and dwelling interpreting and extending Heidegger's thinking.[10] These echoed the first papers from the 1970s by explicating Heidegger's critique of the logic of ecodestruction in the intellectual history of the West, and possibilities for a more harmonious relation to nature. Extending Heidegger beyond philosophy, Pradutt connected Heidegger's work with ecology, and Skocz used him to assess the conceptual foundations of GIS (geographical information systems), an analysis he later applied to reconcile wild animals' lived space and the techno-human space of environmental management. There has never been another conference dedicated entirely to Heidegger and environment, though in 1997, Bruce Foltz and Robert Frodeman, both Heideggerians, founded the International Association for Environmental Philosophy that has hosted many Heideggerian ecophenomenologists.

In 1993, Zimmerman recanted, claiming that Heidegger's involvement with National Socialism tends him toward ecofascism, of which deep ecologists had already been accused.[11] In 1995, Zimmerman had his final word on Heidegger's saving power versus threat by arguing that Heideggerian transcendence supports the will to domination as much as it does benevolence.[12] The question of transcendence figures prominently in Heideggerian approaches to animal issues, but also concerning deeper questions surrounding Heidegger's conception of human being as critics assess whether transcendence, language, and freedom commit Heidegger to a radical distinction between humans and other animals. Since the beginning of animal rights debates, philosophers have argued there is no basis to distinguish humans from other animals that might justify not giving animals the same ethical consideration as people. Heidegger is in a unique position with respect to this debate, because he takes transcendence, whether articulated in terms of being-in-the-world, ek-sistence, or the ek-stases of temporality, as definitive of Dasein yet does not insist that Dasein is necessarily human, and he is strongly critical of the commitment to transcendental subjectivity that characterizes post-Cartesian philosophy. In the lectures on Leibniz and logic, he explicitly states that he has deliberately chosen Dasein and not "'man' . . . for that being which is the theme of the analysis" (GA 26, 172/MFL, 136), and that Dasein is not "the egocentric individual" (GA 26, 173/MFL, 137). Thus his discussion in the *Fundamental Concepts of Metaphysics* brings him directly to the question of animal cognition as he inquires into the metaphysical foundations of thinking. His response is to argue that animals are "poor in world" while humans are "world-forming" (GA 29/30, 263/FCM, 177). As recently as 2012, Hatab notes that the issue of transcendence that Heidegger has engaged since the 1920s remains an open problem in evolutionary biology.[13] Scientists simply cannot explain consciousness, that is, how brain events carry meaning—they dismiss this question as "the hard problem."[14] So for Heidegger, animals are (somewhat vaguely) more worlded than rocks, but less so than Dasein.

Glendinning (1996) argues that Heidegger is anthropocentric in that his focus on language privileges humans.[15] Being anthropocentric (human-centered) is a common criticism in environmental philosophy that accompanies the charge of "speciesism,"[16] that is, the unjustified privileging of the human over other species, analogous to racism, sexism, and other "-isms" of domination. Anthropocentrism reduces nature to its instrumental value for meeting human needs, while biocentrics (who are life-centered) and ecocentrics recognize the intrinsic value of all living beings and take human beings as members rather than overlords of the biotic community. These terms come from deep ecologists, who defend threatened life-forms, species, and/or ecosystems, but have been accused of ecofascism, that is, militant disregard for human welfare, because their biocentrism promotes an egalitarianism in which, for example, the malaria-carrying Anopheles mosquito has as much right to life as anything else.

In Derrida's 1997 lectures, Heidegger's "question of the animal" (Derrida's phrase) is permeated by the issue of language and took a metaphysical turn that Calarco (2008) criticizes as anthropocentric.[17] Since Derrida is interested in "the animal that therefore [he] is," his account could not possibly be non-anthropocentric insofar as it is intentionally Derrida-centric. Yet Derrida is not blind to the limitations of the metaphysics of modernity, and regularly follows Heidegger back to the Greeks. Indeed, Elden (2006) had already argued that Heidegger's *zoon logon ekhon* is not the *animal rationale* of metaphysics.[18] Dombrowski before him in 1994 had also argued for an anti-anthropocentric reading of Heidegger,[19] and McNeill (1999) used Heidegger's historical critique of modernity to demonstrate that he "should not be regarded as another essentialist or humanist" concerning animals.[20] So is Heidegger anthropocentric or biocentric?

Thiele (1995) offers a Heideggerian critique of both biocentrism and sociocentrism, a more nuanced form of anthropocentrism

in terms of societies or social groups rather than the species.[21] Others defend anthropocentrism. Schalow (2002) argues that the capacity for language obliges humans to speak on animals' behalf,[22] but this looks like an instance of the naturalist fallacy in which "is" is taken to imply "ought," or in this case "can" implies "should." More interestingly, Van Buren's (1995) critical environmental hermeneutics argues that Heidegger's account of communicative discourse makes room "for radical heterogeneity and localism in environmental narratives . . . and espouses coexistence, communication, compromise, cooperation, and consensus."[23] In this reading, Heidegger's account of language accordingly precludes ecofascism and instead grounds democratic exchange across disagreements and diverse needs and interests.

Given that mainstream environmental philosophy stalled over the anthropocentric/ecocentric debate, Heidegger's real contribution to ecophenomenology may be not what he brings to specific issues, but how he makes possible new approaches. For example, Swanton (2010) reads Heidegger on dwelling and truth to develop an environmental virtue ethics that avoids both anthropocentric speciesism and biocentric egalitarianism.[24] She claims thereby to escape metaphysical dilemmas in the analytic philosophical tradition of ethics. Ecophenomenology may thus make possible broader Heideggerian contribution to ethics heretofore impeded by his Nazi involvement, and his preference for metaphysics. Such ethics are articulated in "dwelling," Heidegger's alternative to culmination of the intellectual history of the West in the essence of technology.

Manoussakis says Heidegger "had one single thought, Being, as it first appeared in the Greek beginning of philosophy,"[25] that is, as *physis*, nature. Reading Aristotle,

Heidegger confirms that "the word 'nature' . . . contains an interpretation of beings as a whole" (GA 9, 240/PA, 184), and accordingly that "meta-physics is 'physics,' i.e., knowledge of *physis*" (GA 9, 241/PA, 185). He had been coming up against the relation between earth and world, the physical and the metaphysical, for some time, for example, in the 1929/30 lectures on metaphysics (GA 29/30) and the 1935/36 lectures on art. In 1939, reading *Physics* B, 1, he locates the crucial event determining the history of metaphysics in Aristotle's "double concept of *physis*" (GA 9, 273/PA, 209): *physis*, nature, is a way that beings come to be (192b8); but *ta physika*, natural entities, are substances, that is, formed matter. The former is the "last echo of the original (and thus supreme) thoughtful *projection* of the essence of *physis*" of the pre-Socratics (GA 9, 242/PA, 186); the latter is the first interpretation of nature by analogy with production. Definitive of production, *technê*, for Aristotle is the artist's conception of the work prior to its production (640a32; 1140a13). In production, the artist imposes that form onto the material. Heidegger criticized that account in 1935/36 because art is "a bringing forth of beings" (GA 5, 48/BW, 184) that is only possible "in the midst of the being that surges upward, growing of its own accord, *physis*" (ibid.). That is, production is only possible because natural materials are already available of their own accord for appropriation into art. By the mid-1930s, Heidegger already holds that the history of metaphysics following Aristotle interprets art reductively as form imposed on matter. Rather, he argues, art is truth—*alêtheia*, a world-opening event, unconcealment of beings—that can only arise on the ground of earth (GA 5, 31/BW, 168). The creative act is *poiêsis*, and Heidegger will say almost 30 years later, "*physis* is indeed *poiêsis* in the highest sense" (VA, 15/QCT, 10). For as Aristotle knew, *physis* has the "bringing-forth . . . in itself" (ibid.)—nature appears with no artist.

Heidegger is not thereby claiming, however, that nature is like art; rather, art is like nature. Production is a derivative version of the generative power of *physis*. Thus he argues in 1939 that "attempt to clarify the essence of *physis* by way of an analogy with *technê* fails . . . *from every conceivable point of view*" (GA 9, 292/PA, 223). Historically, the medieval account understands natural entities as divine artifacts—an idea in the mind of God that shapes matter—but modern science makes the divine redundant. Glazebrook (2000) explicates how in Heidegger's account, once nature has neither Aristotelian teleology nor divine, Judeo-Christian purpose, nothing stops "the organized global conquest of the earth" (GA 6.2, 358/NIV, 248) by the essence of technology, a mechanistic, materialist way of revealing (VA, 16/QCT, 12) that "sets upon . . . unlocks and exposes" (VA, 18–9/QCT, 15) nature so it can be stockpiled into "standing-reserve" (VA, 20/QCT, 17).[26] Plumwood notes likewise that "a mechanistically conceived nature lies open to, indeed invites the imposition of human purposes and treatment as an instrument for the achievement of human satisfactions."[27] But nature is not mere matter passively standing by for appropriation into human projects. Heidegger names the interpretation of being that turns self-revealing *physis* into the standing-reserve of nature: *Ge-stell*" (VA, 23/QCT, 19); ecofeminists call it the "logic of domination."[28]

Heidegger argues that *Ge-stell*, "drives out every other possibility of revealing" (VA, 31/QCT, 27). Ecofeminists argue likewise that logics of domination privilege the environmentally destructive knowledge practices of modern science over traditional ecological knowledge-systems.[29] In the *Beiträge*, Heidegger argues that "insofar as modern science claims to be one or even *the* decisive knowing" (GA 65, 141/CP1, 98), it determines the abandonment of being, experienced in anxiety that "has never been greater than today" (GA 65, 139/CP1, 97; see GA 9, 337–41/BW, 241–4). The idea of anxiety goes back to *Being and Time* where it is explained as *Unheimlichkeit*, a "not-being-at-home" (SZ, 188/BTMR, 233). But only reading Aristotle's *Physics* on being as *physis* leads Heidegger to the insight that the abandonment of being is not the existential human condition as in *Being and Time*, but the not-being-at-home in nature assessed in the *Beiträge*. Warren likewise describes experience of environmental crisis as "longing for home . . . a troubling, nagging, uncomfortable feeling."[30] Both Warren and Heidegger envision an alternative conception of nature as a home in which human beings dwell.

In the same way that the concept of nature is a historically degraded conception of *physis* derivative from Aristotle's conception of *technê*, science—"the theory of the real" (VA, 42/QCT, 157 et passim)—is for Heidegger a degraded experience of *theoria*. In contrast to the objective indifference of scientific theory, humans can encounter natural phenomena with a sense of wonder. For example, Babich, whose first degree is in biology, describes waterbears as "fascinating, even fun, but little understood to this day . . . alien-seeming, fascinating, and intriguingly intractable."[31] Heidegger argues that etymologically, "theorizing" means "to look attentively on the outward appearance wherein what presences becomes visible and, through such sight—seeing—to linger with it" (VA, 48/QCT, 163). Heidegger identifies such attentive, thoughtful practice with what "the

Greeks" called "*bios theôrêtikos*," the contemplative life. But it has none of the aloofness and restraint of objectivity; rather, it is "the highest doing" (VA, 48/QCT, 164). The pre-Socratics did not experience *physis* as a collection of objects, but as self-revealing provocation to the question, "Why are there beings at all, and not rather nothing?" that ends "What is Metaphysics?" and begins *Introduction to Metaphysics*.

Heidegger identifies "the power of the earth" as a home (GA 39, 88). When the Chipko movement began in India in 1973, the women proclaimed, "The forest is our home!"[32] "Environment" has indeed been famously redefined in the environmental justice movement as "where we live, work and play."[33] Heidegger calls earth "the building bearer, nourishing with its fruits, tending water and rock, plant and animal" (VA, 170/PLT, 178), "the serving bearer, blossoming and fruiting, spreading out in rock and water, rising up into plant and animal" (VA, 143/BW, 351). Glazebrook (2004) argues from experience backpacking in the Canadian Rockies that "Nature gives me all I need to survive, even thrive, but is at the same time an indifferent death trap."[34] Crucial to survival is paying "close attention" (Glazebrook 2004, 89). Heidegger's depiction of earth as nurturer is not mere idealization, but a warning that nature is where humans dwell, on which they depend, and should not be thoughtlessly destroyed. He aims, like ecofeminists, "to honor, cherish, and respect the value of earth as our home."[35]

For Heidegger, humans "dwell in that they save the earth . . . To save properly means to set something free into its own essence . . . Saving the earth does not master the earth and does not subjugate it" (VA, 150/BW, 352). McNeill (1999) explains that "Dwelling means . . . saving the earth and heavens in letting them be."[36] Letting beings be was first hinted at in *Being and Time*'s maxim of phenomenology: "To the things themselves!" In 1930, Heidegger argues that freedom belongs to truth not as a property of human subjects, but "as letting beings be" (GA 9, 188/BW, 125). In 1942, the hospitable host lets the guest "be the one he is" (GA 53, 175–6). In 1951, "to free actually means to spare" (VA, 143/BW, 351), and sparing is "the fundamental character of dwelling" (ibid.). Reading Hölderlin a few months later, ". . . poetically man dwells . . ." when the environment is managed through a "taking of measure" (VA, 196/PLT, 227) that "lets the earth be as earth" (VA, 195/PLT, 227), in contrast to "our unpoetic dwelling [that] derives from a curious excess of frantic measuring and calculating" (VA, 197/PLT, 228). In 1955, *Gelassenheit*, retains the notion of letting as attentive and meditative releasement that frees beings from the "calculative thinking"[37] that reduces them to stockpilable resources. Haar (1993) and Bate (2000) hear song in such ecopoetic listening.[38]

Llewelyn (1991) reads "letting beings be" through the middle voice—a technical term in verb conjugation especially challenging to Anglophones knowing only active and passive voice—to disrupt domination of subject over object, and ground ecological conscience.[39] Heidegger's talk of care in *Being and Time*, with which Heideggerian environmental philosophy began, focuses on how care unifies consciousness (SZ, 193/BTMR, 238). He is still caught in the metaphysics of subjectivity, despite his protests against it. Conscience is the call of care (SZ, 277/BTMR, 322), but that call comes from not-being-at-home (*Unheimlichkeit*) (SZ, 281/BTMR, 325). In dwelling, the thinker experiences not anxiety and homelessness, but wonder. Transcendental subjectivities do

not dwell; dwelling needs community. The situatedness Heidegger identifies as historical is also cultural (once Eurocentric blinders are removed). Every culture is an event of being. Heidegger's "one single thought" is of dwelling together in nature through "cultivating and caring" (VA, 185/PLT, 217). His ecophenomenology is not the wilderness ethics of the deep ecologist, but an agrarian ethics of care.[40]

NOTES AND REFERENCES

[1] Three foundational texts appeared in 1973: R. Sylvan, "Is there a Need for a New, an Environmental, Ethic?" *Proceedings of the XV World Congress of Philosophy*, 1, 205–10; P. Singer, "Animal Liberation," *New York Review of Books*, 20 (5); and A. Naess, "The Shallow and the Deep, Long-range Ecology Movement," *Inquiry*, 16, 95–100. F. d'Eaubonne, *Le féminisme ou la mort* (Paris: Pierre Horay, 1974), the founding text of ecofeminism, appeared the following year.

[2] H. W. Jung and P. Jung, "To Save the Earth," *Philosophy Today*, 19.2 (1975), 108–17, 108.

[3] G. J. Seidel, "Heidegger: Philosopher for Ecologists," *Man and World*, 4 (1979), 93–9; N. J. Holland, "Rethinking Ecology in the Western Philosophical Tradition: Heidegger and/on Aristotle," *Continental Philosophy Review*, 32.4 (1999), 409–20.

[4] G. S. Cave, "Animals, Heidegger, and the Right to Life," *Environmental Ethics*, 4.3 (1982), 249–54.

[5] M. E. Zimmerman, "Toward a Heideggerian *Ethos* for Radical Environmentalism," *Environmental Ethics*, 5.2 (1983), 99–131.

[6] B. V. Foltz, "On Heidegger and the Interpretation of Environmental Crisis," *Environmental Ethics*, 6.4 (1984), 326–42; 338.

[7] L. Westra, "Let it Be: Heidegger and Future Generations," *Environmental Ethics*, 7.4 (1985), 341–50.

[8] M. E. Zimmerman, "Implications of Heidegger's Thought for Deep Ecology," *The Modern Schoolman*, 64 (1986), 19–43.

9 B. Devall and G. Sessions, *Deep Ecology: Living as if Nature Mattered* (Layton, UT: Peregrine Smith Press, 1985); see S. P. James, "'Thing-centered' Holism in Buddhism, Heidegger, and Deep Ecology," *Environmental Ethics*, 22.4 (2000), 359–75.

10 The essays are collected in L. McWhorter, *Heidegger and the Earth: Essays in Environmental Philosophy* (Kirksville, MO: Truman State University Press, 1992); expanded and reprinted, edited by L. McWhorter and G. Stenstad, in 2009 by University of Toronto Press.

11 M. E. Zimmerman, "Rethinking the Heidegger—Deep Ecology Relationship," *Environmental Ethics*, 15.3 (1993), 195–224. See arguments that ecofeminist readings of Heidegger preclude fascism in T. Glazebrook, "Heidegger and Ecofeminism," in eds Nancy Holland and Patricia Huntington, *Re-Reading the Canon: Feminist Interpretations of Heidegger* (University Park, PA: The Pennsylvania State University Press, 2001), 221–51.

12 M. E. Zimmerman, "Ontical Craving versus Ontological Desire," in ed. B. Babich, *From Phenomenology to Thought: Errancy and Desire* (Dordrecht: Kluwer, 1995), 501–23.

13 L. J. Hatab, "From Animal to Dasein: Heidegger and Evolutionary Biology," in ed. T. Glazebrook, *Heidegger on Science* (Albany, NY: SUNY Press, 2012), 93–111.

14 The term was introduced by D. Chalmers, "Facing up to the Problem of Consciousness," *Journal of Consciousness Studies*, 2.3 (1995), 200–19.

15 S. Glendinning, "Heidegger and the Question of Animality," *International Journal of Philosophical Studies*, 4.1 (1996), 75–82.

16 Peter Singer's term from "All Animals are Equal," *Philosophic Exchange*, 1.5 (1974), 243–57.

17 J. Derrida, *The Animal that Therefore I am*, ed. Marie-Louise Mallet (New York: Fordham University Press, 2008); M. Calarco, *Zoographies: The Question of the Animal from Heidegger to Derrida* (New York: Columbia University Press, 2008).

18 S. Elden, "Heidegger's Animals," *Continental Philosophy Review*, 39.3 (2006), 273–91.

19 D. A. Dombrowski, "Heidegger's Anti-anthropocentrism," *Between the Species*, 10.1 (1994), 26–38.

20 W. McNeill, "Life Beyond the Organism: Animal Being in Heidegger's Freiburg Lectures, 1929–30," in ed. H. P. Stevens, *Animal Others: On ethics, Ontology, and Animal Life* (Albany: SUNY Press, 1999), 197–248, 198, following his *Heidegger: Visions of Animals, Others and the Divine* (Coventry, UK: University of Warwick Press, 1993).

21 P. T. Thiele, "Nature and Freedom: A Heideggerian Critique of Biocentric and Sociocentric Environmentalism," *Environmental Ethics*, 17.2 (1995), 171–90.

22 F. Schalow, "Who Speaks for the Animals? Heidegger and the Question of Animal Welfare?" *Environmental Ethics*, 22.3 (2002), 259–72.

23 J. Van Buren, "Critical Environmental Hermeneutics," *Environmental Ethics*, 17.3 (1995), 259–75, 275.

24 C. Swanton, "Heideggerian Environmental Virtue Ethics," *Journal of Agricultural and Environmental Ethics* 23.102 (2010), 145–66. See S. P. James, *Heidegger and Environmental Ethics*. Doctoral thesis, Durham University, 2001 and "Heidegger and the Role of the Body in Environmental Virtue," *The Trumpeter*, 181 (2002), 1–9.

25 J. P. Manoussakis, "The Sojourn in the Light," in eds D. A. Hyland and J. P. Manoussakis, *Heidegger and the Greeks* (Bloomington: Indiana University Press, 2006), 1–8, 2.

26 From *physis* to nature, *technê* to technology: T. Glazebrook, "Heidegger on Aristotle, Galileo and Newton," *The Southern Journal of Philosophy*, 38.1 (2000), 95–118.

27 Val Plumwood, *Feminism and the Mastery of Nature* (New York: Routledge, 1993), 110–11.

28 K. Warren, "The Power and Promise of Ecological Feminism," *Environmental Ethics*, 12.2 (1990), 125–46, 128; see V. Plumwood, *Feminism and the Mastery of Nature* (London: Routledge, 1993).

29 V. Shiva, "Reductionist Science as Epistemological Violence," in ed. Ashis Nandy, *Science, Hegemony and Violence: A Requiem for Modernity* (New Delhi: Oxford University Press, 1988), 232–56; *Staying Alive: Women, Ecology, and Development* (London: Zed Books, 1988), 26; M. Mies, and V. Shiva (eds), *Ecofeminism* (Atlantic Highlands, NJ: Zed Books, 1993) 23; See D. Curtin, "Recognizing

Women's Environmental Expertise," in
D. Curtin, *Chinnagrounder's Challenge:
The Question of Ecological Citizenship*
(Bloomington: Indiana University Press, 1999).

30 K. J. Warren, "Ecofeminism and the Longing
for Home," in ed. L. S. Rouner, *The Longing
for Home* (Notre Dame, IN: University of
Notre Dame Press, 1996), 227.

31 B. Babich, "Towards a Critical Philosophy of
Science: Continental Beginnings and Bugbears,
Whigs, and Waterbears," *International Studies
in the Philosophy of Science*, 24.4 (2010),
343–91, 375.

32 Chipko movement. Uttarakhand Encyclopedia.
Available online at www.apnauttarakhand.
com/chipko-movement/ (Accessed October 12,
2012).

33 See P. Novotny, *Where we Live, Work and
Play: The Environmental Justice Movement
and the Struggle for a New Environmentalism*
(Santa Barbara, CA: Praeger, 2000).

34 T. Glazebrook, *Toward an Ecofeminist
Phenomenology of Nature. Every grain of
sand: Canadian perspectives on ecology and
environment* (Waterloo, ON: Wilfrid Laurier
University Press, 2004), 87–100, 88.

35 Warren, "Ecofeminism and the Longing for
Home," 226.

36 W. McNeill, *Heimat: Heidegger on the
Threshold. Heidegger toward the Turn: Essays
on the Work of the 1930s*, ed. James Risser
(Albany: SUNY Press, 1999), 319–49, 326.

37 M. Heidegger, *Gelassenheit* (Pfullingen: Verlag
Günther Neske, 1992), 12 et passim.

38 M. Haar, *The Song of the Earth: Heidegger
and the Grounds of the History of Being*
trans. Reginald Lilly (Bloomington: Indiana
University Press, 1993); J. Bate, *The Song of
the Earth* (London: Picador, 2000).

39 J. Llewelyn, *The Middle Voice of Ecological
Conscience* (New York: St. Martin's Press,
1991).

40 See P. B. Thompson, *The Agrarian Vision:
Sustainability and Environmental Ethics*
(Lexington: University Press of Kentucky,
2010) on agrarian ethics. See M. Kheel, "The
Liberation of Nature: A Circular Affair,"
Environmental Ethics 6.4 (1985), 339–45;
Warren, "The Power and Promise of Ecological
Feminism";; and, D. Curtin, "Toward an
Ecological Ethic of Care," in ed. Karen Warren,
Ecological Feminist Philosophies (Bloomington:
Indiana University Press, 1996), 66–81 on
ecofeminist ethics of care. See T. Glazebrook,
"Heidegger and International Development,"
in eds Georgakis Tziovanis and Paul Ennis,
Heidegger in the Twenty-First Century (New
York: Springer, 2012); and, V. R. Rao, "Women
Farmers of India's Deccan Plateau: Ecofeminists
Challenge World Elites," in eds David Schmidtz
and Elizabeth Willott, *Environmental Ethics:
What Really Matters, What Really Works* (New
York: Oxford University Press, 2002), 255–62
on ecofeminist agrarian ethics.

55

HEIDEGGER AND GENDER: AN UNCANNY RETRIEVAL OF HEGEL'S ANTIGONE

Tina Chanter

terror is in all cases whatsoever, either more openly or latently, the ruling principle of the sublime. Several languages bear a strong testimony to the affinity of these ideas. They frequently use the same word to signify indifferently the modes of astonishment or admiration and those of terror. . . . [Greek: deinos] is terrible or respectable. Edmund Burke

In order to tackle the question of Martin Heidegger and gender I approach his philosophy through the general problematic of art, with specific reference to Sophocles' *Antigone*. I read Heidegger against the backdrop of G. W. F. Hegel, arguing that Heidegger's understanding of the uncanny sublimates Hegel's rigorously sexualized, representationalist account of Antigone's and Creon's mutually exclusive ethical stances. My approach to Heidegger's reading of *Antigone* is also informed by an intersectional, feminist analysis.

I suggest that feminist responses to Hegel's reading of *Antigone* stand in need of complication, because they remain attached to an understanding of sexual difference that is still too metaphysical. In developing this suggestion, I construe Heidegger's return to *Antigone* as, in its turn, a useful model for feminist intersectional analysis, in the sense that gender needs to be construed in a relationship of fluidity with other political questions, including citizenship and slavery, a fluidity that—much like the question of Being according to Heidegger—has been obfuscated by the rigid oppositions of metaphysical categories. This is not to suggest that Heidegger's apparent disregard for gender is unproblematic. At the same time, I utilize feminist intersectional analyses to complicate Heidegger's not entirely successful effort to overcome Hegel, an effort that nonetheless, paradoxically, returns us to Greek poetry in such a way as to prove Heidegger's interpretation of *Antigone* ultimately more fruitful for contemporary feminist thought than Hegel's—even if Heidegger might not (and, I would say, does not) intend such fruitfulness.

Intersectional analyses problematize the relative isolation in terms of which feminist theory initially broached the concept of gender, insisting that, in order for feminists not to replicate the white, middle class, heteronormative bias of masculinist, patriarchal thinking, specific attention has to be paid to race, class, sexuality, and other sexually salient differences, conceived as intersecting with gender. When Luce Irigaray and Judith Butler, for example, in their very different ways, effect what they intend to be an over-turning or interrogation of the terms in which Hegel approaches *Antigone*, they nonetheless preserve sexual difference as their central cat-egory of analysis. By contrast, intersectional theory insists on construing gender as part of a complex field, striated with a network of social forces. By taking up such analyses and applying them to the ancient Greece out of which *Antigone* emerges, and with which the play engages, I argue that the themes of fam-ily, kinship, and sexual difference need to be thought in relation to—rather than treated in abstraction from—themes of citizen-ship, slavery, and foreigners/outsiders, and that while the play is not typically analyzed in these terms, precisely such an interroga-tion of these interlocking themes permeates Sophocles' *Antigone*.

Taking my cue from an intersectional feminist analysis, I suggest that sexual dif-ference, which remains the dominant vector in both Hegel's reading and in feminist/queer efforts to overturn the naturalized basis in terms of which Hegel interprets ethical life (*Sittlichkeit*), needs to be complicated. Recent, pivotal feminist reclamations of Hegel's figu-ration of Antigone remain, then, I argue, overdetermined by Hegel's oppositional reading of the play, and as such, even as they attempt to overturn his reading they adhere to its terms, remaining at the same time com-mitted to the hierarchical relationship Hegel establishes between art and philosophy in some of its aspects, a hierarchy from which Heidegger's understanding of metaphysics seeks to depart, but in relation to which it also remains captive to some extent.[1]

For Hegel, the tragic form of art presents an early, culturally embedded practice that embodies values that he takes the modern era to have moved beyond, while the ancient Greece out of which the tragic form arose also provides crucial clues for problematiz-ing the legalistic/Kantian direction in which ethics was developed within a metaphysical framework that both Hegel and Heidegger, in different ways, put into question. Hegel's progressive, developmental account of phi-losophy as having surpassed, or sublated the Spirit that expresses itself in a less mediated form in Greek tragedy assumes a relationship between art and philosophy that Heidegger wants to challenge, but to which he remains inadvertently committed, such that he allows the figure of Antigone to continue to perform a preparatory role to philosophy's allegedly more sophisticated conception of the truth of art.[2] Hegel's ambivalent attitude toward the Greeks is taken up as a model for Heidegger's retrieval of the question of Being.

For Hegel, the Greeks serve to provide a lost ideal in some respects, while in other ways they are required to stand for a lack of development. The return to the Greeks effected by both Hegel and Heidegger is a maneuver that is burdened with the meta-physical elaborations that have taken place since the Greeks, and at the same time enriched by those very elaborations, even as metaphysics has led philosophy into cer-tain impasses, which, as they see it, it is up to Hegel and Heidegger themselves to unset-tle, elucidate, or overcome. Thus when Hegel suggests that art for us is not what it was for the Greeks, his judgment harbors an admi-ration for the way in which tragic perform-ances at the theatre of Dionysos constituted part of the cultural fabric of the Athenian polis.[3] Tragedy, for Hegel, depicts heroes who understand and take up their ethical duty not as fully autonomous, individualized moral actors, who choose among an array of moral choices that they are free to embody or discard; rather their stance is assigned to them according to socially prescribed roles, values that proceed from duties embedded and enshrined in culture. Antigone's role as a woman assigns her to the family, to the care of dead, and to the old order of the gods, while Creon's and Polynices's roles as men assign them to the state, the preservation of which Creon understands Polynices to have threatened, and to the new order of the gods.

While the tension between Antigone's and Creon's ethical stances takes center stage for Hegel, the tensions created by his own differential and naturalized assignation of gender remain unexplored by him; sexual difference naturally apportions the female sex to the sphere of the familial, and the male sex to the sphere of the political. The ethics embodied by women are necessary to the state, in providing care for the family (care that not only extends to care of the dead, but in Hegel's reading is epitomized by such care), yet women are themselves not represented in any political capacity by the state. It is left to feminist interpretations to pursue the tensions and difficulties this view entails.

Hegel's admiration of the heroes of Greek tragedy, and of Antigone in particular, is tempered by his progressive, developmental view of history, a history in which the individualization of moral agents has introduced a more sophisticated moral compass into the arena of ethics. If the ethical life (*Sittlichkeit*) for which Hegel makes Antigone and Creon representative in ways that are inevitably partial, since he assigns them to separate, and mutually opposing spheres, according to a naturalized understanding of sexual difference, stands in need of a more variegated

conception of morality, one in which conscience, freedom, reflection, individuation, and choice can play significant roles, it must also be observed that the subject of morality (*Moralität*) into which the custom-based ethics on which Hegel takes *Antigone* to be based devolves, is a morality that is identified with a public sphere that is thoroughly permeated with masculinist assumptions.[4] Women do not count as legal persons (neither for the Greeks nor for Hegel). Women's personhood is subsumed by their husbands (and before that, by their fathers), who, as heads of households, guide families, into which the personhood of women disappears. Women do not have any legal personhood in their own right, and have little, if any, significance outside their familial roles; Hegel considers it women's duty to marry.[5] The peculiar, both quasi-transcendental and abject status that the family plays in Hegel's thought, as both facilitating, yet itself resistant to, dialectical synthesis is explored by Derrida, as is the peculiar status Hegel accords to the sister, to Antigone, whose father, at the beginning of *Antigone*, is dead, and who will never marry.[6] In refusing to marry Haemon, Antigone defies Creon, who is not only her king but who, on Oedipus's death, becomes her familial guardian (*kurios*). Antigone, however, acts as if she is without a guardian; she is *akyron*.

The term *genos*, like the term *Geschlecht* (as Derrida points out) includes among its significations not only family/generation but also race, and as such provides textual evidence for Sophocles' consideration in *Antigone* of a complex and interconnected constellation of concerns, among them the difference between slaves and freemen, that characterize the signifying field that Sophocles is exploring.[7] Yet this complex network of concerns has been oversimplified in the reception of *Antigone*, not least due to the overdetermining influence of Hegel's opposition of family/state, which circumscribes the range of connotations *genos* has by limiting its reference to a narrow conception of family or kinship.

In addition to the polyvalent connotations of *genos*, which Hegelian and post-Hegelian analyses tends to understand restrictively as family/kinship, once one starts to look, textual and contextual evidence abounds for Sophocles' central, but neglected, concern with citizenship/foreignness/slavery not merely in *Antigone* but in the Oedipus cycle as a whole.[8] I restrict myself here to citing only one further detail, a detail, however, that I take to be decisive. Antigone differentiates Polynices from a slave, maintaining that she would not have violated the law in order to bury Polynices had he been a slave.[9] While much ink has been spilled on the issue of irreplaceability vis-à-vis brother and husband, an astounding silence has surrounded Antigone's distinction of Polynices from a slave, a differentiation that grants her brother humanity, while relegating slaves to the murky region of the less than human, or the not quite human.[10] In differentiating Polynices from a slave, Antigone differentiates her family from those whose kin should not be honored in death. She thus appeals to a distinction that sets her familial, generational line, her *genos*, her race, apart from those who would not have deserved a burial that violates Creon's law, those who are thus marked as less than human, those who are deracinated from their families: slaves, who, in ancient Athens, not coincidentally, are, for the most part "barbarians" (nonGreeks). It turns out, then, that any success Antigone might be said to have in inscribing her brother's humanity, and her own existence as an ethical subject—to the extent that we can speak of success in the

case of Antigone, a mythical figure, defined by her incestuous birth and her decision to take on her fate in the form of suicide—is achieved at the expense of writing nameless others out of the history of Being.

Heidegger emphatically—perhaps a little too emphatically—distances himself from Hegel's reading of *Antigone*, rejecting the religion/state opposition in terms of which Hegel reads the play.[11] Yet, in the refusal with which Heidegger greets these Hegelian terms can be read a resounding silence regarding other decisive terms that Hegel opposes to one another in his understanding of Antigone's conflict with Creon, which proceeds not just in terms of the opposition between religion and state, but also in terms of the oppositional claims of *genos* and state, of femininity and masculinity. Hegel's interpretation of Antigone is rigorously sexualized, but, while Heidegger distances himself from the notion of state, insisting that the term *polis* is not to be equated with state, thereby implicitly contesting one side of this Hegelian dichotomy, Heidegger's only response to the question of *genos* and sexual difference is silence.[12] How is this silence to be read? I suggest that Heidegger's highlighting of the notion of uncanny (*unheimlich, deinon*) in *Antigone* can be read as a sublimation of the question of sexual difference, a sublimation in which can also be read the trace of race.

If, at least at the level of his overt interpretation, Heidegger would appear to reject Hegel's reading of *Antigone* entirely, there is one important respect in which his approach to tragedy remains clearly continuous with Hegel's; like Hegel, Heidegger makes Antigone, rather than Oedipus, the privileged hero of his analysis of the Greek tragic form. By construing Antigone as "sublime," Hegel had challenged Aristotle's attribution of pride of place, when it comes to Greek tragic heroes, to Oedipus—with whom Aristotle's *Poetics* associates the "finest recognition (*anagnorisis*)," which "occurs simultaneously with reversal (*peripeteia*)."[13] Hegel's admiration for Antigone, which tends to conflate the empirical category of Athenian women, for which Antigone serves as a symbol, with the mythical, fictional, Theban character of a play written by a male playwright of aristocratic origins, is beset with a series of tensions. Not the least of these, I would argue, is the tension embodied in Hegel's effort to discipline and contain what he construes as Antigone's ethical purity within a (Christian) religious piety at precisely the time at which feminism is beginning to make its demands felt.[14] Yet insofar as Hegel makes Antigone an ethical heroine (albeit one that he does all he can to purify, containing her within the space of domesticity), Hegel implicitly challenges Aristotle's more disparaging attitude to women, which prohibits women from qualifying as fully rounded ethical subjects, and in consonance with this declines to analyze Antigone's significance as a tragic hero, except through omission, neglect, and by intimating her inappropriateness. The sense in which Hegel recognizes Antigone's ethical capacity (even as he limits it, excluding it from the political), embraces a more complex conception of the role of Greek tragedy than Aristotle's, one that anticipates in some ways Jean-Pierre Vernant's assessment of it. Precisely by construing Antigone as an ethical subject, Hegel departs from Aristotle's exclusion of women from ethics, and in doing so construes Antigone as contesting the socially prescribed roles Athens mandated for women.[15] Hegel thereby also gives the significance of tragedy a more political inflection than Aristotle; *Antigone* is the noblest tragedy for Hegel because it explores what Hegel considers to be the most salient political opposition, that between family and state, while *Oedipus Rex* is privileged by Aristotle because the recognition that its plot reversal affords is the most dramatic and complete: we come to know ourselves, paradoxically, only by confronting our failure to know, our ignorance. Aristotle is responding to Plato's Socratic formulation of knowledge that comes from knowing one does not know, a response that champions the self-reflective capacity of an individual, while Hegel's figuring of tragedy understands it as a more collective, civic endeavor, reflecting the pulse of a polity, its performative enactment embodying the tensions of a people.[16]

Although Heidegger follows Hegel in attributing to Antigone, rather than Oedipus, pride of place in the pantheon of ancient Greek tragic, mythical heroes, he follows Aristotle both in depoliticizing Antigone in the wake of Hegel's challenge to Aristotle, and I would conjecture, in highlighting the quality that defines Antigone.[17] I do not think it is too rash to trace, if not a direct causal link, at least some kind of continuity (though not one without reconfiguration) between an observation that Aristotle makes in his *Poetics*, and Heidegger's reading of *Antigone*. Aristotle suggests that it is inappropriate for women to be courageous or clever (*deinen*).[18] The remark is of a piece with the views on women expressed throughout the Aristotelian corpus, and its influence reverberates in a series of references that come to punctuate, not to say determine, a constellation of interpretations of Antigone, including Heidegger's and Lacan's.[19] It also demonstrates that there is a dimension of Aristotle's *Poetics* that fits in seamlessly with his efforts elsewhere to keep women and slaves in their ethical and political place.

What would it mean, then, for Aristotle, who is surely familiar with the use Sophocles makes of the word *deinos* and its derivatives in *Antigone*, to proclaim that it is inappropriate for women to be *deinen*, and for Heidegger to seize upon precisely this term as the lynchpin of his interpretation?[20] Is Heidegger's championing of Antigone as the most uncanny (*to deinotaton*) a celebration of sexual difference, or a taming of it?[21] Is he condoning Aristotle's implication of Antigone's inappropriateness? Is he challenging Aristotle's judgment that it is inappropriate for tragic poetry to characterize women as courageous or clever? Is he championing Sophocles over Aristotle precisely because Antigone crosses the boundaries, mixes up the categories of men and women, public and private? How does Hegel's interpretation, which had accorded Antigone an ethical privilege that Aristotle had implicitly denied her, play into Heidegger's reading of the play? In short, why is Antigone so important in Heidegger's understanding of the play, and what remains of her import as uncanny once it is (at least overtly) shorn of the connotations of sexual difference with which Hegel fuses Antigone's significance?

If Aristotle is surely aware of the use of the term *deinos* in Sophocles' *Antigone*, Heidegger is just as surely aware of Aristotle's use of the term in the *Poetics*. How then should Heidegger's focus on *deinos* be read in the light of Aristotle's judgment? And how should Heidegger's interpretation of *Antigone* be read in the light of Hegel's rigorously sexualized interpretation of *Antigone*, an interpretation that, while glorifying Antigone for embodying in the purest way the ethics of her sex, at the same time circumscribes her in a gesture that I read as a disciplining mechanism, as an effort to contain Antigone within religious, Christian piety,

an effort to contain women within the private, familial, domestic sphere, to keep them in the home, out of which feminism threatens to break them? How should Heidegger's apparent neutralization of the question of sexual difference be read? And how might the determination Heidegger shows in *Being and Time* to maintain Dasein's neutrality with regard to sexual difference—a neutrality that Derrida has suggested in his consideration of *Geschlecht* (a term connoting not just sexual difference but also racial difference), rather than closing down the question of sexuality, productively opens it up—translate into Heidegger's discussion of *Antigone*?[22]

For Heidegger, Antigone's dying is a "becoming homely" (HHTI, 104) that is unhomely in the proper way, that is, "out of a belonging to being" rather than a being unhomely in the improper way, by being "driven about amid beings without any way out" (118). By taking on, enduring suffering (see 103) Antigone becomes supremely uncanny (see 104), she makes the uncanny fitting, that is, she is at home with "being unhomely" (121). As such, for Heidegger, she embodies the truly human, which is to make herself at home in that in which one is not at home, the not-human in the sense of that which is of "no avail" (101). In championing Antigone's uncanniness, her way of abiding in the uncanny, Heidegger recognizes her extraordinariness, yet is too quick to convert this into an exemplary trait of humanity. For Heidegger to elide the difference between the way in which Antigone is not at home in the polis, and the ways others are not at home, short-circuits the question of sexual difference and ignores Antigone's radical exclusion from the polis, ignores that she is not at home in the way that free men are, since they are citizens. Heidegger eclipses this difference, and with it sexual/racial difference, by making Antigone's uncanniness representative of human's uncanniness in general.

Moreover, if, as on Heidegger's reading, Antigone brings out the unfamiliarity at the heart of what it might mean to be human, the limited inscription she achieves for herself as a finite being is accomplished only through the banishment of others to the impossibility of ever being at home. Not only does Heidegger ignore the sense in which Antigone writes herself into the political, from which the *polis* excludes her, and thereby contests the parameters of what constitutes the political, he also neglects (along with an entire tradition) Antigone's endorsing of the inhuman status of those who, in her effort to inscribe herself as a political subject, she stipulates as unworthy of burial, when she differentiates Polynices from a slave. Perhaps, then, it is in the deracination of slaves, their defamiliarization, their uprootedness from families they can call their own, that we should look for a neglected resonance of the meaning of uncanny, since it is in their forced removal from their families in life, that they are also deprived of any possibility of being honored by family members in their death. And in this failure to be honored, they become displaced souls, not quite recognizably human, not quite at home in a world that nonetheless they help to make a world in which others feel quite at home, a world in which others can comfortably qualify as human, and can even safely explore the intricacies of what it might mean philosophically to be wrenched from being at home, wrenched from the secure position of having been at home, yet able to return home. To the extent that Antigone makes herself at home in the world, reconciles herself to that which is "of no avail," it is only by relegating slaves to an uncanniness still more

uncanny than that which Heidegger and others demand that she inhabit.

If Hegel makes the issue of sexual difference decisive for his understanding of *Antigone*, Heidegger obliquely takes up and, despite himself, transforms the issue into a question that brings him into closer proximity with how I am suggesting the nexus of connotations surrounding *genos* resonates in the text of *Antigone*, and how this signifying nexus might have functioned for the variously constituted, ancient Athenian audience of *Antigone*. While Heidegger himself does not prove to be invested in pursuing as problematic the politics at stake in how the discrimination between slaves and freemen takes place, his interpretation of *Antigone* nonetheless, albeit inadvertently, makes more available for interrogation than does Hegel's the neglected Sophoclean themes of citizenship, slavery, and freedom that intersect with those of sexual difference in *Antigone*. In tragedy, Heidegger tells us, in a reference that cannot help but conjure up *Antigone*, as well as fragment 53 of Heraclitus to which Heidegger explicitly refers,

> the battle of the new gods against the old is being fought. The linguistic work, originating in the speech of the people, does not refer to this battle; it transforms the people's saying so that now every living word fights the battle and puts up for decision what is holy and what unholy, what great and small, what brave and what cowardly, what lofty and what flighty, what master and what slave. (GA 5, 29/PLT, 42)[23]

In Heidegger's reading, there might not be a privileging of sexual difference, of who is male and who is female, but in question rather is who is free and who is not, who is master and who slave.

NOTES AND REFERENCES

1 Brilliant as they are, in their different ways, Butler's and Irigaray's interpretations of Antigone might remain too Hegelian in certain respects, but they have also paved the way for going beyond Hegel in crucial regards. While Butler gestures in the direction of expanding kinship in a more racially inflected direction than Irigaray (and while she certainly engages race productively in other works), she only addresses it minimally in her discussion of Antigone. See Butler, *Antigone's Claim: Kinship between Life and Death* (New York: Columbia University Press, 2000) and Luce Irigaray, *Speculum of the Other Woman*, trans. Gillian C. Gill (Ithaca, NY: Cornell University Press, 1985); *Speculum de l'autre femme* (Paris: Minuit, 1974).

2 Heidegger understands Antigone as poetic, but thinks it falls to him to unpack the philosophical meaning of the poetic that she embodies in Sophocles. Antigone "herself *is* the poem of being unhomely in the proper and supreme sense" and the rendering poetic the "potential of human beings for being homely" is the highest vocation of the poet, which Sophocles realizes in *Antigone*. Yet *deinon*, understood as unhomeliness, which is "only through human beings in general being homely in being" is thus named "poetically," without being "thoughtfully unfolded" (HHTI, 91). This latter task, to unfold the poetic thoughtfully, is the philosopher's, Heidegger's. In this way, although Heidegger might appear to privilege the poetic/art, he reinstalls the authority of philosophy over art, making (the female/feminine) Antigone encapsulate the mysterious enigma that the (masculine/male) philosopher must articulate theoretically.

3 In fact, there is a sense in which tragedy, according to Hegel, did not constitute art at all for the Greeks, if we bear in mind that art was not constituted as occupying an autonomous sphere of its own, as it will come to do so from the point of view of the modern regime of aesthetics.

4 The relation between ethics (*Sittlichkeit*) and morality (*Moralität*) referred to here assumes Hegel's understanding in the *Phenomenology of Spirit* rather than the *Philosophy of Right*,

in which the relation is figured differently. See G. W. F. Hegel, *Phenomenology of Spirit*, trans. A. V. Miller (Oxford: Clarendon Press, 1979); *Phänomenologie des Geistes*, ed. J. Hoffmeister (Hamburg: Felix Meiner, 1952). See also Hegel, *Philosophy of Right*, trans. with notes T. M. Knox (Oxford: Oxford University Press, 1967).

5 Hegel, *Philosophy of Right*.

6 See Jacques Derrida, *Glas*, trans. John P. Leavey and Richard Rand (Lincoln: University of Nebraska Press, 1986). As many have pointed out, the temporality of beginning and ends I invoke here is in fact complicated by the order in which Sophocles wrote the Oedipus cycle.

7 Jacques Derrida, "Geschlecht II: Heidegger's Hand," trans. John P. Leavey, Jr. in ed. John Sallis, *Deconstruction and Philosophy: The Texts of Philosophy* (Chicago: Chicago University Press, 1987).

8 I develop this argument in *Whose Antigone? The Tragic Marginalization of Slavery* (Albany: SUNY, 2011).

9 Elizabeth Wyckoff translates "It was a brother, not a slave [*doulos*] who died" Antigone says to Creon in Sophocles' *Antigone* (1954, line 517). See Elizabeth Wyckoff (trans.), "Antigone," in ed. David Grene, *Sophocles I* (Chicago, IL: University of Chicago Press, 1991). David Grene and Richmond Lattimore (ed.), *The Complete Greek Tragedies* (Chicago: University of Chicago Press, 1954).

10 F. Storr translates the line "The slain man was no villain but a brother" (353), while Reginald Gibbons has "It was no slave—it was my brother who died." See F.Storr (trans.), *Sophocles in Two Volumes*, vol. 1. The Loeb Classical Library (Cambridge, MA: Harvard University Press, 1981). See also Reginald Gibbons and Charles Segal, *Antigone, The Greek Tragedy in New Translations*, eds Peter Burian and Alan Shapiro (Oxford: Oxford University Press, 2003).

11 See HHTI, 118.

12 See ibid., 85.

13 Aristotle *Poetics*, Bk. 11, 31–2, ed. and trans. Stephen Halliwell (Cambridge, MA: Harvard University Press, 1995). *Longinus on the Sublime*, trans. W. H. Fyfe, revised by Donald Russell; *Demetrius on Style*, trans.

Doreen C. Innes, based on W. Rhys Roberts. *Loeb Classical Library*, Aristotle, vol. 23 (Cambridge, MA: Harvard University Press, 1995). See also G. W. F. *Hegel's Aesthetics: Lectures on Fine Art*, trans. T. M. Knox, 2 vols (Oxford: Clarendon Press, 1988), vol. I: 464; *Vorlesungen über die Ästhetik*. Suhrkamp Taschenbuch Wissenschaft, b. 13–15 (Suhrkamp: Frankfurt am Main, 1970), b. II: 60.

14 Antigone's attachment to the older order of Greek, chthonic gods is thus doubly purified, first, as it is made to give way to a new order of Olympian gods, with whom Creon is associated, then by the way in which Greek polytheism is made to play the role of precursor to Hegel's Christianity, a religion that provides the Trinitarian structure of Hegel's system of thought.

15 As critics such as Jean-Pierre Vernant have suggested, putting a slightly different twist on Hegel's point by seeing tragedy as a critical inflection of norms, tragic performances were one of the mechanisms by which the Athenian polis put itself on trial and was able to undertake a critical examination of its tensions. See Jean-Pierre Vernant, *Myth and Society in Ancient Greece*, trans. Janet Lloyd (New York: Zone Books, 1990).

16 Hence, for Hegel, *Oedipus Rex*, which is more concerned with self-reflective knowledge, is almost a modern tragedy, while Antigone is more reflective of Greek ethical customs.

17 While Heidegger discusses politics in his consideration of *Antigone*, the gesture is only to distance himself from the idea that everything is political, and to inflect the notion of the polis in the direction of the hearth (see HHTI, 104). As Valerie Reed points out, despite his preoccupation with the senses in which Antigone is both at home and not at home, Heidegger's discussion betrays a conspicuous lack of attention to the notion of *oikos*. See Valerie Reed,

"Bringing Antigone Home?" *Comparative Literature Studies*, 45.3 (2008), 316–40.

18 In maintaining that the characters in tragedy should be good, and having conceded that women and slaves can be good, Aristotle undercuts his concession immediately by adding that women are of an "inferior class" and slaves are "wholly paltry," and then says characters should be appropriate, and "it is inappropriate for a woman to be courageous or clever (*andreion e deinen einai*)" (1995, Bk. 15, 23–4).

19 See Jacques Lacan, *The Ethics of Psychoanalysis 1959–1960: The Seminar of Jacques Lacan*, ed. Jacques-Alain Miller, Book VII, trans. Dennis Porter (New York: Tavistock/Routledge, 1992). It would be worth asking how Freud's reflections on the uncanny might play into Lacan's consideration, and even how those reflections constitute a cultural (if repudiated) background for Heidegger's discussions. But that is another paper.

20 Shortly before Aristotle proclaims it inappropriate for women to be characterized as courageous, in the only direct reference to *Antigone* of the *Poetics* (though he refers to the play elsewhere), he discusses what incidents are "terrible or pitiable" (1995, 75), using the plot of *Antigone* as an example of the "worst" kind of plot, where a character is "about to act knowingly, yet does not do so" (77). The reference is to Haemon and Creon, specifically, in the words of the editor, Henderson, to "Haemon's abortive attempt to kill his father" (ibid.).

21 See GA 40, 114/IM, 159.

22 Derrida, "Geschlecht II: Heidegger's Hand."

23 Thomson also draws a connection between PLT and Heidegger's discussion of death in *Antigone*'s the choral ode in the *Introduction of Metaphysics* (IM, 75–6). See Iain D. Thomson, *Heidegger, Art, and Postmodernity* (Cambridge: Cambridge University Press, 2001). See also Heidegger's discussion of the uncanny in PLT.

56

HEIDEGGER AND POST-CARTESIAN PSYCHOANALYSIS

Robert D. Stolorow

The aim of this chapter is to show how Heidegger's[1] existential philosophy enriches post-Cartesian psychoanalysis and vice versa. Binswanger and Boss were two early pioneers who saw the value of Heidegger's analysis of existence for psychotherapy and psychoanalysis. They both proceeded "from the top down"—that is, they started with Heidegger's philosophical delineation of essential existential structures and applied these to clinical phenomena and the therapeutic situation. Although Binswanger's existential analysis produced some brilliant phenomenological descriptions of the "world-designs"[2] underlying various forms of psychopathology, and Boss's[3] Dasein analysis freed the psychoanalytic theory of therapy from the dehumanizing causal-mechanistic assumptions of Freudian metapsychology, neither effort brought about a radicalization of psychoanalytic practice itself or of the psychoanalytic process.

The evolution of what my collaborators and I call *post-Cartesian* psychoanalysis,[4] by contrast, proceeded "from the bottom up." Born of our studies of the subjective origins of psychoanalytic theories,[5] it developed out of our concurrent efforts to rethink psychoanalysis as a form of phenomenological inquiry

and to illuminate the phenomenology of the psychoanalytic process itself. Our dedication to phenomenological inquiry, in turn, led us to a contextualist theoretical perspective, for which we subsequently found philosophical support in Heidegger's existential analytic.

INVESTIGATIVE METHOD

Post-Cartesian psychoanalytic method is characterized by three closely interrelated features. It is *phenomenological*—its focus is on worlds of emotional experience. It is *hermeneutic*—it seeks interpretively to illuminate the structures of meaning that prereflectively organize such worlds of emotional experience. And it is *contextual*—it grasps emotional experience and its horizons as being constituted within formative relational contexts. Heidegger's investigative method in *Being and Time* is also a unique blending of phenomenology, hermeneutics, and contextualism and thus holds great potential for providing a philosophical grounding for post-Cartesian psychoanalysis.

What enables Heidegger to investigate his subject matter, "the question of the meaning of Being,"[6] phenomenologically? In my reading, it is his choice of the inquirer, *Dasein*, as the right entity to be interrogated as to its Being—that is, as to its intelligibility to itself *as* a human being—that enables him to do so. And this is so because:

> *Dasein* . . . is ontically distinguished by the fact that, in its very Being, that Being is an *issue* for it. . . . [Thus] there is some way in which Dasein understands itself in its Being.[7]

Because this human kind of Being (*existence*) "comports itself understandingly toward that Being,"[8] and an unthematized, pre-ontological understanding of our Being is constitutive of our kind of Being, we humans can investigate our own kind of Being by investigating our understanding (and lack of understanding) of that Being. Accordingly, it follows that Heidegger's investigative method is to be a phenomenological one, aimed at illuminating the fundamental structures of our understanding of our Being.

Heidegger points out, however, that the search for phenomenological access to our kind of Being in our understanding of that Being is a complicated one because, in both our traditional philosophical and our average everyday understanding of Being, Being can be extensively covered up and disguised. Therefore, our Being that is covered up in our understanding of it must be "laid bare" by means of *interpretation* of that understanding. Accordingly, Heidegger's analytic of Dasein is a hermeneutic phenomenology aimed at disclosing or unconcealing the basic structures of our kind of Being, its *existentiality*, which lie hidden within our understanding of it.

For Heidegger, interpreting what is understood means explicitly articulating, unveiling, or thematizing its "as-structure"[9]—for example, our intelligibility to ourselves *as* the human beings we are. Against Husserl, Heidegger insists, "All interpretation . . . operates in the fore-structure,"[10] the system of presuppositions that make up the interpretive perspective the interpreter brings to the act of interpreting.

I see Heidegger's own interpretive perspective as a *contextualist* one, crystallizing contrapuntally from his ongoing dialogue with the philosophers of traditional metaphysics and epistemology—most prominently, Descartes. This feature of Heidegger's thought is of central importance for post-Cartesian psychoanalysis.

CONTEXTUALISM: FROM MIND TO WORLD

In Descartes'[11] metaphysical dualism, mind is ontologically isolated from the world in which it dwells, just as the world is purged of all human significance, and both are beheld in their bare thinghood. Traditional Freudian theory is pervaded by the Cartesian "myth of the isolated mind,"[12] which bifurcates the experiential world into inner and outer regions, severs both mind from body and cognition from affect, reifies and absolutizes the resulting divisions, and pictures the mind as an objective entity that takes its place among other objects, a "thinking thing" that has an inside with contents and that looks out on an external world from which it is essentially estranged. Freud's psychoanalysis greatly expanded the Cartesian mind to include a vast unconscious realm. Nevertheless, the Freudian psyche remained a Cartesian mind, a self-enclosed mental apparatus containing and working over mental contents, a thinking *thing* that, precisely because it is a thing, is ontologically decontextualized, fundamentally separated from its world. Post-Cartesian psychoanalysis, by contrast, is a phenomenological contextualism that investigates and illuminates emotional experience as it takes form within constitutive relational contexts. From a post-Cartesian perspective, all the phenomena that have been the focus of psychoanalytic investigation are grasped not as products of isolated intrapsychic mechanisms but as forming within systems constituted by interacting worlds of emotional experience. This phenomenological contextualism finds solid philosophical grounding in Heidegger's ontological contextualism.

In his hermeneutic of Dasein, Heidegger seeks interpretively to refind the unity of our Being, split asunder in the Cartesian bifurcation. His contextualism is formally indicated early on, in his designation of the human being as *Dasein*, to-be-there or to-be-situated, a term that already points to the unity of the human kind of Being and its context. This initially indicated contextualization is further fleshed out as Heidegger focuses his inquiry on our average everyday understanding of our kind of Being. His aim is to "lay bare a fundamental structure in Dasein: Being-in-the-world,"[13] Dasein's "constitutive state."[14] With the hyphens unifying the expression *Being-in-the-world* (*In-der-Welt-sein*), Heidegger indicates that in his interpretation of Dasein the traditional ontological gap between our Being and our world is to be definitively closed and that, in their indissoluble unity, our Being and our world always already contextualize one another. His analytic of Dasein unveils the basic structure of our human kind of Being as a rich contextual whole, in which human Being is saturated with the world in which we dwell, and the world we inhabit is drenched in human

significance. In light of this fundamental contextualization, Heidegger's consideration of affectivity is especially noteworthy.

FROM DRIVE TO AFFECTIVITY

Heidegger's term for the existential ground of affectivity (feelings and moods) is *Befindlichkeit*. Literally, the word might be translated as "how–one–finds–oneself–ness." As Gendlin[15] has pointed out, Heidegger's word for the structure of affectivity denotes both how one feels and the situation within which one is feeling, a felt sense of oneself in a situation, prior to a Cartesian split between inside and outside. *Befindlichkeit* is disclosive of our always already having been delivered over to the situatedness in which we find ourselves. The concept of *Befindlichkeit*—disclosive affectivity—underscores the exquisite context-dependence and context-sensitivity of emotional experience, a context-embeddedness that takes on enormous importance in view of post-Cartesian psychoanalysis' placing of affectivity at the motivational center of human psychological life.

It is a central tenet of post-Cartesian psychoanalysis that a shift in psychoanalytic thinking from the motivational primacy of instinctual drive to the motivational primacy of affectivity moves psychoanalysis toward a phenomenological contextualism and a central focus on dynamic relational systems. Unlike drives, which in Freudian psychoanalysis were claimed to originate deep within the interior of a Cartesian isolated mind, affectivity is something that from birth onward is co-constituted within ongoing relational systems. Therefore, locating affect at their motivational center automatically entails a radical contextualization of virtually all aspects of human psychological life and of the psychoanalytic process. Nowhere is this contextualization seen more clearly than in the understanding of emotional trauma.

TRAUMA, ANXIETY, FINITUDE

From a post-Cartesian perspective, developmental trauma is viewed, not as an instinctual flooding of an ill-equipped Cartesian container, as Freud[16] would have it, but as an experience of unbearable affect. Furthermore, the intolerability of affect states can be fully grasped only in terms of the relational systems in which they are felt. Developmental trauma originates within a formative relational context whose central feature is malattunement to painful affect—the absence of a context of human understanding in which that pain can be held and endured. Without such a relational home for the child's emotional pain, it can only be felt as unbearable, overwhelming, disorganizing. Painful or frightening affect becomes lastingly traumatic when the attunement that the child needs to assist in its tolerance and integration is profoundly absent.

In addition to providing ontological grounding for trauma's context-embeddedness, Heidegger's existential philosophy—in particular, his existential analysis of anxiety—enables us to grasp trauma's existential significance. Like Freud, Heidegger makes a sharp distinction between fear and anxiety. Whereas, according to Heidegger, that in the face of which one fears is a definite "entity within-the-world,"[17] that in the face of which one is anxious is "completely indefinite"[18] and turns out to be "Being-in-the-world as such."[19] The indefiniteness of anxiety "tells us that entities within-the-world are not 'relevant' at all. . . . [The world] collapses into itself [and] has the character of completely lacking significance."[20] Heidegger makes clear that it is the significance of the average everyday world, the world as constituted by the public interpretedness of the "they" (*das Man*), whose collapse is disclosed in anxiety. Furthermore, insofar as the "utter insignificance"[21] of the everyday world is disclosed in anxiety, anxiety includes a feeling of uncanniness, in the sense of "not-being-at-home."[22] In anxiety, the experience of "Being-at-home [in one's tranquilized] everyday familiarity"[23] with the publicly interpreted world collapses, and "Being-in enters into the existential 'mode' of . . . 'uncanniness.'"[24]

In Heidegger's ontological account of anxiety, the central features of its phenomenology—the collapse of everyday significance and the resulting feeling of uncanniness—are claimed to be grounded in what he calls *authentic* (nonevasively owned) *Being-toward-death*. Existentially, death is not simply an event that has not yet occurred or that happens to others, as *das Man* would have it. Rather, it is a distinctive possibility that is constitutive of our existence—of our intelligibility to ourselves in our futurity and our finitude. It is "the possibility of the impossibility of any existence at all,"[25] which, because it is both certain and indefinite as to its "when," always impends as a constant threat, robbing us of the tranquilizing illusions that characterize our absorption in the everyday world, nullifying its significance for us. The appearance of anxiety indicates that the fundamental defensive purpose ("fleeing") of average everydayness has failed and that authentic Being-toward-death has broken through the evasions that conceal it. Torn from the sheltering illusions of *das Man*, we feel uncanny—no longer safely at home.

I have contended[26] that emotional trauma produces an affective state whose features bear a close similarity to the central elements in Heidegger's existential interpretation of anxiety and that it accomplishes this by plunging the traumatized person into a form of authentic Being-toward-death. Trauma shatters the illusions of everyday life that evade and cover up the finitude, contingency, and embeddedness of our existence and the indefiniteness of its certain extinction. Such shattering exposes what had been heretofore concealed, thereby plunging the traumatized person into a form of authentic Being-toward-death and into the anxiety—the loss of significance, the uncanniness—through which authentic Being-toward-death is disclosed. Trauma, like death, individualizes us, in a manner that invariably manifests in an excruciating sense of singularity and solitude.

THE RELATIONALITY OF FINITUDE

It is implicit in Heidegger's ontological account that authentic existing presupposes a capacity to dwell in the emotional pain—the existential anxiety—that accompanies a nonevasive owning up to human finitude. It follows from my claims about the context-embeddedness of emotional trauma that this capacity entails that such pain can find a relational home in which it can be held. What makes such dwelling and holding possible?

Vogel provides a compelling answer to this question by elaborating what he claims to be a relational dimension of the experience of finitude. Just as finitude is fundamental to our existential constitution, so too is it constitutive of our existence that

we meet each other as "brothers and sisters in the same dark night,"[27] deeply connected with one another in virtue of our common finitude. Thus, although the possibility of emotional trauma is ever present, so too is the possibility of forming bonds of deep emotional attunement within which devastating emotional pain can be held, endured, and eventually integrated. Our existential kinship-in-the-same-darkness is the condition for the possibility both of the profound contextuality of emotional trauma and of the mutative power of human understanding.

Critchley points the way toward a second, essential dimension of the relationality of finitude:

I would want to [emphasize] the fundamentally relational character of finitude, namely that death is first and foremost experienced as a relation to the death or dying of the other and others, in Being-with the dying in a caring way, and in grieving after they are dead. . . . [O]ne watches the person one loves . . . die and become a lifeless material thing . . . [T]here is a thing—a corpse—at the heart of the experience of finitude. . . . [which is] fundamentally relational.[28]

Authentic Being-toward-death entails owning up not only to one's own finitude but also to the finitude of all those we love. Hence, authentic Being-toward-death always includes Being-toward-loss as a central constituent. Just as, existentially, we are "always dying already,"[29] so too are we always already grieving. Death and loss are existentially equiprimordial. Existential anxiety anticipates both death and loss.

Support for my claim about the equiprimordiality of death and loss can be found in the work of Derrida,[30] who contends that every friendship is structured from its beginning, a priori, by the possibility that one of the two friends will die first and that the surviving friend will be left to mourn: "To have a friend, to look at him, to follow him with your eyes, . . . is to know in a more intense way, already injured, . . . that one of the two of you will inevitably see the other die."[31] Finitude and the possibility of mourning are constitutive of every friendship.

In loss, all possibilities for Being in relation to the lost loved one are extinguished. Traumatic loss shatters one's emotional world, and, insofar as one dwells in the region of such loss, one feels eradicated. As Derrida claims, "[D]eath takes from us not only some particular life within the world [but] someone through whom the world, and first of all our own world, will have opened up."[32]

it. So if we are to "leap ahead"[33] of the other, freeing him or her for his or her ownmost possibilities, we must also free him or her for an authentic Being-toward-death and for a readiness for the anxiety that discloses it. Therefore, according to my claims about the contextuality of emotional life, we must Be-with—that is, attune to—the other's existential anxiety and other painful affect states disclosive of his or her finitude, thereby providing these feelings with a relational home in which they can be held, so that he or she can seize upon his or her ownmost possibilities in the face of them. Authentic solicitude—a central component of friendship, love, and a therapeutic attitude—can be shown to entail one of the constitutive dimensions of deep human bonding, in which we value the alterity of the other as it is manifested in his or her own distinctive affectivity.

EXPANDING HEIDEGGER'S CONCEPTION OF RELATIONALITY

Authentic relationality or "Being-with" (*Mitsein*) is largely restricted in Heidegger's philosophy to a form of "solicitude" (*Fürsorge*) that welcomes and encourages the other's individualized selfhood. Here I wish to expand Heidegger's conception of authentic solicitude by showing that it entails the existential kinship-in-finitude that I, along with Vogel, claim is constitutive of our Being-with one another.

Authentic solicitude, in Heidegger's account, frees the other to exist authentically, for the sake of his or her ownmost possibilities of Being. But recall that, for Heidegger, being free for one's ownmost possibilities also always means being free for one's uttermost possibility—the possibility of death—and for the existential anxiety that discloses

CONCLUSIONS: THE ONTICAL AND THE ONTOLOGICAL

Post-Cartesian psychoanalysis and Heidegger's existential philosophy are both forms of phenomenological inquiry. Post-Cartesian psychoanalysis is an ontical discipline; it investigates and illuminates the structures that prereflectively organize the lived emotional worlds of actual particular persons, along with the specific relational contexts in which these structures take form. Heidegger's existential analytic is an ontological inquiry; it lays bare the necessary and universal structures (existentiales) that, a priori, constitute the human kind of Being (existence)—our intelligibility to ourselves as human beings. I have shown that a psychoanalytic phenomenological contextualism finds philosophical grounding in Heidegger's ontological contextualism and that the psychoanalytic understanding of emotional trauma is greatly enriched by an encounter with Heidegger's elucidation of the structures of authentic existing. How did Heidegger view the role of ontical phenomena in the illumination of ontological or existential structures, and how can grasping the interplay of the ontical and the ontological contribute to an enrichment of Heidegger's existential philosophy by post-Cartesian psychoanalysis?

Answers to these questions can be found in the central role that Heidegger gives to moods (affectivity) in the disclosure of our Being-in-the-world: "[O]ntologically mood is a primordial kind of Being for Dasein, in which Dasein is disclosed to itself *prior to* all cognition and volition."[34] Mood discloses Dasein's "'thrownness' ... into its 'there'";[35] it discloses "Being-in-the-world as a whole";[36] and it discloses how "what [Dasein] encounters within-the-world can '*matter*' to it."[37]

Elkholy emphasizes that, for Heidegger, "[M]ood, especially the mood of *Angst*, has the power to reveal the ... whole of how one is in the world and the whole of the world at large."[38] Thus for Heidegger, ontical experiences of certain moods are ontologically revelatory. Anxiety, in particular, is grasped as "a bridge to the truth of Being"[39]—from the ontical or psychological to the ontological.

In his 1929–30 lecture course, Heidegger makes a truly remarkable claim regarding ontologically revelatory moods, which he calls *ground moods* (*Grundstimmungen*) or *fundamental attunements*:

> *Philosophy in each case happens in a fundamental attunement.* Conceptual philosophical comprehension is grounded in our being gripped, and this is grounded in a fundamental attunement.[40]

In the lecture course, Heidegger discusses a number of such ground moods that make philosophizing possible: anxiety, homesickness, turbulence, boredom, melancholy. In later works he emphasizes other ontologically revelatory ground moods, such as awe, wonder, and astonishment.[41]

I cannot recall ever encountering a reference to the mood of shame in Heidegger's philosophical work. It is my view that, just as existential anxiety is disclosive of authentic existing, it is shame that most clearly discloses inauthentic or unowned existing. In feeling ashamed, we feel exposed as deficient or defective before the gaze of the other.[42] In shame, we are held hostage by the eyes of others, belonging not to ourselves but to them. Thus, a move toward greater authenticity, toward a taking ownership of one's existing, is often accompanied by an emotional shift from being dominated by shame to an embracing of existential guilt, anxiety, and anticipatory grief. This is a shift from a preoccupation with how one is seen by others to a pursuit of what really matters to one as an individual, including the quality of one's relatedness to others.

It is precisely here that an encounter with post-Cartesian psychoanalysis has the potential of enriching Heidegger's existential philosophy, in that post-Cartesian psychoanalysis gives an account of the relational contexts that make it possible for one to dwell in and bear the painful emotional experiences, the ground moods, that are revelatory of authentic existing. Experiencing our kinship-in-finitude with one another, thereby finding a relational home or context of human understanding in which the traumatizing emotional impact of our finitude and the finitude of those we love can be held, brought into dialogue, and integrated, helps make authentic existential philosophizing possible. Post-Cartesian

psychoanalysis illuminates the rich relationality of authentic existing.

NOTES AND REFERENCES

1 BTMR.
2 L. Binswanger, "The Existential Analysis School
   of Thought," trans. E. Angel, in eds R. May,
   E. Angel, and H. Ellenberger, *Existence: A New
   Dimension in Psychiatry and Psychology* (New
   York: Basic Books, 1958), 195.
3 M. Boss, *Psychoanalysis and Daseinanalysis*,
   trans. L. Lefebre (New York: Basic Books, 1963).
4 R. Stolorow, *World, Affectivity, Trauma:
   Heidegger and Post-Cartesian Psychoanalysis*
   (New York: Routledge, 2011).
5 R. Stolorow and G. Atwood, *Faces in a Cloud:
   Subjectivity in Personality Theory* (Northvale,
   NJ: Jason Aronson, 1979).
6 BTMR, 19.
7 Ibid., 32.
8 Ibid., 78.
9 Ibid., 190.
10 Ibid., 194.
11 R. Descartes, *Meditations* (Buffalo, NY:
   Prometheus Books, 1989).
12 R. Stolorow and G. Atwood, *Contexts of
   Being: The Intersubjective Foundations of
   Psychological Life* (Hillsdale, NJ: Analytic
   Press, 1992), 7.
13 BTMR, 65.
14 Ibid., 78.
15 E. Gendlin, "*Befindlichkeit*: Heidegger and the
   Philosophy of Psychology," in ed. K. Hoeller,
   Heidegger and Psychology (Seattle, WA:
   Review of Existential Psychology & Psychiatry,
   1988), 43–71.
16 S. Freud, *Inhibitions, Symptoms, and Anxiety*,
   standard edn, vol. 20 (London: Hogarth Press,
   1959).
17 BTMR, 231.
18 Ibid.
19 Ibid., 230.
20 Ibid., 231.
21 Ibid.
22 Ibid., 233.
23 Ibid.
24 Ibid.
25 Ibid., 307.
26 R, Stolorow, *Trauma and Human Existence:
   Autobiographical, Psychoanalytic, and
   Philosophical Reflections* (New York:
   Routledge, 2007).
27 L. Vogel, *The Fragile "We": Ethical
   Implications of Heidegger's* Being and Time
   (Evanston, IL: Northwestern University Press,
   1994), 97.
28 S. Critchley, "*Enigma Variations: An
   Interpretation of Heidegger's* Sein und Zeit,"
   Ratio, 15 (2002), 169–70.
29 BTMR, 298.
30 J. Derrida, *Politics of Friendship*, trans. G.
   Collins (New York: Verso, 1997).
31 J. Derrida, *The Work of Mourning*, ed. P.-A.
   Brault and M. Naas (Chicago: University of
   Chicago Press, 2001), 107.
32 Ibid.
33 BTMR, 158.
34 Ibid., 175.
35 Ibid., 174.
36 Ibid., 176.
37 Ibid.
38 S. Elkholy, *Heidegger and a Metaphysics
   of Feeling: Angst and the Finitude of Being*
   (London and New York: Continuum,
   2008), 4.
39 Ibid., 7.
40 FCM, 7.
41 R. Capobianco, *Engaging Heidegger* (Toronto:
   University of Toronto Press, 2010).
42 J.-P. Sartre, *Being and Nothingness*, trans.
   H. Barnes (New York: Citadel Press, 2001).

57

HEIDEGGER AND ASIAN PHILOSOPHY
Bret W. Davis

ON THE WAY TO THE INEVITABLE DIALOGUE

"Again and again it has seemed urgent to me that a dialogue take place with the thinkers of what is to us the Eastern world." Heidegger wrote these lines in 1969 in a letter to Albert Borgmann, the director of a conference held at the University of Hawai'i on the theme of "Heidegger and Eastern Thought."[1] Since that time, Heidegger's relation to Asian philosophies, and to Daoism and Zen in particular, has been the subject of much commentary and controversy. While some have contended that Heidegger was an inveterate Eurocentrist,[2] others have extolled his efforts to clear a pathway toward what he called "the inevitable dialogue with the East Asian world" (VA, 43/QCT, 158), a dialogue which would enable the development of a radically intertraditional discourse of "planetary thinking" (GA 9, 424/PA, 321).[3] In fact, Heidegger demonstrated a lifelong interest in engaging in such dialogue. It is not without justification that Rolf Elberfeld claims: "Heidegger is the first great European thinker . . . whose entire path of thought has been accompanied by dialogues with Asian philosophers."[4]

Yet, despite the profound interest in Daoism and Zen he often revealed to colleagues and visitors, Heidegger's published references to Asian philosophies are frustratingly few. Gadamer, who has said that "Heidegger studies would do well to pursue seriously comparisons of his work with Asian philosophies," tells us that one reason may be that Heidegger was hesitant to refer to a thought he could not read in the original language.[5] Heidegger himself stated in his letter to Borgmann that, despite the urgency for dialogue with the East, "the greatest difficulty in this enterprise always lies, as far as I can see, in the fact that with few exceptions there is no command of the Eastern languages either in Europe or in the United States."[6] Heidegger frequently expressed such caution and concern about his—and our—ability to understand Asian languages well enough to engage in a dialogue with Asian philosophies. The alterity of East Asian languages in particular was largely responsible *both* for his attraction to East Asian thought as harboring possible alternatives to Western metaphysics, *and* for his wariness regarding our ability to understand it without assimilating it into Western concepts (GA 12, 85, 98/OWL, 4, 15; GA 79, 145–6; LBH, 29).

Indeed, Heidegger would be suspicious of the very title of this chapter, given that he stated, on more than one occasion, that there is no such thing as "Asian philosophy" since "philosophy," properly speaking, is quintessentially Western (GA 55, 3; WhD, 136/WCT, 224; WIP, 31). However, it is important to note that his reasons for saying this are very different from those who, even today, arrogantly and ignorantly presume that only Westerners have thought deeply and rigorously about fundamental questions. When Heidegger says that there is no "Asian philosophy," and that "Western philosophy" is a tautology, he is equating "philosophy" with Western "metaphysics," which Heidegger himself is trying to overcome or recover from. Hence, he speaks of "the end of philosophy and the task of thinking" (ZSD, 61–80/BW, 431–49), and writes: "The thinking that is to come is no longer philosophy because it thinks more originally than metaphysics—a name identical to philosophy" (GA 9, 364/PA, 276). While one can take issue with his restrictive definition of "philosophy," one can hardly doubt Heidegger's interest in and respect for Asian *thinking*.

INDICATIONS OF INFLUENCE ON THE WAY (*DAO*)

While many scholars have pursued fortuitous parallels and resonances (as well as differences and dissonances),[7] some have more recently argued that the development of Heidegger's thought itself was profoundly influenced by his contact with Asian philosophies.[8] While too offhandedly dismissed by some and too eagerly exaggerated by others, it would be difficult to deny some degree of influence, even if its depth and significance remains debatable. Along with the textual evidence assembled (albeit in a rather

prosecutorial manner) by Reinhard May, there exists the following type of anecdotal testimony from the eminent Kyoto School philosopher, Nishitani Keiji. When Nishitani was studying in Freiburg between 1937 and 1939, he presented Heidegger with a copy of the first volume of D. T. Suzuki's *Essays in Zen Buddhism*. It turned out Heidegger had already read and was eager to discuss this book. Nishitani recounted to Graham Parkes "how Heidegger had given him a 'standing invitation' to come to his house on Saturday afternoons to talk about Zen" (HHS, 100). He also told Ban Kazunori that he had often been invited to the Heidegger residence, where he "explained quite a lot about the standpoint of Zen to Heidegger." Nishitani even said that, after taking meticulous notes, "Heidegger would himself repeat these ideas in his lectures, only without mentioning Zen!"[9]

The *ex oriente lux* may indeed go back much further. The term *In-der-Welt-sein* (being-in-the-world), for example, was first coined not by Heidegger but rather in the German translation of Okakura Tenshin's *The Book of Tea*, a copy of which Heidegger reportedly received in 1919.[10] Okakura's expression "being in the world," which appears in a chapter entitled "Taoism and Zennism," was presumably a translation of the term *chushi* (Japanese: *shosei*) from the *Zhuangzi* (e.g. chapter 9).[11] Heidegger was certainly familiar with Martin Buber's 1910 edition of the *Zhuangzi*, at least by 1930, when he refers to chapter 17 of it to elucidate our being-with others.[12] He concludes his 1944–5 *Country Path Conversations* with a reflection on a passage from chapter 26 of the *Zhuangzi* on "the necessity of the unnecessary" (GA 77, 239/CPC, 156–7).

In 1946 Heidegger proposed to cotranslate the *Daodejing* with Paul Shih-yi Hsiao, and, even though the project was abandoned after eight chapters, this work seems to have left a lasting impact on Heidegger (HAT, 93–103). In a text from the 1950s, Heidegger went so far as to write:

> The *Dao* could thus be the Way that moves everything [*der alles be-wëgende Weg*], that from which we might first be able to think what reason, mind, meaning, *logos* properly—i.e., from their own essence—mean to say. . . . [M]ethods . . . are after all merely the runoff of a great hidden stream, of the Way that moves everything, of the Way that draws everything onto its path. All is Way. (GA 12, 187/OWL 92 tm)

Eventually giving his own Collected Edition the motto "ways—not works," Heidegger must have been intrigued by the fact that *dao* can mean both "way" and "to say." For Heidegger, being comes to appear ever again through the saying (*Sagen*) in which "language speaks" (*die Sprache spricht*) (GA 12, 30/PLT, 207). Moreover, the ultimate source of this saying remains, for Heidegger as for Daoism, unspoken. "The Way (*dao*) that can be said (*ke dao*) is not the abiding Way" (*Daodejing*, chapter 1). Heidegger: "Perhaps there is concealed in the word 'Way', *dao*, the mystery of all mysteries of thoughtful Saying, if only we let these names return to that in them which is unspoken" (GA 12, 187/OWL, 92 tm).

In Heidegger's most sustained engagement with Asian philosophy, his "Dialogue on Language between a Japanese and an Inquirer" (dated 1953–4, first published in 1959), he tentatively suggests that the "entirely different" Western and East Asian linguistic "houses of being" may ultimately "well up from a single source" (GA 12, 85, 89/OWL, 5, 8). The dialogue ends by calling

for a shared attunement to an originary silence (GA 12, 144 /OWL, 52–3). Radical crosscultural dialogue would, it is suggested, need to be accompanied by an even more radical diasigetics, a conversing through silence.[13]

HEIDEGGER'S PREPARATION AND JAPANESE ENGAGEMENT

Heidegger's "Dialogue on Language" was rather loosely based on actual conversations he had with Tezuka Tomio and other Japanese visitors. In general, however, Heidegger remained more committed to preparing for the "inevitable dialogue" with East Asian thought than to venturing to engage in it himself. A "dialogue with the Greek thinkers and their language," he wrote, "remains for us the precondition of the inevitable dialogue with the East Asian world" (VA, 43/QCT, 158). According to Heidegger, Westerners, that is to say, those whose language and thinking are determined by the Western "sending of being," are not yet prepared for this encounter. On one occasion he even suggested that this preparation may take another 300 years (LBH, 269)!

Given the swift pace of what Heidegger calls the "Europeanization of human being and of the earth," which is said to "devour the wellsprings of everything essential" (GA 12, 99/OWL 16), centuries of preparation is not a luxury afforded to Easterners themselves. In his "Dialogue on Language" Heidegger admonishes the Japanese to attend to "the venerable beginnings of [their] own thinking" rather than "chasing after the latest news in European philosophy" (GA 12, 124/OWL, 37). Yet, in the *Spiegel* interview of 1966 he claims that "a reversal can be prepared only in the same location in the world where the modern technological world arose, and . . . cannot happen by means of an adoption of Zen Buddhism or other Eastern experiences of the world" (GA 16, 679). Does this mean that Easterners should attend only to their own traditions, even when these cannot help save the world from the problem of technology? Fortunately, this is not all Heidegger had to say on the matter. Indeed, in the *Spiegel* interview Heidegger had already stated: "And who of us can decide whether one day in Russia and in China ancient traditions of a 'thinking' will awaken which will help enable human being to have a free relationship to the technical world" (GA 16, 677). In a foreword written for the Japanese translation of one of his essays in 1968, Heidegger reaffirmed that the *Auseinandersetzung* of Western and Eastern thinking "can assist in the endeavor to save the essence of the human from the threat of an extreme technical calculation and manipulation of human Dasein" (JH, 230).

The Japanese, for their part, have been ardently engaging with Heidegger's thought since the 1920s, when several of Japan's leading young philosophers studied with Heidegger.[14] Indeed, the first article on Heidegger's thought was written by Tanabe Hajime in 1924 (89–108), and the first book on Heidegger was published by Kuki Shūzō in 1933. Moreover, arguably the first substantial critique was undertaken by Watsuji Tetsurō beginning in 1928. Watsuji criticized Heidegger's early emphasis on temporality at the expense of spatiality. By "spatiality" Watsuji meant, on the one hand, a more radical notion of what Heidegger calls "being-with" (*Mitsein*): the originary sociality or "betweenness" (*aidagara*) of human

beings (Watsuji draws here on the fact that the Japanese word for "human being," *ningen*, literally signifies the "betweeness" of "persons").[15] On the other hand, "spatiality" also indicated for Watsuji our originary interconnectedness with the natural environment (in this case he draws on a Japanese word, *fūdo*, which implies both "climate" and "culture").[16] In their own ways, Tanabe and Kuki also criticized Heidegger's early emphasis on temporality at the expense of spatiality.[17]

As it turns out, Heidegger later recanted his earlier attempt to derive existential spatiality from temporality (ZSD, 24/TB, 23), and came to think of time and space as equiprimordially "given" in an originary appropriating-event (*Ereignis*). Moreover, Heidegger's stress on the temporality and historicity of being is increasingly accompanied by the spatial language of the "clearing" (*Lichtung*) and the "place" or "locality" (*Ort*, *Ortschaft*, *Ortlichkeit*) of being, such that he comes to characterize his thought as a "topology of being" (GA 15, 335/FS, 41).

All this invites comparison with Japan's most famous modern philosopher, Nishida Kitarō, who spoke of the self-determination of "the place of absolute nothingness." Parkes has gone so far as to write that "Heidegger's *Lichtung* may be seen as the German version of Nishida's *mu no basho*, or topos of nothingness."[18] Yet Heidegger apparently considered Nishida too "Western" (JH, 170), while Nishida, for his part, did not think much of Heidegger's (early) thought. And so, unfortunately, the potentially historic East-West dialogue between these two great figures of twentieth-century philosophy was not to be—or rather, it is a task they left to those of us who inherit their paths of thought.[19]

BEING: NOTHING: THE SAME

Even if it were not influenced by Nishida's conception of the place of nothingness, Heidegger's thought of the clearing may perhaps have been influenced by the Chinese graph for "nothing" (*wu*, pronounced *mu* in Japanese). One interpretation of this graph entails, to quote a text by León Wieger to which Heidegger may have had access, "A multitude . . . of men acting upon a forest, felling the trees, clearing of wood a tract of land. In the old form [the graph] stated that the wood had vanished."[20] Not only does this resemble Heidegger's later explanations of the clearing (see ZSD, 72/BW, 441), already in his 1936 essay, "The Origin of the Work of Art," we read: "In the midst of beings as a whole an open place occurs. There is a clearing [. . . which . . .] encircles all that is, like the nothing, which we scarcely know" (GA 5, 40/BW, 178). A few years later he sharpens the point: "This emptiness of the clearing is the inceptual nothing" (GA 71, 208).

Although scholars today tend to favor a different etymological account of *wu/mu*, according to which it is related to the graph for "dance" (in this case perhaps a rain dance) and may also depict a person disappearing behind thick vegetation, this interpretation too can be understood to carry strikingly Heideggerian connotations of an interrelation between revealing and concealing. One Japanese scholar recently writes (without reference to Heidegger): "Precisely because 'nothingness' (*wu/mu*) is a hardly perceptible indeterminacy, it contains the idea of anticipating the possible appearance of something. . . . 'Nothingness' contains the etymological ambiguity of 'being going out of being (*Entwerden*)' on the one hand and 'non-being harboring the possibility of being' on the other."[21] In a complementary

vein Heidegger writes: "Even if we mean it only in the sense of the complete negation of anything present, the nothing belongs, in its absencing [*ab-wesend*], to presencing [*Anwesen*] as one of its possibilities" (GA 9, 413–14/PA, 312–13 tm). Yet for Heidegger, as for Daoism and Zen, "the nothing" means much more than merely a negation or privation of what is present.

Dramatically in his 1929 lecture "What is Metaphysics?"[22] and consistently in numerous texts up through the 1966–9 Le Thor seminars, Heidegger links "being" with "the nothing" (*das Nichts*) (GA 9, 105–22, 123, 360, 382–3, 410–20/PA, 84–96, 97, 273, 289–90, 309–18; GA 5, 113/QCT 154; GA 65, §§128–9, 145; GA 66, §§27, 74, 77–8, 84–5; GA 67, 59–61; GA 69, 109; GA 70, 48–50; GA 71, 121, 124, 132–3, 148, 194, 208, 219–20, 223; GA 15, 346–9, 360–2/FS, 48–50, 56–8). According to the "ontological difference," "the being [*Sein*] of beings 'is' itself not a being [*ein Seiendes*]" (SZ, 6/BT, 5); hence, "'being', in contrast to all 'beings', is no 'being' and is in this sense a 'nothing'" (JH, 166). In other words, being "is" no-thing.[23] Or, to put it the other way around: "The nothing itself, however, is being" (GA 71, 121).

Heidegger repeatedly dismisses nihilistic misunderstandings of what he means by the nothing. On the contrary, he retorts, "perhaps the essence of nihilism consists in not taking the question of the nothing seriously" (N2, 53/NIV, 21; see also EM, 155/IM, 217–18). The nothing is not a nihilistic privation of being, but rather "the essential trembling of beyng itself and therefore *is* more than any being" (GA 65, 256/CP2, 209).

In his most terse formulation, Heidegger writes: "Being: Nothing: The Same" (GA 15, 363/FS, 58; see also GA 9, 115, 421/PA 91, 318; GA 66, 294). He sometimes explicates this sameness as an essential inter-play of being and the nothing, such that that "each employs itself for the other in a kin-ship whose essential fullness we have as yet scarcely pondered" (GA 9, 419/PA, 317). Although he does not explicitly cite chap-ter 11 of the *Daodejing*, Heidegger clearly draws an insight from it when he speaks of the emptiness or nothingness of the jug as the ungraspable yet essential element of its being (GA 77, 130–1/CPC, 84–2; VA, 161/ PLT, 167).[24] The *Daodejing* speaks of noth-ingness (*wu*) both as the essential counter-part of being (*you*) (chapter 2) and as the origin of being (chapter 40). For Heidegger, the presencing of being is inseparable from the absencing or nihilating of the nothing. In *Contributions to Philosophy*, Heidegger refers to the nothing as the abyssal char-acter of being (or "beyng"), as the "high-est gift" of its self-withdrawal and refusal (*Verweigerung*); for it is "on account of *this negativity* of beyng itself that 'nothingness' is full of that *assigning* 'power' the endur-ing of which is the origin of all 'creating'" (GA 65, §§128–9/CP2, 193–4; see also GA 66, §§26–7, 84–5; GA 71, 124; GA 5, 113/ QCT, 154).

For Heidegger, it could be said, the noth-ing is the concealedness that always accom-panies the unconcealedness of being. The nothing is the essentially self-withdrawing and self-concealing dimension of being; it is the *lethe* of *aletheia*, the expropriation (*Enteignis*) involved in the appropriating event (*Ereignis*), the mystery (*Geheimnis*) of the forest that surrounds any bounded openness of the clearing. It is not a priva-tion or vacuity, but rather the fullness of the undelimited open-region (*Gegnet*) in which this or that delimited sense of being—this or that horizon of meaning—comes to be formed.

THE NOTHING AND *MU*: RESONANCES

In a letter to Kojima Takehiko in 1963, Heidegger wrote:

> The lecture ["What is Metaphysics?"] was translated into Japanese as early as 1930 and was immediately understood in your country, in contrast to the nihilistic misunderstanding of the terms it intro-duced which remains prevalent in Europe to this day. What is called the nothing [*das Nichts*] in this lecture means that which, in regard to beings [*das Seiende*], is never any one of these beings [*niemals etwas Seiendes*], and which "is" thus the nothing, and yet which nevertheless determines beings as such and thus is called being [*das Sein*]. (JH, 225)

In 1969 he wrote to Roger Munier: "In the far East, with the 'nothing' properly under-stood, one found in it the word for being."[25] In his "Dialogue on Language" Heidegger had already expressed his appreciation for the ability of the Japanese to understand his notion of the nothing, and had his Japanese interlocutor proclaim: "For us, emptiness is the loftiest name for what you mean to say with the word 'being'" (GA 12, 103/OWL, 19 tm).

Heinrich Petzet relates the following 1963 encounter with Bhikkhu Mani, a Theravada Buddhist monk from Thailand.

> Heidegger had spoken of releasement and openness to the mystery, so the nature of meditation is finally discussed. What does meditation mean for Eastern humanity? The monk's response is quite simple: Meditation means "to gather oneself." The more humanity succeeds in gathering itself and concentrating, without exertion of the will, the more it

lets go of itself. The "I" dissolves, until in the end only one thing remains: the Nothing. But this Nothing is not nothing; it is just the opposite—fullness. No one can name this. But it is nothing and everything—fullness. Heidegger understands this and says, "This is what I have been saying throughout my whole life."[26]

At various other times Heidegger expressed similar enthusiasm about the resonances between his own thought and that of Buddhism. He is reported to have exclaimed upon reading a book on Zen by D. T. Suzuki: "If I understand this man correctly, this is what I have been trying to say in all my writings!"[27] Suzuki visited Heidegger in 1953 (see JH, 169–72). Some years later, Heidegger spoke to C. F. Weizäcker of "the deep impression left on him by a visit from a renowned Japanese Zen Buddhist, who spoke of what is decisive in an entirely unmetaphysical manner; it was as if here a door had been opened" for Heidegger (LBH, 29). Heidegger may have had in mind a visit from Hisamatsu Shinichi, a book of whose was later translated into German as *Die Fülle des Nichts*.[28] In 1958 Heidegger concluded a discussion with Hisamatsu by stating: "It has become clear that, with our ideas . . . we can hardly get to where the Japanese already are" (JH, 215).

How close is Heidegger's thought of the nothing to that of Buddhism? While an examination of the various interrelated yet also distinct senses of "emptiness" and "nothingness" in Buddhism and Daoism is beyond the scope of this chapter,[29] some of these senses do indeed resonate with aspects of Heidegger's thinking, and his enthusiasm for pointing these resonances out is not unfounded.

MU AND THE NOTHING: DIFFERENCES

At the same time, Heidegger was also understandably concerned about the differences between his thought and Buddhism. These differences may even undermine some apparent similarities. At one point in *Contributions to Philosophy* (1936–8) he writes: "The less that humans are beings, the less that they adhere obstinately to the beings they find themselves to be, all the nearer do they come to being (Not a Buddhism! Just the opposite)" (GA 65, 170/CP2, 134). However, Heidegger is here presumably following Schopenhauer's and Nietzsche's misinterpretations of Buddhism, as he does later when he speaks of Schopenhauer and Buddhism as both involving a "redemption from the will [that] would amount to redemption from being, hence to a collapse into vacuous nothingness" (VA, 113/NIV, 225). With regard to this passage, Heidegger subsequently admitted to Hellmuth Hecker that he was speaking from the perspective of Nietzsche, and that "Buddhism, and no less Chinese and Japanese thought, were in need of an entirely different interpretation" (LBH, 58).

Even so, important differences between Heidegger's thought and Buddhism remain. In conversation with Bhikkhu Mani Heidegger stated: "In contrast, I believe, to Buddhist teachings, in Western thinking an essential distinction is made between human being and other living beings, [namely] plants and animals. Human being is distinguished by having language, that is, by the fact that he stands in a relationship of knowing to being" (GA 16, 590). Heidegger writes elsewhere: "The human being: 'the placeholder of the nothing' [GA 9, 118, 419/PA, 93, 316; GA 15, 370/FS, 63] and the human being: 'the shepherd (not the master) of being' [GA 9,

342/PA, 260] . . . say the Same" (JH, 225). Following Medard Boss's claim that "Indian thought does not require a guardian for the clearing," Heidegger remarked: "In contrast, it is very important to me that the human being is a *human* being. In Indian thought, the point is 'a giving up of being human' [*Entmenschlichung*] in the sense of Da-sein's self-transformation into the pure luminosity [of being]" (ZS, 178).

In response to these statements, it should first of all be pointed out that in most schools of Hinduism and Buddhism, despite the fact humans are seen as sharing the cycle of rebirth in samsara with other living beings, they are also placed in a unique and privileged position: only in the form of a human being can one attain enlightenment or nirvana. Moreover, some distinctions need to be made, not only between various Hindu schools of thought and Buddhism but also between the Theravada Buddhism represented by Bhikkhu Mani and Mahayana Buddhist schools such as Zen, which proclaim a "non-abiding nirvana" and even the "nonduality of samsara and nirvana." In Zen, when the "I" as an illusory reified and egoistic sense of self is dissolved into the nothing, the "true self" emerges as a self-expression of this creatively self-delimiting nothingness or "emptying of emptiness." In other words, while a false or inauthentic sense of self is to be radically negated in Zen, by way of this "great death" a true or authentic sense of self is born or awakened. From the perspective of the East Asian Mahayana Buddhist school of Zen, so-called Hinayana schools of Buddhism, such as Theravada, along with schools of Hinduism such as Advaita Vedanta, do not sufficiently reaffirm the world of multiplicity and interconnected individuality after negating the illusory ego and its dualistic and reifying discriminations.

Yet Heidegger is still right to point out a difference from Buddhism regarding his conception of the linguistic relation between human being and being. For Heidegger, the essential trait of human being is a responding (*Entsprechen*) or answering (*Antworten*) to the claim (*Anspruch*) or address (*Zuspruch*) or call (*Geheiß*) of being (GA 77, 23–5/ CPC, 15–16; GA 12, 29–30/PLT 206–7; WIP, 68–77; WhD, 80, 152/WCT, 114–15, 124). For Heidegger, the "sameness" (*das Selbe*) of *Dasein* and *Sein*, human being and being, the self and the nothing, thinking and being, is never a distinctionless identity but rather the "belonging together" (ID, 30–2; WhD, 74/WCT, 79; GA 9, 407–8/PA, 308–9) of this call and response. While Heidegger does think being as the nothing, he says that human being is "held out into the nothing" or is "the placeholder of the nothing"; he never goes so far as to identify the nothing with the true self. Zen, on the other hand, urges one to go beyond not only nihilistic and dualistic interpretations of *Mu* (nothingness) but also beyond all linguistic and intellectual discriminations and, by means a holistic practice of seated meditation (*zazen*), to concentrate oneself with one's 360 bones and 84,000 pores into this *Mu* and "*be* 'Mu.'"[30] Only then can one undergo "the great death" and come back to life in a freely creative engagement with things and selflessly compassionate relation with others. Despite some significant resonances with Heidegger's thoughts on death,[31] we do find here a significant difference between his meditative or commemorative thinking (*Besinnung, Andenken*) as a correspondence with being, and the Zen practice of meditation, which involves a more radically nondualistic descent into nothingness by way of a "non-thinking" (*hi-shiryō*) that underlies both thinking and "not-thinking" (*fu-shiryō*).

It is just such a difference that Nishitani has in mind when he criticizes Heidegger's statement: "Da-sein means: being held out into the nothing [*Hineingehaltenheit in das Nichts*]" (GA 9, 115, 120/PA, 91, 95; see also KPM, 162). According to Nishitani, insofar as Heidegger thought of the nothing as an abyss into which Dasein is thrust in a state of anxiety (*Angst*), "traces of the representation of the nothing as some 'thing' [which threatens Dasein from without] still remain."[32] Nishitani's main successor in the Kyoto School, Ueda Shizuteru, traces the development of Heidegger's own understanding of the relation to the nothing, and suggests that the experience of "releasing oneself [*Sichloslassen*] into the nothing," intimated at the end of "What is Metaphysics?" (GA 9, 122/PA, 96), is "radicalized in the later Heidegger's thought into the notion of *Gelassenheit*."[33] Following Ueda's indications we could say that, were one to thoroughly release oneself into the nothing, it would no longer be experienced as "the horror of the abyss" (GA 9, 306–7/PA, 233–4), or as "the anxiety springing from pain, anxiety as experience of the nothing" (GA 71, 220). Rather, in a fundamental attunement of *Gelassenheit* rather than *Angst*, the nothing would be experienced as the essentially concealed dimension of being in its "profoundest sense" of "giving" or "letting be" (*Seinlassen*) (GA 15, 363/FS, 59).

Nevertheless, *Gelassenheit*, for all its resonances with the Daoist and Zen idea of "non-doing" (*wuwei, mu-i*), for Heidegger names a relation to being that entails a "coming-into-nearness to the far," a "going-into-nearness" that also preserves an essential distance from being (GA 77, 116, 152–7/CPC, 75, 99–103). Although both Zen and Heidegger speak of the need to take a radical "step back" (Dōgen: *taiho*,

Heidegger: *Schritt zurück*), for Heidegger "the step steps back before, gains distance from that which is about to arrive" (ZSD, 32/ TB, 30). From the perspective of Nishitani's philosophy of Zen, Heidegger's being maintains an element of externality or "transcendence" that would needed to be "broken through" on the path of a more radical step back or "trans-descendence" to "the absolute near-side," that is, to the field of emptiness that is none other than one's own "original face."[34]

Tsujimura Kōichi was another Zen adept and student of Nishitani's; he was also a leading Heidegger scholar in Japan and principal editor of the Japanese edition of Heidegger's *Gesamtausgabe*. After his stay in Freiburg in 1956–8, Heidegger held him in high regard, and he was asked to speak at Heidegger's eightieth birthday celebration in 1969.[35] Tsujimura has also led the way in plumbing the resonances between Heidegger's thought and Zen. And yet, not only is he critical of the fundamental attunement of *Angst* and what he sees as the "transcendental will" operative in Heidegger's early thought,[36] he also indicates some crucial differences between Heidegger's later thought and Zen. In particular, he contends that the "truth of Zen" is the "absolute nothingness" that "cannot be reached by any kind of thought and cannot be brought to speech as such with any kind of language. . . . By contrast, [Heidegger's] 'truth of being' is a truth that is established thoroughly on the basis of 'thinking' and 'language.'"[37] The "leap into the truth of being" that Heidegger speaks of, according to Tsujimura, does not reach "the origin (*Ursprung*) of thought, which is itself no longer—and not yet—thought." It is for this reason that Heidegger speaks of a "last god" (GA 65, 406–17) or, in the *Spiegel* interview, of a god who is needed to save us (GA 16,

671); these are "the unthinkable origin of thought as it is reflected in the dimension of thought."[38] Tsujimura is careful to point out that Heidegger's thought is not simply confined within the horizon of thought, since it responds to the call of that which is beyond thought, to that which Heidegger names, adopting a term from Schelling, "the unprethinkable" (*das Unvordenkliche*) (GA 77, 146, 231/CPC, 95, 150). The difference is thus that Heidegger's thinking takes place in the in-between of thinking and the unthinkable origin of thought, whereas Zen practice is aimed at becoming that origin itself and speaking from there. Tsujimura concludes: "The 'truth of being' is the 'truth of Zen' insofar as the latter is, as 'the prior to thought', reflected in thought. The truth of being is, as it were, the shadow of the truth of Zen and not the truth of Zen itself."[39]

In short, according to Heidegger, the authentic self and being or the nothing belong together in a linguistic relation of call and response. The nothing is not only a name for being in its difference from beings, it is also the veil separating the concealed or withdrawn dimension of being from human being. Human being is held out into the nothing, is the placeholder of the nothing, but is not the nothing itself. In Zen, by contrast, the nothing is the original face of the true self; as Tsujimura puts it: "This nothing . . . is *this*, *what we ourselves* are."[40]

To be sure, many Zen masters and Kyoto School philosophers suggest that the self is in truth always a twofold self: a being and the nothing. The self is both a finite being standing in relation to other finite beings *and* the field of emptiness in which these relations take place.[41] According to Nishida, "the self is fundamentally a self-contradiction," insofar as that which transcends the self is found within the self as its own basis.[42] On the

"absolutely contradictory self-identity" of the self and this "immanently transcendent" Buddha (i.e. absolute nothingness), Nishida quotes Zen master Daitō Kokushi's famous saying: "For countless eons separated from one another, yet not divided for a moment; standing opposite one another all day long, yet not opposed for an instant."[43]

We may nevertheless conclude with Tsujimura that, while Heidegger's thought can help Zen develop its insights into a historical and critical thinking,[44] Zen can lead Heideggerian thinkers beyond or beneath the limits of thought and language to a more direct experience of their silent origin.[45]

NOTES AND REFERENCES

[1] Winfield E. Nagley, "Introduction to the symposium and reading of a letter from Martin Heidegger," *Philosophy East and West* 20.3 (1970), 221.

[2] Especially Lin Ma, *Heidegger on East-West Dialogue: Anticipating the Event* (New York: Routledge, 2008). See also my review in *Journal of the British Society for Phenomenology* 41.3 (2010), 327–9.

[3] Especially Florian Vetsch, *Martin Heideggers Angang der interkulturellen Auseinandersetzung* (Würzburg: Königshausen & Neumann, 1992); also Reiner Thurnher, "Der Rückgang in den Grund des Eigenen als Bedingung für ein Verstehen des Anderen im Denken Heideggers," in ed. Hans-Helmut Gander, *Europa und die Philosophie* (Frankfurt am Main: Vittorio Klostermann, 1993). For my own examination of this issue, see Bret W. Davis, "Heidegger's Orientations: The Step Back on the Way to Dialogue with the East," in eds Alfred Denker, Holger Zaborowski, Georg Stenger, Ryôsuke Ohashi, and Shunsuke Kadowaki, *Heidegger-Jahrbuch 7: Heidegger und das ostasiatische Denken* (Freiburg/Munich: Alber Verlag, forthcoming).

[4] Rolf Elberfeld, "Heidegger und das ostasiatische Denken: Annäherungen zwischen fremden Welten," in ed. Dieter Thomä, *Heidegger*

Handbuch: Leben-Werk-Wirkung (Stuttgart: Metzler, 2003), 469. Unless otherwise noted, all translations in this chapter are my own. I have marked "tm" where I have modified existing translations.

5 From Gadamer's personal correspondence with Graham Parkes, as related in the introduction to Graham Parkes (ed.), *Heidegger and Asian Thought* (Honolulu: University of Hawaii Press, 1987), 5, 7. This landmark collection will hereafter be cited as HAT.

6 Nagley, "Introduction to the symposium and reading of a letter from Martin Heidegger," 221. See also GA 9, 424/PA, 321, as well as Heidegger's statement quoted in Willfred Hartig, *Die Lehre des Buddha und Heidegger: Beiträge zum Ost-West-Dialog des Denkens im 20. Jahrhundert* (Konstanz: Universität Konstanz, 1997), 15–16. Hartig's book, which collects much of Heidegger's correspondence and reported statements regarding Asian philosophy, will hereafter be cited as LBH.

7 The most important collections are "Heidegger and Eastern Thought," *Philosophy East and West* 20.3 (1970); HAT; Hartmut Buchner (ed.), *Japan und Heidegger* (Sigmaringen: Thorbecke, 1989); LBH; and Denker (ed.), *Heidegger-Jahrbuch 7: Heidegger und das ostasiatische Denken*. Buchner's collection, which includes significant texts by Japanese philosophers as well as correspondence and dialogues with Heidegger, will hereafter be abbreviated as JH.

8 Above all Reinhard May, *Heidegger's Hidden Sources: East Asian Influences on His Work*, trans. with a complementary essay by Graham Parkes (New York: Routledge, 1996); and Graham Parkes, "Rising Sun over Black Forest: Heidegger's Japanese Connections," in Reinhard May, *Heidegger's Hidden Sources: East Asian Influences on His Work* (New York: Routledge, 1996), 79–117. This volume will hereafter be cited as HHS.

9 Ban Kazunori, *Kakyō kara hanarezu: Nishitani Keiji sensei tokubetsu kōgi* [Without Departing from Home: Special Lectures of Professor Nishitani Keiji] (Tokyo: Sōbunsha, 1998), 189–90, 201. Note that Chinese and Japanese names will generally be written in the order of family name first, except in cases where the Western order has been used for publications in Western languages.

10 Tomonobu Imamichi, *In Search of Wisdom: One Philosopher's Journey* (Tokyo: LTCB International Library, 2004), 123.

11 Okakura Tenshin, *Cha no hon/The Book of Tea* (a bilingual edition), trans. Asano Akira (Tokyo: Kodansha, 1998), 92–3; see also Dennis Hirota, "Okakura Tenshin's Conception of 'Being in the World,'" *Ryūkoku Daigaku Ronshū*, 478 (2011), 11, 31. I will cite the *Daodejing* and the *Zhuangzi* by chapter number. Reliable translations include *The Daodejing of Laozi*, trans. Philip J. Ivanhoe (Indianapolis: Hackett, 2003) and *Zhuangzi: The Essential Writings*, trans. Brook Ziporyn (Indianapolis: Hackett, 2009).

12 Heinrich Wiegand Petzet, *Encounters & Dialogues with Martin Heidegger 1929–1976*, trans. Parvis Emad and Kenneth Maly (Chicago: University of Chicago Press, 1993), 18.

13 See the final section of my "Heidegger's Orientations."

14 See the chapter by Yasuo Yuasa in HAT; the chapter by Ryōsuke Ōhashi in JH; Parkes's "Rising Sun over Black Forest"; and Mine Hideki, *Haideggā to nihon no tetsugaku: Watsuji Tetsurō, Kuki Shūzō, Tanabe Hajime* [Heidegger and Japanese Philosophy: Watsuji Tetsurō, Kuki Shūzō, Tanabe Hajime] (Kyoto: Minerva, 2002). While the most prevalent and sustained Asian responses to Heidegger's thought have been in Japan, there have also been important responses made by philosophers from India (such as J. L. Mehta), China (such as Chang Chung-yuan), and Korea (such as Park Chong-Hong, Ha Ki-Rak, and Cho Kah Kyung).

15 Watsuji Tetsurō, *Watsuji Tetsurō's Rinrigaku: Ethics in Japan*, trans. Yamamoto Seisaku and Robert Carter (Albany: SUNY Press, 1996).

16 Watsuji Tetsuro, *Climate and Culture: A Philosophical Study*, trans. Geoffry Bownas (New York: Greenwood Press, 1988).

17 See Mine, *Haideggā to nihon no tetsugaku*, 43, 148–52, 250, 331.

18 Graham Parkes, "Heidegger and Japanese Thought: How Much Did He Know and When Did He Know It?" in ed. Christopher McCann, *Martin Heidegger: Critical Assessments* (New York: Routledge 1992), vol. 4, 394.

19 See Ōhashi Ryōsuke, *Nishida-tetsugaku no sekai* [The World of Nishida's Philosophy] (Tokyo: Chikumashobō, 1995), 179–98; Elmar

Weinmayr, "Thinking in Transition: Nishida Kitarō and Martin Heidegger," trans. John W. M. Krummel, *Philosophy East and West*, 55.2 (2005), 232–56; and John W. M. Krummel, "The Originary Wherein: Heidegger and Nishida on 'the Sacred' and 'the Religious,'" *Research in Phenomenology*, 40 (2010), 378–407.

[20] HHS, 32–3; see also Günter Wohlfart, *Der Philosophische Daoismus: Philosophische Untersuchungen zu Grundbegriffen und komparative Studien mit besonderer Berücksichtigung des Laozi (Lao-tse)* (Köln: edition chōra, 2001), 66.

[21] Mori Hideki, "Dōka ni okeru 'mu' no tetsugaku" [The Philosophy of Nothingness in Daoist Thinkers], *Nihon no tetsugaku* [Japanese Philosophy], 5 (2004), 35–6.

[22] Already in *Being and Time* (1927) Heidegger writes of Angst as bringing Dasein face to face with "the nothingness of [death as] the possible impossibility of its existence" and of "the nothingness of the world" especially when it has "sunk into insignificance" (SZ, 265, 343; see also 187, 308). Shortly thereafter, in 1928, Heidegger writes more positively of the world as a "*nihil originarium*," that is, as "the nothing which temporalizes itself primordially" (GA 26, 272/MFL, 210). In later texts, it remains for Heidegger our mortality that opens us up to being as the nothing. "The nothing, as other than beings, is the veil of being" (GA 9, 312/PA, 238); and "death is the shrine of the nothing" (VA, 171/PLT, 176) insofar as our experience of mortality frees us from our "fallenness" in "running around amidst beings" (GA 9, 116/PA, 92) and opens us up to the no-thing of being. "Death is the purest nearness of the human to being (and therefore to the 'nothing')" (GA 71, 194).

[23] Note that the etymology of *Nichts* is similar to that of "no-thing"; see NIV, 18–19.

[24] See Wohlfart, *Der Philosophische Daoismus*, chapter 2.

[25] Quoted in Ma, *Heidegger on East-West Dialogue*, 238. See also JH, 166.

[26] Petzet, *Encounters & Dialogues with Martin Heidegger*, 180; see also GA 16, 592.

[27] William Barret, Introduction to *Selected Writings of D. T. Suzuki* (New York: Doubleday, 1996), xi.

[28] Hōseki Shinichi Hisamatsu, *Die Fülle des Nichts: Vom Wesen des Zen*, trans. Takashi Hirata and Johanna Fischer (Stuttgart: Neske, 1994).

[29] See Bret W. Davis, "Forms of Emptiness in Zen," in ed. Steven Emmanuel, *A Companion to Buddhist Philosophy* (Hoboken: Wiley-Blackwell, 2013), 190–213.

[30] Zenkei Shibayama, *The Gateless Barrier: Zen Comments on the Mumonkan* (Boston: Shambhala, 2000), 19–20.

[31] See Bret W. Davis, *Heidegger and the Will: On the Way to Gelassenheit* (Evanston: Northwestern University Press, 2007), 56–9.

[32] Nishitani Keiji, *Shūkyō to wa nanika* [What is Religion?], *Nishitani Keiji chosakushū* [Collected Works of Nishitani Keiji] (Tokyo: Sōbunsha, 1987), vol. 10, 108; Nishitani Keiji, *Religion and Nothingness*, trans. Jan Van Bragt (Berkeley: University of California Press, 1982), 96 tm.

[33] Ueda Shizuteru, *Basho: Nijū-sekai-nai-sonzai* [Place: Being-in-the-Twofold-World] (Tokyo: Kōbundō, 1992), 59; see also Davis, *Heidegger and the Will*, 57.

[34] See Bret W. Davis, "The Step Back Through Nihilism: The Radical Orientation of Nishitani Keiji's Philosophy of Zen," *Synthesis Philosophica*, 37 (2004), 139–59.

[35] JH, 159–65; Kōichi Tsujimura, "Martin Heidegger's Thinking and Japanese Philosophy," trans. Richard Capobianco and Marie Göbel, *Epoché*, 12.2 (2008), 349–57.

[36] Tsujimura Kōichi, *Haideggā ronkō* [Heidegger Studies] (Tokyo: Sōbunsha, 1971), 90–5; see also Davis, *Heidegger and the Will*, 35–8, 315 n. 14.

[37] Tsujimura, *Haideggā ronkō*, 44–5; Kōichi Tsujimura, "Die Wahrheit des Seins und das absolute Nichts," trans. Daisuke Shimizu and Ursula Baatz, in ed. Ryōsuke Ōhashi, *Die Philosophie der Kyōto-Schule*, 2nd edition (Freiburg/Munich: Alber Verlag, 2010), 414.

[38] Tsujimura Kōichi, *Haideggā no shisaku* [Heidegger's Thought] (Tokyo: Sōbunsha, 1991), 203.

[39] Tsujimura, *Haideggā ronkō*, 44–8; Tsujimura, "Die Wahrheit des Seins und das absolute Nichts," 413–18; see also Tsujimura, *Haideggā no shisaku*, 359–60.

40 Kōichi Tsujimura, "Ereignis und Shōki: Zur Übersetzung eines heideggerschen Grundwortes ins Japanische," in JH, 82.

41 Nishitani, *Shūkyō to wa nanika*, 170–1, 178, 186; Nishitani, *Religion and Nothingness*, 151–2, 158, 166.

42 *Nishida Kitarō zenshū* [Complete Works of Nishida Kitarō] (Tokyo: Iwanami: 1987–9), vol. 11, 418, 433, 445.

43 Ibid., 399.

44 JH, 165; Tsujimura, "Martin Heidegger's Thinking and Japanese Philosophy," 355; also Tsujimura, *Haidegga ronkō*, 53; Tsujimura, "Die Wahrheit des Seins und das absolute Nichts," 425.

45 Tsujimura, *Haidegga ronkō*, 47–8; Tsujimura, "Die Wahrheit des Seins und das absolute Nichts," 417–18. On the silent origin of language, see GA 65, 36, 79; GA 12, 144, 241–2/OWL, 52–3, 122.

58

HEIDEGGER AND LATIN AMERICAN PHILOSOPHY
Alejandro Arturo Vallega

The reception of Heidegger's thought in Latin America is inseparable from the unfolding of Latin American philosophy.[1] In order to understand the influence of the German philosopher in this development a few historical remarks will serve as a fitting introduction. With the arrival of the conquistadors to the Americas follows the colonization of indigenous cultures and their understanding of existence, through genocide, violence, and exclusion of their thought. At the same time, with the colonization of the Americas and the invention of its other appears the modern European mind. Thus, modern rationality and colonialism appear as inseparable aspects of a single project, the modern revolution or the enlightenment, that is, the development of a single system of economic trade and of production and control of knowledge throughout the world. In light of this entanglement, to speak of Latin American philosophy, and the reception of Heidegger within it, is nothing other than to engage the complex relation of Western thought and Latin American thought in their mutual and yet distinct development. While the Americas participated actively in the development of the enlightenment, the very thought of freedom led to movements in the

nineteenth century that culminated with the independence of most of the Americas from Spain and with the founding of new nations. These movements were philosophically founded on the positivism of such figures as Comte and Spencer. Their ideal of progress through rationalist calculation and growth is well captured in the motto that still appears on the Brazilian flag "Order and Progress." By the beginning of the twentieth century positivism had proven to be a failure in Latin America, and a new generation of intellectuals appeared who rose against positivism and with the aim to developing a thinking grounded on the concrete reality of the Latin American situation. This group of intellectuals known as "the founders" were influenced at first by Bergson's ideas concerning vitalism, by Schopenhauer, Hegel, and later by Ortega y Gasset and Max Scheler. Following the emphasis on life and existentialism, they and the following generation then took up the thought of Husserl, Dilthey, Hartmann, and Martin Heidegger.

Heidegger's influence becomes directly apparent from the 1930s on, through the work of some of the main figures in the development of a situated Latin American thought, whose work was inspired by phenomenology, existentialism, and Heidegger's fundamental ontology, and who went to study with Heidegger. This turn had been prepared and introduced to a great extent by Ortega y Gasset's lectures on phenomenology and eventually on Heidegger's fundamental ontology during his visits to Argentina in 1916 and in 1928, and by the founding of his famous journal "Revista de Occidente" in 1923. Furthermore, the Spanish philosopher Javier Xubiri, who had been a student of Ortega y Gasset and of Heidegger in 1929, would publish in 1932 in one of the first issues of Victoria Ocampo's historical journal *SUR*, the first translation of Heidegger's work to appear in Spanish, Heidegger's "What is Metaphysics?"[2]

Both Carlos Astrada and Alberto Wagner de Reyna studied with Heidegger at the end of the 1920s and in the early 1930s. Carlos Astrada returned to Argentina in 1932 and in 1933 published *El juego existencial* (*The Existential Game*), followed in 1936 by *Idealismo fenomenológico y metafísica existencial* (*Phenomenological Idealism and Existential Metaphysics*).[3] Astrada follows Heidegger´s existential-analytic of *Dasein* in his work, but he criticizes Heidegger's emphasis on the question of being rather than on *Dasein*'s concrete situation. This marks his turn towards Marxism: Astrada develops a synthesis of the thinkers in which he recognizes the praxis that situates *Dasein* without abandoning Heidegger's existential insight. This synthesis finds its strongest form in *El mito Gaucho* (*The Gaucho Myth*).[4] Astrada will continue throughout his career his dialogue with Heidegger's works and their dissemination in the Spanish-speaking world. In 1943 appears his book *Temporalidad* (*Temporality*).[5] In 1949 he publishes the collection of essays *Martin Heideggers Einfluss auf die Wissenschaften* (Bern, 1949), and *Ser,*

humanismo, existencialismo (*Una aproximacion a Heidegger*) (*Being, Humanism, and Existentialism* (*an engagement with Heidegger*)).[6] In 1948, in the first issue of the journal *Cuadernos de Filosofía*, appears Astrada's translation of "The Essence of Truth,"[7] and in 1952/53 in the same journal appears his translation of "Plato's Doctrine of Truth."[8] These works are followed by two essays: "La etapa actual del último Heidegger: Que significa pensar?" (The current stage of the latest Heidegger: What does Thinking Mean?) and "Hölderlin 'los dioses': un paralelo con Heidegger y el humanismo" (Hölderlin "the Gods": a Parallel with Heidegger and Humanism).[9] In 1963 appears another direct encounter with Heidegger's thought in his book *Existencialismo y crisis de la filosofía* (*Existentialism and The Crisis of Philosophy*).[10] In 1968 Astrada dedicates his book *Diálogos* (*Dialogues*) to Heidegger.[11] His proximity to Heidegger is also evidenced by Heidegger's invitation of Astrada to his seminar in 1970 to deliver a lecture titled: "Concerning the Possibility of an historical-existential praxis."[12] In spite of his turn from existentialism to Marxism, Astrada's engagement with his teacher´s work continues to the year of the Argentine philosopher's death in Buenos Aires, with the publication in 1970 of *Martin Heidegger: de la analítica ontológica a la dimensión dialéctica* (*Martin Heidegger: From the Ontological Analytic to the Dialectic Dimension*).[13]

Alberto Wagner Reyna studied with Heidegger in 1935/36, and then went on to complete his dissertation in Peru: Heidegger's Fundamental Ontology, which appeared in book form the following year under the title *La ontologia fundamental de Heidegger: su motivo y significación* (*Heidegger's Fundamental Ontology: Its Themes and Significance*).[14] Out of his analysis of Heidegger's thought Wagner Reyna went on to publish *La filosofía en Iberoamérica*, in which the Peruvian philosopher sought to engage the Latin American situation on its grounding difficulties.[15] In 1954 he published his important work *Destino y vocación de Iberoamérica* (*Destiny and Vocation of Iberoamerica*).[16] In 1958 Wagner Reyna publishes his translation of "Die Zeit des Weltbildes" under the title "La época de la imagen del mundo" (The Epoch of the World-Image). His work on Heidegger will continue to his final days, with the publication of *Ensayos en torno a Heidegger* (*Essays on Heidegger*) in 2000.[17] As another major figure in Heidegger's reception in Latin America has pointed out to the present author, the Venezuelan philosopher Ernesto Mayz Vallenilla, Wagner Reyna (as Astrada) was a major force that brought many others to Heidegger's thought. Walter Reyna recognized the opening provided by Heidegger's work on the ontological sense of historicity (*Geschichtlichkeit*) and a hermeneutics that could lead to a meta-politics that would give articulation to Latin American existence in its specific senses of being. It would be out of his engagement with the work of Walter Reyna and other interpreters of Heidegger that Leopoldo Zea, one of the most important philosophers in the history of Latin American philosophy, would come to call for a Latin American philosophy and no more (*una filosofía latinoamericana sin más*).[18] In terms of this thematic, one must also consider the important work of the Mexican philosopher Samuel Ramos in his famous work *El perfil del hombre y la cultura de México* (*The Profile of Man and Culture of Mexico*).[19] Thereafter Ramos turns to the question of aesthetics. In 1950 he publishes *Filosofía de la vida artística*,[20] and the year of his death appear his translations of

Heidegger's "Hölderlin and the Essence of Poetry" (1936) and "The Origin of the Work of Art" (1934–6).[21]

Another major figure in the reception of Heidegger in Latin America is the Spanish philosopher José Gaos, who in 1938 immigrated to Mexico escaping Franco's regime and became a leading figure in the development of Mexican and Latin American philosophy as a professor at the UNAM in Mexico City. His courses were the inspiration for the next generation of Latin American philosophers. Among his courses is his legendary seminar on *Being and Time*, which he led for ten years, from 1942 to 1952, and in which participated many of those who would become major figures in Latin American thought, including Leopoldo Zea. In 1945 Gaos published *2 exclusivas del hombre, la mano y el tiempo* (Man's Two Exclusives, the Hand and Time).[22] And in 1951 he would publish his famous translation of *Being and Time*,[23] accompanied by his close interpretation of it, titled *Introduccíon al Ser y Tiempo de Heidegger* (*Introduction to Heidegger's Being and Time*).[24] Also worth mentioning is his essay "Heidegger 1956 y 1957."[25] As Enrique Dussel has pointed out, the publication of Heidegger's *Being and Time* in Spanish was itself a major turning point for the development of a philosophy situated in Latin American experience and history. Along with his teaching and interpretation of Heidegger's thought, Gaos would launch a project for a Latin American thought born from the Latin American situation. Already in 1941 Gaos taught a seminar at the UNAM titled, "America en los origenes del mundo moderno y los llamados historiadores de las Indias" (America in the Origins of the Modern World and the So-called Historians of the Indias), and in 1952 he would publish *En torno a la filosofía mexicana*.[26] Ultimately it was Gaos' interest in Latin American philosophy that spurred many of the important figures in the next generation of Latin American thinkers to seek the articulation of its distinct characteristics.

The Argentine philosopher Luis Juan Guerrero closed his studies with Heidegger in 1927 with a dissertation titled "*Die Entstehung einer allgemeinen Wertlehre in der Philosophie der Gegenwart*" (Marburg, 1927). Following his studies Guerrero takes a phenomenological and existentialist approach to philosophy that will eventually lead him to his major work on aesthetics. In 1939 he publishes *Psicología*.[27] In 1942, together with Francisco Romero, he publishes a collection of text from German philosophy aimed to renew the interpretation of German philosophy in the new generation of Latin American thinkers: *Filosofía alemana traducida al español* (*German Philosophy in a Spanish Translation*) (Buenos Aires, 1942). In 1945 in order to become a professor in Buenos Aires he publishes *Tres temas de filosofía en las entrañas del Facundo* (*Three Philosophical Themes in the Guts of Facundo*).[28] In 1949 he presented at the first national congress of philosophy in Argentina two works that mark his future path: "Escenas de la vida estética" (Scenes of Esthetic Life) and "Torso de la vida estética actual" (The Figure of Contemporary Esthetic Life).[29] The years that follow will see the publication of his major works: *Que es la Belleza?* (*What is Beauty?*) (1954); *Ética* (1955); *Estética operatoria en sus tres direcciones I. Revelación y acogimiento de la obra de arte* (*Operatory Esthetics in its Three Directions: Revelation and Reception of the Work of Art*) (1956); *Estética operatoria en sus tres direcciones II. Creación y ejecución de la obra de arte* (*Operatory Esthetics in its Three Directions: Creation and Execution of the Work of Art*) (1956); *and Estética operatoria en sus tres direcciones III. Promoción y requerimiento de la obra de arte* (*Operatory Esthetics in its Three Directions: Promotion and Appropriation of the Work of Art*) (1967).[30] Guerrero's works on esthetics are developed out of Heidegger's sense of the work of art and go further to engage Merleau-Ponty's esthetic thought. Throughout his work Guerrero is clear about the dangers and possibilities for ethics inherent in esthetic experience, and the phenomenological and existential paths that is required for taking up such issues.

Danilo Cruz Vélez studied with Heidegger in1951, and upon his return to his native country, Colombia, founded a landmark group of studies on *Being and Time*, that eventually went on to work on Heidegger's "The Essence of Ground" and "The Essence of Truth." From these years of study results one of his most important books: *Filosofía sin supuestos: From Husserl to Heidegger*.[31] In this work the Colombian philosopher interprets Heidegger's thought as a radicalization of Husserl's understanding of the phenomenological constitution of the knower and the known. For Cruz Vélez, as for many Latin American interpreters of Heidegger's thought, the key moment that happens as thinking is situated in its living context rather than on ideal structures. In 1989 appeared his *El mito del rey filósofo: Platón, Marx Heidegger* (*The Myth of the Philosopher King: Plato, Marx, Heidegger*).[32] His concern with the Latin American situation and with the development of a new humanism appears clearly in *Ortega y Gasset y el destino de América Latina* (*Ortega y Gasset and the Destiny of Latin America*). [33]

The concern with the being of Latin Americans, technology and technique, is the central spurring point for the work of the Venezuelan philosopher Ernesto

Mayz Vallenilla. Mayz Vallenilla studied in Gottingen and Freiburg and was closely acquainted with his teacher Martin Heidegger, who he first met in 1950 and later on visited in the Black Forest. Mayz Vallenilla founded his work on the analysis of Dasein and on the problem of technology as developed by Heidegger. His first work along these themes was *El problema de América: Apuntes para una filosofía americana* (*The Problem of America: Notes for a Latin American Philosophy*).[34] This work is a phenomenological analysis of the being of Latin American *Dasein* in its distinct temporality (given the historical origination of his/her consciousness in the arrival of the conquistadors). He then went on to publish in 1960 *Ontologia del conocimiento* (*Ontology of Knowledge*).[35] Again, taking on Heidegger's work he published *El problema de la Nada en Kant* (*Kant and the Problem of Nothingness*).[36] His concern with the Latin American situation and the role of technology and the possibility of a new humanism in light of Heidegger's thought as a path for interpreting these issues marks his lengthy career, and is apparent in such works as: *Del hombre y su alienación* (*Of Man and his Alienation*);[37] *Técnica y humanismo* (*Technique and Humanism*);[38] *Latinoamérica en la encrucijada de la técnica* (*Latin America at the Crossing of Technique*).[39] His most important later work is *Fundamentos de la meta-técnica* (*The Foundations of Meta-technics*).[40]

Martin Heidegger's work has a founding role for the first philosophy to be distinctly identified with Latin America as its origin and sense, namely the philosophy of liberation. This movement begins in Argentina in the early 1970s, but already in 1968 its most widely known founding figure, Enrique Dussel, offers a course on Heidegger in Mendoza, Argentina. The famous course was titled: *Lecciones de introducción a la filosofía, de antropología filosófica*.[41] The course gives a close reading of *Being and Time*'s *Dasein* analysis as the basis for the unfolding of what will become Dussel's philosophy of liberation, putting emphasis on the idea of a philosophy that arises from *Dasein*'s concrete being-in-the-world. In other words, in this course Dussel interprets Heidegger's work as an anthropological fundamental ontology. He writes: "Man is called by his vocation (*vocare* means 'to call'), by his own pro-ject. This vocation is but the way in which man 'comprehends' himself in the world. . . ."[42] Later he explains, "It is here that in our case philosophy appears, 'anthropological philosophy.' This requires that we overcome the naivete of accepting our very being in the world as something obvious, all of it from the essence of man to the axioms of science . . . 'philosophy will accomplish a more fundamental position . . . a hermeneutical position.' It is here that Heidegger's proposition is situated."[43] Then he concludes:

What we call "philosophical anthropology" is a *fundamental ontological* consideration of man. That is, the sciences will arrive at their unity (as well as the university), not by a synthesis more or less composed accidentally (that is *a posteriori*), but through its foundation, from the root from which they emerge (that is *a priori*). The root from which the sciences arise is man-*already*-in the-world.[44]

Dussel will radicalize Heidegger's insight by turning to Paul Ricoeur and to Levinas' critique of Heidegger. Thus, *Dasein*'s being-in-the-world will become the being-in-the-world of one who tells stories and makes sense of the world, and this being is understood not from the view of Western thought but with Levina's insight, as the other, the excluded, the poor, the exploited. However, Heidegger's insight, the situating of philosophical thought in its originary living situation is a basic pillar for the development of Dussel's work, and for the philosophy of liberation as well.

Another figure present at the very beginnings of the philosophy of liberation was Rodolfo Kusch.[45] Kusch's thought arises in departure from Heidegger's *Dasein* analysis and he is very critical of the German philosopher's later thought. He sees Heidegger's later thought as a turn toward ontological rather than following an anthropological-philosophical path. By contrast, Kusch's own path leads him to think phenomenologically the anthropological reality of indigenous Americans. Indeed, he turns to a concrete analysis that aims to articulate the being of the excluded, forgotten lives of deep America, as the title of his famous book *América profunda* indicates.[46] Kusch thinks out of the *estar* (the concrete existence of the indigenous ways of being in the world) rather than from seeking a general sense of *ser* (being) in light of which an understanding of their existence may occur.[47] His work has begun to gain the attention of North American philosophers, particularly with the translation into English of one of his major works, *El pensamiento indígena y popular en América* under the title *Indigenous and Popular Thinking in America* (*Latin America Otherwise*).[48] We must also mention along with Kusch another major figure in the development of the philosophy of liberation Juan Carlos Escannone, and his critique of Heidegger out of the perspective of the Theology of Liberation, always pointing to Heidegger's turn away from a thinking out of concrete singularity and difference the German philosopher makes possible with his work. Scannone develops in his work a hermeneutical theology of liberation.[49]

The contemporary figures in Latin American philosophy that have continued the legacy of those who studied with Heidegger and brought his thought to bear on the unfolding of Latin American philosophy are as many and bring forth as many complicated issues and new openings for development as is the case with the German philosopher's reception in Europe or North America. Some salient figures must be at least named. The Argentine philosopher Dina V. Picotti C. in departure from Heidegger's later thought in *Contributions to Philosophy* has developed a thinking that engages issues of race and identity in Argentina and Latin America. This unique and powerful work in contemporary philosophy follows her crucial contribution to the reception of Heidegger in Latin America, her precise and clear translation of Heidegger's *Contribution to Philosophy* into Spanish, as well as her translation of *Besinnung*.[50] At the same time contemporary interpreters of Heidegger's have not failed to recognize and problematize his involvement with national socialism. This was already an issue that Pablo Neruda would emphasize in his protests about the publication of Heidegger's works in the famous journal *SUR*.[51] In 1987 appeared *Heidegger et le nazisme* by the exiled Chilean philosopher Victor Farías. This work will open a world-wide discussion concerning the issue.[52] Pablo Feinmann, the Argentine philosopher and writer published his novel *La sombra de Heidegger* in 2005, another work that invited much discussion concerning Heidegger's figure in relationship to Latin American thought.[53] The question of the relationship of Heidegger's thought and National Socialism is distinctly acute in Latin America given the identification in Latin America of his thought as a whole with nationalist populist governments and fascist military regimes. At the same time, as already noted above, Heidegger's thought for a situated thinking invites for the developments of antifascist and diversifying movements like that of the philosophy of liberation. Moreover, with the end of many military dictatorships in the 1990's the question of the role of history in the development of national identities, communities, and subjects becomes central. Again appears existentialism and among the main figures Heidegger in the development of Latin American thought, this time as the call for a hermeneutics that recognizes history and thinks through it, rather than attempting to ignore the violence, exclusion, and destruction of society in the name of focusing on a projection of development and economic growth that must look ahead and forget the past as the only path for the future of Latin America. As a result Heidegger becomes an important figure for rethinking the Latin American situation in light of its hard and dark history of fascist capitalist and neoliberal regimes.[54]

Among later philosophers working on Heidegger appears another crucial figure, the Chilean Eduardo Rivera, a student of Hans Georg-Gadamer and Zubiri, who published a new translation of *Being and Time* in 1997. Thereafter he has followed with an extensive two-volume commentary.[55] The work being done on Heidegger today is too extensive to begin to cover it, but I must mention, although of previous generations, Jorge Acevedo Guerra's work on Heidegger and Ortega in Chile as well as his later work on Heidegger and Technology and, the Venezuelan Alberto Rosales and his work on the ontological difference.[56] Finally I close by mentioning the work of the philosopher Pablo Oyarzún, who has made a fine contribution to the reception of Heidegger in Latin America with respect to the political issues mentioned above with

his little book from 2005 *Entre Heidegger y Celan (Between Heidegger and Celan)*, in which through the tension of reading Celan's poetry and Heidegger's work at the limit of language and sense he explores philosophically the depth and difficulty that affords us the work of Martin Heidegger.[57]

NOTES AND REFERENCES

[1] My discussion will not cover Heidegger's reception in Brazil, which is entirely another fecund field for investigation. Also, I have covered only the principal figures of a history that is too extensive and that reaches to the present in its reception of Heidegger's work. I have based this essay on a previous article: Alejandro Vallega, "Die Heidegger-Rezeption in Südamerika," *Heidegger-Jahrbuch* (Heidegger and Nietzsche), vol. 3 (2006), Verlag Karl Alber Freiburg, Germany.

[2] Along with the translation appeared an essay entitled, "Martin Heidegger before the Shadow of Dostoiewsky" by the poet Benjamín Fondane.

[3] Carlos Astrada, *El juego existencial* (Buenos Aires: Babel, 1933); *Idealismo fenomenológico y metafísica existencial* (Buenos Aires: UBA, 1936). Throughout this chapter I will provide English translation citations when available. The reader should note that almost all of the works on Heidegger from Latin America have never been translated into English.

[4] Carlos Astrada, *El mito gaucho* (Buenos Aires: Ediciones Cruz Azul, 1948. Second edition, 1964).

[5] Carlos Astrada, *Temporalidad* (Buenos Aires: Cultura Viva, 1943).

[6] Carlos Astrada, *Ser, humanismo, "existencialismo". Una aproximación a Heidegger* (Buenos Aires: Kairós, 1949).

[7] Carlos Astrada, "De la esencia de la verdad," *Cuadernos de Filosofía*, Numero Uno, Buenos Aires, 1948. Cuadernos de Filosofía was founded by Carlos Astrada and is now in its third epoch (Obras de Martin Heidegger: según el plan de la Gesamtausgabe, available online at: www.heideggeriana.com.ar/bibiliografia/

gesamtausgabe_1.htm) One of the best sites for information concerning the translations of Heidegger's works into Spanish and for information about Heidegger in Latin America is Heidegger en Castellano, a website kept by Jaime Potel: www.heideggeriana.com.ar/

8 Carlos Astrada, "La doctrina de Platón a cerca de la verdad," *Cuadernos de Filosofía*, 10, 11, 12, Buenos Aires, 1952–3.

9 Carlos Astrada, "La etapa actual del último Heidegger: Que significa pensar?" in *Cuadernos de Filofofía* (Buenos Aires), Numbers 7–9 (1952). "Hölderlin los dioses': un paralelo con Heidegger y el humanismo" in *Aletheia*, Año 1, números 4–5 (1957).

10 Carlos Astrada, *Existencialismo y crisis de la filosofía* (Buenos Aires: Editorial Devenir, 1963).

11 Carlos Astrada, *Diálogos* (Universidad de Puerto Rico) año V, números 11–12 (abril–septiembre, 1968).

12 Original Spanish title: "Sobre la posibilidad de una práctica histórico-existencial."

13 Carlos Astrada, *Martin Heidegger: de la analítica ontológica a la dimensión dialéctica* (Buenos Aires: Editor Juarez S.A., 1970).

14 Alberto Wagner Reyna, *La ontologia fundamental de Heidegger: su motivo y significación* (Buenos Aires: Losada, 1939). The significance of this work for the reception of Heidegger in Latin America is evidenced by its second and third editions in 1945 and in Brazil *Dois problemas na filosofia de Heidegger* (Rio de Janeiro: Imprensa Nacional, 1945).

15 *La filosofía de Iberoamérica* (Lima: Soc. Peruana de Filosofía, 1949).

16 Alberto Wagner Reyna, *Destino y vocación de Iberoamérica* (Madrid: Inst. De Cultura Hispánica, 1954).

17 Alberto Wagner Reyna, *Ensayos en torno a Heidegger* (Lima: PUCP-FCE, 2000).

18 Leopoldo Zea, *La Filosofía Americana como Filosofía Sin Más* (Mexico: Siglo XXI Editores, 2010) *El pensamiento filosófico latinoamericano, del Caribe y "latino" [1300–2000]* ed. Enrique Dussel, Eduardo Mendieta, Carmen Bohórquez (DF, Mexico: Siglo XXI Editores, 2009), 839.

19 Samuel Ramos in his famous work *El perfíl del hombre y la cultura de México*, 2nd edn (Buenos Aires: Espasa-Calpe, 1952).

20 Samuel Ramos, *Filosofía de la vida artística* (Buenos Aires: Espasa-Calpe, 1950).

21 The translation appeared as a book titled *Arte y Poesia* (Buenos Aires: Fondo de cultura económica, 1958).

22 José Gaos, *2 exclusivas del hombre: la mano y el tiempo* (Mexico: Universidad de Nuevo Leon, 1945).

23 Martin Heidegger, *El Ser y el Tiempo*, trans. José Gaos (Buenos Aires: Fondo de cultura económica, 1951).

24 José Gaos, *Introducción a El Ser y El Tiempo* (Madrid: Fondo de cultura económica, 1951).

25 "Heidegger 1956 y 1957," *Dianoia*, 4 (1958), 354–68.

26 José Gaos, *En torno a una filosofía mexicana* (México: Porrúa y Obregón, 1952). Republished in 1980.

27 L. J. Guerrero, *Psicología*, (Buenos Aires: Losada, 1939).

28 L. J. Guerrero, *Tres temas de filosofía en las entrañas del Facundo* (La Plata: Universidad Nacional de La Plata, 1945/Buenos Aires: Docencia, 1981).

29 L. J. Guerrero, "Escenas de la vida estética," en *Actas del Primer Congreso Nacional de Filosofía*, UN Cuyo, Mendoza, 1 (1949) 221–41; "Torso de la vida estética actual," en en *Actas del Primer Congreso Nacional de Filosofía*, UN Cuyo, Mendoza, 3, 1466–74.

30 L. J. Guerrero,¿*Qué es la belleza?*, (Buenos Aires: Columba, 1954). L. J. Guerrero, *Ética* (Mimeo, Buenos Aires, 1955). L. J. Guerrero, *Estética operatoria en sus tres direcciones I. Revelación y acogimiento de la obra de arte* (Buenos Aires: Losada, 1956). *Estética operatoria en sus tres direcciones II. Creación y ejecución de la obra de arte* (Buenos Aires: Losada, 1956). *Estética operatoria en sus tres direcciones III. Promoción y requerimiento de la obra de arte* (Buenos Aires: Losada, 1967).

31 D. Cruz Vélez, *Filosofía sin supuestos. De Husserl a Heidegge* (Buenos Aires: Sudamericana, 1970).

32 D. Cruz Vélez, *El mito del rey filósofo* (Bogotá: Planeta, 1989).

33 D. Cruz Vélez, *Ortega y Gasset y el destino de América Latina* (Buenos Aires: Fundación Banco de Boston, Institución Ortega y Gasset, 1983).

34 Ernesto Mayz Vallenilla, *El problema de América: Apuntes para una filosofía americana* (Caracas: Universidad Central de Venezuela, 1957). *El problema de América* (Caracas: Universidad Central de Venezuela, 1959/ Caracas: Universidad Central de Venezuela, 1969/Caracas: Equinoccio (Universidad Simón Bolívar), 1992).

35 Ernesto Mayz Vallenilla, *Ontologia del conocimiento* (Caracas: Universidad Central de Venezuela, 1960).

36 Ernesto Mayz Vallenilla, *El problema de la Nada en Kant* (Madrid: Editorial Revista de Occidente, 1965/Caracas: Monte Ávila Editores Latinoamericana, 1992; in German: Pfüllingen: Verlag Günther Neske, 1974; in French: Paris: L'Harmattan, 2000).

37 Ernesto Mayz Vallenilla, *Del hombre y su alienación* (Caracas: Instituto Nacional de Cultura y Bellas Artes, 1966/Caracas: Monte Ávila Editores, 1969)

38 Ernesto Mayz Vallenilla, *Técnica y humanismo* (Caracas: Universidad Simón Bolívar, 1972).

39 Ernesto Mayz Vallenilla, *Latinoamérica en la encrucijada de la técnica* (Caracas: Universidad Simón Bolívar, 1976).

40 Ernesto Mayz Vallenilla, *Fundamentos de la meta-técnica* (Caracas: Monte Ávila Editores, 1990/Barcelona: Gedisa, 1993; in Italian: Naples: Istituto per gli Studi Filosofici, 1994; in French: Paris: L'Harmattan, 1997; in German: Berlin: Verlag Peter Lang, 2002; in Portuguese: Lisbon: Edições Colibri, 2004) Published in English under the title, *The Foundations of Meta-technics*, trans. Carl Mitcham (Maryland: University Press of America, 2004).

41 Enrique Dussel, *Lecciones de introducción a la filosofía, de antropología filosófica* (unpublished text, Consejo Nacional de Ciencias Sociales, 1996–2001). From here on sited as LAF, followed by page number.

42 LAF, 38. My translation.

43 Ibid., 49. My translation.

44 Ibid., 50. My translation.

45 He is present and active in the first meetings that give rise to the philosophical movement (at the II Congreso Nacional de Filosofía en Alta Gracia, Córdoba in 1971, and participated in the academic week concerning Latin American thought that took place at the Universidad del Salvador, San Miguel, 1970–3). My following observations about Kusch are founded in part on the fine research done by the contemporary Argentine philosopher Dina V. Picotti C. (see her article on Kusch titled, "Rodolfo Kusch: aportes de una antropología americana," *El pensamiento latinoamericano del siglo XX ante la condición humana* (2003 Coordinador General Pablo Guadarrama González. Coordinador General para Argentina, Hugo Biagini. El pensamiento latinoamericano del siglo XX ante la condición humana. Versión digital, iniciada en junio de 2004, a cargo de José Luis Gómez-Martínez). www.ensayistas.org/critica/generales/C H/argentina/kusch.htm

46 Rodolfo Kusch, *América profunda*, 1st edn (Buenos Aires: Hachette, 1962); 2nd edn (Buenos Aires: Bonum, 1975); and 3rd edn (Buenos Aires: Bonum,1986).

47 Among the many books and writings by Kusch appear his principle works: *La seducción de la barbarie-Análisis herético de un continente mestizo* (Rosario, Argentina: Edit. Fundación Ross, with Prólogues for the 1st and 2nd edn by F. J. Solero and C. Cullen, 1983). *El pensamiento indígena y popular en América* (3rd edn, Buenos Aires: Hachette, 1977). *La negación en el pensamiento popular* (Buenos Aires: Cimarrón, 1975). *Geocultura del hombre americano*, (Buenos Aires: F.García Cambeiro, 1976). *Indios, porteños y dioses* (1st edn, Buenos Aires: Stilcograff, 1966; 2nd edn, 1994). *Esbozo de una antropología filosófica americana* (S.Antonio dePadua: Castañeda, 1978).

48 Rodolfo Kusch, *El pensamiento indígena y popular en América* (3rd edn, Buenos Aires: Hachette, 1977). *Indigenous and Popular Thinking in America* (*Latin America Otherwise*), trans. Maria Lugones and Joshua Price (Durham: Duke University Press, 2010).

49 Among his works are *Religion y nuevo pensamiento: Hacia una filosofía de la religion para nuestro teimpo desde American Latina* (Mexico: Anthropos, 2005); *Discernimiento filosófico de la acción y pasión histórica* (Mexico: Anthropos, 2009).

50 Martin Heidegger, *Aportes a la Filosofía Acerca del Evento*, trans. Dina V. Picotti C. (Buenos Aires: Editorial Biblos, 2003).

Testimony to the excellence of her work is that her translation was one of the few works at times consulted during the translation of Heidegger's work into English (Martin Heidegger, *Contributions to Philosophy (of the Event.)*, trans. Richard Rojcewicz and Daniela Vallega-Neu (Bloomington: Indiana University Press, 2012). *Besinnung* (GA 66) appeared as *Meditaciones* (Buenos Aires: Biblos, 2006).

[51] *This America of Ours: The Letters of Gabriela Mistral and Victoria Ocampo*, trans. Elisabeth Horan and Doris Meyer (Austine: University of Texas Press, 2003), 224–6.

[52] Victor Farías, *Heidegger et le nazisme* (Paris: Editions verdier, 1987), then translated into German under the title *Heidegger und der Nationalsozialismus* (Frankfurt am Main: Fischer Verlag, 1989), and into English as *Heidegger and Nazism* (Philadelphia: Temple University Press, 1989).

[53] Pablo Feinmann, *La sombra de Heidegger* (Buenos Aires: Seix Barral, 2005).

[54] The place of Heidegger's thought in contemporary Latin American philosophy has also been complicated by the fine work on decolonial philosophy by the Puerto Rican thinker Nelson Maldonado-Torres. See Nelson Maldonado-Torres, "On the Coloniality of Being: Contributions to the Development of a Concept," *Cultural Studies*, 21.2–3 (March/ May 2007), 240–70. In a move similar to Dussel's Maldonado-Torres recognizes Heidegger's opening for other ways of thinking and then turns to Levinas and Fanon.

[55] Martin Heidegger, *Ser y Tiempo*, trans. Jorge Eduardo Rivera (Santiago, Chile: Editorial Universitaria, 1997). Jorge Eduardo Rivera y María Teresa Stuven, *Comentario a Ser y Tiempo de Martin Heidegger*, vol. 1, Introducción (Santiago, Chile: Ediciones de la Universidad Católica de Chile, 2008). Jorge Eduardo Rivera y María Teresa Stuven, *Comentario a Ser y Tiempo de Martin Heidegger*, vol. 2, Primera Sección (Santiago, Chile: Ediciones de la Universidad Católica de Chile, 2010).

[56] Jorge Acevedo Guerra, *Heidegger y la época técnica* (Santiago, Chile: Editorial Universitaria, 1999). Alberto Rosales, *Transzendenz und Differenz* (Den Haag, Holanda: Phaenomenologica vol.33, Martinus Nijhoff, 1970)

[57] Pablo Oyarzun Robles, *Entre Heidegger y Celan* (Santiago, Chile: Metales Pesados, 2005). On the question of the limits of language and sense see the article by Juan Manuel Garrido "Una pisca de sentido: acerca de Entre Celan y Heidegger de Pablo Oyarzún," in *Revista de Filosofía*, 64 (2008), 79–88 (Facultad de Filosofía y Humanidades, Universidad de Chile.) For further reading in more detail see "Crónica de la recepción de Heidegger en hispanoamérica," *Revista Santander*, 1 (2006), 102–25.

59

HEIDEGGER'S *BLACK NOTEBOOKS*: NATIONAL SOCIALISM, ANTISEMITISM, AND THE HISTORY OF BEING

Eric S. Nelson*

This new supplementary chapter to the paperback edition of the Bloomsbury Companion to Heidegger *offers a concise critical overview of the recently published* Black Notebooks. *The chapter examines in particular: (1) the* Black Notebooks *in the context of Heidegger's early political engagement on behalf of the National Socialist regime and his growing ambivalence toward its political ideology and tactics; (2) his limited "critique" of National Socialism and its biologically based racism for the sake of his own ontologically oriented ethnocentric vision of the historical uniqueness of the German people and Germany's central role in Europe as a contested "land of the middle" situated between West and East, technological modernity and the Asiatic. The* Notebooks *and related writings reveal that Heidegger remained committed to the vision of history that led to his initial engagement on behalf of National Socialism even as he increasingly criticized it as a missed opportunity for a decisive transformation of history. Heidegger gave National Socialism a derivative role in his narrative of the history of being that concludes in technological modernity after 1935; he relativized it without adequately considering the historical uniqueness of its totalitarian structures and practices and its mass-production of death. Heidegger formulated his own ontologically and geopolitically informed version of ethnocentrism during this period that was intimately interwoven with his understanding of the "history of being." This vision was intensified during and after the Second World War rather than abandoned. Heidegger perceived no difference between the Shoah and the Allied bombing, defeat, and occupation of Germany. Heidegger's postwar philosophy (of home, history, and technology) is shaped by, and remained complicit with, his thinking during this decisive period.*

INTRODUCTION

The controversies surrounding Heidegger's involvement with National Socialism began soon after his early support of the movement and his implementation of its university politics as rector of the University of Freiburg. Adolf Hitler was appointed German Chancellor on January 30, 1933 and Heidegger officially joined the party on May 1, 1933. Heidegger would only serve as rector for one year, from April 21, 1933 to April 23, 1934. It was an eventful year in which the National Socialist policy of *Gleichschaltung* ("coordination"), the subordination of the educational system and all other dimensions of public and private life to party power was enacted across German society. Heidegger's engagement on behalf of National Socialism came as a surprise to his contemporaries, as *Being and Time* and his other writings and lecture-courses had not been understood as supporting fascism. Criticisms of Heidegger's thinking in connection to his politics began in the surprised reaction of his students (e.g. Hannah Arendt, Karl Löwith, and Herbert Marcuse) and young scholars who had been inspired by his philosophy; most strikingly is the case of Emmanuel Levinas who had enthusiastically embraced Heidegger's thought after encountering it in 1929 and criticized the nexus between National Socialism and Heideggerian ontology in "Some Reflections on the Philosophy of Hitlerism" (1934) and *Of Escape* (1935).[1]

The character and scope of Heidegger's commitment to National Socialism has been a reoccurring question since 1933: Günther Anders, György Lukács, Theodor Adorno, and the young Jürgen Habermas, among others, confronted the issue in the 1940s and 1950s; poststructuralist French thinkers such as Jacques Derrida and Jean-François Lyotard engaged the question and its ramifications in the 1980s and 1990s.[2] The publication of the first four volumes of Heidegger's so-called *Black Notebooks* (*Schwarze Hefte*; called

black because of their covers) has reignited smoldering questions concerning the potential authoritarianism and antisemitism of the person and the thought.[3] Although Heidegger distinguished Nazism from fascism and claimed his remarks on the Jews have nothing to do with antisemitism, his reflections remain troubling and problematic.[4] The currently published *Notebooks* consist of *Überlegungen* (*Considerations*) II–XV (written from 1931 to 1941 and published in 2014 in GA volumes 94–6) and *Anmerkungen* (*Notes*) I–V (written from 1942 to 1948 and published in 2015 in GA 97).[5]

The extensive discussion of the *Notebooks* has primarily centered on a few politically charged remarks; most of the content consists of philosophical reflections elaborating on themes found in other writings and lecture-courses from the Nazi era. They neither develop an esoteric political philosophy nor a secret National Socialist vision. Polemical accounts (notably, those of Emmanuel Faye and Richard Wolin) have exaggerated the intrinsic and systematic character of antisemitism and National Socialism operating throughout the entirety of his philosophy.[6] Apologetic tendencies have dismissed political questions as irrelevant to the task of philosophy, established a strict dualistic demarcation between the thought and the person, or characterized questioning and criticism as a denial of the right to read Heidegger. The fact of his commitment to an explicitly totalitarian and racist government that systematically undermined the rights of German citizens while he worked on the regime's behalf and, after Heidegger's withdrawal from active political life, resulted in mass-persecution of minorities and the mass production of human-made death is undeniable. The weight of this fact is sufficient to justify critically questioning both the person and the philosophy. National Socialism and the Holocaust are not negligible historical phenomena to be swept aside as undeserving and unworthy of thought. Heidegger's general silence and few casual remarks during the postwar are indications of a deep—yet not necessarily "great" as Heidegger would later describe it—failure of thinking to confront its finitude and facticity. If such events are not worthy of thought, something has gone wrong with thinking and the defense of Heidegger sacrifices too much and too many.

Is Heidegger's philosophy then "contaminated"—to adopt a word used in some discussions—by National Socialism and antisemitism? The question of Heidegger's involvement is not one of an external contamination but the internal structure and unthought of Heidegger's thinking. It is not so much an issue of whether works associated with the proper name "Heidegger" should or should not be read; they will continue to be. The matter to be thought is how they are interpreted as philosophical works that are bound up with the historical life of a person that Heidegger himself would dismiss as merely biographical and "historiological." It is precisely such an interpretation, however, that the "Heidegger case," and his changing and at times contradictory self-narratives, demands careful contextualization for the sake of philosophical and social–political reflection.[7]

HEIDEGGER'S AMBIVALENCE: THE CONTEXTS OF THE *BLACK NOTEBOOKS*

How then might Heidegger be read in this politically charged context? First, as Jean Grondin notes, the works should be read.[8] As they are read, Heidegger emerges as a complex and ambivalent figure motivated by his perceived failures and sense of crisis.[9] Ambivalence is, however, found throughout the reception of his thought, in which he has been read as both an opponent and proponent of oppression, and in the sources that inspired this legacy. Heidegger's thinking promises an emancipation of ways of being in their multiplicity, especially in the 1920s, and ways of being more experientially attuned and responsive to one's world. Despite his thinking of radical difference, his thought remains obsessed with the ultimate oneness of being (*Sein*) and a schematic and fixated narrative of history that privileges the history of Occidental (*abendländisch*) philosophy and ignores material, social–political, and non-Western histories.[10] Heidegger engages the radical historicity of the human condition while formalizing history into a narrative about the fateful destiny of metaphysics from Greece to Germany.

Heidegger is not a political theorist or thinker in any ordinary sense; he never developed a political philosophy and his political comments reflect a primarily anti-political attitude—which is itself an elitist form of the political, as Habermas has argued concerning Heidegger and the German "mandarins."[11] Politically, mirroring his philosophical stance of the unity of being and the multiplicity of beings, Heidegger shows inclinations toward totalitarianism and anarchism; politics is interpreted through the prism of the history of being and this history relies on a language of destructuring and emancipation in the "other" of history. Historically considered, Heidegger's use of language is—as Adorno has aptly described in *The Jargon of Authenticity*—fundamentally reactionary, shaped by sentiments of nostalgia, home and homeland, and rural life.[12] However, despite Heidegger's own self-interpretation, scholars such as Reiner Schürmann, John McCumber, and Peter Trawny have argued that Heidegger's thought has anarchistic and emancipatory tendencies that destabilize reified conventional and metaphysical concepts. Heidegger deployed a radical language of philosophical contestation, revolution, and liberation that can have anarchistic social–political implications, as it reveals the alterity of the past and present in challenging the conformity and oppressiveness of the conventionally experienced present.[13]

Heidegger's initial support in 1933 and later elitist doubts concerning National Socialism reveal a figure outside of the mainstream of National Socialist politics and ideology while remaining in proximity and in its vicinity. It was widely known by late 1934 in the German-speaking world that Heidegger was "finished," as he had fallen out of favor with the students, professors, and the party.[14] Despite his efforts as rector, Heidegger did not speak in the same way as the National Socialist party philosophers and ideologues and his philosophy could not be embraced by the National Socialist movement. Throughout the *Notebooks*, it is obvious that Heidegger has an elitist "German mandarin" distaste for numerous elements of the National Socialist movement: its vulgar populism, biological and pseudo-Darwinian racism, cultural and media politics, and worship of technology and world-view thinking. He increasingly despises its commitment to the primacy of "organization" and technology, and its use of calculative planning in popular culture, propaganda, and racial eugenics. Central elements of National Socialism are interpreted as symptoms of the crisis of modernity that the movement, as "the confrontation of planetary technology and

modern humanity," was supposed to contest and overcome.[15] Heidegger's failure as rector in Freiburg, as well as his failed embrace of National Socialism, is identified with the being-historical failure of National Socialism to realize its inner promise and potential. National Socialism was in Heidegger's estimation an initially promising response to the nihilism of modernity; its being-historical moment was missed, the opportunity for another beginning lost, and it revealed itself as yet another insidious and derivative version of modernism along with its primary forms that he designated Americanism, Bolshevism, and "Jewry" (*Judentum*).[16] As his initial enthusiasm for National Socialism deteriorated, it is increasingly perceived as a betrayal of the destiny of being and as fated to be surpassed by its superior American and Soviet antagonists with which it is metaphysically the same.[17]

In the *Notebooks*, Heidegger's commitment to National Socialism transitions from initial enthusiasm to disappointment and suspicion. The *Black Notebooks*, like his other unpublished writings and lecture-courses, are full of critical remarks about the movement and his times. Apologists will make good use of these passages; yet they remain insufficient for a social–political critique of National Socialism, which Heidegger never offered, and they can be disturbing in their own ways, since Heidegger's stance toward National Socialism is increasingly "critical" only in a broadly right-wing and elitist manner. Heidegger still maintained in the mid-1934s after his "withdrawal" from politics that National Socialism must still be "affirmed" even though it is not the radical new inception he sought from "1930–1934" (GA 95: 408). National Socialism must be thoughtfully affirmed with necessity as the ultimate late-modern metaphysical movement, at this point, and is not yet considered an "inferior" realization of technological modernity in comparison with Western democracy and Eastern communism as it will be portrayed in the later *Notebooks*.

Heidegger's growing distance from the movement never encompassed political criticisms of the destruction of democracy, citizen rights, and human lives that would be merely ontic and would for him reproduce the same paradigm of modernity. There is likewise no departure from the centrality of the Occidental, and Germany as the decisive land of the middle within the Occident. In contrast to the poetry of Friedrich Hölderlin, which should be exemplary for the renewal of German existence, Heidegger came to believe that National Socialism would ultimately prove to be too inadequate and weak for this challenge and, in the end, must perish to superior forms of modernity. National Socialist Germany had no historical responsibility or uniqueness for Heidegger; it merely conformed to and reproduced Americanism, Bolshevism, and Jewry. This is how Heidegger, in a menacing remark made between 1942 and 1945, can blame Jewry, as the "principle of destruction" that helped unleash the paradigm of technological modernity, for their own self-destruction.[18] Heidegger's problematic remarks are ambiguous and in need of careful interpretation: are Heidegger's anti-Semitic remarks motivated by his anti-Christian polemic, which is a much more central thread throughout the *Notebooks*, or vice versa? Is Jewry the "principle of destruction" in a material sense or in the being-historical sense that Marxism is construed by Heidegger as inverting and destroying the predominant form of modern metaphysics? Is Heidegger blaming the Jews for their own physical self-destruction or maintaining that National Socialism is destroying itself

with the persecution of the Jews? In either case, whether he was committed to vulgar antisemitism or an ontological conception of the Jews, Heidegger was unconcerned with the realities of Jewish suffering. In the fourth volume of the *Black Notebooks*, as in the previously published letter-exchange with his former student Herbert Marcuse, Heidegger is concerned with German suffering at the hands of the Americans and Russians and expresses no concern for victims of National Socialism.[19] "Hitler," who is apparently no worse than Roosevelt or Stalin for Heidegger, does not name historical horror after the end of the war. Hitler—Heidegger remarked in one postwar comment—is the American excuse for the destruction of Europe.[20]

VULGAR AND SUPERIOR RACISM?

Heidegger repeatedly denied that he was antisemitic, and convinced his former student Hannah Arendt after their postwar meeting. As already noted, Heidegger made occasional antisemitic remarks and possibly engaged in antisemitic actions when he was active on behalf of the movement in 1933–34; these include his correspondence, possibly his activities against Jewish faculty enacting the policy of *Gleichschaltung* (coordination) as rector of the University of Freiburg, and the *Black Notebooks* and other writings from the 1930s and 1940s.[21] Heidegger, for instance, commented in the 1933–4 seminar on *Nature, History, State* on "the nature of our German space" and the "Semitic nomads" for whom "it will perhaps never be revealed at all."[22] The *Notebooks* should not be a surprise as other testimonials to his antisemitism and indifference to the fate of the Jews have already appeared in print.[23] They do provide further evidence and context for Heidegger's antisemitism. It might be argued that these remarks are relatively few in number and Heidegger does not make antisemitism the center of his thought in contrast to National Socialist racial ideologues. Probably this is what Heidegger believes when he denied that he is an anti-Semite. Most of the *Black Notebooks* concern his own philosophical thinking; his social–political complaints remain those of a philosopher who fails to engage the concrete structures and mechanisms of social–political life. Even if Heidegger did not engage in public antisemitic polemics, which National Socialists were unafraid to openly pursue, it does not remove the question. It also cannot be solely a question of the quantity of statements. Heidegger's "few" remarks are sufficiently disturbing. They may not express a biological, anthropological, or Social Darwinian racism given his long-standing rejection of racial thinking and dismissal of the rhetoric of blood and soil. Nonetheless, Heidegger's remarks concerning Germans and Jews bear a family resemblance with radical Germanic thinking. They belong to a German-centric, ethnocentric, and folkish (*völkisch*) way of thinking; they evoke the Nazi idea of a world Jewish conspiracy; and they portray Jews (including his own teacher Husserl) in stereotyped ways as calculative, cunning, and criminal.[24] He blames the European Jews for their own self-destruction and for creating the racism and totalitarianism that produced their National Socialist versions.[25]

Perhaps these questionable remarks reflect a "merely" contingent or ontic racism that can be distinguished from the ecstasy and height of Heidegger's philosophical endeavors.[26] Perhaps, according to one line of interpretation, his antisemitic remarks are contingent because of the very character of Heidegger's antisemitism. Heidegger can picture the Jews at most as one part of Western modernity and as an accidental nonoccidental addition to the history of the West that is decisively Greco-German for Heidegger. Heidegger cannot allow a Jewish phase of Western metaphysics, as Jewry is outside of the Occident in its inception and its destiny that will be decided by the Germans.[27] Jews cannot fundamentally define technological modernity, as Wolin and others have maintained, insofar as it is a phase of the history of being from which they are "outside" and excluded. Jewry can only reflect occidental history as the "principle of destruction" such as the Marxist destructive reversal of German idealism.[28] Heidegger maintained that Jewry cannot be creative and innovative, but only destructively enact possibilities given to them by Western, essentially Greek, metaphysics.[29] Consequently, Jewish philosophers from Maimonides to his teacher Husserl cannot, on principle, occupy a significant role in Heidegger's depiction of the history of philosophy.[30] Heidegger's exclusion of Jews as outside and other from the history of Western philosophy and originary thinking is beholden to an ontological rendition of ethnocentrism based in the being-historical priority of Greece-Germany that is reiterated throughout his later works.

Heidegger's few remarks concerning Jews and Jewry, given their relation to the context of his thinking and his consistent avoidance and silence, are enough to indicate that his antisemitism is not accidental or superficial.[31] But given the role of Jewry as one symptom of the history of metaphysics and modernity, which is a consequence of the history of essentially Greek metaphysics, Heidegger's antisemitism is inconsistent with more radical antisemitic visions. Heidegger to this extent should not be classified as a racial ideologue, as he rejected this idea as calculative and reductive throughout the *Notebooks*. He repeatedly criticized racial theory and its anthropological and biologistic (i.e. modern metaphysical) presuppositions throughout his lectures and writings of the 1930s and 1940s.[32] He rejected the racial interpretation of "*Volk*" (the people) maintained by National Socialism without, however, rejecting the notion of the culturally essentialist vision of the unity, truth, and essence of the people (*Volk*).[33] This notion of *Volk* was articulated, after his initial enthusiasm for the National Socialist movement faded, in relation to the history of philosophy and the poetry of Hölderlin.[34] Accordingly, despite his rejection of racial thinking, as part of the problematic of modernity, his thinking remains fundamentally ethnocentric; it remains centered on a Greco-German axis that marginalizes and minimalizes the multiplicity of philosophical perspectives. Heidegger maintained that his thinking is nonsubject-oriented such that the *Volk* cannot be understood as a collective subject that constitutes its world through its will and understanding, much less through its anthropological, biological, and racial characteristics. Nonetheless, the German people are an ontologically and being-historically chosen people who are marked out by the history of being as the ones who pose, decide, and renew the question of being.

Heidegger is committed to a German-centric vision of being from his embrace of National Socialism, as evident in the Rectorate speech, until the end of his life, as visible in the "Spiegel Interview" (1966) that repeats the same themes developed in the 1930s and 1940s. [35] Heidegger undoubtedly abandoned National Socialism in some sense in his own mind in the 1930s and 1940s and retrospectively justified his engagement for National Socialism as "failing greatly." [36] This is evident in his remarks about the movement in the *Black Notebooks*. Heidegger dismissed their vulgar racism and populism, their endorsement of technology and uses of popular culture and politics. He repeatedly expresses distaste for their vulgarity and places National Socialism into the fallenness of the times and the history of being culminating in technological modernity. Nonetheless, Heidegger never questioned National Socialism in a specifically ethical or normative social–political manner. National Socialism failed Heidegger's expectations for a decisive being-historical renewal of German Dasein and this was Heidegger's "failing greatly." Heidegger failed to confront his own personal and intellectual complicity in the postwar period, and his remarks from 1944 to 1948 (in GA 97) show his continuing defiance and resentment in the face of the denazification campaign working against him.

Heidegger's thinking is constitutively unable to respond to much less analyze basic elements of ethical life and social–political reality. There is no care for ethical prophecy that confronts injustice; nor is there concern for the obliteration of democracy and human rights or the destruction of non-German life.[37] After the war, he perceives in democracy a greater form of fascism.[38] When Heidegger mourns war and its death and devastation, he expresses concern only for German life and the only machinery of death mentioned is said to be aimed at Germany.[39] This exclusive focus continues in the postwar period. When Marcuse asked Heidegger about the Holocaust, Heidegger could only respond by countering with German deaths in the fire-bombing of Dresden and the Soviet occupation of Eastern German territories.[40]

Heidegger would never confront his own philosophical–historical conceptions that led to his involvement and complicity with National Socialism. His own collusion in this history is avoided and displaced into a narrative of the history of being such that no discussion of the person Martin Heidegger is permitted. There are no questions of personal individual responsibility and complicity; there are no considerations of repentance, forgiveness, or redemption in Heidegger's vision of being. This banal indifference and refusal toward others is not "erring greatly"; it does not only reveal contingent flaws of personality and character that should be dismissed to remain in pure philosophy. It discloses, to speak in an Arendtian way, a fundamental thoughtlessness and inability to think at the core of Heidegger's thinking.

FURTHER QUESTIONS

There are four constellations of issues in need of further consideration.

(1) The demarcation problem: both apologetic and polemic accounts of the "Heidegger controversy" remain closed to the unavoidable and necessary questions that must continue to be posed and reposed anew. The philosophy and the person cannot be as cleanly separated and demarcated as Heidegger thought or as his most dedicated followers hope. At the same time, the thinking necessarily outstrips the thinker and the philosophy calls for being encountered in its own terms.

(2) Heidegger's questionable understanding of the biographical: Heidegger provided inconsistent self-narratives about his own history and has a questionable understanding of autobiography and biography in relation to philosophy. He rejects the role of biographical interpretation in philosophy. Heidegger's thinking denies local contextual historical and biographical interpretations (which are dismissed as historiographical history) for the sake of interpretation from the history of being (history understood as ontological event); yet it is precisely the former that the "Heidegger case," and his changing at times contradictory self-narratives, demands—careful contextualization for the sake of philosophical and social–political reflection. For Heidegger, it is the history of being and not Heidegger himself that is at stake. Yet the complexities and complicities of his own life and thinking call for such a hermeneutics.

(3) Heidegger's questionable understanding of ethics and politics. Heidegger's "failures" are more than a failure of a person; his philosophy is permeated by structural deficits that need to be addressed at the level of philosophy. There is no thinking of rights of individuals or minorities; there is no concern or care for the suffering of non-German others; democracy and self-organization are reductively taken to be only instruments of organizational planning and technological modernity. His fundamental critique of modernity concerns technology and is addressed through poetry. Ethical–political ideas such as justice, fairness, and equality, and structural problems of capital and bureaucratic power are ignored. All these are necessary for an adequate conception of politics that would challenge the types of power Heidegger leaves unquestioned.

(4) Heidegger's questionable quasi-teleological conception of history stems from Greece and culminates in the German encounter with modernity. Heidegger's conception of occidental history centers on the special ontological and philosophical rank and uniqueness of Germany. This vision is

not identical to that of National Socialism and Heidegger uses it to challenge elements of National Socialism. Still, Heidegger's philosophy of history has its own question-able agenda. The idea of history that led to his engagement for and complicity with National Socialism still shape and are at work in his later thinking.

CONCLUSION

Heidegger wishes to construct a world that can greet and embrace the earth and allow it to flourish and humans to dwell in a more thankful, responsive, and atten-tive way.[41] Such aspects of Heidegger's writ-ing, which are developed throughout the *Notebooks* in intriguing ways, continue to resonate and suggest why Heidegger will be continued to be read even as his more sin-ister thoughts are rightfully criticized and rejected. Heidegger's thinking of history has interruptive and an-archic impulses that can help motivate an encounter with history as event, as suggested earlier; it, nonetheless, is a vision of history without persons and without recognition of genuine suffering.[42] Heidegger's philosophy remains a touch-stone for reflection even as its ethnocentric and depersonalizing tendencies deserve pub-licity and critical reflection.

NOTES

[*] I would like to express my appreciation to François Raffoul and Richard Polt for their comments on an earlier draft of this chapter.

[1] Compare Richard Wolin, *Heidegger's Children: Hannah Arendt, Karl Löwith, Hans Jonas, and Herbert Marcuse* (Princeton University Press, 2003); Samuel Moyn, "Judaism against Paganism: Emmanuel Levinas's Response to Heidegger and Nazism in the 1930s," *History and Memory* (1998), 25–58 and Michael Fagenblat, *A Covenant of Creatures: Levinas's Philosophy of Judaism* (Stanford: Stanford University Press, 2010), 70.

[2] Jacques Derrida, *Of Spirit: Heidegger and the Question* (Chicago: University of Chicago Press, 1989); Jean-François Lyotard, *Heidegger and "the Jews"* (Minneapolis: University of Minnesota Press, 1990).

[3] Questions raised in Karl Jaspers, *Notizen zu Martin Heidegger* (Munich: Piper Verlag, 1978), 57–9.

[4] See GA 95: 408 and GA 97: 159. Martin Heidegger, GA 94–97: *Die Schwarze Hefte*, ed. Peter Trawny (Frankfurt a. M.: Klostermann, 2014–15).

[5] Richard Rojcewicz has titled his forthcoming translation *Ponderings* rather than "Considerations"; Martin Heidegger, *Ponderings II–VI: Black Notebooks 1931–1938* (Bloomington: Indiana University Press, 2016).

[6] A typical example of the former tendency is the work of Emmanuel Faye; on the fairness and accuracy of his account, which does not extend to Faye's more recent treatment of the *Black Notebooks*, see the powerful and insightful critique developed in Thomas Sheehan, "Emmanuel Faye: The Introduction of Fraud into Philosophy?" *Philosophy Today*, 59.3 (Summer 2015), 367–400. On the problematic uses and reception of Heidegger's *Nachlass*, see Babette Babich, "Heidegger's Black Night: The *Nachlass* and its Wirkungsgeschichte," ed. Ingo Farin and Jeff Malpas, *Reading Heidegger's Black Notebooks* (Cambridge, MA: MIT Press, 2016), 59–86.

[7] An alternative conception of interpretation is called for that avoids the dualism between thinker and thinking evident in Heidegger's

hermeneutics I consider this point and examine Heidegger's problematic relationship with biographical interpretation and self-narrative in Eric S. Nelson, "What is Missing? The Incompleteness and Failure of Heidegger's *Being and Time*," ed. Lee Braver in *Being and Time, Division III, Heidegger's Unanswered Question of Being* (Cambridge, MA: The MIT Press, 2016).

8 Jean Grondin, "The Critique and Rethinking of 'Being and Time' in the First Black Notebooks," ed. Ingo Farin and Jeff Malpas, *Reading Heidegger's Black Notebooks* (Cambridge, MA: The MIT Press, 2016).

9 Compare Peter Trawny, *Heidegger und der Mythos der jüdischen Weltverschwörung.* Third edition (Frankfurt a. M.: Klostermann, 2015), 17.

10 On the parameters of Heidegger's ethnocentrism, and his binary opposition of the Occidental/Oriental, see Eric S. Nelson, "Heidegger, Misch, and the Origins of Philosophy," *Journal of Chinese Philosophy*, 39, Supplemental Issue (2012), 10–30.

11 GA 97: 44–45 is an example of Heidegger's global rejection of the category of the political. Heidegger is, according to Habermas, "the very embodiment of the arrogant German mandarin par excellence." Jürgen Habermas, *Europe: The Faltering Project* (Cambridge: Polity Press, 2014), 3. Compare his remark: "what was really offensive was the Nazi philosopher's denial of moral and political responsibility for the consequences of the mass criminality about which almost no one talked any longer eight years after the end of the war. In the ensuing controversy, Heidegger's interpretation, in which he stylized fascism as a 'destiny of Being' that relieved individuals of personal culpability, was lost from view. He simply shrugged off his disastrous political error as a mere reflex of a higher

destiny that had 'led him astray.'" Jürgen Habermas, *Between Naturalism and Religion: Philosophical Essays* (New York, NY: John Wiley & Sons, 2014), 20.

12 Theodor W. Adorno, *The Jargon of Authenticity* (Evanston: Northwestern University Press, 1973).

13 Reiner Schürmann, *Heidegger on Being and Acting: From Principles to Anarchy* (Bloomington: Indiana University Press, 1990); John McCumber, *Metaphysics and Oppression: Heidegger's Challenge to Western Philosophy* (Bloomington: Indiana University Press, 1999); Peter Trawny, *Freedom to Fail: Heidegger's Anarchy* (New York, NY: John Wiley & Sons, 2015).

14 Rudolf Carnap mentioned these developments in his diaries on three occasions in 1934–1935 (VII / 1934; 05.09.1935; and 05.12.1935). Unpublished: Archives of Scientific Philosophy, University of Pittsburgh, Carnap Papers (RC XX–XX). Heidegger's distancing himself from politics in 1934 and subsequent critical remarks about National Socialism present a challenge to the strong account of his involvement with National Socialism. One response, as Jaspers argued in 1949, maintained that a disgruntled Heidegger began to reject the movement in 1934 because it rejected and sidelined him and there was never a decisive break (Jaspers, *Notizen zu Martin Heidegger*, 58).

15 Jürgen Habermas, "Work and Weltanschauung: the Heidegger Controversy from a German Perspective," *Critical Inquiry*, 15:2 (Winter 1989), 452–454. On Heidegger's increasing alienation from National Socialism due to its failure to address the fundamental crisis tendencies of modernity, compare Charles Bambach, *Heidegger's Roots: Nietzsche, National Socialism and the Greeks* (Ithaca: Cornell University Press, 2003), 270.

16 Heidegger uses the German words *Judentum* (which can mean either Judaism or Jewry) and, less frequently, *Judenschaft.*

17 See GA 96: 243.

18 GA 97: 20. For a careful and comprehensive account of Heidegger and the Jews, see Donatella Di Cesare, *Heidegger und die Juden* (Frankfurt am Main: Klostermann, Vittorio, 2015).

19 GA 97; "An Exchange of Letters, Herbert Marcuse and Martin Heidegger," ed. Richard Wolin, *The Heidegger Controversy* (Cambridge, MA: The MIT Press, 1993), 152–164.

20 GA 97: 250. This remark raises the question of Heidegger's changing attitudes toward the figure of Hitler. On Heidegger's early understanding of Hilter, see Richard Polt, "Hitler the Anti-Nihilist? Statehood, Leadership, and Political Space in Heidegger's Seminar of 1933–34," *European Review*, 22.02 (2014), 231–243.

21 For example, there are a number of comments published in his correspondence with his wife: *Elfride: "Mein liebes Seelchen!": Briefe Martin Heideggers an seine Frau Elfride, 1915–1970* (Munich: Deutsche Verlags-Anstalt, 2005).

22 Martin Heidegger, *Nature, History, State: 1933–1934*. Tr. and ed. Gregory Fried and Richard Polt (London: Bloomsbury, 2013), 56.

23 See Richard Wolin, ed., *The Heidegger Controversy.*

24 See GA 96: 46–47, 56–57, 242–245, 262, 266; GA 97: 438; compare Trawny, *Heidegger und der Mythos*, 87.

25 GA 97: 20, 438.

26 On the contrast between philosophical ecstasy and political catastrophe in Heidegger, see David Farrell Krell, *Ecstasy, Catastrophe: Heidegger from Being and Time to the Black Notebooks* (Albany: SUNY Press, 2015).

27 GA 97: 20.

28 GA 97: 20. Heidegger elsewhere denied the Nazi identification of Jewry and Marxism, at least in its "final form" (GA 65: 54).

29 GA 97: 20.

30 Heidegger probably considered earlier forms of Jewish philosophy as derivations of scholasticism. Heidegger barely discussed Maimonides or Spinoza in his works. He remarked in 1936 that Spinoza's philosophy is determined by Cartesianism and Scholasticism and cannot be equated with Jewish philosophy (GA 42: 115).

31 For a critical portrait of the potentially systematic character of Heidegger's antisemitism, see Trawny, *Heidegger und der Mythos*, especially 59–69. If "Bolshevism" and "Marxism" are taken as code words for Judaism, as was frequently the case in Nazi Germany and is clearly the case in some passages in Heidegger, such as GA 97: 20, then antisemitism would be even more deeply ingrained in his thinking of the 1930s and 1940s.

32 Examples include GA 94: 338, 475–476; GA 97: 12.

33 On *Volk*, see GA 38: 65, and compare Trawny, *Heidegger und der Mythos*, 27, 65.

34 For a careful study of Heidegger's ideological context, and its divergence from ordinary National Socialism, see Charles Bambach, *Heidegger's Roots: Nietzsche, National Socialism and the Greeks* (Ithaca: Cornell University Press, 2003).

35 "Der Spiegel's Interview with Martin Heidegger (1966)," ed. Richard Wolin, in *The Heidegger Controversy*, 91–116.

36 This apologetic strategy is developed in the postwar *Notebooks*, see GA 97: 174–179; also compare Trawny, *Freedom to Fail.*

37 Heidegger denounces the prophetic dimension (GA 97: 159), the openness of the public sphere (GA 97: 146–147), ethical judgment and guilt (ibid.) after the war, also in relation to Karl Jaspers.

38 GA 97: 249.

39 GA 97: 148.

40 GA 97; "An Exchange of Letters, Herbert Marcuse and Martin Heidegger," ed. Wolin, ed., in *The Heidegger Controversy*, 152–64.

41 Compare GA 97: 3.

42 On Heidegger's conceptions of historicity and history, see Eric S. Nelson, "Questioning Practice: Heidegger, Historicity and the Hermeneutics of Facticity," *Philosophy Today*, 44 (2001), 150–9; Eric S. Nelson, "History as Decision and Event in Heidegger," *Arhe*, IV: 8 (2007), 97–115; Eric S. Nelson, "Heidegger, Levinas, and the Other of History." ed. John Drabinski and E. S. Nelson, *Between Levinas and Heidegger* (Albany: SUNY Press, 2014), 51–72.

INDEX